OXFORD MEDICAL PUBLICATIONS

Drugs, alcohol, and tobacco:
making the science and policy connections

Drugs, alcohol, and tobacco: making the science and policy connections

Edited by

GRIFFITH EDWARDS

Professor of Addiction Behaviour,
National Addiction Centre,
Institute of Psychiatry,
University of London

JOHN STRANG

Getty Senior Lecturer in the Addictions,
National Addiction Centre,
Institute of Psychiatry/The Maudsley,
University of London

and

JEROME H. JAFFE

Associate Director,
Office for Treatment Improvement,
Rockville, Maryland

Oxford   New York   Tokyo
OXFORD UNIVERSITY PRESS
1993

Oxford University Press, Walton Street, Oxford OX2 6DP
Oxford New York Toronto
Delhi Bombay Calcutta Madras Karachi
Kuala Lumpur Singapore Hong Kong Tokyo
Nairobi Dar es Salaam Cape Town
Melbourne Auckland Madrid
and associated companies in
Berlin Ibadan

Oxford is a trade mark of Oxford University Press

Published in the United States
by Oxford University Press Inc., New York

A catalogue record for this book is available from the British Library

Library of Congress Cataloging in Publication Data
Drugs, alcohol, and tobacco : making the science and policy
connections / edited by Griffith Edwards, John Strang, and Jerome H.
Jaffe.
(Oxford medical publications)
Includes bibliographical references and index.
1. Substance abuse—Government policy—Congresses. 2. Substance
abuse—Research—Congresses. 3. Substance abuse—Treatment—
Research—Congresses. 4. Drug legalization—Congresses.
I. Edwards, Griffith. II. Strang, John. III. Jaffe, Jerome H.
RC563.2.D83   1993   362.29'156—dc20   92-32077
ISBN 0 19 2622579

Typeset by Graphicraft Typesetters Ltd, Hong Kong
Printed and bound in Great Britain by
Bookcraft (Bath) Ltd, Midsomer Norton

Contents

Contributors

Arthur I. Alterman
Veterans Administration Center for Studies of Addiction, Philadelphia VA Medical Center, Philadelphia, USA

Thomas F. Babor
Department of Psychiatry, University of Connecticut School of Medicine, Farmington, Connecticut, USA

Virginia Berridge
Department of Public Health and Policy, London School of Hygiene and Tropical Medicine, London, UK

Sir Walter Bodmer
Imperial Cancer Research Fund, London, UK

Kathleen M. Carroll
Substance Abuse Treatment Unit, Yale University, New Haven, Connecticut, USA

D. Colin Drummond
Addiction Research Foundation, Toronto, Ontario, Canada

Griffith Edwards
National Addiction Centre, University of London, London, UK

Dean R. Gerstein
National Opinion Research Center, University of Chicago, Washington DC, USA

Hamid Ghodse
Division of Psychiatry of Addictive Behaviour, St George's Hospital Medical School, London, UK

Marcus Grant
Programme on Substance Abuse, World Health Organization, Geneva, Switzerland

Steven W. Gust
Department of Health and Human Services, NIDA, Addiction Research Center, Baltimore, Maryland, USA

Ray Hodgson
Department of Psychology, Whitchurch Hospital, Cardiff UK

Jerome H. Jaffe
Office for Treatment Improvement, Alcohol, Drug Abuse, and Mental Health Administration, Rockville, Maryland, USA

Richard Jessor
Institute of Behavioral Science, University of Colorado, Boulder, Colorado, USA

Harold Kalant
Department of Pharmacology, University of Toronto, Toronto, Canada

Robert Kendell
Home and Health Department, St Andrews House, Edinburgh

Herbert D. Kleber
Division on Substance Abuse, Columbia University, New York, USA

Malcolm Lader
Department of Psychopharmacology, Institute of Psychiatry, London, UK

Laurence E. Lynn, Jr
University of Chicago, Chicago, Illinois, USA

A. Thomas McLellan
Veterans Administration Center for Studies of Addiction, Philadelphia VA Medical
Center, Philadelphia, USA

Graham Medley
Imperial College of Science, Technology and Medicine, Department of Biology, London,
UK

David Metzger
Veterans Administration Center for Studies of Addiction, Philadelphia VA Medical
Center, Philadelphia, USA

Roger E. Meyer
The University of Connecticut School of Medicine, Farmington, Connecticut, USA

Robin Murray
Institute of Psychiatry, London

David F. Musto
Yale School of Medicine, New Haven, Connecticut, USA

Charles P. O'Brien
Addiction Research Centre, University of Pennsylvania, Philadelphia, USA

Mary Randall
Veterans Administration Center for Studies of Addiction, Philadelphia VA Medical
Center, Philadelphia, USA

David Robinson
University of South Australia, Adelaide, South Australia

Anders Romelsjö
Karolinska Institutet, Department of Social Medicine, Kronan Health Centre,
Sundbyberg, Sweden

Robin Room
Addiction Research Foundation, Toronto, Canada

Bruce J. Rounsaville
Substance Abuse Treatment Unit, Yale University, New Haven, Connecticut, USA

Marc Alan Schuckit
University of California-San Diego, VA Medical Center, California, USA

Charles R. Schuster
Department of Health and Human Services, NIDA, Addiction Research Center, Baltimore, Maryland, USA

Reginald G. Smart
Addiction Research Foundation, Toronto, Canada

Gerry V. Stimson
The Centre for Research on Drugs and Health Behaviour, 200 Seagrave Road, London, UK

Ian Stolerman
Section of Behavioural Pharmacology, Institute of Psychiatry, UK

John Strang
National Addiction Centre, (The Maudsley/Institute of Psychiatry, University of London), Addiction Sciences Building, 4 Windsor Walk, London, UK

Boris Tabakoff
Department of Pharmacology, University of Colorado Medical Centre, Denver, Colorado, USA

Mark Taylor
Addiction Research Foundation, Toronto, Canada

Robert West
Psychology Department, St George's Hospital Medical School, London, UK

George E. Woody
Veterans Administration Studies of Addiction, Philadelphia VA Medical Center, University Avenue, Philadelphia, USA

Introduction

Griffith Edwards, Jerome H. Jaffe, and John Strang

Different cultures have their unique ways of celebrating important events, but probably none are without a prescribed ritual for welcoming the birth of a baby. When it comes to the birth of a new scientific centre there are no fixed forms to guide us. However, a firm consensus soon emerged amongst the staff of the Institute of Psychiatry's National Addiction Centre (NAC), that the most apt way to celebrate its opening was to convene an international scientific conference to focus on the relationship between science and policy across the broad area of addictions. Conferences of this kind must of course meet certain hard scientific expectations. Their goal is to achieve exchange and updating of information and ideas, and the furtherance and clarification of scientific truth. Conferences are also properly about friendship—new friendships made and old friendships renewed and strengthened, contacts established between one scientific generation and the next, the overcoming of geographical space and national separateness. That fusion of scientific seriousness and celebration of friendship seemed exactly what a newly born centre would require as welcome and blessing from its godmothers and godfathers.

The National Addiction Centre

The inaugural address given at that July 1991 meeting was by HRH The Princess Royal, in her capacity as Chancellor of the University of London. She defined the NAC's mission in the following terms:

Firstly, it brings into effective working partnership a range of research talent, an impressive array of National Health Service clinical services and a very strong teaching base, all dealing with alcohol, nicotine, illicit drugs and the misuse of prescribed drugs, and this in itself is a unique resource. Secondly, an enormously important element of the National Addiction Centre is that it will network its results beyond its own campus, and act as a catalyst and a truly national resource for the UK. Added to which a third and intrinsic part of the NAC is its commitment to serve not only Britain but the needs of the rest of the world. This is particularly true with regard to the training needs of the developing as well as developed countries. We are all learning.

The NAC benefits from what has been accomplished on the Maudsley Institute campus over the last 25 years or more but, as indicated in the

Chancellor's inaugural address, it is now the intention to build on those strengths and establish a major integrated addiction centre of national stature. That does not mean rolling all resources into one monolithic whole, but establishing an effective networked partnership between still autonomous groups, and adding certain further elements. The opening of the NAC's purpose-built Addiction Sciences Building has done much to support this ambition. The NAC places particular emphasis on the strength that comes from integrating the Bethlem Royal and Maudsley's extensive clinical base with the Institute's research efforts through this networking formula. Elements of King's College Hospital and King's Medical School are additional and valued contributors to the partnership, and a National Advisory Panel is being established. The Diploma in Addiction Behaviour and the PhD training programme draw students from around the world.

The conference

So much for a brief description of the NAC, the inauguration of which gave cause for the conference on which this book is based. The structure of the conference was devised at a planning meeting held at the offices of the National Institute of Alcoholism and Alcohol Abuse (NIAAA) at Rockville, Maryland, USA, with the NIAAA's director, Enoch Gordis, kindly acting as host. The members of that group included Dean Gerstein (National Opinion Research Centre), Marcus Grant (WHO), Herbert Kleber (Columbia University), Robert Schuster (NIDA), Reginald Smart (ARF Toronto), Leland Towle (NIAAA), and the editors of this book. It was agreed that the meeting would be structured in terms of its feeding the purposes of a later, internationally useful book, and that plenary papers would be interposed with ample time for discussion. It was also agreed that although the science–policy connection provided a potentially fruitful topic for such a conference, its analysis inevitably set multifaceted and difficult problems. We needed people who were worldly-wise in policy, as well as those who knew about science.

When the planning group sent out the invitations to the plenary speakers and session chairmen, the overwhelmingly positive response gave some assurance that this was indeed an event which could meet a sensed international need, and we are immensely grateful to the speakers, chairmen, and discussants, who made that week in London so rewarding, both in terms of science and friendship. A dinner in the seventeenth century splendour of the Banqueting House in Whitehall, the occasion chosen for Harold Kalant to present the 1991 Jellinek Memorial Award to George Vaillant, provided theatre likely to be remembered in the annals of addiction history.

The book

The meeting was just one week in July, but the purpose of the book is to extend that week's debate to involve a wider audience, and our intention has centrally been to create this sense of shared engagement and debate. We believe that the result is not and cannot be an encyclopedia of easy answers, but an opening up of questions. As the Chancellor said, 'We are all learning'.

In outline, the structure of this volume is as follows: Part I sets the stage by dealing with general issues—the difficult liaison between science and policy. That loaded word 'liaison' may seem, by the end of this particular section and its debates, exactly to encapsulate the mutual dependence, ambivalent love, the occasional distrust, and unfaithfulness of other dangerous liaisons. Part II of the book deals with science and policies as they bear on prevention, while in Part III questioning is directed at what science can, in any truly generalizable sense, say about treatment efficacy. Part IV seeks to put the science and policy connection to a particularly demanding test by exploring what factual basis science can offer to inform debate on the legalization of drugs.

Across this whole book both the strength and tensions which come from trying to consider the science and policy connections in an international, rather than only a parish, forum are evident. Here is an extract from the remarks with which Enoch Gordis welcomed and introduced The Princess Royal:

The meaning of social drinking differs; the view of addiction as a sin or wilful misbehaviour differs; the degree to which coercion is appropriate in treatment differs, the economics of beverage alcohol production and its import differ; the production of illegal drugs and its support differs; the economics of health care; access to treatment, especially for these diseases we're talking about differ, and so we have a wide range of differences between countries, among which we're trying to find common themes of the relation of science and policy. The extent and the support of science in general and of addiction science as a legitimate branch of science also varies among countries . . .

Our ambition is that those who read this book will in some measure share both in the scientific excitement and the sense of friendship which characterized that July meeting. At best one might hope that for scientists and policy makers alike, these chapters and the discussion sessions will offer better understanding of each other's difficult positions. In Chapter 2 Laurence Lynn describes policy in terms of a metaphor of mixed, simultaneous games. If so, this book may do something to illuminate how that game is conducted on the addictions playing field.

The final chapter attempts to sum up the directions in which this conference might be seen to point, but it does not offer a rule book. One thing is certain though: the playing field is seldom a level one.

Acknowledgements

Administrative arrangements for the meeting from which this book derives were handled by Miss Rosamond Wynn-Pope, Director of Action on Addiction, and her staff. Ms Maria Pacan (National Addiction Centre) handled certain on-campus arrangements and has given the secretarial support necessary for the preparation of the text. Generous financial assistance has been provided by Esso.

Part I Science and policy: general issues in a special arena

1. Substance misuse and the uses of science

Griffith Edwards

By any objective reckoning, science has made many and varied contributions to policy formation in relation to the health and social problems set by misuse of mind-acting substances over the post-war decades. That is not to claim that making the science–policy connection is easy, or to argue that either side of the partnership invariably handles its responsibilities to the entire satisfaction of the other partner. The purpose of this book is, indeed, exactly that of exploring how the strengths and quality of the connection can be further enhanced.

We are, however, building on strength. Our knowledge as to the nature and determinants of substance misuse is more advanced than when alcohol was thought to have little or nothing to do with alcoholism (Webster 1984); lung cancer to be a consequence of atmospheric pollution or the spraying of tar on roads; or when heroin dependence was believed in the UK to be best treated by doctors prescribing intravenous heroin and cocaine (Interdepartmental Committee on Drug Addiction 1965), and in the USA by compulsory detention at the Lexington Narcotics Farm (Simbell 1970; Rasor 1978).

The way in which this chapter is structured is as follows. First, issues relating to alcohol, smoking, and drugs are considered separately. Under each of those headings a brief general note will be entered on some leading examples of the way in which science and scholarship have succeeded in being useful to policy decisions over the post-war years, and then in relation to each heading, one particular case example will be selected for more detailed appraisal. On the basis of this three-part review an attempt will then be made briefly to draw together some ideas as to where the main challenges now lie as we aim to strengthen a connection which is centrally about how science and policy are to work together for the common good, and to serve the world's people.

Alcohol, science, and policy

Let us identify a few examples of the way in which research into alcohol has connected usefully with policy over the post-war years. The connection between scientific findings and policy action has, in some instances, been direct (research as an exercise in problem solving), but in other instances the linkage is complex and better perceived in terms of science illuminating our general way of seeing an issue, rather than its offering technical advice of the kind which can bear immediately on the solution of a single problem. Different commentators might nominate different examples, according to their particular background and expertise, but here are five tentative nominations for such a list put forward to stimulate the debate and with ready acknowledgement that other people might choose rather different entries.

Drunk driving

Drunk driving is an example of science speaking with absolute directness to a policy issue (United States Department of Transportation 1968; Ross 1973), so much so that probably by now most members of the public will accept as a matter of folk-wisdom the basic premise that drinking impairs driving ability, and will be surprised when reminded that this contention ever needed a scientific underpinning. Drunk driving legislation, which is now universal in developed countries, constitutes a public health measure which has saved life on a large scale.

Treatment efficacy research

We are in a much better position than 40–50 years ago to say what treatments work or do not work (Miller and Hester 1984; Edwards 1988; Saunders 1989). This is important for our patients, as well as for decisions on the allocation of resources. The treatment system has its entropy, and the research message that many problems should be handled in the primary care, rather than the hospital, setting and by brief, rather than intensive, intervention (Babor *et al.* 1986; Edwards and Guthrie 1967; Orford and Edwards 1977; Drummond *et al.* 1990) is still too seldom reflected in patterns of health care. Later contributors to this book do, however, emphasize that the research policy connection in relation to treatment issues exemplifies the need to scrutinize very critically the relevance, robustness, and generalizability of research findings to policy application.

The two worlds of drinking problems

The phrase being used here was coined by Robin Room (Room 1977). Not long ago the total policy concern in relation to alcohol was focused on the type of drinking problem that was so far advanced that the patient had to be treated by the specialist clinic—the clinical world of alcoholism. The conclusion to be drawn from post-war community survey research is that a second important affected population also exists—the world of mixed, shifting, undramatic, but very prevalent alcohol-related problems, which are in sum enormously costly, but do not resemble the problems with which the clinic conventionally deals (Cahalan *et al.* 1969; Cahalan and Room 1974; Room

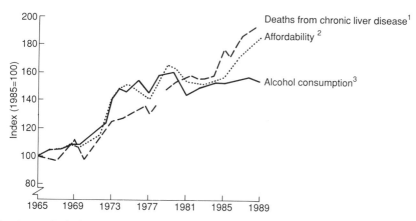

Fig. 1.1 Alcohol consumption, affordability, and deaths from chronic liver disease, UK, 1965–1989.

1977; Clark and Hilton 1991). A health policy which focuses on only one world and neglects the existence of the other is, research tells us, only half a policy.

Natural history of alcoholism

Longitudinal research on the 'natural history of alcoholism' (McCord and McCord 1960; Robins 1966; Jones 1968; Fillmore 1974; Vaillant 1983; Edwards 1989) has helped more understanding of drinking problems beyond the mere snapshot picture to an understanding of life course.

Cultural influences on drinking

There is an enormously varied body of research which has shown that the way people drink is immensely at the play of cultural influence (Pitman and Snyder 1962; MacAndrew and Edgerton; Jessor and Jessor 1977; Babor 1986).

These last two examples are of that kind of research which throws bright and humanizing light on the fundamental nature of the issues with which policy has to deal. Drinking, drinking problems, and what happens to a person with a drinking problem, are all issues which can only be truly comprehended when considered in the context of the individual's life course and the influences of society and culture. A narrowly biological view will not suffice.

Still under the heading of alcohol let us now focus on a particular case example and see what it can reveal about the workings of the science–policy connection. Figure 1.1 is reproduced from a recent publication by the Department of Health (DoH) in the UK (Department of Health 1991). It shows the remarkable closeness with which, over several years, alcohol consumption, the 'affordability' of alcohol, and the death rate from cirrhosis as a marker of alcohol-related harm, are related. The message which Fig. 1.1 conveys is unambiguous: per capita alcohol consumption is a matter of public health concern, and consumption is influenced by price. The position of the DoH has, however, been arrived at only as the result of a tortuous journey. In 1975 Kettil Bruun, working in Finland, crucially brought together colleagues from five different countries to produce what was then a definitive view on *Alcohol control policies in public health perspective*, and that report (Bruun *et al.* 1975*a*) offered the following summary statement:

Changes in the overall consumption of alcoholic beverages have a bearing on the health of the people in any society. Alcohol control measures can be used to limit consumption: thus, control of alcohol availability becomes a public health issue.

In 1979 the UK government's Central Policy Review Staff (CPRS) (Think Tank) offered the following advice on alcohol policies (Central Policy Review Staff, unpublished), much in line with the message in that later DoH figure.

We believe the minimum requirement is that henceforth duty levels should increase at least in line with the RPI [Retail Price Index]. The Government should not actively contribute to increasing alcohol consumption by allowing the value of duty to fall in real terms. No stated wish to reduce alcohol-related disabilities would be credible if it did.

The CPRS report was not published by HM Government, but only offshore in a pirate Swedish edition (Central Policy Review Staff 1982). Shortly afterwards the DoH (or the Department of Health and Social Security (DHSS) as it was called then) published a pamphlet entitled *Drinking sensibly* (DHSS 1981), which put the following gloss on the matter:

Maintaining or increasing the real price of alcohol is not likely to influence many problem drinkers who will probably maintain their consumption by switching to a cheaper drink or reducing their expenditure on other items . . . increasing the real price of alcohol by increasing taxation could play only a limited part in dealing with the problem of alcohol misuse.

The fact that the DoH takes its present unequivocal position on the public health significance of the liquor supply, is no doubt due to the interpretation offered by officials and given to their ministers as a result of an accumulation of scientific evidence, rather than this change of heart being the consequence of any one scientific masterstroke. What though can be learnt from this story about the general processes of the science–policy connection in the substance problems arena? The implications might perhaps be summarized as follows:

1. Giving science its proper application is often a long, slow, cumulative business, rather than a matter of quick fixes, and we should not be discouraged, even if on occasion the political attempt to escape the policy implications of research reaches comic opera proportions.

2. The second conclusion which one might wish to draw here is that an accumulation of data is all very well, but data left to its own devices tends

to mumble in low tones rather than speak with a clear voice. Hence, the significance of the authoritative and integrative scientific review which seeks purposely to make the connection with policy needs. Kettil Bruun's 'Purple book' (Bruun *et al.* 1975) may not have achieved an immediate victory, but it contributed importantly to the process of persuasion.

Smoking, policy, and science

The list of instances in which science has been of significance to policy formation in the tobacco arena must include work which has demonstrated that the cigarette habit is a type of drug dependence, with the drug in question being nicotine (West and Gruneberg 1991). The sad bronchitic does not compulsively light his next cigarette just for the pleasure of watching the upward-curling smoke, but because nicotine relieves a drug craving. This certainly provides an example of science radically changing the perspective within which a health problem is to be approached, and the rhetoric within which it is debated.

Equally basic has been the demonstration that it is the tar in the cigarette which sets the level of carcinogenic danger (US Department of Health and Human Services, 1982). Research which has confirmed the pro-smoking impact of advertising (Laugesen and Meads 1991) has obvious policy implications although one may probably expect to see different governments responding with varied levels of courage and determination. Studies which confirm the damage which can be done to the innocent bystander by someone else's smoke—passive smoking—gives leverage to policies aimed at establishing smoke-free environments at work and in other public places (Russell 1987). Research which has demonstrated that people will stop smoking in response to brief medical advice (especially if aided by nicotine replacement), is a further example of research contributing powerfully to health policies. (Russell *et al.* 1979; Russell 1991).

As a classic illustration of the significance of the science–policy connection within the smoking sector it is, however, inevitable that we should turn to Doll and Hill's paper of 1950—*Smoking and carcinoma of the lung*. The quality of the science in that communication is as evident today as when the report was first published, and it bears witness to that kind of elegant simplicity which led T.H. Huxley to remark that, 'Science is nothing but trained and organized commonsense'. Although the science in that paper is exemplary, what the detailed case study immediately reveals is that here, as with the research on per capita alcohol consumption, the relationship between science and policy did not follow the logical connection between the commissioning of a scientist to solve a problem and the consequent smooth follow-through to the rational application of findings to health policy, which is the favoured model of the management seminar. The link between science and health policy seldom resembles that in the substance problems arena, where the people whose health interests we are seeking to champion are disadvantaged or dispossessed (as with illicit drugs), or where, the substance which wreaks the havoc is the vehicle for profit and the tax take, as is the case with alcohol and tobacco.

Here, in abbreviated form, are the main facts of the story. The lung cancer death rate among men in the UK had risen from 10 per million at the beginning of the twentieth century to an astonishing 198 per million by mid-century (Webster 1984). In January 1948 the Medical Research Council (MRC) commissioned Bradford Hill to carry out epidemiological research with the direct problem-solving goal of determining the cause of this highly sinister development. Bradford Hill engaged Richard Doll as his collaborator (Doll 1991). The investigators applied the case control method, interviewing patients admitted to hospital with lung cancer, patients suffering from certain other types of cancer, and a control group of patients who were not suffering from any malignant disease. What the results showed was that non-smokers or light smokers were more common among the control subjects, while the heavy smokers were over-represented among the lung cancer patients. In regard to one minor detail, habits of scientific reporting have changed over time: Doll and Hill expressed their probability levels with a degree of exactness which today would be unusual. The significance level among males for the differences in the ratio of smokers to non-smokers and comparing lung cancer and control groups, is reported as having been $p = 0.00000064$. Put simply, the likelihood of the observed relationship between smoking and lung cancer being due to chance was less than one in a million. Furthermore, no other factor gave a significant difference. 'Trained and organized commonsense' had thus provided a persuasive answer to a problem of immense policy importance to the then very recently established National Health Service (NHS).

As it subsequently developed, the story of the health–policy connection in this instance proved to be anything but the mythical reflex arc (Webster 1984; Doll 1991). The NHS expert advisory mechanism gave only tepid and equivocal advice to ministers. The Ministry of Health asked for more research, a defensive posture which the MRC rightly treated with contempt. The tobacco industry mounted a counter-attack, although their in-house adviser was before long concluding that the Doll and Hill findings were incontrovertible. It was not until seven years after the publication of the paper in the *British Medical Journal* (Doll and Hill 1950) that a Minister for the first time stood up in the House of Commons and stated in clear terms his agreement with the proposition that smoking causes lung cancer.

There is good news on several fronts: cigarette smoking and the resultant incidence of lung cancer has fallen in Western countries. The European Community is moving toward prohibition of cigarette advertising, with only the UK resisting this action. It is therefore all the more shameful that the Third World is now losing out on many of the gains won from dealing with infectious diseases as a result of targeting by the tobacco multinationals (Crofton 1989; Ball 1990).

One of the conclusions to be drawn from this case example is thus, again, that science does not always find it easy to connect with policy, even when, as in the instance of the Doll and Hill report, the research is directly within the model of commissioned research specially set up to answer a defined problem of great policy importance, with the research giving an answer within a remarkably short time.

If we look more deeply into this story, it becomes evident that what forced the UK to take smoking seriously was the sophisticated campaign organized by a number of doctors and scientists which led in 1962 to the Royal College of Physicians' first report on *Smoking and health* (Royal College of Physicians 1962), and the setting up of Action on Smoking and Health (ASH), as a lobbying and public education group.

Science, policy, and drugs

Now to the third and last major area for review—the misuse of drugs. A list of lead instances of where, over the post-war years, science has served policy particularly well is set out below, with the list, again, intended as no more than starting point for debate.

(1) dependence as learnt drug-seeking behaviour;

(2) drugs and social context;

(3) dependence liability testing.

This list first acknowledges the significance of that mass of work which has moved us away from a model of addiction as a purely physical condition to an understanding of dependence in psychobiological terms as a learnt habit (Goldberg and Stolerman 1986). In some subtle way there has been a revolution in our understanding, not only in terms of the opiate receptor, the brain reward mechanisms, and the behavioural psychopharmacology, but of what drives people to drug-taking. That links very fully, of course, with the second entry in our list and consideration of what research has so richly revealed over the post-war years about the significance to drug-taking of the social context, whether in terms of the inner city and Chein's *The road to H* (Chein *et al.* 1964), a drug using subculture and Becker's *Becoming a marijuana user* (Becker 1953), or Lee Robins's study of returning Vietnam veterans (Robins 1974).

Dependence liability testing, the third entry in the list, constitutes a highly sophisticated area of research endeavour, with direct relevance to national systems of drug control and protection of public health. The traditions and techniques of this largely American speciality have recently been reviewed in

a number of different publications (Adler and Cowan 1990; Erickson *et al.*
1990; Cami *et al.* 1991).

Rather than in this instance risk causing divisiveness by nominating any
one area of scientific research for a special case study, let us turn away altogether from the many kinds of science which we have so far been touching
upon, and take as a case example the significance of historical studies on drug
misuse as an agent for the enlightenment of the policy process.

The importance of the historical analysis of drug use and of society's
response to drug problems, lies in the repeated demonstration that here, as
with alcohol, one cannot understand the substance use or the problem without
close analysis of the large surrounding social play: what has counted as
progress or reform and the influence of political and social movements; fears
of social corruption; the background of economic change, slump and boom;
industrialization; the power play between different professions; the influence
of one nation on another; war and, very literally, the fall of empires. Only
within that kind of perspective can we ever hope to understand Gin Lane,
slaves traded for rum, women factory workers beginning to smoke cigarettes,
alcohol problems among Asian immigrants in Southall; heroin and acquired
immune deficiency syndrome (AIDS) in Thailand; what is happening in Bolivia
and Colombia and thus on the streets of Washington DC; the emergence of
a drug and human immunodeficiency virus (HIV) problem in Eastern Europe,
and much else besides.

At the end of the eighteenth century, Virginia Berridge tells us (Berridge
and Edwards 1981), the Society of Arts offered a prize of £50 to the most
successful British cultivator of home-grown opium. Some experimenters ran
into trouble because of marauding hares who developed a taste for the opium
poppy. In England, child labour was extensively employed in the harvesting
of the opium crop and it was suggested that poppy growing might help to
rejuvenate the depressed state of Irish agriculture. High winds in Scotland
were inimical to the health of the poppy, and the Caledonian Horticultural
Society favoured lettuce opium. In England, some sensible farmers planted
rows of potatoes between the poppies.

What insights does one derive from such historical material? One is, of
course, immediately challenged by the sheer ordinariness of the perspective
within which it was possible to view opium cultivation—opium, as Virginia
Berridge points out, was on a par with turnips and rhubarb. Opium was
needed as the pervasively available over-the-counter remedy for all manner of
ills, at a time when most working people had no access at all to medical care,
and so the situation remained for a large part of the eighteenth century.

Both in the USA, through the work of David Musto (Musto 1973), and in
Britain, with Virginia Berridge's research (Berridge and Edwards 1981; Berridge
1984), scholarship has been well served by the historians. Oriana Kalant's
translation of Maier's *Der Kokainismus* (Maier 1987) has meanwhile made
accessible important material on the history of cocaine. Other outstanding

contributions to drug history have come from Hayter (1968), Lowes (1966), and Bruun *et al.* (1975*b*). Over this period the alcohol field has had its own very distinguished historians (Bynum 1968; Harrison 1971; Levine 1978; Porter 1985).

Science, policy, and the challenges ahead

On the basis of this brief three-part review of what science has done to inform and assist policy in relation to substance problems over the post-war years, what conclusions can now be drawn? On the evidence of what has necessarily been only a cursory examination of a vastly complex field of scientific endeavour and policy action, the general contention that science and policy have, over this period, made many and fruitful connections is well founded, but it would be unwise to give way to triumphalism. If we are now further to strengthen the quality of the science–policy connection, there are tangible challenges to be faced. Here are some suggestions as to what these challenges might be.

The science–policy connection and the developing world

We referred earlier to the assault from the tobacco multinationals from which the developing world is currently suffering, but that is only part of the much wider threat which countries at that stage of development today find themselves facing as a result of problems set by alcohol (Edwards 1979; Cavanagh and Clairmonte 1985; Kortteinen 1988), illicit drugs (World Health Organization 1986), and from the lax control of prescription drugs (Chetley 1990). Those countries need science to support their policy developments as much as the developed world does, but they have few trained researchers, no research infrastructure, and no or vestigal research budgets (Commission on Health Research for Development 1990; Hall 1991). A young doctor who returns to his or her country with a research training will often have to confront the harsh reality that time spent on research will impinge adversely on private practice earnings which are needed to supplement a meagre salary. The plea must be that the developed world, through the WHO and other United Nations agencies, allocate a proportion of funding specifically for research training, and research projects to assist developing countries better to deal with types of problem which are now often of such magnitude as actually to imperil the pace of national development.

Research on transnational issues

At the global level, what seems generally to be happening is that poor countries are exporting their heroin and cocaine to their rich neighbours, while rich countries are sending their alcohol and tobacco to the developing world— a bizarre kind of trade balance. National research budgets are traditionally spent on problems which are deemed to be of immediate national concern. We need now to develop a research capacity which will secure a better understanding of transnational issues, and that again sets a very tangible challenge to those responsible for the organization and funding of research.

The social responsibility of science

The example of per capita alcohol consumption, outlined earlier, showed scientists co-operating to make a powerful international review statement, while tobacco showed the medical profession engaging in very determined activism. The social responsibility of scientists working in this area is an issue which deserves to be debated further. Paradoxically, although science is often expected to be about helping solve policy problems, science in this area repeatedly comes up with findings which create acute problems for the policy maker. Who really wants to know that crime, drug-taking, and poverty are part of the same nexus when it is so much more politically convenient to fight a 'war on drugs' against the pusher and the evil external enemies, rather than focus on the issue of inner city poverty? An independent initiative from the scientific community itself to review the social responsibility of science in this difficult arena would be highly desirable.

Better understanding of the realities of the science–policy connection

The study of how the science base is created and the connection between science and policy best effected, is relevant to every type of scientific activity. Different branches of science do, however, set special problems for the under-standing of this connection, and this type of question has not, up to now, received adequate attention in relation to how science and policy interact in this particular area of concern. Science studies of that kind will help us to learn from experience: the pressures upon us to conduct the next experiment, collect the next portion of data, or make the next set of policy recommenda-tions, rather than to stand back and dispassionately examine the nature and dynamics of the activity in which we are engaged, are always too great. One conclusion might therefore be that if science is to serve the policy expectation better, the major national funding bodies must be willing to invest a proportion of their budgets not just in more science, but in deeper analysis of the science–policy connection.

Better international communication

Neither at the scientific nor at the policy level is there today a satisfactory mechanism to ensure that comprehensive, accurate, and updated exchange of information between countries takes place in relation to research training opportunities, research in progress, research findings, databases, research tech-niques, policy experiences, and the translation of science into policy. Certainly, there often seems to be only minimal communication of experiences across countries. We have not made adequate use of information technology, nor faced up to the language problems. There is again an initiative waiting to be born, and one must hope that some country or some agency will take the lead.

Whenever the science–policy connection is discussed one of the points which is repeatedly and rightly made is that the two sides to the partnership need to strengthen their understanding of each other's positions, working methods, felt constraints, hopes and fears, and sensitivities. There are many consultative, advisory, and informal settings in which that kind of mutual learning is fruitfully taking place on an everyday basis: in reality the degree to which science is involved in policy formation in the substance problem area is therefore already extensive. It would, however, be bland to pretend that these interactions will eventually lead to total unity of purpose between those partners. On the contrary, as well as there being incontrovertible benefit from strengthened and respectful understanding, the relationship between science and policy must always and usefully have within it a place for tension. It is the job of science to advise, to be helpful to, and to support the policy process, but its inalienable responsibility is also to criticize, question, test, and be awkward. Science has to have a larger vision of itself than its being merely a biddable management tool.

References

Adler, M.W. and Cowan, A. (ed.) (1990). *Testing and evaluation of drugs of abuse.* Wiley–Liss, New York.

Babor, T.F., Ritson, E.B., and Hodgson, R.J. (1986). Alcohol related problems in the primary health care setting: a review of early intervention strategies. *British journal of addiction,* **81,** 23–46.

Ball, K. (1990). Exporting death. Britain's malignant epidemic spreads to the developing world. *British Journal of Addiction,* **85,** 313–14.

Becker, H.S. (1953). Becoming a marihuana user. *American Journal of Sociology,* **59,** 235–42.

Berridge, V. (1984). Drugs and social policy: the establishment of drug control in Britain 1900–30. *British Journal of Addiction,* **79,** 17–29.

Berridge, V. and Edwards, G. (1981). *Opium and the people.* Allen Lane, London.

Bruun, K., Edwards, G., Lumio, M., Makela, K., Pan, L., Popham, R.E., *et al.* (1975*a*). *Alcohol control policies in public health perspective.* Finnish Foundation for Alcohol Studies, Helsinki.

Bruun, K., Pan, L., and Rexed, I. (1975*b*). *The gentleman's club.* University of Chicago Press.

Bynum, W.F. (1968). Chronic alcoholism in the first half of the nineteenth century. *Bulletin of the History of Medicine,* **42,** 160–85.

Cavanagh, J. and Clairmonte, F. (1985). *Alcohol beverages: dimensions of corporate power.* Croom Helm, London.

Cahalan, D. and Room, R. (1974). *Problem drinking among American men.* Rutgers Center of Acohol Studies, New Brunswick.

Cahalan, D., Cisin, I., and Crossley, H. (1969). *American drinking practices: a national study of drinking behaviour and attitudes.* Rutgers Center of Alcohol Studies, New Brunswick.

Cami, J., Bigelow, G.E., Griffiths, R.R., and Drummond, D.C. (ed.) (1991). Clinical testing of drug abuse liability. *British Journal of Addiction,* **86,** 12 (Special Issue), 1525–667.

Central Policy Review Staff (1982). *Alcohol policies in United Kingdom.* Sociological Institute of Stockholm University, Stockholm.

Chein, I., Gerard, D.L., Lee, R.S., and Rosenfeld, E. (1964). *Narcotics, delinquency and social policy: the road to H.* Tavistock, London.

Chetley, A. (1990). *A healthy business? World health and the pharmaceutical industry.* Zed Books, London.

Clark, W.B. and Hilton, M.E. (ed.) (1991). *Alcohol in America: drinking practices and problems.* State University of New York Press, New York.

Commission on Health Research for Development (1990). *Health research: essential link to equity in development.* Oxford University Press.

Crofton, J. (1989). Tobacco: world action on the pandemic. *British Journal of Addiction,* **84,** 1397–400.

Department of Health (1991). *The health of the nation.* HMSO, London.

Department of Health and Social Security (1981). *Drinking sensibly.* HMSO, London.

Doll, R. (1991). Journal interview 29. Conversation with Sir Richard Doll. *British Journal of Addiction,* **86,** 365–77.

Doll, R. and Hill, A.B. (1950). Smoking and carcinoma of the lung. *British Medical Journal,* ii, 739–48.

Drummond, D.C., Thom, B., Brown, C., Edwards, G., and Mullan, M.C. (1990). Specialist versus general practitioner treatment of drinking problems. *Lancet,* **336,** 915–18.

Edwards, G. (1979). Drinking problems: putting the third world on the map. *Lancet* ii, 402–4.

Edwards, G. (1988). Which treatments work for drinking problems? *British Medical Journal,* **296,** 4–5.

Edwards, G. (1989). As the years go rolling by: drinking problems in the time dimension. *British Journal of Psychiatry,* **154,** 18–26.

Edwards, G. and Guthrie, S. (1967). A controlled trial of in-patient and out-patient treatment of alcohol dependence. *Lancet,* i, 555–9.

Erickson, C.K., Javors, M.A., and Morgan, W.W. (ed.) (1990). *Addiction potential of abused drugs and drug classes.* Haworth, Binghampton, NY.

Fillmore, K.M. (1974). Drinking and problem drinking in early adulthood and middle age: an exploratory 20 year follow-up study. *Quarterly Journal of Studies on Alcohol,* 35, 819–40.

Goldberg, S.R. and Stolerman, I.P. (ed.) (1986). *Behavioural analysis of drug dependence.* Academic Press, New York.

Hall, A.J. (1991). Health research in developing countries. *British Medical Journal,* **302,** 1220–21.

Harrison, B. (1971). *Drink and the Victorians.* Faber and Faber, London.

Hayter, A. (1968). *Opium and the romantic imagination.* Faber and Faber, London.

Interdepartmental Committee on Drug Addiction (1965). *Second report (second brain report)*. HMSO, London.

Jessor, R. and Jessor, S.L. (1977). *Problem behaviour and psychosocial development: a longitudinal study of youth*. Academic Press, New York.

Jones, M.C. (1968). Personality correlates and antecedents of drinking patterns in adult life. *Journal of Counselling and General Psychiatry*, **32**, 2–12.

Kortteinen, T. (1988). International trade and availability of alcoholic beverages in developing countries. *British Journal of Addiction*, **83**, 669–76.

Laugesen, M. and Meads, C. (1991). Tobacco advertising restrictions, price, income and tobacco consumption in OECD countries, 1960–1986. *British Journal of Addiction*, **86**, 1343–54.

Levine, H.G. (1978). The discovery of addiction: changing conceptions of habitual drunkenness in America. *Journal of the Study of Alcoholism*, **39**, 143–74.

Lowes, P.D. (1966). *The genesis of international narcotics control*. Libraire Droz, Geneva.

Maier, H.W. (1987). *Maier's cocaine addiction (Der Koainismus)*. Translated and edited by O.J. Kalant. Addiction Research Foundation, Toronto.

MacAndrew, C. and Edgerton, R.B. (1970). *Drunken comportment: a social explanation*. Nelson, London.

McCord, W. and McCord, J. (1960). *Origins of alcoholism*. Stanford University Press.

Miller, W.M. and Hester, R.K. (1984). The effectiveness of alcoholism treatment: what research reveals. In *Treating addictive behaviours: processes of change* (ed. W.R. Miller and N. Heather), pp. 121–74. Plenum, New York.

Musto, D.F. (1973). *The American disease*. Yale University Press, New Haven.

Orford, J. and Edwards, G. (1977). *Alcoholism: a comparison of treatment and advice, with a study of the influence of marriage*. Maudsley Monographs No. 26, Oxford University Press.

Pitman, D.J. and Snyder, C.R. (1962). *Society, culture, and drinking patterns*. John Wiley, New York.

Porter, R. (1985). The drinking man's disease: the 'pre-history' of alcoholism in Georgian Britain. *British Journal of Addiction*, **80**, 385–96.

Rasor, R.E. (1978). Reflections on the narcotics farms. In *Drug addiction and the US Public Health Scheme*. (ed. W.R. Martin and H. Isbell), pp. 251–59. Proceedings of the symposium commemorating the 40th Anniversary of the Addiction Research Centre at Lexington, KY US Department of Health, Education, and Welfare, Washington.

Robins, J. (1966). *Deviant children grown up*. Williams and Wilkins, Baltimore.

Robins, L.N. (1974). *The Vietnam drug user returns*. Special Action Office, Monograph Series A, No. 2. Government Printing Office, Washington.

Room, R. (1977). Measurement and distribution of drinking patterns and problems in general populations. In *Alcohol-related disabilities* (ed. G. Edwards, M.M. Gross, M. Keller, and R. Room), pp. 61–88. WHO, Geneva.

Ross, H.L. (1973). Law, science and accidents: the British Road Safety Act of 1967. *Journal of Legal Studies*, **2**, 1–78.

Royal College of Physicians (1962). *Smoking and health*. Pitman Medical, London.

Russell, M.A.H. (1987). Estimation of smoke dosage and mortality of non-smokers from environmental tobacco smoke. *Toxicology Letters*, **35**, 3262–5.

Russell, M.A.H. (1991). The future of nicotine replacement. *British Journal of Addiction*, **86**, 653–8.

Russell, M.A.H., Wilson, C., Taylor, W., and Baker, C.D. (1979). Effects of general practitioner's advice against smoking. *British Medical Journal*, 283, 231–5.

Saunders, J.B. (1989). The efficacy of treatment for drinking problems. *International Review of Psychiatry*, 1, 121–38.

Simbell, E.V. (1970). History of legal and medical roles in narcotic abuse in the US. In *The epidemiology of opiate addiction in the United States* (ed. J.C. Ball and C.D. Chambers), pp. 22–35. Charles C. Thomas, Springfield.

US Department of Health and Human Services (1982). *The health consequences of smoking: cancer*. Office on Smoking and Health, Rockville, MD.

United States Department of Transportation (1968). *Alcohol and highway safety*. Report to the United States Congress. National Institute on Highway Safety, Washington.

Vaillant, G.E. (1983). *The natural history of alcoholism*. Harvard University Press, Cambridge, MA.

Webster, C. (1984). Tobacco smoking addiction: a challenge to the National Health Service. *British Journal of Addiction*, 70, 7–16.

West, R. and Gruneberg, N.E. (1991). The implications of tobacco use as an addiction. *British Journal of Addiction*, 86, 485–8.

World Health Organization (1986). Report of the Conference of Minister of Health on Narcotic and Psychotropic Drug Misuse, London 18–20, March 1986. *British Journal of Addiction*, 81, 831–8.

2. Private behaviour and public policy

Laurence E. Lynn, Jr

Private acts and public consequences

My wife smokes. My doctor is overweight. I seldom buckle up when I drive. The three of us are voluntarily incurring needless risks to our health and well-being. We know the scientific findings concerning the risks, and they are unequivocal.

That is far from the whole story. The neighbourhood in Chicago where I live is surrounded and infiltrated by people who are behaving in ways that are likely to be self-destructive or self-defeating. They abuse alcohol and drugs; they engage in unprotected sexual activity; they have poor diets. Through their behaviour, most of these people are incurring enormous risks to their very life prospects. Whether or not they are aware of the scientific evidence demonstrating these risks, most of them also know better.

So what? My wife, my doctor, and I, as well as our neighbours in Chicago, must face the consequences of our acts. If I am crushed against a steering wheel, if my doctor dies of a stroke, if my wife gets cancer or has premature wrinkles, we have only ourselves to blame. If knowledge of such consequences does not deter our self-destructive behaviour, why not assume that whatever pleasures we are deriving from our vices justify the risks that we incur? Leave us, and those like us, to our fate.

The reason that we do not live and let live is that the consequences of bad behaviour are seldom limited to the culpable individuals. Their behaviours have consequences for innocent bystanders, and these second-hand consequences take a variety of forms. They may be direct: when one person smokes, another may inhale carcinogens; a drunk driver may kill a pedestrian; a drug-abuser may make someone else the victim of his or her desperate search for money; when you bear a child you cannot care for, I may be that unlucky child. Second-hand consequences may be a reflection of specific institutional arrangements: accidents under the influence of drugs or alcohol bear, for instance, on the general level of health insurance losses and premiums. Second-hand consequences may be more diffuse but none the less significant: alcohol, drugs, and tobacco reduce productivity, limit the prospects for economic growth, divert resources to treatment and social control, and, therefore, lead to a poorer society all around.

For reasons such as these, a citizen may choose to concern him or herself with the consequential behaviour of others. He or she may be willing to incur costs to change the drug user's behaviour or to ameliorate the adverse consequences for that citizen. That willingness may take the form of voluntary donations to charities which promise, for example, to prevent and treat substance abuse. A citizen may also be willing to go so far as to invoke the coercive powers of the state to tax income and to restrict freedom to behave badly—drug taking, driving unbuckled, smoking in smoke-free zones, and driving while drunk are illegal in many jurisdictions—even at the expense of taxing him or herself and curtailing his or her own own freedom. Private behaviour thus becomes the subject of public policies.

Willingness to advocate public intervention into private behaviour is contingent, of course, on many factors: on how badly we feel harmed, on financial ability to bear the costs of intervention, on moral convictions concerning the appropriateness of government action or the social acceptability of particular behaviours, on faith in the capacities of charities and state agencies to help in such controversial and sensitive matters, on the nature and attractiveness of other claims on our resources and attention. Thus willingness to act depends on beliefs and circumstances.

Note, too, that even if it is generally agreed that a public policy is needed to control bad behaviour, willingness to intervene in other people's lives may differ considerably from citizen to citizen. Teetotalers and tipplers, smokers and non-smokers, libertarians and liberals, the poor and the rich, the knowledgeable and the ignorant may see the same matter in very different lights and favour very different kinds of intervention. One person may favour regulation, another may favour subsidies. One voter may favour treatment and rehabilitation, another deterrence in the form of laws, enforcement, and punishment.

Finding the aggregate voice

Somehow, we must collectively resolve the problem of whether and how to intervene in the lives of people who are behaving badly by our definition, or who might behave badly, in order to protect society's interests. Thus, we must solve the problems of collective action if we are to create public policies concerning undesirable behaviours and their consequences.

Social scientists have a variety of ways of characterizing and analysing collective action problems. The central problem can be summarized as finding ways of discovering and aggregating the diverse preferences of individual citizens into a collective preference for a coherent public policy concerning, for example, tobacco, drug, or alcohol abuse.

Why are the discovery and aggregation of preferences considered a problem? The kinds of disagreements mentioned above are important obstacles, but there are other, more subtle, ones. Assume for the moment that our citizens are reliably rational. A rational citizen will support any action for which the expected benefit to the citizen exceeds the costs the citizen must incur. But suppose that a public policy's benefits are far beyond the ability of any individual to pay for them, as is the usual case. Suppose, furthermore, that a citizen can enjoy the full benefits of a public policy if someone else pays the bill for the policy. Economists refer to this as enjoying a 'free ride' (Olson 1971; Hardin 1982). With so-called collective benefits, we will observe the well-known phenomena of citizens concealing their preferences for policies so that they are not called upon to pay for them, or expressing support for policies for which they are reluctant or unwilling to vote the necessary taxes.

We relieve ourselves of some of these problems but encounter some others if we abandon the postulate of citizen rationality. People derive benefits from merely contributing to ennobling activities. They enjoy being seen to contribute to good causes (Wilson 1973; Moe 1980). In narrowly rational terms, voting is not rational, since every voter knows that his or her effort to vote cannot influence the outcome. But many citizens nonetheless vote and wish to be known for their good citizenship. They also voluntarily contribute time and money to good causes, even when the benefits to them personally are negligible. So citizens can and will act collectively if they have a conviction that it is right to do so. Entrepreneurship on behalf of good causes, the creation of such convictions, is a major aspect of public policy leadership.

But our willingness to join the cause may depend on how the issue is framed, on how we perceive it, on the symbolic and the intangible aspects of the appeal to our consciences and our purses. If we become afraid, ashamed, infuriated, or appalled, we may be willing to act in ways which seem responsive to our emotional needs. Gusts of panic or fear are often more effective motivators of collective action than appeals to reason or the amassing and dissemination of scientific evidence. Evidence without emotion may produce nothing (Edelman 1988). Long-time activists know these things and use them to their advantage. But, apart from appearing to be nothing more than manipulation, especially to those with a scientific bent, appeals to the so-called irrational and emotional may, in the long run, be an unreliable basis for establishing coherent and consistent public policies. What happens when fear subsides, emotions cool, and citizens lose interest?

Problems of collective action are far more complicated than this consideration of the rationality of individual citizen preferences would suggest. Citizens are not autonomous; they band together into groups and organizations and pool their resources to pursue specific interests. In the USA for example, one can write to a member of Congress and urge him or her to vote in a certain way on smoking control legislation or the elimination of tobacco subsidies. But a letter from the Tobacco Institute or from a legislator representing voters employed by tobacco companies containing threats of political reprisal in the event of a vote unfavourable to their interests will, on balance, be more influential than any single voice. Citizenship and good intentions matter, but so do wealth, power, and economic stakes, and willingness to employ them on behalf of specific interests. Indeed, scientists and specialists are known to support policies that have the peculiar quality of advancing the specific interests of scientists and specialists.

The specialist's voice

To this point, this chapter has been discussing the difficulties of merely creating public policies addressed to collective interests. These difficulties are formidable even if we do not impose demanding criteria concerning quality, or effectiveness, or efficiency, on the public policies we support. But, invariably, those who participate in public policy formation want more than just any public policy; they want good public policy. We care about the content of our policies, about their cost and likely results, about the way these results are achieved (Lynn, in press).

Specialists in a particular policy domain, for example, substance abuse treatment and prevention, invariably want policies that reflect their specialized knowledge and expertise. They invariably want, as well, policies which accord themselves, as the most knowledgeable and involved, privileged roles in formulating and carrying out the policies.

But, who are the specialists in a policy domain, for example the domain of addictions? Are they the field workers, whose daily responsibility it is to serve clients and who believe they know the clients' problems better than anyone? Are they the leadership and members of the professional elites—physicians, licensed practitioners—whose authority legitimates treatment? Are they the scholars and researchers whose work establishes the foundations for training and practice? Are they the addicts themselves and their families? This question presumes that field workers, professionals, researchers, and even addicts, are homogeneous groups. We know, of course, that they are not, and that rivalries among sub-groups, whether based on expertise, position, or ideology, can be intense to the point of destroying common effort. The internecine conflicts of professional groups are often spectacular to see.

There are other specialists who claim influential roles in policy making in the domain of addictions. They range from experts in policy analysis and programme evaluation, whose views tend to be less ideological and more influenced by considerations of efficiency in the use of scarce resources across all policy domains, to experts in law enforcement, criminal justice, and corrections, whose perceptions concerning both need and intervention may differ dramatically from those of research or treatment professionals.

Specialists often have privileged roles in policy debates, especially those concerning programme and treatment design. The authority of specialists legitimates action and provides protective coloration for the non-specialized legislator or bureaucrat. But even in more technical domains, scientific wisdom and practice wisdom, when they are not in conflict with each other, must compete with conventional wisdoms of various kinds, wisdoms founded on religious conviction and scruples, on ideological grounds relating to beliefs concerning human nature and development, on the common experiences and personal observations of laypersons, and on stereotypical views acquired through public media and popular culture. The wisdom of specialists, even when unequivocally supported by science, hardly ever goes unchallenged, nor, most would agree, should it.

From intention to results

Let us suppose that we overcome these various difficulties and reach a collective decision that public policy of a particular content is needed, but now we want a result. A host of fresh difficulties will be encountered in moving from authoritative decisions to results in the field and, beyond results, to the kind of society-wide, collective benefits we are seeking in the first place.

The first difficulty is easy to state. At the level of authoritative decisions, public policies are usually loaded with ambiguity, with conflicts that have been glossed over, with uncertainties that have been ignored, with issues that have been left unresolved, and with goals and definitions that are vague or even inconsistent. Yet these matters must be sorted out somehow, or else there can be no action and no result and no collective benefits. So the mere existence of a policy often does not get us very far.

The sorting out will occur within the usually far-flung network of bureaus and agencies, public and private, national and local, judicial and non-judicial, which must be engaged in the production of specific services and collective benefits.

Command and control arrangements in democracies are notoriously loose and unreliable. Economists identify many of the most common problems of command and control within the framework of what they call a principal-agent model (Arrow 1985). Political authorities, the principals, recruit a network of bureaucratic agents to carry out public purposes. They have power over these agents; they can grant or withhold resources, enforce guidelines and standards, and create expectations concerning performance. But the power of the principals is far from unlimited.

Principals face two common problems. The first is that they may be unable to monitor their agents' behaviour. Agents may operate in distant locations. Their actions may be inherently unobservable, as in the case of an interaction between a counselor and a client, or observable only at unreasonable cost and effort; monitors cannot be everywhere all the time. The second is that, even if agents can be closely observed, the principal may be unable to interpret or evaluate the appropriateness of what is observed. If a counselling session is actually observed, how is the observer to know whether the most appropriate protocol is being followed? These problems of monitoring threaten the achievement of a policy's purposes when agents, such as field workers who owe loyalty to a client, have goals or interests which differ in significant ways from those of their principals, the programme managers who are accountable to higher authority.

The frustrations of attempting to monitor agents often lead to progressively more stringent controls over agent behaviour. Unfortunately, the search for more secure controls is usually doomed to failure because problems of monitoring and enforcement cannot effectively or economically be resolved by requiring more paperwork or reports. Agents are resourceful; they can do one thing and appear to be doing something else.

High game, middle game, and low game

Thus far, this chapter has discussed three different kinds of issues affecting public policy formation and execution. Elsewhere, these clusters of issues, as they are encountered in public policy formation and execution, have been characterized as the high game, the middle game, and the low game (Lynn 1982).

Is there a need for government action at all? If so, what is its purpose? These are the questions addressed in the high game. Debate focuses on the correct thing to do, on philosophies of government and the fundamental responsibilities of institutions, on what kind of nation and society we should be, on social justice and basic principles. Intense controversy is likely because values are at stake. Success in the high game requires an understanding of the broad currents of public opinion, of the larger strategic issues of national politics, and of the influence of large power blocks.

To achieve a purpose, what means or instruments should government employ; for instance, which agencies or branches of government should be authorized to act and how should financial, personnel, and other necessary resources be allocated among them? These are questions associated with the middle game. Debate is about results, about fairness, appropriateness, and consequences, about administrative competence, about costs. Sharp controversies and disagreements are likely to break out, but they are likely to be less intense than high game controversies. Reasoning and evidence will have a larger place in the controversy, and compromises will be easier to reach.

Precisely how shall the means or instruments of government action be designed and used? How shall programmes be organized and administered? What procedures, rules, and routines shall be adopted? This is the low game. Low games tend to reflect the concerns of those with operating responsibilities. To a much greater extent than in high and middle games, the answers will reflect the judgements of specialists, professionals, and technicians. Debate and associated controversies are often highly technical and arcane to non-specialists.

What this chapter has illustrated is the range of difficulties that confronts a participant who wishes to be successful in these various games.

Science and policy, games and gamesmanship

The relationship between science and policy, or between knowledge and power, has been treated at length by a number of scholars and scholarly bodies, and its complexities have been amply vented. Yet the subject of the relationship between science and public policy is still often discussed, especially by scientists, as if policy makers could be regarded as constituting a kind of social engineering firm. As members of the firm, policy makers ought, in this view, to know their science and to apply it instrumentally and skillfully to the production of solutions to society's problems.

But, of course, policy making is not engineering, and policy makers are not social engineers. Policy makers are both agents of wider interests, chosen by a variety of democratically-inspired decision rules, and self-interested actors in social activity which is distinctly game-like. Policy makers can be viewed not as engineers and production workers but as participants in numerous games in the manner of a chess master who simultaneously engages several opponents. In fact, things are even more complicated. Policy making, certainly at senior levels of authority, must be conducted by game masters simultaneously engaged in games of chess, backgammon, bridge, and possibly soccer, each with its unique rules, styles of play, and demands on the players. Arrayed against them are opponents inspired by knowledge and conviction and possessing resources and skill.

What can we say about the relationship between science and public policy in this metaphorically more complex world of games and gamesmanship and levels from high to low? Let us cite an example from the USA selected from the pages of the *New York Times*. Scientists sponsored by the US Environmental Protection Agency (EPA) prepared a report concerning the extent of death and disease caused by second-hand tobacco smoke. The report concluded that second-hand cigarette smoke kills 53 000 non-smokers a year. If true, this finding would justify more stringent controls on indoor air pollution. But release of the report by EPA has been delayed indefinitely. Scientists blame the tobacco industry. The tobacco industry blames the anti-smoking bias of the scientists involved. The EPA's director of indoor air quality has thrown up his hands, and there the matter rests in mid-1991.

One suspects that the scientists have the better case, though estimates such as 53 000 non-smoking deaths a year always convey a spurious precision about which scepticism is warranted. But the policy maker or game master in this case must weigh the consequences of taking action in this controversy in the context of the many other controversies and issues that the indoor air quality office, the EPA, and the Bush administration also face. If a wrong move in this game jeopardizes play against powerful tobacco state legislators in other games, bottling up the report by emphasizing its ambiguities may be a sensible move.

The scientists are unlikely to see it this way, of course. They feel abused, and they accuse the Bush administration of a cowardly sell-out to tobacco interests. Such an accusation can be viewed as part of the game, of course. Therein lies the point with which this chapter will end.

Science and society

Societies founded on principles of democratic participation have concluded that no elite, not the wealthy, not the best families, not the warriors, not the ethnically pure, not the priests, not the workers, not the scientists, and not the wise, shall be able to secure any part of its vision or its interests unless it can play the games of policy formation with skill. For any particular elite, this invariably means recognizing a measure of accountability to the rest of us participants, even though the rest of us may lack the qualifications of the elites.

The implication of this view is that science must connect with society, and with its policy making agents, in all manner of ways: through schools, through the popular media, through official processes of governance, through informal networks of communication and influence. The games are numerous and ongoing, the rules are complex, the demands on the attention, patience, and skill of the participants are intense, and the avenues to success are poorly marked, but there is no easier way. The connection between science and policy is nothing less than the connection between science and society itself.

To scientific communities, this approval of gamesmanship often sounds tawdry and unseemly. But consider the report on second-hand cigarette smoke. Someone is playing this game rather well after all. The controversy has made the pages of the *New York Times*, and the scientists aren't the losers. The findings are out there now, and not only can ambitious critics of the administration use this incident to advantage, even the ordinary citizen may be influenced by science. Science is making its connection.

I am hopeful, for example, that my wife is profoundly moved by scientific evidence, duly reported in the *New York Times*, that she is killing not only herself but me, too. She may even agree that there ought to be a policy against jeopardizing the innocent that way. If so, a small, necessary step forward will have been taken.

References

Arrow, K.J. (1985). The economics of agency. In *Principals and agents: the structure of business* (ed. J.W. Pratt and R.J. Zeckhauser), pp. 37–51. Harvard Business School Press, Boston.

Edelman, M. (1988). *Constructing the political spectacle*. The University of Chicago Press.

Hardin, R. (1982). *Collective action*. The Johns Hopkins University Press, Baltimore, MD.

Lynn, L.E., Jr. (1982). Government executives as gamesmen: a metaphor for analysing managerial behavior. *Journal of Policy Analysis of Management*, 1, 482–95.

Lynn, L.E., Jr. (1992) Policy achievement as a collective good: a public choice perspective on managing social programs. In *Public Management Theory* (ed. B. Bozeman). Jossey-Bass, San Francisco, CA. (In press.)

Moe, T.M. (1980). *The organization of interests: incentives and the internal dynamics of political interest groups.* The University of Chicago Press.

Olson, M. (1971). *The logic of collective action: public goods and the theory of groups.* Harvard University Press, Cambridge, MA.

Wilson, J.Q. (1973). *Political organizations.* Basic Books, New York.

3. Drugs, science, and policy: a view from the USA

Robin Room

A series of small case-studies are presented by Edwards (Chapter 1) of the relation between science and policy in the areas of alcohol, tobacco, and illicit drugs. Primarily these case-studies are success stories for science, examples of where science has made what seems to be a positive contribution to policy making and to human progress. Others have also made collections of such case-studies, including cases in which the knowledge transfer was not so successful (Gordis 1991; Room, 1991), and indeed much useful information can be learned from collecting and analysing such case-studies of the interaction between science and policy making.

How the scientific effort may be maximally useful

Using such material, issues in the relation between science and policy can be tackled from a number of perspectives. The following comments are directed at just one of these perspectives: the issue of how scientific effort might best be organized and managed so that it is maximally useful. So attention is here directed at the science side of the science–policy interface. How can it be better organized to be of use to policy? The starting point is the premise that the primary justification for research in these areas is practical; that however much researchers are fascinated by knowledge and the pursuit of new knowledge for its own sake, their work is primarily justified by, and supported for, its potential to better the human condition.

The following comments are based on, and directed particularly at, the experience in the USA, which is a particularly interesting case for study. The USA has a comparatively large investment in alcohol, tobacco, and drug research; probably in absolute terms the largest in the world. It is an ambitious effort, which aims to cover the entire range of scientific work, and tends to assume that it is 'going it alone'. Thus, in discussions of US research priorities for alcohol and drugs, it is never said that the USA should give a lower priority to a particular line of study because it is already strongly covered in some other country.

Planning to include serendipity

It should be stated at the outset that there is clearly no pat answer to the question of how to organize science for the greatest payoff. The kinds of problems we are facing are multi-level, multi-determined and messy, and there is not going to be a quick technical solution available, such as could be provided by a single-minded Manhattan Project or space-agency task force.

It is also clear that any organization of scientific effort has to allow for serendipity. Quite commonly, the practical relevance of research in the long-term is quite different from its original aim. This is not only a matter of the proverbial happy accidents at the laboratory bench, but also of more far-reaching advances. If the success stories offered by Edwards are examined, the relation between science and the policy payoff is of two main sorts. One kind of relation is quite direct: an epidemiologist is commissioned to find an explanation of the increase in lung cancer mortality, or a new treatment is tried out in a controlled trial. The impetus for doing the research may come from the policy process, it may come from the researcher, or it may come from a clinician or some other third party. The research is a process of filling in a gap, of 'normal science', using Kuhn's term (1962)—although it should be borne in mind that the process looks much more 'normal' and routine in retrospect than it did beforehand. The other kind of relation is much less obvious; this is where the science contributes to changing the whole paradigm by which we understand and attempt to do something about a problem. The reinterpretation of the cigarette habit as a form of drug dependence, or the shift from 'alcoholism' to the broader policy frame of 'alcohol problems', or even the realization that drunkenness was responsible for many road traffic deaths, are examples of this kind of shift in the whole governing image (Room 1973) that the society carries of a problem. Behind such shifts in perspective there is often a whole train of research developments which were not aimed at such a shift at all. These are cases in which the research turns out to have a policy significance which may have been invisible, and indeed unimagined, beforehand.

There is considerable variation in the USA in the extent to which there is room for serendipity and for scientists' self-management of research priorities. The form of support for the scientific effort (and not the source of the funds) largely determines this. Thus, researchers working in positions with security of tenure probably have the greatest scope for serendipity and self-management, but there are relatively few alcohol, tobacco, and drug research positions of this sort in the USA. Only a few state positions (primarily in New York State), the intramural programs of the National Institute on Alcohol Abuse and Alcoholism (NIAAA) and National Institute on Drug Abuse (NIDA), and some positions in the Veterans Administration, resemble the kind of stable research institutions that are the backbone of the research effort in such countries as Finland, Norway, and Canada. All other substantial research support which is specifically for alcohol, tobacco, or drug studies is for identified projects funded for a fixed period, at most five years.

The major source of support for 'investigator-initiated research' in the USA is the federal research grants programme, which includes a variety of support mechanisms, but primarily supports specific time-limited research projects or groups of projects. Proposed projects are subjected to a rigorous peer review, but investigators have considerable discretion in how the research is carried out once they are funded. The funding agency maintains somewhat more control over the research in co-operative agreements, a related federal support mechanism. The following comments mostly concern these federal grant programmes, since they are the primary visible research support mechanism.

There are two other major organizational arrangements for research in the USA. One of these is contractual studies, in which a federal, state, or local government agency specifies a study it wants done. The contracts for such research are modelled on the mechanisms for buying paper-clips or an army tank. Typically, such a study is performed by the winner of a competitive bidding process, and has a relatively short, and often extremely compressed, timetable. The research product is defined in terms of pre-specified 'deliverables', typically a series of progress reports and a final report. A great deal of work on alcohol, tobacco, and drug topics is done under such arrangements in the USA. In the short term, the government presumably gets something which is related to what it wanted. But from the point of view of building cumulative traditions of research findings, the arrangement is highly problematic. Those working in the contract economy often have to zig-zag between topics as the exigencies of the market require. Often the contracting agency has the right to edit out potentially embarrassing or politically problematic findings. There is typically no time and little incentive to publish study results in the journal literature, so the work remains buried in contract reports and other documents. Clearing houses and abstracting services typically resist systematically collecting and indexing such reports, finding that the process is expensive and does not enhance their prestige.

The other organizational arrangement for research in the USA is research performed without specific support by faculty members and advanced graduate students in the university system. Perhaps a majority of doctoral dissertations on alcohol, tobacco, and drug matters in the USA are done without drug-specific funding. The substantial upsurge of historical studies on alcohol and other drugs has had very little in the way of such funding. While qualitative social science studies of illicit drug use have received some grant support, most of the qualitative studies of drinking have been produced by scholars whose research is an adjunct to a university teaching career. Studies produced under these conditions are often relatively isolated efforts not firmly rooted in a cumulative literature. Rather little effort has been made by government alcohol and drug agencies to explore the relevance of these studies to their policy missions.

In-house and contract research financed by the tobacco, alcohol, and pharmaceutical industries has not been included in this consideration. Most such research which would be of policy relevance is not publicly available. Even excluding this, it is apparent that the research scene for the drug field in the USA is extraordinarily polymorphous and diverse. It includes a variety of studies potentially relevant to policy making, such as local needs assessments or programme evaluations, that may not even be thought of as 'research' at all. A great deal of the research is pursued outside the framework of any planned or co-ordinated research programme.

This planning and co-ordination can primarily be found in the programmes of the main federal agencies for research support in the field. For alcohol, this primarily means the NIAAA, and for illicit drugs and psychopharmaceuticals, it primarily means the NIDA, although other agencies in the Alcohol, Drug and Mental Health Administration (ADAMHA) also have some involvement. For tobacco, the responsibility is presently split between several agencies, including the Centers for Disease Control, the NIDA, and such National Institute of Health agencies as the National Cancer Institute. That it is federal agencies that have the primary responsibility for a planned and co-ordinated research programme reflects a general consensus in the US polity about the societal location of responsibility for scientific research. Even those who are most sceptical about government are usually willing to give it some responsibility for supporting scientific research, and particularly medical research; and even those most committed to the 'federalist' policy of keeping central government small tend to see scientific research as appropriately more a federal than a state or local government responsibility.

Deficiencies in current research

There are a number of ways in which the organization and content of the major US research programmes in the drug field may be seen to fall short of being of optimum usefulness from the perspective of providing results useful in policy making.

The problems are not only health problems

The programmes are lodged in agencies operating under a health research rubric, while health problems are only part of the whole spectrum of drug-related problems. The American taxpayer is clearly much more willing to pay for research on medical than on social problems, and the relatively large research commitment in alcohol and drug research is clearly linked in the public mind to a definition of the problems as medical in their nature or their consequences.

Despite their health rubric, the NIAAA and NIDA accept responsibility for research on the whole range of alcohol- and drug-related problems. But their portfolio of research grants is heavily biased towards the health side of the problems. An example of a research area that is largely neglected because of this is the area of alcohol and crime. In the USA, which has a larger proportion of its population in penal institutions than any other industrial country, alcohol is heavily implicated in violent crimes, and a large proportion of all arrests are for alcohol-specific crimes. Yet the federal research portfolio typically includes only one or two research projects in this area.

Alcohol, tobacco, and drugs should often be studied within in a common frame

The research programmes for tobacco, alcohol, and other drugs are separately organized often in separate agencies. Populations of users and of dependent persons, however, overlap considerably, and drugs are often used conjointly or in sequence rather than in isolation. The separation of research programmes facilitates funding priorities for research being decided in terms of the cultural politics of drugs rather than in terms of the relative need for and utility of research. It is also an impediment to research on conjoint use of drugs, and to some extent to comparative studies across drugs.

Alcohol and drug problems are largely local issues

The location of research as a federal responsibility tends to deflect research away from the local level. So does the prestige structure of science, which favours knowledge which has the widest degree of generality, and thus tends to regard local particularities as 'noise' rather than as part of the data. But, as the Temperance Movement and the alcoholic beverage industries well know, alcohol and drug problems are ultimately local problems, and much of the burden of handling and of preventing these problems is inevitably local. Research which would inform policy making and practice in this area includes not only a series of case-studies and evaluations of the effects of particular interventions at the local level, but also meta-analyses across these case-studies of community and situational factors which influence the outcome. In the field of research on the prevention of alcohol problems, the process of accumulating such case-studies has begun (Giesbrecht *et al.* 1990), but research traditions in this area at present seem to be stronger in such countries as Canada, the UK, and New Zealand than in the USA.

Policy-oriented research needs quick-response mechanisms

The research grant review mechanism is ill-adapted to studies of 'natural experiments' (studies of what happens when a new law, regulation, or procedure goes into effect). Since policy making is about the planning of change, and yet policy makers are understandably reluctant to experiment with actual changes at the direction and convenience of scientists, studies of natural experiments in change have emerged as a major field of policy-relevant science.

Such studies require data from before the change has occurred, and, where possible, data also from control sites where no change is planned. Typically, however, changes in laws or regulations happen at short notice, while in the grant review cycle about a year elapses between the decision to write a proposal and receiving funding. In the past, federal agencies have sometimes used *ad hoc* solutions within the grants structure, such as supplementing existing grants to collect the 'before' data, but this solution now seems to have been abandoned.

What is needed is a quick-response capability, which could take the form of a service or centres specifically dedicated to studies of natural experiments as they arise. An alternative which has been fruitfully used in studies of the effects of alcohol supply strikes (for example Mäkelä 1980) is the mobilization of tenured research staff to carry out such studies as a short-term diversion. The paucity of such tenured research positions makes this alternative unlikely for the USA.

The research agenda should not be distorted by prestige considerations

The prestige structure of science tends in a number of ways to disfavour research which is potentially directly useful in policy making. The prestige structure has its effects not only in what individual investigators propose to investigate, but also in the behaviour of the granting agencies. Agencies in ADAMHA tend to define the path to greater prestige for the field in terms of how much their research programme resembles that of an idealized NIH— a cancer institute for example, or one on heart disease. Indeed, a proposed reorganization may very soon split NIDA and NIAAA from ADAMHA's prevention and treatment service and support functions and turn them into NIH institutes (ADAW 1991*a*). Prestige for the field and for its institutions is seen as coming primarily from biological research, and, within biological research, from research conducted at the most microscopic levels. Thus, more prestige attaches to a new finding at the molecular or the gene level than to one at the level of a body organ.

A further tilt of the scientific playing-field comes from commitments to including as much as possible of the phenomena of alcohol and drug problems within a disease framework. Apart from the health rubric under which the research is funded, in the case of alcohol this tilt reflects a continuing societal disposition to keep presumptively unproblematic 'normal drinking' by you and me separate from somebody else's 'alcoholic drinking', defined if possible in terms of biological vulnerabilities in the drinker. This disposition helps to fuel the continuing quest for biological markers and causes of addiction. It is also part of the explanation of prestige differentiations within biological research, by which research on the nature and causes of addiction is favoured over research on the pathways connecting alcohol and drug use to biological harm (see Room 1990). Yet understanding these connective pathways may offer much more practical leverage for prevention of harm than finding a pattern of genes that predispose an individual to addiction. As Gordis (1991) has pointed out, discoveries of ways to identify genetic vulnerability raise difficult problems of public policy around insurance company adverse-risk selection; they may be a case of 'good science, but policy enactment not desirable'.

Across all scientific disciplines, more prestige is attached to 'basic' than to 'applied' research. This is as much true in social as in biological or physical sciences—for instance, within sociology, the study of social problems traditionally has a lower prestige ranking than, say, the study of social theory or social structure. Alcohol and drug research starts, then, with the prestige handicap that it is tied to concrete everyday problems, and is supported by the society not out of a commitment to prestigious science but on the premise that it will come up with practical answers. There is a tendency for alcohol and drug research institutions to try to counter this handicap by identifying with and buying into whatever is perceived as the 'cutting edge' of basic science. In medically-oriented research, following the pattern of the last 200 years, this still tends to mean tying into new machines for measurement at ever more microscopic levels—at present, such techniques as magnetic resonance imaging and positron emission tomography. In scientists' discussions of research priorities for alcohol and drug agencies, this move away from applied research and towards the lure of new measurement techniques is expressed in terms of a counterposition of 'research needs and opportunities'. There are thousands of research needs, the argument goes, and such needs are always present. But what are the research *opportunities*, where the really exciting science can be done? Time after time, the answer tends to be in terms of the exploitation of new measurement technologies—which, of course, is a rather odd way to define what is basic about 'basic science'.

Conclusion

The above discussion has concentrated on identifying some ways in which the research effort in the USA is less than optimally attuned to providing findings useful in policy making and practice, and has left any suggestions for reform implicit. It has entirely omitted discussing the other side of the science–policy interface, where the disjunctions are often severe. The policy process in the USA too often ignores inconvenient science, and on occasion even tries to suppress it.

Today the USA stands at a turning-point in the relation between science and policy and practice. It seems likely that the NIAAA and NIDA will be split off from the service-oriented offices, the Office of Substance Abuse Prevention (OSAP) and the Office of Treatment Improvement (OTI), which will remain in a renamed Alcohol, Drug and Mental Health Services Administration. This provides an opportunity for rethinking the organizational relationship between science and policy. But unless the opportunity is seized creatively, the result of the split is likely to be a further attenuation of the relation between the scientific effort and practical affairs. A summary of the legislation introduced to formalize the change concludes that 'researchers and service providers share a common goal, but they speak a different language and thrive in different professional cultures. The climate at ADAMHA has been competitive rather than collaborative' (ADAW 1991*a*). The director of a Massachusetts treatment service agency put it less diplomatically: 'Sometimes, researchers and clinicians act and talk like they are from other planets. Clinicians feel that researchers engage in a veritable vocabulary of denigration and researchers perceive clinicians as being resistant to research and change. In the proposed new structure, issues of turf, control, and disruption of clinical programs will be minimized' (ADAW 1991*b*).

Acknowledgement

Preparation of this chapter was supported by a National Alcohol Research Center grant (AA 05595) from the US National Institute on Alcohol Abuse and Alcoholism to the Alcohol Research Group, Medical Research Institute of San Francisco.

References

ADAW (1991*a*). Sullivan proposes ADAMHA realignment; institutes to go to NIH. *Alcoholism and Drug Abuse Week*, 3, No. 23, June 19, pp. 1–2.

ADAW (1991*b*). House and senate both take up ADAMHA reorganization. *Alcoholism and Drug Abuse Week*, 3, No. 24, June 26, pp. 1–2.

Giesbrecht, N., Conley, P., Denniston, R., Gliksman, L., Holder, H., Pederson, A., Room, R., and Shain, M., eds. (1990). *Research, action and the community: experiences in the prevention of alcohol and other drug problems*. Office of Substance Abuse Prevention, DHHS Publication No. (ADM) 89–1651, Rockville, MD.

Gordis, E. (1991). From science to public policy: an uncertain road. *Journal of Studies on Alcohol*, 52, 101–9.

Kuhn, T.S. (1962). *The structure of scientific revolutions*, University of Chicago Press.

Mäkelä, K. (1980). Differential effects of restricting the supply of alcohol: studies of a strike in Finnish liquor stores. *Journal of Drug Issues*, 10, 131–44.

Room, R. (1973). Governing images and the prevention of alcohol problems. *Preventive Medicine*, 3, 11–23.

Room, R. (1990) A sociologist looks at biological alcohol research. Paper presented at a session, *Biological and social approaches to alcohol studies: what do we need from each other?*, jointly sponsored by the International Society for Biological Research on Alcohol and the Kettil Bruun Society for Social and Epidemiological Research on Alcohol, Toronto, June 17.

Room, R. (1991) Social science research and alcohol policy making. In *Alcohol: the development of sociological perspectives on use and abuse* (ed. P. Roman), pp. 315–39. Rutgers Center for Alcohol Studies, New Brunswick.

Discussion
Games policy makers play

Chaired by Robin Murray (UK)

Chairman: Dr Kleber, you occupy the middle ground in the USA, in the sense that you are being bombarded with excellent advice from scientists of such quality that you can not properly ignore them, and yet too little seems to happen and governments all too often plough on with damaging policies. I fail to understand that situation.

Dr Howard Kleber (USA): Fortunately, we can find reputable scientists who will take totally opposite points of view, and it is only a question then of to which scientist one wants to listen. For example, one distinguished scientist may tell us of the importance of coercion in terms of getting people into treatment, while other scientists may say that coercion is immoral, does not work, and it then becomes a question of which scientist one chooses to believe. It is like the testimony in criminal cases by psychiatrists as to whether the defendant was insane or not at the time he committed the crime. It is a poor defence attorney that cannot find a reputable psychiatrist to state that his client was insane, and it is a poor prosecutor who cannot find a similarly authoritative expert to say that the defendant was as sane as the judge when he committed the heinous crime. One of the things I have learned about being in government is that there are competing policies, and here I thought Larry Lynn's explanation was perfect in terms of the competing forces, the differing points of view. There is no one right thing to do, everything gets weighed off, action on one bill may cost you certain senators who you need on a more important bill.

Chairman: I wonder if I may come to Dr Jaffe who occupied a similar position within the US government. Is it correct that if you do not want to do anything you can rely on the disunity of the scientists, and you do not have to do anything because they destroy their own case?

Dr Jerome Jaffe (USA): I tend to agree with Dr Kleber, and in general there is this diversity in the scientific community. There are occasions, however, when the preponderance of opinion is so overwhelming that the only way you can put aside the scientific input is by recognizing that it is only one kind of move in a complex set of games. You are always playing more than one game at a time, and the difficulty is that there is no great correlation between scientific skill, and the kind of public maturity that it takes to recognize that there is more than one game to play. So, scientists on a particular issue may go away pouting that you did not believe them, they are unhappy about the way you are interpreting the rules of the game, because they refuse to recognize that there are multiple games. It is a good paradigm, it is a good way of recognizing what goes on in public policy.

Dr John Saunders (Australia): The British government in recent years has placed rather less weight on expert scientific opinion. Have there been phases in which governments in North America have put more or less weight on the opinion of scientific experts?

Dr Laurence Lynn (USA): It could be that the more direct instrumental uses of science occur during periods when we are dealing either with crises or with periods of creativity—when it seems a good time to try things out, a time to listen to voices, when different experiments can be afforded. Extremely difficult circumstances for the use of expert advice or rationalized solutions to problems are when people perceive that resources are scarce and when everything is in competition with everything else.

Dr Charles Kaplan (The Netherlands): The resources may grow but the mechanism of control may also grow, rewarding normal and ordinary work, while discouraging scientific revolutions. The European approach has been to find a moderate formula. In such conditions, science can develop in the way that Huxley said, as nothing but trained and organized commonsense. Commonsense is based on a pragmatic attitude and extremes of any kind are anathema to the European; drug policies coming from both America and Asia seem extreme and fundamentally inapplicable to European conditions. Hard scientific discriminations need to be reformulated about illegal drugs and legal alcohol: we are in a state at present where we permit and socially control some psychoactive substances while criminalizing others, without scientifically knowing quite why. The current popularity in epidemiological and psychiatric circles of ethnography in this field illustrates that both research and training must begin with first-hand experience of drug, alcohol, and social patterns in living communities.

Dr Robin Room (USA): On the general point of the multiple games in which the political process is playing, there are limits on those games and those limits vary from one culture to another. There are limits in any particular culture on what it is appropriate for a politician to be pushing: he or she cannot push beyond a certain point on something that is defined as patriotic. It has been difficult, for instance, for any politician in the USA to push against the tide of the drug war, no matter what the science is showing.

To give one example of this cultural difference issue—Joseph Gusfield is a famous sociologist in the USA who wrote a book called *Symbolic Crusade* about symbolic politics, about how much of the political process is occupied with symbolism rather than with practical matters. I wondered why he was not famous in Scandinavia, where a lot of attention is usually given to American sociologists. My conclusion in the end was that the political process was defined in different terms in Scandinavia, where, far more than in the USA, when they make a law they mean what it says. Conversely, you can find societies where the law means even less of what it says; I remember the former Minister of Health from Panama reporting at a WHO meeting on the laws on alcohol and drugs in Central American countries, and the legislature had been quite happy to pass the laws but there was no particular intent that they were going to be enforced.

We are dealing with great differences from one culture to another in how the political process is defined. A society that sees legislation as a more pragmatic activity will tie the hands of the politicians a little more about the relationship to the scientific findings.

Chairman: As a geneticist one of the things I feel curious about is the credence given in the USA to the increasing stridency of claims that alcoholism is a genetic disease, culminating recently in the publication of a report which said that the gene for alcoholism was the D2 receptor gene of the long arm of chromosome 11. What is the impact of such shifts in scientific fashion on the policy makers? Policy makers struggling to come to terms with making decisions on alcoholism suddenly read in the *New York Times* that there is a single gene for alcoholism, and then subsequently they read a few months later that this was only true for a few weeks.

Unidentified speaker: It is important in our discussions of the science policy connection, to look at it as a two directional process. We have been talking about how science gets into policy, but it is equally important to understand that policy already may be shaping the way in which science is made, and we have to understand that process.

The making of science is a socially organized process, it is dependent upon availability of resources. The very knowledge that is generated and will be available for policy makers, at any given point in time, has already been shaped, its availability has been determined already to a large extent by policy, and we have certainly had this experience in the USA. We remember the time of the Reagan administration when the word 'social research' was anathema, and resources for that kind of work were limited. We see now another kind of development, in which biological research is taking a large part of the resources available for enquiry. Now again if we think about policy makers standing in a position to appraise the knowledge that we as scientists have made available to them, and we have come through a period in which resources for social enquiry have been limited and sources for biological enquiry have been extended, then the kind of knowledge, the balance, the diversity, the comprehensiveness of knowledge that is available is in some sense distorted. That raises the question of the values of scientists entering into the process. Scientists have a responsibility to see that the full range of enquiry is adequately supported.

Dr Griffith Edwards (UK): The analysis which sees policy making as a system of multiple games is intriguing, but carries the danger of our accepting the inference that politicians are always clever and sophisticated fellows balancing one consideration against another, while scientists are *ingenues* who lack the maturity to understand the complexities of the adult world. Worse still, and if we are to believe Dr Kleber, in this clever policy game the scientist is often not much more than a hired puppet who will say 'yes' for one puppet master and 'no' for another. Such pessimism seems to me to be unjustified. It is self-evident that politics is about multiple trade-offs, but within the context of that evidently complex process it is the job of the scientific community fearlessly, resolutely, and persistently to present the truth as best it perceives that truth, with due admission also of ignorance. More daringly still (and with consequently large possibilities for arrogance and betrayal), science is not just about increasing the sum of knowledge but is also concerned with the cherishing and transmission of certain very precious values relating to rationality, integrity, daring to question, and not being bribable. Science does not win its arguments in a day, its findings may often be awkward, but Galileo is more memorable than the papal policy makers who forced his recantation. 'E pur si muove'—but it does move.

4. Science policy from a cancer research setting

Sir Walter Bodmer

Grand policies have a danger of being inflexibe. I also have doubts about what science policy studies can tell us. Can the individual research manager really make much use of citation analysis? Do we not all really know how peer review and the judgement of excellence works, and what remarkable consensus there usually is in grant review committees or appointment boards? Because of these reservations, the best title for this chapter might be 'A personal approach to aspects of science policy in the medical field, with special reference to cancer research and a cancer research charity'.

The Imperial Cancer Research Fund Health Behaviour Unit

The Imperial Cancer Research Fund (ICRF) decided to establish a Health Behaviour Unit in the cancer field at the Maudsley Hospital, Denmark Hill, London, UK, in association with the Addiction Research Unit, with Michael Russell as honorary director. What were the origins of this?

Epidemiological evidence shows that cancer is caused largely by environmental factors and so, in principle, perhaps 80–90 per cent could be prevented if we knew what these factors were and how to manipulate them. However, the practice is far more difficult than the principle.

Cigarette smoking is the one clearly identifiable cause of cancer, and is responsible for about 30 per cent of all cancers in the UK. Thus, as a cancer research organization, placing prevention naturally as the first priority, the ICRF has to ask itself continually what can most profitably be done about cigarette smoking and cancer.

The ICRF has been involved with Richard Doll and Richard Peto and others in pioneering studies on the epidemiology of the association between cigarette smoking and lung and other cancers, and in a continuing monitoring of changes in smoking patterns in the UK and elsewhere and their associations with cancer incidence. We know that there are many harmful chemicals in cigarette smoke which can both initiate cancers and promote them once they are initiated. Further studies to provide more detail about this would not be good value for money. The clear answer was to do research on how to stop people from smoking once they have started, and how to stop them from starting. This is a problem of health education and its associated research, a problem in behaviour analysis and manipulation: that is why the ICRF established collaboration with the Maudsley Hospital, with its well-established, outstanding expertise in research into smoking addiction, the role of nicotine, and approaches to testing different ways of getting across the message about stopping smoking.

There are, of course, other behavioural problems: a major part of the remaining environmental factors must lie with the diet, even though we do not know yet what these factors are. Therefore, understanding what influences people's diet and how to control these influences is another important aspect of health behaviour research for cancer prevention. Secondary prevention—namely screening to detect a cancer at an early stage, when it can still be cured—is also important. What are the factors that motivate a woman to come forward for cervical or breast cancer screening? Why is the response so socio-economically and educationally biased? This is comparable with the remarkable inverse correlation between social class and level of cigarette smoking, no doubt a major contributor to the well-known social inequalities in heath.

This new research unit will take advantage of the wide range of the research activities of the ICRF overall, and will determine where other features of the ICRF's work might be able to contribute to health behaviour research, and vice-versa.

The Imperial Cancer Research Fund

What is the Imperial Cancer Research Fund, and how does it work? It is a cancer research charity founded in 1902, the oldest in Europe and one of the oldest in the world (Bodmer, 1988*a*, 1990*a*). Since its inception it has adhered to the principle of supporting its own work, first in central laboratories and later in extra-mural laboratories and units placed in universities, medical schools, and hospitals. It does not have a grant-giving programme. It is responsible for about one third of all cancer research in the UK. Its policy of supporting its own activities means that it can make long-term commitments to a wide range of research areas, from the most fundamental to the most applied clinical and epidemiological research, and that it can also establish a career structure for all categories of staff, including those with advanced scientific and medical qualifications.

The ICRF's units in universities are like those of the Medical Research Council (MRC). They are mostly in a clinical setting, often based around an endowed chair in clinical oncology. These activities are tripartite collaborations between the ICRF, the National Health Service (NHS), and a medical school, and they take advantage of the medical school and NHS setting, while remaining part of the overall ICRF activity.

The formal ruling body of the ICRF is its Council, which acts as trustee of the charity and provides a check on the chief executive and senior management of the ICRF who run its activities on a day-to-day basis. There is a loose analogy with the board of a company, with a non-executive chairman and non-executive members of the board and executive directors, including the chief executive.

The different components of the ICRF function as an organic whole, contributing to an overall interrelated research programme. This gives advantages of scale, providing a wide range of inter-disciplinary activities within one organization, and enables the efficient provision of central research support resources for both clinical and laboratory work.

Though prevention and treatment of cancer are the goals of the ICRF, the research is very broad-based. The need to support basic research is as important for a mission-oriented cancer research organization as it is for the more broadly-based MRC. It continually has to seek an appropriate balance between basic research and applied clinical and epidemiological studies on treatment and prevention. As basic understanding advances, providing many leads to potential new approaches for prevention, diagnosis, and treatment, the balance between basic and applied work will need to change. It would be as grave a mistake now to miss a real opportunity for practical application of basic research from the laboratory as it would have been when the ICRF began to focus on clinical activities, thereby ignoring the need for fundamental advances at a time when virtually nothing was known about the fundamental nature of cancer.

The balance is delicate: over-enthusiastic support of potential new applications must be avoided, but so must the equivalent of supporting a major development of iron lungs for the treatment of poliomyelitis, with vaccination just around the corner.

The balance of basic and applied research is particularly reflected in the need to find the right way to interface laboratory with clinical and epidemiological studies. Special task forces involving representatives of all relevant areas of work can be helpful. Recently, the ICRF has set up one of these for dietary studies. Clinical research fellowships bring young, bright, and enthusiastic medically qualified people into a high-quality laboratory research environment, and this can be valuable in bridging the laboratory–clinic interface.

Excellence is the key and must be supported at all costs, with rigorous evaluation by peer review of individual scientific groups. Select the right person and let him or her get on with it. He or she may not even believe what he or she is doing is relevant to cancer, but so long as the scientific management believes it is right, that does not matter. I have never met a scientist, however basic his or her work, who is not delighted to see an application, and who does not then get involved to some extent in promoting that application. There is no telling nowadays when the apparently most fundamental piece of work will suddenly become relevant—a DNA binding transcription factor, or a gene critical for the control of cell division from yeast through to mammals may be the latest candidate for an oncogene—one of the key steps in the development of a cancer.

Working for a charity is, on the whole, no different from working for any research organization, but it does give a most valuable sense of purpose. Many of the ICRF's scientists take some part in fundraising, through explaining their work to the public who donate money, and they find this rewarding and stimulating.

Each year the ICRF produces a Forward Plan and tries to look ahead to new opportunities. But how does the ICRF decide what areas to work in and to support? In the basic areas it is not a major problem—aiming for excellence, however fundamental the work, will surely pay off. The best work on transport across bacterial membranes, how bacteria repair their DNA, or how a yeast cell divides, will soon find their application in the problem of cancer, as will fundamental studies on sex determination or on the earliest stages of mammalian differentiation and development. The ICRF looks for and assesses new prospects for applications in the prevention and treatment of cancer as a function of the importance of a disease in terms of its mortality and morbidity incidence. But we only proceed if there is a clear route to a successful outcome based on current research approaches. It is no good throwing money, for example, at more dietary case control studies if these will not yield new answers as to what to do about the dietary control of cancer. What are needed are either new ideas that come from good studies of mechanisms, or a practical attempt at prevention on a large scale—but that is extremely expensive and so needs to be very carefully considered. Of course, fashions determine areas of work, and there is a natural tendency to grow from the interests of the leading scientists in the institution, from the director downwards.

Always remember that the future is, to a large extent, unpredictable and hence the problem of grand policies: they will probably need to be changed, at the current pace of research development, every six months or so. How would I have predicted in my own career that work on incompatibility in primroses would contribute to an interest in the HLA system used for tissue typing to match individuals for transplantation (and now known to be a key factor in controlling susceptibility to many autoimmune diseases), and thence to studies on the immune response to cancer through evidence that comes from abnormalities in the expression of the HLA determinants on cancers?

New opportunities in medical research: the Human Genome Project

Revolutionary new opportunities in medical research in general, and cancer research in particular, have become possible through recent advances in the fundamental understanding of cellular functions and from the technical developments that accompany them, particularly the development of recombinant

DNA techniques—the genetic engineering revolution—together with gene cloning, cell biology, manipulation of cells in culture, and production of monoclonal antibodies. These advances mean that, with increased resources, it is now easier to do valuable work, especially with a strategetic aim, than could have been imagined to be the case 10 or 15 years ago.

A major particular aspect of this revolution is the Human Genome Project, whose aim is to catalogue all the human genes and their DNA sequences, and to identify their arrangement along the chromosomes. This fundamental information is providing, and will increasingly provide, the basis for our understanding of the fundamentals of most diseases, and in particular has made major contributions already to understanding the fundamental genetic basis of cancer (Bodmer, 1988*b*, 1990*b*, 1990*c*). That is why, as a cancer research organization, the ICRF has a major commitment to the Human Genome Project and to providing the resources that allow genes to be mapped and sequenced, and to identifying through this the genetic components of essentially any aspect of human variation. The ICRF, of course, is particularly concerned with specifically inherited susceptibility to cancer and the identification of the genetic changes that take place as the cancer cell itself evolves.

These studies on the human genome will surely make major contributions to the understanding of many aspects of human behaviour, in particular as they relate to mental disease and to problems of addiction, whether to alcohol, smoking, or other drugs. The major problem is environmental control, whatever a person's genetic make-up. But if there are, as we believe, differences, for example in addictability to nicotine, then these will influence the ease with which someone can give up cigarette smoking. And these differences should be identifiable at the genetic level: perhaps they are connected with differences in the way that cigarette smokers metabolize, or in the nature of the nicotinic acid receptors, or even in more subtle but perhaps genetically influenced behavioural differences. There clearly are genetic components to alcoholism, some of them perhaps simply related to metabolic differences, and some of these are known to vary in a major way between population groups, such as Orientals and Caucasians. In this way, the fundamental laboratory studies may soon be applied to the practical problems of understanding at least some aspects of addiction.

In addition, molecular biology can define new receptors and identify heterogeneity in different tissues. Through this it provides the basis for setting up assays to look, in a classical pharmacologist's way, for chemicals that block functions which may help control or counteract addiction in specific ways.

Centres of excellence and scientific management

How can we ensure the highest quality of research that brings together effectively those, for example, at the forefront of basic genetic studies, with those interested in the applications, whether to addiction, or cancer prevention, or the control of heart and mental disease?

There are two essential components. The first, as already emphasized, is the support of excellence. Choose the best scientists in the fields that seem to be most relevant, support them to the hilt, encourage them to collaborate with each other, but leave them to get on with it. Only from time to time monitor rigorously the quality of their work and its progress, and unhesitatingly adjust the level of support to match that judgement.

The second factor is to bring scientists together in centres of excellence. So much of the work at the forefront of modern medical research is interdisciplinary and requires a variety of technologies, from molecular biology and the study of the structure of proteins, all the way to epidemiological and clinical studies, including the contribution of the psychologists and social scientists. The centre of excellence can create appropriate mixtures of people with these different disciplines, provide them with central resources and so encourage the best possible interaction. This can, of course, be achieved in a free-standing research institute. But we have a strong tradition in this country of outstandingly good research work in universities, which brings research together with the teaching which is the ultimate source of the excellent scientists. Thus, it is important to find the right mechanisms for establishing outstanding research groups in universities without overly encumbering them with the problems of university administration and teaching. Too much can be made of the research and teaching link. Of course, an enthusiasm for one's subject, and a scholarly approach and understanding of what is going on at the forefront are needed for good teaching, but not every good teacher needs to be a world-leading researcher at the forefront of his or her subject.

The establishment of research institutes within universities provides one very good solution to this problem. A model is the Institute of Molecular Medicine established by Sir David Weatherall in Oxford, UK. This brings together outstanding research groups, each with some contact with a university department, but loosely connected to it. The Institute is embedded within the university and the medical school and enables a variety of different organizations, including the ICRF, to take part in its activities. This is a model for universities to follow, but there are two provisos. The first is that the quality of the research and monitoring of the resources available to different groups must be as rigorous in this university setting as it is in a free-standing research institute. The second is that the administrative support provided by the university should be comparable to that which can be obtained at the highest level in the support of larger research institutes and organizations, such as the Research Councils and the ICRF and other major medical research charities.

The effective management of scientific research is essential in order to maximize productivity and potential benefits. Management means the provision of support, resources, and an organization, as has been emphasized, that enables outstanding scientists to realize their potential. Management is not to be confused with direction. Good management supports, stimulates, and brings people together, to achieve jointly what they could not do separately, while at the same time controlling the resources so that the best get the most. A university department is not an ideal, or even an adequate, basis in general for acquiring the skills of good scientific management. That is why the universities need to develop procedures for effective research management of organizations such as the Institute for Molecular Medicine.

Research managers should be active scientists. By no means all good scientists can be good managers, but there is no necessary negative correlation between being good at science and being good at management. An active, highly regarded research scientist in a managerial position can provide a model to his or her peers, and remains in touch with the research for which they are responsible. Setting scientific administrators apart in headquarters, such as the UK research councils in Swindon, is not a recipe for good management of science. It is all too easy in the rarefied atmosphere of a somewhat remote head office to float away from the realities of the day-to-day problems of the scientific laboratory.

UK medical research support

There are four major sources of support for medical research and development in the UK. The first is the pharmaceutical industry which spends, at current prices, about £950 million per year, but of which probably no more than a quarter reflects the sort of research that is done in an academic setting. The major government support for such research is from the MRC, which spends about £200 million per year. However, almost uniquely in the UK, an approximately equal amount is provided by the totally private sector, namely the medical research charities. The largest of these are the ICRF, the Cancer Research Campaign, the Wellcome Trust (whose money comes from investment in the Wellcome Foundation and not from normal charitable fundraising activity), and the British Heart Foundation. Lastly, there is support, although still very limited, from the Department of Health. The total in the academically related areas is about £700 million per year, of which the MRC and the medical research charities each provide about 30 per cent.

The medical research charities thus play a major role in the support of medical research, in particular providing a great deal of support within universities. They are able to operate, as is the ICRF, with considerable independence and flexibility in a way that is complementary to the MRC, and absolutely critical for the medical research activities of the UK.

The MRC has, of course, a long tradition of supporting excellent work, including the world-famous Laboratory for Molecular Biology in Cambridge from whence so many discoveries fundamental to the modern medical research revolution have come. Nevertheless, one might ask the question 'Who reviews the MRC itself?'.

There is an increasing amount of collaboration within Europe that involves the MRC and the medical research charities through, in particular, European

Community support. This generates welcome collaboration with our European colleagues, but we must watch carefully the potentially heavy hand of Brussels bureaucracy. Government departments generally determine the membership of European Community committees, including those in science, and it is important that this membership is made up largely of leading active scientists, certainly with experience of management, rather than government scientific administrators. This is the way, it seems, that our European partners operate and we must match them in quality and influence.

There has, in recent years, been much concern about the adequacy of the overall level of support for scientific research including, in particular, medical research. The relative decline of Government support, however, in the medical field has, at least to some extent, been matched by the resilience of the private sector charitable support. A fundamental problem that has developed is that too many people are being supported inadequately by the available sources of support, especially through the Research Councils. It is essential to support scientists adequately, both in terms of salary and, more especially, in terms of the resources available for their research. Only when extra money is available to support new people at the same level that the ICRF is accustomed to would it consider expanding. It is worrying that this has not been the Research Councils' policy. The support per individual, both in terms of salary and research resources, has gradually been eroded to such an extent that it becomes increasingly hard to attract good young people, for example, back from the USA to a position in academic research in the UK. It is, however, difficult to make the case for increasing salaries and the support per individual. It would have been much better to maintain an adequate level of support for fewer people and then argue the case for more in terms of the need for more science to be done at that level.

It is important to find the right mechanism for the different organizations supporting medical research in any given area to work together. The cancer field provides a very good model in the UK Committee for the Co-ordination of Cancer Research. This brings together the MRC, the Departments of Health and the major medical research charities in a forum in which they discuss problems of common interest and which generates many collaborative studies, especially clinical trials, without imposing any undesired constraints on the individual constituent bodies. This is turning out to be the major forum for discussion of cancer prevention and treatment in general, and is proving particularly useful in the interface between academic clinical research and the sort of research—health services research—that is needed on an operational basis for the NHS itself.

Clinical research, as already mentioned, involves an interaction with the NHS, which has traditionally been supportive to research. But the mechanism for costing the component supported by the MRC and by the charities needs to be worked out, so that basic clinical costs are not covered under the guise of research. The new NHS arrangements provide particular challenges for these interactions, namely to ensure that the flow of patients into high quality clinical research and teaching establishments is maintained, for without this there can be no good clinical research. Funding mechanisms that to some extent match external sources of refereed support for a medical school with central Department of Health funding have been proposed.

Another problem arises as the products of research are applied to clinical services or diagnosis and treatment, when there is a gradual transition from research to service. This must be properly managed to anticipate the provision of NHS resources, and to avoid again the use of research for the support of a service which should be provided by the NHS.

An area that is particularly relevant to prevention, and surely must be important to the problems of addiction control, is research involving the general practitioner. As Dennis Pereira-Gray has pointed out, there is a need to find a mechanism for involving general practitioner (GP) practices in research in much the same way as is now the case for hospital medicine. GPs can be at the forefront of appropriate interventions and, apart from contributing to investigations on the origins of disease, they provide a base for trials of different approaches to primary disease prevention (Pereira-Gray (1991)). That is the reason why, in addition to the Health Behaviour Unit, the ICRF supports a General Practice Research Group under Godfrey Fowler in Oxford.

Clinical trials often need to be done on a very large scale to obtain significant results for small differences that may, for a common disease, affect large numbers of individuals. These trials can be very expensive to implement and manage, and must be done in close co-operation with, and often directly within, the NHS. Intervention trials for disease prevention and control, of a sort which must surely be relevant to problems of addiction, may be particularly difficult to plan and support. Close collaboration may be needed not only between the relevant research groups and the NHS, but also, no doubt, with the relevant social services.

Another area in which prevention trials may be particularly important is in the schools. Certainly, this is where cigarette addiction starts and where, if we are to influence the frequency with which people start to smoke, we must be most active.

Public understanding of science

The unfortunate and striking inverse correlation has already been noted between socio-economic levels, and especially educational background, and the incidence of cigarette smoking. There can be no doubt that for health messages to be received and implemented it is essential to have an appropriately educated and scientifically literate population. Public understanding of science is important for a variety of reasons, of which the ability to respond to health messages and advice, and to have some assessment of comparative risks and an understanding of the numbers which lie behind them, are amongst the most important components. The most fundamental underpinning of public understanding of science is an adequate level of science education in the schools (Bodmer, 1986, 1988b). This surely must be the highest of all priorities for any government, anywhere. For without this not only do we not have a public that can take advantage of health messages, and indeed any new scientific discoveries that impact on them, but we will not have the scientists who can continue to push forward the frontiers for the greater benefits of humankind in the future.

In terms of current activity, it is particularly important that the scientists and the medical profession are prepared to speak out and explain their science to the public. This has not been done enough in the past, and now with the Committee on the Public Understanding of Science, sponsored by the Royal Society, The British Association for the Advancement of Science, and the Royal Institution, there is support at the highest level amongst scientific institutions in the UK for scientists to involve themselves in promoting the public understanding of science. Only in this way will scientists be able to allay public concerns about the availability of genetic knowledge of susceptibility to disease. This knowledge will surely be applied in the future to achieve more effective disease prevention, and for that to happen co-operation and understanding from the public at large are essential.

The social sciences

Many of the areas of research involving the problems of addiction must bring together medical research, including epidemiology, with work in the social sciences. The social sciences are the most difficult of all, because they put the complex problems of human society on top of those of biology, which in turn are on top of chemistry, and beneath that, underpinning all, comes the science of physics. Nevertheless, the social sciences must be approached with the same scientific rigour as any of the other sciences. The difficulty that the social sciences face in being accepted as a sister science by the broad community of natural scientists is that they provide an even greater difficulty for analytical approaches in such a complex area than the biological sciences, even at the population level. The prejudices against the social sciences must be overcome. Perhaps the social sciences will be transformed by an influx of scientists from other areas, such as modern biology was in the development of molecular biology by an influx of physicists and chemists. In the case of the social sciences it is perhaps the epidemiologists, population biologists, behavioural scientists, and psychologists, who will migrate to the social sciences and apply some of their techniques in new ways to help the development of the social sciences, just as biology was helped by the physical sciences. Perhaps that integration of the social sciences with medical and biological research is the ultimate challenge for a science policy.

References

Bodmer, W. (1986). The public understanding of science. The Bernal Lecture, *The Royal Society*. Given on 15 October 1986.

Bodmer, W. (1988*a*). Epilogue—the recent past, present, and future. In *A history of the Imperial Cancer Research Fund 1902–1986*. (ed. Joan Austoker), pp. 337–62. Wellcome Unit for the History of Medicine, Oxford University Press.

Bodmer, W. (1988*b*). *Genes and atoms for health and prosperity—presidential address*. British Association for the Advancement of Science. Science and the public. Sept/Oct., pp. 3–8, British Association.

Bodmer, W. (1990*a*). The Imperial Cancer Research Fund in the 1980s *Postgraduate Medical Journal*, **66**(1), S18–22.

Bodmer, W. (1990*b*). The social and political implications of the mapping of the human genome. *Science in Parliament*, **47**(2), 87–93.

Bodmer, W. (1990*c*). Genetic sequences. Fifteenth Fisher Memorial Lecture. *Proceedings of the Royal Society of London, series B*, **241**, 85–92.

Pereira Gray, D. (1991). Research in general practice: law of inverse opportunity. *British Medical Journal*, **302**, 1380–2.

These references also provide general background information.

5. Beyond the invisible college: a science policy analysis of alcohol and drug research

Thomas F. Babor

Early in the seventeenth century, a small group of English scientists, mathematicians, and philosophers began to meet near Oxford University to exchange ideas about astronomy and geometry. Another group, which had begun their weekly meetings in a less academic setting, called themselves the 'Invisible College'. When they eventually merged, these informal groups developed into the world's most influential scientific organization, the Royal Society of London for the Promotion of Natural Knowledge (Bronowski and Mazlish 1986).

The men who founded the Royal Society felt themselves to be part of a broader social movement, a society of scientists exploring the world by means of the modern scientific method. Despite the emergence of formal organizational structures for the promotion of scientific activities, the invisible college did not disappear. Communication, collaboration, and inspiration continued to develop on an informal basis, along with the creation of journals and societies. Since the founding of the Royal Society in 1660, the complementarity between formal and informal structures has been an important indicator of the development of scientific disciplines and the emergence of multidisciplinary areas of knowledge.

The main part of this chapter describes the development of one such area of knowledge, known variously as alcohol and drug studies, alcohology, and addictionology, from its humble beginnings in isolated laboratories in different parts of the world. It focuses on the emergence of an invisible college and the evolution of a scientific infrastructure devoted to the production of knowledge about the use of psychoactive substances. The final part of this chapter discusses how addictions research can be guided by a science policy that will serve the best interests of researchers and society.

Changing times

Over the past century the role of the scientist and the conduct of scientific research have changed dramatically. The nineteenth century stereotype of the basic researcher labouring independently in an isolated laboratory in the search for pure truth bears little resemblance to the current style of science. The emerging image of science is characterized by the mission-oriented multidisciplinary collaborative research team, working harmoniously toward the solution of specific medical and societal problems. While this image may also constitute a stereotype, there is increasing evidence that science has indeed become a mission-oriented, collaborative enterprise. This is reflected in both the trend toward multi-authored scientific publications and the increasing proportion of scientists working in research institutes and organizations. Between 1900 and 1959, for example, the number of multi-authored papers published in biological and chemical journals increased from 25 per cent to 83 per cent (Clarke 1964). Similar observations about the social nature of scientific research have been made with reference to the growth of specialized research organizations (Peltz and Andrews 1976; Committee on Promoting Research Collaboration 1990). Another feature of modern science is its exponential growth. As De Solla Price (1963) has documented, since the end of the Second World War there has been a dramatic increase in the quantity, quality, and influence of almost all areas of science. By 1992, over 12 000 university-related and other non-profit research organizations were operating on a permanent basis in the USA and Canada alone (Hill 1992).

Nowhere are these trends toward collaborative investigation and exponential growth more apparent than in the area of alcohol and drug research. The recognition of addiction as a multidisciplinary problem dates from the late nineteenth century. It is perhaps the first public health problem to have been approached from a holistic perspective (Keller 1975). Long before national and provincial governments began supporting clinical research centres, addiction researchers had established several interdisciplinary, interprofessional institutes to provide a setting for basic and applied research.

The prototypes of this model were the Addiction Research Center, established in Lexington, Kentucky, USA in 1935, to investigate narcotic addiction; the Center of Alcohol Studies, first established at Yale University in 1940 and later moved to its present location at Rutgers University, New Brunswick, New Jersey, USA; and the Addiction Research Foundation established in Ontario, Canada in 1949. The Center of Alcohol Studies was both multidisciplinary and interdisciplinary. From the beginning, its staff included a sociologist, an educator, a lawyer, and a biometrician, all having close ties to physicians, psychologists, and psychiatrists (Keller 1975). The Addiction Research Foundation was developed according to a similar model (Archibald 1990). Both centres have been successful in integrating basic and clinical research, treatment and prevention, as well as professional training and public education.

The idealized image of the scientific researcher is that of a single-minded truth seeker who engages in three primary activities: generating scientific hypotheses, conducting experiments, and interpreting the results of empirical observations. In practice, scientists do much more than these activities, and

Table 5.1 How addictions research is accomplished: scientific infrastructure and process elements

Structures	Mechanisms/processes
Research institutes	Financial support, legal mandates
Research centres	Research management, training
Research laboratories and investigators	Experiments, observations
Professional organizations	Communication, advocacy
Meetings, symposia, conferences	Communication, socialization
Journals, books, newsletters	Communication of ideas, information
Expert committees	Consensus conferences; expert committee reports

many researchers engage in none of them. As sociologists and historians of science have noted (De Solla Price 1963; Brannigan 1981), contemporary science is a much more informal and exploratory process, and the daily work of researchers is often occupied by mundane activities, such as pilot studies, staff meetings, supervision, training, grant writing, and advocacy for the continued survival of their programmes. The following sections of this chapter show that addictions research shares much in common with mainstream science. To understand how addictions research is accomplished, one must examine the underlying foundation of science and describe the basic framework (infrastructure) that has developed during the past 50 years in the industrialized world.

Table 5.1 outlines seven structures as well as the mechanisms or processes that constitute the hardware and software of modern scientific research. The terms science and research are interpreted broadly to include both experimental and non-experimental lines of inquiry; basic and applied investigations; and biological as well as social studies. Research institutes are the primary means of implementing science policy. Superordinate agencies, such as government organs and international organizations, provide a legal mandate to create scientific programmes, typically through the creation of national research institutes. Contrary to the image of the poverty-stricken, eccentric, independent scientist, contemporary science is made possible primarily through the encouragement and support of government agencies. These agencies support individuals and groups of scientists, primarily through direct funding of government programmes, university projects, or private industry. When individual scientists work in organized groups with dedicated facilities and long-term support, the organization can be called a research centre. In addition to the primary affiliation scientists have to their parent institutions and centres, they also affiliate with professional organizations that sponsor meetings for the purpose of scientific communications and continuing education. Research institutes and professional organizations often disseminate information through journals and newsletters to facilitate the scientific process. Finally, scientific researchers are sometimes convened to provide policy makers with expert opinion regarding scientific, social or health issues. It is important to understand how these components of the scientific infrastructure apply to addiction studies, because it has direct implications for both science policy and public policy.

Research institutes

Research institutes are organizations that plan, support, and co-ordinate scientific research on a global, national, or regional scale. Typically they develop and implement research policy with the interests of society and science foremost in mind. Table 5.2 presents, in chronological order of their establishment, the names and locations of research institutes and programmes that have been established in addiction studies by national or international bodies. The geographical distribution indicates that industrialized countries of the northern hemisphere tend to be over represented, with the conspicuous absence of those European countries (for example, Spain, Portugal, France, Germany, and Italy) that have very high per capita alcohol consumption. While several developing countries (for example, Mexico, Costa Rica, and India) have implemented national research programmes, there is little research activity in the southern hemisphere, with the exception of Australia and Brazil.

Table 5.2 also charts the evolution of national research programme capabilities in chronological order by country. While some of the institutes described here function in the more limited sense of a research centre, they are listed as institutes where they play a role in shaping national research policy. One of the first institutional efforts designed to serve the larger needs of society was the World Health Organization's (WHO) programme in the areas of narcotic control, abuse liability, psychiatric classification, and addictions nomenclature. The WHO's initial work during the 1950s and 1960s was conducted in the form of expert committee reports (for example, WHO 1952; WHO 1955). During the 1970s the WHO began the co-ordination of policy studies (Bruun *et al.* 1975; Mäkelä *et al.* 1981), and in the 1980s initiated several cross-national comparative studies (Ritson 1986; Saunders and Aasland 1987). In 1990, most of the WHO's alcohol and drug initiatives were transferred from the Division of Mental Health to the Programme on Substance Abuse, which now has primary responsibility for research policy.

Regarding individual countries, the Addiction Research Foundation (ARF) was established in 1949 by the Canadian province of Ontario to reduce the harmful effects of alcohol through research, education, and service (Cappell 1987; Archibald 1990). Although its original purview was not national in scope, the ARF has made significant contributions to both Canadian and international research policy. The Finnish Foundation for Alcohol Studies is another example of a government sponsored programme having both national and international influence. The Foundation, established in 1950, is funded

Table 5.2 Chronology of national research institutes and programmes

Year*	Country	Institute**
1948/1990	Member States	World Health Organization, Division of Mental Health, and Programme Substance Abuse (Geneva, Switzerland)
1949/1991	Canada	Addiction Research Foundation (Toronto); Canadian Centre on Substance Abuse (Ottawa)
1950	Finland	Finnish Foundation for Alcohol Studies (Helsinki)
1960	Norway	National Institute for Alcohol Research (Oslo)
1967/1991	UK	Addiction Research Unit (London)
1971/1974	USA	National Institute on Alcohol Abuse and Alcoholism; National Institute on Drug Abuse (Washington DC)
1973/1986	Costa Rica	National Institute on Alcoholism and Drug Dependence (San Jose)
1976	Mexico	Mexican Institute of Psychiatry (Mexico City)
1978	Switzerland	Swiss Institute for the Prevention of Alcohol and Drug Problems (Lausanne)
1985	Russia	All-Union Center of Narcology (Moscow)
1987	Australia	National Centre for Research into the Prevention of Drug Abuse (Perth); National Drug and Alcohol Research Centre (Sydney)
1989	Brazil	National Addiction Center (Sao Paulo)
1990	India	National Drug and Alcohol Institute (New Delhi)

* The year that the institute first became functional is given in most cases. In some instances a second year is given to indicate a renewal, expansion or change in status of a particular national programme.
** The word institute is defined broadly to include any governmental agency that plays a national or international role in shaping science policy regarding alcohol and drug research.

by the state alcohol monopoly. It supports research pertaining to policy questions as well as the social and biomedical effects of alcohol (Makala 1988). During the 1960s several other European countries established a national presence in addictions research. In Norway, the National Institute for Alcohol Research was established in 1969 within the Norwegian Research Council for Science and the Humanities (Skog 1987). In the UK, the Medical Research Council funded the Addiction Research Unit (ARU) at the Institute of Psychiatry in London (Russell 1989; Edwards 1989). The ARU's role in national and international addictions research was redoubled in 1991 with the inauguration of a new research facility in London. In the 1970s the US government established two national institutes charged with the development of research, treatment, and prevention activities (Gordis 1988; Schuster 1989; Tabakoff and Peterson 1988). The National Institute on Alcohol Abuse and Alcoholism (NIAAA) and the National Institute on Drug Abuse (NIDA) have developed into the largest addictions research institutes in the world, supporting both basic and applied research in their own intramural programmes as well as other research within a large network of universities and research organizations. During this time smaller research institutes were established in Costa Rica and Switzerland, and in the 1980s Australia established two national research centres devoted to the prevention and treatment of addictive disorders. Other national institutes have been developed in Japan (Suwaaki 1985), India, and Brazil.

The geographic distribution and chronology of research institutes on a global scale might be interpreted as an idiosyncratic development that depends on the particular social and political circumstances of each country. While most of the institutes were established to deal with the problems of alcohol, other substances are now typically included in their mandate. In Mexico, addictions research is still a part of the broader umbrella of mental health. Major differences exist in the way in which these agencies support, organize, and implement research policy. For some (for example, Norway, Finland, and Costa Rica), the institute itself is the primary organ of research in the country. For others (for example, the USA), the institute not only engages in intramural research, it also supports a wide variety of scientific activities at other institutions. One function shared by many of these institutes is that of information dissemination and the interpretation of scientific evidence for the development of public policy. Other functions include research training, public education, and the co-ordination of international activities.

Using the data provided in the first column of Table 5.2, Fig. 5.1 describes the cumulative growth in the number of national research programmes over the past 50 years. The curve indicates that there has been an accelerated growth in national research programmes since the late 1970s, which may reflect a world-wide recognition of addictions as a global public health problem. This trend suggests that there are similarities among nations in the manner and timing of their investment in science, and that government policy has important implications for the development of addictions research.

Research centres, laboratories, and investigators

The core of the addictions research infrastructure is made up of investigators, laboratories, and research organizations. Although the majority of addictions research in many countries is conducted by scientists and clinicians whose primary affiliation is to an academic department or clinical facility, in recent years there has been an expansion of specialized research centres whose

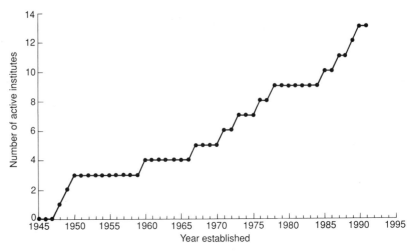

Fig. 5.1 Cumulative growth of national institutes (1948–1991).

primary purpose is to support addictions research and professional training. Because these organizations are more visible and definable, they provide an excellent opportunity to analyse how alcohol and drug research has developed during the past 50 years. More importantly, they account for a disproportionate amount of the addictions research that is conducted world-wide, in part because they employ full-time researchers, in part because they tend to have the most advanced facilities and laboratories.

In the description that follows, a total of 84 research centres were identified in 15 countries by means of published articles, annual reports, programme listings (Hill 1992), and personal communications with a large number of knowledgeable individuals. Although the information pertaining to the size, mission, and year of establishment may be approximate in some instances, the data on which this analysis is based is accurate enough and sufficiently complete to provide a sound basis for the conclusions that will be drawn. (A complete listing of the research centres used in this analysis can be obtained by writing to the author.)

A centre of addiction studies is defined as an organization or organizational subdivision, usually affiliated with a university and having an interdisciplinary staff, devoted to research on psychoactive substances and related problems, and sometimes also engaging in clinical and educational activities (Keller *et al.* 1982). Centres are generally funded by federal or regional governments, although in some countries other sources of support are employed.

Table 5.3 provides information about the geographic distribution of research centres by listing the number of centres located in each country and region. As suggested by the large number of centres located in the USA (n = 58), a large majority (71 per cent) of the currently active centres world-wide are American.

Table 5.3 Geographic distribution of research centres

	Number		Percent Total
North America	60		71
Canada		1	
USA		58	
Mexico		1	
Central America	1		1
Costa Rica		1	
South America	2		2
Brazil		1	
Chile		1	
Europe	13		16
Finland		2	
Norway		2	
UK		5	
Switzerland		1	
Russia		3	
South Asia	2		2
India		2	
East Asia	1		1
Japan		1	
Australia and New Zealand	5		6
New Zealand		1	
Australia		4	
Total		84	

Figure 5.2 shows the cumulative growth in number of research centres according to the year they were established. It indicates an acceleration of growth during the early 1970s. While this trend is strongly influenced by the significant investment in research centres by the US alcohol and drug institutes, it also reflects similar developments in other countries.

Figure 5.3 shows the percentage distribution of research centres according to relative size. The size of the research centre is estimated on the basis of its staff, laboratory facilities, and funding. Large centres generally have five or more laboratories or clinical facilities, and a professional staff of 50 or more scientists. Medium centres have fewer laboratories or clinical facilities, and their staffs range from 10 to 50 professional researchers. Small centres generally have a small group of investigators concentrated in a single laboratory or facility. As indicated in Fig. 5.3, most centres are classified as small, with only five considered large. Those centres are located in Russia (1), Canada (1), Japan (1), and the USA (2).

Figure 5.4 shows that there is a relatively balanced distribution of centres

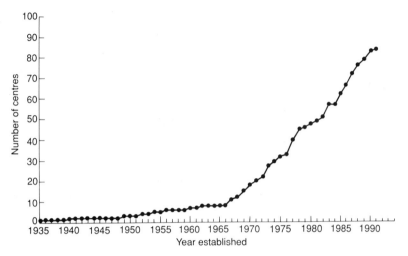

Fig. 5.2 Cumulative growth of alcohol and drug research centres world-wide (1935–1991).

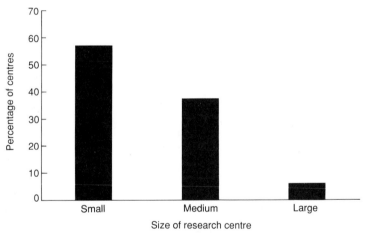

Fig. 5.3 Number of small, medium, and large addiction research centres world-wide.

in terms of their focus on either biomedical research, psychosocial research, or both. This classification was made on the basis on the centre's mission statement, published reports, and, if available, a review of the centre's recent publications. Biomedical research comprises animal studies, pre-clinical investigations, and research on the consequences of drug and alcohol abuse. Psychosocial research comprises studies of anthropological, economic, sociological, and psychological aspects of alcohol use and abuse, including prevention, aetiology, and social consequences.

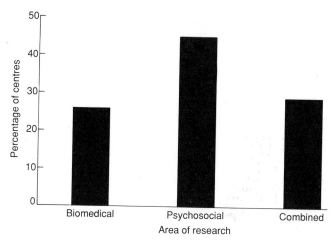

Fig. 5.4 Primary area of research activity: addiction research centres world-wide.

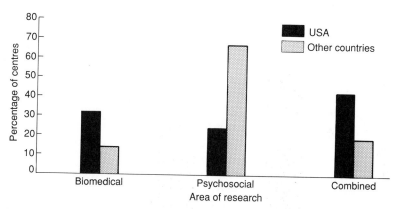

Fig. 5.5 Primary area of research activity, addiction research centres, USA and other countries.

Figure 5.5 indicates that psychosocial research accounts for a greater proportion of research centre activity in countries other than the USA. In the USA the largest proportion of research centres (43 per cent) combine both psychosocial and biomedical research.

Several generalizations are apparent from the information in these figures and from other aspects of this review. First, more than two thirds of the research centres are located in the USA. This may be related to the high value placed on science in the USA, the availability of an extensive system of research universities, the perceived need to reduce alcohol and drug abuse, and the support provided by advocacy groups. Secondly, the majority of research centres have been established in the past decade, with the growth curve representing an exponential rather than a steady linear function. Most centres are based at, or are otherwise affiliated with, academic institutions. In addition, most centres identified in this review reported that clinical service facilities, usually treatment programmes or hospital wards, were directly affiliated with their research programmes. Most research centres are classified as small in size, perhaps reflecting a combination of funding limitations and optimal working conditions. Although it is not difficult to characterize the content and scope of the research conducted at these centres in terms of either a psychosocial or a biomedical orientation, the review revealed a tremendous variety in the disciplinary orientations and the research foci of the different centres. The topics under investigation range from molecular biology to social policy, with a relatively even balance among the biological, behavioural, and social scientific disciplines. In the USA, however, a significantly higher proportion of the centres conducted both biomedical and psychosocial research (43 per cent in the USA versus 19 per cent world-wide), suggesting greater interdisciplinary collaboration in the USA.

The organization, purpose, and functioning of these research centres varies considerably from one location to another. Some are multidisciplinary; others tend to specialize in one disciplinary orientation. The NIAAA-funded research centres are mandated to focus on a central theme, while other centres merely serve as an umbrella organization for independent programme projects. Some centres combine basic science laboratories with clinical treatment facilities in a unified programme. Implicit in this model is the notion that multidisciplinary staff, clinical facilities, research laboratories, and programme projects should be integrated into a unified approach to a common problem.

As the concept of the addiction research centre has developed over the last 30 years, it has taken on a meaning as broad and diverse as the alcohol and drug field itself. Although interdisciplinary collaboration, central administration, and the sharing of facilities seem to be common features of all centres, there is little similarity across centres in the way these elements contribute to the conduct of research. Like all stereotypes, the idealized image of the collaborative research centre is an oversimplification of reality.

A reading of the mission statements of these centres, and a review of the activities they engage in, indicates that they serve a variety of important functions related to science policy and public policy. Many centres, particularly those established by the US NIAAA were created to provide an optimal environment for researchers, one that is free of administrative, clinical, and teaching responsibilities, so that scientists can devote more time to research. This concept of an optimal environment is not only defined by positions dedicated exclusively to research, but also by the provision of long-term support, job security, and the prospect of career advancement. These functions are achieved by establishing centres in institutions that define a clear career path for scientists, and by providing financial support for salaries and research expenses over a relatively long period of time. While certain research centres offer lifetime tenure to their senior scientists, most provide only short-term (3–5 year) contracts. In contrast to independent investigators typically working within academic departments or in government service, scientists affiliated with research centres are expected to develop programmatic research projects that lead to the development of new techniques, methods, and theoretical models.

Another function of research centres is the recruitment and training of new scientists. Because alcohol and drug research is considered a new, if not unusual, career path for scientists in many disciplines, addictions centres often are the only places where younger scientists can become apprenticed.

Research centres typically are invested with core research facilities, such as laboratories, computers, communications equipment, and libraries, that make it possible for collaborating scientists to engage in a variety of scholarly activities. Those activities go far beyond 'bench work' to include travel to scientific meetings, personal communications with other researchers, participation in peer review, journal editing, and the training of other scientists.

A major feature of the ethos of addictions research, particularly as it is practiced at research centres, is the belief that drug and alcohol problems can be addressed through the application of science, reason, and knowledge. This expectation sometimes leads to the imposition of specific conditions on the conduct and direction of research by government funding agencies. Thus, many scientists and the centres they work in are expected to direct their research at specific questions that are asked by policy makers. At times this mission-oriented model of research conflicts with the belief that science is best conducted in an atmosphere of complete intellectual freedom. Nevertheless, there is little in the literature on research centres that indicates that scientists are uncomfortable with the need to make science relevant to social needs. With the exception of a few basic science centres engaged in fundamental biological research, most centres have direct involvement in practical applications of research to the clinical situation or to broader public policy concerns. This is reflected in the large number of clinical facilities affiliated with different research centres, and with the number of studies, particularly in centres conducting social research, that are devoted to policy-relevant issues.

A final role of the research centre is to facilitate the work of science by linkages with the broader community of scholars and with the general public. Research centres are expected to provide leadership, as evidenced by such activities as international collaboration, joint projects with other research centres, and consultation to governments. Many centres report such linkages, both nationally and internationally. In the USA the NIAAA and NIDA have begun to use their research centre networks for collaborative projects and clinical trials.

The WHO has played an important role in the identification of collaborating centres that can participate in joint international projects. According to Sartorius (1988), collaboration between the WHO and an international network of research centres can further the growth of participating centres, broaden researchers' exposure to standardized research methods, explore the cross-cultural generalizability of research findings, and expedite the application of new treatments and technologies.

Professional organizations and meetings

A major source of support and advocacy for scientists working in organizations is the professional societies they have established. Like the medieval guilds, these organizations certify the competency of their members and provide a forum for communication and professional development. What is unique about the field of addiction studies is that organizational ties tend to be established with two different types of professional societies. The first is with the societies representing disciplines engaged in addictions research. Examples include the national organizations representing physicians, psychiatrists, psychologists, biochemists, and biologists. In many cases, these professional societies have developed sections or interest groups that deal specifically with alcohol and drugs. A second type of professional society is concerned with addictions research exclusively, usually in a way that cuts across disciplinary boundaries. Examples of national organizations that are devoted to school and drug research include the British Society for the Study of Addiction to Alcohol and Other Drugs, the French Societé d'Alcoologie, and the American Research Society on Alcoholism. Several international organizations, such as the International Society of Biomedical Research on Alcoholism, and the Kettil Bruun Society for Social and Epidemiologial Research on Alcohol, have been formed to facilitate the work of addictions research across national boundaries.

Professional organizations engage in advocacy for research, distribute news and scientific information to their members, publish journals and newsletters, and at times facilitate collaborative research. A major function is to organize scientific meetings. In recent years the scientific meeting has become a primary vehicle for communication, socialization, and information dissemination. The scope and frequency of scientific meetings, symposia, workshops, and technical reviews organized by professional societies and government agencies has grown tremendously in the past 20 years. The extraordinary advances in telecommunications and air transportation, as well as the increased availability of travel funds for scientists, have facilitated access to scientific meetings and stimulated international exchanges.

Scientific journals and other communications media

Peer reviewed scientific journals are the major medium for the dissemination of research findings. As in the case of scientific meetings and professional

Table 5.4 Scientific journals specializing in addictions research according to year of establishment and language of publication

Year	Language	Journal
1903	English	*British Journal of Addiction*
1940	English	*Journal of Studies on Alcohol*
1949	English	
	French	*Bulletin on Narcotics**
	German	
1954	French	*La Revue de l'Alcoolisme*
1955	English	*Journal of Alcohol and Drug Education*
1965	Japanese	*Japanese Journal of Alcohol Studies and Drug Dependence*
1966	English	*International Journal of the Addictions*
1965	English	*British Journal of Alcohol and Alcoholism*
1967	English	*Journal of Psychoactive Drugs*
1971	English	*Journal of Drug Issues*
1971	English	*Journal of Drug Education*
1973	English	*Journal of Drug and Alcohol Education*
1973	English	*Contemporary Drug Problems*
1974	English	*American Journal of Drug and Alcohol Abuse*
1975	English	*Drug and Alcohol Dependence*
1975	English	*Addictive Behaviors*
1976	French	
	German	*Drogalcool*
	Italian	
1977	English	*Alcoholism: Clinical and Experimental Research*
1978	French	*Alcoologie*
1980	English	*Substance and Alcohol Actions/Misuse*
1983	English	*Australian Drug and Alcohol Review*
1984	Norwegian	*Alcohol Politik*
	Finnish	
1984	English	*Journal of Substance Abuse and Treatment*
1984	English	*Alcohol: An International Biomedical Journal*
1986	English	*Psychology of Addictive Behaviors*
1988	English	*International Journal of Drug Policy*
1988	English	*Journal of Substance Abuse*
1990	Russian	*Problems of Narcology*
1991	English	*American Journal on Addictions*

* Ceased publication.

organizations, addictions research findings are published in both disciplinary journals and journals that specialize exclusively in alcohol and drugs. The latter, called addictions specialty journals, are listed in Table 5.4 according to year of first issue and language of publication. A total of 29 journals were identified. With the exception of one, all are currently active. Seventy-two per cent of these journals are published in the English language, most of them in the USA. As indicated in Fig. 5.6, there has been a significant growth in the number of scientific journals since 1965, thereby providing a ready publication outlet for researchers in the addictions field.

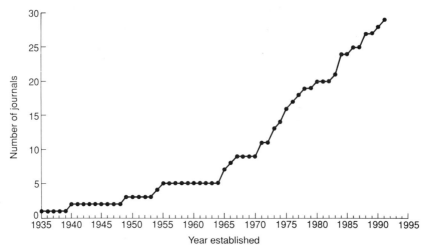

Fig. 5.6 Cumulative growth of specialized journals (1935–1991).

As suggested by the growth curve of speciality journals, there is some evidence that the number of published articles in addiction studies is increasing in proportion to other areas of science. Hughes and Oliveto (1990) conducted a computerized literature search of *Index Medicus* to study the growth of treatment research in alcohol and drug use disorders over a 22-year period (1967–88). They found that the number of articles for alcohol and drug use disorders is growing, especially during the past eight years, relative to the overall growth of the medical treatment literature.

Regardless of the growth in journals and publications, a more basic question is whether this information is being read and utilized. Howard and Howard (1992) traced citation histories of 541 articles published in 12 alcohol and drug speciality journals between 1984 and 1988. Citation counts for individual articles and journals in the drug and alcohol field were found to be quite variable. Citation rates were positively correlated ($r = 0.68$) with circulation size, with the *Journal of Studies on Alcohol* and the *British Journal of Addiction* having the most citations. The mean number of citations to drug and alcohol articles and the percentage of articles cited tend to exceed those generally reported for the social scientific literature as a whole. In addition, citations to addictions studies tend to peak later than in the social sciences generally, suggesting that the impact of drug and alcohol articles is maintained over a longer period of time.

Because alcohol and drug research tends to be interdisciplinary and problem-focused, it might be expected that as specialized publication outlets are developed, they would gradually supplant the more disciplinary-oriented journals as a medium of publication. Figure 5.7 shows that there is a relatively even balance among the addictions specialty journals and disciplinary journals that

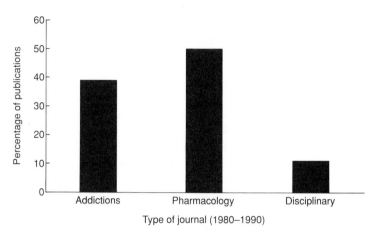

Fig. 5.7 Percentage of addiction research centre publications published in addiction, pharmacology, and disciplinary journals.

are used as publication outlets by addictions researchers. The data for this figure are based on a survey of bibliographies provided by 12 randomly selected centres (six from the USA, six from other countries). The analyses classified more than 700 articles into three categories: addictions specialty journals, journals having a more general disciplinary orientation (chemistry, psychiatry), and those dealing with pharmacology and toxicology, which are considered both disciplinary and, to a lesser extent, focused on psychoactive substances. These findings suggest that addictions researchers still maintain a strong allegiance to their professional disciplines, although they publish with equal frequency in multidisciplinary specialty journals.

In addition to the widespread availability of scientific journals, the addictions field has employed a variety of other tools for communication and information dissemination. The more traditional media are books, technical reports, monographs, and conference proceedings. A complementary medium of information dissemination comprises the newsletters and magazines that are published by professional societies, research institutes, and government agencies. These are directed at a selected group of subscribers or constituents. These media serve to keep scientists informed about new developments, both political and scientific. They also serve to integrate individual scientists with a broader community of scholars who share common interests and beliefs. In addition to desk-top publishing by means of personal computers, the information dissemination explosion that is characteristic of both addiction studies and science in general has been accelerated by advances in telecommunications, the rapid adoption of facsimile transmission machines, and the establishment of inter-institutional computer networks.

A final medium of communication that constitutes an important part of the scientific infrastructure in the addictions field is the expert committee. In recent years there has been a dramatic increase in the sponsorship of consensus conferences, technical reviews, and expert committee reports. The WHO, for example, has used temporary advisers and consultants to develop scientifically based recommendations in the areas of nomenclature (Edwards *et al.* 1981), diagnostic interviews (Robins *et al.* 1988; Wing *et al.* 1990), and alcohol control policy (Bruun *et al.* 1975). In the USA, the National Academy of Sciences has recently issued expert committee reports on treatment (Institute of Medicine 1990, Moore and Gerstein 1981) and research opportunities (Institute of Medicine 1989). The role of the expert committee report is often to summarize research findings in a way that suggests policy implications that can be taken up by governmental agencies or legislative bodies.

Toward a science of addictions science

Having described some of the organizational features and operational procedures that characterize the addiction field, it now becomes possible to identify major trends that have developed in the past 50 years and to offer some observations about the conditions under which addictions research fulfils its promise as a vehicle for learning, science, and public policy. The remainder of this chapter will discuss four major trends and their implications for public policy. The trends are: (1) the rapid transition from 'little science' to 'big science'; (2) the growing importance of social factors in addictions research; (3) the 'internationalization' of addiction studies; and (4) the emergence of an 'invisible college' of addiction scientists.

Rapid transition from little science to big science

Following the Second World War there was a dramatic increase in the volume of scientific research in both the basic sciences and the life sciences. According to De Solla Price (1963), all indicators suggest that this growth has been exponential. Mathematically, the law of exponential growth states that the rate of increase is proportional to the total magnitude already achieved. Evidence reviewed in Fig. 5.1, 5.2, and 5.6 indicates that the law of exponential growth applies equally well to the addictions field. The number of centres, institutes, and journals established in the past 10 years is greater than the number created in the first 40 years. Assuming that there is some relation between the quantity and the quality of addiction research, it might reasonably be concluded that we are witnessing a scientific revolution in addiction studies. The rapid growth of centres, investigators, and publications means that much of what we know about addictions is current, and most of the scientists who have contributed to that knowledge base are still active. Related to this exponential growth is a transition from small science to big science, from part-time independent investigators to career scientists, and from small-scale treatment comparisons to multicentre clinical trials. While these trends may seem encouraging, it should be noted that exponential growth eventually reaches some limit, at which time the process must slacken and stop. Since the resources and manpower of science are finite, a more realistic mathematical function is the logistic curve. The implications of this curve are that addictions research may rapidly be approaching a time, at least in the industrialized countries, when exponential growth is shifting into a more steady state or even a decline. As with the public health movements that accompanied the rise and fall of tuberculosis and polio, addictions science could quickly be relegated to historical artefact by circumstances beyond, as well as within, its control.

The lesson is that it is never too early to pursue the history of addictions science, even though most of its past is alive. And in this analysis it would seem important to study the relation between science policy and social policy, because this may well hold the key to understanding the future as well as the past.

The internationalization of addiction science

The internationalization of addictions science is epitomized by the growing number of international conferences that are sponsored each year by such organizations as the International Council on Alcohol and the Addictions, the Ketteil Bruun Society, and the International Society of Biomedical Research on Addictions. Typically, an international group of social, clinical, and biological scientists, many of whom have known one another for years and even decades, meet together on a common theme, which is freely discussed in a common language. With the emergence of national research programmes, modern communications, and the common language of science, there is a major trend toward the standardization of methods, theories, and agreed upon findings.

One part of this trend that requires special note is the emergence of English as the language of science. A related trend is the emergence of the USA as the engine of addictions research. On the positive side, English is a very rich and adaptable language that is as useful for poetry as it is for science. It is spoken as a first or second language by at least a quarter of the world's population (McCrum *et al.* 1986). It has dramatically improved the ease and immediacy of international communication. The free exchange of ideas and research findings made possible by the implicit acceptance of English has provided a unique opportunity for international collaboration, particularly in the social sciences. Nevertheless, one may wonder about the negative implications of what might well be described as the Anglicizing and Americanization of addictions studies. First, scientists whose native language is not English are at a disadvantage with regard to verbal and written communication. Secondly, to the extent that American values, theories, science policies, and substance use patterns all colour the findings produced by American researchers, a disproportionate part of addiction science is being influenced by a single culture. Although science is a universal language, it is influenced by local biases, such as the selection of topics, methods, and theories. One can question whether the trends, fads, and research priorities of the American scientific establishment (for example methadone maintenance, needle exchange programmes, residential treatment) are relevant to scientists and policy makers in other nations, particularly the developing world.

The social nature of research

Very little is known about the social institutions of science and the social psychology of the scientist. The behaviour of scientists in groups has a different set of determinants than the behaviour of independent scientists. What distinguishes the decisions of the independent scientist from the collaborative researcher is the extent to which decisions are determined collectively. This means that the authority structure, and the formally established system of rules and regulations, must take into account the conditions and interpersonal factors that influence scientific creativity and productivity. Role ambiguity, status inconsistency, inadequate communication networks, personality conflicts, unhealthy competition, maldistribution of rewards (financial or academic), and inappropriate credits for scientific publications can all stifle creativity, poison the decision-making process, and create an atmosphere of rebellion and mistrust. Given the significance of social factors in the management and conduct of addictions research, it is unfortunate that there is no knowledge base to guide the development of addiction studies as a scientific discipline. There is some evidence from research on scientists in organizations that efficient management is best achieved through a system of shared authority and responsibility. Pelz and Andrews (1976) found that scientific achievement and productivity were highest under conditions of 'creative tension' between security, stability, and confidence, on the one hand, and intellectual challenge and even conflict, on the other. Although it is not clear whether these conditions contribute to creativity and performance in addictions research, the issues are worth considering in any attempt to improve the co-ordination and management of addictions researchers in organizations. A major issue in the management of scientific organizations, the training of scientists, and the development of science policy is the formulation of performance criteria. What are the goals of scientific organizations? What distinguishes a good scientist from an ineffectual scientist? What accomplishments should a science policy strive to achieve?

Emergence of an invisible college

The development of institutions, centres, journals, and societies comes about through the diligent work of leaders. These are often people who get together informally to make decisions about the future. Unofficial pioneers in the alcohol research field include men like E.M. Jellinek, Bill W., Brinkley Smithers, and David Archibald, who constitute the first invisible college in alcohol studies. Although these men were based at different institutions during the 1940s, they began to have a greater allegience to the ideas and ideals of one another than they did to their own institutions (Archibald 1990).

Since that time a much more elaborate and complex set of invisible colleges has emerged in the addictions field. Dating back to the founding of the Royal Society in 1660, the term refers to a small groups of leaders, perhaps less than 50 or 100, who exchange papers, do favours, provide support, and collaborate across institutional as well as international boundaries. The function of these assemblages is not to perpetuate an 'old boy' network, but to solve a communications problem. Human beings operate best when they have personal knowledge of each other. The emergence of an invisible college is a sign of the maturity of a discipline. Because the addictions field has grown so rapidly, at present the informal leadership structure in no way resembles an exclusive club.

During a meeting attended by a number of great physicists, the chairman opened the proceedings with the remark: 'Today we are privileged to sit side-by-side with the giants on whose shoulders we stand' (Holton 1961). This statement, which applies equally well to addictions studies, recognizes that a large proportion of the history of science is happening now, within living memory. The peculiar contemporaneousness and relative youth of addictions research is perhaps its greatest asset.

Acknowledgements

The writing of this chapter was supported in part by a grant from the US NIAAA (No. 5P50 AA03510). The author would like to thank Lee Towle, Robin Room, Ernestine Vanderveen, Norman Sartorius, and the many individuals who provided information about specific programmes, facilities and centres.

References

Archibald, H.D. (1990). *The Addiction Research Foundation: a voyage of discovery.* Addiction Research Foundation, Toronto.
Brannigan, A. (1981). *The social basis of scientific discoveries.* Cambridge University Press.
Bronowski, J. and Mazlish, B. (1986). *The Western intellectual tradition.* Dorset Press.
Bruun, K. *et al.* (1975). *Alcohol control policies in public health perspective.* Vol. 25. The Finnish Foundation for Alcohol Studies, Forssa.
Cappell, H.D. (1987). The Addiction Research Foundation of Ontario. *British Journal of Addiction*, 82, 1081–9.
Clarke, P.L. (1964). Multiple authorship trends in scientific papers. *Science*, 143, 822–4.
Committee on Promoting Research Collaboration (1990). *Interdisciplinary research*

promoting collaboration between the life sciences and medicine and the physical sciences and engineering. National Academy Press, Washington.

De Solla Price, D.J. (1963). *Little science, big science.* Columbia University Press, New York.

Edwards, G. (1989). The Addiction Research Unit of the Institute of Psychiatry, University of London—I. The work of the unit's drug and alcohol section, and general issues. *British Journal of Addiction,* 84, 715–25.

Edwards, G., Arif, A., and Hodgson, R. (1981). Nomenclature and classification of drug- and alcohol-related problems: a WHO memorandum. *Bulletin of WHO,* 59(2), 225–42.

Gordis, E. (1988). National Institute on Alcohol Abuse and Alcoholism. *British Journal of Addiction,* 83, 483–93.

Hill, K. (ed.) (1992). *Research centers directory,* Vol. 1, (16th edn). Gale Research Inc.

Holton, G. (1961). On the recent past of physics. *American Journal of Physics,* 29, 805.

Howard, M.O. and Howard, D.A. (1992) Citation analysis of 541 articles published in drug and alcohol journals: 1984–1988. *Journal of Studies on Alcohol,* 53, 427–34.

Hughes, J.R. and Oliveto, A.H. (1990). The growth of treatment research in alcohol and drug use disorders: a computerized literature search. *Drug and Alcohol Dependence,* 26, 81–4.

Institute of Medicine (1989). *Prevention and treatment of alcohol problems research opportunities.* National Academy Press, Washington.

Institute of Medicine (1990). *Broadening the base of treatment for alcohol problems.* National Academy Press, Washington.

Keller, M. (1975). Multidisciplinary perspectives on alcoholism and the need for integration: an historical and prospective note. *Journal of Studies on Alcohol,* 36, 133–49.

Keller, M., McCormick, M., and Efron, V. (1982). *A dictionary of words about alcohol* (2nd edn). Rutgers Center of Alcohol Studies, New Brunswick.

Mäkelä, K. (1988). The Finnish Foundation for Alcohol Studies and the Social Research Institute of Alcohol Studies. *British Journal of Addiction,* 83, 141–8.

Mäkelä, K., Room, R., Single, E., Sulkunen, P., and Walsh, B. (1981). *Alcohol, society, and the state. Vol. 1: a comparative study of alcohol control.* Addiction Research Foundation, Toronto.

McCrum, R., Cran, W., and MacNeil, R. (1986). *The story of English.* Elisabeth Sifton Books, Viking, New York.

Moore, M.H. and Gerstein, D.G. (ed.) (1981). *Alcohol and public policy: Beyond the shadow of Prohibition.* National Academy Press, Washington.

Pelz, D.C. and Andrews, F.M. (1976). *Scientists in organizations: productive climates for research and development.* (Revised edn). University of Michigan, Ann Arbor.

Ritson, B. (1986). *Community responses to alcohol-related problems. Review of an international project.* World Health Organization Public Health Papers, Geneva, Switzerland.

Robins, L.N., Wing, J., Wittchen, H.U., Helzer, J., Babor, T.F., Burke, J., *et al.* (1988). The composite international diagnostic interview. An epidemiological instrument suitable for use in conjunction with different diagnostic systems and in different cultures. *Archives of General Psychiatry,* 45, 1069–77.

Russell, M.A.H. (1989). The Addiction Research Unit of the Institute of Psychiatry University of London—II. The work of the unit's smoking section. *British Journal of Addiction*, **84**, 852–63.

Sartorius, N. (1988). Experience from the mental health programme of the World Health Organization. *Acta Psychiatrica Scandinavica*, **344**, 72–74.

Saunders, J.B. and Aasland, O.G. (1987). *WHO collaborative project on identification and treatment of persons with harmful alcohol consumption. Report on Phase I. Development of a screening instrument.* WHO Offset Publication No. 86.3, World Health Organization, Geneva.

Schuster, C.R. (1989). The National Institute on Drug Abuse (NIDA). *British Journal of Addiction*, **84**, 19–28.

Skog, O.J. (1987). Norway: National Institute for Alcohol Research. *British Journal of Addiction*, **83**, 495–504.

Straus, R. (1986). Alcohol and alcohol problems research 10. The United States. *British Journal of Addiction*, **81**, 315–25.

Suwaki, H. (1985). Alcohol and alcohol problems research 2. Japan. *British Journal of Addiction*, **80**, 127–32.

Tabakoff, B. and Petersen, R.C. (1988). Intramural research program of the National Institute on Alcohol Abuse and Alcoholism. *British Journal of Addiction*, **83**, 495–504.

World Health Organization (1952). *Expert Committee on Mental Health, Alcoholism Subcommittee, Second Report.* World Health Organization Technical Report, Series, No. 48, World Health Organization, Geneva.

World Health Organization (1955). *Alcohol and alcoholism, report of an expert Committee.* WHO Technical Report Series, No. 94, World Health Organization, Geneva.

Wing, J.K., Babor, T.F., Brugha, T., Burke, J., Cooper, J.E., Giel, R., *et al.* (1990). SCAN: Schedules for Clinical Assessment in Neuropsychiatry. *Archives of General Psychiatry*, **47**, 589–93.

Discussion
The optimum conditions for making science happen

Chaired by Boris Tabakoff (USA)

Panel members: Irina Anokhina (USSR), Ilana Glass-Crome (UK), Frederick Goodwin (USA), David Hawks (Australia), Yedi Israel (Canada), and John Shanks (UK), with further contributions from the floor.

Chairman: When one launches into such a discussion one has to take at least a few minutes to reflect on what is science and what is it that we are wanting to happen. Griffith Edwards mentioned that science is an illumination. He also mentioned Huxley's perception that science is trained and organized commonsense.

My perception may differ a little from either of these views. Science is a process of seeking answers to questions that produce objective information. It is that objective information that we need to have for policy decisions to be properly formulated. The question of putting together optimal conditions for science to happen should take into account that not all science is the same. Science is not a homogeneous endeavour, and in fact there are great differences in the optimal organization and resource requirements, as well as motivational requirements, for the different types of sciences that are going on.

Basic science, which seeks to understand the nature and workings of humans and the universe, is different in its requirements from the quantification of phenomena needed for sound business decisions, and that is, in turn, different from the type of science that is done in response to public health or other crises, or space science. That was emphatically emphasized in the USA, in response to the Sputnik launch. I am reminded also of Einstein's reflections on his most productive years of thinking, and he seemed to believe that these were while he was a patent clerk in an office in Berne, Switzerland. When one is considering the optimal conditions for science maybe we should work to increase the number of patent offices and the number of staff with PhDs working within them. I am not being absolutely facetious in this example, because during this meeting we have heard laudatory comments about centres of excellence as the way to do science. Whether big science is the way that we should go is perhaps one of the issues to be brought up in this panel discussion, and whether that is the best way to integrate science into policy.

Dr David Hawks (Australia): If objectivity is a scientific virtue so is persistence, and persistence has to do with the motivation for doing research. While some scientists are indeed motivated by the goal of an elegant solution or a parsimonious model of explanation, some of which do of course turn out to have great practical significance, for others it is the possibility of influencing the world and particularly the welfare of people, which lends their endeavours persistence.

While not wanting to wake up one morning to find that I am running the country, I at least want to think that I am influencing the way the country is being run. So while respecting the democratic conventions whereby science is properly only one of the influences impinging on policy, I, and I suspect others, would want to think that our endeavours were considered relevant. While not expecting to win all of the arguments as to what should be policy, my ability to sustain scientific endeavour at least partly depends on the sense that I have of being part of the debate, part of the argument. My education in this matter was furthered by a Minister of Health who replied to me after I had attempted to explain a difficult concept to him, that I was probably right but I had only one vote, and it was a matter of me persuading others before he had to be persuaded himself.

Now, as to whether commissioned or free-rein research is likely to be more or less relevant, or tenured or contractual positions the more productive, or even egalitarian or hierarchical structures the most motivating, there is in fact no simple or single answer. Some commissioned research, despite the pretence of ownership, and despite at times having clear implications for policy is thoroughly ignored. Some free-rein research turns out fortuitously to be profoundly influential. There is a lot of noise in the system. Those of us who agonize about what makes a research environment productive or creative are in any case only able to influence the margins, the two per cent of difference, and what principally determines the matter is the people appointed to do the work, and in this I find myself in happy agreement with Sir Walter Bodmer. Discerning creativity in others and then promoting it is a difficult art, made easier of course if they have already demonstrated creativity, but more difficult when it is merely a potential to be ascertained. Getting that right is perhaps the thing that distinguishes a good environment for scientific endeavour from a merely ordinary one.

Dr Irina Anokhina (USSR): I would like to speak about the conditions which are needed to make science productive and effective. First, it is important to have good access to the literature. Unfortunately not all countries have a good system of information, including the USSR, but only after analysis of this background can an idea arise for concrete scientific investigation.

This idea, in fact, arises on the basis of the knowledge of the leader of this research, his or her education, personal opinion, and so on. It is well known that in the same experiment in the same circumstances, different people see different things and make different conclusions. Karl Popper said that there is no poor observation, each observation is on the basis of individual experience, an individual type of thinking, and the individual approach. So in this situation it is important to have a leader of quality. When you have the ideas you must then choose the adequate research methods, and here science needs financial support, equipment, chemical reagents, and much else.

The next step is when this idea guw produces experiments. I do not know what the situation is in other laboratories, but unfortunately in our Institute's laboratory, sometimes one person produces accurate experiments but often he or she does not understand the place of this experiment in the overall scientific research. At the stage of analysis and synthesis the role of the leader is again crucial. After this analysis and synthesis comes the conclusion, and a new idea further to continue this investigation. To accomplish these steps the most important person is the leader of research work, and his or her qualifications, position, ideology, and capacity to make a serious and fundamental analysis and synthesis.

Dr Frederick Goodwin (USA): When one considers stability, which is that Sir Walter Bodmer emphasized as the main requirement for nurturing that delicate flower of creativity that we call research, at least in the USA, we have arrived at a more informed consumer-oriented society, in which the general public wants to be supportive toward the creation of that stable environment.

Now in the drug abuse area there are some special issues about how public attitudes lead to instability, which has to do with tracking the peaks and valleys of drug epidemics so that we attract an enormous amount of public attention briefly. Sometimes we are at fault for stimulating too much public attention to our drug problem, and then the public attention shifts, and then the research budget slumps. Everyone has heard about the incredible growth and achievements of the US biomedical scientific establishment.

But we have a paradox, for at the same time that we are having explosive growth in our knowledge base, we are also having a growing uneasiness in the public about what science is doing. Secretary Sullivan has referred to this unease in terms of the four Cs: biomedical research is too costly, too cruel, too corrupt, and too closed. If you look at the roots of those uneasy public attitudes which are now being played upon and amplified by some dangerous anti-science movements, they go back to the mid-1960s, when we had a series of nationally traumatic events triggered by the Kennedy assassination, the Vietnam War, the failure of some of the programmes of the Great Society, and the Watergate fiasco, which lead to a culture of mistrust. What we then saw from 1965 to 1985 and which affected a whole generation of our country, was a sharp decrease in long-term and a shift towards short-term investment. We saw a decrease in investment in education, and our country shifted away from first to thirteenth, and from first to last in science education in the developed world. We saw a shift in the percentage of our gross national product that goes into civilian research and development, from a high of 2.7 per cent after Kennedy to a current low of 1.7 per cent, although it has stabilized in the last five years. These attitudes, the shift towards short-term views and particularly the culture of mistrust which was fermented by Watergate but which has continued, particularly in our new mistrust of media, has distorted the public debate, and particularly the capacity to educate consumers about science in a way that we are having to do.

The area that has brought this into sharpest relief is the animal rights movement, which has focused specifically on drug addiction research because it knows that it can play on the public perceptions of drug addiction as really not being a bio-medical problem, but simply a behavioural problem or an environmental problem. Indeed, whenever you deal with the brain and behaviour you are coming up against strong public prejudices against biological determinism—we are messing around with the human soul, we are messing around with free will. If we examine the animal rights attack on drug addiction research, which has resulted in a rather significant decline in the number of investigators willing to work in primate studies in drug addiction areas, we can see both a model for some of the problems we face, and a paradigm for what is wrong with our response. The academic community tends to be more reflective than reactionary, and the lack of a capacity for action orientation in the academic community was nowhere more evident than it was recently in the failed response to the animal rights movement, and hence our defensive and apologetic tone.

We progress so rapidly in generating new information that we are now completely overwhelmed by it, and there is little time for scholarship any more, little time for mentorship, little time for what we used to call scientific citizenship. If you look at just one piece of scientific citizenship, which is setting out to educate the public and to educate children in schools, we need to do something about this. We need to shift the incentives in academia, because at this moment in our academic environments there is virtually no incentive to do anything other than generate and publish data and write grants. There is a tendency for people who are active in public education to be vaguely seen as self-promoting.

Unless we foster in our young scientists some coterie of people who are willing to defend the infra-structure of science we can no longer assume the kind of public support that has been prevalent in the period since the Second World War in Western cultures. We have in the Alcohol, Drug Abuse and Mental Health Administration started some initiatives to try to shift that incentive. We have, for example, initiated a scientific education partnership award which is a two million dollar programme in grants to individual scientists to form partnerships with school programmes and to get out and educate young people about science. We have done the same thing for some public education initiatives. And if you look at what is happening in the USA, there are now some subtle shifts in public attitudes that are beginning to come in our direction, but the question is are we going to direct those shifts and shape them or are we going to be bystanders? If you examine what happened in the post-Gulf War climate for example, there has been an increase in confidence in technology, an increase in confidence in long-term investments, an increase back to the Kennedy era levels in altruism, and increased attention at the national level to our serious problems in the educational system. We need to get scientists more involved in these policy issues, get them out of their laboratories and clinics, get them involved in things which in the past have been thought of as second class things for a scientist to do. We should not wait until people are senior members of their professions, when they can rest on their laurels, but get them out there when they are young, as educators and public spokespeople. We scientists are the only enterprise that I can think of in Western society that does not systematically attempt to develop its own defenders, and its own people who help and protect the infrastructure. Science will not survive unless these policy issues which support the stability of our work, are seriously and sustainedly addressed.

Dr Ilana Glass-Crome (UK): I would like to ask the other panel members what they think about defining productivity. We have heard Tom Babor talking about productivity in terms of number of citations. This is a relatively easy way of measuring productivity, but measurement needs to be extended into the quality of the science.

Dr Frederick Goodwin (USA): One possible way in which to refine the citation index would be simply to eliminate self-citation.

Dr Irina Anokhina (USSR): The quality of science poses difficult questions, but several opinions are better for deciding opinion is really true. It is one of the main goals of scientific meetings to discuss different opinions, different results, different approaches, and after several years it will be clear who is right.

Dr David Hawks (Australia): I agree with the idea that we need to broaden the definition of productivity. To determine whether or not one's research is enacted in policies, is however a severe test. To be made responsible for the intransigence of governments seems too heavy a burden to lay on researchers. Yet on the other hand the relevance of what you do is a measure of your productivity, and some test of that kind needs to be applied.

Dr Frederick Goodwin (USA): Does one have to be in the mainstream at all times to be considered productive or valuable to science? That is one of the issues when one considers the value of centres versus science conducted at a more individual level. Both are necessary, because centres sometimes become too monolithic in their approaches.

Chairman: The topic of science managers is an important issue. Good science needs nurturing, and who are the individuals who will nurture science and how do you develop a motivation for those individuals to nurture science?

Dr Juan Carlos Negrete (Canada): One of the curses that scientists experience is being known for having developed a theory. Someone who has developed a theory is recognized as somebody who has made a particular contribution, but once you have a theory then you are no longer so prepared to test it any more, you have to defend it. Your prestige and your identity goes with it. That is one major problem for leadership; there are some centres that become known because of a theory, rather than a finding. The other question in relation to our field which is growing so quickly, is the disregard for history. Many people start research without knowing what has been done, not 50 years ago, but just five years ago, because the literature bank gives them a print-out for three years and that is enough.

Dr Charles Kaplan (Netherlands): My question is directed to Dr Goodwin. Given the great impact of US biomedical science, what is the future for social medicine and the psychosocial approach?

Dr Frederick Goodwin (USA): In the USA the historical traditions of psychosocial research and purely biological research, have been much more integrated in the training of individuals than they have been in some Western countries. In my own field of psychiatry, for example, the psychoanalytical and biological traditions grew out of the same individuals rather than constituting separate traditions as in many countries in Europe. The neurosciences are the fastest growing area of all biomedical science in the USA and among the neuroscientists supported by my agency, most are psychologists. The neurosciences in our arena are behaviourally sophisticated and invest as much care in behavioural measurements and behavioural theory, as in the biological. In terms of the larger social context, the biggest problem with marrying research to societal issues is the ethical constraints around conducting controlled experiments. It is difficult to conduct prevention projects in which you control all the variables because you are dealing with individual lives. There has been a fair amount of progress in translating some of the techniques of clinical trials into large community based programmes. That is one of the things that Enoch Gordis at NIAAA and Charles Schuster at NIDA are much involved in. My general perception for future science in the USA is optimistic, if science gets out of its ivory tower.

Dr Ilana Glass-Crome (UK): I tend to think of the problems that are confronting us today in the following way. Identifying the characteristics of a scientist is one category. Identifying the characteristics of a team or institution which may best foster science is another. Looking at the supportive contribution that society may provide yet another. And then finding the right balance.

If you talk to scientists and try to identify why they went into science, they will always say that there is that curiosity, the pleasure, the delight in more knowledge and more discovery. In our field, of course, we hope very much that this will lead to practical application. Along with this is creativity, but this must be based in the ability to persist, to commit oneself. Another factor which we might discuss is whether luck and chance and timing play a part, or are the good scientists the ones who come by the luck and chance and good timing more often? I also tend to think that youth is on the side of a good scientist, who will be unencumbered by mistakes and administration. A centre needs to be a community with a common purpose and a shared vision where collaborators are in healthy competition. The leadership is there to teach modes of thinking and techniques, but a career structure is necessary to provide security and status. Management is necessary but in moderation and planning is necessary so as to choose effective, worthwhile enterprises. There needs to be a democratic atmosphere in which there is dialogue, and, as one scientist said to me, you have to have the confidence to talk complete nonsense. An atmosphere is needed which is not overloaded by bureaucratic administration or an autocratic leadership. Clinical exposure in this arena is almost imperative. We need to find a balance between tradition and innovation so that tradition does not stifle innovation. Because we are working as multi-disciplinary teams we need to be able to speak a common language so that we can talk with our colleagues.

Now what about society? I think society should be educated to value science, rather than to feel hostile towards it. We need to educate people so that they avoid having the distorted image of that one single brilliant experiment, which is going to put everything right, because clearly they are disenchanted with that view because it does not happen very often. They need to recognize that science needs funding because it is credible, and there needs to be the long-term support for complex problems. Funding should not be dependent on fashion. All scientists value having a degree of freedom and independence, as much of it as possible. We need better to understand the properties of research-producing institutions. What is the best size? What is the best mix of disciplines? What is the best measure of productivity? What is the best balance between competition and collaboration? What is the best balance between science and managerial skills? How do we integrate various disciplines? How do we avoid unnecessary duplication, but replicate when we think we have to? We cannot programme novel ideas to appear, we need to find a mechanism, as Sir Walter Bodmer has said, to recruit able people to give of their best in an atmosphere of freedom and independence which is curiosity led. The process of science for policy, and policy for science, is an interactive one. And finally, although I am not a feminist, we need more women in this business.

Dr John Shanks (UK): I am a part-time civil servant and a part-time doctor in the NHS, and so perhaps represent something of a hybrid between policy making and one type of science. When I joined the civil service I discovered a curious phenomenon, which was that there were jokes in it. There is such as thing as government humour, and one of the aphorisms which I discovered early on in my career was that experts should be on tap not on top. That phrase may represent either some of the mutual suspicion or the healthy scepticism, between policy making and science. There are a number of ways in which public policy can influence science, the most obvious of which is direct support; the money is counted and that is taken to be the value which that particular institution or the public body attaches to science. That may not be the most important way of actually supporting science and it certainly is not the only way.

There are aspects of policy that can create a need for science that goes well beyond the institution itself. We are subject to a recent example of this in the UK, where there have been major changes to the NHS and community care which have made all those authorities which purchase services assess in a systematic way the needs for care of their populations. Suddenly a whole lot of people who regarded epidemiology as pure research and as only marginally more interesting than counting the number of angels who could dance on the head of a pin, find that they actually require epidemiological data to go about their daily work. It is important that sometimes both scientists and the rest of the world can see science making a visible difference, actually making something happen that manifestly could not have happened without scientific endeavour.

Again, looking back to our own UK experience of addiction services, the establishment of syringe and needle exchange schemes is an example of a hotly contentious issue, which probably could not have been implemented if it had not been recast as a scientific experiment that would be evaluated, with an outcome which would decide whether or not there would be continuing public support for the venture.

There has to be the right climate, and policy has a role here, but when we are establishing the micro-climate within policy making organizations themselves, the other aphorism is that the best antidote to a hot debate is to throw a few cold facts on it. Policy makers themselves can establish that as being the climate within their organization, that facts are looked for when an argument becomes heated.

Perhaps more importantly, but most difficult of all, is establishing the right macro-climate in society at large, the notion that ordinary people who are not scientists and will never become scientists, should nevertheless appreciate and acquire something of the scientific cast of mind, should develop that healthy scepticism which is the best aspect of scientific enquiry, and learn to ask what is the evidence, how do we know this? When Dr Goodwin was speaking about the difficulty that some scientists are experiencing at the moment in being sure of public support, it occurred to me that perhaps we should neither be too surprised nor be too annoyed. Is it not the case that the public are posing the null hypothesis for science and the scientific method, asking us to bring forward evidence to refute the notion that there is no value in science or in the scientific method?

Dr Yedi Israel (Canada): We have heard the lovely quote that science is nothing but trained and organized commonsense, and now we hear that objectivity is to be added to the definition, and I agree. I would like to add that predictability or generalizability also would be important. All of that is child's play compared with what we have heard about the need to connect with public policy. In fact there is much simplicity in the elements that are needed for trained and organized commonsense. Allow me to single out only three of these elements; talent, priorities, and motivation. It is difficult to explain the simple, and in doing that one usually dresses in heavy robes, but let me try. In talking about talent I mean creativity, or as Albert Saint Georgi put it, the ability to see what everybody has seen but to think what nobody else has thought. The greatest impact of a science leader is in the recruitment of talent. The recognition of talent is simple, you know it because in its presence many pieces of a large puzzle suddenly fit into place. The problem is not how to recognize it, but how to attract it to your institution. Thus, in the matter of recruitment it is important to understand what motivates scientists. More often than not scientists are motivated by a critical mass of other accomplished scientists. If your institution does not have a critical mass, it is better to team up with an institution that has it. Part of an excellent scientist is better than the whole of a mediocre one. Offer whatever you must to attract the very best. Your facilities, support services and compensation, should match the quality of your recruit. Often this means several trips for negotiation to your human resources department, which has develop guidelines to compensate individuals in the middle range, which are precisely the ones you must avoid. The task of the science leader is continuously to look for these outstanding individuals and to be sufficiently aware of the potential of other peripheral disciplines to enhance his or her field. Even as the chief administrator in an organization is the person at the interface between the organization and society, the science leader is at the interface between his or her field and the many other areas of knowledge that he or she has to bring into it.

Allow me then to enter into the area of defining priorities, which is, or should be, one of the most exciting challenges for the scientific leader. Priority setting should be seen as the marriage between needs on one side and opportunities on the other, so crisply defined by the Nobel Laureate, Otto Warburg, who taught his student, Sir Hans Krebs, that excellent research stems from the art of asking good questions that can be answered. The best scientific leader is actually a broker between needs and opportunities. The mechanism of priority definition should however be seen as an empowering mechanism to your scientist, never an encumbering one. While it is clear that the scientific leader will contribute most importantly in formulating priorities, we should also remember that science is in a sense that purest form of democracy, where no votes are counted, but any single voice can have veto power. In priority setting there are no ranks beyond that of the power of reasoning.

The question is then sometimes asked how much deviation from priority research should be accepted. In my mind that is the wrong question. The proper question is how much deviation from priority directed research should be required. It is only through a continuous flow of information from other disciplines that we can gather fresh concepts to apply them to our own field. Here I can only give my own recipe, I take the attitude that about 20 per cent of the scientist's time should be devoted to non-priority research. However, I have no problem in accepting 50 per cent for the individual who delivers 140 per cent.

Let me now move on to motivation. Here that you hope is that you have done such a good job in priority setting that motivation now fits like a natural glove. I am sure that I will find that fit in my next life. For this one I employ the tools used by most of us, emphasizing seminar series, presentations to learned societies, publications in excellent journals, and peer review funding. But most importantly I keep current on the progress of the people I work with. I celebrate their successes and I grieve with them at their failures. Back into full circle, talent, priorities, and motivation. Indeed, science is organized commonsense.

Dr David Hawks (Australia): I would like to respond to one aspect of Dr Glass-Crome's analysis which I found very astute, and it is her suggestion that clinical exposure is imperative in furthering the research enterprise. That is a controversial view, and many of the people who pursue research in this area have no clinical experience, but I would agree with her for two reasons. Clinical exposure aquaints one with the complexity of the phenomena one is attempting to study, and it also motivates one to do something about the pain. I suspect that if one is going to persist with scientific endeavour it is important to have that gut involvement which often only comes from a commitment to the solving of problems of a human kind.

Dr David Grahame-Smith (UK): My immediate approach to quotations from the scientific establishment of Great Britain is that they make me rather sceptical. As to this business of science as just commonsense, well, I have to turn it around and say that commonsense actually is science, because it is the collection and correct interpretation of observations that have been empirically made by somebody during their experience. That is in fact what commonsense is, so I don't think we can necessarily split the two. They are integral to each other.

Chairman: The only comment I have in response is that commonsense to one individual may not be the same commonsense to another.

Dr David Grahame-Smith (UK): That is absolutely right, and then there will be controversy. I was struck by something that John Shanks said about the null hypothesis. In many areas we have been talking about the trust which public, politicians, and so on have in science, but as scientists we have a peculiar way of thinking because we are extremely sceptical, and go about our business by trying to prove what we think is right, wrong. Now if the businessman or a politician did that, the businessman would be bankrupt and the politician would be out of office before you could say Jack Robinson, whereas that approach is in fact the absolute basis of our scientific method.

Dr Roger Meyer (USA): As I was listening to these themes I was thinking of Plato and the Athenians, and the arguments go back quite some time. But there are some other general comments. In a world which seems increasingly obsessed by ethnicity, scientists are the quintessential cosmopolitans and that gets in the way of our ability to influence policy. Secondly, I think we often miss the point of boundaries: when we move too far into the role that is legitimately policy we get our hands slapped by other constituencies.

In the substance abuse field we are often perceived as just one more interest group, and we need to accept that limitation. The other issue about boundaries is not only the boundaries between science and government, but the boundaries within science itself. The boundaries that exist for instance in the laboratory between the manager and the scientists so that scientists can be creative, and the boundaries between the mentor and the trainee, so that the trainee can in fact develop and not simply serve as the creature of the mentor. That is a critical issue that we often do not address. We feel that because of our concern about knowledge we should be entitled to do research with animals and we do not appreciate the fact that we are vulnerable because of our arrogance. The most critical issue that we have to address is to get away from the arrogance of what we feel is our special place, and respect these limitations in terms of boundaries.

Dr Dorothy Black (UK): Taking up the question of scientific arrogance, science must accept that it is a servant of the society in which it lives.

Dr Dean Gerstein (USA): My own view is that science is clearly an unstable mixture of commonsense, scepticism, and imagination. It is the instability that comes of this mixture that creates the fragility that we see, and the desire for stable centres and support. At the same time as science engenders suspicion and uncertainty in our environment, and that combination of arrogance and uncertainty amongst ourselves, we are tied by these different components to different elements. The commonsense ties us to our applications, and those who apply science in the clinical and other realms. The scepticism ties us individually to our own sense of novelty and of wanting to create something new. Imagination, I suppose, ties us only to divinity.

Dr Herbert Kleber (USA): One thing we should not forget is that scientists are also humans who often have liberal values, and often they let the values get in the way of properly analyzing their science. It is not simply that science is commonsense: very often science should be examining what commonsense is, and showing that scientifically it does not work. Take needle exchange. Everyone seems to be saying that needle exchange is a great idea, but if you look at the science, the finding is that the great majority of the people who initially make contact drop out, and of those remaining most were not needle sharers to begin with. Meanwhile, work from Dr O'Brien's group in Philadelphia has shown that people who share are more likely to have serious depression. You can correlate sharing with increases in the Beck depression inventory, so that when we start getting liberal and saying that it is a good idea to get addicts not to share needles, we sometimes forget that we also need to be scientists and look at what the data show. If the data show things that we as kind, compassionate human beings may not like, we still need to be honest about those findings. Otherwise we forfeit the respect of the public who see us no longer as scientists but just as fallible human beings.

Chairman: One of the things that comes through loud and clear in terms of the optimal conditions to make science happen, is that scientists have to look after science. Scientists have to concern themselves with societal values and try to improve the relationship between science and society, and gain an acceptance for science in society. This particular issue is too often neglected when discussing the proper climate for science to happen. Another critical issue is that we must not forget that we need to maintain a proper cadre of scientists, of individuals interested in doing science. Science is time consuming, it is a creative process, it cannot be turned on and off as needed by the policy maker, and thus one needs to concern oneself that there is an infra-structure for doing science and that infra-structure is maintained. Another issue is prestige, and that plays an important role in what kind of science is conducted. When one considers science and policy, the ability of a scientist to influence policy is an important prestige factor for people going into science, and that relationship when maintained will encourage good science. Finally, I would like to think of another optimal condition for good science to happen, and that is asking the right question. One of the obligations of scientists is not only to answer the questions that are posed to them by policy makers but to make sure, as much as they can at least, that proper questions are being asked by the policy makers and by the public at large.

Part II Prevention: science and policy connections in different substance fields

6. Tobacco-related disease

Robert West

When medical science established beyond all doubt that cigarette smoking kills large numbers of people one might naïvely have supposed that politicians in democratic countries would have made urgent and strenuous attempts to reduce the death toll. It is now clear, however, that this was not what happened.

Extensive inaction

It would be unfair to say that there have been no attempts by governments to control tobacco use. For example, there have been restrictions on the promotion of cigarettes, and occasionally taxation has been used to raise prices with the stated aim of deterring use (Warner 1985). However, there has (with the exception of Norway, Canada, and communist countries) been no ban on promotion, no punitive taxation policy, and no attempt to ban the sale of cigarettes to adults. Bans on cigarette sales to children have been widely flouted and little effort has been made to prevent this (Jarvis and McNeill 1990), although recently the UK government did try to ban Skoal Bandits®, a form of oral smokeless tobacco, although there were virtually no users in the country anyway.

There appear to be several reasons for this unenthusiastic response to the health threat posed by tobacco. The first is concern on the part of governments that a dramatic decline in tobacco manufacturing and sales would have a damaging effect on their domestic economies, at least in the short term. Secondly, there may be implications for public finances. Weighing heavily in the economic balance sheet would be the increased demand for retirement pensions at a time when there is already concern about how the ever-growing elderly population is to be supported. Thirdly, there is the problem of infringing upon the civil liberties of smokers. Severe pressure on smokers to give up, or bans on the sale of tobacco would, it is argued, take away an important element of choice in people's lives. Fourthly, in the case of a complete ban on manufacture and sale, there would be the problem of enforcement. A black market might quickly develop, and attempts to control it would place an intolerable burden on enforcement agencies.

Evidence of some action

The above considerations are likely to be highly persuasive in deterring governments from taking active steps which would cause a dramatic fall in tobacco consumption. On the other hand, many countries have vociferous anti-tobacco lobbies, and governments are reluctant to be seen to be doing nothing at all about the death toll resulting from tobacco use. Therefore some governments may be prepared to take modest and indirect steps gradually to reduce the prevalence of tobacco use over a period of years or decades. A gradual reduction may permit adjustments to be made to compensate for the loss of a major sector of the economy. Fiscal policy could also be adjusted gradually to take account of the loss of tax revenue and the increased expenditure on pensions. Such a gradual reduction might in principle be achieved in several ways:

(1) helping smokers who wish to give up to achieve that aim;

(2) persuading more smokers to try to give up smoking;

(3) persuading teenagers not to take up smoking;

(4) changing the smoker's environment, primarily by increasing the price of cigarettes and/or banning cigarette promotion.

Consideration will now be given to each of these areas, exploring the extent to which scientific findings could help governments to achieve this rather modest goal. Consideration will then turn to the role that taxation or bans on tobacco promotion might play; and finally an alternative approach to reducing tobacco-related disease will be discussed.

Helping smokers to give up smoking

The majority of smokers (some 70 per cent in the UK and the USA) state that they wish they could stop smoking (Action on Smoking and Health 1991; Glass 1990), yet they continue to smoke nonetheless. In fact, only about 40 per cent of adults in the UK who have ever been regular smokers become ex-smokers by the time they reach 60 years of age (Jarvis 1991).

One way of achieving a reduction in the prevalence of smoking may be to take smokers at their word when they say they would like to give up cigarettes, and provide them with the help they need to do so. In fact there have been numerous attempts to devise such smoking 'treatment' programmes over the years. However, with one exception, none has been shown to be have any long-term effect over and above what can be achieved through simple support and advice (Raw 1986). Despite the claims of many treatment programmes, the typical smokers clinic achieves one-year abstinence rates of around 15 per cent.

The one treatment which has been shown to work is nicotine replacement therapy. The recognition that addiction to cigarettes is in large part attributable to nicotine led to the development of a chewing gum containing nicotine to be used as an adjunct to psychologically-based smokers clinic treatments (see US Department of Health and Human Services 1988 for a recent review of the role of nicotine in cigarette dependence). Use of the gum has been shown to double the long-term success rates of smokers clinics in placebo-controlled trials (Fagerstrom 1988). It also reduces the severity of withdrawal symptoms. Recent trials of other nicotine replacement therapies, including a skin patch and a nasal spray have shown similar success rates to nicotine gum (Russell 1991). Also, several other drugs are being tested as aids to smoking cessation, including the alpha-2 adrenergic antagonist, clonidine, the anti-depressant, fluoxetine and the anxiolytic, buspirone (see Sachs 1990). Glucose tablets have recently been shown to reduce craving for cigarettes (West *et al.* 1990). It is possible that these too might improve the success rates of those giving up smoking. However, the efficacy of any pharmacological aids other than nicotine has yet to be established.

Even using nicotine gum, long-term abstinence rates of smoking treatment programmes only average about 30 per cent. Moreover, only a very tiny minority of smokers seem prepared to seek help from these programmes in giving up smoking. As things stand, therefore, such programmes are unlikely to affect smoking prevalence to a significant degree. This does not of course mean that they are not worthwhile. They tend to attract highly addicted, heavy smokers, who are at a greater than average risk of contracting a smoking-related disease, and every smoker who is helped to give up is potentially a life saved.

Recent moves in the UK to make nicotine gum available over the counter, rather than on prescription only, may mean that more smokers will use it when trying to give up by themselves. However, it is not yet clear whether this will help to reduce prevalence by improving their success rates.

Persuading more smokers to try to give up smoking

It is possible that smoking prevalence could be reduced by encouraging more smokers to try to give up smoking (Daube 1983). Mass-media campaigns, national non-smoking days, etc. are difficult to evaluate properly because of the problem of finding adequate controls. However, where specific campaigns have been evaluated, the results have tended to be disappointing (for example Dyer 1983). Also, it is primarily lighter smokers who appear to give up in response to such campaigns (Gritz *et al.* 1988).

Russell *et al.* (1979) reported that simple advice to smokers from a general practitioner in the course of a routine consultation could lead to some 5 per cent giving up smoking. If a prescription of nicotine gum is offered in addition to this, the percentage of patients quitting appears to rise to about 8–10 per cent (See Sachs 1990). Although it is not yet clear whether in this context nicotine gum amounts to anything more than a placebo (Hughes *et al.* 1989), a 5–10 per cent reduction in smoking prevalence would still be well worth achieving.

Unfortunately, the results of these kinds of interventions on prevalence may be more modest than had been hoped. Russell *et al.* (1988) evaluated the effects of a district-wide intervention against smoking involving general practitioners. Advice from general practitioners to their patients to give up smoking, coupled with the offer of a prescription for nicotine gum had no detectable effect on prevalence in their practice populations compared with controls. In practices where advice to stop smoking and offer of nicotine gum was coupled with an offer of referral to a smokers' clinic, there was a drop in prevalence of 2.6 per cent over a 30 month period compared with controls. However, prevalence was measured by self-report and it is possible that a higher proportion of smokers in the clinic referral practices claimed to be non-smokers (see Russell *et al.* 1987). Also, the practices which undertook the more intensive intervention were a minority of those approached and may have been more than averagely enthusiastic in their attempts to reduce smoking among their patients.

In general, it appears that specific programmes aimed at persuading smokers to give up may have only a very small impact on prevalence. However, it must be remembered that smokers in the countries where these programmes have been tested—primarily the USA and UK—are already constantly exposed to warnings about the health risks from tobacco, and few would argue with the view that wide publicity about the health risks from cigarette smoking has contributed to the decline in smoking prevalence in these countries (Warner 1989). The problem is that we do not know whether the same, or even an increased level of publicity would reduce prevalence still further.

Persuading teenagers not to take up smoking

Given the difficulty which many smokers have in giving up smoking, it makes some sense to try to prevent teenagers from taking it up in the first place. There have been countless studies examining how this might be done. Techniques that have been tried range from simple education, to role-modelling and social skills training. The results have typically consisted of modest but significant short-term reductions in the number of teenagers taking up smoking, but with the effects dissipating over time (Flay *et al.* 1989; Murray *et al.* 1988). As yet, there is little evidence that specific interventions aimed at teenagers can contribute to a sustained reduction in prevalence.

New ideas for more effective interventions are being developed (Leventhal *et al.* 1991), but as yet no clear results have emerged. Future designs of programmes aimed at adolescents may well need to take into account the fact that within a year of starting smoking they are already inhaling a similar dose of nicotine per cigarette as adults (McNeill *et al.* 1989), and many of them report experiencing some cigarette withdrawal symptoms when they try to abstain (McNeill *et al.* 1986).

Thus, as with campaigns aimed at adults, there is little hard evidence that specific programmes aimed at persuading children not to smoke will contribute significantly to a progressive reduction in smoking prevalence. There is an argument that as long as cigarette smoking is prevalent among the adult population, many children will still consider it to be important to their sense of identity as they approach adulthood. Therefore, it could be argued that a reduction in smoking prevalence in children may depend on a reduction in smoking among adults.

Changing the smoker's environment

The above analysis suggests that there is little scientific backing for the proposition that programmes aimed at persuading or helping smokers to quit and persuading children not to take up smoking will have much impact on smoking prevalence in the foreseeable future. That is not to say that such campaigns are totally ineffective—only that any effect has been difficult to detect. Let us consider, therefore, whether governments have it in their power to change the smoker's environment in such a way that smoking prevalence is reduced in the kind of steady fashion that might be deemed acceptable.

Two main instruments for smoking reduction have been considered—(1) raising tobacco taxes; and (2) restricting or banning the promotion of tobacco products.

Raising tobacco taxes   Econometric analyses have shown very consistently that the overall demand for tobacco is influenced by its price, other things being equal (Lewit 1989). In general, studies in countries such as the UK and the USA indicate that a 10 per cent increase in the price of cigarettes would result in a 4 per cent fall in smoking prevalence in the short term. In the longer term, a larger drop in prevalence may occur because the effect of price rises on adolescent smoking is much greater than that on adults—a 10 per cent rise in prices would be expected to result in at least a 10 per cent fall in smoking in those under 20 years old. Given that almost all smokers start in their teenage years, it is possible that a price rise would markedly reduce the proportion of people who ever take up smoking.

Although using taxation to influence smoking prevalence sounds attractive, its importance should not be overstated. It would not be feasible to continue to raise excise duty on an annual basis above the increase in level of earnings for more than a few years. A point would quickly be reached at which the taxation level would be so high that it would be tantamount to a ban, something which governments would probably wish to avoid.

Restricting or banning the promotion of tobacco   The other main way of influencing the smoker's environment is to restrict or ban the promotion of tobacco products. Very recently the European Community proposed a complete ban on the advertising of cigarettes and on the use of cigarette brand names in sponsorship. This is a move which the UK government has indicated it will oppose, and it remains to be seen whether this ban will come into force.

The evidence on whether a ban on tobacco advertising (either directly or through sponsorship) would affect smoking prevalence is unclear. There have been econometric studies showing a small but positive association between expenditure on print tobacco advertising and overall tobacco sales on a quarterly basis (Tether and Godfrey 1990). However, when the figures are aggregated on an annual basis the relationship ceases to hold.

However a separate, and perhaps the main, argument for a ban on promotion is that, as long as cigarettes are being actively promoted, children see them as being a normal part of life and indeed smoking may still possess a positive image. Banning tobacco advertising and promotion of all kinds might change this. It could contribute to a social view of smoking as deviant and outside the bounds of normal behaviour. This might in turn lead fewer children to take it up. Indirect support for this argument comes from a survey by Marsh and Matheson (1983), who found that 44 per cent of smokers believed that smoking could not really dangerous because the government still permitted its advertising.

Safer alternatives to smoking

Science may have yet to provide firm guidance to policy makers about how to achieve a steady reduction in the prevalence of smoking. However, the task is sufficiently important that it is essential that efforts continue, including follow-up of the leads that have been provided by the research to date.

In the meantime, perhaps other ways could be found of helping to reducing smoking-related disease. It has been shown that it is components in the tar in tobacco smoke that contribute to lung cancer and other forms of lung disease (US Department of Health and Human Services 1982, 1984). In contrast, there is evidence that the ingredient which smokers are mainly seeking is nicotine (US Department of Health and Human Services 1988). There is currently no evidence that nicotine is a major cause of death and illness in the doses obtained by smokers (Benowitz 1989; Levy and Martin 1989; Roe 1989). If tobacco users were to switch wholesale from tobacco to pure nicotine products, then perhaps a dramatic reduction in smoking-related disease might result.

The technology of administering pure nicotine to the body is still relatively crude. A large proportion of swallowed nicotine is metabolized to an inactive form in the liver before it reaches the central nervous system. Therefore, simple nicotine capsules are probably not a suitable method of administration. The first widely-used nicotine product has been nicotine chewing gum. This allows absorption through the lining of the mouth (Fagerstrom 1988). Nicotine gum has its limitations, however. Many smokers find the taste unpleasant; they do not like to be seen chewing gum; and the nicotine dose obtained is typically quite small. In addition, the rate of absorption via the buccal mucosa is slow and may not match the smoker's need for instant-aneous nicotine shots.

More recently, other nicotine products have emerged which offer some promise. As mentioned earlier, clinical trials are in progress on a nicotine transdermal patch (see Russell 1991). However, absorption of nicotine is slower than from the gum and patches may be unsuitable for lifetime use because of skin irritation. Nicotine nasal drops and sprays have been in-vestigated and show some promise (see Russell 1991). They provide more rapid absorption of nicotine, but they irritate the mucosa in the nose, and users may be slightly embarrassed to use them in public.

The most efficient method of nicotine delivery must be one that mimics cigarettes. The objective is to produce an aerosol with droplet sizes small enough for the vapour to travel to the lungs where it can be absorbed rapidly over a large surface area. This has proved difficult to achieve, but progress is being made. R.G. Reynolds developed a cigarette which delivered nicotine and carbon monoxide but no tar. However, there was considerable opposition to its introduction from public health campaigners, and there was also some consumer resistance because of its taste characteristics. Another product, a device shaped like a cigarette with nicotine-impregnated material in the tip, has been tested as an aid to giving up smoking (Hajek *et al.* 1989). Despite the fact that it was very inefficient as a means of nicotine delivery, it successfully reduced craving for cigarettes.

Much more research needs to be done before a nicotine product will be commercially available to replace cigarettes, and questions remain about consumer acceptance of a product which is overtly a drug delivery system—smokers may be reluctant to make so obvious a statement that they are drug users. Consumer resistance to R.G. Reynolds' tar-free cigarette suggests that the sensory aspects of smoking cannot be ignored.

Considering the opposition to action

Tobacco manufacturers are unlikely to commit the necessary resources for the development of cleaner nicotine products as long as the likelihood is that governments and public health agencies will make it impossible for them to be marketed. Therefore, an important first step must be a commitment on the part of governments at the very least to allow nicotine products to be sold and marketed as freely as cigarettes. Russell (1991) has even argued that it may be worthwhile for governments actively to discriminate in favour of nicotine products to aid the process of switching away from tobacco. There could, for example, be tax incentives. Alternatively, governments could gradu-ally tighten up restrictions on the concentrations of harmful components in cigarette smoke, forcing tobacco companies to move in the direction of pure nicotine products in order to sell their wares. In may be in the interests of both governments and the tobacco industry to adopt this approach—

governments because they could continue to derive considerable tax income from nicotine, and the tobacco industry because tobacco is likely to be the main source of nicotine for the foreseeable future.

The idea that pure nicotine products should be promoted as an alternative to cigarettes is likely to be controversial. The extent to which it takes hold will depend on whether nicotine can be exonerated from the charge of playing a significant role in smoking-related disease. At present we do not know what component of cigarette smoke causes the smoking-related increase in cardiovascular disease. The two main candidates at present are nicotine and carbon monoxide (Levy and Martin 1989). If it is found that nicotine contributes substantially to the increased risk of cardiovascular disease, then active promotion of nicotine products will be difficult from a political point of view, and a judgement will also have to be made as to whether it might lead to an overall increase in usage which would offset the reduction in cancer and lung disease caused by a switch away from cigarettes. Therefore it could reasonably be argued that the most urgent priority for research in tobacco is to determine the extent to which nicotine contributes to cardiovascular disease.

Conclusion

Increases in taxation of tobacco would reduce the prevalence of tobacco smoking, but repeated increases in the real price of cigarettes could not be sustained for long because a point would be reached relatively quickly when a further price increase would be tantamount to a ban. Other methods of reducing tobacco prevalence through bans on promotion, media campaigns, general practitioner interventions, and specialized treatment programmes may have an effect in reducing the prevalence of smoking, but there is currently little hard evidence for this.

Lung diseases associated with tobacco smoking result from components in the tar of cigarette smoke, whereas smokers are primarily seeking nicotine. Therefore, it has recently been suggested that, in addition to a continued search for measures to reduce the desire of individuals to smoke tobacco, alternative cleaner forms of nicotine delivery should be developed and made available to the public as an alternative to smoking. The extent to which this line can be promoted depends on whether nicotine itself is shown to have some role in causing heart disease. This must be an urgent priority for research in the next few years.

References

Action on Smoking and Health (1991). *NOP omnibus survey* 11 March.

Benowitz, N.L. (1989). Central nervous system toxicity of nicotine. In *Nicotine, smoking and the low tar programme*, (ed. N. Wald and P. Froggatt). Oxford University Press.

Daube, M. (1983). Public information programmes. In *Proceedings of the 5th world conference on smoking and health*. Canadian Council on Smoking and Health.

Dyer, N. (1983). *So you want to stop smoking: results of a follow-up one year later*. BBC, London.

Fagerstrom, K.O. (1988). Efficacy of nicotine chewing gum: a review. In *Nicotine replacement: a critical evaluation*, (ed. O. Pomerleau and C. Pomerleau). Alan R. Liss, New York.

Flay, B.R., Koepke, D., Thompson, S.J., Santi, S., Best, A., and Brown, K.S. (1989). Six year follow-up of the first Waterloo school smoking prevention trial. *American Journal of Public Health*, 79, 1371–6.

Glass, A. (1990). Blue mood, blackened lungs: depression and smoking. *Journal of the American Medical Association*, 264, 1583–4.

Gritz, E.R., Carr, C.R., and Marcus, A.C. (1988). Unaided smoking cessation: great American smokeout and New Year's Day quitters. *Journal of Psychosocial Oncology*, 6, 217–34.

Hajek, P., Jarvis, M.J., Belcher, M., *et al*. (1989). Effect of smoke free cigarettes on 24h cigarette withdrawal: a double blind placebo-controlled study. *Psychopharmacology*, 97, 99–102.

Hughes, J.R., Gust, S.W., Keenan, R.M., Fenwick, J.W., and Healey, M.L. (1989). Nicotine v. placebo gum in general medical practice. *Journal of the American Medical Association*, 261, 1300–5.

Jarvis, M.J. (1991). A time for a conceptual stocktaking. *British Journal of Addiction*, 86, 643–8.

Jarvis, M.J. and McNeill, A.D. (1990). Children's purchases of single cigarettes: evidence for drug pushing? *British Journal of Addiction*, 85, 1317–22.

Leventhal, H., Keeshan, P., Baker, T., and Wetter, D. (1991). Smoking prevention: towards a process approach. *British Journal of Addiction*, 86, 583–8.

Levy, L.S. and Martin, P.A. (1989). Toxicology of nicotine—its role in the aetiology of cancer due to cigarette smoking and cardiovascular disease. In *Nicotine, smoking and the low tar programme* (ed. N. Wald and P. Froggatt). Oxford University Press.

Lewit, E.M. (1989). US tobacco taxes: behavioural effects and policy implications. *British Journal of Addiction*, 84, 1217–35.

Marsh, A. and Matheson, J. (1983). *Smoking attitudes and behaviour*. HMSO, London.

McNeill, A.D., West, R., Jarvis, M.J., Jackson, P., and Russell, M.A.H. (1986). Cigarette withdrawal symptoms in adolescent smokers. *Psychopharmacology*, 90, 533–6.

McNeill, A.D., Jarvis, M.J., Stapleton, J.A., West, R., and Bryant, A. (1989). Nicotine intake in young smokers: longitudinal study of saliva cotinine concentrations. *American Journal of Public Health*, 79, 172–5.

Murray, D.H., Davis-Hearn, M., Goldman, A.I., Pirie, P., and Luekper, R.V. (1988). Four and five year follow-up results from four seventh grade smoking prevention strategies. *Journal of Behavioral Medicine*, 11, 385–406.

Raw, M. (1986). Smoking cessation strategies. In *The addictive behaviors, Vol. 2, Processes of change*. (ed. W.R. Miller and N. Health). Plenum, New York.

Roe, J.C. (1989). The toxicity of nicotine: cancer. In *Nicotine, smoking and the low tar programme*, (ed. N. Wald and P. Froggatt). Oxford University Press.

Russell, M.A.H. (1991). The future of nicotine replacement. *British Journal of Addiction*, **86**, 653–8.

Russell, M.A.H., Wilson, C., Taylor, C., and Baker, C.D. (1979). Effects of general practitioners' advice against smoking. *British Medical Journal*, **2**, 231–5.

Russell, M.A.H., Stapleton, J., Jackson, P., Hajek, P., and Belcher, M. (1987). District programme to reduce smoking: effect of clinic-supported brief intervention by general practitioners. *British Medical Journal*, **295**, 1240–4.

Russell, M.A.H., Stapleton, J., Hajek, P., Jackson, P., and Belcher, M. (1988). District programme to reduce smoking: can sustained intervention by general practitioners affect prevalence? *Journal of Epidemiology and Community Health*, **42**, 111–15.

Sachs, D. (1990). Advances in smoking cessation treatment: state of the art. *Current Pulmonology*, **12**, 139–97.

Tether, P. and Godfrey, C. (1990). Tobacco advertising: In *Preventing alcohol and tobacco problems*, Vol. 2, (ed. C. Godfrey and D. Robinson). Avebury, Aldershot.

US Department of Health and Human Services (1982). *The health consequences of smoking: cancer.* Office on Smoking and Health, Rockville, MD.

US Department of Health and Human Services (1984). *The health consequences of smoking: chronic obstructive lung disease.* Office on Smoking and Health, Rockville, MD.

US Department of Health and Human Services (1988). *The health consequences of smoking: nicotine addiction.* Office on Smoking and Health, Rockville, MD.

Warner, K.E. (1985). The consumption impacts of a change in the federal cigarette excise tax. In *The cigarette excise tax*, Harvard University Institute for the Study of smoking behavior and policy, Cambridge, MA.

Warner, K.E. (1989). Effects of the anti-smoking campaign. *American Journal of Public Health*, **79**, 144–51.

West, R., Hajek, P., and Burrows, S. (1990). The effects of glucose on craving for cigarettes. *Psychopharmacology*, **101**, 555–9.

7. Alcohol prevention

*Reginald G. Smart**

The difficulty of making connections between science and policy is well-recognized. Consider the example of scurvy in the British Navy (Mosteller 1981). In 1601, when the East Indian Company first went to India, deaths from scurvy were reduced by serving three teaspoons of lemon juice per day to the sailors. About 150 years later, the same experiment was conducted again, but it took another 48 years for the British Navy to introduce a 'citrus juice policy', that is to give it to sailors on a regular basis. It took another 70 years—until 1865—until this policy was generally applied in the British mercantile Navy—a total of 264 years. What happened during all that time? The scurvy science experts and the Navy policy experts did not agree, they failed to communicate: in fact, they showed distrust and maintained unreasonable expectations of each other. Perhaps that is what sometimes happens in the field of alcohol research and policy.

There are some major successes for scientific influence on alcohol policy. Some examples would be the increased drinking age laws in North America, the drinking driving legislation, or 0.08 laws, and the provision of alcoholism treatment in many countries. Perhaps in the field of alcohol studies it is not possible to give examples of missed influence over 264 years but some long delays can certainly be identified. For example, no country seems to have introduced an alcohol control policy based on the single distribution theory, nor has any country tried to tie reduced consumption to increased levels in real prices for alcoholic beverages, despite the scientific support for these policies. No country seems to have introduced policies which favour the exclusive development of out-patient treatment for alcoholics on the basis that it is cheaper and just as effective as in-patient care. In this chapter consideration is given to the problems which make it difficult for science and policy to influence each other in the proper way, and how this situation might be remedied. (For this chapter, the consideration is based on the role and viewpoint of the scientist.) The main problems may be identified as follows:

* The views expressed in this paper are those of the author and do not necessarily reflect those of the Addiction Research Foundation.

1. Scientists and policy makers rarely meet and probably form two cultures.

2. Scientists have unpopular and sometimes equivocal results.

3. Lack of knowledge about how and when policy decisions are made.

4. Scientists, and perhaps policy makers, have unreasonable expectations.

5. Wrong models of scientific influence are being used.

The two cultures: science and policy

It seems that alcohol research scientists and policy makers form two cultures which rarely interact. Most scientists are career-oriented and keen to make use of their scientific background: few become policy makers. At the senior level few policy makers are scientifically trained and many are political appointees with political science or management backgrounds. They have interests which are different from those of scientists; they read different material and they probably belong to different clubs. They do not attend the same scientific or professional conferences. One rarely meets people from the government alcohol control agencies at any scientific conference on alcohol. Scientists do not often go to the meetings of alcohol control people. This could be changed, of course, if there were more joint sessions and more effort to have integrated meetings.

Few senior policy makers want to read long scientific reports, and there is thus probably a need for 'research brokers' (Sundquist 1978). They would repackage information for decision makers in a form which is more readily digested. To some extent the daily newspapers may perform this function: decision makers often read several newspapers a day. At the Addiction Research Foundation (ARF), broad media coverage is solicited for any important scientific findings and this is usually provided. The findings are also made available in brief summaries of different types. These efforts are probably as successful as most in getting the scientific findings to the policy makers.

Scientific findings: unpopular results

Poor communication is not the only problem between scientists and policy makers. Scientists who study alcohol problems often have unpopular results which are difficult to turn into policies without alienating important groups in society. Those same findings may be equivocal or disputed by other scientists. For example, the finding that alcohol problems and alcohol consumption are related is difficult for policy makers to use. It means that efforts should be made to reduce alcohol consumption by reducing alcohol availability and increasing real prices. Of course, taxes accrued from alcoholic beverages could be affected by these decisions. In many Western countries alcohol consumption has been stable or declining for the past ten years. With that decline, less money has come into many government treasuries. Few governments will want to take a major step which may cause even further declines.

When social scientists argue that taxes should be raised on alcoholic beverages, not all scientists agree. Also, they are but one of many constituencies interested in the issue. There are many thousands of owners and workers in bars, restaurants, and the hotel industry who have an interest too. There are also the grape growers, and the farmers who grow wheat and barley for distilled spirits, in addition to the brewers and distillers themselves. A few years ago when public hearings were held on changing the liquor licence laws in Ontario, Canada, more than 100 briefs were submitted. Only a very few of these briefs were from people or agencies interested in health: almost all were from the current sellers of alcoholic beverages or those who wanted to start selling them. The weight of the arguments presented to the Liquor Licence Commission was that alcohol control laws should be relaxed in as many ways as possible.

It is to the credit of the Liquor Licence Commission that they did not agree to an overall relaxation of controls. Part of the reason is that an ARF scientist, Eric Single, had been seconded to the Commission for almost a year. His daily presence allowed scientifically based arguments to be put urgently and forcefully to the Commission. He became a research broker and an insider, and he helped to bring the two cultures of science and alcohol policy together. In order to create and preserve the proper influence, scientists and policy makers should find more ways of getting together via secondments, sabbaticals, inter-agency committees, and the like. Much research on how policy is made shows that decisions depend more on inside champions or promoters of a position than on technical experts (Glaser *et al.* 1983).

We do not know how decisions are made

It is surprising that there have been so few case studies of how major decisions are made on alcohol policy. Just how and why are such decisions really made? For example, the US Congress and Senate through various committees debated the issue of warning labels on alcoholic beverages for almost 20 years. In 1988 the situation changed suddenly, so that legislative and beverage industry opposition disappeared. However, there has been no detailed study of how and why that happened and what the special influences were. Many people predicted that alcohol warning labels would soon be introduced in Canada, but three years later there is no sign of interest among legislators. Again—why?

In Canada, legislators tend to prefer to focus on restricting or controlling alcohol advertising, rather than variables such as price or opening hours. This occurs despite the general finding that advertising is at best a weak influence on consumption or problems (Smart 1988). Recently, there was a surprising announcement that the government of Ontario would soon control sexist

themes in alcohol advertising, and later other forms of advertising were included as an afterthought. It would appear that too little is known of how
alcohol policy areas are chosen for scientists to influence the outcome. Often
policy makers depend upon trusted advisers: new ideas are rarely accepted on
their own merits but because an adviser argues for them (Fairweather *et al.*
1974). For example, outside pressure groups, such as citizens against drunk
driving, can be very effective in arguing for some alcohol policies, and the
leaders of these groups have sometimes become trusted advisers to alcohol
policy makers.

Great difficulty is encountered in attempting to predict what is coming next
or what alcohol controls will be most salient in the next few years. Social
scientists should embark on more study of why certain policy areas have been
important in the past, what ones will soon be important, and how to influence
the decisions made.

Timeliness in research

If alcohol policy shifts cannot easily be predicted it will be difficult to have
the right policy advice and research available at the right time. Usually when
governments want to make a change in alcohol policy they want to do so
quickly. Policy makers want scientific results to be available when they need
them and are not usually willing to wait several years while the correct
studies are undertaken. Unfortunately, existing results based on research done
a few years ago may be dismissed as 'out of date' or 'irrelevant'.

Researchers on alcohol policy have the difficult situation of predicting what
policy-relevant research results will be needed a few years from now. It is safe
to predict that a few policy areas will be a surprise (such as sexism in alcohol
advertisements) but there are some perennial issues (such as advertising, price,
hours of sale, and types of selling establishments) which will all still be
relevant. To be effective in influencing policy, ongoing research in all of these
areas is needed—but it is difficult to obtain funding for policy research when
the area is dormant politically.

Sometimes policy makers will accept arguments based on research from
other research areas. For example, when the US Congress approved alcohol
warning labels there was no research demonstrating their effectiveness.
However, it was possible to draw on some good research on labels of prescription and over-the-counter drugs and dangerous household products, and
this seemed to be influential. Perhaps alcohol policy advice should more often
involve research-based arguments drawn from a variety of sources when
nothing totally relevant exists.

Scientists have unreasonable expectations

Alcohol researchers are often disappointed about the influence which their
work has on policy making. Scientists seem to believe in a 'sellers versus

buyers', model, with themselves as the sellers of scientific information and policy makers as the buyers. However, this is not the reality which is usually found. When it comes to alcohol policy, decision makers usually have willing, even aggressive, inputs from a wide variety of people. These will include beverage manufacturers, hotel owners, parents and citizens groups, other politicians, and sometimes even the general public. It is unrealistic for scientists to expect decision makers to 'buy' their results and make them directly into policy, when so many other forces exist.

Another force which must be taken into account is 'public opinion'. Decision makers often make public opinion (whether known or surmised) the reason why alcohol control measures are accepted or rejected. In Ontario, a majority of citizens are in favour of controlling alcohol advertising and that surely contributes to the politicians' belief that advertising controls should be pursued. A few years ago a political party in Ontario campaigned with a promise that beer and wine would be sold in local grocery stores. However, when it became obvious that public and some professional opinion was very much against the idea, it was quietly dropped. Frequently, it is not at all clear which ideas for alcohol controls are supported by the general public. Greater understanding of public opinion and its formation may make it easier to get political support—at least for the most popular proposals.

Scientists often forget that science is just one factor in the considerations of policy makers. Policy makers are not a *tabula rasa* on which scientists can expect to write their research findings. Rather than a model of buyers and sellers, a model is required which emphasizes more frequent interaction or networking between policy makers and scientists.

There is a need for policy makers who are open to scientific arguments and innovations based on them. Research on innovators in government shows that they are often younger, more cosmopolitan, and newer at the job. They get around more, have more sources of information and more social networks than do non-innovators (Glaser *et al.* 1983). There may be merit in encouraging 'research brokers' to get information informally to decision makers, if social scientists are unable or unwilling to do so.

The problem-solving model and its problems

There is a tendency to look for the direct impact of research on decisions. This has been described as the problem-solving model (Bucavalas unpublished 1978) and it exists in the alcohol field. Researchers often believe that their results should change or determine policy. When they fail to do so, an undercurrent of discontent develops and researchers lament that policy makers do not use their results. If the results of a particular study are expected to lead automatically to a particular decision, policy or programme, then there will be many disappointments. It took 20 years of research on drinking and driving before 0.08 laws were introduced in most countries, and this stands out as one of the most successful areas of influence.

It is much better to adopt a conceptual approach to the use of scientific results in policy making. In this approach scientific findings provide concepts, understandings, and enlightenment for policy makers: they do not just deliver a clear decision. Research on alcohol policy would then be seen as material that helps the decision maker to think about and conceptualize the problems of making particular decisions. There would then be a shift in the relationship: research demonstrating the link between alcohol consumption and real prices would not be expected to lead directly to a government decision to increase prices. Rather, the research on price, along with other research on availability, would raise issues that must be considered in the decision about whether prices should be raised or not. It should introduce concepts and points of view which have not been considered before. Research on alcohol policy should provide what Orlans (1973) has called a 'language of discourse'.

In the conceptual model, use of research is less dependent upon having a single right answer. Findings from various studies, from different countries and time periods, can all be called upon to provide a conceptual understanding. These policy analyses must be up to date and focused on the questions that policy makers find most important. Very few research organizations carry out such policy analyses of alcohol control issues until they are requested to do so by some level of government. At the ARF, a series of 'best advice' documents have been developed which examine policy issues, such as alcohol treatment, alcohol advertising, beer and wine in grocery stores, etc. However, it is very difficult to keep the content and range of policy analyses both up to date and timely. If the shift (described above) towards a conceptual view of alcohol policy research were to occur, then there would be merit in further development and increasing the number of policy analysis or best advice documents.

What can we do to make things better?

An attempt should now be made to summarize the above suggestions for improvements in relationships between alcohol researchers and policy makers:

1. Look for more ways to break down the two cultures of science and policy.

2. Make scientific results more available to policy makers by getting newspaper coverage and by making results available in brief, highlight types of reports.

3. Use 'research brokers' to bring scientific results to policy makers from the inside, and in informal settings.

4. Learn more about how alcohol policy decisions are actually made and what influences them.

5. Generate an on-going programme of policy relevant research and policy analysis of help to policy makers in the near future.

6. Reduce expectations (from scientists) that scientific findings will solve problems directly.

7. Accept the conceptual model which says that scientific findings promote enlightenment, understanding, and new insights, but rarely lead to a particular social policy.

References

Bucavalas, M.J. (1978). *Certain myths about the use and usefulness of social science research*. Paper prepared for Conference on Social Policy and Drug Use, Washington.

Fairweather, G.W., Sanders, D.W., and Tornatzky, L.G. (1974). *Creating change in mental health organizations*. Pergamon, New York.

Glaser, E.M., Abelson, M.H., and Garrison, K.N. (1983). *Putting knowledge to use*. Fossey-Bass, New York.

Mosteller, F. (1981). Innovation and evaluation. *Science*, **211**, 881–6.

Orlans, H. (1973). *Contracting for knowledge: values and limitations of social science research*. Fossey-Bass, San Francisco.

Smart, R.G. (1988). Does alcohol advertising affect overall consumption? A review of empirical studies. *Journal of Studies on Alcohol*, **49**, 314–23.

Sundquist, J.L. (1978). Research brokerage: the weak link. In *Knowledge and policy. The uncertain connection*, (ed. L.E. Lynn) National Academy of Sciences, Washington.

8. Licit psychotropic drugs

Malcolm Lader

Licit psychotropic drugs comprise those medicines affecting the mind whose use is sanctioned by society. This entails a value judgement by society that a drug is sufficiently useful to be worth having available for the use of at least some of its members. These perceptions can change—not long ago, stout (a form of beer) was prescribable in some hospitals in the UK as a tonic! The data upon which such a value judgement is based concern both the expected benefits of the drug and possible risks, both of which are related to the severity of the indication for which the drug seems appropriate. Much effort has been expended in drawing up guidelines for the estimation of this risk–benefit ratio, but precision remains elusive.

Dependence potential with its attendant complications is an obvious risk with a psychotropic drug. Sometimes the risk is regarded as totally unacceptable and the drug is banned, as with lysergic acid diethylamide (LSD), and more recently with triazolam (Halcion). Often the risk is regarded as acceptable in relation to the benefits, but precautions are necessary, as with most drugs in less severe schedules. Occasionally, as with diamorphine, opinions and policies vary from country to country.

The establishment of the risk–benefit ratio is the scientific aspect of this topic; translating it into policy involves administrative steps in which much wider politico-economic considerations come into play (see also the consideration of alcohol by Smart, Chapter 7). With illicit drugs, the policy adopted can be translated into practical restrictions quite easily. With licit drugs, the legitimate interests of the patient and prescriber have to be brought into the equation and the whole process is much more complex.

In this chapter, these various areas are reviewed, but the quantification of risk is restricted to those problems related to dependence. The benzodiazepine tranquillizers are widely used and will serve as the main example. However, the general principles are similar for all the other licit psychotropic drugs attended by dependence problems, such as the sedatives, stimulants, and analgesics. The mechanisms of policy formation and implementation will be outlined.

The risks

Society's perception of the risks of technological advances, amongst which can be included most new drugs, changes rapidly (Louis Harris and Associates

Table 8.1 Assessing abuse potential of an hypnotic

Animals
1. Reinforcement of drug
    seeking behaviour
    self-administration
    place preference
2. Drug discrimination
3. Ability to produce tolerance

Normal subjects and casual misusers
1. Preference studies
2. Reinforcement
3. Subjective assessment

Patients
1. Case reports
2. Post-marketing surveillance
3. Casualty reports (for example, DAWN)
4. Polydrug abusers 'street-lore'

1980). In the past few decades much concern has been expressed and many organizations set up to lessen such hazards. The conditions in Western civilization today are the safest that have ever existed, as reflected by life expectancy figures, but despite this, concerns mount. This is partly the result of the extent and complexity of technological advances which have been introduced. Computer and communication technology is an obvious example; in the health sphere the advances due to molecular biology are probably even more significant. Many minor risks have been controlled, yet major disasters continue unabated. Higher powers or magic are no longer invoked to explain these disasters, because it is assumed that all events have discernible (and therefore ultimately avoidable) causes—a view not always shared by the experts. New drugs have not been an exception to this, the best example being, of course, the thalidomide disaster.

Society divides into those who would like to revert to a state of nature (some primeval ideal state of innocence) and others who expect science and technology to improve matters by solving the problems which they create. The pharmaceutical industry engages in these 'technological fixes', endlessly trying to introduce improved products without necessarily exploring all of the implications. The drug manufacturers have concentrated on communicating to the prescriber and the public the benefits of a new medication, while often downplaying the frequency, severity, and implications of side-effects.

Risks can be objective or perceived. The former relies on data to establish the probability and nature of a risk, the latter is related to the education of those exposed to that risk. The techniques for establishing the dependence and abuse risks of a tranquillizer are listed in Tables 8.1 and 8.2. They all provide useful data on which a value-judgement can be made. The perception

Table 8.2 Assessing dependence potential of an hypnotic

Animals
1. Physical withdrawal syndrome, spontaneous or induced
2. Suppression of withdrawal to known dependence-inducing drugs
3. Negative reinforcement during withdrawal
4. Cross-tolerance to known dependence-inducing drugs

Normal subjects
1. Short-term studies of rebound
2. Cross-tolerance to known rebound-inducing drugs

Patients
1. Short-term studies of rebound
2. Suppression of rebound to known rebound-inducing drugs
3. Long-term studies of withdrawal
4. Suppression of withdrawal to known withdrawal-inducing drugs
5. Case reports
6. Post-marketing surveillance
7. Epidemiological surveys
   prescription
   usage
8. Evaluation of special groups, for example, the elderly

---

of that risk has changed immensely, from the benzodiazepines being regarded as safe, effective drugs by both prescriber and public, to being dismissed as dangerous poisons (Gabe and Williams 1986).

Some of the factors which influence the perception of risk have been identified. Involuntary risks are perceived as much greater than those which one can choose whether to confront or not. Unknown or covert risks are regarded as more substantial than the familiar risks all about us. Threat to self is perceived differently from assaults on society, and there is also the time element, the single catastrophe versus the chronic hazard. Unprecedented risks are perceived as more threatening than those which we have encountered before. Overall, however, the difference between objective and perceived risk is that between a statistical concept and a culturally learned response to uncertainty (Sills 1985).

These factors can be examined for the risks of tranquillizers. One of the most contentious topics has been the claim, now generally accepted, that tranquillizers could cause dependence, as manifested by a characteristic physical withdrawal reaction, *even in normal dosage* (Petursson and Lader 1981; Tyrer *et al.* 1981). Patients did not need to escalate their dosage to become dependent. Thus, the risk of dependence in users on prescribed tranquillizers was originally unknown and exposure to it involuntary. It is hardly surprising that the patients felt that they had been betrayed by the medical profession and by the pharmaceutical industry. An inevitable consequence has been that some 15 000 claimants have launched claims against the benzodiazepine manufacturers alleging negligence in developing these drugs. Members of the medical profession will no doubt also be sued.

Now that the dependence risk of the benzodiazepines is known, patients are reluctant to expose themselves to that risk, and this adverse perception has been generalized to some extent to other drugs, such as the antidepressants.

The benefits

The benefits of psychotropic drugs can be divided into clinical, the psychosocial, and the economic. Modern methods for measuring clinical benefits date back only about 40 years (Hunt *et al.* 1985). Before then, many forms of therapy were considered beneficial on the basis of the status, authority, and assertiveness of the proponents, rather than on any scientific assessments. The application of controlled trial technology, with random allocation to treatments, double-blind procedures, and appropriate experimental design and analysis has revolutionized the assessment of clinical benefit. Furthermore, the need to characterize patients has led to the adoption of pragmatic nosologies. Finally, regulatory agencies have issued various guidelines on measuring the clinical effects of drugs, thus standardizing the conduct of such trials (Food and Drug Administration 1978).

Nevertheless, problems arise in quantifying the usefulness of the clinical benefit conferred, despite it being significant. Such caution has led to a reappraisal of the efficacy of many prescribed licit drugs. The obsolescence and desuetude of the amphetamines and the barbiturates are cases in point.

Psychosocial benefit is even more difficult to assess. It refers to the general psychological and social functionings of the individual, both very difficult aspects to measure accurately. Recently, attention has focused on the patient's perception of his or her functioning, and subsumed under the vague rubric of 'quality of life' (Alexander and Willems 1981). This can be equated with the WHO definition of perfect health as a state of complete bodily, mental, and social well-being.

Consideration of economic benefit is confined in this chapter to that accruing to the individual and society because of the efficacy of a drug: hence it does not include the benefit to the pharmaceutical industry (Agran and Martin 1985). Such indices as reductions in hospital bed-occupancy, out-patient and general practitioner attendances, and days lost from work provide part-estimates. Reduced morbidity may also result in enhanced productivity and many other less easily quantifiable measures. Even more complex issues include, for example, the savings accruing from increased safety in overdose of a psychotropic drug.

The benefits of the tranquillizers may be examined under these three headings. The clinical benefit of these drugs has been reviewed many times in general terms. More useful is the critical assessment, including a meta-analysis, carried out as part of a Quality Assurance Project (1985) under the aegis of the Royal Australian and New Zealand College of Psychiatrists. An analysis of more than 80 comparative studies suggested that placebo treatment was fairly effective in patients with generalized anxiety disorder, and that the benzodiazepine anxiolytics had about double that effect. Nevertheless, the overall drug effect was really quite modest. As often happens in psychiatry, the clinical benefit is proportionately greater in the more seriously ill. Indeed, in the mildly ill and in the elderly, clinical benefit may be nugatory.

Psychosocial benefit is probably greater but more illusory. Many patients derive only partial clinical benefit from tranquillizers, but this may be sufficient to enable them to function at home, at work, and in society. It is illusory because such drug-induced re-adaptation may render the individual unwilling or incapable of tackling the personal problems which underlie his or her stress responses and anxiety. In turn, many patients' problems emanate from unsatisfactory and ultimately intolerable politico-economic circumstances. Then tranquillizers can be stigmatized as a way of suppressing attempts to protest against those conditions of poverty and deprivation. How does one quantify the dubious 'benefits' accruing to society in subduing its disadvantaged minorities? (Gabe and Lipshitz-Phillips 1984).

Risk–benefit decisions

The risk–benefit decision has to be made against the background of other factors, such as the severity and chronicity of the proposed indication, the expected duration of use, and the type of patient population, for example, the elderly. The availability of alternative methods of treatment, their usefulness, and the need for new therapies also influences this assessment. The stage of the development programme dictates the type of information available. Early on, animal data preponderate; late on, much clinical experience should have accrued (Teeling-Smith 1983).

Evaluation of the risk–benefit ratio is usually almost entirely a value judgement by experts although more formal cost–benefit analyses are sometimes feasible. Assessments against other therapies may allow comparative rankings without precise quantification of the individual ratios.

It is the task of the regulatory authorities to assess new drugs from the point of view of safety, efficacy, and quality (see, for example, Medicines Act 1968). Furthermore, licences are reviewed regularly or on demand and can be modified or revoked if the risk–benefit ratio is perceived to have changed. Thus, both data prior to launch and data garnered post-marketing are used in this exercise.

The misuse potential of a drug is not considered by the UK licensing authority, except within its stated indication. In other words, the misuse potential of a benzodiazepine by anxious patients for whom it is prescribed is a legitimate concern, whereas the abuse by people who obtain it illicitly is not taken into account in the initial licensing or review process. However, this may change.

Assessment of misuse potential

The responsibility for assessing the misuse potential lies with the Advisory Council on the Misuse of Drugs (ACMD), a statutory body set up under the Misuse of Drugs Act 1971 'to keep under review the situation in the United Kingdom with respect to drugs which are being or appear to them likely to be misused and of which the misuse is having or appears to them capable of having harmful effects sufficient to constitute a social problem . . .' The Council then advises the responsible Ministers on appropriate measures, such as restricting the availability of such drugs. The whole panoply of Controlled drugs and the classification and scheduling relates to these restrictions.

A committee of the ACMD, the Technical Committee (currently chaired by the author) is charged with the task of reviewing the data on drugs of misuse and potential misuse and advising the full Council accordingly. With prescribed drugs such as the benzodiazepines, the scope for review is limited to misuse potential constituting a potential social problem and does not include such factors as physical withdrawal syndromes and use within the therapeutic context. The therapeutic usefulness of a drug inevitably gets drawn into the arguments. It would not be advisable to control strictly a drug which was widely used and only occasionally misused by individuals obtaining illicit supplies. To that end, soundings are taken of professional organizations representing doctors, dentists, pharmacists, and so on. The opinions received relate to the perceived efficacy of the drug, its usefulness, the perceived side-effects and drawbacks and also the practical implications of restricting the availability of a licit drug by scheduling it.

Ultimately, the decision revolves around a value-judgement of a complex risk–benefit assessment. The complexity arises out of the need to balance the benefit accruing to legitimate users of the drug against the risk to society posed by the illicit abusers. With the benzodiazepine tranquillizers, an additional complication concerns the dependence potential in normal usage. However, this does not constitute a social problem—old ladies do not mug passers-by in order to sustain their 5 mg of diazepam twice-a-day habit. General practitioners still prescribe these drugs to regular users, albeit more reluctantly than previously, and it is hoped with more careful monitoring. Consequently, concern about dependence, as opposed to abuse, potential has expressed itself in official pronouncements from the Medicines Division (now the Medicines Control Agency) of the Department of Health rather than the Drugs Section of the Home Office. The relevant Act is then the Medicines Act 1968 rather than the Misuse of Drugs Act 1971.

The steps in warnings about tranquillizers

The earliest warning came from the Committee on the Review of Medicines (CRM), which in 1980 published a review of the benzodiazepines in the *British Medical Journal* (Committee on Review of Medicines 1980). The CRM was a committee set up under Section 4 of the Medicines Act 1968 to review all medication marketed under Licences of Right at the implementation of the Act. After exhaustive review of the data, the CRM expressed concern about the extensive long-term use of tranquillizers. At that time, the existence of normal dose dependence was disputed and abuse potential appeared low but the CRM warned against unnecessary long-term use and also emphasized the need for gradual tapering to minimize the withdrawal syndrome. Nearly 10 years later, the evidence had become so compelling that both the Royal College of Psychiatrists and the Committee on Safety of Medicines (another Section 4 Committee) issued recommendations that benzodiazepines should be reserved for the short-term treatment of moderate of severe anxiety.

Scheduling of benzodiazepines

The problem of the abuse of benzodiazepines is dealt with as a separate issue, in this instance under the Misuse of Drugs Act 1971. They are included in Class C substances and are in Schedule 4, subject to minimal control. Thus, controlled drug prescription requirements do not apply, and these drugs are not subject to requirements for safer custody. Schedule 4 contains benzodiazepines only.

The UK is a signatory to the United Nations Convention on Psychotropic Substances 1971 and therefore is obliged to implement the decisions of the Commission on Narcotic Drugs of the Economic and Social Council of the United Nations, as based on the evidence provided by the World Health Organization (WHO). The WHO works through specialist advisory committees who assess the dependence potential, adverse effects and abuse potential, and the 'evidence that the substance is being or is likely to be abused so as to constitute a public health and social problem' (United Nations 1977).

With the benzodiazepines, as licit drugs, provision was made by the WHO for representations to be made by the manufacturers. They pointed out that usefulness of these drugs and argued that this outweighed the abuse potential, which they regarded as limited. The representatives of Third World countries in the WHO drew attention to the extent of abuse in their countries, where easy availability had often led to major social problems. The benzodiazepines were scheduled, but at a level of rigour which meant little change in those countries in which the benzodiazepines were available only on prescription.

There was originally some reluctance on the part of the UK authorities to schedule the benzodiazepines, as it was thought that the problem of abuse, as opposed to dependence, was uncommon and that as these drugs were already available only on medical prescription, further restrictions were superfluous. However, the UK now has a major problem with temazepam which is injected intravenously. Most of the problem concerns polydrug abusers but some individuals are known who abuse temazepam only. In view of the risks of intravenous drug usage, warnings have been issued to the medical profession to be careful with prescribing of these compounds (Grahame-Smith 1991).

Conclusions

Licit drugs cover several types of compound of varying degrees of usefulness. Some, such as the barbiturates and amphetamines, are obsolescent, others, such as the benzodiazepine anxiolytics and hypnotics, are being severely criticized and their use limited. These changes in usage reflect changing perceptions of the risk–benefit ratio in relationship to the severity of the indication. The development of better alternatives is a major aim of the pharmaceutical industry. Assessment of the dependence potential is an important part of the development of a new medicine.

Assessment of abuse potential is more difficult, and sometimes the extent of the problem is only apparent when the drug has been available for some time. Scheduling of a potentially abusable drug is a complex matter calling for a value-judgement in which the legitimate needs of the patient and prescriber are balanced against the overall risks to society.

The benzodiazepines provide an example of drugs with double problems— normal dose dependence leading to long-term use; and intravenous use by injecting drug abusers. The former problem is dealt with the education of doctors and their patients. The latter, however, requires the same approach as other drugs of intravenous abuse.

References

Agran, M. and Martin, E.E. (1985). Establishing socially validated drug research in community settings, *Psychopharmacology Bulletin*, 21, 285–90.

Alexander, J.L. and Willems, E.P. (1981). Quality of life: some measurement requirements. *Archives of Physical Medicine and Rehabilitation*, 62, 261–5.

Committee on the Review of Medicines (1980). Systematic review of the benzodiazepines. *British Medical Journal*, 1, 910–12.

Food and Drug Administration (1978). Obligations of clinical investigators of regulated articles. *Federal Register, Washington*, Aug. 8, 1978.

Gabe, J. and Lipshitz-Phillips, S. (1984). Tranquillisers as social control. *The Sociological Review*, 32(3), 524–46.

Gabe, J. and Williams, P. (1986). Tranquilliser use: a historical perspective. In *Tranquillisers. Social, psychological and clinical perspectives* (ed. J. Gabe and P. Williams), pp. 3–17. Tavistock Publications, London.

Grahame-Smith, D.G. (1991). Letter to the Editor. *British Medical Journal*, 302, 1210.

Hunt, S.M., McEwen, J., and McKenna, S.P. (1985). Measuring health status: a new tool for clinicians and epidemiologists. *Journal of the Royal College of General Practitioners*, 35, 185–8.

Louis Harris and Associates: (1980). *Risk in a Complex Society—a Marsh and McLennan Public Opinion Survey*. Marsh and McLennan, New York.

Medicines Act, (1968). *Her Majesty's Stationery Office*, London.

Misuse of Drugs Act, (1971). *Her Majesty's Stationery Office*, London.

Petursson, H. and Lader, M. (1981). Withdrawal from long-term benzodiazepine treatment. *British Medical Journal*, 283, 643–5.

Quality Assurance Project, (1985). Treatment outlines for the management of anxiety states. *Australian and New Zealand Journal of Psychiatry*, 19, 138–51.

Sills, D.L. (1985). Hazards beyond number. *Nature*, 317, 117–18.

Teeling-Smith, G. (1983). In *Measuring the social benefits of medicine*, (ed. G. Teeling-Smith), pp. 163–6. Office of Health Economics, London.

Tyrer, P., Rutherford, D., and Huggett, T. (1981). Benzodiazepine withdrawal symptoms and propranolol. *Lancet*, i, 520–22.

United Nations (1977). Convention on psychotropic substances, 1971. New York.

9. The US anti-drug prevention strategy: science and policy connections

Herbert D. Kleber

In order for public policy to be maximally effective, it should be based on a scientific examination of the nature of the problem and of programmes that work. Unfortunately, in the area of prevention of the use of illicit drugs, policy makers are faced both with inadequate epidemiological data on the nature of the problem, and insufficient controlled studies on which prevention programmes work best. This was certainly the situation prevailing in the USA in 1989 when the government set about devising a national anti-drug strategy. Unfortunately, even when there is good information available, it is not always used for policy, as Gunne and Gronbladh (1984) have pointed out in the response of the Swedish government to a very successful methadone maintenance study in the early 1980s. This chapter will detail the prevention strategy in the USA and the rationale behind it. It is recognized that countries with a different magnitude or type of drug problem, or a different historical relation with drug use, might have chosen a very different path.

Overall US drug control strategy

In the USA, it was the problem of an escalating cocaine epidemic and the lack of a co-ordinated national effort to fight it that brought about the creation in 1988 of the Office of National Drug Control Policy (ONDCP), and the subsequent development of a National Drug Control Strategy. The creation of the ONDCP by the US Congress was unprecedented in the history of the US government, a cabinet-level office created for the purpose of co-ordinating all federal efforts focused on a single goal.

The two major components of the ONDCP, are the Offices of Supply Reduction and Demand Reduction. The Director of Demand Reduction is charged with overseeing that portion of the National Drug Control Strategy concerned with prevention and treatment efforts, as well as serving as chairperson of a co-ordinating committee of high-level representatives from 19 federal agencies that work to ensure that federal anti-drug prevention efforts are working in concert with each other and within the guidelines of the National Drug Control Strategy.

One important emphasis of the US National Drug Control Strategy is the need to take the long view, to realize that significant progress will not be made until the government and the people stop giving in to the same temptation as the drug user—the search for the quick fix. There is neither a painless nor a quick solution to the complex problems involved in the fight against drug use: time and much effort are required.

The National Drug Control Strategy also stresses that if citizens rely solely upon the federal government, failure is certain. Substantially reducing drug use requires the involvement in the struggle of an entire nation, including States, communities, schools, religious groups, and families.

In consequence, the ONDCP devised a national, not just a federal strategy, a blueprint for unified action on all fronts. The strategy seeks to co-ordinate in a coherent, integrated, and much-improved programme, the initiatives of criminal justice, drug treatment, education, the workplace, research, public awareness, community prevention campaigns, international activities, and efforts to interdict smuggled drugs before they reach the country's borders. It is believed that no single initiative or programme can solve the problem alone. In an all-out anti-drug effort, the whole may truly be greater than the sum of its parts.

Prevention and epidemiology

Let us begin by examining the area of prevention. It is in many ways more difficult than treatment, since less is known about it. The body of knowledge is, however, expanding significantly.

One way to conceptualize the drug problem is to think of a pipeline. At one end are the non-users, at the other end, the heavy users and addicts. In between are so-called casual or controlled users, individuals who by definition are able to stop their drug use (if not, they move on to the next category of heavy users or addicts). The role of prevention is to persuade the non-users not to start and those who have started to stop before they get into trouble. For those already addicted, prevention is no longer the issue, and treatment, either voluntary or compulsory via the criminal justice system, is often required. It appears obvious that decreasing the number of individuals entering the pipeline, or getting those already in to stop before they become addicts, will ultimately decrease the number of addicts. Since treatment, although it can certainly be successful, does not work as often or as well as one would like, prevention becomes essential if we are to lower the numbers of addicts and the social pathology they convey.

A scientific approach demands that prevention policy begins with epidemiological data as to the nature of the problem. Demographic data, such as the size and characteristics of the population at risk of using drugs, the type of drugs being used, etc., is critical to effective policy making.

In 1989 when the ONDCP was begun, good data was not readily available.

There were limited statistics available from the High School Senior Survey and the National Household Survey. The High School Senior Survey, while conducted yearly, was limited because it did not include younger students or those who dropped out of school. The National Household Survey was a sampling of 8000 people, taken only every three years usually with a lag of at least a year before results were available, and did not include critical subsets of drug users: the homeless, those in prisons, jails, shelters, those in college dormitories, etc.

Through co-operative efforts between the ONDCP and the National Institute for Drug Abuse, special surveys have been initiated in the USA that also include eighth and tenth grade pupils (14 and 16 years olds) as well as school drop-outs. The frequency of the National Household Survey has been increased to once a year and the number of people being surveyed has increased to 20 000. Major metropolitan area surveys, street epidemiologists, and other methods are increasing our knowledge base. So-called 'quick response surveys', while not yet in place, hold out the promise of providing some data on a timely basis that would help policy makers in knowing whether they are on the right track.

Without appropriate data the policy maker is at a disadvantage for devising appropriate responses. For example, it is a common misconception in the USA that most drug occurs among the poor and disadvantaged, a notion fostered in part by the media. Newspaper articles and television programmes depict primarily African–American and Hispanic addicts. It is easy to lose sight of the fact that most of the people in African–American and Hispanic neighbourhoods are not using drugs, that most people who use drugs are not poor, and most of the poor do not use drugs.

Normalization and denormalization

The history of the recent escalation of illegal drug use in the USA began during the decades of the 1960s and 1970s, when American society became very tolerant of drug use, a major change from the preceding decades. This resulted in large increases in the use of illegal drugs, especially marijuana in the 1960s and 1970s, and cocaine in the 1970s and 1980s. Drug use in the USA essentially became 'normalized'. From the use of d-lysergic acid diethylamide (LSD) and marijuana in high schools and colleges; to the use of amphetamines by medical students to help them study; to the use of cocaine in professional sports, workplaces, and parties; it became 'normal' to use drugs.

Consequently, one of the first prevention themes of the National Drug Control Strategy in the USA was the denormalization of drug use. The dramatic changes in attitude regarding drugs, and the substantial decreases in the number of children and adults using drugs over the past 5 years speaks to the success of this approach which pre-dated the formation of the ONDCP, and is a tribute to numerous grass roots efforts as well as the Media Partnership for a Drug-Free America. The ONDCP's strategy attempts to expand and improve upon these efforts.

One of the important means in the approach to denormalizing drug use is to hold the user accountable. The theory behind this is as follows. Observation of how individuals begin drug use shows that the carrier, or vector, of this disease is the casual drug user, not the addict. The burned-out addict, or the psychotic cocaine abuser who has lost his or her health, possessions, and families. The role model is the person who is using drugs at work or at school, who sends the message by his or her behaviour that you can have it all: you can enjoy the pleasurable effects of drugs and still keep your health, your possessions, your family, and your job.

That is how most individuals start taking drugs—they do not buy drugs the first time. Rather, they are given drugs by older siblings or friends and acquaintances at school, at work, or at parties. A useful prevention strategy is to target these casual users, and work to deter those who have never used drugs from ever starting.

User accountability

That is why one of the foundations of the National Drug Control Strategy is user accountability, which means holding both 'casual' and 'heavy' drug users accountable for their drug use. User accountability laws and policies provide clear consequences for the possession or use of illegal drugs. For example, laws have been passed that lead to the suspension of drivers' and pilots' licences, etc., for using illegal drugs; and drug testing has been implemented for bus drivers, train engineers, etc. Some State licensing agencies hold professionals, such as doctors, lawyers, and real estate agents, accountable by suspension or revocation of licences for drug use, restoring them only after successful rehabilitation. Public housing projects and neighbourhood block coalitions have turned 'free-drug zones' into 'drug-free zones' by evicting and forcing out drug users, and by establishing resident patrols to enforce no-use policies.

A user accountability strategy is appropriate in a situation such as that in the USA where, by 1988, 74 million Americans—one-third of the population—had taken illegal drugs. It might not be appropriate in a country with a relatively small level of drug use. Since both children and adults spend most of their time either at school or at work, user accountability school and workplace policies and procedures can have an important impact on deterring drug use. Law enforcement programmes, such as 'No Drugs, Do Time' in Phoenix, Arizona, USA, give those arrested for simple use or possession of illegal drugs a choice: pay a fine and undergo treatment or risk serving time in prison.

User accountability measures are helping to denormalize the use of drugs and are innovative means by which Americans are reducing drug use. However, efforts to compel current users to give up drugs is only one part of the prevention strategy. Education has an important role in preventing drug use as well.

The role of education in a prevention strategy

Although some individuals use the terms prevention and education synonymously in relation to illegal drug use, it is clear that they are not the same. While education may be a necessary part of prevention, it is clearly not sufficient. What is needed is a comprehensive approach that includes parents, the community, the workplace, and the media, in conjunction with education. When this happens, as in Project STAR in Kansas City, USA, drug use can be shown to drop compared with control groups (Pentz *et al.* 1989).

The good news is, according to the 1990 High School Senior Survey, drug use by teenagers in the USA fell by 13 per cent from 1988 to 1990. Cocaine use by teenagers declined by 49 per cent during the same period and 28 per cent more teenagers disapproved of drug use. This does not mean that the situation is improving everywhere at the same rate, and in fact, it may be getting worse in some areas. Nevertheless, it is improving overall. The bad news is that there are still far too many people using drugs. More needs to be done.

Education is only one part of the prevention activities that need to be targeted at children. There is, however, a growing consensus that merely providing cognitive knowledge about drugs does not work. It is not surprising that knowledge is cure active only so far as ignorance is the disease. That is why a number of schools are adopting different approaches. The most promising is often called 'refusal skills training' or 'resistance training'. It grew out of previous efforts to teach youngsters how to say 'no' to smoking. Resistance training has had success because it correctly recognizes the enormous role peer pressure plays in influencing decisions to try drugs. The training method is summarized in four basic points: (1) identity pressures to use drugs; (2) counter these pro-use arguments; (3) learn how to say 'no'; (4) provide the motivation to say no by explaining current rather than future negative effects on daily life and social relationships, and by dispelling the belief that drug use is widespread, desirable, or harmless. The US Department of Education gives more than $500 million to local school districts for drug-free programmes, and innovative programmes, such as DARE, (Drug Abuse Resistance Education) have been developed at the local level.

High-risk and low-risk youngsters

Prevention will be most successful if it is appropriate, targeted, and recognizes the diversity of the problem. One approach to segmentation is to conceptualize four groups: high-risk and low-risk youngsters growing up in high-crime or low-crime areas. A different kind of prevention programme is needed for the high-risk youngsters in the high-crime areas than for the high-risk youngsters in the low-crime areas. The latter group is often comprised of the children of alcoholics, children from troubled or single parent families, and those with psychological problems, especially learning problems, such as attention deficit disorder, combined with anti-social personality disorder. Numerically, although not by rate, these youngsters make up the majority of drug users. They need attention directed to these issues just like the high-risk youngsters in the high-crime areas may need academic tutoring, adult male role models, and after-school recreational activities. Both of these groups need different strategies from low-risk youngsters in low-risk areas, for whom a 'just say no' method with appropriate resistance strategies often may be sufficient.

As mentioned earlier, schools must also develop clear and firm policies regarding drug use. The Anne Arundel School district in Maryland, USA, as cited in the National Drug Control Strategy, combines a good drug education programme with firm policies. The first time you are caught selling drugs, you are expelled; the first time you are caught using or in possession of drugs, you are suspended for a few days, your parents are notified, and you have to attend specialized drug education counselling. When you return to school, a second offence leads to expulsion and being sent to an alternative school. School attendance is still required, but you do not attend with your former classmates as a vector, a carrier, spreading drug use. The student needs to earn his or her way back to regular classes by appropriate behaviour.

After instituting those policies, there was an 80 per cent decline in the number of youngsters who had to be expelled from school for drug use. Combining effective drug education with firm and unambiguous policies is more likely to lead to a better outcome than just one or the other alone.

It is important also that institutions of higher learning adopt clear and firm approaches to drug use on campus. These institutions, dedicated to the life of the mind, too often do not have or enforce anti-drug policies. They prefer to ignore the problem, but have an important obligation to do more. Drug use is as inconsistent with scholarly endeavours as plagiarism. It not only extols present over future gratification, it can also interfere with learning via the physiological effects of the drugs.

In order to help prevention and treatment of drug use by college students, the National Drug Control Strategy (1989) proposed, and Congress passed, a new law requiring all schools to develop and make available for review detailed descriptions of drug prevention programmes and policies. The overarching goal is, again, to denormalize drug use on campus. The law and its regulations—described well in the US Department of Education's Guide for College Presidents—states that institutions of higher education must:

(1) develop clear policies concerning alcohol and drugs;

(2) enforce substance abuse regulations;

(3) provide drug education programmes;

(4) ensure intervention and referral for treatment of students, faculty, and staff;

(5) assess attitudes and behaviour toward drugs.

The role of the workplace

For the adult, a key target area is the workplace. Employers should have drug-free workplace policies, including, where appropriate, drug testing, supervisor training, and employee assistance programmes. Federal law requires firms that have government grants or contracts of over $25 000 a year to develop a drug-free workplace with four components. The first component is clearly enunciated drug-free workplace policies that spell out the company's policy on drug use, including consequences. One study has found that 70 per cent of all drug users are employed. Workers are often more concerned about losing their job than they are about losing their spouse. Drug use in the workplace is also associated with higher absenteeism, more accidents, and poorer quality of work. Thus the workplace becomes a natural setting upon which to focus.

The second is training and education about drug abuse to supervisors and employees. If someone is using drugs, it is more likely to be known by their co-workers, than their supervisors. Whether they do something about it, whether the co-worker puts pressure on his or her colleague to get help, or reports him or her to the employee assistance programme if not, is likely a function of what the co-worker thinks will happen. If the perception is that the drug user will immediately be fired, the co-worker will not report his or her colleague. He or she is much more likely to report it, however, if he or she thinks the colleague will get help. Such help not only benefits the drug user, but also helps the co-worker, since drug use related to the job makes work more dangerous for everyone and the company less competitive, which could lead to job layoffs. Again, firm policies are needed, but rehabilitation programmes are just as important so that individuals can get help.

The third is employee assistance programmes. These can be very effective. A number of such programmes has been studied, and they commonly show a success rate for drug and alcohol problems up to 65 per cent or higher. They are both a cost-effective and a humane way of approaching the problem. Drug-free workplaces are an important part of a national policy—an important place for early intervention with the person who is already an addict, and a crucial place to hold the casual user accountable for his or her use.

The fourth component is appropriate drug testing. There are essentially four kinds of drug testing: pre-employment, post-accident or for cause, upon suspicion, and random. The first three are relatively uncontroversial, and businesses find them useful in deterring use and identifying those with drug problems who need help. The last kind, random, is more controversial, but it is encouraged at least for those employees in safety-related or sensitive positions, and some companies, such as the Motorola Corporation, have found random testing of all employees, from the president of the company to line workers, to be effective. (A fifth kind of drug testing involves the random but relatively frequent testing of individuals who have been through rehabilitation and have now returned to work.)

The role of the community

Ultimately though, the most important part of the prevention effort may be at the community level. All segments of the community need to be involved: parents, law enforcement and health professionals, the faith community, service clubs, businesses, and government officials—entire communities must organize and work together to fight drugs. While the federal role is limited in terms of what needs to happen within communities, there are ways in which it can help.

For example, the Robert Wood Johnson Foundation sponsored a $26 million initiative in which communities of between 100 000 and 250 000 people had the opportunity to receive up to $3 million for community-organized efforts to combat drug use. Although only eight communities will eventually receive grants, over 700 indicated some interest in applying, and 300 of these organized themselves enough to send in the demanding application. This example led the National Drug Control Office to the development of the Community Partnership initiative, working together with the US Department of Health and Human Services (DHHS). The Office of Substance Abuse Prevention in the DHHS will devote $50 million in 1990, and over $100 million in 1991 to fund such community coalition-building efforts. Eventually, the Federal Government will fund more than 200 such communities.

To complement this programme and other community efforts, a National Volunteer Training Center has been developed to train volunteers as to what has been successful in other communities. Trained drug prevention volunteers in every community will bring effective techniques within the reach of all the millions of Americans who, in poll after poll, indicate their desire and willingness to become involved in the fight against drug abuse. The center opened in the autumn of 1991.

In addition, there are a number of groups supporting community volunteer efforts: service groups, such as the Lions, and fraternal orders, such as the Masons. The latter have started innovative programmes in a number of states to help high-risk youngsters. A programme started in 1989 in New York State called 'Bank on Prevention' is run by the association of independent banks. They raise money for anti-drug efforts in a number of local communities, with a local banker acting as trustee. There are many ways in which the private sector can become involved in the crucial efforts at the community level.

The National Drug Control Strategy also calls for the federal government to put greater resources into research that will identify the most effective means of preventing drug use. Carefully monitored demonstration projects—with control groups, independent testing, and follow-up research—will be funded to determine what kinds of prevention programme work best, and why. More basic prevention research that examines both biological factors (for example serotonin levels) and psychological ones (for example learning and attention disorders) that put individuals at higher risk will receive continued funding priorities, as will the role of psychiatric disorders.

Role of the media

Thorough and thoughtful media campaigns can work together with schools and communities to help shape public opinion and attitudes about drugs. The anti-smoking campaign of the 1970s and the recent emphasis on the dangers of passive smoking may have had a great deal to do with the reductions in teenage and adult smoking during the past decade. In the last few years, we have seen similar media attention toward drugs.

Practically every American has been a television or print advertisement produced by the Media Partnership for a Drug-Free America, created in 1986. The organization set a target in 1989 of raising $1 million dollars in advertising a day from the private sector for three years—more than $1000 million to continue and enhance this media effort. Not only is the space and time for these advertisements donated, but the creative work is provided free of charge as well. Surveys have shown that in the areas of higher media saturation by the Partnership, changes in attitudes toward drug use and users have been greater.

The media campaign recognizes that it is necessary to focus on both potential 'consumers' and 'influencers'—parents, peer groups, health care professionals, opinion leaders, and teachers. The primary 'influencer' messages have three components: informational, to arm them with facts so that discussion with users and potential users can occur on a credible basis; responsibility inducing, to point out that control is possible and the need to exercise it; and finally, to upset the cost-benefit balance by communicating to the public the costs on a personal and societal basis. The primary 'consumer' messages also focus on three elements: motivation, dispelling the mythology that one can benefit from illegal drug use; countering misinformation, highlighting the true negative effects; and values, stressing responsibility to oneself and society, and how drug use can undermine this. Another way to view this is to postulate that one can influence the decision to use drugs, either alone or in combination, by providing the individual with information and moral persuasion to help shape his or her attitudes and desires, or by making an individual fear the consequences and penalties. The quantity of the advertisements and their superb creative quality are a tribute to the efforts of the Media Partnership staff, the concern and generosity of the media, and the creative genius of the advertising companies.

These and similar advertisements are examples of efforts to encourage negative attitudes toward drugs, to 'denormalize' their use. Such efforts are more effective when they are part of a consistent approach in which not only advertisements but regular television programmes and films, sports, entertainment stars, and other role models convey an unambiguous anti-drug message. In a democratic society, such efforts, will, of course, not be universal and society needs to avoid the enforced silence about drugs that occurred in earlier decades and is cited by historians such as Musto as paving the way eventually for the drug use explosion in the 1960s and 1970s.

Prevention efforts appear to be most successful when parents, schools, service and religious groups, communities, law enforcement, media, and employers act as a unified front. Community policing, as pioneered in cities such as Charleston, South Carolina, USA, can help communities reclaim the streets and make the task of prevention easier.

Prevention happens too late for the estimated 4–6 million Americans who are problem users or addicts. Changing their deeply ingrained destructive behaviour is a task not for media campaigns or educational efforts, but for treatment programmes.

Conclusions and predictions

To summarize, more money, attention, thinking, research, legislative and government action, co-operative effort, and manpower are being applied to the drug problem now than probably at any time in American history. In every relevant area, more efforts are underway: against drug production and trafficking overseas; against smuggling at our borders; against drug crime in our streets and communities; against the medical problems of addiction; and against the encroachment of drugs into our schools, families, and neighbourhoods.

There appears to be cautious reason for optimism. Casual drug use began to decline around 1985 and continues to decline (Johnson *et al.* 1990; NIDA, 1990). Heavy drug use increased from 1984 to 1989 as crack hit the USA, but even that appeared to be declining by 1990, as measured by emergency room data. By 1991 numbers had increased, back to the 1989 peak, so it is not clear at this time what is happening to the level of heavy drug use. Since the casualty curve lags behind the incidence curve by at least 3 years, it is not surprising that such heavy use did not turn down at the same time as the more controlled use did. Nor is it surprising that use is not down uniformly, that certain sections of our biggest cities do not show the improvement seen in other neighbourhoods or in other cities. These communities should eventually catch up as the expanded treatment, widespread community organization against drugs, and improved policing techniques take hold.

Conclusions

A prudent and cautious judgement on the present circumstances in the USA would be that the drug problem, nationwide, is no longer getting worse, and in some very significant respects is now getting better.

Keeping the pressure on over time—both organized government and private sector effort—is the key. The drug problem is still far too big. Too many communities, families, and individuals still suffer the terrible consequences of drug use and drug crime. The drug situation in too many neighbourhoods has not improved, and now is precisely not the time to reduce effort or cut funding. The evidence of the past year suggest that progress is possible—not that it is inevitable. Continued national and international support of anti-drug efforts will make a definitive and lasting difference. While the goal of an entirely drug-free America is utopian and not likely to be reached, it is realistic to strive for earlier eras—such as the 1950s—when drug use was a small problem on the American scene.

What about the future? What is on the horizon for Europe? If present trends continue, by 1995, or so, heavy cocaine use in the USA could decline by 50 per cent from 1988 levels. Unfortunately, this probably will not be the case in Europe.

Heroin use appears to be increasing in the USA, but at a much lower rate than the decrease in use of cocaine. The ONDCP estimates that there are about two million cocaine addicts in the USA, so that number may drop by about one million, and perhaps 100 000 to 200 000 of those will switch over to heroin. So there will be some rise in use of heroin, but far smaller than the decline in use of cocaine. Most of the new heroin addicts will be people switching over from cocaine, not new drug users. Cocaine seizures in Europe have sharply increased, and the rate appears to be climbing. This increased supply will probably translate into sharply increased use. In short, there may be a reversal in what is driving the use of illegal drugs. In the 1980s demand drove supply; in the 1990s supply will drive demand. There will be a glut of cocaine in the world, looking for users. This could lead to sharp rises in cocaine use in western Europe, Japan, and the Andean nations themselves. These countries will need to study the best prevention efforts most relevant to their populations to lessen this impact.

As these trends unfold, or unexpected ones develop, it is critical that the scientific and research communities be prepared to provide the kind of data that will improve the making of public policy, and that governments be prepared to provide resources to these groups to do so.

References

Guide for College Presidents (1990). U.S. Department of Education. Supt of Documents, US Government Printing Office, Washington.

Gunne, L.M. and Gronbladh, L. (1984). The Swedish Methadone Maintenance Program. In: *Social and Medical Aspects of Drug Abuse* (ed. G. Serban), pp. 205–13, Spectrum, New York.

Johnson, L.D., O'Malley, P., and Bachman, J.G. (1990) *Illicit drug use, smoking, and drinking by America's high school students, college students, and young adults: 1975–1990.* National Institute on Drug Abuse (NIDA).

National Drug Control Strategy. The White House (1989). Supt of Documents, US Government Printing Office, Washington.

National Institute on Drug Abuse (NIDA), (1990). *National Household Survey on Drug Abuse. 1990.* DHHS Pub. No. (ADM) 91–1732. Supt of Documents, US Government Printing Office, Washington.

Pentz, M., Dwyer, J., Mackinnon, D., *et al.* (1989). A multicommunity trial for primary prevention of adolescent drug abuse: effects on drug use prevalence. *Journal of the American Medical Association* **261**, 3259–66.

10. Commonalities and diversities in the science and policy questions across different substances

Marcus Grant

First, the record must be put straight. It is not, of course, the function of intergovernmental bodies to tell countries what they must and must not do. This is as true in the area of policies on substance use and abuse as it is in any other. However, what can be done is to assemble previous relevant experience from countries that have, in one way or another, attempted to introduce national policies. Guidelines can then be derived from those examples, and, through appropriate advice and support, intergovernmental bodies may assist those countries that request it.

It is important to recognize, however, that some countries may choose not to develop policies at all and that others may choose to develop them without seeking advice from international organizations. Others may choose to control only some categories of substances, such as illicit drugs, leaving tobacco and alcohol to the vagaries of market forces. In maintaining an ability to respond to a range of different requests from different countries, but mindful of the danger inherent in clinging to concepts that are deteriorating through lack of use, international organizations can legitimately act in two ways. They can, through an advocacy role, encourage countries to develop their own policies; and they can, in promoting appropriate technology, offer advice that will enable countries that *do* decide to act, to make their policies as effective as possible.

Influences on national policy

A serious and sustained commitment is required from the countries concerned. This needs both imagination and a great deal of hard work. The delicate act of balancing the demands of public order, public health, and the public purse is perhaps the central obstacle, but it is certainly not the only one. Co-operation among many different interest groups, within and outside government, will be necessary. Ministries with responsibility for justice, defence, education, agriculture, trade, employment, and social affairs, among others, will need to be involved. The ministry of finance must be deeply involved in the fiscal implications of any proposed policies. In some countries, it is more than likely that the head of state may take a personal interest in this area. Thus the impetus to develop policy may well stem from some part of government other than the ministry of health—often with the ministry of health playing a part in its development.

Equally, however, interested bodies outside government will have a part to play. Treatment agencies, self-help organizations and other voluntary bodies, churches, and teachers and parents' organizations, will want to contribute to the process of policy development, and in some countries the list will be longer still. In addition, not only the pharmaceutical, tobacco, and alcoholic drinks industries, but other industries, including catering, tourism, advertising, and the media generally, will have essential contributions to make. The exclusion from the process of policy development of any significant interested party is likely to prejudice the subsequent successful implementation of the policy. A special case may be that of organized criminal networks involved in illicit drug trafficking, but even these will need to be acknowledged as the important force that they are in any major producer, trans-shipment or consumer country. Only alongside these other players does one find another key player, namely the scientific community.

It would be naïve to suppose that all the different interest groups will have compatible points of view. Even within government, there will be conflicts between some ministries, as well as agreements between others. Nor will the areas of agreement or disagreement be the same in every country. When it comes to the influence of any interest group external to government, the potential for conflict over priorities and principles becomes even more marked. The scientific community is no exception to that rule. There is potential for disagreement, not only between the scientific community and government, or between the scientific community and other special interest groups, but also, of course, within the scientific community itself, since this is a community characterized by intense rivalry between champions of competing hypotheses.

In any case, policy, once developed, will not be immutable; as circumstances change so the policy will need to change with them, just as the existence of the policy will itself be likely to change a variety of contingent circumstances. Nor should the ingenuity of consumers be forgotten. Scientists and policy makers alike tend to be a long way behind consumers when it comes to the identification of new psychoactive substances. The waiting list of such substances includes natural plants, pharmaceuticals, and industrial products, whose mind-altering properties are well known to those who consume them, but whose adverse health and social consequences have never been assessed. The process of developing national substance abuse policies is therefore continuous, and should not be seen as a static position of any kind. The key players in the policy debate cannot afford to rest upon their laurels; whatever influence they bring to bear, they must be prepared to keep bringing it to bear.

Diversity in national policies

So far, the consideration has been conducted as if integrated and comprehensive national policies on alcohol, tobacco, and drugs were the norm. In
fact, such policies are extremely rare. Most countries have quite different
mechanisms for dealing with the control of tobacco products, alcoholic beverages, pharmaceuticals, and illicit drugs. What exists in most countries is a
muddle of different responses which have arisen from all sorts of historical
and cultural circumstances and which reflect the interests of many key players
(see above). Logical or operational linkages between national responses to
alcohol, tobacco, pharmaceuticals, and illicit drugs, are conspicuous by their
absence in most countries. Yet this confusion is itself the very subject of study
in the search for commonalities and diversities across different substances;
and this is the area in which intergovernmental bodies are expected to be
offering consistent advice based upon the best available scientific evidence.

Whilst this piecemeal approach to policy formulation may seem to be
illogical and unsatisfactory, it may actually provide opportunities for those
outside government, such as the scientific community, to influence the direction
of policy development. The capacity to introduce telling data, intended to
change national policy, depends on the access by the scientific community to
the processes of policy formulation. And these opportunities might be less
frequent if the whole process was enshrined in a single rigid procedure,
relevant to all psychoactive substances.

The scientific community has, on the face of it, impeccable credentials; an
allegiance to the promotion of truth, not to the pursuit of political or economic gain, and a commitment to objectivity. It would be a bold government
that chose to ignore the suggestions of those who appear to have so little to
gain and whose motives seem so pure. Yet the scientific community often
complains that its views are ignored; and ignored consistently, not just by
governments which have a traditional disrespect for the facts, but also by
those who pretend to have great openness and transparency in their affairs.
In part, this may reflect the diversity of views within the scientific community,
since there is no single voice which is truly representative. It may, however,
also reflect the tendency of governments to be selective in the scientific views
which they choose to hear, as well as their preference for hearing such views
in private rather than in public.

Towards a logical approach

One logical approach to policy formulation in this area might be to base it
on the relative danger of different psychoactive substances. Such an approach
would have the advantage of consistency and comparability, as well as encouraging independent validation through an examination of the empirical
data available about the use and abuse of each substance. There are efforts

in that direction; for example, the two relevant International Conventions, one on Narcotic Drugs and the other on Psychotropic Substances, both require the World Health Organisation (WHO) to review drugs for their abuse potential and dependence liability on the one hand and for their therapeutic usefulness on the other. Thus, a recommendation on the level of international control appropriate for a particular drug should be based on a balanced view, which takes into account all relevant information. It is, in that sense, a scientific judgement, made by a group of independent experts and transmitted by an intergovernmental organization to an intergovernmental forum—the United Nations Commission on Narcotic Drugs—where representatives of governments vote on it. It is a process which is carefully monitored and one which allows for the danger (and usefulness) of substances to be compared with each other. It also allows for adjustments to be made in the light of new evidence.

Necessary caution

However, are there really grounds for satisfaction when a critical gaze is cast over the *relative* levels of control currently applied to tobacco products, alcoholic beverages, industrial solvents, petrol, khat, and betel-nut, to say nothing of marijuana, benzodiazepines, heroin, and cocaine?

Tobacco, alcohol, solvents, and a number of other substances are not covered by the current international drug conventions. Nor does there seem much likelihood at present that the relevant conventions will be modified to include them or that new conventions covering those areas will be introduced. But it is important to remember that the decision to exclude these substances was made with the benefit of scientific advice. It was, of course, a political decision, expressed in the form of international law, but the decision was based in considerable part on what was taken to be the best scientific advice available.

It is necessary to recognize, therefore, that the idea of a single and immutable scientific truth is certainly not the case in the area of substance abuse. This observation does not refer to great unanswered questions of the addictions field, but to the many differences of opinion which exist, based upon interpretations of empirical data. Sometimes the differences can be explained by the underlying assumptions of particular scientific disciplines, or by cultural factors which influence the way in which research is conducted or reported. There are, however, many instances in which it has to be recognized that the available data do not lead to a single conclusion which could form the basis for policy determination.

Equally, research must often be concerned with the verification of details, whilst policies have to address the creation of a broad context for social action. It is little wonder, in such circumstances, that policy makers are reluctant to look to the scientific community for final guidance on priorities or principles. When the political moment is right, it is cold comfort to be informed that there is conflicting evidence or that insufficient information is available. Scientists should not be too surprised by the scepticism of policy makers who, when they ask for advice, are frequently advised that they should recommend more research. In other words, the motivation of the scientific community is perhaps not quite as selfless as it might seem. How rare is the meeting of experts which does not recommend that they should meet again, though seldom at their own expense.

The necessary relationship between science and policy

Edwards has recently gathered together interviews that have appeared over the years in the *British Journal of Addiction*, (Edwards 1991). The final nine interviews were gathered under the general heading of 'The Wide World'. At first glance, the only thing these interviews had in common was that their subjects were not members of the usual Anglo-Saxon mafia that dominates international journals and international meetings in the addictions field. However, on closer study, another commonality emerged—namely, that all the interviews explored the relationship between individual scientists and the political events in which they had become involved, whether willingly or reluctantly.

Not that there was any convenient consensus between them. That these individuals represented the highest standards of scientific enquiry is apparent from the extent to which they questioned the field in which they were working and their own place in it. Wald talked of it as 'a field . . . overpopulated with people who were active but not always competent'. Although he was describing a particular moment in history and a particular national situation, it is surely not too difficult to echo these words in other times and other places. Looking across substances and looking across different cultures, it is possible to examine how the scientist has related to the troubled world of policy development. Beaubrun, for example, spoke of 'influencing the public to do what needs to be done', whilst Mardones stated that 'the worst thing a scientist can do is to pollute the scientific environment with data of poor value'. The pragmatist and the purist: or so it seemed at first sight. In the end, however, what united them and what informed the debate on the connections between science and policy, was what Soueif referred to as 'intolerance of intellectual frustration'. That may be the final position of the scientist, faced with the compromises and inconsistencies of the policy-making process.

Yet there is a need for action, nationally and internationally; and there is a real sense in which action either derives from or creates policy. It is not a sufficient response to allow events to play themselves out. On whichever side of this debate one stands, as individuals or collectively, there is an obligation to play one's part. If we are not part of the solution, then we are part of the problem.

It is surely not necessary to re-state that substance abuse causes individual suffering and leads to the break-up of families and communities; but it must not be forgotten that it also causes substantial economic loss to society as a whole. These problems are by no means diminishing, especially in developing countries, and there is an urgent need to take action. When it comes to devising policies and programmes to deal with the health and social problems associated with substance abuse, there exist already the means to arrest and even to reverse these trends. This does not mean that there is a magic formula for solving all problems; rather, there is an array of public health measures which have shown sufficient evidence of effectiveness to be promoted with some confidence. The challenge is to find the right combination of measures to suit the particular needs of each country. And it is the role of WHO to bring to the attention of Member States scientific evidence that will help them to do just that.

Conclusion

The emphasis of this discussion has been on the vast public health challenge posed by current trends in substance use and abuse, and the special role that WHO can play in confronting and reversing those trends. This is an area in which WHO has been active since 1948 and has taken the lead in documenting the nature and extent of alcohol-related problems, in promoting the exchange of national experience in dealing with those problems, and in developing guidelines for effective national and international action. There is now a need to focus on the specific technology available, so that countries can make choices on the basis of their needs and capabilities. In this sense, perhaps the best role for WHO is that of honest broker, trying to match the stringent requirements of the scientists with the urgent needs of governments confronted with a moral and political obligation to do something to alleviate the human misery caused by substance abuse.

In this chapter, there has been a deliberate avoidance of the fashionable vocabulary of the *war* against drugs or of the need to *combat* alcohol abuse, because success in this area is likely to depend on the ability to build partnerships rather than to find enemies. Of all the partnerships which need to be built, the most important is between the scientific community, which is committed to expanding our understanding, and the policy makers, committed to enhancing our well-being. WHO has an essential role to play in helping to forge and sustain that partnership. There exist, already, a commitment to increase both understanding and well-being, and a willingness to see science in its sociocultural context (and to promote its findings, even when they are not likely to prove popular), but there must be other guiding principles as well, which it is important for the scientific community to recognize. These include the sovereignty of Member States; the need to help to sustain economic and social development; and the need to ensure the protection of individual human rights. That surely, is our collective challenge.

References

Beaubrun, M. (1991). Interview, in *Addictions: personal influences and scientific movements*, (ed. G. Edwards), Transaction Publishers, New Brunswick and London.

Edwards, G. (1991). *Addictions: personal influences and scientific movements*. Transaction Publishers, New Brunswick and London.

Mardones, J. (1991). Interview, in *Addictions: personal influences and scientific movements*, (ed. G. Edwards), Transaction Publishers, New Brunswick and London.

Soueif, M. (1991). Interview, in *Addictions: personal influences and scientific movements*, (ed. G. Edwards), Transaction Publishers, New Brunswick and London.

Wald, I. (1991). Interview, in *Addictions: personal influences and scientific movements*, (ed. G. Edwards), Transaction Publishers, New Brunswick and London.

Discussion
What future for prevention?

Chaired by Hamid Ghodse (UK)

Dr Juan Carlos Negrete (Canada): This is a session about prevention, the contribution that science should make towards that goal, and how much use has been made of the available evidence. Within the health sciences, that would seem almost an irrelevant question, because the public health model of prevention was of course possible and was so effective precisely because of scientific knowledge. Aetiological agents, modes of transmission, and risk factors over which there was control were discovered, and the solutions were there to be shown as a result. However, health sciences now extend well beyond infectious diseases and we now have problems which may be defined as illnesses and are indeed a process of disease in many people, but certainly do not follow the model of the infectious diseases. No single group of aetiological agents has so far been defined. The process of transmission and the vulnerabilities are still being explored.

We have a problem when prevention is being undertaken: is it being undertaken with the help of scientific evidence, with no regard to scientific evidence, or sometimes even against whatever scientific evidence would suggest? One thing that both scientists and policy makers must still learn is that there seems to be a spontaneous course for 'epidemics' of drug abuse. Dr Musto and Dr Berridge describe the ups and downs of drug problems through the ages.

Why do drug epidemics get bad and then improve? Dr Kleber has described the cocaine epidemic in the USA. Since the early 1980s and particularly since 1985, the data collected in the USA indicate that fewer and fewer people are using cocaine. Dr Kleber also candidly admitted that he had nothing to do with it, that his national programme had nothing to do with it, and that this turnabout was related to the spontaneous course of the epidemics and occurred before such measures were effected or started to become effective. As prevention scientists who are going to advice policy makers, we have to understand that there is such a thing as a spontaneous course for some of these problems.

We have heard about tobacco, which is an entirely different picture, a well accepted habit, believed to be harmless, until the scientists started to measure the harm. It seems fair to assume that the decline in tobacco consumption and the progress in tobacco prevention were started with the strong contribution from scientists but have you ever talked with people who do not start smoking or have opinions about smoking right now? None of the youngsters say 'Oh, I don't want people to smoke because it causes cancer'. They talk mostly in almost aesthetic terms, 'Oh, it smells, it stinks, its ugly, look at your teeth'. Its decline may have been started by the strong impact on society by scientific evidence, but has now been taken over by changes in social attitudes.

With marijuana, there.is a similar social component that we do not adequately understand and which is not necessarily influenced by scientific evidence. Marijuana was a major problem in North America in the 1960s and 1970s, but the extent of use of this drug is now also declining. Why? During the 1960s and early 1970s, the drug was identified with a social attitude of staying apart, dropping out. In the 1980s cocaine took over, also because of an attitude. Cannabis was not appropriate to the new social attitudes.

Finally, with prescription drugs, we have a field that surely should be the subject of prevention campaigns based on scientific information. These drugs become available through scientific work and they are made known to the prospective user mostly through the work of professionals. Society is convinced by scientists that those drugs are to be approved, and the pharmaceutical industry produces them, makes them available, and then promotes them.

As a society, we are now more ready to modify brain function in order to feel comfortable. There is a question of ethical choice, and there is a question of political choice as well, allowing so much of mood altering exercises being practised. And there is also a choice of a professional and scientific order.

Dr Griffith Edwards (UK): I wanted to put one very specific question on the science-policy connection, vis-à-vis prevention; but the question may go broader. Mr Grant was really suggesting that the scientific community are a muddle-headed lot. He was not actually saying that, but he was not actually not saying that either. He was suggesting that the scientific community didn't always speak with one voice. It is the same criticism that is made of doctors in the phrase 'doctors disagree'. If you ever appear on a television show where there is an advocate of the tobacco industry, he will rubbish you if you are not careful and he will usually get the last word. 'Thank you very much' the presenter will say and with a laugh against you, all will fade as he says 'well, of course you chaps never agree among each other'. That is a very damaging allegation—it has an element of truth in it. But I want to ask the group here what we should do about it. Sometimes, of course, we appear not to be speaking with one voice because dissension has actually been planted by the said tobacco manufacturer who has hired someone purposely to muddy the water and to prove that cigarette advertising really prevents children from smoking. For a fee, someone is probably willing to produce a paper of that sort. You may think I'm exaggerating (at least to a mild extent), but what mechanisms really are in place for developing the voice of science, the credible authoritative review? Clearly there are some national mechanisms, the US Surgeon-General's report on smoking, the UK College of Psychiatrists with benzodiazepines. There are other similar reports, such as the Wootton Report on cannabis and some of the other cannabis reports: there have been many examples. Are you satisfied that at a national and international level we are investing sufficient in analysis and mete-analysis to make sure that hot foot from the laboratories the authoritative voice of integrative research is carried to the policy maker?

Mr Marcus Grant (WHO): I will try to answer very briefly. Consensus has become a little less fashionable, but I think consensus is probably a key concept here. It's the way that things must move internationally if we are to avoid conflict and it's the way in which the scientific community can perhaps achieve a more coherent perspective with regard to policy makers. The differences that exist in the pronouncements of the scientific community are often legitimate; data are in conflict, the evidence does not point only one way—but if you wish your influence to be brought to bear, then maybe sometimes you have to be prepared to guard a little less jealously the results of your particular laboratory, of your particular general population survey, in order to communicate a larger truth. The scientific community finds that a bitter pill to swallow. Their nature is to strive for the greatest accuracy possible. You may need to put the emphasis on the word 'possible' rather than on the word 'accuracy' and be prepared to agree that your colleagues, whilst not absolutely right, may be jolly close to being right. I think that's something which the scientific community, like five-year-olds in the playground, find hard to do.

Dr Jerome Jaffe (USA): I find this all a little curious. Perhaps Dr Kleber can enlighten us a little about the full range of the issue of prevention. So much of supply availability efforts are undertaken in the name of prevention. Yet within that whole range of activities (crop substitution, crop eradication, arresting people on the street, breaking up large cartels), there are many areas for necessary policy analysis. We are obsessed often with whether in-patient or out-patient care is more effective and how to maximize resources, and yet this critical perspective is rarely seen with the supply side efforts. One rarely hears whether an aircraft carrier off the coast of South America is more effective than some other technique applied in some other sphere. Is there anything that you would call scientifically-directed policy analysis of the cost-benefit of these various approaches to supply control? Is there anything like the kinds of things that science here seems to be obsessed about and where we are expected to speak in one voice with consensus on the very best way to do this. We seem to have two standards of expectation, even though the expenditures on controlling supply of illicit drugs are far greater than on demand reduction. I just want to call people's attention to the fact that nobody is talking about that range of policy analysis, or policy influence.

Dr Herbert Kleber (USA): If you take bread out of the oven before it's ready it will be half-baked, and the issue of scientific consensus can be half-baked if you do it prematurely. Consider the scientific consensus on cocaine in 1975: if you had just taken a poll of scientists, the view would probably have been that cocaine was harmless. Certainly our leading textbooks said so. If they had brought in people like Dr Musto they may have been reminded that cocaine was dangerous 80 years ago, and maybe that would have changed the consensus. But the majority of people would have asked 'Why are you recommending such draconian solutions for such a harmless drug, when the best people in London do it'. So a consensus of people in London in 1987 may also have been, 'it's a harmless drug'. I think we need to be careful about scientific consensus and not arrive at it before the evidence is there. I would rather see lack of consensus than a forced or premature consensus.

Let me move on to Dr Jaffe's provocative question about the balance of expenditure between the supply side and the demand side. He well knows the generals and admirals, one of whom recently said, 'We spill more in one day than you guys spend in a year'. That's accurate: our total drug control budget now is 11.5 billion dollars, of which my office controls 8 billion. Certainly my counterpart, the Deputy for Supply Reduction, is trying to introduce efficiency measures, looking at whether it is better to have an aerostat over Panama or off the coast of Mexico, and what are the number of seizures you get per number of flying hours. At $25 000 an hour, how much cocaine do we seize? How much do we prevent? Do we simply shift routes from that part of the country to coming in through tunnels between the border between Mexico and Arizona, for example?

I don't think that there will ever be the same attempt to be as rigorous, we have the scientists on the demand side, whereas they have the generals and the admirals on the supply side. We should try to get more rigour into it, I am not that optimistic that we will succeed. Even if we succeeded, I am not sure that it would do anything to change funding priorities. I have argued that the only part of the war that's been successful so far is demand reduction: therefore I should get some of that 8 million dollars to use for increased prevention and treatment. I met with incredulous looks. 'Does that mean you want to close down certain bases or throw five hundred DEA agents out of work?'

Finally, would progress have occurred without the Office of Demand Reduction? Is progress inevitable? Our first Director, Bill Bennett, said that progress is possible but not inevitable. We are ourselves part of the historic inevitability that ends epidemics. The epidemic probably ended at the turn of the last century, when society got involved in the churches in the community groups in the government, when cocaine came to be seen as the worse public health hazard this country had ever experienced. That is what it takes to end epidemics. So you cannot sit back and say it is going to run its course. Somehow, even though you know that it will run its course, it will not run its course unless you fulfil your role in trying to end it.

Dr Hamid Ghodse (UK): Whenever you quote those figures, it is depressing from a European perspective because your budget for one year is probably equivalent to the European budget for the next two hundred years.

Dr Harold Kalant (Canada): I would like to put forward a contrary point of view— that to talk of a rational policy is an oxymoron. There is no such thing as a rational policy in a field such as drug use or drug control policy. As scientists we may be troubled that our scientific advice is not used in the formulation of policy, but it is not a justified complaint for the simple reason that when we give advice on policy as scientists, we are not being scientists. Policy is never just a matter of purely rational cost-benefit analysis. There are always implicit or explicit value judgements, and when, as scientists, we advance recommendations on policy, we are failing to declare the value judgements that underlie our recommendations. The great debate years ago between Oppenheimer and Teller for example, illustrated beautifully that the debate, the difference of opinion was not really about facts. I am sure that the two of them could easily have agreed on the force that would be generated by a nuclear weapon of certain size, on how many buildings would be destroyed within a certain radius, on how many people would be killed, etc. The difference was purely a judgemental difference—was it better to be red than dead, or better to be dead than red. In making recommendations for policy about drugs we also (without stating it usually) build in our own biases as to whether we think that the social value of individual freedom is more or less pressing than the social value of preservation of health, or social function, and of economic well-being, for example.

If we want to offer those judgements, we are doing so as citizens, not as scientists. Once we have outlined the facts, the knowledge as it now stands, we can then disagree from now till Doomsday about which is better or worse. Policy is all about which is better or worse. If, as scientists, we are asked to say what is the best way of achieving a particular objective, we can probably agree on facts relating to one or another proposal. What if we ask what is the more important objective to be achieved? Then what do we do? We are no longer talking science; we are talking social values. Unless we constantly remind ourselves of this underlying fact, we will always be dissatisfied and we will be dissatisfied without justification. It is not our role as scientists to say what is good. It is certainly our role as citizens to say what is good, but it is the role of every other citizen to say that too. This may be devil's advocacy, but I would like us to consider that perhaps a purely rational policy cannot exist when the objectives are defined by social values.

Dr Malcolm Lader (UK): There is a quick answer and there is a longer answer. The quick answer is 'Yes, I agree', the longer answer is 'Yes, but . . .'. I think the 'but' is the scientist making a value judgement on his own data. We all do that.

Let us go back to the question about consensus. You cannot have a premature consensus. You have to sense when a consensus is possible and then get together the people who are going to provide you with that consensus. It always requires somebody who has a purpose in life. The consensus about the data should contribute to the general well-being of the particular population it is devised to serve. I take a Tolstoyan view of this: there are waves in human endeavour, in human belief, which you have to use, and if you can ride the crest of that wave and make it look as if the science is there, then that is fine. Occasionally, science just has to take a back seat. With cigarette smoking science took a back seat for many years. The evidence that cigarette smoking produced lung cancer was incontrovertible scientifically. You could argue about the mechanism, but the association was there. Not only was the association there, but soon we found that if you reduced the cigarette smoking, then you also reduced the lung cancer. Indeed, the medical profession was the guinea-pig. Policy is something which has to fit in with the public's perception of its own good.

Dr Crewe (UK): The presentations have focused on the contribution of science to public policy but there is also the contribution of scientists to institutional and local policy. Many of us work in institutions. As an example, scientists working in the teaching institution can contribute to the thinking of a whole generation of students, maybe 30–40 000 students in a professional career. The scientist can also contribute to the development of institutional policies, for example with relation to smoking. What are the possible contributions to this sort of local or institutional policy?

Dr Malcolm Lader (UK): There are two aspects here. First, there is the scientist and what data he or she provides; but secondly and much more important, is the way the scientist thinks. Scientists are born, not made, and perhaps science is the ability to tolerate uncertainty but to be as precise as possible in doing so.

Dr Michael Russell (UK): Dr Negrete seemed rather sanguine about what is being done about smoking. Just because it is declining, does not mean that all is fine. It is indeed declining in some developed countries, but it is declining extremely slowly, one of the problems being that the advertizing and promotion is doing all it can for the tobacco companies, all it can to maintain the demand side. As the demand in developed countries is declining, they are building up the demand in developing countries at an absolutely alarming rate. Peto, a statistician at Oxford who worked with Doll, has forecast that the 1990s figure of three million deaths per year in the world from smoking, will escalate, so that by 2025 it will be 10 million per year. He has forecast that 200 million of today's young children and teenagers are, on present trends, going to be killed by the year 2025. Perhaps we should be less complacent about the progress being made.

I wish to turn now to the subject of dependence. Consider the little old lady who takes her three tablets of diazepam today. Is that in itself harmful? Is that harmful other than slight intoxication, perhaps requiring the avoidance of machinery or driving. The dependence itself is surely not harmful. Dependence itself is not a clinical condition, but a concept. What is harmful is if the little old lady goes on taking her tablets, starts to lose her tolerance and ends up in the back ward of a mental hospital mislabelled as a demented old fool. That is the danger, and that is where people are not being careful enough. That is why usage ought to be monitored.

Dr Alex Wodak (Australia): The figures in Dr Kleber's presentation covered a lot of data on consumption, but there was really no data on other parameters of harm, such as morbidity, mortality, or social and economic parameters. Would you like to give some indication of whether you think consumption figures on their own are of importance and are of greater importance than direct parameters of harm? Do you have any data on morbidity and mortality related to the drugs you mentioned—preferably population adjusted? For instance, do you have heroin-related deaths (population adjusted over the last couple of decades perhaps) or cannabis deaths?

Dr Herbert Kleber (USA): A quick answer; the data is not as good as one would like. There is an ongoing study that NIDA has of medical examiner data which looks at emergency room data related to use of illicit substances. But it is an imperfect measure because it is mainly the mortality that would show up in an emergency room or an overdose where you die in the street. If you are driving a car under the influence of cocaine and you crack up, then that will not usually end up in any of the mortality figures, yet a study that was reported about a year ago indicated that in 25 per cent of all automobile fatalities in New York city, the drivers had cocaine in their blood. Yet we have no good way of capturing that data on a national basis.

Turning to the economic impact, there was a major study that has just been funded by NIDA and NIMH, looking at the total economic impact of drugs, mental illness, etc. So there are studies, albeit imperfect, that try to get to the data but it is still incomplete data.

Dr Richard Jessor (USA): I am surprised at the relative lack of attention to social differentiation in developed societies. This differentiation has implications for the kinds of policies that ought to be developed or can be developed. When Dr Kleber refers to Black and Hispanic changes, it separated those groups out from the larger patterns and that is not actually defensible.

I am also surprised that we rarely consider whether policy should be derived from an analysis of the determinants of the behaviour. If we consider cigarette smoking and provision of alternatives for cigarette smoking, we learn that there are possible alternatives routes for the administration of nicotine, but not a substitute for smoking behaviour. It is so important that we understand why it is that people smoke. The same issue is true with regard to heroin and cocaine use. The up-market executive who is sniffing a line of cocaine then gets scared by the 'war on drugs': this person might lose their job. The minority member in an inner city may have no job to lose, and the question of prevention is then a very different issue. Why is it that people get into the pipeline, and why is it that they stay in the pipeline? We should not just wage a 'war on drugs' in an attempt to stamp out behaviour: rather we should look to provide alternatives to the behaviours that are used.

Dr George Vaillant (USA): I just want to offer an analogy that I think underscores Dr Kalant's remarks. Here at our meeting in London, we are near to Greenwich. As soon as the Greenwich clock was invented, the world policy was that the zero meridian would run through the middle of Greenwich. Here is an example of science profoundly influencing policy. This was not half-baked science. The quality of this clock was such that it told the real time and was absolutely accurate. But it also profoundly influenced celestial navigation. And we shall bear in mind there is nothing in the Greenwich Observatory that tells anybody where they ought to go.

Part III Substance misuse: how good is science in responding to suddenly changing policy demands?

11. The impact of AIDS on the research agenda

Gerry V. Stimson and John Strang

Infections come and go, and it could be argued that acquired immune deficiency syndrome (AIDS) is but a passing distraction in the longer term course of research into addictive behaviours. Nevertheless, AIDS is forcing major changes in the drugs research agenda—at least for today and a good few tomorrows. This may prove to be but a hiccough, a short-lived modification to our hierarchy of concern and interest. Alternatively, it may prove to be a new order, with effects which may extend even beyond the human immuno deficiency virus (HIV) epidemic itself. Drug research may never be the same again.

The last few years have seen major review and change in the response to, and thinking about, drug problems. The challenges posed by AIDS have cut across all sectors of society and they demand a creative response from politicians and policy-makers, from those in prevention and those in treatment, as well as from those whose research both serves the new questions and helps put new issues on the agenda.

New areas of study

AIDS has brought several new areas to the research agenda.

Mapping the spread of HIV

The presence of HIV infection amongst people who inject drugs has now been identified in more than 5 countries. Drug injectors now form the second largest, and in some places the fastest growing, group of AIDS cases in developed countries (Carballo and Rezza 1990). In Europe AIDS cases from drug injecting have been reported from 22 of the 32 countries, and the proportion of cases attributed to drug injecting has risen from 15 per cent to around 40 per cent. The number of new cases of AIDS from drug injecting now equals those from sex between men.

The time lag from HIV infection to AIDS is now calculated as a mean of around 10 years. This means that attention must now be turned to levels of HIV infection in order to plot the trends in the epidemic.

Several studies have noted the rapid spread of HIV infection in some cities. Places like Edinburgh, UK (Robertson 1990), Bangkok, Thailand and New York, USA (Des Jarlais and Friedman 1990) show what can happen when things go wrong. They also serve as a baseline for assessing AIDS prevention measures elsewhere. However, the scientific evidence to explain such rapid spread is still distinctly lacking; and there is also a lack of good explanation for the levelling of prevalence in some cities, and the continued low prevalence in others.

Prevalence rates vary dramatically, even within one country. In the USA there is evidence of distinctly 'hot' spots in parts of the North East and in Puerto Rico. In the UK, the high rates found in Edinburgh and Dundee by 1985 have not so far been repeated elsewhere. However the most recent data from London (Crosier 1991, personal communication) indicate a rising prevalence to around 13 per cent, but it is not yet known whether this is an artefact of the particular study or represents a real change.

Some cities have sustained level prevalence but with a high incidence of cases, indicating the need for both prevalence and incidence studies (see Moss and Vranizan 1992). Research has been facilitated by changes in the technology of testing: for example the HIV saliva test has opened up new possibilities for behavioural and other scientists to engage in such work. However, there are still major methodological problems associated with attempts to sample adequately populations of injecting drug users, many of whom remain in various 'hidden populations' (Lambert 1990).

Mapping the spread of injecting

Drug injecting is found throughout the world in countries with very different social conditions and levels of development. There is a need to map the prevalence of drug injecting and to plot trends and changes. Mapping the size, location, and changes in the drug injecting population, which was important enough before AIDS, is now vital. Few countries have a clear idea of the extent of drug injecting or of changes in the drug injecting population. Lack of such information hinders projections about the scale of the HIV and AIDS problems. It also hinders assessment of the effect of HIV prevention measures on drug injecting.

The need for monitoring may be particularly valuable in countries with widespread drug use, but where drug injecting is still uncommon. In such regions there is the possibility that the predominately non-injecting relationship with the drug may change. Widespread transitions in route of administration do occur (Strang et al. 1992), and hence there may be important opportunities for study. For example in Madras, India, a change may currently be taking place with a shift from the smoking to the injecting of black market heroin. On-going assessment of the local drug injecting population is important for developing properly targeted interventions.

Study of HIV risk factors

A more perceptive understanding of the risk factors for HIV infection is required. A substantial body of knowledge now exists about the individual risk factors for HIV infection, and the research agenda has turned to the minutiae of some of these practices, for example the question of *how* people share syringes. The social relations (for example order of injection, who owns the syringe) and the detailed sharing sharing practices (how drugs are mixed, what equipment is shared, what happens to discarded syringes) are areas which still need more detailed investigation.

Some practices can already be identified as particularly high risk, but there is a continuing lack of context in which to place the concern about this high risk. For example, the injecting of drugs in shooting galleries, places where people can buy or rent needles and syringes and inject drugs. To what extent are these shooting galleries a significant part of the life of most regular or occasional injectors? And, if not widespread, what factors influence the extent of occasional or regular use of these venues; and to what extent might it be possible to alter behaviours within these shooting galleries even while they continue?

Detailed investigation of drug injecting and sexual behaviour were not, until recently, major topics for research with drug injectors. Though scientists have described the individual behavioural factors, few have addressed in detail and explained the different risks of HIV infection for different social groups by gender, race, and culture. For example, in the UK, women have higher levels of syringe sharing than men, and higher levels of HIV infection. More speculatively it has been suggested that UK Afro-Caribbean and Asian groups may be subject to stronger taboos against injecting than their Caucasian contempories (Strang *et al.* 1992). In many parts of the USA (but not necessarily elsewhere) there is a marked association between HIV infection and race. In the Bronx, New York, for example, HIV seroprevalence is higher for Blacks and Hispanics than for Whites. Other ethnographic data from several countries show marked variations in injecting and sexual practices in different social groups. These differences may not only warrant study in their own right, but may also open up possible avenues for the development of new interventions.

New importance for old areas of study

The interrelationship of individual, socio-cultural, and economic factors

Individual risk factors appear to be related to social, cultural, and economic factors, and research on this relationship requires specific study. The particular conjunction of factors will vary by city and country. In the USA, areas with a high prevalence of HIV have high levels of other social problems, such as in sexual behaviour, housing, employment, and lack of services. Whether one is considering the social conditions of Brasilia, of Birmingham, or of the south Bronx, the social conditions are intimately tied up with the kinds of risks that people face, and with the kind of care that can be provided for people who have HIV disease. In the UK, the social conditions and circumstances of people's lives have been identified as correlates of risk behaviour (Donoghoe *et al.* 1992). For example, high risk needle sharers are likely to be in unstable living conditions, to be unemployed, and have illegal sources of income.

Another level at which these issues might be considered, is at the macro level of the factors that facilitate both drug use and HIV infection in a particular society. For example, as is well known, Thailand has seen a major outbreak of HIV infection amongst people who inject drugs. Whilst this may be understood through an anatomy of the risk behaviours, some reflection on the situation in Thailand may suggest other levels at which the situation may be understood. To understand HIV and injecting drug use in Thailand, there must first be an understanding of why Thailand and the Golden Triangle became drug producing areas, the impact of local and international policing practice, the development of injecting drug use in slums, and introduction of HIV through drugs and sex tourism. Changes in international drug markets and production were facilitated by international and national politics and conflict, by international and national laws and policing, and by international inequalities in income. This suggests that research needs to extricate the links between social conditions, injecting drug use, and HIV, and in turn may suggest new levels for intervention, as a result of which there may be lessons here for other developing countries.

Influences on change in behaviour

The study of behaviour change has always been generally relevant to the addictions field, but may now be studied in the context of AIDS. An area of particular study is that of individual behaviour change.

The empirical evidence from a variety of sources and countries, using a variety of methodologies, is that many people who inject drugs have changed their behaviour in order to reduce their risk of HIV infection and their risk of transmission to others. The baseline for this might reasonably be studies conducted before the onset of AIDS, which tend to show high levels of syringe sharing. Unfortunately, few such studies have been conducted, but a reasonable estimate is that before the onset of AIDS about 70–90 per cent of injectors regularly shared syringes. There is now considerable evidence from countries such as the UK, the Netherlands, and Australia, that this is now around 20–25 per cent or less among sharers in contact with services.

No single study has yet shown conclusively that risk behaviours have changed. However, triangulation of data from various sources using various techniques, gives some confidence that behavioural changes have indeed occurred. Such speculation is more usually associated with the research and development work in the competitive climate of industry, where missed imaginative leaps are missed opportunities, and hence missed income. In the field of AIDS research, there is a similar requirement for vision so as to enable short-cuts to be taken in research evolution in this new subject.

Street level research and evaluation of specific interventions shows that many injectors have adopted a variety of protective strategies. Ethnographic studies in England (Burt and Stimson 1990) show that the social etiquette of drug use has changed: many people who inject no longer view sharing of syringes as normal behaviour. However, there have been many fewer changes, if any, in sexual behaviour. The new research agenda should address not only the existing empirical evidence, but the lack of theoretical understanding of health behaviour.

The evaluation of specific interventions

Whereas for many years abstinence has usually been the main target for drug treatment programmes, many are now setting targets which fall far short of this. They may target changes in behaviour which have an impact on the risk of HIV infection and transmission, but not on continued drug use, or even on drug injecting itself.

The themes and the terminology may now be well known. One is the idea of harm minimization (Buning 1990; O'Hare *et al.* 1992; Stimson, in press). This idea has been around in British drugs policy for many decades, occasionally resurfacing, and at other times being pushed aside by more avid treatment approaches. It was developing in the late 1970s and early 1980s with, for example, risk reduction for glue-sniffers (Institute for the Study of Drug Dependence 1976, 1980; Lifeline Project 1982). It also surfaced as a central theme to the Prevention report from the Advisory Council on the Misuse of Drugs (1984) which drew attention to two levels of prevention: preventing drug use and preventing harm associated with drug use. However, harm minimization comes to the fore with the idea of risk reduction and prevention for continuing drug injectors—those who are unable or unwilling to stop injecting drugs.

For the research agenda, the measurement criteria must change with the identification of new treatment goals. Success may be measured first by the number of contacts that are made, and then, secondly, in terms of what may be made of those contacts. Earlier research work which may have focused on abstinence as a criterion for treatment success may no longer be so relevant. The AIDS and Drug Misuse report from the Advisory Council on the Misuse of Drugs (1988) promoted the value of working towards 'intermediate goals'. These are changes in the nature of continued drug use which are associated with reduced risk (especially HIV/AIDS risk) and may be seen as significant half-way stations in the longer journey of treatment. Measures are required for these intermediate goals and for smaller changes in behaviour that may be encouraged through drug treatments, such as methadone maintenance, or through public health measures such as outreach, bleach, and syringe distribution (see, for example, Samuels *et al.* 1992).

Many of the new intervention strategies place great importance on their characteristic of being innovative and 'user friendly', for example the syringe-exchange scheme, or the outreach caravan for drug injecting prostitutes. But the problem exists: how can research be undertaken, when research itself may inadvertently make the service unfriendly? The challenge is to develop methodologies appropriate for low threshold settings, where the conditions for strict scientific trial are usually absent.

New alliances

Finally, there are now new alliances which are being formed, and these are already having a profound influence on the way in which researchers operate in an AIDS epoch.

The researcher and the policy maker as allies

The first alliance is between research and the development of policy, with resulting support for evaluation of prevention and treatment strategies. This has meant the possibility of real policy relevance for scientists' work.

The most dramatic impact has been on behavioural science. HIV disease is essentially a behavioural disease, and so the behavioural sciences now occupy a central position where once they may have been to be on the periphery. This central position of the behavioural sciences is due to HIV's spread through quite specific behavioural practices (the intimate social practices involving the exchange of body fluids through the sharing of drug injecting equipment or through sexual intercourse), and perhaps because the spread of HIV disease can be prevented only by encouraging behavioural change. These social behaviours are intricately associated with factors operating at an individual, community, and societal level. As such, research and prevention questions must be asked at the level of the individual, the community, and society.

There are also other reasons why it may be judicious to consider HIV as a behavioural disease. There are short-term limits regarding the possibility of palliative and curative medical interventions, and hence the care of those with HIV disease necessitates the development of networks of support within social and medical services, and in the community. In the case of people who inject drugs who have HIV disease, one can see the enormity of this challenge.

The drug-taker and the service-provider as allies

The second alliance is the necessary alliance between people who inject drugs and those who are trying to facilitate change in their behaviour. People cannot be made to change their behaviour: it is no longer justifiable (if it ever was justifiable) to offer services only to the deserving and well-motivated. Public health as well as personal health considerations require a broadening of our constituency of concern.

The challenge facing researchers is similar to the challenge facing prevention and treatment workers—that is to develop an honest relationship with people who inject drugs. This may mean recruiting drug users themselves as prevention workers and conducting research which is for their benefit and which is not merely exploitative. Drug users should see themselves and their peers as potential beneficiaries, and not just as subjects for study. Behavioural science again offers a model. Community ethnography and anthropology, with their insights into the working of communities and cultures, and their understanding of the importance of social networks, provide a model for both research and community outreach prevention work. Research work cannot just be conducted from the safety of the clinic.

Alliances across traditional research boundaries

The third alliance is within the new research community. The traditional division of labour and knowledge has begun to crumble. AIDS research needs specialists in virology, immunology, epidemiology, modelling, behavioural and social science, economics, social policy, public health, and many other disciplines. It requires that each specialist rapidly acquires the knowledge of parallel fields. The breadth of knowledge required and the speed with which that knowledge must be transmitted, have been remarkable features of the scientific response.

The urgency of the situation has mean that it is often too long to await results in the scientific literature. Publication delays can have serious consequences for public health. Traditional forms of dissemination have, to some extent, been replaced, as AIDS researchers have developed their global network of colleagues exchanging pre-publication findings. By the time they appear in print, it is old news.

Conclusion

The first decade of the AIDS epidemic has now passed. A provisional new research agenda has been formed and has already made a major contribution to the present understanding of, and response to, this epidemic. The interplay between individual, community, and societal levels in the understanding of drug use is now more widespread, and there is frequent acknowledgement in the new analyses of AIDS and drug misuse to the importance of research.

It would however be a mistake to assume that scientific endeavour has proceeded independently of policy: in this field, it has usually been driven by policy. Attention has been drawn above to the new alliance between science and policy which is crucial in developing appropriate national responses to AIDS and drug injecting, but this alliance has not always worked well. It is incumbent upon senior scientific administrators to put the scientific case to governments, and governments must have the courage to listen and act. It is disappointing when senior scientific colleagues are obliged to promote one preventive strategy over another, not on the basis of the available scientific information, but for political expediency. It is likewise disappointing when governments prevent scientific enquiry into specific areas (as has happened recently in the UK and the USA), or when scientific results become distorted for political ends. In some countries, then, the obstacles are not the lack of scientific evidence, but the lack of political will to apply the findings from scientific work.

The challenge for the research community may then be to assist in the re-formulation of the hierachy of concerns, to explore critically the resulting priority areas of research, and to enter actively into these new alliances without losing touch with an essential independence and objectivity of view. The need is great and the opportunity exists for the research community to accept the responsibility of a strengthened influence on policy and practice, and to assume a more significant and influential position in the science–policy relationship.

References

Advisory Council on the Misuse of Drugs (1984). Report on *Prevention*. HMSO, London.

Advisory Council on the Misuse of Drugs (1988). Report on *AIDS and drug misuse: Part I*. HMSO, London.

Buning, E. (1990). The role of harm-reduction programmes in curbing the spread of HIV by drug injectors. In *AIDS and drug misuse: the challenge for policy and practice in the 1990s* (ed. J. Strang and G.V. Stimson), pp. 153–61. Routledge, London.

Burt, J. and Stimson, G.V. (1990). *Strategies for protection*. Health Education Authority, London.

Carballo, M. and Rezza, G. (1990). AIDS, drug misuse and the global crisis. In *AIDS and drug misuse: the challenge for policy and practice in the 1990s* (ed. J. Strang and G.V. Stimson), pp. 16–26. Routledge, London.

Des Jarlais, D. and Friedman, S.R. (1990). The epidemic of HIV infection among injecting drug users in New York City: the first decade and possible future directions. In *AIDS and drug misuse: the challenge for policy and practice in the 1990s* (ed. J. Strang and G.V. Stimson), pp. 86–94. Routledge, London.

Donoghoe, M.C., Dolan, K.A., and Stimson, G.V. (1992). Lifestyle factors and social circumstances of syringe sharing in injecting drug users. *British Journal of Addiction*, 87, 993–1004.

Institute for the Study of Drug Dependence (1976). Not to be sniffed at? *Druglink*, 6, 1–2, ISDD, London.

Institute for the Study of Drug Dependence (1980). *Teaching about a volatile situation: suggested health education strategies for minimising casualties associated with solvent sniffing*. ISDD, London.

Lambert, E. (ed.) (1990). *The collection and interpretation of data from hidden populations*, NIDA Research Monograph no. 98. National Institute on Drug Abuse, Rockville, MD.

Lifeline Project (1982). *Sniffing for pleasure?* Lifeline Project, Manchester.

Moss, A. and Vranizan, K. (1992). Charting the epidemic: the case study of HIV screening of injecting drug users in San Francisco, 1985–1990. *British Journal of Addiction*, 87, 467–72.

O'Hare, P.A., Newcombe, R., Matthews, A., Buning, E., and Drucker, E. (1992). *The reduction of drug related harm*. Routledge, London.

Robertson, R. (1990). The Edinburgh epidemic: a case study. In *AIDS and drug misuse: the challenge for policy and practice in the 1990s* (ed. J. Strang and G.V. Stimson), pp. 95–107. Routledge, London.

Samuels, J., Vlahov D., Anthony, J. and Chaisson, R. (1992). Measurement of HIV risk behaviours among injecting drug users, *British Journal of Addiction*, 87, 417–28.

Stimson, G.V. (1992) Minimising harm from drug use. In *Responding to drug abuse: the 'British System'* (ed. J. Strang and M. Gossop), Oxford University Press (forthcoming).

Strang, J., Des Jarlais, D.C., Griffiths, P., and Gossop, M. (1992). The study of transitions in the route of drug use, *British Journal of Addiction*, 87, 473–84.

12. Cocaine: challenges to research

Charles R. Schuster and Steven W. Gust

What are the important research issues which have been stimulated by the recent epidemic of cocaine use in the USA? A useful starting point may be a consideration of the broad array of challenges, from the molecular level to the socio-political level, which have emerged from this epidemic.

Changing perceptions of cocaine as a problem drug

Coca, and its principal psychoactive ingredient cocaine, has shown wide swings in its reputation and acceptability by the many civilizations that have encountered it. In the ancient Incan civilization coca was avoided by the leaders of some generations and venerated by others (Kennedy 1985). In the late nineteenth century, Sigmund Freud extolled the pharmacological effects of cocaine. Indeed, he cited a broad variety of beneficial effects, including counteracting fatigue, increasing physical work capacity, acting as a sexual stimulant, relieving a variety of gastrointestinal disorders, asthma, and even anaemia, as well as suppressing alcohol and morphine intake (Byck 1974). Although Freud later changed his mind about the benefits of cocaine, his pronouncements, along with many others, helped to popularize the use of coca-containing products, such as Vin Mariani and Coca-Cola. There were others at the same time, however, who denounced coca and cocaine as the third scourge of the world, joining the ranks of opium and alcohol (Erlenmeyer 1887; Lewin 1964). Despite these concerns, literally hundreds of tonics containing cocaine were sold in the USA as cures for every conceivable ailment from addiction to opiates to fatigue and general malaise. Concern about the widespread use and abuse of cocaine and cocaine-containing products, along with the disappointment about its properties as a panacea, led to its inclusion as a narcotic in the 1914 Harrison Narcotic Act, which limited its availability to physicians for a few medical indications.

For many years this action succeeded in decreasing the use of cocaine in the USA. As part of the drug revolution of the 1960s, cocaine began to re-emerge as a drug of abuse through illegal distribution networks. That the public and even public health authorities had forgotten the potential dangers of widespread cocaine use is shown by the fact that as recently as 1974 authorities such as Dr Peter Bourne (the drug advisor to President Carter) stated that 'Cocaine is probably the most benign of illicit drugs currently in widespread use' (Education Newsletter 1974). A decade and a half later pollsters reported that the US public felt that drug abuse, most notably of cocaine, was the number one social and public health problem facing the nation (Gallup 1989; ABC Poll 1989).

These widely varying views about the usefulness, acceptability, and safety of cocaine set the context for cocaine research, and may have had an important influence over the nature of the research which was conducted. During periods of societal acceptability, the possible beneficial effects, or at least the absence of harmful effects of cocaine, were the subject of research. For example, the eloquent description by Freud on the performance-enhancing effects of cocaine was written during such a time (Byck 1974). Once cocaine began to fall out of favour with society, studies of its adverse consequences on physical, psychological, and social functioning became more frequent. It is also interesting to note that, at least for the recent surge in cocaine use, the volume of scientific research, as indicated by the number of published research reports, closely tracks the prevalence of use (Budney *et al.* 1992).

Making sense of the diversity of opinion

How to account for the great divergence in the opinions regarding the safety and acceptability of cocaine is one of the many challenges that this drug poses. There are, of course, obvious reasons for some of the differences in opinion that are based upon moral and ethical concerns over the use of any mood-altering drug unless it is justified by therapeutic reasons.

The safety of any drug is, of course, a function of dose, route, and frequency of administration, as well as individual differences in sensitivity to its toxic effects. It is of interest to note, therefore, that in the early 1970s, when many authorities felt that cocaine was a recreational drug that posed little, if any, public health threat to the nation, that the price of cocaine was comparable to the price of gold, reflecting its scarce availability.

Furthermore, the principal route of administration of the drug at that time was through nasal insufflation (snorting) which, because of the vasoconstrictive properties of cocaine, slows and limits the absorption of the drug. Given the price of cocaine at that time, it is likely that the dosage and frequency of cocaine administration used by most were relatively low, thus lessening the chance for toxic effects of cocaine to be observed. The price also prevented the widespread use of cocaine and thereby decreased the probability that individuals who were especially vulnerable to the toxic effects of cocaine would be exposed to the drug.

All of this changed dramatically as the price and availability of cocaine put it within easy reach of virtually the entire population. Reflected in estimates from NIDA's National Household Survey on Drug Abuse (NHSDA) this popularity sustained robust increases for nearly a decade in the USA—from 1.6 million users in 1977 to more than four million both in 1979 and 1982.

With the emergence of 'crack' cocaine—a relatively inexpensive, smokable form of the drug in the mid 1980s two of the major obstacles imposed by the powdered form of the drug were suddenly removed. More affordable, and ingestible in a manner considered to be more 'acceptable' or 'familiar', cocaine's prevalence further soared to unprecedented levels (an estimated 5.8 million users in 1985) (National Institute on Drug Abuse 1987).

Sustained prevention efforts aimed at youth and the casual user, as well as a growing emphasis on 'user accountability' during the last decade, have contributed to bringing prevalence rates downward in the USA since 1985. However, despite these encouraging trends in overall rates of past month cocaine use, frequent or more intense use has unfortunately not shown a parallel decline.

Cocaine was once the 'drug of choice' among the elite, media, and sports celebrities, and members of groups of upper socioeconomic status. However, in recent years, cocaine use has become more prevalent in very different populations. The cocaine 'epidemic' of the late 1970s and early 1980s has today gradually evolved into one primarily afflicting those of lower socio-economic and educational status. Cocaine use among unemployed 18–34-year-olds in 1991 was over $2\frac{1}{2}$ times that among the employed of this age group (4.9 per cent versus 1.8 per cent). Similarly, high school drop-outs were found to be considerably more likely to be cocaine users (3.6 per cent) than high school graduates (1.6 per cent) (National Institute on Drug Abuse 1992b). This presents another challenge to research, since it is these populations that are not only most vulnerable to drug abuse but most resistant to traditional methods of reducing or preventing it.

Moreover, objective evidence is steadily accruing which definitively dispels the myth once surrounding cocaine's safety. Substantial numbers of emergency room cases involving cocaine continue to be reported by NIDA's Drug Abuse Warning Network (DAWN) system, demonstrating the extent of medical consequences affecting those who are involved in using cocaine. Coupled with the development of the smokeable product, crack, the number of emergency room mentions associated with cocaine use rose dramatically and at its peak exceeded even those reported for alcohol in combination with other drugs (National Institute on Drug Abuse 1991). That the problem is not abating is demonstrated by some recent data showing that cocaine-related mentions increased 31 per cent from 19 381 in the fourth quarter of 1990 to 25 370 in the second quarter of 1991 (National Institute on Drug Abuse 1991, 1992a).

Studying the toxic effects of cocaine

It has long been established from both clinical reports and laboratory experimental evidence in animals that both acute and repeated administration of cocaine can produce a wide variety of toxic effects (Johanson and Fischman 1989). Unfortunately, this evidence did not reach the American public, or at least did not seem to concern the millions of people who experimented with street cocaine during the 1970s and 1980s. It was not until the cocaine-related death of a young superstar basketball player named Len Bias following a night of partying with cocaine that concern for the toxic consequences of cocaine became widespread. Although it was later contested, the first reports concerning the death of Len Bias stated that this was the first time that he had used the drug. This was shocking to the public, many of whom believed that cocaine was a relatively harmless recreational drug if it was not used regularly. One of the major challenges facing drug abuse prevention programmes is the ability to portray the results of animal research and the experience of past generations in a manner that is credible to the youth of succeeding generations who are faced with the decision of whether or not to use cocaine or any other drug of abuse.

Behavioural toxicity

Cocaine has many toxic effects, but it is its behavioural toxicity which is perhaps of most importance. One of the most striking consequences of repeated use of high doses of cocaine is the development of a toxic psychosis characterized by mounting anxiety, paranoia, stereotyped behaviour (which can include the repetitive use of the drug until supplies are exhausted or other forms of toxicity preclude further drug taking), and auditory, visual, and tactile hallucinations. Once an individual has developed a cocaine-induced toxic psychosis it has been suggested that they become sensitized to these actions of cocaine and will develop the psychosis more readily when reinitiating drug use even after prolonged periods of cocaine abstinence (Ellinwood 1979). Although these effects could be obtained by the abuse of cocaine by any route of administration, the induced toxic psychosis was reported to increase in frequency in the Bahamas when coca base smoking became popular (Manschreck *et al.* 1987). Recent findings of extremely high arterial levels of cocaine following smoking (Evans, personal communication) have made it clear that previous studies, in which intravenous cocaine levels were measured following smoking the drug, grossly underestimated the levels reaching the heart and brain (Perez-Reyes *et al.* 1982). Thus, the greater toxicity of smoked cocaine is most likely attributable to pharmacokinetic factors. The repeated administration of cocaine at lower doses produces more subtle forms of behavioural toxicity, including excessive psychomotor activation, paranoid thinking, irritability, hypervigilance, and disruption of normal eating and sleeping patterns (Gawin and Ellinwood 1988). Given the irritability and paranoia associated with cocaine abuse, its association with violence becomes more understandable. In addition to the behavioural toxicity directly produced by cocaine, epidemiological as well as clinical reports have implicated cocaine use as a risk factor for the development of panic disorder (Anthony *et al.* 1989) and has been reported to exacerbate a number of other mental disorders (Regier *et al.* 1990).

Cardiovascular complications

Numerous clinical reports have implicated cocaine in a wide variety of potentially fatal disorders of the cardiovascular system (myocardial infarction, ventricular arrhythmias, decreased pacemaker activity, ischemic and haemorrhagic stroke) and recent animal research has begun to provide some insights into the underlying mechanisms (Kaku and Lowenstein 1990; Thadani 1991). Particularly noteworthy are the reports of individual differences in the myocardial effects of cocaine in squirrel monkeys which may be genetically determined (Tella *et al.* 1991) and the interaction of diet and cocaine on the production of injury to the walls of the aorta in rabbits (Langner and Bement 1991). Furthermore, the potentiating effects of exercise in rats (Conlee *et al.* 1991) and the stress of performance testing in humans (Foltin *et al.* 1988; Foltin and Fischman 1990) on the cardiovascular effects of cocaine are of importance to understanding its toxic effects. Cocaine also produces increased body temperature which would be exacerbated by physical exertion and could contribute to the development of seizures (Ritchie and Greene 1985).

Complications of pregnancy

One of the major concerns of public health officials is the use of cocaine by women during pregnancy. Unfortunately, at the present time, the estimates of the prevalence of this problem vary widely (Chasnoff 1988, 1989; Dicker and Leighton 1991) and it is increasingly difficult to obtain accurate estimates as more states threaten to impose criminal sanctions on women who use cocaine during pregnancy (Reproductive Rights Update 1989). Furthermore, studying the effects of *in utero* exposure to cocaine on the developing fetus and its longer term post-natal consequences is extremely difficult because cocaine users are usually poly-drug abusers, nutritionally deprived, often have sexually transmitted diseases, and rarely obtain adequate prenatal care. These factors must be taken into account when interpreting the studies which have shown an association between cocaine use and increases in premature labour and delivery; spontaneous abortions and fetal death; low birth weight and small head circumferences; genitourinary malformations; and neurobehavioural deficits as revealed by the Brazelton Neonatal Behavioural Assessment Scale and Apgar scores (Finnegan *et al.* 1992; Kilbey and Asghar 1991). Furthermore, the mother's use of cocaine and its deleterious consequences to child development does not stop with birth but rather may be responsible for continued neglect and/or child abuse.

There are a number of significant challenges to obtaining reliable answers in this area. Animal research would seem to be the obvious answer to many of these methodological problems if it were clear how best to model this phenomenon. There are a variety of issues which must be considered in the use of animals to investigate the impact of cocaine use during pregnancy. What species should be used? By what route should the cocaine be given?

How often and at what dosage levels? During the entire pregnancy or at critical developmental periods? Can we model post-natal maternal negligence or abuse of the neonate? Is it obvious that no single animal model is going to be useful to address all of the relevant questions. Rather, a variety of animal models must be developed, each of which may complement human studies better to define the complications of pregnancy caused by cocaine.

Studying the mechanisms of toxicity

A final caveat concerning the use of animals for modelling the toxicity of cocaine comes from the results of a study in which the toxicity of cocaine in rats was compared in animals who self-administered cocaine with yoked controls who passively receive identical doses of cocaine. When rats were allowed to self-inject low doses of cocaine (0.33mg/infusion) by pairing a lever press with a drug injection thus giving the rats control over when they received injections, few rats died; whereas, over 50 per cent of the yoked controls who received exactly the same doses at exactly the same time but who did not control the injections, died within a few weeks (Dworkin 1991). The reasons for the difference in toxicity between the two groups are as yet unknown, but the results of this study clearly indicate the complications in determining the way in which cocaine toxicity should be studied in animals.

Looking for evidence of physical dependence

A long-standing challenge to research stems from the debate on whether cocaine should be considered an addicting drug or whether it produces only 'psychological dependence'. There are several important issues raised by this question. First, does cocaine produce physical dependence? Secondly, why is physical dependence considered to be such an important consideration in assessing the 'addictiveness' of a drug?

Unlike the opiates, sedative hypnotics, and alcohol, humans and animals repeatedly administered cocaine do not show any obvious signs of withdrawal when cocaine administration is stopped. For this reason, it has been generally believed that cocaine does not produce physical dependence (Jones 1984). However, Gawin and Kleber (1986) carried out a naturalistic study of 30 cocaine users and described three phases which they characterize in cocaine withdrawal: the 'crash' phase which lasts for approximately nine hours to four days; the 'withdrawal' phase which lasts for one to ten weeks; and the 'extinction' phase which lasts indefinitely. Maximum probability of relapse to cocaine use occurs during the withdrawal phase, when patients reported strong craving for cocaine. Although the craving diminishes during the extinction phase, environmental cues associated with cocaine can induce craving and relapse to drug use. Recent animal research has shown that there is a disruption of food maintained responding for several days when cocaine administration is terminated which can be reversed by administration of the drug (Woolverton and Kleven 1988). Unfortunately, this study was not designed to determine whether cocaine abstinence increased drug-seeking behaviour.

This brings us to the heart of the question—why is physical dependence an important issue? Obviously, if the withdrawal of cocaine following long-term administration produced a medical crisis, as is the case with sedatives and alcohol, methods for detoxifying cocaine users would be essential. Clearly, this is not the case. The second reason why physical dependence may be of importance is if the withdrawal state has motivational properties leading to a marked increase in drug-seeking behaviour. This has been clearly established with opiates (Schuster and Johanson 1973) and has been reported anecdotally to occur with cocaine (Gawin and Kleber 1986). More definitive research is needed in this area.

The study of new approaches to treatment

Use of cocaine is decreasing overall, but there is still a burgeoning need for drug abuse treatment for cocaine users. An analysis of state alcohol and drug abuse profile data shows a dramatic six-fold increase in cocaine client treatment admissions reported over a recent six-year period—from 38 000 in 1985 to 235 000 in 1990 (Butynski *et al.* 1991). One of the key challenges faced by NIDA is the development of effective treatment strategies specifically for cocaine abuse.

At the present time there is no generally accepted pharmacological, behavioural, or psychodynamic treatment for cocaine dependence, although partial success with all of these approaches has been reported (Johanson and Fischman 1989). The development of a pharmacological agent for the treatment of cocaine dependence has been guided by the evidence suggesting the critical importance of dopamine, one of several important brain neurotransmitters, in the reinforcing actions of cocaine. The demonstration by Kuhar and his colleagues of the high correlation between the reinforcing effects of a series of cocaine analogues, and their binding strength to the dopamine uptake transporter, strongly suggests that it is this specific action which initiates the cascade of neurochemical events underlying cocaine reinforcement (Ritz *et al.* 1987). The recent cloning and sequencing of the dopamine transporter molecule (Shimada *et al.* 1991) permits the study of the possibility of developing a specific cocaine blocker which could be useful for the treatment of cocaine dependence. Experience with methadone and naltrexone for the treatment of heroin dependence has shown that a medication would be unlikely to be a 'magic bullet cure' for cocaine dependence. Nevertheless, like methadone or naltrexone, a medication for the treatment of cocaine dependence could be useful as a component of a comprehensive treatment and rehabilitation programme.

Conclusion

The multiple social and public health problems created by the epidemic of cocaine abuse that began in the USA in the 1970s sparked tremendous public concern and led in the 1980s to major increases in the funding for research into the aetiology, prevention, and treatment of cocaine dependence. Today, there is a tremendous decline in the incidence of cocaine use in large segments of the population in the USA (National Institute on Drug Abuse 1992*b*; Johnston *et al.* 1992), although it is significantly higher in school drop outs and the unemployed (National Institute on Drug Abuse 1992*b*). Excellent progress is being made in understanding the biological, behavioural, and social factors leading to cocaine abuse and dependence. It is to be hoped that the research initiatives begun during the period of great societal concern will not be prematurely phased out as the current cocaine epidemic wanes. This would be particularly tragic if, as in the past, the problem of cocaine abuse is only on a temporary holiday.

References

ABC Poll (1989). Reported in the *Washington Post*, August 29, 1989.

Anthony, J., Tien, A.Y., and Petronis, K.R. (1989). Epidemiologic evidence on cocaine use and panic attacks. *American Journal of Epidemiology*, 129, 3, 543–9.

Budney, A.J., Higgins, S.T., Hughes, J.R., and Bickel, W.K. (1992). The scientific/clinical response to the cocaine epidemic: a Medline search of the literature. *Drug and Alcohol Dependence*, 30(2), 143–9.

Butynski, W., Reda, J.L., Canova, D., McMullen, H., Bartosch, W., Fitzgerald, C., Nelson, S., and Ciaccio, M. (1991). *State resources and services related to alcohol and other drug abuse problems, fiscal year 1990. An analysis of state alcohol and drug abuse profile data*. National Association of State Alcohol and Drug Abuse Directors, Inc. Washington.

Byck, R. (1974). *Cocaine papers*. Stonehill, New York.

Chasnoff, I.J. (1988). News release on the first National Hospital Incidence survey conducted by the National Association for Perinatal Addition Research and Education (NAPARE).

Chasnoff, I.J. (1989). Drug use and women: establishing a standard of care. In *Prenatal abuse of licit and illicit drugs*, (ed. D.E. Hutchings). Annals of the New York Academy of Sciences, 562, 208–10.

Conlee, R.K., Barnett, D.W., Kelly, K.P., and Han, D.H. (1991). Effects of cocaine on the physiology of exercise. In *Cardiovascular toxicity of cocaine: underlying mechanisms* (ed. P. Thadani). National Institute on Drug Abuse research monograph 108, DHHS Pub. No. (ADM) 91–1767, pp. 167–80. US Government Printing Office, Washington.

Dicker, M. and Leighton, E.A. (1991). Trends in diagnosed drug problems among newborns: United States, 1979–1987. *Drug and Alcohol Dependence*, 28, 151–65.

Dworkin, S.I. (1991). Evaluation of the neurotic effects of self-administered cocaine.

Final progress report submitted to the National Institute on Drug Abuse, Contract No. 271–87–8118.

Education Newsletter (1974). *Drugs and Drug Abuse*, **3**, 5.

Ellinwood, E.H. (1979). In *Handbook on drug abuse*, (ed. R.L. DuPont, A. Goldstein, and J. O'Donnels), pp. 221–31. US Government Printing Office, Washington.

Erlenmeyer, A. (1987). *Die morphiumensucht und ihre behandlung*, (3rd edn), p. 154. Heusser, Berlin.

Finnegan, L.P., Mellott, J.M., Williams, L.R., and Wapner, R.J. (1992). Perinatal exposure to cocaine: human studies. In *Cocaine pharmacology, physiology, and clinical strategies*, (ed. J.M. Lakoski, M.P. Galloway, and F.J. White), pp. 391–409. CRC Press, Boca Ratan, FL.

Foltin, R.W. and Fischman, M.W. (1990). The effects of combinations of intranasal cocaine, smoked marijuana, and task performance on heart rate. *Pharmacology, Biochemistry, and Behaviour*, **36**, 311–15.

Foltin, R.W., McEntee, M.A., Capriotti, R.M., Pedroso, J.J., Pearlson, G.D., and Fischman, M.W. (1988). Effects of cocaine on the talk elicited physiological response. *Pharmacology, Biochemistry and Behaviour*, **31**, 387–91.

Gallup Poll (1989). July and August reports in *USA Today*.

Gawin. F.H. and Kleber, H.D. (1986). Abstinence symptomatology and psychiatric diagnosis in cocaine abusers—clinical observations. *Archives of General Psychiatry*, **43**, 107–13.

Gawin, F.H. and Ellinwood, E.H. (1988). Cocaine and other stimulants: actions, abuse, and treatment. *New England Medical Journal*, **318**, 1173–82.

Johanson, C.E. and Fischman, M.W. (1989). The pharmacology of cocaine related to its abuse. *Pharmacological Reviews*. **41**(1), 3–52.

Johnston, L.D., O'Malley, P.M., and Bachman, J.G. (1992). Results from the 'Monitoring the Future' survey (Vol. 1), DHHS Pub. No. (ADM) 93–1920. US Government Printing Office, Washington.

Jones, R.T. (1984). The pharmacology of cocaine. In *Cocaine: pharmacology, effects, and treatment of abuse*, (ed. J. Grabowski). National Institute on Drug Abuse research monograph 50. DHHS Pub. No. (ADM) 87–1326, pp. 34–53. US Government Printing Office, Washington.

Kaku, D.A. and Lowenstein, D.H. (1990). Emergence of recreational drug abuse as a major risk factor for stroke in young adults. *Annals of Internal Medicine*, 133(11), 821–7.

Kennedy, J. (1985). *Coca exotica, The illustrated story of cocaine*. Associated University Presses, Inc., Cranbury, NJ.

Kilbey, M.M. and Asghar, K. (ed.) (1991). *Methodological issues in controlled studies on effects of prenatal exposure to drug abuse*. National Institute on Drug Abuse research monograph 114. DHHS Pub. No. (ADM) 91–1837. US Government Printing Office, Washington.

Langner, R.O. and Bement, C.L. (1991). Cocaine-induced changes in the biochemistry and morphology of rabbit aorta. In *Cardiovascular toxicity of cocaine: underlying mechanisms*, (ed. P. Thadani). National Institute on Drug Abuse Research Monograph 108, DHHS Pub. No. (ADM) 91–1767, pp. 154–66. US Government Printing Office, Washington.

Lewin, L. Phantastica (1964). In *Narcotic and stimulating drugs, their use and abuse*, translated by P.H.A. Wirth, pp. 75–88. Routledge & Kegan Paul, London, and E.P. Dutton and Co., New York.

Manschreck, T.C., Allen, D.F., and Neville, M. (1987). Freebase psychosis: cases from a Bahamian epidemic of cocaine abuse. *Psychiatry*, 28, 555–64.

National Institute on Drug Abuse (1987). *1985 national household survey on drug abuse, population estimates, (1987)*. DHHS Pub. No. (ADM), 87–1539, US Government Printing Office, Washington.

National Institute on Drug Abuse (1991). *1990 annual emergency room data from the drug abuse warning network (DAWN)*. Statistical report series I, Number 10, DHHS Pub. No. (ADM) 91–1839, US Government Printing Office, Washington.

National Institute on Drug Abuse (1992a). *1991 annual emergency room data from the Drug abuse network (DAWN)*. Statistical Report Series I, Number II, DHHS Pub. No. 93–1955, US Government Printing Office, Washington, in preparation.

National Institute on Drug Abuse (1992b). *National household survey on drug abuse: Population Estimates 1991*. DHHS Pub. No. (ADM) 92–1887, US Government Printing Office, Washington.

Perez-Reyes, M., Diguiseppi, S., Ondrusek, G., Jeffcoat, A.R., and Cook, C.E. (1982). Free base cocaine smoking. *Clinical Pharmacology*, 32, 459–65.

Regier, D.A., Farmer, M.E., Rae, D.S., Locke, B.Z., Keith, S.J., Judd, L.L., and Goodwin, F.K. (1990). Comorbidity of mental disorders with alcohol and other drug abuse. Results from the epidemiologic catchment area (ECA) study. *JAMA*, 264(19), 2511–18.

Reproductive Rights Update (1989). American Civil Liberties Union/Reproductive Freedom Project, New York 1(7), 7.

Ritchie, J.M. and Greene, N.M. (1985). Local anesthetics. In *The pharmacological basis of therapeutics*, (ed. A.G. Gilman, L.S. Goodman, T.W. Rall, and F. Murad). pp. 302–21. Macmillan Publishing Company, New York.

Ritz, M.C., Lamb, R.J., Goldberg, S.R., and Kuhar, M.J. (1987). Cocaine receptors on dopamine transporters are related to self-administration of cocaine. *Science*, 237, 1219–23.

Schuster, C.R., and Johanson, C.E. (1973). Behavioural analysis of opiate dependence. In *Opiate addiction: origins and treatment*, (ed. S. Fisher and A. Freedman), pp. 77–92. Z.H. Winston and Sons, New York.

Shimada, S., Kitayama, S., Lin, C.L., Patel, A., Nanthkumar, E., Gregor, P., Kuhar, M., and Uhl, G. (1991). Cloning and expression of a cocaine-sensitive dopamine transporter complementary DNA. *Science*, 254, 576–8.

Tella, S.R., Schindler, C.W., and Goldberg, S.W. (1991). Cardiovascular effects of cocaine in squirrel monkeys. In *Cardiovascular toxicity of cocaine: underlying mechanisms*. (ed. P. Thadani). National Institute on Drug Abuse research monograph 108, DHHS Pub. No. (ADM), 91–1767, pp. 74–91. US Government Printing Office, Washington.

Thadani, P. (ed.) (1991). *Cardiovascular toxicity of cocaine: underlying mechanisms*. National Institute on Drug Abuse Research Monograph 108, DHHS Pub. No. (ADM) 91–1767, US Government Printing Office, Washington.

Woolverton, W.L. and Kleven, M.S. (1988). Evidence for cocaine dependence in monkeys following a prolonged period of exposure. *Psychopharmacology*, 94, 288–91.

13. Research, policy, and the problems set by rapid social, economic, and political change

Robin Room

My fundamental intellectual interest is in the study of change, but when I first got a job in alcohol studies, in 1963, the field seemed far from these interests. At that time, the underlying epistemological assumption in the USA about drinking was that things did not change much; that what you found out about patterns at one time would be equally valid 10 years later. In fact, if some indicator, such as the Jellinek formula, was showing evidence of change, that was presumed by one well-known scholar to be evidence that the indicator was no longer working, that it needed to be fixed. This underlying assumption actually was a fairly good fit to drinking in the USA of the 1950s, when per capita consumption stayed more or less level; it might be argued that the assumption also reflected something about American society more generally in the 1950s.

Some years later, after Jerome Jaffe and I had become acquainted at a meeting in London in 1972 ('Epidemiology' 1973), I was precipitated by him into the literature on illicit drug epidemiology. Here, there was the opposite underlying epistemological assumption: everything was always changing, what had been true last year could not be assumed to apply this year, and new data was collected not so much for what it could tell us about the present status as for what it could tell us about trends. It might be added that for US society generally, by the early 1970s there had been a number of rude awakenings from the apparent changelessness of the 1950s.

Change and scientific laws

We live in a world which is both ever-changing and unchanging. Whether we see change or constancy depends considerably on where and how we look at the world. The habit of mind of science is to look for what is constant, even amid apparent change. In this habit of mind, variability and change are often seen as surface 'noise', potentially obscuring the unchanging mechanisms below. The research questions are posed in absolute, timeless terms: what is the dependence potential of this benzodiazepide, what are the metabolic pathways of ethanol, what is the action and effectiveness of this potential remedy? The scientific enterprise is seen in terms of discovery, in the most literal meaning of the term: unwrapping the timeless secrets of the natural world.

One should not imply, of course, that this frame of mind ignores change. Change is often, indeed, the object of study: the motions of the planets, the evolution of life forms, the natural history of a disease, are all classical matters for scientific study. But the aim of the scientific enterprise is to find and specify the unchanging laws which underlie and explain the observed changes. The recurrent habit of thought is to assume that when such a regularity is found it will be universally applicable. It has often been a long and painful process for science to recognize that there may be limits on a law's universality. The classic resolution at the end of this process is to discover a new, more general law. With this discovery, order is again restored to the universe: now there is a new universal law, at a new level of generality, within which the old law is nested as an application in limited conditions. The consistent concern of the scientific enterprise, then, is to find universal and unchanging laws that underlie and explain observations of change.

This search for the unchanging and universal is a large part of the appeal of the scientific enterprise for our kinds of societies, and the promise of discovery of universal laws is an important part of the implied social contract between science and the society. The idea that something can be discovered, and after that it more or less stays discovered, means that science can be seen as producing durable goods, both in the sense of permanent intellectual property and, our societies hope, in the sense of permanently useful inventions. The idea that the discovery is universally applicable means that it has been made and paid for once and for all, so that every new circumstance does not require further research. Paying for science, in this perspective, is not a mere running cost for today, like providing clinical or social services, nor even just an upkeep cost for the near future, like teaching the young, but instead is an investment which will pay permanent dividends. Even if new discoveries eventually supersede the scientific knowledge, they will be built on its base. No other societal investment promises this kind of permanence, uncorrupted by moth, rust, or shifting fashion. If the scientific promises of permanent advances and of substantial generality wear thin, it becomes much harder to argue for a special societal investment in science: science retreats to being one more branch of knowledge, alongside the humanities and vocational knowledge, whose adepts are mainly paid to pass on this form of cultural capital by teaching the young.

Change, science, and human drug use

This frame of reference of cumulative and generalizable scientific knowledge has been the primary frame of reference for modern medical research. In the

UK and the USA, at least, alcohol and other drug research has primarily been conducted under such a medical research rubric. And in some aspects of alcohol and drug studies, work pursued in this frame can point to great and permanent success, in terms of the advancement of knowledge. What we have learned in the last 40 years about tobacco and lung cancer, about opiates and brain receptors, or about the detailed effects of drinking on performance decrement, for instance, will be reflected in the textbooks of the next century, even if only as a base underlying further advances.

But when we try to transfer this general scientific epistemology to the practical prevention of drug, alcohol, and tobacco problems, we find ourselves in trouble. The application of the cumulative and generalizing frame of physical and biological science to human society and behaviour was precisely the ambition of nineteenth century social science. But the search for universally applicable laws of human behaviour that were not trivial proved a humbling experience. By and large, twentieth century social science has retreated from this ambition to more modest aims. The problem is that human social behaviour is too complex, multi-layered, and multi-determined. Our predictions of the future from a particular set of observations may be quite good for the next moment, but their accuracy tends to decay fairly rapidly over time. Human behaviour cannot be predicted in detail as solar eclipses can, hundreds of years in advance.

With respect to any science of prevention and intervention, the problem of prediction is further complicated by the fact of human cognition and ingenuity. If policy makers raise an obstacle to a desired behaviour, commodity or event, some minds are likely to set to work on the task of overcoming the obstacle. The long-term net effect of the intervention, then, does not simply consist of its immediate and direct effect, but rather of this effect less any neutralization of it that ingenious minds have managed.

These problems do not invalidate efforts to build a scientific base for prevention policies and programmes, but they do suggest starting with modest aims and a certain degree of humility. There are in fact some generalizations that can be made about the human response to particular policies and interventions, but they are often of limited specificity, and of bounded applicability. Indeed, part of the scientific task involved in accumulating knowledge about the effects of specific measures is not only to specify the relationship involved but also to specify the boundaries of its applicability.

These general points can be illustrated with the particular example of the effect of changes in taxes—which translate into changes in prices—on levels of alcohol consumption in a population. This is one of the most frequently studied potential prevention measures; there are numerous estimates of the price elasticity of demand for alcoholic beverages. A few general conclusions can be made from this literature.

1. There is some negative elasticity in the demand for alcoholic beverages; that is, if the price goes up, the consumption will go down.

2. In economist's terms the demand tends to be relatively inelastic—that is, a 10 per cent rise in price will usually cause a fall in consumption of less than 10 per cent.

3. The elasticity for the main alcoholic beverage in a culture—for instance, beer in the UK, wine in Italy—tends to be less than the elasticity for other alcoholic beverages.

4. Heavy drinkers as well as light drinkers show some price elasticity—their drinking behaviour is not immune to price (we still need a wider range of evidence concerning this point).

The generalizations that can be made beyond these would be relatively few. And even the generalizations that can be made have hidden boundaries, which need to be made explicit. As an outer limit, discussions of elasticity assume a market economy, where alcoholic beverages have an exchange value relative to other goods and services. The estimates tend to be based on relatively small-scale variations in the price of alcohol, and it may well that the effects of drastic changes in price cannot be extrapolated from the effects of small changes. Elasticity estimates are abundant for a small group of industrial countries with a strong historic concern with alcohol issues, and much sparser in other industrial countries; this may affect the generalizability of the conclusions from the literature. Elasticities often vary over time in a given society, so that a set of elasticities computed on the basis of the immediate past cannot be assumed to be good for the indefinite future. It would be difficult to identify any model or theory of variations in a particular society in the price elasticity of alcoholic beverages, and neither is there a clear theory of the determinants of cross-cultural variations in elasticity. There is also the issue that conventional econometric estimations of elasticity assume that the effects of rising prices are simply the reverse of falling prices, while an addiction concept would make the opposite assumption. In this connection, we need more detailed studies of changes in the buying behaviour of different classes of drinkers when prices go up and down.

This example, drawn from the literature on a relatively well-studied measure, suggests how limited is the base from which we are starting if we set out to develop a scientific basis for policy making and prevention programming—that is, if we wish to understand how rates of drug-related problems change and can be subjected to change.

So what are some of the steps forward we need to take in building such a base of knowledge? The tasks we face can usefully be divided into two parts: building knowledge on how to manage, and if possible reduce, alcohol and drug problems in a relatively stable situation and society; and building knowledge on how to understand, respond to, and if possible, bring about large-scale change. These issues are not really distinct, of course: large-scale changes are often the result of the aggregation of small changes. But the distinction is still worth making, from two points of view: the methods of study of the two kinds of situation tend to be distinct; and policy makers and professionals tend to play a larger role and have more control over the situation in a case of incremental change than in the case of large-scale change.

Studying small-scale purposive change

Most of the systematic literature which we have available deals with the small-scale change end of the spectrum. This is the home territory of the classical quantitative outcome evaluation study, with prior and post measurements in the study site and in a control site. Three major types of such studies have emerged. One type, full-scale experimental policy studies where a control measure is changed in one community or set of communities but not in another, has primarily been a specialty of Nordic countries experimenting with alcohol policies. A second type, 'natural experiment' or 'legal impact' studies, differs in that the policy change or intervention is not under the control of the researchers. Frequently, researchers have to scramble to find the resources to carry out the prior measurements. A subclass of this tradition consists of 'strike studies', studies of sudden perturbations in the supply of a drug, for instance from a strike of employees of state liquor stores (see review by Smith 1988).

The third type of evaluation study is the community intervention study. This type of study compares the effects of a programme or programmes in one or more target communities with trends in matched control communities. In this type of study, there is typically a professionally-provided intervention or set of interventions: it may be a mass media campaign, school or after-school education programs, or training or brief therapy for heavy users. Less typically, the intervention may be a community organizing effort around local tobacco, alcohol or drug policies.

Full-scale evaluation studies take considerable time and effort—particularly the community intervention studies. They tend to be carried out in a relatively small roster of countries—primarily, the Nordic and Anglophone countries. Well-done studies of this type provide some of the most convincing evidence we have on which measures have what effects under what circumstances. But the boundary around their generalizability must remain quite tight, in a global perspective, so long as they are confined to such a restricted range of countries. It would be a brave planner indeed who would predict, on the basis of Saturday-closing experiments in Norway and Finland, what would happen if alcohol sales were halted on Saturday in Italy or Nigeria.

According to the usual scholarly norms, only the outcome results from such studies typically find their way into the abstracted literature. But from the point of view of cumulating the results of the studies into a broader picture of the conditions of a measure's effectiveness, the outcome results of a study often constitute only a single case in what is, as a result, a rather small population of case studies. Usually, however, the researchers involved in the study learned a great deal more about the potential for, and hazards in, introducing change in the course of the study. Our understanding of the conditions for success of purposive change efforts is potentially greatly enhanced when the process data on the studies also becomes broadly available. This was the major rationale behind a 1989 conference on evaluated community action projects in the alcohol field (Giesbrecht *et al.* 1990), and a follow-up conference held early in 1992.

So far, efforts to cumulate the knowledge from these experimental and quasi-experimental studies have primarily taken the form of review articles, usually dealing with one drug class at a time. While there are probably not enough cases yet for a formal meta-evaluation, it would be interesting to examine the variation by drug in results with a given intervention. For instance, it seems that educational approaches in US schools in the current era more often can show positive effects, compared with control sites, for tobacco than for alcohol.

From the point of view of making this literature more broadly useful to policy discussions, the primary need is to increase the number and particularly the spread of cases studied. One avenue for increasing the case file is to reach back into the past. An alternative to prior/post evaluation studies is the use of autoregressive time-series methods (ARIMA) to study the effect of some policy change on indicators of drug use or of drug-related problems. Such analyses still require a substantial investment of energy; one case study can take the time of an experienced analyst for three months. But this is still a small investment of resources compared with carrying out a full experimental study. And usable social and health statistics data are available for a considerably broader spread of time and of societies than can be covered with experimental studies. As we move towards a greater number of scholars being competent in ARIMA and related analytical techniques, it would be worthwhile to open discussions internationally on developing a list of interesting cases for study.

Even where data are probably insufficient for formal ARIMA techniques, collecting case studies of change is a worthwhile effort. It would be particularly interesting to study variations in the effects of the same policy change in different subpopulations—for instance, the Muslim and wine cultures as well as spirits cultures of the former Soviet Union.

It must be recognized that there are limits to what can be concluded from studies of small-scale purposive change. Designers of experimental studies face a Hobson's choice between testing a single intervention and testing a package of interventions. While testing a single measure gives the most determinative results, there is good reason to believe that measures are often mutually reinforcing, so that measures which individually are ineffective may become effective as an aggregation. Evaluation methods are also inherently better attuned to measuring short-term change than to measuring long-term change. In the long run, history has a way of intruding or at least happening, and the long-term effects of a particular change in policy become progressively harder to separate out as time passes.

Studying big changes

Big changes do happen in the use of and problems from legal drugs as well as illicit ones. Although tobacco smoking has been well entrenched in Europe for about four centuries, cigarette smoking, which we now know hugely increased the morbidity and mortality associated with tobacco use, is largely a phenomenon of this century. The 1830s and early 1840s saw a truly big change in alcohol consumption in the USA, with very little government involvement: it is estimated that per capita consumption of ethanol for those aged 15 and over fell from about 17 to about 7 litres per annum (Rorabaugh 1979, p. 233).

Some big changes, particularly big declines in consumption, happen in a situation of national crisis—in wartime, as a result of revolution, or during a major depression. Government action is frequently involved, as in the swingeing increases in spirits taxes in Denmark in 1917, but the spirit of national crisis validates and provides support for the action that would not have been there in normal times. Otherwise, big declines in use of deeply entrenched drugs tend to have been borne by major social or religious movements. The decline in alcohol consumption in the 1830s and early 1840s in the USA was associated with a religious revival called the Second Great Awakening. In countries like Finland and Iceland, temperance became caught up with social movements for national independence and nationbuilding. Big increases in use, on the other hand, are often a generational phenomenon. The carriers of the rise in US alcohol consumption after the 1920s were middle-class youth, in revolt against their parents' Victorian morality, just as counter-cultural youth of the late 1960s and 1970s were major carriers of an upsurge in illicit drug (as well as alcohol) consumption.

As we study big changes in drug use and problems, then, with attention to policy makers' particular interest in what governments can do to help or hinder them, there is a need to adopt a broad perspective, with attention to a range of social trends in the society. At the moment, the study of big changes is at the stage of compiling case studies; thus Esa Österberg, Norman Giesbrecht, and Jacek Moskalewicz are currently compiling a book of such studies for alcohol, under the auspices of the Kettil Bruun Society. The skills of historians as well as social scientists will be needed to increase our stock and range of case studies. It is not too early, too, to begin making comparisons—across societies, across historical epochs, across drugs.

A programme of research with a global scope

What is being proposed here is, then, that we undertake two very ambitious programme of work. In both cases, the challenge is to be comparative, on at least three dimensions.

1. Across cultures and populations: from this we can get some sense of how similar or different outcomes can be under different conditions.

2. Across time: looking at different time periods in the same society to some extent controls for the kind of hidden variation built into cross-cultural comparisons.

3. Across drugs: here we are examining not only differences in the psycho-pharmacology of the drugs but differences in their social definition and position. It is striking how different the assumptions and epistemologies often are in separate discussions of the science and policy connections for nicotine, alcohol, illicit drugs, and licit psychotropic drugs.

The studies of small-scale purposive efforts at change and of big changes are being proposed as separate efforts, but we also need explicit attention to the relation between the two. When and under what circumstances do small-scale change efforts cumulate into a big change, and when may they have perverse effects, setting off a generational rebellion against the 'nanny state'?

How are these programmes of work to be carried out? The most likely answers are probably both true in a way, though they contradict each other: they won't be carried out, and they are already being carried out. They are already being carried out in the sense that we are beginning to build up a substantial literature of studies of the effects of policy and prevention efforts, and a substantial historical literature on big changes in drug use and in societal responses to drug use. They won't be carried out, on the other hand, in the kind of systematic way suggested here, without some substantial innovations in the way we carry out research.

The problem is several-fold. Ironically, much of the work involved is presently seen as too far from policy significance to be fundable, at least with alcohol- and drug-specific funds. Historical work has thus largely depended on the passion or self-sacrifice of individual scholars, or has been carried out in little protected niches of the funding structure for research. Conversely, evaluations of purposive change efforts are often too much under the thumb of their policy significance. Frequently, the funding agency can suppress the results if it doesn't like them, or the results are buried in the fugitive literature of project reports and conference presentations.

The most serious problem with the current literature is its narrowness of coverage. As has been noted, the currently available work is heavily bounded—by time and to some extent by type of drug, but in particular by societal setting. The bounds are multi-determined. Does the society have a tradition of evaluation studies and of strength in the requisite research traditions? Does it problematize the drug enough to create a specific research tradition? Is it rich enough to support a substantial research base? All of these are true for the societies which have contributed the bulk of the current literature. With a few exceptions, the present pattern is for explicitly policy-attuned studies to be carried out only in the society which is funding them. The main literatures where a scholar often works on a society outside his or her own have been anthropology and history, where the tradition of the small-scale enterprise of the individual scholar still holds sway.

It is important that we find ways to transcend these limitations. Interesting changes, big and small, are going on all around us, and going unstudied or less than fully studied. Much can be learned, for example, from studying the huge transitions in Eastern Europe, from studying the rise of markets for drugs and attempts to control the markets in developing societies, and from studying community control efforts in village societies. Work of this sort will need to be carried out collaboratively with the participation of local scholars, but it is going to take some commitment of resources by societies with the resources and the interest to undertake the kinds of research here discussed.

The proposed programme of research is of clear practical significance. But it is important to be modest and realistic about what we are likely to be able to offer the policy process. We cannot expect to end up with scientific laws which apply in general across the sway of time and circumstance. Instead, we can hope for conditional probabilities for particular sequences of events under specific conditions: if X happens, Y is very likely to follow, particularly if Z is also true. Part of the researcher's task, as earlier noted, is to specify the boundaries within which we have evidence for these generalizations.

Lastly, it should be kept in mind that science is always potentially inconvenient and even subversive (Gusfield 1975). It may establish relations that from an immediate practical point of view are useless. For instance, while recent studies have suggested that alcohol rationing systems reduce the drinking of heavy drinkers, rationing of alcohol as a public health intervention is presently politically inconceivable in most industrial societies. It is likely that researchers will insist on including within the scope of their studies dimensions that policy makers are uneasy about subjecting to scrutiny—notably including the actions of the policy makers themselves (Bruun 1973). And the findings of the research may well be disconcerting. Those involved in the policy process are well advised to keep in mind that the true heroes, for scientists, tend to be those who succeed in disproving what they set out fervently believing in.

Acknowledgement

Preparation of this chapter was supported by a National Alcohol Research Center grant (AA05595) from the US National Institute on Alcohol Abuse and Alcoholism to the Alcohol Research Group, Medical Research Institute of San Francisco.

References

Bruun, K.E. (1973). Social research, social policy, and action. In *The epidemiology of drug dependence: report on a conference, London 25–29 September 1972*, pp. 115–19. Copenhagen: WHO, Regional Office for Europe, EUR 5436 IV.

'Epidemiology' (1973). *The epidemiology of drug dependence: report on a conference, London 25–29 September 1972*, Copenhagen: WHO, Regional Office for Europe, EUR 5436 IV.

Giesbrecht, N., Conley, P., Denniston, R.W., Gliksman, L., Holder, H., Pederson, A., Room, R., and Shain, M. eds. (1990). *Research, action, and the community: experiences in the prevention of alcohol and other drug problems*, OSAP Prevention Monograph 4, Rockville: Office of Substance Abuse Prevention, DHHS Publication No. (ADM) 89–1651.

Gusfield, J.R. (1975). The (f)utility of knowledge? The relation of social science to public policy toward drugs. *Annals of the American Academy of Political and Social Science*, 417, 1–15.

Rorabaugh, W.J. (1979). *The alcoholic republic: an American tradition*. Oxford University Press, New York and Oxford.

Smith, D.I. (1988). Effectiveness of restrictions on availability as a means of preventing alcohol-related problems. *Contemporary Drug Problems*, 15, 627–84.

14. Action at the local level: aids to strategic thinking

David Robinson

During the 1970s, those concerned with alcohol, tobacco, and other drugs concentrated, quite understandably, on the definition and classification of problems, the search for better ways of assessing their extent, range, and impact, and the development of treatment facilities. The key concern for the 1980s was to shift the focus of attention from epidemiology, aetiology, and service provision to a consideration of how best to prevent and control specific problems: a matter which was usually referred to as 'everybody's business'. This shift in emphasis was both accompanied and stimulated by the increasing involvement of social, economic, and political scientists. And a sub-theme running through much contemporary debate was a recognition of the need to mobilize concerted 'action at the local level'.

While the 1980s certainly took seriously the issue of prevention and control, stimulated in no small part by the WHO, there is no denying that much of the policy debate was little more than the exchange of slogans under the guise of recommendations. This chapter will indicate some examples of recent social science work which could act as 'aids to strategic thinking' for those who would seek to translate the enthusiasm and exhortation of the 1980s into well-founded action in the 1990s. The emphasis is on 'action at the local level' addressed in relation to the key thrust of this book, namely: what can we learn of the contribution of science to the demands and development of policy? The science is the social sciences, and the issue is discussed under four headings: localities in context, guides to local action, assessing service requirements, and costing packages of care provision.

Localities in context

All problems are local in the sense that everywhere is local. But, of course, local problems may be initiated and exacerbated by nationwide or international activity. And again, local groups, agencies, and organizations are not free to act as they please. They act in a context. This section will touch on 'localities in their context': that is, the issue of the political and other structures which need to be appreciated by those with any responsibility at the local level in relation to alcohol, tobacco, and other drugs. National structures and international relations will be mentioned.

Of those who call for national control policies, some do not appear to appreciate the range and complexity of existing policies and activities. In fact, they appear to believe that there is, in their country, no national policy at all. But, of course, every country in which there is any alcohol, tobacco or other drug has its national policy. We may or may not like that policy, but that is a separate matter. Anyone claiming to be serious about taking local action must attempt to understand the nature and impact of national policy: made up of the activities, rules, and relationships of the wide range of statutory, commercial, voluntary, professional, service sector, and other agencies involved in some way with alcohol, tobacco or any other drug.

Tether and Harrison (1988) have produced for one country and for one substance the kind of detailed analysis which could serve as a model for those concerned with other places and substances. For alcohol policy in the UK, they have mapped out the policy complexity within 16 government departments. They give a fascinating outline of the departmental alcohol responsibilities and then describe where these responsibilities are located within departmental structures, trace out the principal intra- and inter-departmental links and, finally, indicate each department's contacts with those key non-departmental organizations which contribute to the alcohol policy process.

Just as much action at the local level is ill-informed about its national context so, similarly, much national policy in relation to alcohol, tobacco or other drugs is discussed and debated as though it existed in isolation, not merely from local activities, but from the interests and activities of other nations. The internationality of the illicit drugs market is, of course, well recognized, and there is increasing effort being made through international co-operation to detect and deter drug trafficking. Similarly, the inter-relation between illicit drug supply reduction through multinational activity, and demand reduction within national boundaries is obvious and itself international. As George Shultz, the then US Secretary of State, acknowledged on his visit to Bolivia in 1987, there is no point in criticizing that country for not reducing the production and export of cocaine if the USA, the main market, does little to reduce the demand for its import.

All that is uncontentious in relation to illicit drugs, but there are equally important international dimensions which tend to be overlooked or played down by those who call for national control policies for alcohol or tobacco. In particular, there are those who do not acknowledge the impact of their own national actions on the development of problems in other countries. Yet, for alcohol and tobacco no less than for illicit drugs, they cannot be considered in isolation.

Even if that international issue is taken seriously, there is another problem, namely; the implicit assumption in much debate about alcohol, tobacco, and other drugs, that nations can actually control key aspects of their national life. The 1970s and 1980s in the UK, for example, saw the production of many reports and recommendations from government departments, professional associations, and other bodies calling for, among other things, the manipulation of taxes and more and better education and information. Rarely, however, did there appear to be much appreciation of the question of how much control the UK could actually exercise in these areas. These issues have been addressed by Powell (1988), who spelled out the restrictions which membership of the European Community places on the UK's room for tax and excise manoeuvre, and Harrison (1989), who indicated the many recent technological and associated political and economic developments which curtail the ability of any nation to determine the amount and content of the information to which its population is exposed.

Guides to local action

An appreciation of the national and international context and its constraints should not deter those with interest and responsibility at the local level. What it should do is to make local action more realistic and focused and, therefore, more likely to be successful. Philip Tether and I have spent time over recent years encouraging the development of alcohol policies and programmes at the local level, of a kind which reflect and reinforce national action. For action at the local level is not a substitute for national policy. Not only that, but local activities, developed in light of a clear understanding of context—such as existing legislative and organizational frameworks—can set the agenda for further national action by identifying specific problems, generating information, raising awareness, and providing models of good practice.

In Tether and Robinson (1986), Philip Tether and I took seriously local resources and organization, local initiative and interest, and local goals and priorities. Any guide to local action is based on the assumption that in every area of everyday life there are people getting into difficulties to a greater or lesser extent because of alcohol, tobacco or other drugs. It follows, therefore, that in every area of everyday life there is a potential for prevention. The task is to identify those opportunities for action at the local level. Key areas of concern and opportunity can be grouped under five headings which reflect structures of organization and relationships. These are: advertising and the media, education and training, employment and the market, health and safety, and law and order. Within these constellations of issues there are, of course, numerous specifics. Within 'law and order', for example, there are, among other things, matters to do with: illegal possession, illicit production, illegal sale or purchase, product and purchase-related theft, trade and tax offences, liquor licensing and public disorder, and drinking, drugs, and driving.

Yet even this is too simple a level for mapping the fine detail of real policy issues which provide opportunities for action at the local level. Within the 'drinking, drugs, and driving' issue, for example, there is a multitude of policy strands, such as apprehension procedures, police record systems, court practice, social work facilities, general public safety, driver education, highway construction, road surface markings, and lighting.

Guides to action would take each of these areas of potential for good practice and identify resources, map out the context of regulation and procedure, gather examples of innovation from other localities, indicate complementary issues where other groups and organizations might be mobilized, emphasize the importance of adapting routine records and procedures to take account of the alcohol, tobacco or other drug dimension of organizational practice and procedure, and stress the importance of a locally relevant system of information exchange, support, and co-ordination of mutual effort.

In relation to alcohol (Robinson and Tether 1990) we suggest that in each section of any nation's guide to local action would: introduce a particular constellation of issues in a succinct and readable way; identify the individuals, groups, and organizations which are in a position to play a significant prevention role; and describe clearly, and in as much detail as possible, what these prevention activities are, how they might be carried out, and the sources of materials, information, and additional help which are available. The eight sections in our 'guide to guides' cover: educating the public about alcohol; alcohol promotion; alcohol and safety; alcohol outlets and their staff; alcohol and work; alcohol, education and young people; alcohol, the helping professions and Alcoholics Anonymous; and alcohol and the law.

Assessing service requirements

Although prevention is vital, there are those for whom prevention activity at the local level, or anywhere else, is just too late. They already have a problem, which requires immediate attention.

One of the key problems for those charged with planning for, delivering, financing, and assessing the value of services for those with alcohol, tobacco, and other drug-related problems is to have a clear idea of the size of the local need, the flow of people into the overall system of services and facilities, and the range and changes in demand for particular kinds of therapeutic attention, financial, and other practical assistance, and emotional and social support.

As we know, most service provision and its development is driven by shifts in clinical fashion, the political muscle of competing professions and service providers, the ill-thought-out plans of overworked administrators, and, just occasionally, the results of clinical and service-based research. All of this is tempered by the constriction of declining real-value budgets, and the physical bounds of buildings of the wrong size, with the wrong facilities and, with population drift and new ideas of community care, which may be in the wrong place too. Most staff, of course, are dedicated to their patients and clients, and muddle through as best they may with more or less concern, success, and heartache.

An interesting strand of social science work has developed over recent years which attempts to put some order, or at least insert some systematic thinking, into this area. Much has come out of the Addiction Research Foundation in Ontario, Canada. Rush (1990) presented a model for estimating the required capacity of alcohol treatment systems at the local or regional level. Although Rush is modest about it, the model could apply to services related to drugs other than alcohol and to services quite other than those for the treatment of drug problems of any kind. This section will merely describe, in the briefest terms, the systems-based approach underlying Rush's work.

In contrast to a demand-based approach to forecasting the pattern and range of facilities required in any locality which reflects how things are, a system-based model projects what requirements should be. It is a zero-based procedure. As Rush puts it:

Following an estimate of the size of the population in need and an estimate of the proportion of this population which should be treated in a given year, the resulting number of treatment cases is apportioned into the treatment system according to specific percentages for the different types of care.					(Rush 1990, p. 50)

Rush presents in outline the assumptions and associated decision rules for defining what counts as a population or locality, for estimating the number of problem drinkers and dependent drinkers in each population—the 'in need' population, the number of people in need who should be treated in any year—the 'demand' population, and the number of people from the demand population that will require service from each component of the treatment system. The components of the system for which estimates were made ranged across the whole continuum of care from assessment and referral, via detoxification, case management, out-patient, day, short-term and long-term residential treatment, to aftercare (Fig. 14.1).

The flow through the system is planned, with proportions estimated at each point. The estimates for allocating individuals to the various treatment categories 'was made with varying degrees of confidence' (Rush 1990, p. 54) on the basis of published research literature, a client monitoring system, trienniel surveys of existing programmes, other system-based forecasting models, and 'informed opinion', with reliance wherever possible on empirical research:

As new research data emerge concerning, for example, the matching of clients to treatment or the cost-effectiveness of different treatment settings, the model is flexible enough to incorporate this information immediately into the planning process . . . (and) . . . (j)ust as this approach provides a direct link from research to planning, it also shows how the planning process should contribute to the research agenda. For example, estimating the percentage of cases that should be treated on an in-patient or out-patient basis requires information about the client characteristics that are predictive of success in these different settings . . . and the distribution of these characteristics in the treatment population.					(Rush 1990, p. 56)

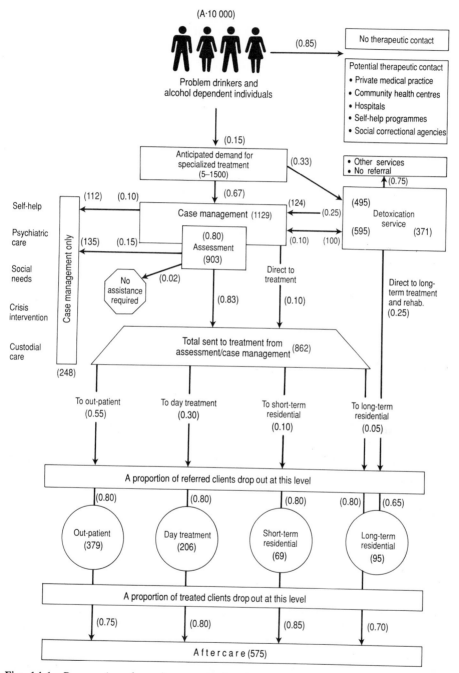

Fig. 14.1 Progression through a comprehensive continuum of care. (Reproduced, with kind permission, from Rush (1990)).

The model is now being applied in various parts of Ontario and is making a significant contribution to the identification of needs and the systematic reordering of service priorities and facilities at the local level.

Costing packages of care provision

Closely associated with the question of how to order local services to best meet estimates of local need is the issue of the cost to a locality of providing appropriate packages of care. For any social and health problem, such as those connected with alcohol, tobacco or other drugs, there will be a wide range of statutory, voluntary, private, self-help, and informal sources of help and support.

Two aspects of a project concerned with HIV-AIDS and social care (Tolley *et al.* 1991), which was based at the Universities of Hull and York, UK, will be outlined here. The funders, the Department of Health and the Scottish Education Department, were particularly interested in two financial issues: the cost of local authority responses to HIV-AIDS, and the cost of packages of social care for people at different stages of their HIV-AIDS career. Clearly, this project was not concerned with alcohol, tobacco or other drugs, except in so far as either the route to infection was drug-related or where people with HIV-AIDS or their intimates were seeking help and support from a drug-related agency. The Hull-York project does, however, provide a way of approaching issues of provision cost in a way which might be of interest to those concerned with addiction problems.

A simple framework helped us to analyse differing profiles of UK local authority social care activity across localities. The components of the framework were:

(1) service management and co-ordination (MC);

(2) training (T);

(3) prevention and education (PE);

(4) housing (H);

(5) direct social care and support (SC);

(6) monitoring and evaluation (ME);

(7) voluntary sector (V).

Inputs to each component had to be specified clearly and rules for defining and timing them determined. Costings could then be arrived at. For example, three simple rules were employed for estimating the Source Service Department–Social Work Department time input (and, therefore, cost) of line management involved in HIV-AIDS related work;

Table 14.1 Social care provision in five localities, 1989–90

Components*	Hammersmith and Fulham (%)	Kensington and Chelsea (%)	Lothian (%)	Manchester (%)	Westminster (%)	Total (%)
MC	14.8	8.9	6.6	20.0	5.3	10.4
T	8.0	8.9	6.1	15.5	11.3	9.2
PE	10.4	10.1	15.3	22.3	12.7	13.6
H	—	1.7	—	3.9	0.5	1.3
SC	40.4	53.2	28.8	11.2	60.7	39.0
ME	3.4	1.8	0.5	0.5	3.1	1.7
V	23.1	15.4	42.9	26.5	6.3	24.8
Total (£m)	1.5	1.4	1.9	0.7	1.0	

* See list in text for key to components.

(1) 100 per cent of the time of HIV-AIDS specialist staff providing line management;

(2) 10 per cent of the time of non-specialist line managers to whom full-time HIV-AIDS specialists are responsible;

(3) 5 per cent of the time of line managers with generic staff with HIV-AIDS responsibilities.

Estimates were arrived at for the resources devoted to each strand of each relevant component of social care. Table 14.1 shows a total for five study authorities of just over £6.5 million for 1989–90.

The Hammersmith and Fulham authority's broad profile of activities reflect most closely the aggregate picture across the five authorities, with approximately 10 per cent of resources being devoted to each of management and co-ordination, staff training, and public education and prevention, 40 per cent to direct social care and support, and 25 per cent grants to the voluntary sector.

The differing patterns of input to the various components of the social care supply model reflect variations in the numbers of people with HIV-AIDS, the availability of central government funds, and legitimately different service strategies. For example:

1. The high MC, T, and PE percentages in Manchester reflect their early stage of service development and low number of people with HIV-AIDS in comparison with the London boroughs.

2. The high V percentage for Lothian in 1989–90 reflects, among other things, the £300 000 granted toward the construction and revenue costs of a hospice development.

Table 14.2 Use of care packages and cost per user

Care packages	HIV+ (%)	ARC (%)	AIDS (%)	Average weekly cost per user (£)
Social worker	30	66	63	10.22
Home support:				
Voluntary + SSD-SWD	10	26	23	74.86
Informal care	18	31	53	66.05
Practical goods and services	24	54	55	13.37
Health maintenance, therapy, treatment	26	37	50	10.11
Advice, emotional support	74	89	75	0.74
n	106	35	40	

3. The low V percentage for Westminster reflects the reluctance of that authority to provide or contribute to services for users from other boroughs.

Turning from the patterns of resources used by local authorities to the range of resources used by individuals with HIV-AIDS; social care and support was provided by statutory, private sector, voluntary, and informal cares. For the purposes of analysis and costing this was brought together into five packages of care.

Clearly, according to need and the appropriateness of the service provided, each person with HIV-AIDS uses aspects of all, some, or none of these packages. Table 14.2 indicates the percentage of each diagnostic category using each care package, together with the average weekly cost per user.

This is a very simple amalgamation of a wealth of detailed costings. The cost per user varied widely between diagnostic group. For example, the average weekly cost per user of £75 for voluntary and Source Service Department–Social Work Department home support is made up of £17 for those who are HIV positive only, £66 for people with ARC (symptomatic HIV, pre AIDS), and £168.00 for those with AIDS. These were high cost estimates. Each sub-component was given a high and a low cost estimate.

As an indication of the sub-components:

1. The social worker package included both community and hospital based workers.

2. Home support included home help provision and informal care, which was costed at the rate of a non-HIV-specialist home help and included only four tasks—shopping, cooking, house work, and laundry.

3. Practical goods and services included such things as home equipment and adaptations; grants for accommodation, household bills and clothes; travel, taxi cards, and bus passes; and private services for removals, gardening, and cleaning.

Table 14.3 National social care cost estimates

	Low estimate	High estimate
1. AIDS		
Average cost (£ per week)	88	106
Aggregate cost (£) (n = 1776 at 17 Dec 1990)		
per week	156 288	188 256
per year	126 976	789 312
2. HIV		
Average cost (£ per week)	17	19
Aggregate cost (£) (n = 14 723 at 30 Sept 1990)		
per week	250 291	279 737
per year	13 015 132	14 546 327
3. AIDS + HIV		
Aggregate cost (£ per year)	21 142 108	24 335 636

4. Health maintenance, therapy, and treatment included all non-NHS services, such as massage and aromatherapy, whether provided privately or received through a voluntary agency.

5. Advice and emotional support included advice on diet, sex, housing, etc., provided by a range of medical, local authority, and voluntary bodies, with costs based on salary, direct costs, and overhead costs associated with the assessed time used. Helpline services, for example, were based on the hourly cost of an HIV-specialist volunteer related to a cheap rate local call lasting 30 minutes (high cost) and 10 minutes (low cost).

It is a mass of detail, but it is only by conducting this kind of exercise that we can begin to make any kind of realistic assessment of the resources devoted to social care for those with HIV-AIDS, or with any other problem such as those associated with alcohol, tobacco or other drugs.

Using the UK figures for HIV-AIDS and extrapolating from the Hull-York data, Table 14.3 shows some high and low estimates of national social care costs.

Again, if we are really interested in having serious debate about the cost of any nation's overall alcohol, tobacco or other drug problem, it must be built up from this kind of detailed work 'at the local level'.

Conclusion

This chapter has concentrated on work by social and political scientists which may make some contributions to the difficult task of those who have prevention or treatment responsibility for alcohol, tobacco, and other drug-related problems. The work cited may also stimulate us to shift some of our attention from the perennial issues which have dominated addiction studies for the past two decades. The basic position is that no amount of biomedical, social-psychological, and treatment research—however excellent and right— can begin to make any real impact on the world of addiction problems unless it is complemented by an understanding of the socio-political and economic context and the processes of policy formation and implementation.

The modest 'aids to strategic thinking' which have been highlighted in this chapter on 'action at the local level' are focused, specific, extant, and may repay a modicum of consideration. They are:

1. The analysis of national government roles and responsibilities which places local action in context (Tether and Harrison 1988).

2. The guides to local action which indicate the range of resources and possibilities for prevention (Robinson and Tether 1990).

3. The model for assessing service requirements at local level, which estimates what ought to be, rather than perpetuates what is (Rush 1990).

4. The framework for costing packages of provision which allows for local comparison and national extrapolation (Tolley *et al.* 1991).

References

Harrison, L. (1989). The information component. In *Controlling legal addictions*, (ed. D. Robinson, A. Maynard, and R. Chester), Macmillan, Basingstoke, pp. 183–202.

Powell, M. (1988). Data note 15: alcohol and tobacco tax in the European Community. *British Journal of Addiction*, 83, 971–8.

Robinson, D. and Tether, P. (1990). *Preventing alcohol problems: local prevention activity and the compilation of 'guides to local action'*. WHO/MNH/ADA/90.4 World Health Organization, Geneva.

Rush, B. (1990). A systems approach to estimating the required capacity of alcohol treatment services. *British Journal of Addiction*, 85, 49–59.

Tether, P. and Harrison, L. (1988). *Alcohol policies: responsibilities and relationships in British Government*. Monograph, Addiction Research Centre, Universities of Hull and York.

Tether, P. and Robinson, D. (1986). *Preventing alcohol problems: a guide to local action*. Tavistock, London.

Tolley, K., Maynard, A., and Robinson, D. (1991). *HIV-AIDS and social care*. Monograph. Universities of Hull and York.

Part IV Science and treatment policies

15. The nature of the target disorder: an historical perspective

Virginia Berridge

In 1952, Lincoln Williams, psychiatrist at the West End Hospital for Nervous Disease, London, UK, succinctly expressed the optimism of a section of the post Second World War medical profession about the treatment of alcoholics. It was 'the dawning of this new humanitarian conception that addiction is an illness and not a moral failing . . .' (Williams 1952). Just 60 years earlier, James Stewart, speaking at a quarterly meeting of the Society for the Study of Addiction, had made much the same point:

> We are not here as moralists or as social reformers. We are not banded together in this Society to discuss such questions . . . as Sunday closing or prohibition . . . here we assemble as scientific physicians to discuss the disease of inebriety, not the vice of drunkenness. (Stewart 1892)

Historical memories are short in this, as in other areas of health policy. The tendency has been for each change in the conceptualization of the condition, each paradigm shift, to be hailed as an advance, as a breakthrough. From inebriety to addiction, on to dependence and problem drug and alcohol use, particular sections of what would now be termed the alcohol (or drug) 'policy community' have proclaimed ideological progress and practical advantage in terms of treatment, management, or the social response to the condition.

The purpose of this chapter is not to add a further celebration of the 'march of progress'. As various historians have argued elsewhere, definitions of alcoholism and drug addiction are historically constructed, are the products of particular historical sets of circumstances and interrelationships; just as they are for insanity in general (Berridge and Edwards 1987; Scull 1981). Disease concepts, for example, may have been common to the 1890s and the 1950s, but the components of the theoretical basis were very different in those decades. History does not repeat itself, nor is it an upward graph of progress. Certain continuing themes can, however, be identified over the last two centuries, certain definitions, sometimes competing, sometimes coalescing, which have served both to underpin discussions of the basic condition and to structure the responses which are considered appropriate.

The purpose of this chapter is to examine those themes historically and then to focus on their inter-relationship in the period since the Second World War. Three themes can be identified: the impact of voluntarism and self-help, as the expression of forms of Christian and moral concern; the input from medical and clinical science; and definitions and responses within a public health context. All have had practical implications in terms of the response to the condition, but to picture them as sharply differentiated definitions would be too simple; there have been dialectical interrelationships over time.

Christian and moral concern: the Temperance Movement

Voluntarism, self-help, and moral concern formed the classic nineteenth century expression of self-help, of the approach to alcohol as a moral crusade, and came in the form of the temperance movement, common to many European countries. Originally, Temperance (as an anti-spirits movement) was not committed to the principle of total abstinence, but sought simply moderation in alcohol consumption and to confirm the sobriety of the sober. It was an elite movement, based on the philanthropic lobbies and the Evangelical Christianity of the early decades of the nineteenth century. But in the UK the defeat of working class political radicalism saw a change of focus and a descent down the social scale. Total abstinence, or 'teetotalism' was adopted by young 'labour aristocrats'; the focus shifted to individual betterment and self-help, rather than to the radical social and political change which movements such as Chartism had advanced. In terms of the practical response to the condition, and its conceptualization, this change of focus had dramatic consequences, as Harrison has noted,

Once the temperance movement had adopted the reclaiming of drunkards as its leading objective it had to transform its local structure. Regular meetings alone could keep the drunkard out of the drinking place . . . only by regular visitation, by 'pairing off' with reformed drunkards, and by creating a new framework of life for its members could the teetotal movement secure the ground it gained. Only by putting the reformed drunkard in office, by keeping him in good company, and by encouraging him publicly to announce his changed life could the incentives to sobriety be adequately reinforced . . .   (Harrison 1971)

Alcohol abuse was an individual moral vice and its solution lay in individual reformation, but also in reform of the licensing laws, or even in prohibition.

The Temperance approach remained distinct, however, from the classic environmentalist public health approach of the nineteenth century. Individual alcohol reformers (Lord Shaftesbury among them) and some Medical Officers of Health did stress the need for better housing conditions and water supplies as necessities for the reform of drinking habits: but alcohol missed the mainstream of nineteenth century public health policy. As Wohl has noted, 'The teetotal movement was always more of a moral crusade than an integral part of the public health movement' (Wohl 1983). That moral crusade continued into the late nineteenth century and beyond. Drink remained a continuing component in a debate which accepted the traditional distinction between the deserving and underserving poor. The crusade against alcohol was part of Christian Socialist concern for 'darkest England' in the 1870s. In the 1880s, it was part of the theory of urban degeneration, the belief that generations of the poor who had been born and lived in such conditions would inevitably 'degenerate' both physically and morally. Drink was now not a cause, but a symptom of the decline of the race and was part of the emergence of an urban 'residuum' (Stedman Jones 1971).

Medical and clinical science: the emergence of addiction

The 'degeneration of the race' was set within an hereditarian framework of thought. And it was in the 1880s, that a clinical and medical formulation with an hereditarian approach was also established. Disease theory in the form of inebriety had practical implications in terms of the establishment of treatment structures in the late nineteenth century. But the 'discovery of addiction' has traditionally been located earlier in the nineteenth century, or even earlier, in the eighteenth century. Levine, for example, has argued that at some point in that century, drunkenness, from being a sin became conceptualized as a habit or a disease (Levine 1978). Benjamin Rush in the USA and Thomas Trotter in England both made important individual statements of the new position. But, as Porter has argued, the concepts of tolerance and of withdrawal were not new (Porter 1985). In fact, little in Trotter's text was new, either in terminology, concepts, or therapeutics. Trotter's skill, according to Porter, lay in his effective publicity for ideas which were already commonplace. And what allowed the concepts to attain prominence was a particular conjunction of social, cultural, and political forces which gave them hegemony. Disease theories were established from a matrix of philanthropic pressure groups, churchmen and the strategies of the emergent psychiatric profession. In the earlier decades of the century most conceptual development took place in continental Europe and not in the UK. The 'new dawn' of medical thinking focused on the condition as a disease. In his inaugural Presidential address to the Society for the Study (and Cure) of Inebriety, in 1884, Norman Kerr said that:

Inebriety is for the most part the issue of certain physical conditions, is an offspring of maternal parentage, is the natural product of a depraved, debilitated, or defective nervous organisation. Whatever else it may be, in a host of cases it is a true disease, as unmistakably a disease as is gout or epilepsy or insanity.   (Kerr 1884)

There has been much discussion of the dimensions of the concept in the context of late nineteenth century psychiatry and of theories of insanity. Two themes should be stressed. Inebriety, as conceptualized, stressed individual responsibility for disease; and it also had clear implications for a practical response. In line with contemporary theories of insanity, it was a physical hereditarian concept. Physical disease was conceived within a degenerationist paradigm. This, as Bynum has noted, provided a secular, scientific, yet still ultimately moral reading of human behaviour; it enabled physicians to preach in the name of science (Bynum 1984). Its appeal, too, was particularly to doctors active in the Temperance Movement. Many of the early medical specialists were also temperance supporters; for disease and the scientific approach was not separate from the moral position.

Nor was the concept of disease distinct from a legislative response to alcohol. The medical specialists wished to distinguish themselves from the advocates of Sunday closing or prohibition; but they themselves also looked to the state to provide a structured treatment system. This was the other important strand emanating from disease. As MacLeod has noted, 'The concept of making government provision for chronic alcoholics added a new dimension to the developing relationship between medicine and the state' (MacLeod 1967). It was an early illustration of the potential role of government in health policy and of the key policy role of the medical profession. But the advocates of state intervention to control disease in this area ultimately achieved little in the late nineteenth century. The role of the inebriates acts never advanced much beyond the possible incarceration of non-criminal inebriates on a voluntary basis. By the outbreak of the First World War, the institutional option for treatment was in total disarray.

Public health definitions

The idea of the relationship between medicine and the state had focused exclusively on the concept of early treatment. This strand of thinking bore almost no relationship to the environmentalism of the nineteenth century public health movement. Nor, as has already been noted, did the strand of Christian and moral concern. In its incarnation both as 'scientific' and as 'social reform' issue, alcohol remained distinct from traditional public health. But public health itself did not remain an unchanging absolute. As Lewis has noted, the mandate of public health has narrowed in the twentieth century (Lewis 1986). Scientific advances in bacteriology, germ theory in particular, redefined the type of intervention appropriate for public health. The 'new concept of dirt' was narrower and, increasingly health and welfare were conceived of separately.

From the early years of the twentieth century, public health focused on what the individual should do to ensure personal hygiene and on the individual's responsibility for the prevention of disease. This was the 'new public health' of the early 1900s. The late nineteenth century fear of urban degeneration and physical deterioration was re-established through the concepts of social hygiene and the concern for the future of the race which animated Edwardian enquires, including the Royal Commission on Physical Deterioration.

Alcohol, distinct from public health in the nineteenth century, fitted neatly into a more individual set of concepts. The focus on individual responsibility so far as drink was concerned was epitomized in the Lees and Raper Memorial Lecture given in 1908 by McAdam Eccles, a prominent Temperance supporter. At that time, statistics in the UK, from Glasgow and Edinburgh, had shown the connection between poor physical condition and living conditions. For Eccles, the explanation lay in individual morality.

... life in one room means want of growth; and a single living room often means rent-money spent on drink ... The connection between drink and one room is obvious ...

(Eccles 1908)

The redefinition of public health encompassed both the scientific and the social reform perspectives as applied to alcohol. The crisis of insanity and of inebriety treatment in the late nineteenth century was in part resolved by the adoption of new professional strategies, the concept of prevention among them.

The temperance focus was also changing towards an embryo social science perspective, marked by reference to research and to 'scientific' management and investigation of the issue. Temperance and clinical science coalesced to bring alcohol to a central position in the debates around national efficiency. Concern focused on the classic 'risk group' of women in their role as mothers; alcohol was part of the 'maternal ignorance and incompetence' school which continued its argument in the face of evidence which stressed the importance of environmental factors.

The political imperative for this more limited public health mandate was as important as changes in medical science. The particular role of crisis in stimulating a public health conception should be noted; it was when the threat appeared to be to the whole community that the terminology of public health was invoked. It was the poor condition of British recruits in the Boer War which drew attention to the crisis of the race. The national crisis of the First World War allowed the discussion and partial adoption of more extensive measures, state purchase of the drink trade among them.

Post Second World War: 'new dawns' and new definitions?

At the time of one period of crisis, then, the conceptual strands had been subsumed under the banner of the public health approach, an approach which favoured appeal to the national interest. But how can these strands be perceived after another period of crisis in the Second World War? The final section of this chapter will briefly sketch out how the three key themes have fared in the post war period, and what the practical implications have been.

In the years immediately following the Second World War there was a sense of a 'new dawn' in terms of concepts and of practice. But it is also clear that much derived from the past. The key approaches outlined at the beginning of this chapter were being redefined and the relationships between them re-ordered under the impact of more general political and medical imperatives. The late 1940s and the 1950s were the high points of technological and scientific medicine; one fundamental tenet of the newly established British NHS, for example, was a faith in hospital based clinical science.

The initial resurgence of the disease theory of alcoholism was primarily American in origin. The establishment of the Yale Centre for Alcohol Studies, the *Quarterly Journal of Studies on Alcohol,* and E.M. Jellinek's work there and, most significantly, in Geneva at the WHO—the story has often been told (Room 1983). On both sides of the Atlantic however, doctors discovered, or rediscovered, the disease theory of addiction. The central concept was of physiological addiction to alcohol reacting on an individual who was predisposed. William Burroughs' treatment by Dr Dent in London in the late 1950s exemplified one variant of the physicalist approach.

The doctor explained to me that apomorphine acts on the back brain to regulate the metabolism and normalise the blood stream in such a way that the enzyme system of addiction is destroyed over a period of four or five days . . . I saw the apomorphine treatment really work . . .   (Burroughs 1959)

It was the legitimation of disease at the international level through the WHO which gave the concept widespread acceptance. However, as Room has noted, the 'WHO definition of alcoholism' had a dual focus; alcoholism was both a disease and a social problem. The voluntary, moral impulse of the nineteenth century still coexisted with disease. In England, for example, the focus on the homeless alcoholic in the 1950s and 60s paralleled the medico-moral concerns of the late nineteenth century. The Anglican priest, Ken Leech, in his recent autobiography, has described how London's East End based Christian social concern of the 1880s and 90s revived in the 1950s and focused in the 1960s on vagrant alcoholics and crude-spirit drinkers (Leech 1990). As in the 1880s such concerns found allies in the medical profession. The crusade for the homeless alcoholic and for hostel provision united clinical and moral concern.

The 1960s were the last decade when the strands of thinking identified in this paper could unite; when disease, voluntarism and social problem/public health concepts provided a unified approach. The report of the second Brain Committee, responding to the rapid increase in drug addiction in England in the 1960s exemplified the interrelationship. Again, the impact of a perceived crisis stimulated the rhetoric of public health. But this was public health, clinical science, and, to a lesser extent, social concern combined. Addiction was a 'socially infectious disease' and the proper response was one of quarantine and compulsory treatment (the line taken in the report) and of notification (Brain Committee 1965). Some commentators saw distinct advantage in this type of interrelationship. Archer Tongue, director of the International Council on Alcohol and the Addictions, and a long-time observer of the addictions scene, regretted the decline of the disease concept after the 1960s precisely because of its unifying nature and because it had attracted public support and understanding (Tongue 1984).

The 1970s and 1980s have seen a firmer separation of the component strands. The 1977 WHO re-definition of alcoholism separated the central core of the 'alcohol dependence syndrome' from the concept of 'alcohol-related disabilities'—the 'dependence approach' from the 'problems approach'. In the 1970s and 1980s behaviourally-oriented psychologists and psychiatrists have offered a reformulation of disease in the 'dependence approach'. The psychological input had been of growing although varied importance since the First World War and has been fully integrated into the biological model.

The social reforming, voluntary strand has increasingly separated itself; alcoholism in this context has become a set of alcohol related problems. Some advocates of the 'problems approach', while critical of the claim from advocates of the 'disease theory' that it illustrates medical progress have lapsed into parallel progressivism about their own concept. 'Problem drug use' and 'problem alcohol use' are thus another 'new dawn'. But the concerns of the 'problems approach', as this chapter has indicated, also have strong historic antecedents. They derive from the social hygiene concerns of crime, disease, and mental illness, and from a concern for the relationship between ill-health and economic efficiency (which had also been a major temperance argument). More immediate contributory factors include the emergence of a 'professionalized', non-medical cadre of researchers around alcohol, most significantly sociologists and epidemiologists; and the establishment of parallel non-medical practitioners as professionals, with social workers as the obvious example (Collins 1990; Room 1983). Psychologists have provided a bridge between the 'dependence approach' and the 'problems approach', but in general the overall conception of the target disorder has fragmented.

Conclusion

Few historians would use the past, even the very recent past, to predict the future. But the 1980s have seen some interesting conceptual and consequent practical developments—albeit limited both in terms of substance and country-specificity. In the UK the advent of AIDS as a perceived crisis once again stimulated the language of public health so far as drugs were concerned. The rhetoric of the nineteenth century underpinned an approach initially based in practice on the social hygiene focus on individual responsibility for health. Recently, there have been some moves to locate this stance within a broader environmentalist and social reforming perspective (Berridge, 1993). The crisis of the 1980s has led to a response which stresses both 'harm reduction' and 'treatment'; once again crisis and the public health approach have provided cohesion. Social and moral concern, public health, and medicine have reacted in the 1980s and 1990s as they did in the 1900s. As in that decade, the importance of political imperatives for the approach need to be recognized, as well as developments in medical, psychological, and social science.

References

Berridge, V. (1993) AIDS and British drug policy: continuity or change? In *AIDS and contemporary history*, (ed. V. Berridge and P. Strong) pp. 135–56. Cambridge University Press.

Berridge, V. and Edwards, G. (1987). *Opium and the people. Opiate use in nineteenth century England.* Yale University Press, London.

Brain Committee (1965). *Inter-departmental Committee on Drug Addiction. Second report.* HMSO, London.

Burroughs, W. (1959). *The naked lunch.* 1982 edn, Paladin, London.

Bynum, W. (1984). Alcoholism and degeneration in nineteenth century European medicine and psychiatry. *British Journal of Addiction*, **79**, 59–70.

Collins, S. (ed.) (1990). *Alcohol, social work and helping.* Tavistock/Routledge, London and New York.

Eccles, W. McAdam (1908). The relation of alcohol to physical deterioration and national efficiency. *British Journal of Inebriety*, **5**, 197–217.

Harrison, B. (1971). *Drink and the Victorians: the temperance question in England.* Faber and Faber, London.

Kerr, N. (1884). President's inaugural address. *Proceedings of the Society for the study and cure of inebriety*, **1**, 1–16.

Leech, K. (1990). *Care and conflict. Leaves from a pastoral notebook.* Darton, Longman and Todd, London.

Levine, H.G. (1978). The discovery of addiction: changing conceptions of habitual drunkenness in American history. *Journal of Studies on Alcohol*, **39**, 143–74.

Lewis, J. (1986). *What price community medicine? The philosophy, practice and politics of public health since 1919.* Harvester/Wheatsheaf, Brighton.

MacLeod, R. (1967). The edge of hope: social policy and chronic alcoholism 1870–1900. *Journal of the History of Medicine and Allied Sciences*, **22**, 215–45.

Porter, R. (1985). The drinking man's disease: the pre-history of alcoholism in Georgian Britain. *British Journal of Addiction*, **80**, 385–96.

Room, R. (1983). Sociological aspects of the disease concept of alcoholism. In *Research advances in alcohol and drug problems*, Vol. 7, pp. 47–91. Plenum Press, New York and London.

Scull, A. (1981). (ed.) *Madhouses, mad-doctors and madmen. The social history of psychiatry in the Victorian era.* University of Pennsylvania Press, London.

Stedman Jones, G. (1971). *Outcast London. A study in the relationship between classes in Victorian society.* Oxford University Press.

Stewart, J. (1892). Prevention of the development of inherited inebriety, *Proceedings of the Society for the Study of Inebriety*, **31**, 1–9.

Tongue, A. (1984). Conversation with Archer Tongue. *British Journal of Addiction*, **79**, 245–9.

Williams, L. (1952). Informal discussion following Presidential address. *British Journal of Addiction*, **49**, 16–20.

Wohl, A. (1983). *Endangered lives. Public health in Victorian Britain.* Dent, London.

16. Prospects, politics, and paradox: pharmacological research and its relevance to policy development

Roger E. Meyer

The disease concept of addiction was first elaborated for alcoholism by Benjamin Rush (Rush 1790). For Rush, alcohol was the causal agent, loss of control over drinking behaviour was the characteristic symptom, and total abstinence was the only effective cure for the disease. In the nineteenth century, with the building of inebriate asylums to house and treat alcoholic patients for prolonged periods of time away from their homes, alcoholics were treated like the mentally ill, the impoverished, and the tubercular. Toward the end of the nineteenth century, the Temperance Movement began to focus its goal on Prohibition in North America, with a concern about alcohol's influence on social problems. While this has been seen as a turning away from the disease construct of addiction, it was also, at some level, compatible with the then contemporary public health view of disease prevention. Removal of, or restricting access to, 'the agent' has been applied to the prevention of some epidemic infectious diseases, as well as alcohol (Prohibition) and other drugs of abuse (through laws governing the practice of pharmacy and medicine, as well as laws defining drug possession or trafficking as illegal). In these policies, one senses the primary concern with the power of the agent, and relatively little concern about risk factors associated with the host or his or her environment (apart from drug/alcohol availability).

Research in the shadow of the Temperance Movement

In this century, the introduction of Prohibition in the USA reflected the triumph of the morally based Temperance Movement, and alcohol became a problem for law enforcement. With the closing of the morphine clinics in the USA in the 1920s, the status of opiate addiction was also consigned to the judicial system. Not surprisingly, the interest of the medical profession in the treatment of addictive disorders declined during this period in the USA. Addiction became a focus of research with the establishment of the Addiction Research Center (ARC) at the Narcotic Treatment Farm at Lexington, Kentucky in the late 1930s. For much of its early history, the rationale behind the research at the ARC was the search for non-addicting analgesic drugs. Again, even the research was driven by a concern about prevention through the elimination of addictive drugs in the pharmacopoeia. Testing of drugs for the treatment of opiate addiction at the ARC did not really begin in earnest until the mid to late 1960s, with a major focus (at that time) on narcotic antagonists. Yet, research done at the ARC identified important areas of dysfunction in the abstinent opiate addict which could contribute to relapse. 'Protracted abstinence' (Martin and Jasinski 1969) and 'conditioned abstinence' (Wikler 1965) suggested pathophysiological models of dysfunction which might be modified by pharmacological treatment. Surprisingly, there has been little systematic research on a pharmacotherapy to ameliorate these sources of persistent residual dysfunction in the abstinent addict.

In the alcohol field, with the end of Prohibition, the disease concept was most explicitly stated in the writings of Jellinek, a non-physician, and in the tenets of Alcoholics Anonymous, a non-medical self-help organization. Jellinek traced many of his ideas to the work of nineteenth century physicians and their interest in the disease of alcoholism and its sub-types (Jellinek 1960). Elsewhere, the evolution of psychiatry's view of alcoholism (and other drug dependencies) in this century has been described (Meyer and Babor 1989). During the period of psychoanalytical ascendancy in the USA, these disorders were viewed as self-medication for underlying mood, thought, or personality disturbances, rather than diseases in their own right. With the introduction of DSMIIIR (APA 1987) in particular and the work of Edwards and Gross (1976), the disease concept seems to have returned to where it started with Benjamin Rush.

Since the end of Prohibition, the most outspoken advocates of a 'disease' concept of alcoholism have been members of Alcoholics Anonymous (AA) and related 'Twelve Step' programmes. Yet the various self-help groups that have developed around addictive disorders in the USA are not monolithic (Meyer 1972). They vary from ambulatory and brief in-patient programmes based upon the 12 steps to recovery enunciated first by AA, to longer term residential programmes that have incorporated a variety of psychological techniques designed to change the 'sickness' that 'led' the individual into an addicted lifestyle. While a number of distinguished physicians, including psychiatrists, have worked well in conjunction with AA, there is some antipathy towards psychiatry within the recovering community. Indeed, despite a strong belief in the disease concept of alcoholism, AA and its offshoots have developed apart from the medical community. In the USA, where support for biomedical research for specific diseases often depends upon the level of advocacy offered by those with the disease or by members of their families, there has been little visible support for biomedical or behavioural research on the disease 'alcoholism' from members of AA or their families. There is real interest in the findings from genetics research, but little support for biomedical and behavioural research that might lead to more effective treatment for the alcoholic. Twelve step programmes and long-term residential drug treatment programmes also share an antipathy toward psychotropic drug prescription. The occasional exceptions that have been made for the treatment of some patients with co-morbid bipolar disorder or schizophrenia seem simply to be exceptions that help to define the rule.

With certain exceptions, this negative attitude toward a pharmacotherapy of addictive disorders has had a strong influence on policy makers in the USA. It has also led to regulation of physicians and their prescribing habits, which suggests that there is a concern that doctors function like 'tainted wells', fuelling a drug abuse epidemic. Indeed, regulations which discourage benzodiazepine prescription (for example, triplicate prescription) are less costly and more easy to implement than effective interdiction of illicit drug supplies, or successful drug abuse prevention among at-risk populations. Recent studies suggest that where triplicate prescription has been implemented, there has been an increase in emergency room visits for overdosage with other, more dangerous, hypnotic sedative drugs (Schwartz in press). Incidentally, there is no good evidence that triplicate prescription prevents the development of primary benzodiazepine dependence. Finally, a negative or ambivalent view of psychotropic drug use has also complicated the politics and prospects for pharmacological research on addictive disorders, even as the wars on drugs (circa 1971–1976 and 1989–present) stimulated research on new pharmacotherapies influenced by the model of methadone maintenance treatment.

Research in the era of methadone maintenance

Methadone maintenance treatment of heroin addiction was developed by Dole and Nyswander at Rockefeller University, USA between 1963 and 1965 (Dole and Nyswander 1965). It is the most successful pharmacotherapy that has yet been developed for an addictive disorder. Despite its relative success, methadone maintenance has drawn intense and emotional opposition. In a paper written nearly a decade ago, Kleber quoted an early opponent of methadone treatment as follows: 'I think methadone maintenance is a great idea; they ought to give money to bank robbers, women to rapists, and methadone to addicts' (Kleber 1983). For a rational pharmacotherapy, methadone treatment has generated some emotional opposition, some ethical questions, and some significant policy ramifications. Opposition has come from advocates of drug-free treatments for opiate addicts, from communities (and their representatives) opposed to drug treatment clinics in their midst, and from some individuals (sometimes government officials) concerned about funding long-term treatment for patients, which diverts scarce resources away from other community needs (Meyer 1972). For advocates of drug-free treatment, methadone represented drug substitution, of one narcotic for another.

If 'addiction' is the disease, then it was difficult to conceptualize another addiction as the treatment. If the problem which really underlies the addiction is psychological, then the treatment may seem to be 'covering up' the real problem, and interfering with the opportunity for a 'real cure'. Since only a minority of patients who are put on methadone maintenance treatment are able to sustain eventual drug-free status, is it ethical to use methadone maintenance as a treatment of first resort? Since methadone treatment is necessarily long-term, whose responsibility is it to fund these programmes? What are the essential elements in treatment? Most importantly, the introduction of methadone treatment raised the most critical questions regarding the goals of addiction treatment and the definition of what constitutes the disorder. If physical dependence is the disorder, then methadone maintenance is not an appropriate treatment. If drug-seeking behaviour, and the psychological and social consequences of illicit opiate use are the problem, then methadone can play an important role in rehabilitation. If chronic heroin use has altered physiology to the extent that the patient has come to 'require' ongoing opiates to feel and function normally, then methadone maintenance becomes a treatment of choice.

Many of the essential elements of methadone treatment were described in the context of the original programme developed by Dole and Nyswander, including the need for urine monitoring; general medical, and psychiatric services; adequate staffing; careful patient selection; and rigid control of dispensing to prevent diversion to illicit sale. The importance of these programme elements has recently been confirmed in the findings of Ball and Ross (Ball and Ross 1991). Clinical research conducted over the past 25 years has supported the efficacy of out-patient induction into treatment, the relationship between dose and risk of continued injecting drug use, and the characteristics of patients and of clinical facilities associated with the most favourable treatment outcomes (Ball and Ross 1991; Cooper *et al.* 1983). The best programmes continue to struggle with the challenges presented by the substantial minority of patients who continue to abuse alcohol and/or other drugs of abuse, suffer from significant psychiatric disturbances (particularly antisocial personality and/or other impulse-laden personality disorders), or choose to terminate treatment for a drug-free lifestyle. While the literature suggests some approaches to these issues, each individual case presents distinct clinical problems. As Ball has observed, programmes differ substantially in their ability to meet the needs of their patients.

While Ball's work has attracted substantial interest in the clinical research community, its policy ramifications have not been applied to government policy or funding requirements. Between 1967 and 1981, the federal government funded community-based drug treatment programmes across the USA. In 1971, the Special Action Office for Drug Abuse Prevention established a capitated model for funding methadone treatment, which took into account the service requirements of these programmes. In 1981, the federal government converted its support for drug abuse treatment into block grants to the states, which were free to set up their own criteria for disbursing funds. Moreover, the absolute funding level for these programmes by the federal government was reduced. At this juncture, as the present administration is involved in reorganizing its efforts at funding drug abuse treatment and prevention, the policy ramifications of Ball's research, 25 years of clinical experience, and the original work of Dole and Nyswander need to be translated into some mechanism for programme oversight. If the programmes are well-managed, and the patients provided with essential psychological and social services, the benefits to patients and their families are real. Moreover, in this era of AIDS, an effective treatment programme reduces the risk of infection and its consequences. Indeed, an expansion of methadone treatment would be the single most effective public health measure to prevent the spread of AIDS in the intravenous drug using community. It is unclear why activists lobby for programmes for needle exchange or bleach in areas that having waiting lists for methadone treatment. That they do, and that such waiting lists exist, is one of the paradoxes of our societal response to methadone, and to addicts. Moreover, issues of dosage continue to be studied, bearing in mind that most data suggest that as dosage decreases below 50 mg per day, there is increased likelihood of some continuing intravenous drug use.

Methadone maintenance treatment opened the door to the pharmacotherapy of other addictive disorders, even as the issues in treating these disorders have turned out to be more complex. Dole postulated that chronic exposure to heroin caused persistent residual changes in cellular function that obliged addicts to resume opiate self-administration (after detoxification) in order to maintain normal function (Dole and Nyswander 1967). In principle, methadone maintenance represented, on the one hand, a treatment for the 'drug hunger' associated with protracted abstinence, as well as a treatment which could block the reinforcing efforts of injected heroin, thereby leading to extinction of heroin self-administration behaviour. (By using high doses of methadone, addicts were tolerant to the effects of injected street heroin). Methadone maintenance may represent a uniquely successful example of same-class drug substitution treatment for an addictive disorder.

One of the problems of same-class drug substitution is that drugs which have the same discriminative stimulus properties as the original drug of abuse may paradoxically increase the likelihood of relapse. Animal experiments suggest that low doses of same-class drugs serve as powerful cues for drug self-administration (Steward *et al.* 1984). In the early phase of the present cocaine epidemic, methylphenidate was proposed as a treatment for cocaine addiction (Khantzian 1983). Unfortunately, this treatment was ineffective and may have increased craving for cocaine. Similarly, Kissin had proposed that chlordiazepoxide might represent an effective treatment of alcoholism, somewhat analogous to methadone treatment of opiate addiction (Kissin 1975). He proposed three criteria for effective pharmacotherapy: (i) the drug should help to increase the retention rate of patients in treatment; (ii) it should have low potential for abuse; and (iii) it should not potentiate the effects of alcohol. Unfortunately, benzodiazepines potentiate the impairments of cognition and motor performance with alcohol, and the similarity in the respondent, discriminative, and reinforcing stimulus properties of this class of drugs and alcohol increases the likelihood of cross-dependence patterns of addiction (Meyer 1986). In summary, attempts to develop treatments for other addictive disorders by analogy to methadone maintenance treatment of heroin addiction have not worked well.

For policy makers, the 'magic bullet' quality of methadone treatment has seemed to be a seductive answer to the cocaine problem. In the USA, Senator Biden has proposed a $300 million drug development programme for the treatment of cocaine addiction, based largely on the example of methadone and heroin addiction. In our free society, informed by 'sound bites' of less than 30 seconds of television exposure, the slogan outweighs the caveat. What should the role of science and scientists be in helping to inform policy? If a scientifically-based programme of research emerges from the drug development programme, might we not learn more about the central nervous system manifestations of protracted cocaine abstinence that might lead to other approaches to pharmacotherapy? Conversely, will the public and the government hold the scientists accountable for their failure to deliver a 'magic bullet' for cocaine addiction, after spending $300 million or more? As the pace of the cocaine epidemic fades, and the problem of use reverts to endemic patterns in poor urban environments, will the government be able to sustain its support for the scientists to develop an adequate base of information from which new treatments can emerge? Finally, is there a chance that scientific research designed to find cures for addiction could yield even more dangerous drugs to tease the human proclivity for pleasure-seeking? In these questions reside the prospects, the politics, and the paradox of policy development.

The new climate for research

The research for new pharmacotherapies for the treatment of alcoholism, cocaine, and other drug dependencies has been fuelled by the relatively high failure rate in traditional treatments, and by the growing knowledge base in the neurosciences. The improved technology of clinical trials in this field is also a very significant development (IOM 1989). The progress in reliably characterizing patients' psychiatric diagnoses and addictive disorders, and in defining the non-pharmacological components of treatment, are now considered to be state-of-the-art for such studies. Assessment of treatment compliance and multiple parameters of outcome (including biological and self-report measures of drug/alcohol use, psychological symptomatology, and social function) are essential. Controlled treatment trials comparing active medication with placebo (or a comparison treatment) are required before a new drug treatment can be considered effective. Adequate sample size, and rigorous statistical methodology which can account for the problem of drop-outs, should be planned in advance of data collection. In the field of alcohol research, efforts to operationalize criteria for treatment efficacy have focused on abstinence or moderation of drinking (as measured by self or significant other report, and/or biological markers associated with drinking). In the case of illicit drugs, both criteria have also been employed, although abstinence is the a priori gold standard of efficacy. Many investigators have asked subjects to record their 'desire' or 'craving' for their preferred substance on a visual analogue scale. Some studies ask subjects to record this on a retrospective basis, while other studies ask subjects to record 'craving' or 'desire' on the day of examination, or daily while in treatment. The validity of the visual analogue scale (relative to the probability of substance use) has not been systematically examined. Because 'craving' or 'desire' is at best only an imperfect correlate of drug or alcohol consummatory behaviour, it is not, by itself, a useful measure of treatment outcome. Moreover, there are at least four different circumstances that have been associated with an increase in craving or desire: (i) acute drug or alcohol withdrawal; (ii) the period of protracted abstinence following acute withdrawal; (iii) the presentation of drug- or alcohol-related stimuli; and (iv) drug or alcohol administration.

In conceptualizing a pharmacotherapy for the long-term treatment of drug or alcohol dependence, 'protracted abstinence' and conditional responses to drug/alcohol-related stimuli represent potential targets of opportunity. If the new medication is designed to affect 'craving' associated with protracted abstinence, it would seem prudent to secure other subjective and physiological measures associated with protracted abstinence. The latter has been most thoroughly described from a clinical research perspective in alcoholics, where it includes persistent anxiety and depressive symptoms (in the absence of a co-existing anxiety or mood disorder); abnormalities of sleep architecture and subjective complaints of insomnia; neuroendocrine abnormalities, such as non-suppression in the dexamethadone suppression test; persistent alterations in the gating of auditory evoked potentials; and neuro-psychological deficits (Meyer 1989). As is true of other addictive disorders, there is increased risk of relapse in the first 3–6 months after withdrawal—suggesting a relationship between the symptoms of protracted abstinence and an increased probability of relapse (Meyer 1989). Potential targets of drug treatment in the alcoholic include central nervous system hyperexcitability, anxiety and depressive symptoms, altered circadian rhythm, cognitive impairment, and insomnia.

If a new medication is developed which may reduce the likelihood of relapse associated with drug- or alcohol-related environmental cues, it will be important to assess behavioural concomitants. For example, does the patient fail to experience the usual 'craving' in familiar drinking or drug-using settings or in association with specific negative mood states previously associated with substance use? Does he or she find it easier to avoid 'high risk' situations? Does the medication enhance the patient's coping ability in high risk situations? Recent evidence suggests that certain drugs may moderate drinking among heavy drinking subjects. Serotonin uptake inhibitors (Naranjo *et al.* 1987) and the narcotic antagonist, naltrexone (Volpicelli *et al.* 1989), have been reported to produce modest reductions in alcohol consumption when these medications are administered in the absence of non-pharmacological therapies. Do these drugs reduce drinking as part of a general effect on consummatory behavior? Do they affect the discriminative stimulus properties of alcohol that usually trigger heavy drinking? Do they affect appetitive mechanisms, or do they reduce the reinforcing properties of ethanol? Finally, do they affect satiety mechanisms that previously failed to limit alcohol consumption?

What are the policy ramifications for the alcohol field of drugs which moderate drinking behaviour, or drugs which facilitate coping with high risk situations? Is moderate drinking an acceptable treatment goal? Is moderation of illicit drug use ever an acceptable treatment goal? Is it possible to study systematically the efficacy and mechanism of action of drugs which appear to moderate drinking or affect coping with high risk situations if one is not able to administer alcohol to alcoholics or abuse drugs to drug addicts in the laboratory? In all of these issues and questions of clinical research methodology, there are policy complications for journal editors, manuscript reviewers, clinicians and clinical investigators, as well as federal drug regulators.

The importance of drug self-administration studies in the development of new pharmacotherapies for addictive disorders was highlighted by the development of narcotic antagonist drugs for the treatment of heroin addiction. Wikler had proposed that the administration of a narcotic antagonist to a heroin addict who was allowed to self-administer heroin would lead to the extinction of drug self-administration and drug-seeking behaviour (Wikler 1971). In order to test this hypothesis a study was conducted of heroin self-administration in patients/subjects treated with naltrexone (a narcotic antagonist) or placebo (Meyer and Mirin 1979). Most of the naltrexone treated subjects quickly determined that they were not going to get 'high' from their heroin injections, and stopped 'craving' and self-administering the opiate. Clearly naltrexone was pharmacologically efficacious (it blocked the effects of injected heroin), but its clinical utility would depend upon the patient's compliance in taking it. While some information regarding efficacy will emerge from standard controlled clinical trials of new medications in the community, an understanding of mechanism of action in these behavioral disorders will require studies in the clinical laboratory in which alcoholic subjects can consume alcohol, and drug addicts can consume their preferred drug in studies not unlike the above study by Meyer and Mirin.

These studies raise important ethical issues that need to be addressed sensitively. Surely it should be ethical to permit alcoholics to administer alcohol (and addicts to administer abused drugs) in this type of research, if efforts are made to assure state-of-the-art treatment and follow-up, and other rules governing human studies are rigorously followed.

Six possible approaches to the development of a rational pharmacotherapy of alcoholism have previously been described (Meyer 1989). The same general approaches apply to other types of drug dependence. The following represent six areas of opportunity for new pharmacotherapy initiatives: (1) drugs that may reverse or ameliorate the central nervous system signs and symptoms of protracted abstinence; (2) drugs that may have a primary effect on the desire to consume alcohol as part of a general effect on consummatory behaviour; (3) drugs that may improve the cognitive capacity of patients with alcohol-induced impairments; (4) drugs that appear to block the reinforcing effects of alcohol; (5) other types of forms of antidipsotropic agents, which may be less problematic than the present formulation of disulfiram (one can envisage development of analogous medications that would threaten to produce aversive reactions to other abused drugs), and (6) specific psychotropic drugs for the treatment of co-morbid psychiatric disorders that can be administered in conjunction with standard alcohol treatment.

One critical element in developing new pharmacotherapies is the availability of relevant animal models of the human disorder. In this respect, the DSMIIIR model of alcohol and drug dependence is compatible with animal models of alcohol and drug self-administration that have been developed over the past 25 years. While no specific animal model of alcohol consumption fully satisfies all dimensions of human alcoholism, it is clear that ethanol consumption can be significantly affected by schedules of reinforcement and/or association with other reinforcers; and that ethanol consumption is significantly affected by pharmacogenetic factors (Meyer and Dolinsky 1991). Proposed pharmacotherapies of human alcohol dependence need to be tested in animal models that approximate DSMIIIR criteria for alcohol dependence. In addition, animal models of protracted abstinence, alcohol-induced cognitive impairment, and co-morbid psychopathology and alcohol dependence need to be pursued.

In the drug field, where animal models of drug dependence more closely approximate the human disorder, it is somewhat easier to relate animal data to prediction of abuse liability and pharmacological efficacy than to the complexities of clinical application. Naltrexone will suppress opiate self-administration in the animal laboratory demonstrating the kind of pharmacological efficacy observed by Meyer and Mirin. While, the animal data did not anticipate the problems of clinical efficacy in this area, they are critical to drug development. In this respect, the range of methodologies available suggest additional scientific questions—with substantial clinical significance. Buprenorphine appeared to suppress cocaine self-administration in monkeys (Mello *et al.* 1989), but it facilitated the acquisition of place preference associated with cocaine administration in the rodent (Brown, *et al.* 1991). In recent acute clinical trials in human beings, humans behaved more like the rat than the monkey, in that the acute combination of buprenorphine and cocaine was a more powerful reinforcer than cocaine alone (Kosten, personal communication). The conclusion is that animal models will be essential for the development of new pharmacotherapies for addictive disorders, even as anti-vivisectionists in North America have specifically targeted this area of research involving animals for special attention. Policy makers will have to develop laws to protect the continuity of science in this area—or there will be no new pharmacotherapies for addictive disorders. Already, research with non-human primates has been severely curtailed, and all addictive disorders research with animals is under siege.

Conclusion

With the rapid pace of research in neurobiology, and the continuing concern about substance abuse, the next decade should see the introduction of new pharmacotherapies that may improve the treatment of alcoholism and other drug dependencies. How might this change clinical practice? Optimally, we will see the development of specific pharmacotherapies for specific aspects of the disorders, rather than the present generic approach to treatment. In the best of circumstances, we will see the blending of pharmacotherapy with other treatment modalities. These are, after all, behavioural disorders and not infections. We will need to provide our patients with the coping skills to modify their behaviours. 'Twelve Step' programmes offer patients hope and a framework of values for living: can these groups accept the possibility of pharmacological treatment of disease for individuals who also wish to embrace their fellowship? Can physicians offer pharmacotherapy and recognize the needs of their patients that can be bet met through self-help programmes? Can cognitive behavioural therapists accept that alcohol or drug-consuming behaviours have a biological dimension that might be modified by pharmacotherapy? Can one envision phases of pharmacotherapy commencing in the earliest stages of withdrawal, proceeding through the treatment of protracted abstinence, with additional treatments designed to enhance coping with high-risk situations and conditional stimuli, and psychotropic drug treatment of co-morbid psychopathology?

The true student of health and science policy will not be content with this horizontal survey approach to the many policy ramifications of pharmacological research in the addictions field. Any of these areas deserves a fuller hearing in some depth: a vertical approach as it were. Unfortunately, the field is beset by a broad range of policy choices, each of which can limit or enhance the prospects for progress. For too long, the field has been burdened by overly simplistic thinking and ideology. The disease concept of addiction that was developed by Benjamin Rush was a product of the age of enlightenment. Implicit in the message of that time was a belief in the power of reason and the idea of progress. Progress in this case will not come from 'magic bullets' or ideologies. The challenge to politicians, policy makers, and scientists will be to harness the findings of basic research to well-characterized human disorders whose social and psychological consequences may be ameliorated by new therapies stemming from new knowledge.

References

APA (American Psychiatric Association) (1987). *Diagnostic and statistical manual of mental disorders*, (3rd edn, revised). American Psychiatric Association, Washington.

Ball, J.C. and Ross, A. (1991). *The effectiveness of methadone maintenance treatment: patients, programs, services, and outcome*. Springer-Verlag, New York.

Brown, E.E., Finlay, J.M., Wong, J.T.F., Damsma, G., and Fibiger, H.C. (1991). Behavioral and neurochemical interaction between cocaine and buprenorphine: implications for the pharmacotherapy of cocaine abuse. *Journal of Pharmacology and Experimental Therapeutics*, **256**, 119–26.

Cooper, J.R., Altman, F., Brown, B.S., and Czechowicz, D. (ed.) (1983). *Research on the treatment of narcotic addiction: state of the art*, DHHS publication, number (ADM) 83–1281.

Dole, V.P. and Nyswander, M.E. (1965). A medical treatment for diacetylmorphine (heroin) addiction. *Journal of American Medical Association*, **193**, 646–50.

Dole, V.P. and Nyswander, M.E. (1967). Heroin addiction—a metabolic disease. *Archives of Internal Medicine*, **20**, 19–24.

Edwards, G. and Gross, M.M. (1976). Alcohol dependence: provisional description of a clinical syndrome. *British Medical Journal*, **1**, 1058–61.

IOM (Institute of Medicine) (1989). *Prevention and treatment of alcohol problems: research opportunities*. National Academy Press, Washington.

Jellinek, E.M. (1960). *The disease concept of alcoholism*. Hillhouse Press, New Brunswick.

Khantzian, E.J. (1983). Cocaine dependence: an extreme case and marked improvement with methylphenidate treatment. *American Journal of Psychiatry*, **140**, 784–5.

Kissin, B. (1975). The use of psychoactive drugs in the long-term treatment of chronic alcoholics. *Annals of the New York Academy of Sciences*, **252**, 385–95.

Kleber, H.D. (1983). Critique. In *Research on the treatment of narcotic addiction: state of the art*, (ed. J.R. Cooper, F. Altman, B.S. Brown, and D. Czechowicz) DHHS publication, number (ADM) 83–1281, pp. 530–38.

Martin, J.R. and Jasinski, D.R. (1969). Physiological parameters of morphine dependence in man—tolerance, early abstinence, protracted abstinence. *Journal of Psychiatric Research*, **7**, 9–17.

Mello, N.K., Mendelson, J.H., Bree, M.B., and Lukas, S.E. (1989). Buprenorphine suppresses cocaine self-administration by rhesus monkeys. *Science*, **25**, 859–62.

Meyer, R.E. (1972). *Guide to drug rehabilitation: a public health response*, pp. 61–82; 127–54, Beacon Press, Boston.

Meyer, R.E. (1986). Anxiolytics and the alcoholic patient. *Journal of Studies on Alcohol*, **47**, 269–73.

Meyer, R.E. (1989). Prospects for a rational pharmacotherapy of alcoholism. *Journal of Clinical Psychiatry*, **50**, 403–12.

Meyer, R.E. and Babor, T.F. (1989). Explanatory models of alcoholism. In *Annual*

Review of psychiatry, (ed. A. Tasman, R.E. Hales, and A.J. Frances), pp. 273–92. American Psychiatric Press, Washington.

Meyer, R.E. and Dolinsky, Z. (1991). Alcohol reinforcement: biobehavioral and clinical considerations. In *Neuropharmacology of ethanol: new approaches*, (ed. R.E. Meyer, G.F. Koob, M.J. Lewis, and S.M. Paul), pp. 251–64. Birkhauser, Boston.

Meyer, R.E. and Mirin, S.M. (ed.) (1979). *The heroin stimulus: implications for a theory of addiction*. Plenum Press, New York.

Naranjo, C.A., Sellers, E.M., Sullivan, J.T., Woodley, D.V., Kadlec, K., and Sykora, K. (1987). The serotonin uptake inhibitor citalopram attenuates ethanol intake. *Clinical Pharmacology and Therapeutics*, **41**, 266–74.

Rush, B. (1790). *An inquiry into the effects of spiritous liquors on the human body*. Thomas and Andrews, Boston.

Schwartz, H. (1992). An empirical review of the impact of triplicate prescription of benzodiazepines. *Hospital and Community Psychiatry*, **43**, 382–6.

Stewart, J., DeWit, H., and Eikelboom, R. (1984). Role of unconditioned and conditioned drug effects in the self-administration of opiates and stimulants. *Psychological Reviews*, **91**, 251–68.

Volpicelli, J.R., O'Brien, C.P., Alterman, A.I., and Hayashida, M. (1989). Naltrexone in the treatment of alcohol dependence: initial findings. In *Opioids, bulimia, alcohol abuse and alcoholism*, (ed. L.B. Reid). Springer-Verlag, New York.

Wikler, A. (1965). Conditioning factors in opiate addiction and relapse. In *Narcotics*, (ed. D.M. Wilmer and G.G. Kassebaum), pp. 85–100. McGraw Hill, New York.

Wikler, A. (1971). Requirements for extinction of relapse-facilitating variables and for rehabilitation in a narcotic antagonist treatment program. In *Narcotic antagonists*, (ed. M.C. Braude, L.S. Harris, J.P. Smith, E.A. May, and J.E. Viallareal), pp. 399–414. Raven Press, New York.

17. Psychological treatments: the research and policy connections

Ray Hodgson

The main emphasis of this chapter will be upon treatment research in the field of alcohol dependence. Before considering the large number of clinical trials in the field of alcohol misuse, it should be emphasized that there are many people consuming excessive amounts of alcohol who are not ready for change. Motivation to change is a key concept in the field and will be considered briefly. Brief interventions will then be discussed, since their proven effectiveness has important policy implications.

Motivation to change

It is often assumed that there are just two types of addict. There are those who are desperate to change, and those who have absolutely no intention of changing. According to this view, the former group is given help, whereas the latter group is confronted with the facts about drug misuse until they are sufficiently motivated to accept help. In fact, this view is not supported by the evidence. Motivation to change is complicated and fluctuating. Furthermore, confrontation is not usually the best method of encouraging change.

Prochaska and DiClimente (1986) have carefully researched the way in which changes occur and concluded that there are at least four stages. In the *pre-contemplation stage* the drug user does not intend to change in the near future. This could be because the perceived benefits of drug use still outweigh the perceived costs, often because the costs are played down through ignorance or denial. Drug users who try to change but fail sometimes slip back into this stage. The *contemplation stage* covers that period when the costs and benefits are being reappraised and ability to cope with behavioural changes are being assessed. This stage can last a few minutes or a few years. In the *action stage* a pledge has been made and positive steps are being taken. Finally, the *maintenance stage* begins a few months after successful change. In this stage vigilance is still relatively high in an attempt to prevent relapse. There is not usually an orderly progression from one stage to the next and stable changes are only achieved after many unsuccessful attempts.

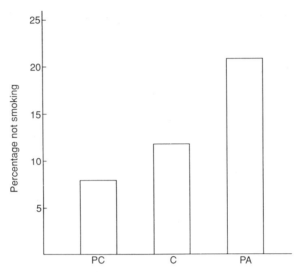

Fig. 17.1 Percentage of smokers who reported that they were not smoking at six-month follow-up. Subjects were categorized at the start of the study into pre-contemplators (PC), contemplators (C), and preparing for action (PA).

A great deal of work in this area has been carried out on smokers under-going self-help programmes (Prochaska *et al.* 1988). It is clear from this work that the stage of change at the start of a study predicts successful outcome. For example, the results displayed in Fig. 17.1 indicate that good outcome at the six-month follow-up point is three times more likely in those who are preparing for action at the start of the study than in those who are pre-contemplaters. Furthermore, a movement from one stage to the next during treatment is also an important predictor. For the pre-contemplators who progressed to contemplation at one month, 7.4 per cent took action by six months. This compared with only 3 per cent for the pre-contemplators who had not progressed to the next stage. Similarly, contemplators who had pro-gressed to the ready-for-action stage were twice as likely to have taken action at six months compared with those contemplators who had not progressed (41 per cent versus 20 per cent).

The stages of change approach has important implications for psychological treatments, since less than 20 per cent will be ready for action at any one time (for example Abrams *et al.* 1988). If only a small number of people are ready for action then there is no point in attempting to provide action oriented programmes for every smoker, alcoholic or addict identified in a community survey or a primary care screening programme. Brief interventions at this level must be tailored to the stage of change and, furthermore, primary care workers should remember that facilitating movement from one stage to the next doubles the probability that action will be taken.

Brief interventions

The fact that a number of studies have now demonstrated the effectiveness of relatively brief interventions suggest a particular approach to the treatment and prevention of alcohol-related problems. Before discussing the implications of this research three of these studies will briefly be described.

One important investigation carried out in Malmo, Sweden by Kristenson *et al.* (1983) studied a group of middle-aged male heavy drinkers (age 46–49 years) who had been identified as a result of a general health screening project. The 585 men having a raised gamma-glutaryltransferase (GGT) on two occasions were randomly assigned to an intervention group and a control group. The control group were simply informed by letter that the test indicated a liver problem and that they should reduce their consumption of alcohol. They were invited for further tests after two years. The intervention group were given a physical examination and a detailed assessment of alcohol consumption and alcohol-related problems. They were then offered an appointment with a doctor every three months, as well as monthly appointments with a nurse for repeated assessments of GGT. The emphasis of the brief monthly intervention was upon simple advice and regular knowledge of results through GGT feedback. Progress was evaluated at two and four years after the original screening and the intervention was observed to lead to a very significant reduction in days sick and days in hospital.

This study clearly demonstrates that a relatively low-cost intervention, which focuses upon a biochemical marker of liver dysfunction, can have a very significant beneficial effect. The results indicate that a team set up by a health authority to carry out this type of intervention could quickly pay for itself by reducing hospital admissions.

A study carried out by Chick *et al.* in a rather different setting has reached very similar conclusions (Chick *et al.* 1985). This study involved men who were admitted for a medical condition to the Edinburgh Royal Infirmary Edinburgh, UK. Again, at one-year follow-up, the intervention group were drinking less than the control group, had lower levels of gamma-GT, and obtained better scores on a global rating of improvement.

In a more recent study of a brief intervention (Miller and Sovereign 1988) the impact of therapist style was investigated. In the *directive* style clients were encouraged to accept that they were alcoholic and were urged to seek treatment. The *client-centred* style, in contrast, tended to elicit and reflect a client's own concerns and no attempt was made to impose a label or to encourage formal treatment. There were very striking differences in client responses within these two groups. Clients in the directive condition showed significantly higher levels of resistance (arguing, interrupting, and changing the subject) as well as denial (minimizing the problem). Furthermore, analysis of taped records of the sessions demonstrated that the more the therapist confronted the client the more the client was drinking during follow-up. Therapist support and listening responses, on the other hand, predicted good outcome.

This work provides relatively strong evidence to support the view that early identification and intervention is a cost-effective way of preventing alcohol-related problems. One of the difficulties encountered in this approach to secondary prevention is to give the intervention at the right time. As a result of work in Cardiff, UK, carried out in both a District General Hospital (DGH) and a general practice, it was concluded that the DGH emerges as an ideal setting for early interventions. On a hospital ward patients ruminate about their health and have plenty of time to listen to advice. Equally important, the 'change agents' believe that great job satisfaction would be derived from being a member of a prevention or health promotion team covering alcohol, smoking, drug use, nutrition, exercise, and stress. Such a team, composed of a nurse, a health education officer, and a psychologist, could help to transform the way in which a DGH provides a comprehensive health promotion service. Furthermore, the research described above strongly suggests that such a health promotion team would pay for itself.

Controlled studies of treatments

One important question to ask is whether there are any reasonably well controlled studies of alcoholism treatments which consider the effectiveness of different treatment modalities. The answer is 'Yes', and two recent reviews have summarized the relevant findings (Miller and Hester 1986; Holder *et al.* 1991).

Holder *et al.* (1991), in their most recent publication, reviewed randomized clinical trials as well as those studies in which a matched comparison group had been formed. Positive findings were counted when a particular treatment resulted in significantly better drink-related outcomes than another treatment condition. From more than 200 comparisons some treatments turned out to be clear winners and others were clear losers. Holder *et al.* (1991) devised a simple weighted index, by subtracting the number of negative findings from the number of positives and then adding an extra point for every positive finding greater than two. This weighted index takes into account the fact that positive findings are more difficult to obtain than negative findings and that, for example, a treatment with five positives and five negatives is more impressive than a treatment with just one positive and one negative.

A health policy board, a health authority, or a funding agency want to know in which of four categories a particular treatment falls, namely:

(1) treatments with good evidence of their effectiveness;

(2) treatments that are promising but not proven;

(3) treatments with insufficient evidence to judge one way or the other;

(4) treatments that are·reasonably well researched but no good evidence of effectiveness has emerged.

Table 17.1 displayed the results of the review carried out by Holder *et al.*, adapted slightly to fit the four categories described above. Descriptions of all 34 treatment approaches are provided in the original article. The following are very brief descriptions of the more psychological approaches.

Social skills training

The drinker is taught specific behavioural skills for forming and maintaining interpersonal relationships. Assertiveness training is a common focus. Such training is usually conducted in a group format.

Self-control training

Specific self-management skills are taught, individually or in groups, to help the client reduce or avoid alcohol consumption. Strategies commonly include specific goal-setting, self-monitoring, rate reduction, self-reinforcement, functional analysis, and learning of alternative coping skills. Treatments limited to environmental contingency management are not included here, but are reported separately in the section below on behaviour contracting.

Brief motivational counselling

Brief counselling for alcohol problems has typically consisted of 1–3 sessions of motivational feedback and advice. The drinker is typically given an assessment of alcohol-related impairment, and is advised to change his or her drinking pattern. Explicitly confrontational interventions are not included in this category.

Marital therapy

Marital therapy involves both the problem drinker and the spouse and may be conducted with individual dyads or in groups of couples. Behavioural marital therapy seeks to improve communication and problem-solving skills, and to increase the exchange of positive reinforcement. Other, non-behavioural approaches to marital therapy have also been tested.

Community reinforcement approach

This broad-spectrum behavioural approach seeks to change the drinker's environment so that abstinence becomes more rewarding than drinking. Daily doses of disulfiram are monitored and reinforced by a significant other.

Table 17.1 Evidence of treatment effectiveness. Table adapted with permission from Holder *et al.* (1991). This table displays the total number of controlled studies of a particular treatment, number of positive outcomes, and the weighted index

	Number of studies	Number of positive studies	Weighted index
Good evidence of effectiveness			
(weighted index +6 or higher)			
Social skills training	10	10	+18
Self-control training	17	12	+17
Brief motivational counselling	9	8	+13
Marital therapy, (behavioural)	7	7	+12
Community reinforcement approach	4	4	+6
Stress management training	10	6	+6
Treatments that are promising but not proven			
(weighted index 0 to +5)			
Aversion therapy, covert sensitisation	7	4	+3
Behaviour contracting	4	3	+3
Disulfiram, oral	10	5	+3
Psychotropic medication, antidepressant	4	3	+3
Disulfiram, implant	5	3	+2
Marital therapy (non-behavioural)	3	2	+1
Cognitive therapy	7	3	0
Hypnosis	4	2	0
Psychotropic medication, lithium	7	3	0
Treatments with insufficient evidence			
(fewer than 3 studies)			
Acupuncture	1	1	+1
Calcium carbimide	1	1	+1
Residential/milieu, Minnesota Model	1	1	+1
Residential/milieu, Halfway House	1	0	−1
Alcoholics Anonymous	2	0	−2
Aversion therapy, apnea	2	0	−2
Psychotropic medication, antipsychotic	2	0	−2
No evidence of effectiveness			
(weighted index −2 or lower)			
Aversion therapy, electrical	15	5	−2
Aversion therapy, chemical (nausea)	5	1	−3
Confrontational interventions	4	0	−4
Educational lectures/films	9	2	−5
Psychotherapy (individual)	9	2	−5
Psychotropic medication, psychedelic	9	2	−5
Videotape self-confrontation	5	0	−5
Psychotropic medication, antianxiety	10	2	−6
Counselling, general	9	1	−7
Metronidazole	10	1	−8
Group psychotherapy	13	2	−9
Residential/milieu treatment	14	1	−12

Additional behavioural counselling is directed toward job-finding, problem-solving, improving relationships, and increasing involvement in sober and enjoyable leisure activities.

Stress management training

The individual is taught methods for reducing personal tension and stress. These have included relaxation techniques, systematic desensitization, and cognitive strategies.

Aversion therapy

Aversion therapies are designed to induce a conditioned avoidance of alcohol. The images or drinking of alcohol are paired with unpleasant experiences, to create an aversion to alcohol. A variety of unpleasant experiences have been used, including electric shock, nausea and vomiting, respiratory paralysis (apnea), and imagined adverse consequences (covert sensitization).

Behaviour contracting

This approach includes explicit arrangement of environmental contingencies, such as behaviour prompts, reinforcement of new behaviours incompatible with problem drinking, and extinction or punishment of heavy drinking.

Cognitive therapy

This approach seeks to identify and modify maladaptive thoughts or beliefs that contribute to problem drinking. Included here are relapse prevention strategies that target cognitive mediational processes, such as expectancies and self-efficacy. Other 'relapse prevention' approaches that teach behavioural coping skills are included in separate categories (for example social skills training).

Hypnosis

A hypnotic trance is induced, and the drinker is then given specific instructions intended to alter future drinking. Some treatments have relied upon post-hypnotic suggestion, while others have induced relaxing or aversive imagery during trance.

Having considered a summary of the available evidence, a health policy board will want to know how much confidence they can place in these results. Were all the studies of equal methodological rigour and are there any other issues that should be considered? It must be admitted that, although all of these studies were of an acceptable standard, it is possible that some were more rigorous than others. It should also be noted that a badly done study with inaccurate measures might not identify real differences between treatments. Another very important issue that must be borne in mind is that a particular treatment approach might be effective only for a particular subgroup of drinkers. For example, it could be argued that residential/milieu treatment is helpful for a few patients who are severely dependent and lack social supports. Such a beneficial effect on a small group will not be observed if the study includes the less severely dependent or those who will be returning to good social environments. Bearing in mind these methodological issues the following advice can still be given to a health policy board with a fair degree of confidence.

1. Psychological approaches which are directed towards improving social and marital relationships are very effective and should be included in a comprehensive service for people with alcohol-related problems. This research is very convincing. If we combine the work on social skills training, behavioural marital therapy, and community reinforcement, there are 21 studies, all of which are positive. Furthermore, investigations of those factors which predict relapse and recovery suggest that family stability, cohesion, and social support are among the most important (Orford and Edwards 1977; Billings and Moos 1983).

2. There is good evidence that psychological approaches directed towards self-control and stress management training are effective. A total of 27 studies have investigated these approaches and 18 (67 per cent) were positive. These methods usually involve the identification of high risk situations or cues as well as the rehearsal of coping strategies. There are reasons to believe that these very good results could be improved if cue exposure was incorporated into self-management approaches (Hodgson 1989).

3. A few psychological approaches look promising and should be subject to further research before being used widely and routinely in clinical practice. These approaches are as follows (percentage of positive outcomes in brackets): covert sensitization (57 per cent), behaviour contracting (75 per cent), non-behavioural marital therapy (67 per cent), cognitive therapy (43 per cent), and hypnosis (50 per cent). These approaches are very broad, and an important research question is where the focus should be when dealing with alcohol related problems. For example, exactly what instructions or images are likely to be effective in conjunction with hypnosis.

4. There are some psychological approaches which are still commonly used even though there is no evidence of effectiveness. The possibility of diverting resources into more effective approaches should be seriously considered. Electrical and chemical aversion therapy, confrontational interventions, educational lectures and films, individual and group psychodynamic therapy, are all suspect and should not be included in a comprehensive approach unless there is a very good reason. There is also no evidence at all that watching a videotape of one's own intoxicated behaviour can have a positive effect. Of most significance when considering cost-effectiveness, there is no evidence that spending time away from drinking environments and temptations (residential/milieu treatments) is of any value at all for the majority of clients.

Cost-effectiveness

Holder *et al.* (1991) were able to get a first approximation of the costs of the range of treatments shown in Table 17.1 by taking the following steps:

1. Compiling an extensive database of average costs from providers, insurance carriers, state alcohol and drug abuse authorities, and self-insured employers. Costs ranged from $6 per visit for neighbourhood recovery programs to $585 per day for general acute care hospital treatment (1987 prices).

2. Questioning 29 expert respondents about the settings in which a particular treatment is usually offered, the types of personnel who usually provide the treatment and the recommended time necessary to complete the treatment for the average patient.

3. Using this information to estimate the minimum total cost for each treatment.

Table 17.2 summarizes their findings by placing each treatment into one of five cost categories.

A number of conclusions can be drawn from Table 17.2 which should be of some interest to a health policy board. First, there are a number of treatments which are low–medium cost with good evidence of effectiveness. These treatments emphasize coping skills and relationships. Secondly, there are some treatments which are in the high cost categories for which there is no evidence of effectiveness. These include insight psychotherapy, residential milieu therapy, and some drug treatments. What is very clear is that effectiveness does not increase as costs increase.

Of particular importance is the conclusion that in-patient treatment (residential/milieu therapy) should not be a routine response to alcohol dependence. It is a very high-cost treatment and yet there is no evidence of effectiveness from the combined evidence of a range of studies from different research centres (Miller 1990). For example, a recent randomized clinical trial carried out by Chapman and Huygens (1988) found no advantage for in-patient treatment when compared with six sessions or one session of community out-patient counselling. This confirms the findings of the first of these studies carried out 25 years ago (Edwards and Guthrie 1967). It is also interesting that private alcoholism hospitals in the USA tend to retain patients in treatment for twice as long as the publicly funded hospitals, even though there is no evidence that length of stay increases effectiveness (Templer and Kauffman 1988). If in-patient treatment is of any value, then it will be only for a particular group of patients and a health policy board will need further evidence to support this view.

In conclusion, three main policy implications can be derived from this extensive body of research. First, most people dealing with alcohol related problems should be able to administer an appropriate brief intervention,

Table 17.2 Treatments by cost and effectiveness categories

	Minimal cost ($0–99)	Low cost ($100–199)	Medium cost ($200–599)	High cost ($600–999)	Very high cost (≥$1,000)
Good evidence of effectiveness	Brief motivational counselling	Self-control training, stress management	Social skills training, community reinforcement, marital behavioural therapy		
Treatment that are promising but not proven		Behaviour contracting	Aversion, covert sensitization, psychotropic, antidepressants, other marital therapy, cognitive therapy, psychotropic, lithium	Disulfiram (oral), disulfram (implant), hypnosis	
Treatments with insufficient evidence	Alcoholics Anonymous		Aversion, apnea	Calcium carbimide, psychotropic, antipsychotic, acupuncture, Halfway House	Residential, Minnesota
No evidence of effectiveness		Educational films and lectures	Confrontational intervention, aversion, electrical video, self confrontation, group therapy	Psychotropic, antianxiety, psychotropic, psychedelic, metronidazole, counselling, general	Aversion, nausea residential milieu insight psychotherapy

depending upon the stage of change. Secondly, there is good evidence that some psychological interventions are effective. These include approaches directed towards social and marital relationships as well as self-control and stress management. Finally, these successful approaches are also the most cost-effective.

It should be added that our knowledge is still very primitive and certainly, during the next ten years we must continue to ask which approaches are the most effective, for which people, with which therapists at what cost?

References

Abrams, D.B., Follick, M.J., and Biener, L. (1988). Individual versus group self-help smoking cessation at the workplace: initial impact and twelve month outcomes. In *Four National Cancer Institute-funded self-help smoking cessation trials: interim results and emerging patterns* (Chair T. Glynn). Symposium conducted at the Annual Association for the Advancement of Behavior Therapy Convention, New York.

Billings, A.G. and Moos, R.H. (1983). Psychosocial processes of recovery among alcoholics and their families: implications for clinicians and program evaluators. *Addictive Behaviors*, 8, 205–18.

Chapman, P.L.H. and Huygens, I. (1988). An evaluation of three treatment programmes for alcoholism: an experimental study with 6- and 18-month follow-ups. *British Journal of Addiction*, 83, 67–81.

Chick, J., Lloyd, F., and Crombie, E. (1985). Counselling problem drinkers in medical wards. *British Medical Journal*, 290, 965–7.

Edwards, G. and Guthrie, S. (1967). A controlled trial of inpatient and out-patient treatment of alcohol dependency. *Lancet*, i, 555–9.

Hodgson, R.J. (1989). Resisting temptation: a psychological analysis. *British Journal of Addiction*, 84, 251–7.

Holder, H., Longabaugh, R., Miller, W.R., and Rubonis, A.V. (1991). The cost effectiveness of treatment for alcohol problems: a first approximation. *Journal of Studies on Alcohol*, 52, 517–40.

Kristenson, H., Ohlin, H., Hulten-Nosslin, M., Trell, E., and Hood, B. (1983). Identification and intervention of heavy drinking in middle-aged men: results and follow-up of 24–60 months of long-term study with randomised controls. *Alcoholism: Clinical and Experimental Research*, 7, 203–9.

Miller, W.R. (1990). Emergent treatment concepts and techniques. In *Annual review of addictions research and treatment*, Vol. 1 (ed. P.E. Nathan, J.W. Langenbucher, B.S. McCrady, and W. Frankenstein).

Miller, W.R. and Hester, R.K. (1986). The effectiveness of alcoholism treatment: what research reveals. In *Treating addictive behaviors: processes of change.* (ed. W.R. Miller and N. Heather), pp. 121–74. Plenum Press, New York.

Miller, W.R. and Sovereign, R.G. (1988). The check-up: a model for early intervention in addictive behaviors. In *Addictive behaviors: prevention and early intervention*, (ed. T. Loberg, W.R. Miller, P.E. Nathan, and G.A. Marlatt), pp. 219–31. Swetz and Zeitlinger, Amsterdam.

Orford, J. and Edwards, G. (1977). *Alcoholism: a comparison of treatment and advice.* Maudsley Monograph No. 26. Oxford University Press.

Prochaska, J.O. and DiClemente, C.C. (1983). Stages and processes of self-change of smoking: towards a more integrative model of change. *Journal of Consulting and Clinical Psychology*, 51, 390–5.

Prochaska, J.O. and DiClemente, C.C. (1986). *Toward a comprehensive model of change*. In *Treating Addictive Behaviors: Processes of Change*, (ed. W.R. Miller and N. Heather), pp. 3–27. Plenum Press, New York.

Prochaska, J.O., DiClemente, C.C., and Velicer, W.F. (1988) Comparative analysis of self-help programs for four stages of smoking cessation. In *Four National Cancer Institute funded self-help smoking cessation trials: interim results and emerging patterns*, (Chair T. Glynn). Symposium conducted at the Annual Association for the Advancement of Behaviour Therapy Convention, New York.

Templer, D.I. and Kauffman, I. (1988). Exploitation or neglect. *American Psychologist*, 43, 200–1.

Woody, G.E., McLellan, A.T., Luborsky, L., and O'Brien, C.P. (1987). Twelve-month follow-up of psychotherapy for opiate dependence. *American Journal of Psychiatry*, 144, 590–6.

18. Implications of recent research on psychotherapy for drug abuse

Kathleen M. Carroll and Bruce J. Rounsaville

Although Parloff (1982) likened the evidence from psychotherapy research in the face of current policy concerns to '. . . a quixotic Bambi planted firmly in the path of the onrushing Godzilla of cost-containment policies', there is a broadening middle ground between the top-down analysis of the policy maker and the bottom-up perspective of the psychotherapy researcher. The development of the technology model of psychotherapy research, which allows for greater standardization and specification of psychotherapies in a manner analogous to the specification of pharmacotherapies in controlled clinical trials, dramatically improved researchers' ability to rigorously evaluate and contrast different forms of psychotherapy. This has allowed psychotherapy researchers increasingly to address issues of interest to the policy maker. In this chapter, the policy implications of empirical evidence on psychotherapy as treatment for drug abuse are explored from the following perspectives: (1) the efficacy of psychotherapy and its role in the treatment of drug abuse, (2) policy implications of the specificity versus non-specificity dilemma in psychotherapy research.

The efficacy of psychotherapy

It is now widely recognized that the undifferentiated question, 'Does psychotherapy work?' is no more useful than the question 'Does surgery work?'. Surgery is not indicated for all clinical disorders, nor is a single surgical procedure appropriate for diverse conditions—the same is true for psychotherapy. For many years psychotherapy researchers have sought to evaluate the specificity of psychotherapy; that is, 'What psychotherapies, delivered under what conditions, work for what particular disorders?'.

The role of psychotherapy

Early work on the treatment of drug users suggested that psychotherapeutic approaches, used alone, had disappointingly little effect on keeping addicts in treatment or reducing their illicit drug use (see Brill 1977; Nyswander *et al.*

1958; O'Malley *et al.* 1972). The development of pharmacological interventions, such as methadone maintenance, demonstrated previously unseen ability to keep drug users in treatment and reduce their use of illicit drugs, and so provided the conditions under which psychotherapeutic treatments could be more productively implemented. Hence, most research on psychotherapy for substance abuse has evaluated the efficacy of psychotherapy in combination with pharmacological or environmental interventions, and psychotherapy has been evaluated for its capacity to: (1) facilitate compliance with, or response to, pharmacological interventions, (2) broaden or enhance addict's improvements in treatment beyond substance use alone, such as addressing symptom or problem areas that would not be expected to improve through pharmacological intervention, or (3) foster greater durability or robustness of gains made in treatment.

Overall, the addition of psychotherapy to pharmacological interventions has been shown to improve outcome across several treatment modalities with some consistency. Among opiate addicts, the provision of psychotherapy has been found significantly to increase rates of successful naltrexone induction (Anton *et al.* 1981; Resnick *et al.* 1981), foster greater retention in methadone-assisted ambulatory detoxification (Rawson *et al.* 1983), and improve programme attendance in methadone maintenance (Ramer *et al.* 1971; Senay *et al.* 1973). Studies which have attempted to withhold psychotherapy in methadone maintenance have often been unsuccessful (Ramer *et al.* 1971; Senay *et al.* 1973). Ball *et al.* (1988) suggest that outcome in methadone maintenance may be strongly mediated by the psychosocial aspects of the programme in which it is administered.

Among cocaine abusers, the role of psychotherapy for cocaine abuse is still controversial (Kang *et al.* 1991). However, there is as yet no established pharmacotherapy for cocaine abuse, and psychosocial interventions currently constitute the core of treatment for cocaine abuse. Preliminary evidence from ongoing trials suggests some unanticipated findings, including (1) psychotherapy may be sufficient as the sole treatment for some cocaine abusers, particularly those with lower severity, (2) psychotherapy may play an important role in fostering treatment retention among cocaine abusers, and (3) heavier users of cocaine may differentially respond to more structured and directive psychotherapeutic approaches (Carroll *et al.* 1991).

The strongest evidence to date for the value of psychotherapy in drug treatment comes from a study evaluating psychotherapy as an adjunct to methadone maintenance (Woody *et al.* 1983). This study included important design features, such as random assignment to treatment conditions, specification of treatment in manuals, use of experienced therapists who were committed to the type of approach they administered, extensive training of therapists, ongoing monitoring of therapy implementation, multi-dimensional ratings of outcome by independent raters, and adequate sample size. A total of 110 opiate addicts entering a methadone maintenance programme were randomly assigned to a six-month course of one of three treatments: drug counselling alone, drug counselling plus supportive-expressive psychotherapy, or drug counselling plus cognitive-behavioural psychotherapy. While the two groups receiving psychotherapy did not differ significantly from each other on most measures of outcome, subjects who received either form of professional psychotherapy evidenced greater improvement in more outcome domains than the subjects who received drug counselling alone. Furthermore, gains made by the subjects receiving professional psychotherapy were sustained over a 12-month follow-up, while subjects receiving drug counselling alone evidenced some attrition of gains (Woody *et al.* 1987). Differential responsiveness to treatment by patient type was also seen. Addicts with low levels of psychopathology tended to improve regardless of types of treatment received, whereas those with higher levels of psychopathology were likely to improve only if they received professional psychotherapy (Woody *et al.* 1983).

To date, only one major study has failed to demonstrate the efficacy of psychotherapy as an adjunct to methadone maintenance. Rounsaville *et al.* (1983) found no differences in outcome between methadone maintained addicts who were randomly assigned to weekly interpersonal psychotherapy versus a low contact condition, in which the patient met with a therapist for one 20-minute session per month. In contrast to the study of Woody *et al.*, however, there were important differences in implementation of the study treatments that may have accounted for the failure to show a psychotherapy effect, such as offering psychotherapy well after the patient had the opportunity to become fully engaged with other programme staff, and poor integration of the psychotherapy into the methadone programme. This resulted in a recruitment rate of less than 5 per cent of eligible subjects and thus a preponderance of poor prognosis patients entering the study (for example, as a 'last resort' before being administratively discharged).

Implications of the evidence

Despite major advances in recent years, studies evaluating the efficacy of psychotherapy have been undertaken only recently and as yet offer few clear guidelines for programme policy. This may be for a number of reasons, including: (1) well-designed studies of psychotherapy as treatment for drug abuse are still rare, (2) those which have been completed have not yet been replicated, (3) direct contrasts of psychotherapy with other forms of treatment (particularly behavioural interventions such as contingency management) have not been done, and (4) the types of psychotherapies which are among the most widely used in general clinical practice have not yet been evaluated in randomized controlled trials. Nevertheless, the preponderance of evidence to date suggests that psychotherapy has value in the treatment of some forms of drug abuse. In particular, the Philadelphia study (Woody *et al.* 1983, 1985, 1987) indicates that the addition of psychotherapy can enhance the magnitude, breath, and durability of outcomes over drug counselling alone.

The Woody study is especially compelling in that its major findings—the superiority of professional psychotherapy relative to drug counselling, but the equivalence of both types of psychotherapy—parallel the findings of the bulk of psychotherapy research in other areas of psychiatry. Meta-analyses, such as those conducted by Smith *et al.* (1980), the box-score approach of Luborsky *et al.* (1975), as well as important multi-site collaborative clinical trials which pioneered the use of the technological approach to psychotherapy research (Elkin *et al.* 1989), all '. . . have shown, with almost monotonous regularity, that all forms of psychological treatments—be they psychodynamic, behavioral, or cognitive—are comparably effective in producing therapeutic benefits with particular disorders. Moreover, such benefits are reliably superior to those found in comparable groups of patients in the no-treatment or other control conditions' (Parloff 1982).

The general support for the efficacy of psychotherapy can be conceived of as both good news and bad news for the psychotherapy researcher and the policy maker alike. For the psychotherapist, the good news is that 'nobody loses'; psychotherapy appears to be effective in the treatment of drug abuse, particularly under certain circumstances and more so with particular types of patients. The bad news in that nobody wins, either. No form of psycho-therapy or type of practitioner (psychiatrist, psychologist, social worker, substance abuse counsellor) has emerged as superior in effectiveness. This is not particularly encouraging to clinicians who have spent years honing very specialized skills.

For the policy maker, the good news is that psychotherapy appears to enhance the effectiveness of drug treatment. The strongest empirical evidence suggests that psychotherapy is an effective adjunct to pharmacotherapies, such as methadone maintenance. However, even in out-patient drug-free programs, where few randomized clinical trials have been done, large-scale programme evaluations suggest that outcomes from the primarily psychosocial treatments provided in these settings are comparable to those of methadone maintenance programmes (National Institute on Drug Abuse 1984; Sells *et al.* 1977; Simpson *et al.* 1978), although interpretation of these findings is com-plicated by differences in sample severity.

The bad news for the policy maker is that the available research findings provide few guidelines other than 'all psychotherapies seem to work about equally well' and 'psychotherapy provides added benefit over drug counsel-ling for the more psychiatrically impaired addicts'. Furthermore, Luborsky *et al.*'s (1975) restatement of the Dodo bird verdict ('everyone has won and all must have prizes') largely holds for the psychotherapeutic treatment of drug abuse. There has been virtually no strong negative findings against the use of psychotherapy, any particular form of psychotherapy, or type of practitioner. No type of psychotherapy can be eliminated, restricted, or deemed less worthy of support based on current empirical evidence.

From a policy maker's perspective, however, professional individual psychotherapy, whatever its efficacy, is far too labour-intensive to be a viable treatment adjunct for all substance users. So, although everybody wins, the policy maker will no doubt be reluctant to give everyone prizes.

How then, should· decisions be made regarding the allocation of psychotherapy services in drug treatment? Consideration will now be given to the implications of the statement 'Everybody wins and all must have prizes' from the perspective of the two current major research directions in psychotherapy research: (1) non-specificity, the theory that general effectiveness of diverse psychotherapies results from curative elements common to all psychotherapies, and (2) specificity, which holds there is marked individual variation in response to psychotherapy, but failure to identify patient-treatment interactions results in apparent equivalence of all psychotherapies.

Implications of non-specificity: if everyone deserves prizes, the prizes have to be smaller

A major conundrum of the Smith *et al.* (1980) work was the finding that behavioural therapy and more traditional dynamic psychotherapies were roughly equivalent in effect size despite well-documented and convincing differences in theoretical underpinnings and the therapeutic interventions themselves. This was paralleled in both the NIMH Treatment of Depression Collaborative Research Project and the Philadelphia studies, where therapists conducting different types of psychotherapy demonstrated considerable technical diversity, but differential efficacy of treatments was not seem (Elkin *et al.* 1989; Luborsky *et al.* 1982).

This has led some researchers to conclude that the curative elements of psychotherapy are not the unique 'active ingredients' of particular therapies; instead, the therapeutic effect lies in the non-specific elements that are common to all psychotherapies, such as provision of support, empathy, persuasion, the skill of the therapist, and the quality of the therapeutic relationship (Rozenzweig 1936). For example, process analyses of the Woody *et al.* data indicated that not only were the ratings of the helping alliance the strongest predictors of outcome, but that they were also far better predictors than the level of the therapists' conformity to interventions outlined in the treatment manuals (Luborsky *et al.* 1985).

How do these findings relate to cost and other policy concerns? Figure 18.1 describes three hypothetical curves depicting the relationship between treatment costs and effect size. Curve A illustrates the most commonly assumed relationship, increasing effectiveness with the highest levels of cost. Curve B illustrates the inverse relationship, with effectiveness increasing as costs decrease, and curve C illustrates constant effectiveness of treatments, regardless of cost.

Curve C is the most compatible with current empirical evidence from psychotherapy research in substance abuse, which suggests fixed levels of effectiveness across different treatment types, with some variation in cost, due to

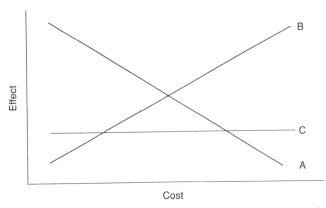

Fig. 18.1   Cost versus effectiveness. (Reproduced from Holder *et al.* (1991)).

differences in length of treatment, type of therapist, and the setting in which psychotherapy is provided. From a policy perspective, if it is the non-specific elements common to all psychotherapies that are curative, the least expensive psychotherapy that contains the minimum effective dose of the non-specific elements and which has evidence of efficacy would be the most desirable.

Assuming that most substance users benefit from psychotherapy and that widely different forms of psychotherapy are equivalent in effectiveness, briefer psychotherapies would appear to have advantage over more long-term ones, as more substance abusers can be exposed to the potential benefits of psychotherapy at lower cost.

What evidence is available for the effectiveness of brief psychotherapies? The Woody *et al.* studies demonstrated robust psychotherapy effects after only 26 weeks of treatment. Meta-analyses of psychotherapy, such as the Smith *et al.* (1980) work, have generally failed to find significant association of treatment length and effectiveness. Howard's (1986) analysis of the dose–response relationship in psychotherapy suggests that most patients show measurable improvement after only eight therapy sessions. Moreover, evidence from alcoholism treatment research suggests that not only are brief interventions sufficient for many alcoholics, but changes seen after brief interventions are often comparable in strength and durability to long-term approaches (Miller and Hester 1986).

Implications of specificity: give prizes only to those who benefit from them

The second major theory explaining the failure of any single type of psychotherapy to emerge as superior is that differential effectiveness of psychotherapies is masked by the failure to identify patient–treatment interactions, as illustrated by Fig. 18.2. If patient uniformity is assumed and patient characteristic

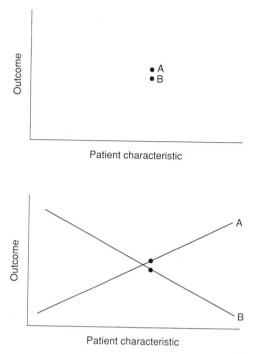

Fig. 18.2 Patient–treatment matching. (Reproduced from Finney and Moos (1986)).

X is not evaluated as a mediator of outcome, treatments A and B appear equivalent in efficacy. However, when treatment outcome is evaluated with respect to variability in characteristic X, treatment A emerges as superior for those with higher levels of X, and treatment B is superior for those with lower levels of X. Furthermore, if A is a more expensive treatment than B, policy makers might consider whether treatment A should be reserved only for those individuals at the very highest levels of X.

The major advantage of pursuing this line of research is identification of patient types who will or will not benefit from particular forms of treatment (for example, patient types for whom low-intensity treatments may be sufficient versus those who require more intensive interventions), as well as identification of patients who differentially respond to one form of treatment over another (for example, to a behavioural versus a psychodynamic approach). Patient-treatment matching is particularly attractive from a policy perspective, as the identification of promising patient-treatment matches should both enhance the effectiveness of treatments and reduce costs, through providing the least expensive form of treatment to which the individual will respond, as well as avoiding exposure to treatments to which an individual may not respond or may have a negative reaction.

Again, the Woody *et al.* studies provide the most favourable guidelines to date on the type of drug abusers who may benefit from psychotherapeutic intervention. While methadone-maintained opiate addicts with lower levels of psychopathology tended to improve *regardless of* whether they received professional psychotherapy or drug counselling, those with higher levels of psychopathology tended to improve *only if* they received psychotherapy. As many substance abusers have concurrent psychiatric disorders (Rounsaville *et al.* 1982) which are associated with higher levels of impairment and poorer outcome (McLellan *et al.* 1983; Rounsaville *et al.* 1986), the Woody *et al.* findings are particularly important, in that psychotherapy offers a means of enhancing outcome in a group of patients with particularly poor prognosis. Moreover, this study provides indications on differential response to psychotherapy by concurrent psychiatric disorder: for example, depressed addicts improved with psychotherapy, while addicts with antisocial personality disorder tended to show little or no improvement unless they were also depressed (Woody *et al.* 1985).

Conclusions

Available evidence consistently suggests that outcomes in substance abuse treatment can be broadened, strengthened, and made more durable by the addition of psychotherapy. Yet there is a continuing absence of effective co-ordination of psychotherapy in order to maximize treatment benefits. We are just beginning to understand the complex interactions of patient, therapist, treatment, and setting that affect outcome in psychotherapy. Increasing precision in the specification of each of these variables is furthering our efforts, but much more research is needed. Where are we now, while awaiting more data to come in? The current evidence suggests that professional psychotherapy should be given primarily to substance abusers with concurrent psychopathology and those with higher severity of drug use. Brief, less intensive approaches may be sufficient for many drug users without concurrent psychopathology.

Psychotherapy works; few today would treat substance abusers without some form of psychosocial intervention. Individual psychotherapy or counselling is available in 99 per cent of drug treatment units in the USA (Onken and Blaine 1990). Furthermore, very often psychosocial interventions represent the core of treatment; since for many classes of drug abuse (marijuana, stimulants, hallucinogens, benzodiazepines, and barbiturates), no established pharmacological intervention exists, and psychotherapy is the only available treatment alternative.

Even for those classes of drug abuse for which there are effective pharmacotherapies, the availability of methadone, naltrexone, and antabuse have by no means cured drug abuse. Pharmacotherapies work only if drug abusers see the value of stopping drug use, and drug abusers have consistently found ways to circumvent these pharmacological interventions. These very powerful agents tend to work primarily on the symptoms of drug abuse that are time-limited and autonomous, but have little impact on the enduring behavioural characteristics of drug use. It is unlikely that a pharmacological intervention will be developed that gives addicts that motivation to stop using drugs, helps them see the value in renouncing drug use, improves their ability to cope with the day-to-day frustrations in living, or provides alternatives to the rein-forcements drugs and drug-using lifestyles provide. Psychotherapy will con-tinue to be necessary to foster compliance with our treatment system and to 'warm up' our pharmacotherapies, but also to help addicts to work, to love, and to see that they may have lives beyond drug abuse.

References

Anton, R.F., Hogan, I., Jalali, B., Riordan, C.E., and Kleber, H.D. (1981). Multiple family therapy and naltrexone in the treatment of opiate dependence. *Drug and Alcohol Dependence*, 8, 157–68.

Ball, J., Corty, E., Bond, H., Myers, C., and Tommasello, A. (1988). The reduction of intravenous heroin use, non-opiate abuse, and crime during methadone main-tenance treatment: further findings. In *Problems of Drug Dependence, 1987*, (ed. L.S. Harris), (NIDA Research Monograph Series No. 81, pp. 224–9). National Institute on Drug Abuse, Rockville, MD.

Brill, L. (1977). The treatment of drug abuse: evolution of a perspective. *American Journal of Psychiatry*, 134, 157–60.

Carroll, K.M., Rounsaville, B.J., and Gawin, F.H. (1991). A comparative trial of psychotherapies for ambulatory cocaine abusers: Relapse prevention and interper-sonal psychotherapy. *American Journal of Drug and Alcohol Abuse*, 17, 229–47.

Elkin, I., Shea, M.T., Watkins, J.T., Imber, S.D., Sotsky, S.M., Collins, J.F., *et al.* (1989). National Institute on Mental Health treatment of depression collaborative research program: General effectiveness of treatments. *Archives of General Psychiatry*, 46, 971–82.

Finney, J.W. and Moos, R.H. (1986). Matching patients with treatments: Conceptual and methodological issues. *Journal of Studies on Alcohol*, 47, 122–34.

Holder, H.D., Longabaugh, R., Miller, W.R., and Rubonis, A.V. (1991). The cost effectiveness of treatment for alcohol problems: A first approximation. *Journal of Studies on Alcohol*, 52, 517–40.

Howard, K.I., Krause, M.S., and Orlinsky, D.E. (1986). The attrition dilemma: To-ward a new strategy for psychotherapy research. *Journal of Consulting and Clinical Psychology*, 54, 106–10.

Kang, S.Y., Kleinman, P.H., Woody, G.T., Millman, R.B., Todd, T.C., Kemp, J., and Lipton, D.S. (1991). Outcomes for cocaine abusers after once-a-week psychosocial therapy. *American Journal of Psychiatry*, 148, 630–35.

Luborsky, L., McLellan, A.T., Woody, G.E., O'Brien, C.P., and Auerbach, A. (1985). Therapist success and its determinants. *Archives of General Psychiatry*, 42, 602–11.

Luborsky, L., Singer, B., and Luborsky, L. (1975). Comparative studies of psycho-therapies: is it true that 'everyone has won and all must have prizes'? *Archives of General Psychiatry*, 32, 995–1007.

Luborsky, L., Woody, G.E., McLellan, A.T., O'Brien, C.P., and Rosenzweig, J. (1982). Can independent judges recognize different psychotherapies? An experience with manual-guided therapies. *Journal of Consulting and Clinical Psychology*, 50, 49–62.

McLellan, A.T., Luborsky, L., Woody, G.E., O'Brien, C.P., and Druley, K.A. (1983). Predicting response to alcohol and drug abuse treatments: role of psychiatric severity. *Archives of General Psychiatry*, 40, 620–25.

Miller, W.R. and Hester, R.K. (1986). The effectiveness of alcoholism treatment methods: What research reveals. In *Treating addictive behaviors: processes of change* (ed. W.R. Miller and R.K. Hester), pp. 121–74. Plenum, New York.

National Institute on Drug Abuse (1984, January). *The treatment outcome prospective study (TOPS): an overview of study features*, NIDA Research Notes. National Institute on Drug Abuse, Rockville, MD.

Nyswander, M., Winick, C., Bernstein, A., Brill, I., and Kaufer, G. (1958). The treatment of drug addicts as voluntary outpatients: a progress report. *American Journal of Orthopsychiatry*, 28, 714–27.

O'Malley, J.E., Anderson, W.H., and Lazare, A. (1972). Failure of outpatient treatment of drug abuse. I. Heroin. *American Journal of Psychiatry*, 128, 865–8.

Onken, L.S. and Blaine, J.D. (1990). Psychotherapy and counselling research in drug abuse treatment: questions, problems, and solutions. In *Psychotherapy and counselling in the treatment of drug abuse*. (ed. L.S. Onken and J.D. Blaine), NIDA Research Monograph Series No. 104. National Institute on Drug Abuse, Rockville, MD.

Parloff, M.D. (1982). Psychotherapy research evidence and reimbursement decisions: Bambi meets Godzilla. *American Journal of Psychiatry*, 139, 718–27.

Ramer, B.S., Zaslove, M.O., and Langan, J. (1971). Is methadone enough? The use of ancillary treatment during methadone maintenance. *American Journal of Psychiatry*, 127, 1040–44.

Rawson, R.A., Mann, A.G., Tennant, F.S., and Clabough, D. (1983). Efficacy of psychotherapeutic counselling during 12-day ambulatory heroin detoxification. In *Problems of drug dependence, 1982*, (ed. L.S. Harris), NIDA Research Monograph Series No. 43. National Institute on Drug Abuse, Rockville, MD.

Resnick, R.B., Washton, A.M., and Stone-Washton, N. (1981). Psychotherapy and naltrexone in opioid dependence. In *Problems of Drug Dependence, 1980*, L.S. Harris (ed.), (NIDA Research Monograph Series No. 34, pp. 109–15). National Institute on Drug Abuse, Rockville MD.

Rounsaville, B.J., Weissman, M.M., Kleber, H.D., and Wilber, C.W. (1982). Heterogeneity of psychiatric diagnosis in treated opiate addicts. *Archives of General Psychiatry*, 39, 161–6.

Rounsaville, B.J., Glazer, W., Wilber, C.H., Weissman, M.M., and Kleber, H.D. (1983). Short-term Interpersonal Psychotherapy in methadone maintained opiate addicts. *Archives of General Psychiatry*, 40, 629–36.

Rounsaville, B.J., Kosten, T.R., Weissman, M.M., and Kleber, H.D. (1986). Prognostic significance of psychopathology in treated opiate addicts. *Archives of General Psychiatry*, 43, 739–45.

Rozenzweig, S. (1936). Some implicit common factors in diverse methods of psychotherapy. *American Journal of Orthopsychiatry*, 6, 412–15.

Sells, S.B., *et al.* (1977). Evaluation of present treatment modalities: Research with the DARP admissions-1969–1973. Paper presented at the Conference on Recent Developments in the Chemotherapy of Narcotic Addiction, Washington, November 3–4, 1977.

Senay, E.C., Jaffe, J.H., DiMenza, S., *et al.* (1973). A 48-week study of methadone, methadylacetate, and minimal services. *Psychopharmacology Bulletin*, **9**, 37.

Simpson, D.D., *et al.* (1978). *Evaluation of drug abuse treatments based on first year follow-up of admissions to drug abuse treatments in the DARP during 1969–1972.* Publication No. (ADM) 78–701. US Department of Health, Education, and Welfare, Washington.

Smith, M.L., Glass, G.V., and Miller, T.I. (1980). *The benefits of psychotherapy.* Johns Hopkins, Baltimore, MD.

Woody, G.E., Luborsky, L., McLellan, A.T., O'Brien, C.P., Beck, A.T., Blaine, J., Herman, I., and Hole, A. (1983). Psychotherapy for opiate addicts: Does it help? *Archives of General Psychiatry*, **40**, 639–45.

Woody, G.E., McLellan, A.T., Luborsky, L., and O'Brien, C.P. (1985). Sociopathy and psychotherapy outcome. *Archives of General Psychiatry*, **42**, 1081–6.

Woody, G.E., McLellan, A.T., Luborsky, L., and O'Brien, C.P. (1987). Twelve-month follow-up of psychotherapy for opiate dependence. *American Journal of Psychiatry*, **144**, 590–96.

19. Appropriate expectations for substance abuse treatments: can they be met?

A. Thomas McLellan, Mary Randall, David Metzger, Arthur I. Alterman, George E. Woody, and Charles P. O'Brien

Drug abuse is widely recognized as one of the most serious social, legal, and medical problems facing the USA today. There is some evidence that recent efforts to reduce casual drug use have been successful. However, by all indications, serious drug use is not reducing, especially in the inner cities of the USA, where it appears to be intimately related to other serious social problems, such as crime, unemployment, and AIDS. Many people in the USA have called for additional drug abuse treatment efforts, with the view that this will be the most effective way to deal with this complex and pervasive problem; but, while some segments of the public are demanding greater availability and more public financing of treatment, there are those in government, health care financing, and the public at large who question the efficacy of substance abuse treatment, and whether treatment is 'worth it'. If society is asked to support and even expand treatment efforts then it has a right to know that its efforts and resources are well spent. In turn, it is the responsibility of the treatment establishment and the scientific community to devote focused effort toward sound, comprehensive, and sophisticated examinations of the overall value and impact of substance abuse treatments. In this respect there have been evaluation studies indicating that at least the most common forms of standard substance abuse treatment can work (Miller and Hester 1986; Rua 1989; Sisk *et al.* 1990; Saxe *et al.* 1983; Simpson and Savage 1980). Despite this encouraging evidence, it is equally clear that these treatments do not always work optimally or even well for all patients.

What are reasonable expectations regarding a substance abuse intervention?

What might an effective intervention (regardless of whether it is a treatment intervention) for substance abuse be expected to do? Is treatment for substance abuse effective in terms of these expectations? In this chapter, 'appropriate expectations' for substance abuse treatments are proposed and some recent data are presented that are pertinent to these expectations. A second, and equally important, question is whether substance abuse treatments are better and/or more cost effective than other potential types of interventions in meeting these 'appropriate expectations'. This is directly pertinent to the efficacy and 'worth' of substance abuse treatments. For further examination of this question, to and for comparative data on the relative efficacy of treatment, no treatment, and two non-treatment alternatives for substance abusers, see McLellan *et al.* (1991).

In many ways the public provides the most demanding standards against which to judge the value of substance abuse treatments. A list of common public expectations of substance abuse intervention is shown below:

(1) safe, complete, detoxification;

(2) reduced use of medical services;

(3) eliminate crime;

(4) return to employment/self-support;

(5) eliminate family disruption;

(6) no return to drug use.

As can be seen, these expectations go far beyond the goals of simply reducing or even eliminating the excessive alcohol and drug use seen in these patients. In fact, with the exception of the last criterion (which will be discussed separately), the major interests of the employers, insurers, law enforcement personnel, and family members who come into contact with substance abusers, are no the excessive use of public resources (treatments, welfare, criminal justice system, etc.) and the associated disruptions to the family and society that so often occur in association with alcohol and drug abuse. Why are the expectations regarding treatment effects so broad? Are they reasonable and should substance abuse treatments even attempt to meet goals that go beyond the simple reduction of alcohol and drug use? These are critical questions that address the basic goals of substance abuse treatments, the appropriate type of staffing and of course, the appropriate methods for evaluating the efficacy of these treatments.

Empirically, it is a fact that substance abusers who present for treatment rarely suffer exclusively from excess alcohol or drug consumption. The large majority of treatment-seeking patients also have serious additional medical, family, employment, and/or psychiatric problems (see Rounsaville *et al.* 1982; McLellan *et al.* 1981). These problems have come to be called 'co-morbid' conditions by insurance and medical personnel, since they complicate the treatment plans and post-treatment prognoses of these patients.

The type of relationship between the addiction and the 'co-morbid' problems has been debated. Many in the field have argued that the medical, economic, and social problems seen among substance abusers at treatment admission are the *result* of prolonged, excessive alcohol and drug use. In contrast, others in the field have argued that these problems are the *underlying reasons* for the initiation and continuation of substance abuse. These views make different assumptions regarding the philosophy of and the appropriate methods for rehabilitation. However, since these problems are often the 'precipitating conditions' leading to treatments admission, it is only natural for families, employers, courts, and others outside the substance abuse treatment field to assume that these problems will resolve with 'effective' substance abuse treatment. It seems unlikely that there will ever be convincing evidence regarding the *original* chronological order or causal role of excessive substance use and the co-morbid 'addiction-related' problems. However, regardless of the *pre-treatment* relationship between the excessive substance use and the associated psycho-social problems, there is very clear and widely replicated evidence that *post-treatment* relapse is regularly produced by unresolved problems in the areas of work, family, medical, and psychiatric conditions (for example, see Marlatt 1983).

Thus, for reasons of clinical philosophy regarding the origins of substance abuse, public expectations regarding the desired benefits from treatment and the practical reality that unresolved medical, family, and social problems can lead to post-treatment relapse, there is every reason to broaden a definition of 'effective treatment outcome' beyond the narrowly focused question of whether or not the treated abuser is abstinent. Given this background of expectations the premise is proposed that '. . . addiction must be considered in the context of those treatment problems which may have contributed to and/or resulted from the chemical abuse' (McLellan *et al.* 1980, p. 27). In turn, this premise has determined the selection of measurement domains used to evaluate the efficacy of substance abuse treatments, as listed below.

(1) Alcohol and drug use;

(2) Employment, self-support;

(3) Crime;

(4) Family, social relations;

(5) Medical and psychiatric status.

To this end, a measurement instrument has been developed to effectively characterize the nature and severity of the alcohol, drug, and other problems of patients admitted to substance abuse treatments. This instrument, the Addiction Severity Index (ASI) (McLellan *et al.* 1980, 1985) is a structured, 45-minute clinical research interview designed to assess problem severity in seven areas commonly affected among substance abusing individuals. In each of these areas, questions measure the number, frequency, intensity, and duration of problem symptoms in the patient's lifetime and during the 30 days before the interview. Using data collected from the 30-day periods prior to admission and the follow-up point, it has been possible to assess the nature and extent of improvements shown by patients in treatment and to compare different types of treatments across all of the seven problem domains.

Can a substance abuse treatment meet these expectations?

Previous publications have included evaluations of various substance abuse treatments using these measurement domains and these expectations (McLellan *et al.* 1982, 1985, 1991). In the remaining pages of this report analyses are presented of four new samples of substance abuse patients treated in three different settings. These samples were selected to represent the most common drugs of abuse (alcohol, opiates, and cocaine) and the most common forms of treatment (both public and private). Using these samples an attempt has been made to evaluate the efficacy of substance abuse treatment in terms of the full range of measurement domains presented in the list above and against the expectations listed previously using a pre-to-post treatment comparison design. There have been many pre-to-post treatment studies performed over the years and space does not permit even a partial discussion of the findings. (The interested reader is referred to studies by Simpson and Savage (1980) using the DARP data, Hubbard *et al.* (1989) using the TOPS data, DeLeon (1984) studying therapeutic communities and Anglin *et al.* (1989) studying methadone maintenace). It is important to state at the beginning that simply finding status improvements following treatment discharge does not constitute evidence that treatment has been the causal factor. At the same time, evidence of positive change following treatment is a minimal condition for further exploration.

There have been substantial advances over the past decade in the methodologies associated with pre-to-post treatment comparisons. It is now standard for subject interviews and data collection to be completed by independent evaluators not associated with the provision of the intervention, thereby reducing the likelihood of 'demand effects' Rigorous studies do accept subjective reports of post-treatment status but also collect breathalyser and/or urine screening tests and/or collateral reports to validate those reports. Finally, a high rate of patient follow-up contact is necessary to ensure representative information from the treated sample. It is possible to interview a minimum of 85 per cent of patients at a six month follow-up and studies reporting contact rates that are less than this should be evaluated critically. Although the choice of a six-month post-treatment interval to evaluate improvement is admittedly arbitrary, data from several studies of alcohol, opiate, cocaine, cigarette, and poly substance abusers indicate that the large majority of relapses occur within 3–6 months after treatment cessation (Woody and Cacciola 1991). Thus, while a six-month interval may not necessarily be the optimal measurement interval, it is at least one appropriate evaluation point.

Table 19.1 illustrates selected demographic and background status variables for each of the four patient samples. Even from cursory examination, it is evident that these samples of patients were different on most of the dimensions measured. The methadone programmes were both publicly funded (Veterans Administration and Philadelphia City) providing maintenance (modal dose 60 mg) and social services to caseloads of 250–300 patients. Two public (VA) alcohol and cocaine programmes were included, an in-patient pragramme and a partial hospital (27 hours per week) programme, each lasting 30 days. Each treated alcohol and cocaine dependent individuals together in a total abstinence approach utilizing group therapy to reduce denial and referral to Alcoholics Anonymous or Narcotics Anonymoth. The private programmes (two in-patient and two out-patient) each treated approximately 30 alcohol and/or cocaine dependent patients together in 30-day, abstinence oriented programmes that were very similar to those at the VA. Again, space limitations prevent further description but the programmes selected for study represent the most common treatment philosophies, settings, and funding sources.

All patients were evaluated at admission to treatment and at six-month follow-up by independent research technicians. Patients were consecutive admissions to these treatment programmes. The only exclusion criterion was failure to complete at least five days or five visits. No programme had more than 8 per cent of patients excluded and 3 per cent was the average exclusion rate across programmes. Therefore, this study included an average of 97 per cent of all patients admitted to the programmes during the study period, and consequently represents a conservative, realistic, and comprehensive estimate of treatment efficacy at these programmes.

Follow-up contact rates were not less than 89 per cent and averaged 91 per cent across the four groups. Urine and breathalyser reports were collected on random samples of patients to verify outcome reports. Comparison data from the ASI were compared for the 30-day periods preceding admission to treatment and the six-month follow-up point. Summary measures of overall status in each problem area (factor scores) were calculated by combining unweighted sets of individual items. While these factor scores are statistically reliable measures (range 0–1.0; higher scores equal worse severity; see McLellan *et al.* 1985), they offer little clinically relevant information. Therefore additional individual items from each of the problem areas are presented to provide a more basic indication of the changes that occurred.

A comparison of the admission measures among the four groups (see Table 19.2) reveals major differences among the groups in all the problem areas. In general, the methadone maintenance sample had the worst pre-treatment status in most areas, while the private cocaine/alcohol group showed generally the best admission status. Despite the obvious differences in background status among these samples, the comparisons shown in Table 19.2 indicate substantial improvements in alcohol and drug use for all groups. An average of 70 per cent of patients were abstinent from all drugs over the 30 days prior

Table 19.1 Background status variables for four groups of substance abusers

	Public methadone maintenance	Public alcohol rehabilitation	Public cocaine rehabilitation	Private alcohol/cocaine rehabilitation
Number of patients	98	81	65	122
Age (Mean and SD)	42 (6)	42 (6)	33 (6)	38 (6)
Race (%)				
Black	77	73	96	67
White	20	25	3	33
Marital status (%)				
Never married	12	24	37	22
Married	24	25	23	33
Divorced/separated	46	51	40	31
Living situation (%)				
With sexual partner	32	44	47	52
With family or friends	38	38	34	32
Alone	17	16	14	14
No stable arrangement	13	2	5	2
Years of (Mean and SD)				
Alcohol abuse	11 (6)	20 (9)	10 (3)	11 (4)
Opiate abuse	13 (5)	<1 (1)	<1 (2)	<1 (3)
Cocaine abuse	4 (1)	<1 (1)	4 (3)	1 (3)
Depressant abuse	2 (1)	2 (4)	1 (2)	<1 (4)
Longest abstinence (monthly)	23 (19)	7 (12)	28 (12)	37 (22)
Years education (Mean and SD)	12.1 (4)	11.2 (3)	12.3 (4)	12.7 (3)
% With skill or trade	67	80	83	83
% Employed past year	64	49	57	91
% Received welfare past year	18	7	2	<1
Ever incarcerated (%)	52	16	2	11
Psychiatric problems (%)				
Lifetime depression	47	68	59	40
Made suicide attempt	8	11	8	10
Trouble cont. violence	24	42	33	24
Prior treatments (Mean and SD)				
Alcohol abuse	<1 (5)	4 (2)	1 (1)	3 (2)
Drug abuse	4 (1)	<1 (1)	1 (2)	3 (2)
Psychiatric disorder	1 (2)	2 (1)	<1 (1)	2 (1)
Medical condition	3 (5)	3 (3)	2 (2)	3 (3)

Table 19.2 Admission and six-month outcome in four substance abuse treatments

Variable	Public methadone maintenance (n = 98)			Public alcohol rehabilitation (n = 81)			Public cocaine rehabilitation (n = 65)			Private alcohol/cocaine rehabilitation (n = 122)		
	Treatment admission	t-test	Six-month follow-up	Treatment admission	t-test	Six-month follow-up	Treatment admission	t-test	Six-month follow-up	Treatment admission	t-test	Six-month follow-up
Number of patients												
Medical factor @	0.322	*	0.267	0.274		0.291	0.241	*	0.122	0.131	*	0.092
Days medical problems	8		5	8		9	5	*	2	3		2
Employment factor	0.633	**	0.554	0.666	**	0.549	0.674	**	0.547	0.344		0.361
Days worked in past 30	11	**	14	10	**	14	9	**	14	17		17
Employment income ($)	483.73	**	729.98	431.27	**	689.33	398.32	**	687.55	1,186.50		1,181.26
Welfare income ($)	62.24		74.54	48.23		39.57	36.67		28.64	6.50		16.31
Drug factor	0.300	***	0.211	0.032	*	0.015	0.248	***	0.072	0.138	***	0.027
Days opiate use	14	***	2	<1		0	2		1	1		<1
Days stimulant use	5	*	3	2		1	13	***	3	5	**	1
Days depressant use	3		3	2		1	2		0	1		1
Per cent abstinent	2	***	46	23	***	81	6	***	77	16	***	76
Alcohol factor	0.131	*	0.094	0.629	***	0.165	0.273	**	0.091	0.451	***	0.124
Days alcohol use	7	*	4	19	***	5	9	**	3	15	***	3
Days drank to intoxication	4	*	2	18	***	3	6	**	2	14	***	2
Per cent abstinent	12	**	38	9	***	71	12	***	86	11	**	58
Legal factor	0.122	*	0.051	0.064	*	0.014	0.076	*	0.037	0.046	*	0.009
Days illegal activity	3	**	1	2	*	0	3	*	1	1		<1
Illegal income ($)	164.62	**	7.05	38.23		0.00	71.32	*	19.11	57.21		13.66
Family factor	0.206		0.176	0.231	**	0.113	0.258	**	0.118	0.187	**	0.121
Days of conflict	1		1	2	*	0	3	*	<1	2		1
Psychiatric factor	0.195		0.154	0.245	***	0.146	0.211	***	0.081	0.139	**	0.094
Days psychological problems	7		6	9	**	6	7	**	3	6	**	3

@ All variables reflect the 30 day periods prior to treatment admission and six-month follow-up.

ASI factor scores are general measures of problem status. Scores range from 0 to 1.0 with higher scores indicating greater problem severity.

*$p<.05$, **$p<.01$, ***$p<.001$ by paired t-test.

to follow up and 63 per cent were abstinent from alcohol. Furthermore, improvements were not confined to the alcohol and drug use but included most of the areas of adjustment listed on p. 000. Seventy-two per cent of patients were employed during the month preceding follow-up, less than one per cent were incarcerated, 3 per cent received welfare income and 4 per cent were in medical, psychiatric or substance abuse treatment. All but the methadone maintenance sample showed significant improvements in family relations and psychological functioning. In fact, medical status was the only problem area where few significant changes occurred. These findings and the substantial body of additional evaluation data available from other treatment outcome studies suggests, but does not conclusively prove, that substance abuse treatments can be quite effective in '. . . producing significant, pervasive, and sustained positive change in the lives of these patients' (McLellan *et al.* 1982, p. 1427).

Conclusion

Two conclusions can be drawn from this consideration. First, the data suggest that patients who enter substance abuse treatment typically show improvement in, if not elimination of, their alcohol and drug use, lasting at least six months following completion of treatment. Secondly, improvements following substance abuse treatments are not confined simply to the areas of alcohol and drug use, but are seen in the important medical, self-support, and social problem areas. The data presented here and elsewhere (McLellan *et al.* 1982, 1991), indicate that *substance abuse treatments can be effective in terms of the broad goals that the public, the press, and the funding agencies have come to expect.*

The only area where substance abuse treatment fails to live up to public expectation is the area of relapse. It is this important and pervasive fact of addiction that leads to dissatisfaction with substance abuse treatment. Yet rates of relapse for substance abuse appear to be approximately equal to those of other medical disorders, such as diabetes, hypertension, and depression, and are produced by many of the same causes. In this regard, substance abuse providers need to educate the public regarding the realistic expectations associated with all relapsing diseases (see also Maddux and Desmond 1986). In addition, treatment providers must reduce emphasis on short-term, in-patient programmes rather than protracted, out-patient treatments that can retain patients in interventions for significant periods of time (at least 6–9 months) as a hedge against relapse.

Acknowledgement

This work was supported by grants from NIDA, NIAAA, and the Department of Veterans Affairs.

References

Anglin, M.D., Speckart, G.R., and Booth, M.W. (1989). Consequences and costs of shutting off methadone. *Addictive Behaviors*, **14**, 307–26.

DeLeon, G. (1984). *The therapeutic community: study of effectiveness* NIDA Treatment Research Monograph No. 84–1286, USGPO, Washington.

Hubbard, R.L., Marsden, M.E., Rachal, J.V., Harwood, H.J., Cavanaugh, E.R., and Ginzburg, H.M. (1989). *Drug abuse treatment: a national study of effectiveness*. University of North Carolina Press, Raleigh, NC.

Maddux, J.F. and Desmond, D.P. (1986). Relapse and recovery in substance abuse careers. In *Relapse and recovery in drug abuse* (ed. F.M. Tims and C.G. Leukefeld), pp. 26–44. NIDA Research Monograph Series 72, DHHS Pub. No. (ADM) 86–1473, USGPO, Washington.

Marlatt, G.A. (1983). Relapse prevention: a self-control program for the treatment of addictive behaviors. In *Adherence, compliance and generalization in behavioral medicine*, (ed. R.B. Stuart), pp. 323–61. Brunner-Mazel, NY.

McLellan, A.T., Luborsky, L., O'Brien, C.P., and Woody, G.E. (1980). An improved evaluation instrument for substance abuse patients: the addiction severity index. *Journal of Nervous and Mental Diseases*, **168**, 26–33.

McLellan, A.T., O'Brien, C.P., Luborsky, L., Woody, G.E., and Kron, R. (1981). Are the addiction related problems of substance abusers really related? *Journal of Nervous and Mental Diseases*, **169**, 232–9.

McLellan, A.T., Luborsky, L., Woody, G.E., and O'Brien, C.P. (1982). Is treatment for substance abuse effective? *Journal of the American Medical Association*, **247**, 1423–7.

McLellan, A.T., Luborsky, L., Cacciola, J., and Griffith, J.E. (1985). New data from the addiction severity index: reliability and validity in three centers. *Journal of Nervous and Mental Diseases*, **173**, 412–23.

McLellan, A.T., O'Brien, C.P., Metzger, D., Alterman, A.I., Cornish, J., and Urschel, H. (1991). Is substance abuse treatment effective: compared to what? In *Advances in alcohol and drug dependence*, (ed. C.P. O'Brien and J. Jaffe), pp. 101–41. New York Academy of Science Press.

Miller, W.R. and Hester, R.K. (1986). Inpatient alcoholism treatment: who benefits? *American Psychologist*, **41**, 794–805.

Rounsaville, B., Weissman, M., Wilber, C., and Kleber, H. (1982). The heterogeneity of psychiatric diagnosis in treated opiate addicts. *Archives of General Psychiatry*, **39**, 161–6.

Rua, J. (1989). *Treatment works: the tragic cost of undervaluing treatment in the drug war*. Paper presented at the 'What works: an international perspective on drug abuse treatment' conference. New York State Division of Substance Abuse Press, NY.

Saxe, L., Dougherty, D., Esty, K., and Fine, M. (1983). *The effectiveness and costs of alcoholism treatment*. Health Technology Case Study 22. Office of Technology Assessment, USGPO, Washington.

Simpson, D. and Savage, L. (1980). Drug abuse treatment readmissions and outcomes. *Archives of General Psychiatry*, **39**, 896–901.

Sisk, J.E., Hatziandreu, E.J., and Hughes, R. (1990). *The effectiveness of drug abuse treatment: implications for controlling AIDS/HIV infection*, Office of Technology Assessment, USGPO, Washington.

Woody, G.E. and Cacciola, J. (1991). Report of the APA. Remission from substance dependence. In *DSM IV Sourcebook*, (ed. T. Widiger, A. Frances, and H. Pincus). American Psychiatric Association Press, Washington.

20. Short-term views will not do for long-term problems

Anders Romelsjö

Consideration will be given to two particular areas in this chapter. First, the policy implications of the research and reviews of secondary prevention in primary health care will be discussed. This area is important and has great potential, as many more people visit general practitioners than specialists for the treatment of alcohol dependence. Secondly, the rapid growth of new kinds of treatment facilites outside hospitals which seem to attract new social strata of people with alcohol problems, and the simultaneous increase in compulsory care for more severe addicts in Sweden will be analysed.

The role of primary health care

More than 15 years have passed since Wilkins (1974) carried out a pioneer study on the hidden alcoholic in general practice, and since Murray concluded that 'numerous authorities have stated that the family physician is ideally placed to detect alcoholics, but there have been remarkably few investigations of such an approach' (Murray 1977).

During the last 5–10 years the number of studies in general practice has increased considerably and there are a number of good reviews (Babor *et al.* 1986). Those studies have generally supported the contention by Wilkins and Murray. A considerable proportion of patients attending the general practitioner have an indication of high alcohol consumption and/or alcohol-related problems. King reported that 13.6 per cent of male and 1.3 per cent of female patients at a London health centre were high consumers of alcohol and yet revealed few indicators to alert the general practitioner (King 1986). In a questionnaire study of 25496 men and 36657 women from 47 group practices in Great Britain, Wallace *et al.* (1987) found that 7.6 per cent of the males admitted to a weekly alcohol consumption of 35 units or more, while 2.7 per cent of the females were drinking 21 units per week or more. Baxter *et al.* found that 25 per cent of 202 consecutive general practice subjects were likely excessive drinkers—probably the highest figure reported from general practice (Baxter *et al.* 1981). In a register study from a small industrial town in Sweden, around 300 'problem drinkers' were identified during one year in

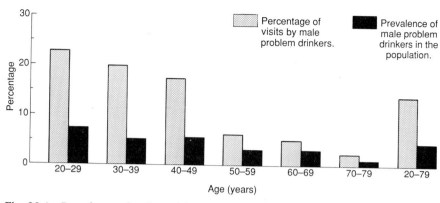

Fig. 20.1   Prevalence of male problem drinkers (%) distributed by age: percentage of visits to the general practitioners by male problem drinkers in relation to all visits by males.

at least one of about 20 registers, approximately ten times as many as were known at the district health centre before the study (Romelsjö 1988). Those 'problem drinkers' accounted for 53 per cent of all males aged 20–49 years who made six or more visits to the district health centre in 1980, while they constituted 6 per cent of the male population the same year, and also had an increased consumption of other kind of care, especially among young males (see Fig. 20.1).

Almost 15 years ago, Edwards *et al.* reported that simple advice seemed to be as effective as a more comprehensive treatment programme among male alcoholics (Edwards *et al.* 1977). Kristenson subsequently reported good results from supplying simple support and advice, a few times a year to middle-aged males with an increased level of alcohol-related gamma-glutamyltransferase (GGT) who attended a general health examination and generally were at an early stage in their potential drinking career (Kristenson 1982). There was a reduction in sick-listings, in-patient stays, and mortality in the intervention group compared with the control group, which was still evident 6 years later. Kristenson used the level of GGT as a tool in a feedback approach. Chick *et al.* (1985) reported that consistent advice given by a nurse about alcohol consumption to high consumers among in-patients on a medical ward after exclusion of more severe cases led to a reduction in alcohol-related problems and levels of GGT in the intervention group, and a significant reduction in self-reported alcohol consumption, compared with the control group.

The randomized studies by Edwards *et al.*, Kristenson, and Chick *et al.* drew attention to the astonishing results obtained with simple supportive treatment of early high alcohol consumers, and have inspired randomized secondary preventive trials in primary care. The most comprehensive study, by Wallace *et al.* (1988), shows results comparable with the best results from specialists.

Included from 47 group practices were 919 males and females who admitted a higher-than-recommended alcohol consumption (35 units or more for men and 21 units or more for women) during the last seven days. Subjects randomized to the intervention group were contacted by their ordinary general practitioner, who had received a brief training session. Subjects were shown how their weekly consumption compared with that of the general population, were given advice about the potentially harmful effects of their current level of consumption, and received a drinking diary. Males were advised to drink not more than 18 units a week and females not more than 9 units a week. They were offered new appointments after one, four, seven, and 10 months. The subjects in the control group received no advice about drinking, except at their own request. At one year follow-up, a mean reduction in the consumption of alcohol of 18.2 units per week had occurred in 'treated' men, compared with 8.1 units in controls. The proportion of men with excessive consumption had dropped by 43.7 per cent in the 'treatment' group, compared with 25.5 per cent in the control group. The reduction among females was of similar magnitude, and the differences between the groups were significant. At one year, the mean value for GGT had dropped significantly more in 'treated' males than in male controls, which was not the case among females. The reduction in consumption in both sexes and the reduction in GGT activity among males increased significantly with the number of general practitioner interventions.

Scott and Anderson (1991) reported similar results in a comparable study with group practices in the Oxfordshire area of the UK. Heather *et al.* (1987) and Romelsjö *et al.* (1989) found a marked reduction in alcohol consumption, alcohol-related problems, and/or alcohol-related GGt in both intervention and control groups after one year, but no difference in change between the groups in randomized studies. The subjects in the control groups in those two studies were informed, or could easily get the impression that, their current alcohol consumption was too high. The authors separately contended that this probably meant a kind of minimal intervention also among the subjects in the control group, which might explain the lack of differences between the intervention and the control groups.

To conclude, there is every reason to support the policy advocated by Wallace *et al.*, that 'general practitioners and other members of the primary health care team should be encouraged to include counselling about alcohol consumption in their preventive activities'. Those authors have calculated that intervention by general practitioners could reduce to moderate levels the alcohol consumption of some 250 000 males and 67 500 females if the results of this study were applied to the UK. What are the results of treatment of that many 'ordinary' alcoholics and what are the costs?

The seemingly straightforward policy implication would presumably be to spread and market those studies and results by whatever means throughout society, among decision-makers and general practitioners. There are, however, real problems. One problem is the low level of interest in alcohol problems among many general practitioners and other personnel in primary health care. There are many reasons for this, such as the legitimate interest in other areas of the widespread field of health and diseases that the general practioner is supposed to harvest. Studies have shown that interest in primary health care for patients with alcohol problems generally is not very great. Studies of around 300 employees at 15 district health centres in the Stockholm area in Sweden showed reluctance, especially among nurses and nurse assistants, to work with alcoholics perhaps because they see more of the negative aspects of alcohol problems in some patients than the general practitioners do (Sandberg and Romelsjö 1985). However, it is interesting to note that 91 per cent wanted more education about alcohol and 98.5 per cent thought that it is essential to reach high consumers of alcohol at an early stage. The attitudes were generally more positive at those district health centres which had received a limited education about alcohol in connection with a primary health care based health examination and the secondary prevention trial. It should be easier to obtain understanding and support for secondary preventive activities nowadays, when definite results are available of successful results from brief interventions by general practitioners.

Also, Drummond *et al.* found, after an initial detailed assessment and advice session by a specialist, the treatment provided to 'ordinary' problem drinkers by the general practitioners was at least as effective as that from a specialist clinic (Drummond *et al.* 1991).

The general practitioner in the primary health care setting has a great potential role, especially in the finding and treating of early stage problem drinkers for certain reasons:

1. The general practitioner meets a large segment of the general population.

2. Subjects with alcohol-related problems are over-represented.

3. A potentional alcohol-related problem is a good starting-point.

4. The general practitioner can use the best methods.

5. The general practitioner and nurse know about the patient.

6. Scientific basis.

7. The costs are low.

This policy is not a short-term view for a long-term problem. To realize the potential will, however, need long-term and enduring education and policy changing initiatives. The policy implications may be controversial if it is suggested that there should be changes in the distribution of resources within the health care sectors based on a positive interpretation of those results from primary health care. Instead, a way forward may be the closer collaboration between specialists and general practitioners on equal terms and with respect for each other's domains and qualifications.

The increase in compulsory care of addicts and the rapid growth of treatment resources for new social strata in Sweden

There has been a simultaneous increase in compulsory care for certain groups of alcoholics and drug addicts and a great increase in new treatment ideologies and treatment facilities for largeliy new social groups with alcohol problems, at a time when there has been a profound decline in alcohol-related problems in Sweden. This development raises important questions: is there any basis in treatment research for those trends? Are other societal forces and factors more responsible for those trends in ideology, and policy? Is compulsory care compatible with medical ethics? This development and questions like those have attracted great interest and vigorous debate in Sweden, this issue appears to be more difficult, more challenging, and more controversial than the question of the role of primary health care.

Compulsory care of alcoholics has always been allowed in Sweden and is based on laws approved by the Parliament. It is widely recognized that Sweden, for many decades, has had a rather restrictive set of policies in the field of alcohol, and this has also had an impact on treatment policy. The first public referendum in Sweden in 1922 concerned alcohol policy. A proposal from a Governmental Commission prohibited sales and consumption of alcoholic beverages. A more liberal movement headed by the young physician Ivan Bratt won the referendum by a slight majority with 50.5 per cent, compared with 49.5 per cent for the prohibition line. Alcohol rationing was then introduced and lasted until 1955. Alcoholic beverages can still only be bought at state owned retail monopoly stores, which are only open in the daytime from Monday to Friday, and at restaurants, where 12 per cent of the alcohol is sold, at high prices. The referendum in 1922 also meant that Temperance Boards were established in all the thousands of municipalities in Sweden. They were empowered to take actions against subjects who misused alcohol. Compulsory measures (treatment at institutions and coercive supervision) were by law effected by decision of the public Temperance Boards, elected political bodies in the municipalities, and based on investigations and suggestions by the social welfare agencies. The alcohol ration book could also be taken away from those subjects or their ration could be reduced. This was, in fact, rather common. This period has been analysed by Bruun and others (Bruun and Frånberg 1985).

After the abolition of alcohol rationing in 1955, alcohol-related consequences increased rapidly, and much more than alcohol consumption, which increased by approximately 60 per cent from 1964 to a peak of 7.6 litres of 100 per cent ethanol per annum per capita aged 15 years or more in 1976. The increase was especially great among young people and women.

A more liberal climate of opinion had begun to question the Temperance laws and their implementation and the number of compulsory measures

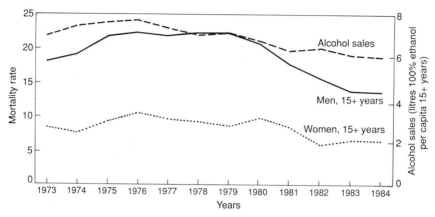

Fig. 20.2   Mortality in liver cirrhosis (underlying cause of death) in Sweden during 1973–84, ages 15+ years. Age-standardized rates per 100 000 inhabitants.

decreased. The Temperance Movement, which was very strong at the beginning of the century has been weakened profoundly since the Second World War. The disease model had grown, and there was a tremendous increase in the number of subjects with an alcohol abuse diagnosis under the hospital care. The organization of the social welfare agencies changed. An organization with specialized bodies for child welfare, economic support, alcohol abuse, and implementation of the Temperance laws was replaced by a more unified organization. The social welfare offices were supposed to deal with all the client's problems from a holistic perspective. This also meant a weakening of special competence, that is in the alcohol abuse field. The idea that alcohol abuse and addiction were caused by social circumstances and thus a symptom of deficiencies in society acquired strong support among social workers and in society as a whole. The societal concern over reports of alcohol abuse, especially among young people, increased. In 1977, it was declared in Parliament unanimously among the political parties that the goal of Swedish alcohol policy was 'to reduce alcohol consumption and hence alcohol-related problems'. Several restrictive alcohol policy measures were undertaken, and the alcohol question was really on the political and societal agenda in the latter part of the 1970s and the beginning of the 1980s. Alcohol consumption declined by 22 per cent in eight years, more among young people, and the rates of alcohol-related consequences even more (Romelsjö 1987) (see Fig. 20.2).

In this situation, in 1982, three laws came into force as a result of an investigation by a Government Commission. The most important was the new 'Social services act', a framework law which emphasized the rights of citizens to many forms of help from their local borough councils. The law also declared that those in need should be treated on the basis of respect for their self-determination and integrity. Section 11 in that law states:

The social welfare committee is to work for the prevention and 9-counteraction of the use of alcohol and other habit-forming agents. Particular attention is to be paid to measures on behalf of children and young persons in this connection. The social welfare committee is to disseminate knowledge concerning the harmful effects of abuse and concerning the help available by means of information supplied to authorities, groups and individual persons and by means of activation measures. The committee is also to support the individual alcoholic or addict and to ensure that he recieves the assistance or care which he needs in order to overcome his abuse.

The emphasis of the new Act was upon a voluntary partnership between social services and their clients.

The 'Care of alcoholics and drug abusers act' (LVM) concerns compulsory care of adult alcoholics and drug addicts. Some of the members in the Commission had wanted to dispense with the compulsory care of adults completely, based on a strong opinion among social workers and their chiefs. There remained others who were convinced that compulsory care could be neccessary. The LVM was thus a compromise. It was made clear that LVM should only be used as a last resort when alcoholics or addicts behaved in such a way as to put their health in serious danger, or to seriously damage themselves or their kin to the extent that there was an urgent need for care. In such cases proceedings could be started which could result in individuals being taken into care for up to two months with a possibility of a further extension of two months. It was argued that such a period would be sufficient to wean somebody off drink or drugs and motivate them to accept help voluntarily thereafter.

The introduction of the LVM resulted in a marked reduction in the number of subjects being taken into compulsory care. The Commission behind the new law was asked to monitor the operation of the new act and report back to the government. In 1987 (five years after the introduction of the LVM) the Commission's report on LVM was published, together with a set of proposals for a new law with the same title—'The misusers, the social services and compulsory care' (Governmental Commission 1987). The Commission was concerned about the situation of those alcoholics and drug addicts who were the target group for the LVM, that is, the most severe cases. In the 1960s, most alcoholics had a job but now the majority were unemployed and lived either on a state pension or on social assistance. More were becoming homeless. The death rata of alcoholics was higher than for the general population. This was a especially true for young alcoholics. Drug addiction was increasingly associated with crime, sickness, and prostitution. At around this time, the first cases of infection with HIV and of AIDS also appeared.

Although most people left LVM-homes in a better physical and mental state than when they entered, the long-term prognosis for them keeping off drugs and drink was not good. Almost half of the alcoholics and 70 per cent of the drug addicts inmates absconded. None of this led the Commission to question the desirability of compulsory care. The poor recovery rate was

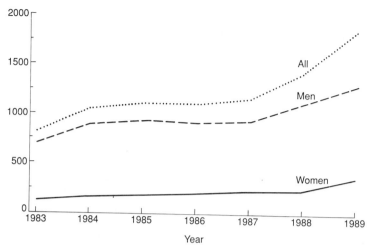

Fig. 20.3 Number of persons subject to compulsory care on ground of abuse in Sweden during 1983–89.

attributed to inadequate follow-up care by the social services. The Commission recommended that the scope of the LVM should be widened, which also became the result (Fig. 20.3). It was suggested that a social indicator clause be added so the law could be applied to those with seriously worsened living conditions. It was felt that these changes would enable the authorities to intervene at an earlier stage in the career of an alcoholic or an addict, particulary the young. The Commission based its arguments not upon the increase in misuse so much as the worsening health and social conditions of existing misusers.

The Commission suggested that the law should place an obligation on the authorities to intervene, not simply empower them to do so. They also suggested that the maximum duration of compulsory care should be increased to six months instead of two months. The local social welfare committees as well as the police should be given the power to take somebody into immediate custody when the circumstances were particulary acute. The local welfare committees were identified as having the responsibility of ensuring that alcoholics and addicts received long-term follow-up treatment after their stay at a LVM-home and that they were helped to find jobs, accommodation, education, and training. The social services committees were advised to take a more active role in preventive work. A cut-back had already been made in resources to the social services, while they thus were given more tasks.

Gould has described the vigorous debate around the Commission's report (Gould 1989). The Government's proposal for legislation was approved by the Swedish Riksdag (Parliament) in June 1988. Almost all of the Left Communist Party, four social-democrats and one liberal voted against the proposal. This means that the vast majority of the members of the SAP (Social Democratic

Workers' Party) which held the Government, the entire Conservative Party, all but one of the liberals and the whole Centre Party voted for the new version of the LVM. The debate and the decision show that there was an alliance between authorities and elements on the political left and right, and libertarian elements across the political spectrum. Gould makes the intepretation that it seemed to be possible, in the same ideological framework, to unite those who felt that something drastic should be done for the weakest members of the society and those who wished to discipline the lumpenproletariat or malingerers.

Parliament also concluded that research into compulsory care had been too much neglected and claimed that it was important to follow the implementation of LVM with qualified research and to assess the changes in law. A report was published in the end of 1989, about one year after the introduction of the widened LVM (Delegation for Social Research 1989), by a working party including Swedish scientists. This report shows that very little is known about the effects of compulsory care. There seems to be no scientific support for the idea that two or six months of compulsory care is superior to two weeks of compulsory care. There were no studies available showing that subjects are more motivated towards voluntary care after compulsory care. Statistics for 1989 show that only 20 per cent of those subjects with severe alcoholism and/or drug addicts continued with voluntary care. The average duration of stay was 131 days in 1989, an increase of 55 days, or 72 per cent, compared with 1988. The average duration of stay was 128 days for men and 140 days for women. A total of 76 per cent of the 1803 persons subjected to measures under the LVM were men and 24 per cent were women. Thus, the decisions by Parliament on compulsory care do not seem to be based on scientific studies.

It is not yet known if there is an association between changes in the extent of compulsory care and rates of severe alcohol-related problems in society. Around 50 per cent of the applications to the County Courts are abandoned. Those subjects could constitute a control group to other addicts given care under the LVM—admittedly not perfect, but an acceptable control group for some studies.

Compulsory care and ethics

The change in the LVM provoked vigorous debate about a fundamental ethical issue in the Swedish Medical Association. One paragraph in the LVM states that a patient who is voluntarily cared for at a hospital, while at the same time sentenced to compulsory care due to addiction, could and should be prevented from leaving hospital. On behalf of the Swedish Psychiatric Association, the World Psychiatric Association assessed this paragraph in the LVM, found that it was not compatible with paragraph 7 in the Hawaii declaration 'par 7.. if a patient or some third party demands actions contrary

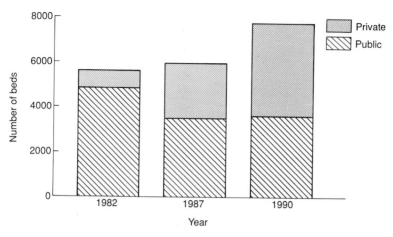

Fig. 20.4 Institutional care of abusers in Sweden at public and private institutions in 1982, 1987, and 1989. (Reproduced from Johansson (1991)).

to scientific knowledge or ethical principles the psychiatrist must refuse to cooperate'. The debate was not silenced by this assessment by the World Psychiatric Association. Some psychiatrists were of the view that the international criticism of the LVM could be explained by incorrect translation from Swedish to English, while one professor in psychiatry felt sympathetic to use of 'loving or tender compulsion' as he put it, in certain cases. This view probably reflected a widespread opinon among Swedish psychiatrists.

Statistics on voluntary and compulsory care

The number of treatment or residential homes has increased from 186 at the introduction of the LVM in 1983 to 326 in 1989 (Statistics Sweden 1989), an increase of 72 per cent in seven years, while the number of admissions has increased by 18 per cent and alcohol consumption by 7 per cent during this period. There has especially been a rapid growth of private facilities. Most well known are, perhaps, treatment facilites based on the Minnesota model since the middle of the 1980s (Cook 1988; Keso 1988), recruiting new social strata to treatment and treatment facilites organized by a free church. This is a new situation in Sweden, also because of the professional marketing and the profit interest. In 1982 there were a total of 737 beds in private institutions, while by 1990 there were 4158 beds in such institutions, an unplanned increase of 464 per cent in 8 years (Fig. 20.4) (Johansson 1991). During the same period, the number of beds in public institutions decreased from 4857 to 3622. Those institutions came to rely heavily on public interest and support. In 1988 a survey conducted among all the Minnesota model institutions in Sweden showed that the municipal social services paid for the treatment of

81 per cent of the patients. Treatment in the privately owned institutions is generally substantially more expensive than in the public ones. Thus, at the end of the 1980s there were, in Sweden, two major trends in treatment: a widening of the scope of compulsory care for severe, often non-working, alcoholics and addicts, and a growth of facilities, also attracting new middle-class social strata. This change in treatment policy was neither based on new treatment research, nor on a consensus conference with all established specialists. It remains to be seen whether this development will mean more than short-term solutions for long-term problems.

Conclusion

The two dominant trends in treatment in Sweden are the increase in the compulsory care of alcoholics and drug addicts between 1983 and 1989, and the rapid growth of new kinds of treatment facilities, mainly based on the AA model, which may attract new social strata. These developments, can neither be understood as an indicator of advances in treatment or treatment research, nor as an indicator of increase in the rates of very serious alcohol- and drug-related problems. Is this development instead an indicator of failure on the part of social policy and/or an indicator of changes in the societal attitudes to respond to, or care for, people with severe problems, and to alcohol as a common cause of illness? Is there a link between those two developments? Is this development—compulsory care for deterioriated people and more resources to institutional care of people with a better prognosis—sound, or an indication of reduced interest in some of the weakest members of society?

References

Babor, T., Ritson, B., and Hodgson, R. (1986). Alcohol-related problems in the primary health care setting: a review of early intervention strategies. *British Journal of Addiction*, 81, 23–46.

Baxter, S., Fink, R., Leader, A.R., and Rosalki, S.B. (1981). Laboratory tests for excessive alcohol consumption evaluated in general practice. *British Journal on Alcohol and Alcoholism*, 15, 164–6.

Bruun, K. and Frånberg, P. (ed.) (1985). *Den svenska supen.* (The Swedish snaps). Prisma, Stockholm, (in Swedish).

Chick, J., Lloyd, G., and Crombie, E. (1985). Counselling problem drinkers in medical wards. *British Medical Journal*, 290, 965–7.

Cook, C. (1988). The Minnesota model in the management of drug and alcohol dependency: miracle, method or myth? Part I. The philosophy and the programme. *British Journal of Addiction*, 83, 625–34.

Delegationen för social forskning (1989). (The Delegation for Social Research). *Research about abusers and the care, with special reference to compulsory care.* Stockholm: Delegationen för social forskning. (The Delegation for Social Research). (En rapport från LVM-gruppen). (A report from the LVM Group), (in Swedish).

Drummond, D.C., Thom, B., Brown, C., Edwards, G., and Mullan, M. (1991). Specialist versus general practitioner treatment of problem drinkers. *Lancet*, 336, 915–18.

Edwards, G., Orford, J., Egert, S., Guthrie, S., Hawker, A., Hensman, C., *et al.* (1977). Alcoholism: a controlled trial of 'treatment and advice'. *J. Stud. Alc.*, **38**, 1004–31.

Govermental Commission (Socialberedningen) (1987). *Missbrukarna, socialtjänsten och tvånget.* (The misusers, the social services and the compulsory care). Socialberedningen, Stockholm. (Betänkande av socialberedningen). (SOU 1987:22). (in Swedish).

Gould, A. (1989). Cleaning the people's home: recent developments in Sweden's addiction policy. *British Journal of Addiction*, **84**, 731–41.

Heather, N., Campion, P., Neville, R., and Maccabe, D. (1987). Evaluation of a controlled drinking minimal intervention for problem drinkers in general practice (the DRAMS scheme). *Journal of the Royal College of General Practitioners*, **37**, 358–63.

Johansson, G. (1991). *Privat och offentligt i vården.* (Private and public in care). National Board of Health and Welfare, Stockholm, (in Swedish).

Keso, L. (1988). Inpatient treatment of employed alcoholics: a randomized clincial trial on Hazelden and traditional treatment. Helsinki Central University Hospital, Helsinki.

King, M. (1986). At risk drinking among general practice attenders: prevalence, characteristics and alcohol-related problems. *British Journal of Psychiatry*, **148**, 533–40.

Kristenson, H. (1982). Studies on alcohol-related disabilities in a medicial intervention programme in middleaged males. Malmö. (Thesis). Lund University.

Murray, R. (1977). Screening and early detection instruments for disablties related to alcohol. In (ed. G. Edwards, M.M. Gross, M. Keller, J. Moser, and R. Room) *Alcohol-related disabilities.* (WHO Offset Publication No. 32) WHO, Geneva.

Romelsjö, A. (1987). *Epidemiological studies on the relationship between a decline in alcohol consumption, social factors and alcohol-related disabilities in Stockholm County and in the whole of Sweden.* (Thesis). Karolinska Institutet, Sundbyberg.

Romelsjö, A. (1988). Consumption of care among problem drinkers in a small industrial town in Sweden. *Family Practice*, **5**, 271–7.

Romelsjö, A., Andersson, L., Barrner, H., Borg, S., Granstrand, C., Hultman, O., *et al.* (1989). A randomized study of secondary prevention of early stage problem drinkers in primary health care. British Journal of Addiction, **84**, 1319–28.

Sandberg, P. and Romelsjö, A. (1985). *Inställningen till alkoholmissbrukare inom primärvården i Stockholms län.* (The attitudes to alcohol abusers in primary health care in Stockholm county). Sundbyberg: landstingets hälsovård. (Grön rapport nr 111). (In Swedish).

Scott, E. and Anderson, P. (1991). Randomized controlled trial of general practitioner intervention in women with excessive alcohol consumption. *Drug and Alcohol Review*, **10**, 313–22.

Statistics Sweden (National Central Bureau of Statistics) (1990). *Insatser för vuxna missbrukare 1989.* (Measures for adult abusers). Statistics Sweden, Örebro, (in Swedish).

Wallace, P.G., Brennan, P.J., and Haines, A.P. (1987). Drinking patterns in general practice. *Journal of the Royal College General Practice*, **37**, 354–7.

Wallace, P.G., Cutler, S., and Haines, A.P. (1988). Randomised controlled trial of general practitioner in patients with excessive alcohol consumption. *British Medical Journal*, **297**, 663–8.

Wilkins, R.H. (1974). *The hidden alcoholic in general practice.* Elek Science London.

21. Interpretation of addiction treatment outcome research: skill or racket?

D. Colin Drummond

Being a line judge at Wimbledon is a difficult and thankless task. A tennis ball is delivered somewhere in the direction of a thin white line at over 100 miles per hour. A decision must be made in a split-second, about whether the ball was in or out based at best on the most minimal data. After many hours of being ignored by the crowd, that little patch of grass where the ball lands, for a couple of milliseconds, belongs to the line judge. He or she faces public humiliation at the hands of professional tennis players' temper tantrums in front of an audience of millions if the decision is wrong, and sometimes even when it is right! That split-second decision will undergo micro-dissection by armchair critics who, unlike the line judge, have the benefit of slow-motion video replay.

So it is with treatment outcome research in the addictions. While clearly operating at a much slower pace, treatment services are delivered by therapists with varying degrees of drive and skill. Patients present highly variable returns of service and often leave the court before the end of the first set. To the humble research line judge the interpretation of such a therapeutic encounter is at best an extremely difficult business. How can one hope to succeed under such adverse playing conditions?

This chapter will explore three difficulties in the life of the hapless treatment researcher. In doing so, the intention is to bring greater precision to the practice of treatment research. And for non-players who like to follow the game, it is hoped that some insight can be made into the complexities of the problems involved. First, it is important to examine why this might be an important activity to engage in.

What policy makers want to know

The question most often asked of the researcher by the policy maker is 'does treatment work?' On the face of it, this is a perfectly reasonable question to ask of the researcher, in that this is the implicit aim of most treatment outcome research. However, in spite of, or perhaps as a consequence of, the large body of available research literature on the subject, the answer to such a question is likely to be less than straightforward. The researcher is, then, faced with three options:

1. Lie: 'of course it works'. This is probably the easiest option, and that which is likely to bring the most favourable policy outcome for the treatment community. It may not, however, rest easily on the researcher's scientific integrity. Furthermore, the scientifically aware policymaker may not be satisfied until evidence to support this claim is presented, or more embarrassingly, they may be aware of evidence to the contrary.

2. Tell the truth: 'probably' or 'yes and no'. This option risks the researcher being branded as vague and of having an inability to come to terms with the demands of the real world of policy.

3. Ask 'how long have you got?' This risks losing the attention of the world-weary policy maker. It is important, however, adequately to inform those whose responsibility it is to develop rational treatment policies of the complexities in interpretation of treatment outcome research. We also need to take stock of the extent to which the technology we have available at present addresses the important policy questions. Without an adequate understanding of the difficulties in the interpretation of treatment outcome research we will be unable to improve the effectiveness of treatment, and the methods of treatment research will not improve.

The complexity of treatment outcome research

Treatment is a complex business

The treatment of people suffering from addictive disorders is not comparable to giving an injection and expecting instant cure. Would only that it were so simple. This may seem such a facile statement as to be hardly worth making. However, it is necessary constantly to remind ourselves that the reductionistic way in which we use the shorthand terms 'treatment' and 'addiction' may easily be misconstrued by the unwary policy maker as being akin to the process of treating infection with antibiotics.

Clearly, treatment, even within our current limited understanding, is a complex and interactive process. Patients bring to treatment different motivations, expectations, past experiences, and may have very different wishes and needs. Similarly, therapists work with markedly differing views of the nature of the disorder and of the treatment required. They may operate with differing degrees of flexibility and may have different levels of skill and training. The way in which these two individuals interact and the extent to which they form a positive therapeutic alliance may crucially determine outcome.

We understand, at present, little of the nature of 'motivation' and its influence on treatment. There are, however, strong theoretical reasons to expect that a wide range of both patient and therapist characteristics may interact in such a way as to influence treatment effectiveness (Brickman *et al.* 1982; Institute of Medicine 1990). Patient attributions and degree of dependence, as well as social stability and support, have already emerged as important factors of this type. While there is some empirical evidence to support this notion (Miller 1991; Annis 1990), the search for such treatment matching effects is likely to continue for some time and will require considerable research investment.

The treatment process is often of long duration, involving multiple contacts with the same or different therapists before lasting improvement in the patient's condition occurs. This will be important in assessing treatment efficacy. Most often we study the effects of a single treatment episode on a group of people who are at varying points in a drinking or drug taking career, rather than trying to understand the possible cumulative effects of treatment in the context of the individual's life history. The nature of the patient's disorder, and hence their treatment needs, are also likely to covary with their stage of psychosocial development (Scaturo 1987). This underlines the importance of studying addictions in the long term (Vaillant 1983; Edwards *et al.* 1983).

Even within one treatment episode it may be difficult to disentangle the 'non-specific' factors which influence outcome from the 'specific' factors which we originally set about trying to evaluate. Two treatments may differ, not only in terms of their specific modality, such as methadone maintenance compared with detoxification, or group versus individual therapy, but also in terms of the amount of contact between patient and therapist, or the quality and commitment of the therapist in the two treatment modalities. This problem is common to all areas of the evaluation of psychotherapy (Bergin and Lambert 1978); the 'placebo effect' is also a recognized problem in the testing of pharmaceutical agents. The development of methods of understanding and evaluating the process of treatment are likely to be crucial in this respect. In addiction treatment research the precise process of change is often not specified or measured, favouring simply a crude global measure of outcome, such as alcohol consumption or problems at the follow-up point. In this sense the cue exposure paradigm particularly lends itself to such a process analysis, in that it is possible to monitor extinction of responses to repeated exposure to an alcoholic drink (in the case of an alcoholic), during the course of treatment (Drummond *et al.* 1990*a*). This process research conducted more at a micro level of analysis needs to be developed, rather than assuming that a move towards more or larger-scale controlled trials is likely to bring improvements in understanding.

Outcome is a complex business

What do we mean by 'outcome'? The answer to this question may appear obvious, but the more one explores this issue, the more complex it becomes. It is perhaps because of this complexity that researchers have tended to view outcome in rather narrow terms, for example by categorizing subjects in a treatment study as being either 'abstinent' or 'relapsed', or as being in a 'good' or 'bad' outcome category at the point of follow-up. Such an approach certainly makes the results of such studies easier to interpret, but such categorizations are often arbitrary and oversimplistic.

There are four ways in which our current knowledge counsels against viewing treatment outcome in simplistic, black-and-white terms. First, we know that outcome is statistically multi-dimensional, as indeed is the nature of addiction itself (Babor *et al.* 1988; Drummond, 1990). It is possible, at least in certain cases, to experience a significant reduction in the number and severity of problems associated with the use of drugs or alcohol following treatment without necessarily being completely abstinent. Similarly, abstinence or reductions in the use of a drug to an objectively low level does not guarantee the resolution of problems. Treatment may help to enhance an individual's adaptation to the environment without necessarily altering the quantity of use of the substance to a significant degree. This underlines the importance of the measurement of multiple dimensions of outcome. However, having done so, it is highly questionable whether one treatment can be assumed to be truly better than another simply on the basis that one out of a whole range of outcome measures is found to be significant in a statistical analysis. If we are going to make multiple outcome measures, we should routinely employ multivariate statistical analysis, as has become commonplace in other areas of basic and applied research (Drummond *et al.* 1991).

Secondly, outcome is not a categorical phenomenon, it is a dynamic process. Just as many individuals move in and out of episodes of heavy drinking prior to treatment, the same is true of the post-treatment period. Taylor *et al.* (1985) have graphically demonstrated such an effect in their 10-year follow-up study of 68 alcoholics. Figure 21.1 is a barycentric plot which shows the relative length of time spent by each individual in each of three outcome categories during the follow-up period ('abstinent', 'troubled', and 'social drinking'). It can be seen that only one individual spent the whole follow-up period in a state of continuous social drinking. The majority are distributed between periods of complete abstinence or troubled drinking. Similarly, in a follow-up study of heroin addicts, Gossop *et al.* (1989) found that while 71 per cent resumed drug use within 6 weeks of discharge from treatment, by 6 months 46 per cent were abstinent. The implication of these findings for future research is that outcome is a more subtle and dynamic phenomenon than is implied by categorical cumulative survival indices.

On a related point, the length of follow-up may crucially determine whether treatment effects are detected by a particular study. Differences in outcome between two treatment groups might only exist for a brief period following the end of the treatment episode, only later to disappear before follow-up is completed. It is a moot point whether such short-lived treatment effects signify any real advantage of one treatment over another. In terms of the scientific method as applied to addiction treatment, it would be most appropriate to

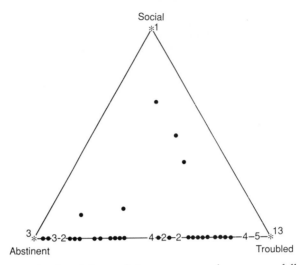

Fig. 21.1 Barycentric plot of the total time spent over the ten years follow-up in each behaviour category for the 68 individuals. Each point represents one individual and the numbers indicate superimposed points. (From Taylor *et al.* 1986. Published with permission.)

specify in advance of hypothesis testing what extent and duration of differences are required to reject the null hypothesis.

Thirdly, it would be erroneous to assume that treatment is the only determinant of outcome. Many other factors, including patient characteristics, such as social background, can be more important determinants of outcome than is treatment itself. With the aid of path analysis, Cronkite and Moos (1978) have elegantly demonstrated the individual contribution of variables which will confound treatment outcome studies. Outcome is therefore not only multi-dimensional but also multi-determined.

Finally, there is the question of the extent to which measures of outcome are true reflections of events in the real world. There is an extensive literature surrounding the evaluation of validity of self report measures in the alcoholism treatment field (for example Midanik 1982; Watson *et al.* 1984). While this issue is discussed in more detail in another chapter (see McLellan, Chapter 19), it would appear that the validity of outcome measures will to a large extent be determined by the sophistication of the methods used. It has been discovered, for example, that interview methods which involve asking subjects to recall their pattern and quantity of drinking in the context of other more readily recalled events, such as in the 'time line follow-back' method (Sobell *et al.* 1988) will provide better estimates of drinking than less sophisticated methods. There is a need to standardize measures used across different studies to allow comparisons to be made.

So, in summary, in common with treatment (and indeed addiction itself), outcome is a complex phenomenon. It would be wrong to suggest, however, that the difficulties in finding an adequate means of measuring outcome should discourage efforts to evaluate treatment. Such research needs to be strengthened and the measures improved and standardized. The aim is more to discourage simplistic notions of outcome which may lead to the erroneous interpretation of treatment studies.

Research is a complex business

Much of what has been said so far will make the thrust of this statement only too apparent. A few additional points about the nature of treatment research, however, should be made. There is little doubt that the controlled trial is the best means at our disposal to assess treatment effectiveness. Uncontrolled studies, while of interest in other respects, cannot adequately answer the policy maker's effectiveness question. There are a number of factors which may limit the interpretation even of controlled studies: some representing limitations of controlled trials in general, while other difficulties specifically attend the evaluation of addiction treatment.

Random assignment to different treatment conditions increases the likelihood of establishing groups with similar characteristics. Where sample sizes are small, as is often the case in addiction treatment trials, the possibility of chance differences occurring between the groups increases, however. This may present significant difficulties when the characteristic with which the groups differ by chance also happens to be one which is known independently to influence outcome. Efforts should therefore be made to ensure that, as far as possible, treatment groups are adequately matched at intake.

Even if we are able adequately to match the groups, it is possible that the patients may have their own view of which treatment group they would like to be in. Following randomization, patients may not follow the prescribed treatment course or may cross-over into a different treatment group by seeking treatment from another agency. The extent to which the treatment groups in reality receive different treatment should be monitored during follow-up (for example Drummond *et al.* 1990*b*).

A further problem in relation to small scale treatment trials concerns the detection of patient–treatment matching effects. This should be seen as distinct from group matching at intake, discussed above. While there may be no difference in outcome overall between two treatment groups, it is possible that such a finding conceals important interaction effects. Certain subgroups may fare better in one treatment compared with another. For example, Orford *et al.* (1976) found, in a controlled trial of intensive treatment versus advice in a group of alcoholics, that while there was no difference in outcome overall the more severely dependent patients had a better outcome in the more intensive treatment. Several interactive or matching effects have been found in other sudies, as described above. One must therefore be cautious in dismissing an overall negative result as truly representing no difference in outcome.

The final point concerns the generalizability of findings of treatment studies. To what extent does a research trial reflect treatment in the 'real world'? Such research is often conducted in well staffed centres by motivated clinical researchers. Many patients may be excluded from research studies by virtue of presenting special problems or may simply refuse to give their consent to participate. Furthermore, there may be a reluctance on the part of both journals and researchers to publish negative findings.

Conclusions

While methods of evaluating treatment outcome in the addictions have improved in recent years they remain less than perfect. Just as the line judge at Wimbledon faces a difficult task, many pitfalls also attend the interpretation of treatment outcome research. Rather than hanging up one's blazer and dismissing treatment research as one big racket, or alternatively taking the easy option and blindly exercising the eye of faith, I have proposed several ways in which greater precision could be introduced into treatment research and its interpretation.

Before embarking on the next treatment trial, or briefing the policy maker on the question of 'does treatment work', we need to tackle some of the problems raised in this chapter. We need to know more about the process of treatment and of recovery. In doing so, we need to take a longer-term view than is typical of treatment research at present. The nature of addiction and outcome needs to be viewed in a more sophisticated and multi-dimensional way. Most of all, like the Wimbledon line judge, we need to worry more about getting our interpretation of research wrong.

References

Annis, H.M. (1990). Effective treatment for drug and alcohol problems: what do we know? In: *Institute of Medicine. Broadening the Base of Treatment for Alcohol Problems*. National Academy Press, Washington.

Babor, T.F., Dolinsky, Z., Rounsaville, B., and Jaffe, J. (1988). Unitary versus multidimensional models of alcoholism treatment outcome: an empirical study. *Journal of Studies on Alcohol*, **49**, 167–77.

Bergin, A.E. and Lambert, M.J. (1978). The evaluation of therapeutic outcomes. In *Handbook of psychotherapy and behavior change: an empirical analysis*, (2nd edn), (ed. S.L. Garfield and A.E. Bergin), pp. 233–45. Aldine, Chicago.

Brickman, P., Rabinowitz, V.C., Karuza, J., Coates, D., Cohn, E., and Kidder, L. (1982). Models of helping and coping. *American Psychologist*, **37**, 368–84.

Cronkite, R.C. and Moos, R.H. (1978). Evaluating alcoholism treatment programs: an integrated approach. *Journal of Consulting and Clinical Psychology*, **46**, 1105–19.

Drummond, D.C. (1990). The relationship between alcohol dependence and alcohol-related problems in a clinical population. *British Journal of Addiction*, **85**, 357–66.

Drummond, D.C., Cooper, T., and Glautier, S.P. (1990*a*). Conditioned learning in alcohol dependence: implications for cue exposure treatment. *British Journal of Addiction*, 85, 725–43. ˙

Drummond, D.C., Thom, B., Brown, C., Edwards, G., and Mullan, M. (1990*b*). Specialist versus general practitioner treatment of problem drinkers. *Lancet*, 336, 1583–4.

Drummond, D.C., Taylor, C., and Edwards, G. (1991). Analysis of treatment outcome in problem drinking. *Lancet*, 337, 295–6.

Edwards, G., Duckitt, A., Oppenheimer, E., Sheehan, M., and Taylor, C. (1983). What happens to alcoholics? *Lancet*, ii, 269–71.

Gossop, M., Green, L., Phillips, G., and Bradley, B. (1989). Lapse, relapse and survival among opiate addicts after treatment: a prospective follow-up study. *British Journal of Addiction*, 154, 348–53.

Institute of Medicine (1990). *Broadening the base of treatment for alcohol problems*. National Academy Press, Washington.

Miller, W.R. (1991). Alcoholism treatment outcome. Paper presented to the 36th International Institute on the Prevention and Treatment of Alcoholism. ICAA, Stockholm, Sweden.

Mindanik, L. (1982). The validity of self-reported alcohol consumption and alcohol problems: a literature review. *British Journal of Addiction*, 77, 357–82.

Orford, J., Oppenheimer, E., and Edwards, G. (1976). Abstinence or control: the outcome for excessive drinkers two years after consultation. *Behaviour Research and Therapy*, 14, 409–18.

Scaturo, D.J. (1987). Toward an adult developmental conceptualization of alcohol abuse: a review of the literature. *British Journal of Addiction*, 82, 857–70.

Sobell, L.C., Sobell, M.B., Leo, G.I., and Cancilla, A. (1988). Reliability of a timeline method: assessing normal drinkers' reports of recent drinking and comparative evaluation across several populations. *British Journal of Addiction*, 83, 393–402.

Taylor, C., Brown, D., Duckitt, A., Edwards, G., Oppenheimer, E., and Sheehan, M. (1985). Patterns of outcome: drinking histories over ten years. *British Journal of Addiction*, 80, 45–50.

Watson, C.G., Tilleskjor, C., Hoodecheck-Schow, E., Pucel, J., and Jacobs, L. (1984). Do alcoholics give valid self-reports? *Journal of Studies on Alcohol*, 38, 344–8.

Vaillant, G.E. (1983). *The natural history of alcoholism*. Harvard University Press, Cambridge, MA.

22. Limits to generalizability in treatment research

Marc Alan Schuckit

There was a time when the invocation of clinical experience to 'do the best possible' was all that medicine and psychology had to offer. With few data, limited funds, and subsequent modest results, therapeutic efforts inched forward using a haphazard reliance on philosophical beliefs and the charisma of the practitioner.

Today, behavioural medicine is expected to function as a science (Goodwin and Guze. 1989; Institute of medicine 1990). The decision to offer treatment and the selection of a specific intervention cannot be justified solely by the large number of relevant patients, but optimally rests with data that demonstrate that the regime successfully accomplishes the relevant goals with a beneficial ratio of assets to liabilities (Helzer *et al.* 1991; Institute of Medicine 1980). While an estimated 600 evaluations of therapeutic interventions in the substance use area have been published prior to 1990 (Institute of Medicine 1990), many clinicians and scientists have the impression that few of these research results have had a direct impact on health care policy.

This assumption should be placed in perspective. First, treatment issues in the substance use field are not alone, as other areas of research regularly question the general applicability of published reports. One example is the ongoing disagreement about the relationship between modest drinking and the risk of heart attack (Shaper *et al.* 1988). Secondly, some research results in alcoholism treatment have proven to be replicable and, while not universally accepted, do appear to have had an impact on the policy used in many therapeutic settings. These include the large scale and carefully conducted evaluations demonstrating a general lack of efficacy for disulfiram and lithium in treating the average alcoholic (Fuller *et al.* 1986; Dorus *et al.* 1989). Research has also consistently demonstrated that no specific discipline for therapists nor any specific counselling technique is essential for successfully treating alcoholics (Armor *et al.* 1978). Admittedly, however, these might be considered as relatively unimpressive fruits of such an extensive treatment literature dating back over 90 years.

This chapter explores some factors that might limit the generalizability and subsequent implementation of results from studies of treatments for alcohol use disorders. A perspective is selected that might be relevant to a policy maker (for example an insurance executive or politician) who is trying to make some sense out of the alcohol treatment literature. After listing potential problems, some suggestions are made for improving the impact that clinical researchers might have on relevant policy decisions.

Problems with definitions

The optimal conditions for implementing scientific results require that a policy maker understands how important issues are defined. Unfortunately, there are many relevant definitions and serious disagreements in several key definitions related to studies of treatment of alcoholism.

Problems with defining the disorder

The definition of alcohol treatment could include efforts to control a broad range of problems, including drunkenness, occasional lapses such as absences from school or work, or driving when even modestly intoxicated, and the severe repetitive problems of alcohol dependence. For the problems of alcohol dependence, multiple definitions have been developed in the past several decades, with some outlining more mild difficulties with little certainty of continued problems, and others focusing on severely impaired men and women (Schuckit 1989; Boyd *et al.* 1983). Less demanding criteria are appropriate for general population surveys where under-reporting is a potential problem, while the more restrictive rubrics are more relevant for decisions regarding treatments that demand relatively large expenditures of resources.

Optimal conditions for the development of treatment policies demand, at a minimum, reliable guidelines for labelling severe impairment. However, the criteria for alcoholism from the second Diagnostic and Statistical Manual of the American Psychiatric Association (DSMll) were changed dramatically in 1980 in the third version of that manual which uses a concept of alcohol abuse and dependence, only to have yet another criteria set presented in 1987 as the third revised edition (DSMlllR) (Rounsaville and Kranzler 1989; Schuckit *et al.* 1990). Labelling becomes even more confusing because of the differences between the American schemes and the Ninth and Tenth versions of the International Classification of Diseases (Schuckit *et al.* 1990). Thus, a treatment trial carried out in 1979, another completed in 1983, and yet another initiated in 1987 might incorporate relatively important differences in the diagnostic criteria for alcohol abuse or dependence (alcoholism). This presents a bewildering array of results to the policy maker and could, by itself, jeopardize generalizability and the confidence with which research results might be translated into policy (McGuire 1981).

Problems with defining treatment

Treatment researchers focus on aspects of alcohol interventions that range from educational lectures for individuals involved in a single drunk-driving arrest through extended in-patient rehabilitation for alcoholics with severe social, health, and legal problems. Thus, it is important for any investigation to carefully define the focus of the study, a step which, unfortunately, is often missing. A recent report defined treatment as 'a broad range of services with the goal of decreasing or eliminating the contribution of alcohol to physical, psychological, or social dysfunction' (Institute of Medicine 1990; p. 46). Such a definition, while useful, still includes a diverse range of actions addressing disparate populations, making it difficult at times for other scientists and policy makers to study the treatment literature and identify generalizable results (Institute of Medicine 1990; Tuchgeld and Marcus 1982).

The need to specify the level of care

Varied elements remain even within the concept of in-patient care. Thus, the careful reader must distinguish between acute interventions (including screening, confrontation, detoxification, and optimizing physical as well as psychological functioning), rehabilitation efforts (including further evaluation, efforts at enhancing motivation, and interventions aimed at helping to readjust to a new lifestyle), and programme components aimed at maintenance (including aftercare, relapse prevention paradigms, and domiciliary care (Institute of Medicine 1990; Schuckit 1989).

Specifications of who delivers the treatment

Complicating the issue further is the fact that treatment efforts are often delivered by a wide variety of personnel. These range from teachers in drunk-driving programmes, to personnel working in prisons, to recovering alcoholic counsellors, individuals with a variety of counselling degrees, social workers, psychologists, psychiatrists, and non-psychiatric physicians. While it appears that no single discipline is obviously superior in the delivery of care (Armor *et al.* 1978; Blane 1977), it is possible that the characteristics of an individual therapist (for example, the level of empathy or his or her cultural background) correlate with treatment response.

Problems with defining outcome

When one considers the variety of alcohol problems that might be addressed and the host of possible therapeutic efforts, it becomes obvious that no single definition of outcome is appropriate for all interventions in all settings (Institute of Medicine 1990). One might, however, expect some homogeneity for outcome goals for in-patient rehabilitation. However, even here most practitioners recognize the importance of diverse social legal, and interpersonal problems, not just abstinence (Armor *et al.* 1978; Babor *et al.* 1988; Mandell *et al.* 1979; Pomerleau *et al.* 1976). While the correlation between abstinence and improvement in other areas of life functioning is estimated to be as high as 0.7, there is not a one-to-one relationship.

After considering this section, the policy maker who attempts to translate scientific results into policy will require some level of sophistication about the definition of a case, the parameters of therapeutic interventions, and relevant outcomes. Heterogeneity in all three areas as they relate to alcohol treatment creates a potentially bewildering array of results that both limit the generalizability of research and undermine efforts at comfortably translating science into social action.

Problems resulting from the variable clinical course of alcoholism

The problems, however, do not stop here. Even after diligent efforts have been made to gain expertise about the multiple levels of relevant concepts, the results of treatment research must be placed into another important perspective. In the ideal situation, therapeutic interventions are applied to a group of people with a disorder that has a highly predictable clinical outcome. The results can then be compared with what was likely to happen without treatment.

Unfortunately, the clinical course of alcohol problems, even carefully diagnosed alcohol dependence, is highly variable (Ludwig 1972; Vaillant and Milofsky 1982; Fillmore and Midanik 1984; Vaillant 1983). People tend to come to the attention of health care deliverers at a time of crisis when alcohol-related difficulties are at their peak, with the natural swings in the intensity of the disorder contributing to the likelihood that a second evaluation at any randomly chosen point is likely to produce evidence of improvement. In addition, between 20 per cent and 50 per cent of individuals identified as having alcohol problems develop long-term abstinence as either spontaneous remission or a response to non-specific life events (Institute of Medicine 1990; Schuckit 1989; Mandell 1979; Vaillant and Milofsky 1982; Vaillant 1983).

An additional complicating factor is the probability that not all patients enter treatment with the same chances for recovery (Institute of Medicine 1990; Schuckit, 1989; Schuckit *et al.* 1986). In general, men and women with higher job functioning, fewer arrests, a more extensive social support system, and higher levels of cognitive functioning are likely to be doing better at follow-up (Blane 1977; Schuckit *et al.* 1986; Moos *et al.* 1990). There are estimates that perhaps one third of the variance related to outcome can be explained by patient characteristics alone (Schuckit *et al.* 1986).

Another set of factors that influence the clinical outcome among alcoholics relates to the presence of pre-existing major psychiatric disorders. Most investigations have demonstrated that men and women with severe antisocial problems in multiple life areas beginning before the age of 15 years and before the onset of severe life difficulties related to alcohol (i.e., those with the antisocial personality disorder) have poor prognoses for their substance-related problems no matter what treatment is used (Schuckit 1985, 1989; Helzer 1987). Interestingly, some alcoholics with pre-existing and independent severe depressive episodes that occur unrelated to periods of heavy drinking have been reported in some studies to have better prognoses for their alcohol problems, perhaps reflecting additional efforts by clinicians to deal with the mood disturbance (Schuckit 1985; Rounsaville *et al.* 1987).

This section has drawn attention to the fact that the fluctuating intensity of symptoms inherent in the natural history of alcoholism, spontaneous remission, differences in prognosis associated with patient characteristics, and the impact of pre-existing major psychiatric disorders combine to contribute to a highly variable course of problems in alcoholics. Two treatment evaluations might, thus, reveal marked differences that relate to the characteristics of the patients, results that might have nothing to do with the efficacy of the programme. This has added variability to results and made simple interpretations difficult (Institute of Medicine 1990; Blane 1977; Mandell 1979).

Problems related to research methods

By this point, many policy makers are likely to have thrown up their hands in frustration and decided that scientific results are too complex to assimilate readily. However, they are asked to become conversant with at least one additional level of input—the scientific methods involved.

The impact on outcome of factors unrelated to the characteristics of the treatment programme has produced a lively discussion in the literature about the optimal research procedures for evaluating alcohol treatment. Many scientists feel that results cannot be appropriately interpreted unless steps are taken to minimize the influences from patient selection procedures and the fluctuating course of the disorder. Typically, these researchers call for the careful selection of both treatment and control groups, with the two populations having similar prognostic characteristics and apparent levels of motivation, but differing levels of exposure to the therapeutic intervention (Jeffrey 1975; Nace 1989). Without such controls, including the random assignment of comparable patients to relevant treatment groups, it may be difficult to establish whether any improvements observed were related to the intervention itself (McGuire 1981; Nace 1989). One study reported the enthusiasm felt by researchers when 42 per cent of the treated subjects appeared to be doing well at 1 year, and the subsequently disappointment when similar positive results were observed in 38 per cent of the controls (McGuire 1981).

Other investigators, however, point out a number of deficiencies inherent in these randomized controlled studies (Institute of Medicine 1990). First, this research approach tends to screen subjects so carefully that it can be difficult to determine how results might apply to the usual patient. Secondly, it is difficult to establish controlled trials in a setting where clinicians enthusiastically believe that their therapeutic interventions are essential for good outcome and are, thus, reluctant to see treatment withheld from anyone. Thirdly, these controlled trials of programme effectiveness tend to occur in highly specialized clinics, with results that might be difficult to generate outside of university affiliated institutions.

Therefore, a number of alternatives have been proposed. These include accepting results from systematic monitoring of how patients do on follow-up, placing greater emphasis on individual case descriptions, surveys of consumer satisfaction, and using follow-ups to demonstrate the characteristics of patients most likely to benefit from a particular programme which in turn guide the clinic in subsequently selecting those patients who seem to have the best chances of benefiting from the specific intervention (Institute of Medicine 1990). Many scientists are not convinced that these approaches provide adequate answers.

Policy planners cannot glibly accept the tables or summary section of a treatment evaluation study, but must read the relevant methodologies carefully. This requires intense study and some level of expertise with research methodologies, factors that contribute to the reluctance of policy makers to accept treatment study results as generalizable.

Additional problems that limit generalizability

A variety of factors related to the history of alcohol treatment, political battles, and financial competition add increasing levels of complexity that threaten the efficient translation of even clear-cut results from treatment evaluation research into policy.

First, it can be difficult to engender high levels of enthusiasm for any intervention when the impact of that treatment is likely to be relatively modest. Despite all of the problems outlined above, there are data indicating that between one-third and two-thirds of the usual patients entering care are likely to do well at follow-up (Institute of Medicine 1990; Blane 1977; Babor *et al.* 1988; Nace 1989; Helzer *et al.* 1985). Improvements are likely to be observed in most aspects of life functioning, not only in abstinence. Conversely this range of results can be bewildering to policy makers and even those studies that indicate that interventions appear to be superior to no treatment have problems convincing readers that the response rates are dramatically different from those that would be observed from non-specific life events. Therefore, it is not possible to point to a specific number of lives saved and severe costs avoided which, in turn, make it difficult for the policy maker and politician to assign financial resources to therapeutic efforts instead of competing social programmes.

A second problem relates to the reluctance of care deliverers to admit that their treatment efforts might be of limited impact. Perhaps reflecting the abrogation of interest in alcohol treatment evidenced by many health specialists prior to the 1960s, care deliverers in this field were left on their own to decide the importance of a specific intervention. Many arrived at the pragmatic notion that because something makes sense it must work, or felt that their own personal improvement after a treatment indicates that the intervention is of general importance. These contributed to subsequent feelings that withholding a treatment element is unethical. Adding to these problems are the consequences of inertia and reluctance to change, along with the fear that physicians and other professionals might be carrying out research in an effort to disprove the effectiveness of less highly trained personnel.

A third factor limiting the generalizability of research is the high cost of studies that incorporate optimal controls. Not only must comparable subjects be assigned at least to two types of interventions, but active efforts must be made to be certain that men and women in group A are denied the treatments that were assigned to group B. As a result, an evaluation of in-patient versus out-patient rehabilitation for relatively severely impaired alcoholics might find that a consequence of half of the patients getting the less intrusive out-patient care is an increased number of empty beds during the trial. Few programmes can afford these financial losses, and few, if any, funding agencies are willing to make up such costs.

Finally, reflecting many of the factors described above, medical scientific results are difficult for the non-expert to extract from the published literature (Haynes 1990). The careful reader must wade through studies that often offer only preliminary results and others that are highly technical and ridden with jargon. Indeed, the process of translating results into practice is very hard work.

A recapitulation and some suggestions

This chapter has focused on how a policy maker might view some problems that limit the ease with which results from research evaluating alcoholism treatment can be translated into action. The review has demonstrated how broad and complex treatment research in the alcohol field is and that policy makers must pay careful attention to the details of research methods. Much of the problem for the policy maker results from the level of expertise needed to assimilate these complex results fully. Other difficulties are the result of our desire to simplify a complex picture and find ready answers to help us address the needs of society.

If alcohol treatment research in the future wishes to impact optimally on policy, a number of important steps need to be considered. The first is the need for researchers to carefully describe the type of alcohol problem being treated, consider which of the carefully defined therapeutic interventions might be appropriate for which projected outcome, and make better efforts to match patient characteristics and needs with the therapeutic intervention involved (Institute of Medicine 1980; 1990). This manoeuvre is likely to yield the most clearly-specified methods, with results that might be interpreted more easily by policy makers and subsequently incorporated more readily into treatment efforts in the future.

A second suggestion is to help the non-scientist to a better understanding of the essential aspects of the results by taking special care in the writing of the abstract (the section of the manuscript most accessible to non-scientists). This requires a succinct statement of the problem being studied, a brief description of the essential research parameters, a bold presentation of the most important single result, and a reminder of essential caveats. This might take a total of perhaps six sentences.

Thirdly, if scientists want to have a say in policy decisions, advantage must be taken of every available opportunity to translate results into more accessible forms. This includes developing relevant columns about policy in major journals and sponsoring appropriate policy-oriented newsletters. A variation on this theme is the need to be willing to participate in expert panels for government bodies or the National Academy of Sciences (or parallel institutions) that work to develop consensus statements or monographs on the state of a field.

Fourthly, it should be recognized that the politicians who help to set policy regard the electorate as their major influence group. The officeholder who gets too far out in front of his or her constituents on an issue is likely soon to be unemployed. Therefore, one important step in altering public policy is to reach out to the populace. This involves, among other things, helping to educate them by being readily available to talk to reporters from newspapers, television, and radio.

Another important step results from the recognition that the combination of multiple definitions of problems, a panoply of potential therapeutic efforts, and a wide range of relevant outcomes produces a multi-dimensional grid with an almost infinite number of combinations. Following up on a suggestion made in an earlier Institute of Medicine report (Institute of Medicine 1980) optimal advances in treatment research probably require a systematic effort to control definitions, interventions, and outcome evaluations across studies. Thus, researchers in multiple locales must agree on the client or patient population, the definition of the parameters of the specific treatments being invoked, and the appropriate controls, so that results can be compared. One possible framework for this approach would be a single centrally-funded panel to which treatment researchers apply. After agreeing to incorporate standardized definitions and methodologies, patients can be assigned to treatment groups, and the results generated in one clinic can be adequately compared with those demonstrated in another. Optimally, this co-ordinated series of contracts would have to be carried out over a decade or more.

Conclusions

Treatment research in the alcoholism field has taught us many important lessons about the fluctuating nature of this disorder, the broad array of problems that might be addressed, and potentially important interventions. At the same time, a number of factors have combined to limit the generalizability of treatment research from one setting to another. These, in turn, have hampered attempts to translate science into policy in this field. Future gains in treatment research, with results that optimally impact on policy, require a co-ordinated effort with a relatively long-term mandate. With such commonsense steps we can look forward to the possibility of optimal translation of science into policy beyond the year 2000.

Acknowledgement

This work was supported by NIAAA grants numbers 05526 and 08401 and The Veterans Affairs Research Service.

References

Armor, D.J., Polich, M., and Stambul, H.B. (1978). *Alcoholism and treatment.* Wiley, New York.

Babor, T.F., Dolinsky, Z., Rounsaville, B., and Jaffe, J. (1988). Unitary versus multidimensional models of alcoholism treatment outcome: An empirical study. *Journal of Studies on Alcohol*, 49, 167–77.

Blane, H.T. (1977). Issues in the evaluation of alcoholism treatment. *Professional Psychology*, 8, 593–608.

Boyd, J.H., Weissman, M.M., Thompson, W.D., and Myers, J.K. (1983). Different definitions of alcoholism, l: Impact of seven definitions on prevalence rates in community survey. *American Journal of Psychiatry*, 140, 1309–13.

Dorus, W., Ostrow, D.G., Anton, R., Cushman, P., Collins, J.F., and Schaefer, M. (1989). Lithium treatment of depressed and nondepressed alcoholics. *Journal of the American Medical Association*, 262, 1646–52.

Fillmore, K.M. and Midanik, L. (1984). Chronicity of drinking problems among men: A longitudinal study. *Journal of Studies on Alcohol*, 45, 228–36.

Fuller, R.K., Branchey, L., Brightwell, D.R., Derman, R.M., Emrick, C.D., Iber, F.L., et al. (1986). Disulfiram treatment of alcoholism: a Veterans Administration cooperative study. *Journal of the American Medical Association*, 256, 1449–55.

Goodwin, D.W. and Guze, S.B. (1989). *Psychiatric diagnosis*, (4th edn). Oxford University Press, New York.

Haynes, R.B. (1990). Loose connections between peer-reviewed clinical journals and clinical practice. *Annals of Internal Medicine*, 113, 724–8.

Helzer, J. (1987). The co-occurrence of alcoholism with other psychiatric disorders in the general population. *Journal of Studies on Alcohol*, 49, 219–24.

Helzer, J.E., Robins, L.N., Taylor, J.R., Carey, K., Miller, R.H., Combs-Orme, T., and Farmer, A. (1985). The extent of long-term moderate drinking among alcoholics discharged from medical and psychiatric treatment facilities. *New England Journal of Medicine*, **312**, 1678–82.

Helzer, J.E., Burnam, A., and McEvoy, L.T. (1991). Alcohol abuse and dependence. In *Psychiatric disorders of America*, (ed. L.N. Robins and D.A. Regier), pp. 81–119. The Free Press, New York.

Institute of Medicine (1980). *Alcoholism, alcohol abuse, and related problems: Opportunities for research*. pp. 165–86. National Academy Press, Washington.

Institute of Medicine (1990). *Broadening the base of treatment for alcohol problems*, pp. 23–162. National Academy Press, Washington.

Jeffrey, D.B. (1975). Treatment evaluation issues in research on addictive behaviors. *Addictive Behavior*, **1**, 23–36.

Ludwig, A.M. (1972). On and off the wagon: reasons for drinking and abstaining by alcoholics. *Quarterly Journal of Studies on Alcohol*, **33**, 91–6.

Mandell, W. (1979). A critical overview of evaluations of alcoholism treatment. *Alcoholism: Clinical and Experimental Research*, **3**, 315–23.

McGuire, F.L. (1981). Alcohol rehabilitation: fact or myth? *American Journal of Drug and Alcohol Abuse*, **8**, 131–5.

Moos, R., Finney, J., and Cronkite, R. (1990). *Alcoholism treatment: context, process and outcome*. Oxford University Press.

Nace, E.P. (1989). The natural history of alcoholism versus treatment effectiveness: methodological problems. *American Journal of Drug and Alcohol Abuse*, **15**, 55–60.

Pomerleau, O., Pertschuk, M., and Stinnett, J. (1976). A critical examination of some current assumptions in the treatment of alcoholism. *Journal of Studies on Alcohol*, **37**, 849–67.

Rounsaville, B.J., Dolinsky, Z.S., Babor, T.F., and Meyer, R.E. (1987). Psychopathology as a predictor of treatment outcome in alcoholics. *Archives of General Psychiatry*, **44**, 505–13.

Rounsaville, B.J. and Kranzler, H.R. (1989). The DSM-III-R diagnosis of alcoholism. In *Review of psychiatry*, Vol. 8, (ed. W. Tasman, R.E. Hales, and A.F. Frances), pp. 323–40. American Psychiatric Press, Washington.

Schuckit, M.A. (1985). The clinical implications of primary diagnostic groups among alcoholics. *Archives of General Psychiatry*, **42**, 1043–9.

Schuckit, M.A. (1989). *Alcohol and drug abuse: a clinical guide to diagnosis and treatment*, (3rd edn), pp. 45–67. Plenum, New York.

Schuckit, M.A., Schwei, M.G., and Gold, E. (1986). Prediction of outcome in inpatient alcoholics. Journal of Studies on Alcohol, **47**, 151–5.

Schuckit, M.A., Helzer, J.E., Crowley, T.J., Woody, G., and Nathan, P.E. (1991). Deliberations of the substance use work group for DSM-IV. *Hospital and Community Psychiatry*, **42**, 471–4.

Shaper, A.G., Wannamethee, G., and Walker, M. (1988). Alcohol and mortality in British men: explaining the u-shaped curve. *Lancet*, ii, 1267–73.

Tuchfeld, B.S. and Marcus, S.H. (1982). Methodological issues in evaluating alcoholism treatment effectiveness. *Advances in Alcoholism*, **2**, 1–4.

Vaillant, G.E. and Milofsky, E.S. (1982). The etiology of alcoholism: a prospective viewpoint. *American Psychologist*, **37**, 494–503.

Vaillant, G. (1983). *The Natural History of Alcoholism*. Harvard University Press, Cambridge, MA, pp. 120–33.

Discussion
Science and treatment: what message for the policy maker?

This section puts together two sessions which were chaired, respectively, by Robert Kendell (UK) and Mark Taylor (Canada).

Panel members included Karl Mann (Germany), Martha Sanchez-Craig (Canada), Charles O'Brien (USA), Jim Orford (UK), Miguel Casas (Spain), Nikolai Ivanets (USSR), and Timothy Stockwell (Australia).

Dr Karl Mann (Germany): In discussing treatment efficacy and outcome we should take account of the toxic damage which alcohol exerts on the brain, and the reversibility of brain changes through abstinence. Changes on a morphological level are likely to be the basis of improvements at a functional level, and we now know that we are not only dealing with, as it were, a software problem, but with a hardware problem as well, with possibilities of improvement at both levels. These provide a better basis to understand what happens during abstinence and thus they are helpful in motivating patients to join, and policy makers to support treatment programmes.

What kind of treatment for what kind of patient? I would like to give you two examples on how this question is being handled at present in Germany. We're living in a period of transition in Germany and in central Europe, we are having a dual system for a restricted period of time, for a year or two, with the result of 40 years of communism on the one side and the benefit of 40 years of capitalism on the other side. In the West we have a standard treatment programme for alcoholics which consists of six months of in-patient treatment, and in the East we have a quite succesfully functioning treatment programme which is founded on out-patient treatment and day clinics.

The second example is the threshold to be used for drunk driving. In the West we have 80 mg% blood alcohol concentration, in the East we have 00 mg%. Both problems seem to be resolved by moving toward the Western way, and we are already building huge hospitals in the East to have 200–300 beds for alcoholic patients to be treated in this western manner for half a year, and I am sure that the 80 mg% threshold will be introduced into the whole country without asking or any scientific advice.

Dr Jim Orford (UK): Why have we not got a clear enough answer to give to the policy maker? We have been at it for some time, this business of inventing and trying out treatments. I think the reason we have not got a simple enough answer yet for the policy makers is that we are trying to give them too simple answers. We are trapped into such over-simple questions as is social skills treatment the answer, is methadone treatment the answer, does psychotherapy hold the answer, and so on. That makes the serious mistake of simplifying the process of giving up an addictive behaviour. The process is in reality highly complicated and it often takes people many years to think through the decision to change their behaviour, and we are trying to reduce the matter down to finding *the* treatment.

We need to borrow from what is going on in the wider literature of psychotherapy research. As Kathleen Carroll has been telling us, that shows very clearly that there may be important interaction affects and it also shows us that there may be important non-specific effects. If people who are undergoing treatment have a choice available to them so that they can match their needs to the treatment, that may be an important factor. Another issue which needs to be considered is that it is no good perhaps devising treatments that are incompatible with the things that are being said to you or the interactions you are having with your nearest and dearest when you go out of the therapy room.

Another way in which we are simplifying things is in terms of seeing treatment as something we as experts do to people. Our model of treatment seems to be one in which we as experts devise treatments, we package them, we call them things, we write manuals about them. The psychotherapy literature is really going quite the wrong way in manualizing everything.

Another aspect of complexity lies with sex differences. There is evidence that women on the whole have a different causal explanation of why they come to be addicted than do men. That is obviously to generalize broadly, but there is for instance evidence to suggest that women who have an addiction problem and a marital problem, tend to say that the addiction problems were reactive to their marital problems. Men who have addiction problems and marital problems tend, on the other hand, to say that their marital problems are responsive or secondary to their addiction. Similarly, there is evidence that with alcohol problems and depression, women who have that combination tend to think that depression preceded the alcohol problem, men tend to see it in the reverse. If what men and women are differently saying is right, then that suggests that the type of treatment that suit the average man and the average woman is going to be different, and there is just one more type of interaction.

We have to ask ourselves, surely, not whether it is social skills training that is the treatment of choice, but what is common to Dr Hodgson doing social skills in Cardiff in the 1990s and the strategies of the Bradford Temperance Union in the 1840s. Both those approaches appear in their historical and social context to be quite effective ways of helping addictive behaviours. It is the commonalities that we have got to dissect out and then seek to understand in interactive context.

Dr Charles O'Brien (USA): In terms of what we have to say to policy makers, I think of the experience that I have had as someone who has been doing treatment research in the mental health field, mainly, but not only, in substance abuse, for more than 20 years now. In those years I have contributed many hours to sitting down with policy makers, some of them Congressmen and Senators that were engaged in an annual meeting that Roger Meyer arranges for research centre directors in Washington. The other group of policy makers, with which we have had dealings, are people in the insurance industry. The health insurance industry in the USA are very important policy makers and they help to shape the way treatment is delivered. We spend all of this time in discussion with policy people and we never know when it is going to have a beneficial effect: it is almost like playing the lottery. We spend hours on the telephone or in someone's office and it may lead to nothing. Then sometimes just a few minutes at the right time and an idea winds up in legislation. One of the biggest problems we encounter is that all these people have in their own personal experience some friend, relative, neighbour, or employee who has been in treatment and that treatment seemed to be a failure. 'We sent my nephew down to X clinic in Y State, a very famous clinic and he spent 28 days there and he said they said he did well, but he relapsed while he was changing planes in Atlanta.' That causes them to feel negative about all treatment, and of course we know that these 28 day in-patient programmes are shown by research to be not particularly effective.

There is too great a tendency for people automatically to think of substance misuse as an acute illness, like a fractured bone or pnuemonia, and we have to dispel that concept. We should instead use the model of arthritis or diabetes. A 60-year-old man develops a bad case of arthritis, and he goes to an arthritic specialist, he is not cured but life is more bearable and he has 50 per cent more mobility at his joints. He can walk better, but periodically the condition gets worse and he comes back in to see the doctor and they change his medication. He is not abstinent, is not drug free, is not cured but he is happy with his doctor, and his neighbours and his friends and his senator are happy with the doctor. Nobody is saying this is ineffective treatment. That is the same way in which we ought to regard alcoholism and other kinds of drug dependence. Abstinence is a great goal and I am not against it, but we are doing ourselves a big disservice if we only focus on abstinence. If I impart to my patients, not to mention the people funding my work, that it is a failure if you relapse, I am disregarding all the benefits patients get from treatment in terms of their physical health, their family life, their psychological health, their ability to work and pay taxes and take care of their family even if they may slip periodically.

Another thing that we have to tell our policy makers is that all addiction is not alike. There are sub-categories—not only can the wrong treatment be ineffective, but it may be toxic. We could show you data for opiate addicts where if they go to a drug free therapeutic community, they get worse at follow-up, compared with those with the same kind of psychiatric severity who go to methadone maintenance.

In Philadelphia we study not only our ivory tower clinics where we have excellent and well-trained staff, but we go out into the community and study patients being treated in private practice, and in public programmes where they get free treatment or treatment based on public assistance. One of the really sad things is that the level of sophistication of the staff in these programmes is so poor that they are not able properly to implement even the methadone treatment, a pharmacologically easy approach. If we take something much more sophisticated and complicated like naltrexone, there is no way that this could be properly used in these programmes. They are underfunded and in a way it is waste for us to be doing research and developing new and more sophisticated treatments if in fact the people who are going to apply these treatments have not been trained to know how to apply them.

Finally, there is a tendency for us to over promise things to our legislatures. A good example of this tendency was the discovery of the opiate receptors and the endogenous opiodes. That was beautiful basic research with a tremendous impact on neurobiology, and it was sold to Congress at that time that we were near some kind of a cure or breakthrough for opiate addiction. Now we have the situation with regard to cocaine dependence where Congress wants a solution quickly so they are pouring a lot of money into this area, and one of our most intelligent Senators actually recently sent a letter to NIDA and said 'look we have more than doubled your budget, we gave you all these millions of dollars eighteen months ago, but you have not come up with a methadone for cocaine yet'. When we talk to our legislators we have to spend enough time with them to educate them about the real complexities.

Dr Martha Sanchez-Craig (Canada): I would offer a cautionary tale about the difficulties of translating research findings on the treatment of alcohol problems into rational policies. In almost 20 years that I have been a researcher at the Addiction Research Foundation I have witnessed two attempts by the government of Ontario to implement research based innovations in the provision of treatment services.

The first of these is generally acclaimed as a significant success: non-medical detoxification for persons with alcohol problems. This approach has been succesfully adopted across the province and also has been succesfully exported. In settings similar to Ontario non-medical detoxification has worked very well, however it is an empirical question whether such an approach could flourish in places like Glasgow, where DTs seem to be much more common than in Canada.

The second example of research based policy adopted by the government of Ontario has a more troubled history which is still unfolding. Our Ministry of Health was persuaded that the bulk of scientific evidence indicated that in general residential treatments had not proved superior to briefer interventions, for example out-patient treatment or even one session of advice. Accordingly, the Ministry resolved to give deliberate priority to the establishment of out-patient services without cutting back on available residential treatments. This was not a radical adoption of the apparent implications of the research but rather a shift in emphasis influenced directly by the research findings.

You should be aware that in Ontario, we embody the demon of the American Medical Association, namely socialized health care. The government foots the bill for citizens whether treated in Ontario or elsewhere. South of the border, in the USA, treatment programmes had empty beds and began aggressive marketing in Ontario offering substantial case finding fees to their agents. Distraught clients and their families are easily persuaded that immediate admission to residential care is desirable, especially when an agent is already prepared with airline tickets to sun-blessed treatments in the sophisticated USA. The drain on funds from the province became a major political issue when it was revealed that one of our citizens in a fairly short period of time incurred charges in excess of $450,000 for this wonderful US treatment. This sum could fund an out-patient treatment service for a year or longer. Research data are not going to clarity or resolve this issue; it has moved into the realm of value based political decisions.

Dr Miguel Casas (Spain): AIDS has forced society and the policy makers to accept that it is correct that a group of heroin addicts, those perhaps who otherwise relapse often, those that destroy our statistics, must be treated for a long time, or maybe for all their lives, with methadone or bupranorphine. Every effort that we can make in order to stop AIDS, this terrible epidemic, is necessary. Methadone by itself cannot though give all the answers. We are now in Barcelona, Spain, running a small project in which every time that we have a new young heroin addict we ask who his friends are. If we can convince his friends, and the friends of his friends to come into treatment, that is worthwhile.

Dr Nikolai Ivanets (USSR): I am a psychiatrist working in addiction as a clinician and as a scientist for more than 20 years. Every clinician understands that the therapeutic process is a very difficult process. Usually the therapeutical programme must consist of three parts, medication, psychotherapy, and rehabilitation. However, different specialists use these approaches in different ways. It is well known that you can treat diseases only if you know the mechanism of their development. Now we know the principal biological mechanism of dependence. The main disturbances are in neuromediator and neuromodulator systems. We began to use a new method in the clinic which is able to normalize the functions of this system. These disturbances are the basis of pathological craving for psychoactive substances.

Dr Robert Kendell (UK): I would like to invite you to think about this legislator whom we are trying to influence. He is almost certainly male, middle-aged, and middle-class. He has a great deal of confidence in his own judgement, he is suspicious of all experts and he is probably more suspicious of social scientists than he is of, let us say, engineers or nuclear physicists. As Dr O'Brien reminded us he almost certainly has got a nephew or a wife or a daughter who has had treatment for some kind of addiction and he has a strongly held personal view about the efficacy or otherwise of treatment, based on that one relative or friend. I suspect that if our legislator had been sitting here today nothing that he had heard would persuade him to alter the views which he held at the beginning of the day based on his personal experience of one relative. It is very important that we recognize this otherwise we will remain powerless. At the stage at which we do try to influence legislatures we have got to have agreed amongst ourselves what we want to say. We have got to have an agreed message. It has got to be fairly simple, it has got to be backed up by what looks like convincing evidence but is also fairly simple, and it has got to be accompanied by a realistic estimate of the likely cost to the public purse.

Dr Tim Stockwell (Australia): I would liek to draw together some threads from the presentations in this section. One is the need to simplify the great complexity that exists in scientific studies without doing them an injustice or misleading policy makers. The second theme is the unanimous agreement that the simple question, does treatment work?, is absurdly over-simple. The whole process of treatment, who is the agent providing the treatment, who is receiving it, the context in which it is done, the time and place and culture in which it is taking place, are all too variable to permit simple questions. I am reminded of how I used to feel attempting to carry out the difficult business of treatment research and comparing notes with a friend who was a market gardener. He used to perform wonderful scientific experiments on how best to grow cabbages. He had neat rows of cabbages all lined up, and he would give treatment A to one lot of cabbages, and treatment B to the other. He would measure leaf size to see which produced the best results and I was green with envy about the situation that he had in comparison with mine. For one thing, when he decided to do a treatment trial his cabbages did not mysteriously vanish and leave the allotment. When he measured leaf size they did not fluctuate wildly from day to day or even hour to hour like patients' symptoms are apt to do. Furthermore, they all attended for their follow-up appointments. Treatment research is in contrast very difficult.

Marc Schuckit gave us many ideas as to how we can simplify the complex business of treatment and how there are ways in which we must somehow end up with that half piece of A4 paper, conclusions which as a scientific community we have agreed are the best statement we can make at the moment, and failure to do that is abnegating our responsibilities.

We need here to study very carefully the process of interaction between science and policy, and that is an issue worthy of study in its own right. Maybe we need to look at a state of change model for policy makers, how many of them are at a pre-contemplation stage and have not considered the possibility that alcohol and drugs are a significant problem that they should deal with. Then there is the contemplation stage, when they may realize that there is a problem but they do not believe it is their responsibility or that they have community support to do anything about it, and perhaps they do not believe there is anything effective that could be done about it anyway. If we are lucky, and this sometimes happens, we get policy makers who are at an action stage: unfortunately, of course, they then often act swiftly after a two minute phone call to a person they happen to know, and they set up a school education programme, or introduce intensive treatment programmes all over the country. It is hoped that there is a point at that stage at which we might be able to influence them far better. Finally, there is the maintenance stage of ensuring resources for monitoring the effectiveness of the programmes that have been instigated. Our research has much to offer at each of those stages, but we should assess whether the policy makers we deal with are pre-contemplators, contemplators, actors or maintainers. Furthermore, we have a moral imperative to make sure we are doing the best we can to communicate as clearly and as effectively the best information we have available, and that is relevant at whichever stage the policy maker happens to be.

Dr Robin Room (USA): I want to pick up on the issue of compulsory treatment. This is an important policy issue that gets played out in different ways in different countries, and it was interesting to see that the Swedish movement is towards a greater use of compulsion. That is a historic break with the position of Swedish doctors in the early part of the century when they were clear about there being social problems from drinking which were the responsibility of social work and the penal authorities, and then there were medical problems from drinking which were the responsibility of doctors. I remember a quotation from a Swiss psychiatrist who was visiting Sweden, and was quite surprised by the distinction that the doctors in Sweden were exploying, which was different from the Swiss situation. These days you can find similarly different assumptions between the UK and the USA, reaching through the whole underlying epistemology around how we are going to define dependence. For instance, ICD-10 under the influence of British traditions has kept the social consequences out of the definition, whereas DSM-III-R has the social consequences not fully removed and they may be put back in even more firmly in the DSM-IV as part of the psychiatric condition.

The issue of compulsion changes the frame all the way through when we are talking about treament evaluation studies and their implications for policy. Let me give you an example, Dr McLellan's statement about the ethics of random assignment. Random assignment feels a little different when somebody is actually being compelled into treatment. The ethics of denying compulsion are different from the ethics of denying something which somebody is voluntarily seeking. The issue is complicated by the fact that little treatment is really entirely voluntary in our field: most people are in one way or another under some sort of pressure. At the point when a court is telling someone 'Well as a condition of probation you can go into treatment instead of going to jail', then that seems rather different from having a family that is fed up with that person. It seems that in the USA the drug treatment system is largely composed of clients who are there under that kind of court pressure, and more and more of the alcohol treatment system is composed of people who are there under that same kind of court pressure. And that really needs to be thought about in our treatment designs, and in our estimations of the usefulness of treatment and its justifiability.

If, as Marc Schuckit says, the impact of treatment is modest, at what point are we justified in putting people through that treatment process on an involuntary basis? It struck me forcibly when I was comparing the two Institute of Medicine reports, one on drug treatment and one on alcohol treatment, that there was a different perspective between those two reports. The drug treatment literature assumes, really on the basis of one study in California, that compulsory drug treatment is effective. The alcohol treatment evaluation literature is much more sceptical about the effectiveness of compulsory treatment. It seems unlikely that the empirical situation is going to turn out to be so different between the two sectors if more studies are carried out to look at this issue carefully.

Mr Mark Temple (Canada): It may be that if early intervention gives more positive results, early intervention and coercion at the same time would work better. If that were the case we would expect to see, for instance, the drinking driver who is arrested more often put into some kind of an intervention programme right at the onset.

Dr Juan Carlos Negrete (Canada): I would like to focus on an issue that seems to have become increasingly salient. The thrust which comes from several of our presentations is that as regards the question 'Does treatment work?', we have to tell the politicians 'don't ask such a silly question, it doesn't make any sense to put it that way'. But in fact we cannot have the cake and eat it too. If we have fought so long to make this particular field of endeavour the same as other health care endeavours, and have been saying to colleagues within hospitals 'Look, it is as legitimate to think about alcoholism in terms of health service needs as it is for any other disease, please do not exclude us, we do not belong out there with the Salvation Army, we belong right here among all of you' then we cannot tell them 'don't ask such silly questions as whether treatment works'.

I remember time and again when we started to be accepted within Medical and even Surgical Rounds, at the end of a discussion there was always a question, what is the rate of success in your clinic? And of course I used the psychiatric trick, I turned the question back to them—'What do you mean by success?' But there was a feeling that we did not have an answer, and that was the flavour that was left after the question. We should change a bit the terms of our answer to that question. My wife is an oncologist and at her professional meetings, I heard oncologists answering similar questions. Everybody feels comfortable to report success so long as it is a modification of the otherwise negative course of events, and they have invented terms such as 'local control' or 'site control', 'survival rate from 2 years to 3 years', making the best of a very difficult situation. When a cancer therapist says 'I've obtained very good local control for this particular cancer', it does not matter whether the person dies within five years anyway, it means that there is local control and there is no recurrence in the breast. So we have to learn that kind of perspective in giving our answers. But of course we want so much to make people believe that we have a solution to the problems with which we deal, that we propose the abolition of the problems completely and we cannot come out with that kind of success. The basic question is, however, not silly. It is logical, and our answers have to change in perspective so that they can more accommodate what we are able to do for these people.

Dr Griffith Edwards (UK): I find Robin Room's reminder of the sense of history useful. On the question of attitudes to compulsion, he is probably aware that the Society for the Study of Addiction founded in London in 1884 as the Society for the Study and Cure of Inebriety (the society which to this day publishes the British Journal of Addiction), was intrinsically a lobbying organization which pressed for compulsory treatment. That was seen as a benign approach in Victorian England. The similar society which briefly flourished but went out of existence before the Great War in the USA, had very much the same programme. But what I would like to test further is where do we stand in the face of history as regards the overall question of treatment research?

I would like someone to look at the historical evolution and describe the trajectory of treatment research on dependence problems. There have been scattered case series reports since the last century, some of them well worth looking at: case series on withdrawal for instance, where clinicians were discussing the use of tapering approaches as opposed to abrupt withdrawal. It is not until 1956 in the USA that one sees Wallersteins's Meninger Clinic study and the first attempt at a controlled trial—a classic study still worth getting off the library shelves. But what one then largely sees is the evolution of entirely empirical studies, nearly always conducted by psychiatrists, which were first of all uncontrolled studies, then empirical but controlled studies, but still guided by no theory. As Colin Drummond was picking up, such studies are intrinsically in some ways weak because it is difficult to generalize from them: it is difficult to make of them any incremental science when they are not theory based and you do not understand the change process. But one then sees a wave of research developing which is theory-led and marks the arrival of the psychologists: that is very exciting, but where is the trajectory now leading, where is the next move?

What one might perhaps hope to see would be movement in two directions, firstly with longitudinal treatment research taken more seriously. There is an awful arbitrariness in the 12 months of the calendar: why are follow-ups nearly always six or 12 months? Ten or 20-year follow-up studies give insights very different from anything our 12-month treatment studies tell us. It is an almost wilful conspiracy of treatment researchers to persevere with short-term studies. If I were a policy maker I might put my finger on the emperor's new clothes of the researcher who insists on doing only short-term research on what is manifestly a life course problem.

The second direction which might now be beginning to open up would be concerned with the interaction between treatment and natural processes. At present we tend, for instance, to ignore that strange things may be happening to people just before they come to treatment. What are the happenings and feelings which drive people into treatment? What are the things which cause them to co-operate in treatment? What are the life events, the crises, the terrible despairs or the new hopes which move people in the treatment direction? What one seldom sees, either described or measured or matched, is an attempt to take into the reckoning the homes from which people come or to which they return. Some patients go home after a period in a treatment centre to a loving spouse, the flags out from the neighbours, a job waiting for them, a golf course at the door, the sun is always shining, and the environment invites and supports recovery. Others go back to sleep under railway arches, or they go back to antagonism. When one looks at the work done by social psychiatrists who have researched schizophrenia or depression, when one sees their acute awareness of the influence of the family and social environment on those conditions, it really does seem very strange that our research community has not caught up with what the social psychiatrists have taught us in those other arenas. Thus, if we believe that our research endeavour is an evolving tradition, what today are the directions for that evolution?

Dr Roger Meyer (USA): Long-term and short-term outcome may involve very different processes. On a broader scale I think we have a major disconnectedness between research and policy in the treatment world which exceeds that in the oncology community. Just to give some brief history, NIAAA funded public alcohol treatment programmes in the USA up until 1981, roughly from 1971 to 1981, under the Hughes Act. We then had a period of mandated insurance coverage and this encouraged in-patient treatment, three to four week treatment programmes, and we had a burst of in-patient programmes unrelated to research with many of them based on the Hazleded model. These programmes continued and were highly profitable: they were highlighted in the Wall Street Journal. Then the DRG's began to discourage longer in-patient stays in the alcohol and drug area, but were not applied in the case of mental illness. Now we are dealing with something called managed care in the USA, which is reducing in-patient treatment to a virtual impossibility, except paradoxically for Medicaid in certain states. It is very, very difficult to get insured patients into in-patient care. Again, none of this is based on any research findings. What we have in this field is thus an extraordinary disconnection between research and treatment communities, and that is a real problem for the insurance industry. We have many providers besides physicians and psychologists, we have providers who are authorized drug or alcohol counsellors, we have every kind of provider out there. In that situation the insurers are terrified. We cannot even give them information as to how they can differentiate one kind of provider from another. That is a major policy problem, it does not have anything to do with whether treatment works, it has to do with a huge array of services that are waiting to be paid for, and that is what is driving this process.

What we do not have is an orderly way of integrating research findings into new treatment developments. And that is one of the exciting things about what Tom McLellan and the group at Penn have been doing. My only objection to his reports are that he continues to talk about his treatment as out-patient care, but in reality it is a partial hospital programme. Studies have demonstrated that approach to be as effective as, or more effective than in-patient care, not only for dependence but in the wider field of mental illness. But again the issue of how you incorporate new findings into practice is complex. The behavioural psychologists are extremely enthusiastic about their results, but for the most part they are not dealing with alcoholics but heavy drinkers, and the results are not generalizable and in my experience do not inform practice. The exciting thing about the Philadelphia group and also the group at Yale, is that they are truly inter-disciplinary and they are trying to advance the broader practice of treatment in these fields. That involves medicine, psychology, and drug counselling.

But, at present, all the insurance side see is many hungry mouths waiting to be fed on the service providers' side. The policy makers see this huge number of providers and they do not want to pay for it.

Dr Thomas Babor (USA): I would like to introduce the concept of an expert committee as an intermediary process between the isolated researcher or scientist and the isolated policy maker, and often that is the way that one speaks to the other and both speak to a broader public. There are some examples. The Royal College of Physicians in 1962 and the Surgeon General's report in the USA in 1964, had a profound effect on first communicating the simple idea that there is a connection between cancer and smoking, and secondly that there is a policy implication stemming from that evidence, and action that should be taken. In the area of drugs, there was an influential report in the 1970s from the US National Marijuana Commission, the title was *Marijuana— a signal of misunderstanding*. That stimulated a lot of sympathy for de-criminalization and a much more open and tolerant attitude towards marijuana. From the WHO and the National Academy of Sciences in the USA you had expert reports, one on *Alcohol control policies in public health perspective*, the other *Beyond the shadow of prohibition*. Both of these attempted to translate a relatively simple idea that came out of research about the connection between per capita consumption and alcohol problems, into policy implication. More recently in the treatment area in the USA, we have had two other National Academy of Science's reports, one on drug abuse, the other on alcoholism treatment.

The ideas that we have heard about the scientific evidence for the effectiveness of brief interventions delivered to heavy drinkers and problem drinkers, people at less severe levels of problems and often in primary care settings, that research could be translated into a mandate to reach out to this larger population. All of these reports and commissions suggest that there is a policy mechanism here that has been well tried. There is also a game that is often played; in many cases the conclusions are almost pre-conceived, somebody says here is the idea that has been around for a while, let's get a commission to certify it, present it to the public. If the exercise is orchestrated properly the policy makers will be ready to take the idea and run with it, and do something. In other cases such a report presents a completely new idea and nobody is ready for it, so they bury the report and pull it out ten years later when things have changed. But by studying this process we may be able to come up with a set of conditions under which policy can benefit from research in an optimal way— mechanisms through which research can deal with public opinion and with a little bit of luck, influence the policy making process.

Dr Tom McLellan (USA): Just to return to a mundane issue regarding follow-up, the choice of six months is not completely arbitrary: George Woody did a review of published studies of alcohol, cigarette, and opiate addiction, and found that between 60 and 80 per cent of relapses, that is return to use, occurred within four to six months following cessation of treatment. I would not claim that it is the best measure of outcome, but at least it is not crazy.

The other issue, I think is an excellent one: the importance of the pre-treatment characteristics of the patient that predict outcome, particular things like psychiatric problems, family problems, employment problems, all that has been confirmed by many centres. I put that together with some of the material that we have been looking at with regard to the provision of professional services during treatment in the following way; it seems to me that you can affect an individual's post-treatment environment. If he or she is provided with family therapy whilst in treatment, you might affect his or her post-treatment family environment.

Dr Jerome Jaffe (USA): I want to respond to Dr Meyer's implicit suggestion that there ought not to be conflict between research and the providers. I think that there is a danger in glossing over real problems: if we do not see problems because they do not please us, then we will not try to find solutions to them. One of the great lies of the world is, 'I'm from the government and I'm here to help you': it ranks along with 'the cheque is in the mail'. The point is that when science conducts evaluation on treatment and draws inferences, it may very well be that there is pain to be distributed. When people in the USA decided that perhaps the military establishment was bigger than it had to be, recognizing the changes in the world, the people surrounding the bases that were recommended for closure did not stand up and say we are delighted that the world is peaceful, please close down the bases and take away our jobs. When we find that one treatment is more effective than the other or more cost effective, the people who are now rendering those services which come off less well in the research will not stand up and thank you, they will lobby for what has become their life's work and their livelihood. So it is a problem for policy to think not only how we can communicate the findings to the legislatures, but how also we might be able to suggest ways in which they can deviate from the usual policy that 'everybody wins, everybody gets a prize', and make it possible to distribute a little bit of the discomfort.

Part V The legalization debate: finding the scientific basis for productive discussion

23. The great legalization debates

Harold Kalant

Policies can never be wholly rational. The reason for such an assertion, however, is inherent in the process of policy formulation itself. Except for those based on dogma or fanaticism, policies are normally formulated by a process that involves either explicit or implicit cost–benefit analysis, and this in turn inevitably implies value judgements that are, by definition, subjective and non-rational. Sometimes it may appear possible to make such judgements by a wholly rational process. For example, a number of chapters in preceding sections of this book have dealt with the evaluation of methods for the treatment of drug dependence. They described objective techniques for evaluating the results of different types of treatment programme, so that these programmes could be compared with respect to the benefits obtained in return for the money expended. Such comparisons could then contribute to the rational formulation of policy options with respect to the types and amounts of treatment services to be provided to a given population. Selecting from among these options, however, departs from the rational process. How much improvement in treatment outcome is worth how much extra expenditure? Since funding for treatment programmes is always limited, any additional amount spent to improve treatment outcome must be at the expense of some other service or function (for example, education, road construction, and unemployment benefits), for which the extra money could have been used. Once again, the comparative evaluation of these competing claims for resources is based finally on subjective values that can not be in themselves purely rational.

The complexity becomes much more obvious when we examine the input of research on broad social, legal, cultural, or economic issues. The great legalization debate about drug use provides a particularly striking example. To be more accurate, we should refer to the legalization debates, because this century has already witnessed at least three such debates: in the 1920s the debate was about the repeal of alcohol prohibition in North America, in the 1960s and 1970s it had to do with the legalization of marijuana, and the current debate was provoked primarily by concerns about cocaine. In all three cases, however, the issues and arguments have been fundamentally similar. Proponents of legalization have, in each case, drawn attention to the huge costs to society that are incurred by attempts to enforce legal prohibition of the drug, and that could be avoided if the drug were made legal. Opponents of legalization, conversely, have emphasized the magnitude of the costs resulting from drug use itself.

It is instructive to examine these arguments in a little more detail, because such an examination may make the distinction between the rational and non-rational elements in the formulation of policy clearer. It is argued that legalization of drugs that are now illicit would eliminate the huge monetary costs of the police activities, courts, and prisons, that are now spent on efforts to suppress the use of these drugs. It is also claimed that legalization and sale of the drugs at moderate prices would eliminate the costs of property crimes committed to obtain money to purchase expensive illicit drugs, and of violent crimes related to competition among drug traffickers. Furthermore, if the drugs were legal, much better quality control would be possible, so that secondary toxicity due to contaminants could be eliminated. All of these claimed effects are potentially quantifiable with more or less accuracy, so that they could be fitted into a reasonably objective cost–benefit analysis. However, it is also argued that legalization would eliminate the personal harm suffered by those who are imprisoned and left with a criminal record as a result of conviction for possession or trafficking. This is not nearly as readily quantifiable, because a high proportion of young drug offenders have prior histories of antisocial behaviour and offences unrelated to drug use. Thus, the harm that can result, at least in theory, from loss of eligibility for certain types of employment, or for visas to enter certain countries because of conviction on drug-related charges, may have little or no consequence for somebody who already has an earlier criminal record for offences unrelated to drugs.

Finally, it is argued that drugs should be legalized because drug use does not warrant application of the coercive power of the state to suppress individual freedom of choice when this freedom does not impinge upon the freedom of other persons. Undoubtedly, many moderate users of drugs do not demonstrably cause harm to others by such use, but clearly some users do. Therefore, it has been argued that drug use, or at least heavy use, is not a 'victimless crime' because it *does* impinge in many ways on the rights and freedoms of other individuals and of society collectively. However, even if we assume that most drug use does not affect non-users adversely, the value placed on the personal freedom to use or not use is clearly an element that differs fundamentally from the others, and is virtually impossible to weigh in the same balance.

Similarly, the arguments *against* legalization are of qualitatively different kinds. It is argued that increased ease of availability of drugs will increase the extent of their use, and thus increase the numbers of medical, psychological, and behavioural problems directly caused by drug use itself. Furthermore, if one of the goals of legalization is to eliminate the illicit traffic in drugs, the price of the licit drugs will have to be low enough to make illicit drugs unattractive, and low price has been shown to be another important stimulus to increased use. It is therefore argued, that the increased costs to the health care system and social services resulting from increased use as a result of legalization could offset the revenue generated by legal sale of the drugs, and the reduced costs of law enforcement. These are all potentially quantifiable consequences that can, at least in theory, be compared on the same scale as the claimed savings that might result from legalization. However, another argument against legalization is that it is not in accord with the moral values and ethical standards of the great majority of citizens of the societies that might consider it, and that it would thus change the character of the society in a way which was at odds with their wishes. This is a very different type of argument, which again can not be weighed in the same balance with the other considerations mentioned above.

Some of the specific claims on both sides are indeed legitimate topics for research. Good research has already been done, and more is desirable, on such topics as: the effects of price, and of ease of accessibility, on levels of drug use and frequencies of different types of adverse effect of use; the consequences of earlier drug policy changes in various societies; economic analyses of the relations between drug use and economic productivity, crime, health costs, etc.; the influence of public attitudes, values, beliefs, and knowledge, on drug use and on social policies about it.

However, no matter how much research is done on these and other questions, and how much accurate and objective knowledge is garnered about them, the final decisions about policy rest on value judgements made both by the public and by the politicians acting in the name of the electorate. It is noteworthy that the 'legalization debate' is being conducted just as much, or more, in the popular media as in the scientific literature. Objective information can not answer questions such as how much personal freedom is worth how much extra social cost, or how much individual dissent from social consensus is desirable or permissible in a given society. It is self-evident that total individual freedom of action is incompatible with the existence of a functioning society, but societies differ with respect to how much individual latitude they are willing or able to tolerate. These are value judgements. Research can ensure that they are made on the basis of the most accurate information, but can not decide the values themselves. We will have to take full conscious responsibility for our own value judgements, and recognize that we act as citizens, not as scientists, when we advocate the adoption of these values, and of the policies that flow from them, by the rest of society.

24. The rise and fall of epidemics: learning from history

David F. Musto

To draw lessons from history is an admirable goal, but one of the lessons of history is that the effort is rarely successful. Proffered 'lessons' often turn out to be deeply held convictions for which a study of history has been only a search for illustration. Some of these 'lessons', for example, those that promise a solution to the drug problem if only some simple, dramatic action is taken, attempt to extract from history more than history has to offer. I have a prejudice against this kind of extrapolation from the past, but subscribe to Richard Hofstadter's observation that although history 'tends to deny that high state of expectation, that hope of ultimate and glorious triumph, that sustains good combatants . . . there may be comfort in it still'. (Hofstadter 1970). This has certainly been my experience after 25 years of studying drug and alcohol issues.

My research has focused on the history of drugs and alcohol in the USA, and on entering this field it seemed that, in general, the previous histories had been constructed by those 'good combatants' whom Hofstadter mentions. The record proved to be more complex and, occasionally, more interesting than the slogans and simplifications that had described the past of this controversial subject. At this point several observations may be offered for consideration.

National climate and the rating of a drug problem

The promotion or restriction of a particular drug is strongly influenced by the specific social history and environment of a nation, as well as by the physiological characteristics of the drug. Although this may seem obvious, the history of drug policy suggests otherwise. This observation is particularly important from the American perspective for two reasons.

First, Americans critical of the prohibitory approach to non-medical drug use in the USA have long had a habit of looking to the drug policies of other nations for models to imitate, while ignoring the context in which those foreign policies existed. Calls for adoption of what has been termed in the

USA the 'British system' illustrate the conviction that a given form of law will lead to similar consequences in different nations.

Secondly, when the USA initiated the world anti-narcotic movement 80 years ago, the beliefs held at that time by the US government (and the vast majority of its citizens) regarding drugs were presented as the standard by which other nations should measure their laws and attitudes (Musto 1987, pp. 35–7). These American policies were related to specific drugs. The standard put more emphasis on a drug's intrinsic dangers and its presumed inherent social effects, than on the societal context or the particular form in which the drug might be available. It advised, therefore, wherever and however the drug might exist, anywhere in the world, its use should be restricted to unquestioned medical purposes. Later, in the 1920s, the US government went further and demanded international elimination of heroin and prohibition of any medical use (Musto 1987, pp. 200–2).

Thus, both those who would liberalize American drug laws in conformity with what they perceived as, say, the 'British system', and those who would demand prohibition of certain drugs in any form everywhere in the world, share a faith in the uniformity of societies which is unwarranted.

The story of the 'British system' in the American debate about drug policy is instructive. In 1920 the Dangerous Drugs Act became law in the UK. Provision was made for the continued prescribing of opiates to those who could not successfully become abstinent. By the 1930s British authorities knew of only a few heroin addicts, while US authorities estimated the number of domestic opiate addicts to be in the tens of thousands. Some American students of the drug problem suspected that the British provision of heroin to the addicted—in contrast to criminal justice procedures in the USA—accounted for the contrasting circumstances (Lindesmith 1947). In recent years the lengthy study published by the Consumer's Union in the USA, *Licit and illicit drugs*, echoed this explanation for the low number of addicts and declared that 'the results can best be described as magnificent . . . by 1935 . . . there were only 700 addicts left in the whole country' (Brecher 1972). The problem with this interpretation is that there were very few addicts in Britain *before* the Act. A distinguished British expert once estimated the number before 1920 as about 75. In conversation with persons who held that the Act exercised great power to reduce addiction, one learns that they assumed that a serious opiate addiction problem prompted the drug law, as had happened in the USA. This, however, was not the case in the UK: the Act was required by the Versailles Treaty. The Hague Convention of 1912 had been made a part of the Versailles Treaty at the suggestion of Great Britain and the USA, and a ratifying nation had 12 months in which to enact the required domestic legislation to implement the Hague Treaty.

One observation to make about this American perception of British drug policy is that advocacy of the 'British system' failed to put the law into historical context. That the law was required by the Versailles Treaty—and did not represent a response to a raging opiate epidemic—was known at the time of passage (Berridge 1978). This was no secret. The earliest stage of historical inquiry would have revealed this.

The full historical context of the Dangerous Drugs Act of 1920, however, would have carried no impact in American debate over drug policy: it could neither be dramatically presented as a panacea for the American problem, nor as a simple and astounding refutation of the policies that did evolve in the USA after the First World War. A reasonably thorough description of the British policies would instead have raised the complex question of differing cultures and the envelopment of drugs deep within a particular nation's social history. It is not easy to offer a solution to changing a nation's social attitudes and traditions: it is much easier to propose a new law.

Even when history becomes a weapon in the war over drug policies, it is rarely considered central to the issues. In fact, the drug problem in the USA is a social problem that to its participants seldom seems to have a history: it just is. The past is brought in more to add colour and anecdotes buttressing a deeply held conviction regarding drug control, than to clarify policy questions.

The size of the problem influences social perceptions

A driving force behind this pressure to simplify the past for purposes of debate is the reality that the drug question touches our deepest beliefs about the control of social problems, and the nature of the society in which we wish to live. The drug problem can assume such proportions in public life that it overshadows everything else. A few years ago in the USA, the drug problem was the leading concern of the public over all other social and political questions. The most important decisions of an entire nation appeared to rest on the fulcrum of drug policy. To the 'good combatants' society itself was at stake, and the controversy over drugs was a debate on the large questions of polity: the limit of freedom and the extent of social control.

One aspect of the situation in the USA that is often ignored is the impact of the number of drug abusers on policy decisions. When drug use was low, local and state laws in the USA often allowed maintenance and left to health professionals the provision of opiates, and even of cocaine when it was initially introduced in the 1880s and 1890s. The lack of any national controls over medical or pharmaceutical practice, and the complete freedom to sell and advertise these drugs, helped spread drug use in the USA at the turn of the century. Subsequently, restrictions were tightened and, after overcoming great constitutional obstacles, national legislation controlling opiates and cocaine was achieved. When the level of drug use in the USA was low, the attitude toward the problem had characteristics that later advocates of the 'British system' admired: drugs were obtained from physicians, addiction was treated in sanitaria or clinics or by the local physician, and penalties were modest or non-existent. Later, when drug use appeared to be out of control, the government reacted by establishing—with strong public support—the more familiar policy of drug prohibition except for strictly medical purposes. Many factors were at work in creating this transition to a fear of drugs, but one which deserves consideration is the role of numbers in formation of policy. One wonders whether this parameter of drug use is little considered because it is too pragmatic for the moral judgements that dominate debate.

International relations and the perception of drug problems

Thus far we have examined policies in the USA. Let us conclude by examining an international aspect of drugs. The drug issue, as crucial and paramount as it may be described by governments to their citizens, is secondary—or even tertiary—to larger international forces, and is not infrequently employed as an instrument to further those national goals. That is, international drug policy is as enmeshed with larger and disparate issues as domestic policy.

The Cold War provides an excellent example of the way in which the larger concerns of great powers find in the narcotics issue an instrument to promote national interests. The example which we will take here is the accusation that 'the People's Republic of China (PRC)' officially engaged in heroin trafficking.

During the UN Commission on Narcotic Drugs (UNCND) meeting on 5 May 1952, the US Narcotics Commissioner, Harry J. Anslinger, Chairman of the US Delegation, launched an attack on the PRC. Anslinger stated that he had copious evidence that the PRC was currently 'the biggest source of the illicit traffic in narcotic drugs in the world'. Evidence from arrested traffickers, Anslinger said, revealed that 'profits from the smuggling were used to finance the activities of the Communist Party and to obtain strategic raw materials' (Anslinger and Tompkins 1953, pp. 73,70). At a later meeting of the UNCND in April 1953, Anslinger continued the attack which can be summarized by his statement that the 'United States is a target of Communist China to be regularly supplied with dollar-earning, health and morale-devastating heroin' (Anslinger and Tompkins 1953, p. 92).

The USSR and the PRC angrily denounced these charges as slanders against the people of China. In a meeting in May 1952 the Soviet delegate explained the slander as attempts by the USA to divert attention from the 'poison gases and bacterial warfare' used by US troops in Korea (Anslinger and Tompkins 1953, p. 72). Later that month the Foreign Ministry of the PRC echoed these charges and stated that the US allegations arose from 'the severe censure by world opinion of the bacterial warfare unleashed by the United States' (United Nations 1952).

Attack and defence continued for years thereafter. The importance the USA attached to the narcotic charges against the PRC can be seen in their frequent attempts to justify the PRC's exclusion from the UN. Anslinger argued in

1956 that the PRC 'needs this new badge of prestige badly if she is to protect and expand her $1 billion a year traffic in narcotics' (US House of Representatives 1956). In 1961 the US Senate passed a resolution opposing the PRC's admission to the UN on several grounds, including 'its export of narcotics to non-communist countries in collaboration with criminal elements in these countries, on a scale that makes it the major source of the international illicit narcotic traffic' (US Senate 1961).

In the mid-1960s, however, remarkable changes took place in great power relationships, and the attitudes of the USA and the USSR regarding Chinese opium traffic underwent an astounding alteration.

After the death of Stalin in 1953, tensions arose between the USSR and the PRC. The PRC, under Mao Zedong, sought not only leadership of the Communist world, but also had sensitive requests, such as adjustments to the Sino-Soviet border that would transfer disputed areas currently under Soviet rule. Khrushchev's rise to the premiership of the USSR in 1958 failed to resolve these differences, and by 1964 the Soviets and the Chinese were at loggerheads.

Drug problems and an international volte-face

In September 1964 *Pravda* published a startling essay entitled 'Traders in narcotics'. The article charged that the dissident government of the PRC financed a 'system of lies and slander' against the USSR 'in large measure by money received from sale of drugs'. The argument continued, 'The smuggling of drugs annually yields $500 million to the present Chinese leaders. . . . This trade has become one of the main sources of convertible currency for the leadership of the Chinese Communist Party' (Ovchinnikov 1964).

This echo of American charges was met with outrage from the PRC, which reminded the Soviets that the USSR had defended the Chinese against similar American accusations as recently as May 1963. At that time, the Soviets had called the attacks 'false and unjustified accusations made for purely political reasons' (Survey of China Mainland Press 1964). While Beijing sent volleys of epithets at both the USA and the USSR, the official statements by the USA were muted. Changes were stirring in the USA, also.

In the mid-1960s a re-evaluation of the PRC was forming in the USA. The possibility was slowly entertained that the PRC, now an enemy of the USSR, could become a recognized entity with normal diplomatic relations. One of the first signs that the wind had changed direction was a statement on narcotics by Henry Fowler, US Secretary of the Treasury. In May 1967, Fowler announced that only about 5 per cent of the heroin smuggled into the USA 'might' come from the Far East (*Los Angeles Times* 1967). More concessions were to follow.

In July 1971, President Nixon announced that he would visit the PRC (as he did in February 1972) and 'seek the normalization of relations'. Less noticed was a statement the US State Department had issued two weeks earlier: 'So far as we are aware, opium is not grown legally in the People's Republic of China and none is exported by the Chinese Communist authorities' (US House of Representatives 1971). In October 1971, the PRC was admitted to the UN and assumed its seat on the Security Council. Two days later the State Department spokesman stated: 'There is no reliable evidence that the Communist Chinese have ever engaged in or sanctioned the illicit export of opium or its derivatives. Nor is there any evidence of that country exercising any control over or participating in the Southeast Asia opium trade' (US House of Representatives 1972).

While the USA officially retracted almost two decades of detailed charges against the PRC, the USSR hugged its new line and persisted in alleging that the Maoists were producing and distributing opium. The Soviets must have taken some pleasure in quoting the many US media reports on the PRC's complicity in narcotics trade back to an American government now denying that the PRC 'ever engaged' in the nefarious traffic.

When we examine this prolonged example of the Cold War's impact on international narcotics policy we cannot determine just where the truth lay, but we can be reasonably confident that the switch in solemn and detailed official statements about the PRC was related to realignments among the great powers and not to changes in the narcotics activities (or inactivities) of the Chinese mainland government.

History, policy, and reasonable judgements

In conclusion, a review of the history of dangerous drugs in the last century reveals that what at first appears a discrete problem caused by substances that can be seen, weighed, and held, is entwined with society, culture, politics, and international rivalries. The drug question operates at many levels, from that of an individual who may or may not as a result of socialization become a drug user, to the great arena of international politics, in which the drama and fear of drugs may be enlisted for purposes totally unrelated to drugs. The more we know of this history, the more likely it is that citizens will make reasonable judgements about drug policy.

Acknowledgements

My understanding of the controversy among the governments of the US, PRC, and USSR was aided by Allison B. Spadone's Yale College senior essay: *Chasing the dragon: two decades of American accusations against communist China and its role in the illicit narcotics traffic*. I also thank Jennifer Spiegel for assistance in the preparation of this chapter.

References

Anslinger, H.J. and Tompkins, W.F. (1953). *The traffic in narcotics.* Funk and Wagnalls, New York.

Berridge, V. (1978). War conditions and narcotics control: the passing of defense of the realm act regulation 40B. *Journal of Social Policy,* 7, 285–304.

Brecher, E.M. (1972). *Licit and illicit drugs, the Consumers Union report on narcotics, stimulants, depressants, inhalants, hallucinogens, and marijuana—including caffeine, nicotine and alcohol.* Little, Brown, Boston.

Hofstadter, R. (1970). *The progressive historians, Turner, Beard, Parrington.* Vintage Books, New York.

Lindesmith, A.R. (1947). *Opiate addiction.* Principia Press, Bloomington.

Los Angeles Times (1967). Illicit U.S. narcotics traffic does not provide communist China with any significant amount of American dollars. 28 May 1967.

Musto, D.F. (1987). *The American disease: origins of narcotic control* (expanded edition). Oxford University Press, New York.

Ovchinnikov, V. (1964). Traders in narcotics. *Pravda,* 13 September 1964.

Survey of China Mainland Press (1964). Has Pravda no sense of shame? asks Jen-min Jih-pao, Observer. Peiking. 21 September 1964.

United Nations (1952). *Narcotic drugs: statement circulated at the request of the delegation of the U.S.S.R.* UN Economic and Social Council, 14th session, agenda item 19, 27 May 1952.

US House or Representatives (1961). *Congressional Record.* 17 February 1961.

US House of Representatives (1971). *Congressional Record.* 7 June 1971.

US House of Representatives (1972). *Congressional Record.* 29 March 1972.

US Senate (1961). *Senate resolution No. 34.* 87th Congress, 31 August 1961.

25. Behavioural pharmacology of addictive drugs: cost, availability, and individual differences

Ian Stolerman

Psychopharmacological evidence is one of several inputs to policy decisions. This chapter considers some studies in behavioural pharmacology that relate to the impact of variations in cost and availability on the extent of substance use. It goes on to highlight possible future contributions pertinent to the regulation of availability, and suggests that individual differences should be studied more extensively.

Drugs as reinforcers

The central insight of the behavioural approach to addiction has been the realization that drugs can serve as positive reinforcers in a manner much like conventional, non-pharmacological stimuli. Thus, experimental models in which animal or human subjects self-administer drugs have been developed so that drug-seeking responses may be examined under defined and controlled conditions. This work places drug-seeking behaviour in the context of other instrumental behaviours in which learning factors play an important role at all times. Most frequently, animal subjects have been used and the drugs have been made accessible through chronic venous catheters. This technology is used because the short interval of time between a behavioural response and the onset of effects with intravenous delivery facilitates learning. Using parenteral routes for administering drugs also eliminates effects associated with the taste of the drugs, an important factor if drug solutions are made available for oral consumption.

Extensive studies of the reinforcing effects of many different drugs have established an impressive correlation between the ability to maintain self-administration behaviour above control rates in the laboratory and addiction liability in the community. While amphetamines, cocaine, opioid agonists such as morphine, heroin and codeine, dissociative anaesthetics, ethanol, nicotine, barbiturates, and benzodiazepines can serve as positive reinforcers and are addictive, conversely, antidepressants, neuroleptics, narcotic antagonists, and aspirin are neither reinforcing nor addictive in normal circumstances. This is an impressive relationship and there are few exceptions. Procaine is reinforcing but seemingly not addictive, whereas lysergic acid diethylamide (LSD) is abused but has not been found to serve as a reinforcer in studies to date (results of self-administration studies with tetrahydrocannabinols have been inconclusive).

Nicotine and cocaine compared

The question of whether self-administration studies can quantify the reinforcing efficacy of drugs needs to be considered because the propensity for abuse is relative; policy has to balance the risks of abuse against the dangers of excessive criminal penalties. Katz (1990) has reviewed methods for comparing the relative reinforcing efficacy of different drugs and has concluded that quantification is very difficult with existing methods. Nevertheless, comparisons between nicotine and cocaine may be illuminating.

Both nicotine and cocaine can serve as positive reinforcers, but when direct comparisons have been made, nicotine has appeared to have the weaker effect (Ator and Griffiths 1980; Goldberg and Spealman 1982; Griffiths *et al.* 1979; Risner and Goldberg 1983). For example, in studies of intravenous drug self-administration, dogs would emit up to 1000–4000 pedal-pressing responses to obtain cocaine (Risner and Goldberg 1983) (Fig. 25.1). The same dogs would emit no more than 300–500 responses to obtain nicotine (at optimal doses in each case), although this was above the non-drug control level of about 100 responses for infusions of saline. Thus, nicotine and cocaine can maintain self-administration through similar behavioural processes, but the effect of nicotine is weaker than that of cocaine except under narrowly circumscribed conditions (Goldberg and Spealman 1982).

The preceding comparison between nicotine and cocaine indicates clearly the important role of availability and social factors on the extent of drug use. The relatively weak reinforcing effect of nicotine contrasts markedly with the relative frequency of use among the general population. For example, the US Household Survey and other surveys discussed by Goldstein and Kalant (1990) reported that their respondents were 20–100 times more likely to have used nicotine than cocaine in the preceding month. This apparent dissonance between relative reinforcing efficacy and patterns of use reflects not a disagreement but a striking convergence of laboratory and clinical findings; a recurring and often repeated theme in the experimental literature of the last 25 years has been the malleability of reinforcing stimulus properties of drugs as a function of environmental factors, prime among which has been availability of a substance as defined by behavioural factors, such as schedules of reinforcement. Factors such as drug dose per reinforcer presented, duration of access to drugs, and schedule-associated factors (such as the amount of work required to obtain each dose), have all been shown to influence profoundly

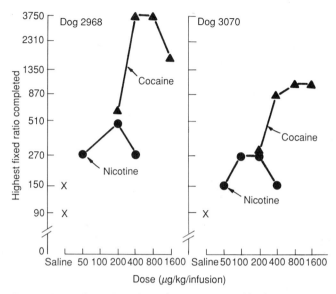

Fig. 25.1 Comparison of nicotine (●) and cocaine (▲) self-administration in two dogs with chronic venous catheters. Ordinates, largest numbers of lever presses made to obtain the doses shown (numbers of lever presses required to obtain infusions were increased progressively until responding ceased). Crosses (X) represent lever presses emitted to obtain saline control solutions. Each point shows result of a single determination for the dose shown (dog 2968 was tested twice with saline). Note the logarithmic scale used for the ordinate. (Reproduced from Risner and Goldberg (1983)).

the amounts of drug-taking seen in laboratory self-administration studies with a wide variety of drugs. Although direct laboratory analogues for social factors have been studied rarely, there is no incompatibility between the reinforcement-based behavioural model and a key role for social factors as a determinant of use. Thus, social factors may modulate the relative reinforcing efficacy of different drugs. Furthermore, variations in the response requirements to obtain drugs in the laboratory provide a viable model for price-related factors in clinical situations.

Behavioural economics of self-administration

Laboratory data on drug self-administration have been re-analysed recently in a novel and provocative manner from the point of view of behavioural economics (Bickel *et al.* 1990). This approach determines the relationship between unit price and consumption in studies of drug intake by subjects under controlled conditions. It complements traditional analyses of the cost/consumption relationship in community studies, and aids their interpretation.

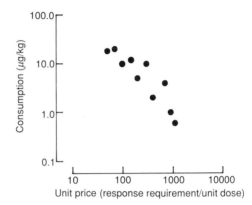

Fig. 25.2   Consumption of cocaine by a squirrel monkey, as a function of unit price, based on the re-analysis by Bickel *et al.* (1990) of data from Goldberg (1973). The monkey pressed a response key to self-administer the drug through a chronic venous catheter under fixed-ratio schedules of reinforcement.

It may help to strengthen links between laboratory studies, clinical practice, and policy.

Many studies of drug self-administration yield a similar outcome when analysed in this way; consumption increases when unit price decreases. Figure 25.2 shows the re-analysis by Bickel *et al.* (1990) of data from Goldberg (1973) and illustrates how even the consumption of cocaine, which is probably the most powerful of all pharmacological reinforcers, is sensitive to variations in price. Unit price is defined here as the work (operant responses) required to obtain each dose of the drug (response requirement/unit dose). Consumption is measured as the total amount of drug taken (unit dose × number of doses taken).

Much the same relationship has been seen for a variety of drugs (for example cocaine, nicotine, methohexital, ketamine, and phencyclidine), embracing three routes (oral, inhaled, and intravenous), and several species (rat, squirrel monkey, rhesus monkey, and human). All these data suggest that, other factors being equal, reducing the price and thus accessibility of drugs will encourage the tendency for their use. This principle seems likely to apply to both licit and illicit substances. The relationship demonstrated has been clear and powerful enough to be seen in individual subjects, it holds across a reasonable range of conditions, it is based on precise measurements under well-defined conditions where other variables could not have co-varied with unit price and confounded the outcome. Although most of the data are from studies in animals, the similarity of outcomes across different species suggests that the findings are not species-specific. When laboratory science yields a conclusion like this, it is perilous to ignore its implications.

The application of the ideas of behavioural economics to drug self-administration needs further development. Although the general form of the relationship between unit price and consumption seems quite consistent across different drugs, existing studies do not allow for comparisons of the slope of the cost/consumption curves for different substances. Thus, it is difficult to compare the relative risks involved in decreasing the unit prices of heroin, cocaine, nicotine, and alcohol. Studies enabling such comparisons to be made may be scientifically valuable because they suggest an approach to quantifying the relative reinforcing efficacy of different drugs, at present a difficult undertaking (Katz 1990).

Individual variation: self-administration

In many laboratory studies, it appears that all subjects self-administer drugs and various factors combine to obscure individual differences. First, procedures are commonly set to maximize acquisition and performance of the behaviour for the largest number of subjects. Secondly, most studies seek to reach general conclusions and adopt methods to minimize individual variability. For example, inbred strains of animals are used wherever possible, and environmental factors are held constant to ensure that as far as possible all subjects have a similar history prior to commencement of experimentation. Thirdly, many experiments study only variations in self-administration performance after the behaviour has been acquired; in such cases, subjects that do not reach a criterion of performance are removed from the study.

However admirable these experimental strategies may be, in many instances they have tended to direct attention away from the practically important questions of why some subjects with access to drugs sample them and others do not, and why it is that some people maintain patterns of relatively light use over long periods of time whereas others in similar circumstances become heavy users. Studies of the role of behavioural and pharmacological history in determining effects of addictive drugs may help to shed light on these questions. Some recent studies have yielded provocative results.

Piazza *et al.* (1989) compared rates of amphetamine self-administration in two populations of rats selected according to their basal levels of locomotor activity. Rats that had previously exhibited large amounts of locomotor activity increased their rates of operant responding when solutions of amphetamine were available under a simple schedule of reinforcement, and thus acquired drug-seeking behaviour readily. In contrast, rats that had exhibited smaller amounts of activity did not increase their rates of operant responding above baseline levels; these rats could be induced to self-administer amphetamine after five daily priming injections of the drug given without any requirement for operant responding. The differences in the propensity to self-administer amphetamine were thought to be related to individual differences in the status of the dopamine system that is known to play a major role in mediating both the locomotor activity and the reinforcing effects. How these differences in the dopamine system came about was unclear, but findings such as these indicate one route that is open for studying individual differences in addiction liability.

Individual differences: drug discrimination

Other studies have shown that previous behavioural history of subjects can markedly influence and sometimes even reverse the effects of addictive drugs on rates of operant responding (Barrett *et al.* 1989). The exact significance of these findings for understanding of addiction is unclear but other work has shown that the way that drug discriminations are established can greatly influence their characteristics. Such drug discrimination work is directly pertinent to addiction because it is arguably the closest approximation to assessing in animals a process functionally related to subjective effects of drugs in humans (Preston and Bigelow 1991). Recent studies on the discrimination of mixtures of amphetamine plus pentobarbitone illustrate this point.

Rats were trained to discriminate mixtures of amphetamine plus pentobarbitone under two different procedures, and the characteristics of the discriminations were then compared. Training procedures were then equated and the discriminations were compared again. The first group of rats was trained simply to discriminate between the mixture and the undrugged state, a standard procedure (Mariathasan *et al.* 1991). When tested, these rats showed strong dose-related discriminative responses to amphetamine and pentobarbitone separately, as well as to the mixtures, suggesting that the mixtures were perceived in terms of their component drugs rather than as a unique and distinctive entity (Fig. 25.3, left section). The second group of rats was trained to discriminate between the mixture and either amphetamine or pentobarbitone given separately, a novel procedure (Stolerman and Mariathasan 1990). When tested, these rats exhibited a strong dose–response curve with the mixture, but little response to any dose of either amphetamine or pentobarbitone administered separately; in other words, the mixture behaved as a unique entity that was totally distinguishable from its components. Furthermore, when these rats were placed on the standard training regimen (mixture versus undrugged state), the altered response persisted for at least several weeks (Fig. 25.3, right section).

These results suggest that a history of experimenting with single drugs prior to using them as mixtures may change an individual's perception of the effects of the mixture. One can speculate that the circumstances surrounding the use of the drugs, such as information or misinformation given about them, may influence their perceived effects and thus the tendency to continue taking them (i.e. their reinforcing effects).

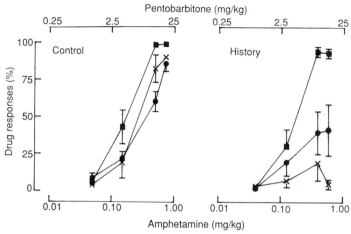

Fig. 25.3 Discriminative stimulus effects of amphetamine (X) and pentobarbitone (●) separately and as mixtures (■) in two groups of rats (n = 8–10). Left section shows results for control rats trained to discriminate a mixture of (+)– amphetamine (0.5 mg/kg sc) plus pentobarbitone (12 mg/kg sc) from saline throughout their experimental history (mixture versus saline training). Right section shows results from rats with a previous history of training to discriminate a mixture from either drug alone, followed by instatement of mixture versus saline training 3 weeks before collection of the data shown. (Modified from Stolerman and Mariathasan (1990) and Mariathasan *et al.* (1991).)

Individual differences: reinstatement effects

Other studies also indicate a possible influence of discriminative drug effects on drug-seeking behaviour. Stretch and Gerber (1973) reported that in monkeys that had been trained previously to self-administer amphetamine, the self-administration response could be reinstated after periods of extinction by administering doses of the drug without any response requirement. Experiments of this type suggest that perception of the drug effect may act as a cue triggering further bouts of drug-taking. Later work suggested that these effects were dependent on the previous history of the subjects. Thus, in rats with a previous history of heroin intake, morphine, but not cocaine, cued further drug-directed responding, whereas in rats with a history of cocaine intake, cocaine, but not morphine, cued responding (De Wit and Stewart 1981, 1983). Discriminative effects of previously used substances may therefore encourage further intake of substances in a pharmacologically selective manner. However, these priming effects of drugs on self-administration behaviour have not been studied extensively and much more work is needed to strengthen and extend the existing findings.

Conclusions

From the beginning of the era of laboratory studies of drug self-administration, right through to the present day, it has been apparent that availability is a major factor determining the amounts taken. Animals with continuous access to large doses of drugs may self-administer them to the extent of producing serious toxicity and even death. Controlling availability by means of schedules of intermittent reinforcement powerfully influences the doses obtained, the amounts of drug-seeking behaviour and its temporal patterns. Reducing the 'price' of drugs (defined in terms of work requirement per unit of dose) increases consumption of several drugs self-administered by different species via various routes of administration. Thus, laboratory studies indicate clearly that making drugs more easily available by decreasing their price or by reducing sanctions against their use will have the inevitable effect of increasing consumption. Decisions on the issues of legalization and decriminalization must therefore balance the adverse effects of increased drug use against the claimed advantages of such measures. How such a balancing equation can be formulated is a question that needs to be addressed.

The next decade of laboratory studies will highlight new facets of drug-seeking behaviour. One important way in which such studies may contribute to the legalization debate is by determining whether the consumption of certain drugs is increased in a particularly marked manner by reductions in price. Another increasingly active area of research relates to individual differences that have for so long been largely ignored or thrust aside in many studies. Investigations now beginning are likely to illuminate the roles of both genetic and environmental factors as determinants of intake. Laboratory studies can complement and support the endeavours of social scientists in this field by evaluating the way previous history interacts with current circumstances in the genesis of drug-seeking behaviour. Laboratory studies will not succeed either on their own terms or as a source of information for policy makers if they ignore hypotheses derived from social science. Similarly, social science will not advance if it formulates its hypotheses and collects its data in such a way that the psychopharmacology of addiction and the biological effects of drugs are ignored. The way ahead, through multi-disciplinary research, requires mutual respect and understanding between all participants.

References

Ator, N.A. and Griffiths, R.R. (1980). Intravenous self-administration of nicotine in the baboon. *Fed. Proc.* 40, 298.

Barrett, J.E., Glowa, J.R., and Nader, M.A. (1989). Behavioral and pharmacological history as determinants of tolerance- and sensitization-like phenomena in drug action. In *Psychoactive drugs: tolerance and sensitization*. (ed. A.J. Goudie and M.W. Emmett-Oglesby), pp. 181–219, Humana Press, Clifton, N.J.

Bickel, W.K., DeGrandpre, R.J., Higgins, S.T., and Hughes, J.R. (1990). Behavioral economics of drug self-administration. I. Functional equivalence of response requirement and drug dose. *Life Sci.*, **47**, 1501–10.

De Wit, H. and Stewart, J. (1981). Reinstatement of cocaine-reinforced responding in the rat. *Psychopharmacology*, **75**, 134–43.

De Wit, H. and Stewart, J. (1983). Drug reinstatement of heroin-reinforced responding in the rat. *Psychopharmacology*, **79**, 29–31.

Goldberg, S.R. (1973). Comparable behavior maintained under fixed-ratio and second-order schedules of food presentation, cocaine injection or *d*-amphetamine injection in the squirrel monkey. *J. Pharmac. Exp. Ther.*, **186**, 18–30.

Goldberg, S.R. and Spealman, R.D. (1982). Maintenance and suppression of behavior by intravenous nicotine injections in squirrel monkeys. *Fed. Proc.*, **421**, 216–20.

Goldstein, A. and Kalant, H. (1990). Drug policy: striking the right balance. *Science*, **249**, 1513–21.

Griffiths, R.R., Brady, J.V., and Bradford, L.D. (1979). Predicting the abuse liability of drugs with animal drug self-administration procedures: psychomotor stimulants. In *Advances in Behavioral Pharmacology*, Vol. 2, (ed. T. Thompson and P.B. Dews) pp. 163–208. Academic Press, New York.

Katz, J.L. (1990). Models of relative reinforcing efficacy of drugs and their predictive utility. *Behavioral Pharmacology*, **1**, 283–301.

Mariathasan, E.A., Garcha, H.S., and Stolerman, I.P. (1991). Discriminative stimulus effects of amphetamine and pentobarbitone separately and as mixtures in rats. *Behavioral Pharmacology*, **2**, 405–15.

Piazza, P.V., Deminière, J.-M., Le Moal, M., and Simon, H. (1989). Factors that predict individual vulnerability to amphetamine self-administration. *Science*, **245**, 1511–13.

Preston, K.L. and Bigelow, G.E. (1991). Subjective and discriminative effects of drugs. *Behavioral Pharmacology*, **2**, 293–313.

Risner, M.E. and Goldberg, S.R. (1983). A comparison of nicotine and cocaine self-administration in the dog: fixed-ratio and progressive-ratio schedules of intravenous drug infusion. *J. Pharmac. Exp. Ther.*, **224**, 319–26.

Stretch, R. and Gerber, G.J. (1973). Drug-induced reinstatement of amphetamine self-administration behaviour in monkeys. *Canadian Journal of Psychology*, **27**, 168–77.

Stolerman, I.P., and Mariathasan, E.A. (1990). Discrimination of an amphetamine-pentobarbitone mixture by rats in an AND-OR discrimination paradigm. *Psychopharmacology*, **102**, 557–60.

26. Projections of the health consequences of illicit drug use: what contribution to the legalization debate?

John Strang and Graham Medley

The search for scientific truths

What does the study of the health consequences have to contribute to the formation of policy in the area of use of drugs that are currently prohibited from popular consumption? One might have thought that policy would be heavily influenced by science: and that of all areas of science the study of health consequences would weigh particularly heavily in the balance, when policy makers consider health and social policies, and control and legal sanctions. What a disappointment to find that the relationship is not so intimate or uncorrupted. Moore and Gerstein (1981) describe it thus:

In a democracy, government policy is inevitably guided by commonly shared simplifications. This is true because the political dialogue that authorises or animates government policy can rarely support ideas that are very complex or entirely novel. There are too many people with diverse perceptions and interests and too little time and inclination to create a shared perception of a complex structure. Consequently influential policy ideas are typically formulated at a quite low level and borrow heavily from commonly shared understanding and conventional opinions.

An orthodox approach to this subject might be to catalogue (drug by drug, or organ by organ) the health consequences of illicit drug use. However, an alternative approach is employed in this chapter: first, an examination is undertaken of the relationships that may exist between drug use and health consequences (including consideration of mathematical models of the epidemics which may be constructed), following which consideration is given to the extent to which cognizance of the health consequences has informed and influenced (or failed to influence) the debate about national drug policy, and hence the legalization debate.

Different types of scientific truth

The health consequences of drug use for the individual and the population are different. Traditionally, medicine (and hence policy) are rightly concerned with the individual's welfare, but policy and the monitoring of policy usually occur at the community or population level. In most cases, the health of individuals and population are benefited by the same policy changes, but occasionally this is not so. Discussions about health and health policy are usually clearer if it is made explicit whether it is the individual, population or both that is under consideration.

Different relationships exist between use of a drug and potential health consequences to individual and population. One important distinction is the extent to which the relationship is either *stable* or *changing* at both levels. With some drugs, such as alcohol or tobacco, there is a reasonably stable relationship over time between the individual's use of the drug and risk of identified health consequences. However, population morbidity is affected not only by per capita consumption, but also by the manner in which this consumption is distributed through the community. The profile of the prevalences of different health consequences will then vary according to the different patterns of drug use: for example, the different patterns of alcohol-related morbidity in North European and Mediterranean countries. Nevertheless, the charting of changes in the extent of use of the drug acts as a reasonable handle on the likely levels of current or future health consequences.

To what extent can it be assumed that the use of illicit drugs in the late twentieth century has a stable relationship with associated harm? When considering injectable drugs, the relationship has been changed by hepatitis B, and more recently by HIV. In contrast to direct toxicity and septicaemia, which are more quantifiable and less subject to change, the risks associated with HIV are uncertain and changing faster. In considering the drugs/HIV relationship, a more complex model is required. The extent and nature of the drug use itself will have a changing relationship with the health consequences as sero-prevalence levels increase. This consideration is further complicated when one considers varying degrees of infectivity during the natural history of HIV progression. If infectivity is found to be mainly associated with viraemia around the period of original infection and then again at the time of HIV disease manifestation, then the relationship between drug use and health consequences will vary greatly according to the stage of HIV disease of either the individual or the group under study. It is as if an attempt was being made to consider the relationship between alcohol and cirrhosis, or between tobacco and carcinoma of the lung, at a time not only prior to the discovery of the nature of the relationship, but when the relationships themselves were only developing. Furthermore, the relationship acts both ways: HIV spread is both influenced by and influences injecting drug use. Changes induced by the HIV epidemic will alter the pattern of spread, and these changes occur on a time scale which is faster than both policy and research, making the study even more complicated.

Different models of health consequences

How might an attempt be made to project the health consequences associated with, for example, HIV infection in injecting drug misusers? The projections of the exponential explosion in the spread of HIV in society are now familiar, but what is required is an examination behind these graphs so as to tease out the factors associated with the slope and eventual level of such epidemic curves. It is necessary to emphasize that HIV is transmitted through injecting and sexual behaviour. As with all infectious diseases, the degree of spread of the epidemic in the population is greatly influenced by the behaviour of those who are, as yet, uninfected, and those already infected. Indeed, it is the transmission process (i.e. behaviour) which has the most influence on the dissemination of any infectious disease in a population, be it measles, malaria, or cholera (Anderson and May 1991). But it is not enough simply to quantify the behaviour involved: we must also know how behaviour is influenced by the epidemic, and also how the transmission is influenced by behaviour.

These interrelationships are almost always counter-intuitive, and belie attempts to think about them without some quantitative framework. This is because the relationships are complex and non-linear: a halving of the number of shared syringes will not simply halve the number of people who become infected with HIV. A useful tool in these situations is the construction of mathematical models to assess the interactions of these myriad processes.

Different mathematical methods have been developed for making projections of the health consequences of HIV infection and AIDS. Some are specialized to consider different transmission groups, for example, homosexual men, injecting drug users, and sex workers, while some are more general methods which allow data from the epidemic to be analysed, regardless of the route of transmission. For reviews of this subject see Anderson (1988 1989) and Anderson and May (1992). There are three broad catagories of model which have proved useful in this respect.

With the first method (Fig. 26.1), an examination is made of the past trends so as to assign a simple mathematical function to the course of the epidemic to date, following which there is the exercise of extrapolating the curve into the future. Problems inherent in this approach include the practical task of identifying the correct mathematical function at such an early stage in the unfolding course of the epidemic; to which must be added the uncertainty as to whether the future course of the epidemic will necessarily follow the mathematical function which described the early part of the curve. Figure 26.1 demonstrates the results of such an exercise for injecting drug users in England and Wales.

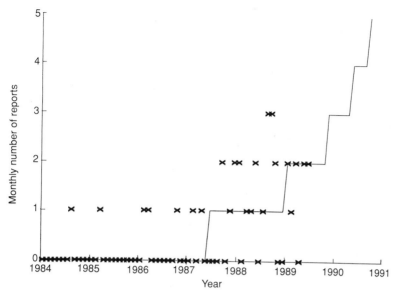

Fig. 26.1 Methods of evaluating future patterns in the AIDS epidemic. The results of fitting a simple exponential curve to the monthly reports of AIDS cases among intravenous drug users in England and Wales (points). (Data supplied by the Communicable Disease Surveillance Service, PHLS, Colindale, London. Method given in Cox and Medley (1989).)

The second approach is that of 'back calculation': this involves an examination of actual AIDS cases and the distribution of the incubation period of AIDS for these subjects, from which a calculation can be made of the number of HIV infected individuals in the population from which the AIDS cases have emerged (Fig. 26.2). However, not only is the accuracy of this method dependent on the quality of information provided, but it is also complicated by the introduction of study contaminants, such as the arrival of an effective treatment which arrests or slows down the rate of disease progression. It is also important to note that due to the form of the incubation period (only a small percentage of infections progress to AIDS in the first four years), estimates of HIV infection incidence in the most recent years are very uncertain.

The third approach requires more complex mathematical modelling so as to accommodate the different biological and epidemiological processes within different populations and with different risk behaviours and co-morbidities (see Fig. 26.3). For any such approach, detailed information is required on the transmission dynamics: for example, what are the sexual or drug injecting and drug sharing behaviours of different groups, and the extent of overlap or interference between sexual and injecting behaviours?

It is evident that a different epidemic curve will be seen with injecting drug

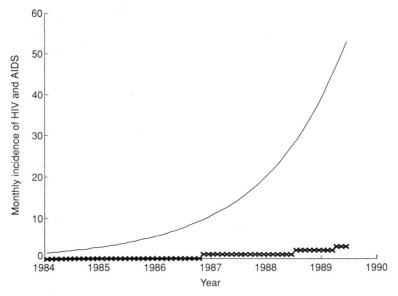

Fig. 26.2 Methods of evaluating future patterns in the AIDS epidemic. An example of the back-calculation method in which the monthly HIV incidence (upper curve) is inferred from the assumed exponential pattern of AIDS diagnoses used in Fig. 26.1. (The method used is due to Becker *et al.* 1991)

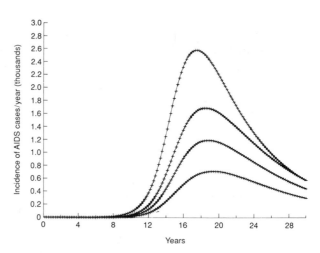

Fig. 26.3 Method of evaluating future patterns in the AIDS epidemic. An example of a simple transmission model used to examine the effects of heterogeneity in sexual behaviour (the lines show increasing heterogeneity from highest to lowest). (Reproduced from Anderson *et al.* (1986).)

users from the curve seen with homosexual and bisexual men. At present (1991) in the UK, the epidemic among injecting drug users is still undergoing a steep exponential rise while that among homosexual men has slowed to a constant number of new notifications per year. In the UK and in many other countries and cities around the world, the HIV epidemic amongst drug injectors is currently at a fascinating point, where there are substantial variations in the slope of attack of the epidemic curve. The epidemics among drug injectors in the infamous HIV cities of New York, USA (Des Jarlais and Friedman 1990), Edinburgh, UK (Brettle *et al.* 1987; Robertson 1990), Milan, Italy (Tempesta and Di Giantonio 1990), and Bangkok, Thailand, have been described with rapid spread extensively through the drug injecting populations within a year or so. However, the rate and extent of spread has been much less in some cities, such as San Francisco, USA (Moss 1990; Moss and Vranizan 1992), Amsterdam, the Netherlands (Buning 1990), Glasgow, and London, UK. Why should there be such marked international and inter-urban variations? Time will tell whether there may also be changes in the *eventual* extent of penetration of the virus into populations of injecting drug misusers.

There is a 'lente' nature to the impact of this lentevirus. Even if further transmission were to stop today, the health consequences will only become evident over the course of the next decade or so, or over an even longer period once treatments become available which result in a delaying of illness manifestation and a slowing of subsequent disease progression. The speed with which there may be cessation of transmission of the virus will have a major impact, not so much on the year of peak incidence of AIDS cases, but more markedly on the size of the peak and the cumulative total of infected individuals.

In a separate modelling exercise, Anderson and colleagues examined the impact of AIDS on changes in sexual behaviour amongst homosexual men, and plotted the predicted quarterly AIDS incidence rate according to three possible circumstances: either no change in frequency of change of sexual partner, or a 50 per cent reduction in frequency of change of sexual partner from 1986 onwards, or a 50 per cent reduction in 1986 followed by a further halving in 1989 (Fig. 26.4). The strikingly different resulting courses of the unfolding epidemic are evident. The evidence now emerging of change in the shape of the epidemic amongst homosexual men suggests that the unfolding curve is most closely represented by the bottom trajectory in this figure, consistent with self-report data of substantial behavioural change by 1989 (supported by evidence at that time of accompanying reductions in incidence rates, for example, of anal gonorrhea). But again, it has not yet been possible to tease out the relative contribution of behaviour change and saturation effects: that is, the point in the unfolding epidemic when contacts which would have resulted in transmission are between individuals already infected. For example, does the infection prevalence of 20–30 per cent of homosexual men attending clinics for sexually transmitted disease in central London, UK

Drugs, alcohol, and tobacco

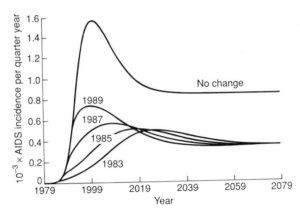

Fig. 26.4 The importance of early reduction in sexual behaviour on the future pattern of the AIDS epidemic. The years indicate when sexual behaviour was reduced from an average of 8.7 different partners per year to 5 partners per year. (Reproduced from Anderson *et al.* (1989).)

represent a success with regard to changing behaviour? What would the prevalence have been without any change, or with a different change or at a different time: 70 per cent as in San Francisco, USA? The same question put more pertinently might be as follows: if the supposed change is reversed, by how much will prevalence rise?

Neither homosexual men nor injecting drug abusers are so obliging to behave as if they were a homogeneous group. Perhaps the change might only occur in a susceptible fraction of the total population; or perhaps only in new recruits into injecting; or perhaps in all individuals. Such change of behaviour as does occur may be insufficiently robust to be sustained over time: for example, recent evidence on sexually-transmitted diseases suggests a slipping-back to earlier patterns of behaviour, as evidenced by an upturn in rate of surrogate markers, such as anal gonorrhoea, by 1990, indicating either 'relapse' amongst pre-existing group members or a re-emergence of former patterns of behaviour amongst new entrants to the behaviour group. The influence of this different distribution of behavioural change has a marked impact on both the peak of the epidemic and the longer-term endemic patterns within the population.

Modelling of the HIV/'drug' interaction

How might modelling help us to anticipate the various possible unfolding courses of morbidity and mortality amongst drug users? Against a shifting baseline of changing prevalence (far more rapidly variable than for most health considerations), it may nevertheless be possible to extrapolate and make projections according to different sets of presumptions. Projections within confidence bands can be made if the prevalence of illicit drug use remains constant and the extent, frequency, and nature of needle-sharing and sexual behaviours do not change. Likewise, the exercise can be conducting against a shifting baseline if it is given that illicit drug use will increase annually by a constant proportion (or according to any other such given function). For an example of an attempt at this, see the work of Blower and colleagues (Blower *et al.* 1991; Blower and Medley 1992).

From this position it is then possible to consider the input of various behavioural changes. What would be the impact if all injectors were to stop any further sharing of needles and syringes? Or if the extent of sharing was halved? And, if halved, what would be the different impacts if this was evenly spread across the injecting population, or alternatively was achieved by cessation of injecting in one half of the population but not changed with the other half? What influence might be anticipated by factors which increased or decreased the geographical mobility of drug injectors (for example travel across, or between, countries in response to different perceived treatment availability)? And what different influences on the epidemic might occur with public or personal health measures which seek either to achieve major reductions in risk behaviour in a small proportion of those at risk, or alternatively minor reductions in the majority of those at risk?

Studying the relationship between injecting and HIV without including sexual transmission is building on the shifting sands of uncertain data. The interaction between injecting and sexual transmission is an additional, probably crucial, complication. Statistics collected nationally and locally may show the number of infected, injecting people, but what proportion of these were actually infected by the sexual route: 1 per cent, 10 per cent, or 50 per cent? Sex is the route of transmission to which most people are exposed, so that policy designed to alter injecting behaviour must consider the implications to individual injectors, their sexual and non-injecting partners, and hence the wider population.

Additional efforts have included consideration of different networks of choice of sexual partner: and here there may be merit in the application of mathematical modelling to consideration of choice of partner for sharing of needle and syringe. When mixing or sharing is occurring at a high level but entirely within group, the epidemic curve not only peaks at a lower level but also reachers a lower plateau, although it may be necessary to consider a multi-peaked curve as different rates of transmission are seen between high-sharing and low-sharing individuals within these groups (for example see Fig. 26.5.)

Thus, the original simple epidemic curve for the spread of HIV (see Figs. 26.1, 26.2 and 26.3) may actually be more complex, representing the cumulative total from different groups. Clearly all is not what it seems at first sight.

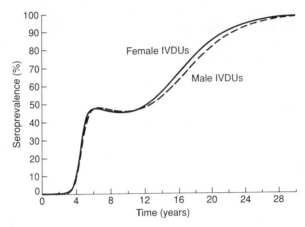

Fig. 26.5 An example of the results of a model of HIV and AIDS amongst intravenous drug users (IVDUs) in New York City, USA. The levels of infection in female and male IVDUs are shown. (The details are given in Blower *et al.* (1991).)

Health consequences and the consideration of legalization

What are the issues which relate to the health consequences which we might consider when looking at legalization? For example, to what extent is there evidence of variability within drug taking behaviour so that it must be considered as something other than an all or nothing phenomenon; and to what extent is there evidence of malleability of the behaviour? Today's choices of policy and practice will have an influence at the public and personal levels tomorrow's health consequences.

Firstly, there is a need to consider the nature of the consequences which are the subject of concern. Does the concern relate to the use of the drug itself, or perhaps to hazardous consequences of impairment resulting from the drug use, or perhaps to hazard or harm accrued almost incidentally as a result of the method of administration? Various attempts have been made to provide terminology to help in the journey through this minefield. The 1981 Memorandum from the WHO provided three possible terms in addition to unsanctioned use: dysfunctional use (in which use of the drug leads to impaired psychological or social functioning); harmful use (in which use of the drug may cause direct tissue damage or mental illness); and hazardous use (in which use of the drug increases the likelihood of subsequent dysfunction or harm). In a document considering the broader goals of prevention, the UK Advisory Council on the Misuse of Drugs (1984) identified two goals for prevention, the prevention of a drug's use, and the prevention of harm consequent upon the use of the drug. Thus there are health consequences which are *substance-specific* (deficits which are directly attributable to effects of the drug itself); and health consequences which are *technique-specific* (being related, for example, to the mode of administration (such as hepatitis B infection, with its subsequent expanded complications of delta coinfection and hepatitis C; and also the similar subsequent picture with HIV infection). The 1990 report from the Institute of Medicine on *Treating drug problems* suggests that there are two simplifying strategies which have popular appeal. If there is overriding concern about a particular health consequence, then strategies can be developed and measured according to the extent to which they suceed or fail in reducing the level of pathology that would overwise have been evident. The alternative approach is to look behind these mani-festations or health consequences, to identify the causes which are most important in generating the adverse consequences. Here again one might reasonably look for evidence of change in the extent of pathology consequent upon the drug use as a measure of the effectiveness of the approach, and also look for earlier evidence of change in the key aspects of the behaviour to which causal responsibility has been assigned (Gerstein and Harwood 1990).

Looking for evidence of variability and malleability

To what extent can variability in drug taking behaviour be identified, even within consideration of a single substance? Although it may suit politicians and policy makers to resort to a simple concept of the phenomenon being either present or absent, there is abundant evidence of marked variability in behaviour within and between populations at any particular time, within individuals over time, and also more broadly within a particular society over time.

Separate consideration may need to be given to the extent of processing or refinement of the drug which may also have a substantial influence on the health consequences. Major changes in the extent of dependence and extent of problems have occurred with the production and active promotion of shredded leaf ready make tobacco cigarettes, and a similar change in the relationship between humans and drugs is seen with the appearance of the refined product when a long established co-existence with an opium market or coca leaf market is accosted by the arrival of refined heroin or cocaine (Strang 1990). Cigarette smoking is an example from which it may be possible to extrapolate to consideration of the consequences of use of other drugs, for here it has been possible to identify the different causal agents implicated in the development of dependence (nicotine), and the development of many of the life-threatening physical sequelae (tar).

Within this variability, consideration must also be given to the extent to which achievable variations in the drug use may leave some health conse-quences entirely unmodified, whilst in other instances the harm may be substantially reduced or eliminated. Thus, if the cigarette smoker can find a method of continued delivery of nicotine without exposure to the tar, if the heroin addict can avoid use of needle and syringe, if the amphetamine or cocaine snorter can maintain a pattern of snorting without progression to injecting, then each of these individuals may be able substantially to alter the health consequences which they encounter, despite their continued use of, and even dependence on, the drug.

However, despite the abundant evidence of the variability of the drug taking behaviour, critical enquiry is required into the extent to which there may be *malleability* of this behaviour—the extent to which the individual or the group may be able to bring about beneficial changes in the nature of their continued drug use so as to reduce the health consequences, and the extent to which these changes, when they have been achieved, may be robust or transient changes. At the macro level of economic analysis, there is certainly evidence that, for at least some drugs, demand is price-elastic: and following from this evidence, there is the possibility of a strange alliance, a collaboration between clinician and economist in studying the individual applicability of the price-elasticity or inelasticity of demand for a particular drug. As relative price goes up so that the drug is less affordable, so the per capita consumption decreases, with corresponding decreases in harm to the population as a whole. Whilst such preliminary analyses may require consideration of the population as a homogeneous whole, there must be scope for more specific study of different individuals and groups within the population, as has been described earlier in this chapter with the work from Anderson and his colleagues on the mapping of HIV transmission. The clinician may be more likely to see individuals for whom demand has lost its price-elasticity, for whom the overriding drive to repeat the administration of the drug is dominant, with a consequently greater likelihood of accepting the risk consequent upon use.

The deficient framework of the legalization debate

Neither the debaters nor society benefit from increasing polarization of the legalization debate in which only extremes are considered, and hence prohibition is pitched against legalization. Only the media benefit. The absurdity of this polarized debate is matched by the unreality: there is a danger that such polarization may serve an unhealthy public function and distract attention from real issues and consideration of more realistic and implementable changes in our reponse to drugs.

The legalization debate is taking place largely outside any discussion of the possible health consequences. This is surprising as it should be one of the central issues. One important reason for this omission must be the difficulty in assessing the outcome of legalization on health. Legalization will alter behaviour, but how and when are not clear. The individual and population health will be affected by the change in behaviour, but as has been discussed these issues are not open to simple interpretation. Until some progress is made in these directions, health issues will continue to be at the margins of any legalization debate.

Public opinion and policy on the different currently illicit drugs have changed over the years. Gerstein and Harwood (1990) give a visual representation of these changes over the last century in the USA. The contour of this curve for different countries would of course be different, and would presumably vary according to the particular substance under consideration. Indeed, an interesting exercise in today's HIV-conscious climate would be to conduct a similar exercise on governing ideas about needle and syringe availability.

Thus, one might need to consider the possibility that there may be benefit to one section of the population, whilst another is exposed to the likelihood of greater harm. Although the clinician may be driven by consideration of the impact on his on her individual patient, or on the impact of the patient population as a whole, the policy maker may adopt an approach of 'therapeutic Benthamism' in which the aim is to obtain maximum benefit to the maximum number of individuals, which may involve an acceptance of greater harm to a smaller number if it is sufficiently offset by benefit to the greater number.

Flexing the lexicon

How useful is consideration of the consequences that might follow legalization? Certainly, consideration is handicapped by the poverty not only of the debate but also of the language. What do the various discussants mean by legalization? The issue has perhaps been explored more fully with illicit drugs in Australia in recent years. In a review paper, Rolfe identified at least six options that might need to be considered, and not just the extremes of total prohibition or total legalization: harsher penalties, prescription supplies, licensing, regulation, decriminalization, and free availability. If the lexicon could be expanded to include these terms in the debate, then the value of the debate to policy formation may be enhanced considerably.

Natural experiments are forever taking place in the arena of drug policy which would never be supported if merely proposed by the research scientist. Sadly, the impacts of these changes are rarely studied, so that one is left with retrospective reconstructions of what might have taken place, such as the diverse opinions which can now be elicited on the impact of changes in the control policy with regard to cannabis in the Netherlands. Scientific fact becomes something which more closely resembles a scientific Rorshach, in which the percieved reality is influenced by the personal and policy position of the ink-blot itself. Whatever else, it is essential that there is careful contemporary documentation of the changes that may follow in the wake of natural experiments of changes in national policy. There is great danger that the political and policy rhetoric may be received uncritically, and may interfere with the truly independent perspectives of detached observers and critical scientists.

Both scientist and policy maker must also acknowledge that changes in policy may not be reversible (certainly not reliably reversible), and that a move to legalization may not be simply reversible if the results are disastrous. In the days of Thomas de Quincey, the contemporary hypothesis appears to have been that working people were taking opium because of their economic and social disadvantage, and as an anodyne to 'taedium vitae'.

(With) wages rising, it may be thought that this practice would cease: but as I do not readily believe that any man having once tasted the divine luxuries of opium will afterwards descend to the gross and mortal enjoyments of alcohol, I take it for granted: that those eat now, who never ate before; and those who always ate, now eat the more. (de Quincey 1821)

AIDS *or* drug misuse; or AIDS *and* drug misuse?

Finally, it may be appropriate to consider the much quoted statement from the UK Advisory Council on the Misuse of Drugs (1988) that: 'HIV is a greater threat to public and individual health than drug misuse'. A similar statement was made in the US Watkins Report. Commentators who have subsequently quoted this statement may have, on occasion, misused this quote. The statement has both had a major impact on policy and has also been abused by policy makers who have sought a quasi-scientific justification for the changes in policy and practice which they have covertly endorsed. The contexts in which this statement has been quoted have generated an unintended adversarial component, as if it were necessary to subscribe *either* to concern about AIDS *or* concern about drug misuse. Indeed, one of the unfortunate side effects of this statement has been that some policy makers would appear to believe that an abandonment of concern about the consequences of drug misuse is a *necessary* part of expressing proper concern about HIV.

Thus, whilst the literal accuracy of the scientific statement may be sound, there is nevertheless legitimate cause for concern about the language of the communication with policy makers, or to be more specific, with the selective nature of the listening. Perhaps the risk of this misuse is increased when single short sentences are pulled out in this way as policy 'sound bites'. It is possible that if the authors were re-drafting this section today, they might place greater emphasis on the still-developing nature of the relationship between HIV and drug misuse, as a result of which they could identify an opportunity for the policy maker to influence the phenomenon which science might then study.

Conclusion

In conclusion, it would seem that science is only poorly informing policy with the present polarized legalization debate. Likewise, policy is failing to promote scientific enquiry into the broader area of the possible influences of a range of control options on the extent of use of the drug(s) in question, and into the extent of harm to individuals and across populations. The present forced dichotomy between prohibition and legalization may suit the zealot, the tabloid journalist, and the politician approaching date-expiry, but is an unworthy simplification of the necessary broader consideration that should be undertaken collaboratively by scientist and policy maker.

Acknowledgement

Graham Medley is a Royal Society University Research Fellow.

References

Advisory Council on the Misuse of Drugs (1984). Report on: *Prevention*. HMSO, London.

Advisory Council on the Misuse of Drugs (1988). Report on: *AIDS and Drug Misuse—Part One*. HMSO, London.

Anderson, R.M. (1988). The role of mathematical models in the study of HIV transmission and the epidemiology of AIDS. *Journal of AIDS*, 1, 241–56.

Anderson, R.M. (1989). Mathematical and statistical studies of the epidemiology of HIV. *AIDS*, 3, 333–46.

Anderson, R.M. and May, R.M. (1991). *Infectious diseases of humans: dynamics and control*. Oxford University Press.

Anderson, R.M. and May, R.M. (1992). Understanding the AIDS pandemic. *Scientific American*, 226, 58–63.

Anderson, R.M., Medley, G.F., May, R.M., and Johnson, A.M. (1986). A preliminary study of the transmission dynamics of the human immunodeficiency virus (HIV), the causative agent of AIDS. *IMA Journal of Mathematics Applied in Medicine and Biology*, 3, 229–63.

Anderson, R.M., Blythe, S.P., Gupta, S., and Konings, E. (1989) The transmission dynamics of the human immunodeficiency virus type I in the male homosexual community in the United Kingdom: the influence of changes in sexual behaviour. *Philosophical Transactions of the Royal Society of London*, 325, 45–98.

Becker, N.G., Watson, L., and Carlin, J. (1991). A method of non-parametric back-projection and its application to AIDS data. *Statistics in Medicine*, 10, 1527–42.

Blower, S.M. and Medley, G. (1992). Epidemiology, HIV and drugs: mathematical models and data. *British Journal of Addiction*, 87, 371–9.

Blower, S.M., Hartel, D., Dowlatabadi, H., Anderson, R.M., and May, R.M. (1991). Drugs, sex and HIV: a mathematical model for New York City. *Philosophical Transactions of the Royal Society of London*, Series B, 321, 171–87.

Brettle, R.P., Bisset, K., Burns, S. *et al.* (1987). Human immunodeficiency virus and drug misuse—the Edinburgh experience. *British Medical Journal*, 295, 421–4.

Buning, E. (1990). The role of harm-reduction programmes in curbing the spread of HIV by drug injectors. In *AIDS and drug misuse: the challenge for policy and practice in the 1990s*, (ed. J. Strang and G. Stimson), pp. 153–61. Routledge, London.

Cox, D.R. and Medley, G.F. (1989). A process of events with notification delay and the forecasting of AIDS. *Philosophical Transactions of the Royal Society of London*, 325, 135–45.

De Quincey, T. (1821). *Confessions of an English opium-eater*. Penguin edition, 1971. Penguin, Harmondsworth.

Des Jarlais, D. and Friedman, S.R. (1990). The epidemic of HIV infection among injecting drug users in New York City: the first decade and possible future directions. In *AIDS and drug misuse: the challenge for policy and practice in the 1990s*, (ed. J. Strang, and G. Stimson), pp. 86–94. Routledge, London.

Gerstein, D.R. and Harwood, H.J. (ed.) (1990). *Treating drug problems: a study of the evolution, effectiveness and financing of public and private drug treatment systems*. National Academy Press, Washington.

Moore, M. and Gerstein, D. (1981). *Alcohol and public policy: beyond the shadow of prohibition*. National Academy Press, Washington.

Moss, A. (1990). Control of HIV infection in injecting drug users in San Francisco. In *AIDS and Drug Misuse: the challenge for policy and practice in the 1990s*, (ed. J. Strang and G. Stimson), pp. 77–85. Routledge, London.

Moss, A. and Vranizan, K. (1992). Charting the epidemic: the case study of HIV screening of injecting drug users in San Francisco, 1985–1990. *British Journal of Addiction*, 87, 467–71.

Robertson, R. (1990). The Edinburgh epidemic: a case study. In *AIDS and drug misuse: the challenge for policy and practice in the 1990s*, (ed. J. Strang and G. Stimson), pp. 95–107. Routledge, London.

Strang, J. (1990). Heroin and cocaine: new technologies, new problems. In *Addiction controversies*, (ed. D.M. Warburton), pp. 201–11. Harwood Academic Publishers, Reading.

Tempesta, E. and Di Giantonio, M. (1990). The Italian epidemic: a case study. In *AIDS and drug misuse: the challenge for policy and practice in the 1990s*, (ed. J. Strang and G. Stimson) pp. 108–17. Routledge, London.

27. Estimating the social and economic costs and benefits of drug policies

Dean R. Gerstein

This chapter will discuss the social and economic costs and benefits of drug policies. There are not yet enough studies to proffer a formal meta-analysis (Glass *et al.* 1981; Wachter and Straf 1990), but then, there are not yet any meta-analytic formalisms suitable for use with simulations and non-experimental data. In this chapter, the primary concerns are: first, to define clearly the nature and variations of drug policies within a historical perspective; and secondly, to locate cost–benefit thinking within the general framework of policy, clarifying its institutional role and making a particular case for its support. This discussion is based largely on work that has focused on the evolution of alcohol, tobacco, and illicit drug policy in the USA (Attewell and Gerstein 1979; Besteman 1992; Committee on Substance Abuse and Habitual Behavior 1982; Courtwright 1982, 1992; Gerstein and Harwood 1990; Kaplan 1970, 1983; Moore and Gerstein 1981; Musto 1987; National Commission on Marijuana and Drug Abuse 1972, 1973; Parsons and Gerstein 1977; Room 1974; Schelling 1984).

The nature of drug policies

Policy may be defined as the legitimate actions of an organized group that involve collective objectives, as well as the preferred means chosen by leaders for achieving them. It is salutary to distinguish and include both ends and means—objectives and instruments—in the definition of policy. A familiar example in the field of alcohol or tobacco is the policy objective of reducing the level of consumption across the population as a whole, perhaps even by a specific titre of regular smokers per capita, drink units per week, or litres of ethanol per year. A clear objective is not, however, enough; there must be a means to achieve it. A preferred set of instruments might be taxation, accompanied by restrictions on advertising practices or on the placement or the hours-of-sale of outlets; while other conceivable instruments, such as outright prohibition, might be entirely outside the policy.

Drug policy is a highly complicated matter, because:

(1) there are many psychoactive drugs, and the pharmacopeia is growing constantly;

(2) each drug is simultaneously an article of commerce, a pharmacological agent, and a cultural symbol;

(3) drug users are distributed across different social groups;

(4) collective agencies responsible for implementing policies—such as governments—are imperfect instruments; and

(5) societies change.

Therefore, drug policies, as an empirical matter, are very complicated equilibria of competing values, agendas, and programmes. The result is not necessarily to make policies unstable, but when they do become vulnerable to change, the forces for change and the forces for continuity align themselves in terms of simple rhetorical oppositions under which policy directions are promoted or denounced. For example, drug policy preferences become associated with slogans, self-selected or pasted on by opponents or the press, such as 'legalization', 'demand reduction', 'sealing the borders', 'user accountability', 'normalization', 'non-smokers' rights', 'neo-prohibitionism', 'the alcohol bill of rights', and 'responsible drinking'.

These slogans represent applications to contemporary circumstances and sensibilities of a handful of enduring, simple ideas, whose significance has been stated as follows:

In a democracy, government policy is inevitably guided by commonly shared simplifications. This is true because the political dialogue that authorizes and animates government policy can rarely support ideas that are very complex or entirely novel. There are too many people with diverse perceptions and interests and too little time and inclination to create a shared perception of a complex structure. Consequently, influential policy ideas are typically formulated at a quite general level and borrow heavily from commonly shared understanding and conventional opinions.

(Moore and Gerstein 1981, p. 6)

Although such simplifications do not capture all the important aspects of a problem, and mask ambiguous possibilities of success, hard trade-offs, and unanticipated results, which often bedevil policy implementation, they have the merit of focusing attention clearly on some significant dimensions of a problem and concerting social attention and action toward it—something that more complicated ideas cannot usually achieve.

The most successful policy ideas tie together a selected major effect or objective of policy and a judgement about the principal instrumentality for affecting it, to form a neat conceptual bundle. A few such bundles have had widespread, durable appeal in US society because they proved compatible with common social views, evolving social experience, and the interests and purposes of organized groups. These cognitive bundles are referred to here as governing ideas. They provide the crucial context for understanding the nature of drug policy.

A series of policy reports (Gerstein and Harwood 1990; Moore and Gerstein 1981; Olson and Gerstein 1985) undertaken at the US National Academy of Sciences over the past decade or so—therefore old enough in American terms to have already acquired the patina, if not the rust, of tradition—has evolved the concept of a spectrum of governing ideas, which define and dominate the realm of alcohol and drug policy. Although a spectrum is continuous, with one idea shading imperceptibly into its neighbours, simplification demands that sharper boundaries be drawn. The ideas, which for convenience are arranged from the least restrictive in approach to the most restrictive, can be grouped under three headings: libertarian, medical, and criminal. Of course, the placement of ideas along this continuum does not necessarily refer to the actual consequences of policies, but only to the character of the ideas that inform them. The determinants of policy consequences are more complex than ideas alone, embracing economic conditions, political mobilization, religious movements, and the educational level and degree of alienation or frustration of the population.

With each idea comes a different vision of policy. The classical libertarian ideal, as formulated by utilitarians from Locke to Mill, is minimal interference by government. It envisions a relatively small government apparatus concerned for the most part on the domestic level with protecting property rights and maintaining civil order. Libertarian policies are intended to achieve a situation in which relatively open consumer markets are viewed as the primary arena of policy. At its least restrictive, this idea approbates freewheeling markets limited at most to purity inspections and controls; in a more moderate mode, markets may be legislatively taxed as a means of compensating for 'market failures' due to external costs. At the most restrictive end of libertarian ideas are regulatory schemes to improve the achievement of limited social welfare goals, such as the protection of children or safety of transportation systems.

Medical policies may range from aggressive prescribing practices to conservative medical maintenance to psychotherapy. The medical idea arose in the late 1800s, when physicians began to observe significant numbers of citizens, mostly middle class, 'respectable' women, who were becoming addicted to oral morphine and other opiates. Opiates were very much a staple of nineteenth century medical (including folk-medical) practice—one of the few truly effective medicines of the day, that is, manifestly able to reduce the suffering of many patients for whom no other useful medical intervention was known. There was widespread prescription, promotion, and sale of opiates for a variety of ailments and as routine 'tonics'. It gradually became clear to observant practitioners that individuals who had become accustomed to using these compounds became ill, agitated, and despondent if they tried to do without them; yet these same individuals functioned reasonably well with continued regular doses, even though these doses often reached high levels.

As a result, this observation of the addictive effects of chronic use was viewed as regrettable but not catastrophic, particularly because so many of those affected were older women, many of whom had begun using the habit-forming drugs under medical or pharmaceutical advice or supervision and who, on the whole, seemed harmless. One standard medical response to this problem was maintenance on a prescribed dose, with the goal of continuing the patient on a course of normal, comfortable functioning. A variety of detoxification therapies, some sensible and some quite exotic, were also attempted, but relapse to habitual use was common, making maintenance appear even more reasonable as an alternative.

Of much greater concern were 'opium habitues' of the lower social classes whose lives centred around multiple, daily periods of intoxication achieved through the opium pipe, the needle, or tinctures of high opiate (and alcohol) content. These individuals were quite different from respectable middle-class users—but their agitated responses to a threatened loss of access to the drug were quite similar. From these observations, physicians formulated the medical view of narcotic drugs: whatever the origins of opiate use or the prevailing moral judgement regarding it, individuals invariably display an addiction withdrawal syndrome and craving for further dosing (which abolishes withdrawal, among other effects) if they have consumed powerful intoxicants, such as narcotics, for a long enough period. The similarity between the alcohol and narcotic addiction syndromes was recognized in many quarters.

The initial explanation developed for these phenomena was an extension of psychiatric theory of the period. The middle-class people who sought opiates seemed to belong to the 'neurasthenic' personality type—people of weakened and unstable temperament who needed pharmacological assistance to endure the rigours of modern life. In the 1920s, as physicians saw more and more urban 'pleasure users', a darker assessment arose: these users seemed more and more to be afflicted not with temperamental weakness but psychopathic dispositions. In the 1950s and 1960s, a median position became prominent, that prolonged exposure created a neurobehavioural or neurological abnormality equivalent to a chronic disease or disability, controllable through treatment but possibly no more curable than diabetes or cirrhosis.

In the criminal view of the drug problem, families, with churches and schools as social support, are fundamentally responsible for teaching children to behave responsibly and morally, behaviour that includes shunning intoxicating drugs. The presence of moral anchors—most generally, the capacity for self-control in the face of temptation and a generalized respect for the law—is the vital element that separates the good citizen from the pleasure-seeking drug user. If the family or school, for whatever reason, fails in its responsibility to provide moral education, the problem must be dealt with by another authority. The main such agencies are the police, the courts, and prisons;

there may, however, be room for intermediate socializing agencies (guidance counselling or social work) to supplement, or substitute for, the family, especially in co-operation with the juvenile justice system.

The criminal view dominated drug policy in the USA for more than 40 years from the 1920s to the 1960s, and non-medical users were arrested at virtually every opportunity. Nevertheless, the criminal view of drug problems was affected by changing times and changing ideas about controlling criminal behaviour. Within this fundamental view of drug use as a criminal problem and users as moral derelicts deserving of retribution, several variants have arisen that correspond to philosophies reflected in the broad streams of modern criminological thought (Blumstein *et al.* 1978). The idea of rehabilitation—that criminals may be redeemed by appropriate arrangements, incentives, and lessons fashioned within the penal environment—is the basis of prison as a place of penitence, or 'penitentiary' (it is explicit as well in the official term, 'corrections'). Evidence of its diffusion is also found in widespread acceptance of probation—a period of testing to discover the true character of the offender—as an appropriate response to first or minor offences. The concept of deterrence draws a sharper line: the lesson conveyed by punishment is intended not only for the individual but also for the community as a whole, or at least for all others who might consider similar deeds. Finally, incapacitation takes the bleakest view of the criminal, putting little stock in the possibility of redeeming or deterring criminal behaviour. Instead, this school of thought calls for protecting society by isolating the criminally inclined for the longest period consistent with community standards of 'just deserts' for the crime, or crimes, committed (in the extreme, a sentence of life—or death).

Within the framework of governing ideas of drug policy, one can look not only at snapshots of policies in place but at the moving picture of policy shifts. Legalization, for example, is shorthand for a complex shifting of social objectives and policy mechanisms in the direction of the libertarian idea. Yet the debate over legalization in any jurisdiction is heavily shaded by its particular history, the association of drugs with different population segments, and by other political positions. For example, the most common aim of exponents of 'drug decriminalization' in the USA during the 1970s was simply to reduce the weight of procedures and severity of penalties for simple marijuana possession, including 'accommodation' or transfer of small quantities, from the felony track (arrest, booking, and possible long prison terms) to a programme of citations and fines similar to those associated with traffic infractions (Committee on Substance Abuse and Habitual Behavior 1982; Kaplan 1970; National Commission on Marijuana and Drug Abuse 1972). Since there was not a well-formed medical opinion on marijuana—there was substantial dissensus about its therapeutic value, addictive potential, degree of physiological toxicity, and suitability of treatment—there was a vacuum in the middle of the policy spectrum. Therefore, any move away from the criminal idea was taken for a leap into wholesale 'legalization'.

Regarding heroin, decriminalization more clearly took the form of medicalization. There was some lessening in the application of penalties in some areas, but all aspects of heroin remained heavily criminalized. There was, however, a successful move to incorporate therapeutic concepts into the policy matrix, including legalization of a particular opiate prescribing pattern to treat addiction, methadone maintenance. The relatively smooth adoption of methadone maintenance in the UK, which already had a medicalized policy, is in stark contrast to the highly contentious climate around methadone and the tenuous position of this therapy in many places, as reflected in the prevalence of low-dose and term-limited regimens which seem clinically indefensible but are politically and ideologically far more palatable to those willing to accept the medical idea only as hybrid with the criminal idea.

Elsewhere in this volume, reference has been made to the statement of the advisory committee on drug misuse in the UK, which concluded that: 'the spread of HIV is a greater threat to the public health that the misuse of drugs'. A US committee looking at US mortality and morbidity statistics would be forced to exactly the same conclusion, although there might be some uncertainty over the present value of future costs of fetal cocaine exposures. Nevertheless, this conclusion would have policy force only to the extent that threats to public health count highly in drug policy formation, and this force is quite limited. The USA now outspends every continent in the world, to the tune of a breathtaking $800 billion annually, on health care services, a figure that is growing, even adjusting for inflation, at a steady pace that exceeds 7 per cent per year. However, one other element in the economy is also growing almost as relentlessly—the size of the population residing in prisons or under parole or probation. Most US citizens and policy makers associate drugs much more with crime than with health issues. In order significantly to shift the momentum of US drug policy, an appropriately charged advisory committee would have to come to the conclusion that the spread of firearms is a greater threat to public safety than the misuse of drugs. Such is the power of a governing idea.

The role of cost–benefit analyses

Over time, we know that rather large shifts in consumption behaviour have occurred, and that important consequences tend to be pulled along by the level of consumption if other structural elements remain relatively undisturbed or move in step. So what are the underlying causes of 'long cycles' in consumption? There are numerous attempts to answer this question, which have grown more knowledgeable and sophisticated over time, although not necessarily more conclusive.

Two points must be mentioned here. First, there is reason to believe that waves of waxing and waning consumption are rather resistant to policy interventions, which can at best accelerate or decelerate them but not shift their direction—rather like the business cycle. Secondly, there is evidence of an underlying social learning curve; as consumption increases and its accumulating (often lagging) adverse consequences become evident across society, this cumulative evidence acts as a brake and then a thrust reverser. Yet, as consumption falls and the evidence of harm recedes, it is as though social immunities wear off and vulnerability grows toward a new wave of increase. The same may operate in terms of supply: as drug marketing efforts (legal and illicit) expand, those wanting to undermine this expansion with regulatory, public health, or law enforcement instruments become combat-wise and efficient on the terrain, and seek out applications of cost–benefit thinking to improve their work. Once the tide is turned and the troops retire or move on to other engagements, these close-in skills fall into disrepair. Yet cost–benefit issues remain; most critically, are educational 'inoculations' or measures of market prophylaxis capable of maintaining social immunity, or do they become ineffectual or irrelevant when the threat fades?

Policies are seldom, if ever, univalent; they always involve sets of objectives and sets of instruments. The relations between members of these sets are best understood as trade-offs, and cost–benefit estimation as the assessment of trade-offs that occur in moving from one bundle of policy emphases to another or in shifting the selection or relative intensities of the instruments being employed—in other words, a shift along the spectrum of governing ideas. It is therefore sensible to speak of the costs and benefits of moving across the spectrum from point A to point B at a certain point in time and place, rather than the costs and benefits of policies A, B, and C in isolation. We can not setp out of history or culture, imagining that to please our policy preferences the impossible will happen—at least, not if we wish to be of any use to policy makers, or to comprehend their behaviour. Ends are realized only through means that are practically at the disposal of the collectivity, with some attention to factors that are not ours to call forth, which amount to the luck of history.

Given this understanding of policy, it should not be surprising that estimating the costs and benefits of drug policies is a multi-dimensional problem on which progress has been slow. The most fruitful avenue is to view cost–benefit estimation as the analysis of marginal differences, net effects of policy changes relative to the baseline of existing policies, however happy or unhappy we are with those. This work takes advantage of 'natural experiments' in policy change to assess the current range of policy limits, and to extend these relatively small increments imaginatively but systematically to estimation of changes of greater magnitude, or to project these changes on to environments or circumstances differing moderately from those in which they were observed.

The first analytical necessity is always to characterize the present policy objectives accurately and to see what changes in circumstances might have a bearing on their adequacy. It is then, secondly, necessary to define the desired changes in policy with precision, which generally means in terms of the detailed shifts in emphasis being advocated. The most important specific question is what the advocates of change are willing to lose in order to reap the gains they seek. (There are no free lunches in policy, just good and bad bargains. For example, in the 1970s there was a general agreement across many states in the USA that is was worthwhile accepting rather than trying to reverse a fairly large increase in marijuana use, in exchange for keeping large numbers of marijuana-using middle class youths out of the criminal justice system. This was not a relevant concern in the 1950s or early 1960s, when there were few middle class users of marijuana to be worried about.)

Thirdly, it is necessary to define the differences between the current and proposed mix of policy instruments and their relative costs of deployment. Finally, one can derive estimates of the effects of the new mix *vis-à-vis* the old. It is important here to recognize that there is more than simply comparing the merits of a present policy with an alternative one; also to be considered are the costs of getting from here to there. The cost of change, in terms of upsetting vested interests, junking previous investments and training, and realigning whole systems that include drug policy as an element, may be so high as to mean that a less desirable policy can be maintained more easily than a more desirable policy can be achieved.

This rather complicated agenda requires an expansive base of information and expertise. Vital to it is an occupation that has been given the name of 'knowledge brokerage', which is performed sometimes as an amateur effort but is largely the province of a growing corps of professionals. Generally, in the relation between knowledge and policy, the key development is not the individual scientist calling attention to the policy ramifications of his or her own work. (This can occur before or after the research is performed, that is, as an argument for funding a specific proposal or as an expression of scientific responsibility to take one's work a step beyond scholarly publication). Rather, the policy-effective analysis is the persuasive pulling together for policy makers of multiple finished empirical results with packages of well-rehearsed scientific ideas; such syntheses themselves derive from orchestrating varieties of political interests to finance projects that may not pay off immediately but do so over the longer run—investments in fundamental long-term research programmes (Study Project on Social Research and Development 1978).

Brokerage functions needs to be competitive and open, subject to inspection and validation of the methods and the results. The mobilization of research knowledge for policy can not be entrusted to a sole scientific judge. This lesson is not always respected. For example, the US National Household Survey on Drug Abuse has been conducted and summarily reported every two or three years since 1972. But only within the past year, for the first time, has anyone outside the National Institute on Drug Abuse (NIDA) and its closely tied contractors been given direct access to these survey data—for the single year 1985. Over the next year or more, other years' data will become available, and broader scientific imaginations and judgements can be brought to bear on these data resources. This sustained long-term monopolization of a major resource for producing policy knowledge is contrary to NIDA's general policy of disseminating preclinical and clinical research, but not uncharacteristic of its approach to epidemiological research.

By and large, the USA has been fortunate to have available some institutionalized counterweights within the federal government—the Office of Technology Assessment and the General Accounting Office, which lie within the legislative branch—and the quasi-independent National Academy of Sciences complex outside the government, as balances to the executive agencies. Moreover, the mission of the Department of Health and Human Services as divergent from the Department of Agriculture and Department of Justice has sometimes permitted open debates over central drug policy issues. However, drug policy makers in the federal and other levels of government by and large would have been well served during the drug crises of the 1980s had there been much more effort to support strong independent centres of knowledge brokerage and a more aggressive policy of public release of pertinent data.

Conclusion

This chapter has briefly considered drug policy analysis and the role of cost–benefit estimation within it. It has intended to convey the sense of the problems addressed, rather than to stress any specific findings. The accretion of research in this field, at least in the USA, seems likely to accelerate dramatically over the next several years as large amounts of new data come on line and tidal shifts occur in the broader political and economic realms; this combination should provide a dramatic stimulus to new thinking and new results. I look forward to reading, or writing, a very different chapter with this title five or eight years hence.

References

Attewell, P. and Gerstein, D.R. (1979). Government policy and local practice. *American Sociological Review*, **44**, 311–27.

Besteman, K.J. (1992). Federal leadership in building the national drug treatment system. In *Treating drug abuse, Volume 2*, (ed. D.R. Gerstein and H.J. Harwood), pp. 63–88. National Academy Press, Washington.

Blumstein, A., Cohen, J. and Nagin, D. (ed.) (1978). *Deterrence and incapacitation: estimating the effects of criminal sanctions on crime rates*. National Academy of Sciences, Washington.

Committee on Substance Abuse and Habitual Behavior (1982). *An analysis of marijuana policy*. National Academy Press, Washington.

Courtwright, D.T. (1982). *Dark paradise: opiate addiction in America before 1940*. Harvard University Press, Cambridge, MA.

Courtwright, D.T. (1992). A century of American narcotics policy. In *Treating drug abuse, Volume 2*, (ed. D.R. Gerstein and H.J. Harwood), pp. 1–62. National Academy Press; Washington.

Gerstein, D.R. and Harwood, H.J. (ed.) (1990). *Treating drug abuse, Volume 1*. National Academy Press, Washington.

Glass, G., McGaw, B., and Smith, M. (1981). *Meta-analysis in social research*. Sage Publications, Beverly Hills, CA.

Kaplan, J. (1970). *Marijuana: the new prohibition*. World Publishing Company, New York and Cleveland.

Kaplan, J. (1983). *The hardest drug: heroin and public policy*. University of Chicago Press, Chicago and London.

Moore, M.H. and Gerstein, D.R. (ed.) (1981). *Alcohol and public policy: beyond the shadow of prohibition*. National Academy Press, Washington.

Musto, D.F. (1987). *The American disease: origins of narcotic control*, (2nd edn). Yale University Press, New Haven.

National Commission on Marijuana and Drug Abuse (1972). *Marijuana: signal of misunderstanding*. US Government Printing Office, Washington.

National Commission on Marijuana and Drug Abuse (1973). *Drug use in America: problem in perspective*. US Government Printing Office, Washington.

Olson, S. and Gerstein, D.R. (1985). *Alcohol in America: taking action to prevent abuse*. National Academy Press, Washington.

Parsons, T. and Gerstein, D.R. (1977). Two cases of social deviance: addiction to heroin, addiction to power. In *Deviance and social change*, (ed. E. Sagarin), pp. 19–57. Sage Publications, Beverly Hills, CA.

Room, R. (1974). Governing images and the prevention of alcoholism. *Preventive Medicine*, **3**, 11–23.

Schelling, T.C. (1984). *Choice and consequence*. Harvard University Press, MA.

Study Project on Social Research and Development (1978). *The federal investment in knowledge of social problems*. National Academy of Sciences, Washington.

Wachter, K.W. and Straf, M.L. (ed.) (1990). *The future of meta-analysis*. Russell Sage Foundation, New York.

28. Psychosocial issues in drug policies: implications for the legalization debate

Richard Jessor

The primary impetus for recent discussions about whether to legalize illicit drugs has come from the growing conviction that current policy for controlling drug abuse is fundamentally inadequate. In the USA, the failure of the 'war on drugs', with its emphasis on interdiction of supply and its heavy reliance on law enforcement, is evident on the streets of the inner cities, in the statistics on drug-related violence and crime, and in the editorial columns of major newspapers. There is a sense of urgency that alternatives to current drug policy be explored, and it is in this context that the legalization of illicit drugs has received renewed attention.

The arguments for and against legalization

Proponents for legalization have articulated compelling arguments in its favour. Legalization of illicit drug use would lift an enormous and unmanageable burden from the shoulders of the criminal justice system. It would lessen the damage to health that results from unregulated impurities in drugs and from the sharing of contaminated needles. And, perhaps most importantly, it would assimilate illicit drugs into the same regulatory system that societies use for licit drugs, such as alcohol and nicotine, whose costs and dangers in terms of morbidity, mortality, and damage to the social fabric far outweigh those of any of the currently illicit drugs.

Those who oppose the legalization option have been able to summon equally persuasive arguments. By eliminating the threat of sanctions and by bringing drug prices down, legalization would make drugs more available, which would result in a significant increase in the incidence and prevalence of drug use. In addition, since currently illicit drugs, such as heroin and cocaine, and especially crack cocaine, are considered to be extremely addictive, the expected increase in drug use would result in more people becoming addicts. Equally significant in the objections to legalization are concerns, widely-shared in the society as a whole, about the moral legitimacy of such a policy action. The main concern is that legalization would be taken as an endorsement of drug use, or, at least, as the abandonment of opposition to it. And that, in turn, is felt to pose a serious threat to fundamental societal values, about responsibility and commitment, about work and striving to get ahead, about an other-regarding ethic of social involvement, and perhaps more subtly, about the unacceptability of mere pleasure-seeking as an end in itself.

In the exchanges that have taken place, in venues ranging from the pages of scientific journals to the stages of television studios, there has been frequent recourse to lessons drawn from history and from examining the diverse ways in which various drugs have been dealt with by different societies and by different subgroups within societies. The long-term, secular changes in attitudes and policies about opiates in American society, and America's twentieth century experience with Prohibition have been closely examined. The experience with decriminalization of marijuana for personal use in Alaska and Oregon are often cited as are, of course, the 'harm reduction' approach in the Netherlands and the earlier British experiment with heroin maintenance.

Other lessons have been sought in the ethnographic legacy handed down to us by anthropologists and sociologists, textured accounts of the ways in which various drugs have been integrated into societal practices and social relationships to reflect cultural values and shared images of appropriate behaviour. We know about the acceptance of and even delight in the social-convivial use of alcohol among Jews and Italians, their simultaneous proscription of drunkenness, and their repudiation of the *shikker* and the *ubriacone*, respectively. We know also about the use of marijuana in Jamaica and the chewing of coca leaves in Peru—both socially benign and personally facilitative of work and routine tasks. The entire range of drug behaviour—from the socially-organized and expected inebriety on Saturday evenings in Scandinavia, to the regular sharing of 'joints' among jazz musicians, to weekend 'chippers' of heroin, to, more recently, the up-scale cocaine sniffing of harried executives—has been extensively reported. The literature is instructive in revealing the vast diversity of ways in which drugs have been used throughout history and across cultures, often for integrative purposes, including religious rituals, or as benign adjuncts of ongoing role performance, and generally in consonance with the values and norms of the larger society or those of some particular reference group.

With current circumstances so different historically, socially, economically, and politically, however, it is difficult to argue that the lessons drawn from any of these examinations or from any of the ethnographic accounts constitute compelling guidance for new policy initiatives. Despite the acknowledged shortcomings, if not the failure, of present illicit drug control policy, the legalization alternative has not been able to overcome the arguments of its critics nor its basic inconsonance with the prevailing moral ideology about the nature and meaning of illicit drug use.

Getting beyond the impasse

It appears that getting beyond this impasse requires that two steps be taken. The first would entail acknowledging that many of the assumptions made in conventional discourse about illicit drugs, even by scientists, have actually served as impediments to understanding or have, indeed, been misleading. For example, too much of the discussion about drug use and its consequences has focused on the substance itself, as if its consequences were merely an unfolding of its immanent properties. Yet we know that this is not true of any drug, and that attaching the causal vector to the substance rather than to the interaction between the dispositional properties of the drug and the conditions of its use (both user and context) is logically untenable. No drug 'causes' anything by itself, any more than a gene by itself causes a particular phenotype. This failure to deal with substances in an interactionist framework is a kind of pharmacological reductionism: it denies the obvious diversity we just reviewed in the ways in which drugs have been used in different cultures at different times; it denies also the obvious individual differences that exist in outcomes of use of any given drug; and, perhaps most importantly, it imbues substances with the aura of inherent power that is so central, and so misleading, in the lay concept of drug addiction.

Furthermore, too much of the discussion has focused solely on the harm that is associated with the ways in which drugs are used. While harm is obviously an important concern, such a focus does need to be qualified in several ways. First, it is important that illicit drug use behaviour be recognized as functional and instrumental, behaviour that can provide a wide variety of satisfactions (other than mere pleasure), such as a sense of social solidarity and group membership, a way of coping with frustration and anxiety, a feeling of efficacy and competence, etc. Instead of a singular focus on drug-related harm, a cost/benefit perspective is much more illuminating of the underlying dynamics involved. Secondly, harmful outcomes are not restricted to illicit drugs alone but are associated with the use of licit drugs as well. None of the illicit drugs, in fact, can match the havoc wreaked on the roads by drivers who have been drinking, or can equal the mortality rates from cardiovascular disease and lung cancer that follow after years of tobacco smoking. Thirdly, harmful consequences are, of course, often associated with non-substance use behaviours—eating, sex, gambling, driving, climbing step-ladders, etc. The main point here is that the mere demonstration that some kind of harm is associated with illicit drug use—a key orientation of US policy—fails to distinguish such behaviour from that associated with licit drug use, or from behaviour that does not involve drugs at all.

Finally, too much of the discussion has relied on a model of addiction that is biologically-defined, a model that fails to consider addiction, also, as 'a way of being in the world'. It is a model that ignores the social factors that initiate and sustain excessive involvement with drugs, and a model that, as

Peele (1987, 1990) has reminded us, divests persons of any measure of auto-nomy and responsibility in respect of their manifest commitment to involve-ment with drugs. Such a model has difficulty, therefore, in explaining the evidence for the sudden abandonment of long-term reliance on cigarette smoking (Schachter 1982), or the case reports of autoremission from chronic dependence on alcohol or on heroin (Klingemann 1991; Stall and Biernacki 1986), or the 'maturing out' of heroin addiction with age (Winick 1962) or with the return of soldiers from Vietnam (Robins *et al.* 1974), or the remark-able example of recovery from chronic alcoholism by the 45-year-old, out-of-work carpenter, found drunk on a doorstep in Deptford High Street, that Griffith Edwards describes with his usual hermeneutic flair. Edwards writes, 'From the day of that encounter in the Emergency Clinic he has been entirely, resoundingly, and continuously sober' (Edwards 1989, p. 24).

The first requirement, then, for supervening the impasse in the legalization debate is for all parties to adopt a more scientific perspective in place of the more conventional 'wisdom' that has too often been relied upon. This is especially critical in relation to the way in which drugs are thought about, the properties that are assigned to them, and the connotations that the term 'addiction' is intended to convey. Most basic, perhaps, is the urgent need to understand that drug abuse, whatever else it may also be, is instrumental behaviour in a social context.

The second requirement for getting beyond the impasse, is that the perimeter drawn around the legalization debate be enlarged. Thus far, the debate has been confined to such issues as the expected reduction in crime versus the expected increase in access to drugs. What has been missing has been both theory and research on the determinants of drug abuse, especially among the urban disadvantaged populations toward whom the legalization initiative has primarily been directed. The legalization option could then be appraised as a strategy for reducing drug abuse by eliminating its determinants. Equally important, other policy options for eliminating or weakening the determinants of drug abuse would also become apparent.

The determinants of drug abuse

What is evident in the scientific literature about the determinants of drug abuse? The research has shown that variation in both licit and illicit drug abuse can be accounted for, and to a substantial extent, by a combination of social environmental and individual difference characteristics. At the environ-mental level, such factors as limited access to opportunity, the breakdown of normative consensus about appropriate behaviour, the attenuation of in-formal social controls, and the disintegration of regulatory institutions, such as family and community, are all implicated in the greater likelihood of problem behaviour, including the abuse of drugs. These are the social at-tributes, that, when positive, serve a regulatory function over behaviour: first, by providing a stake in and reward for commitment to the larger society, and secondly, by providing a set of controls and regulations against behaviour that would depart from society's norms and values. At the individual level, scientific research has implicated attenuated values on achievement, a sense of personal inefficacy and alienation, and personal attitudes of tolerance toward normative and legal transgression as among the factors that are related to drug abuse. Such individual-level characteristics, it can be seen, reflect the characteristics of the social context, mentioned above. Both sets of factors are, of course, clearly associated with the poverty that is endemic in the urban ghetto.

In enlarging the perimeter around the discourse on legalization, we have introduced a psychosocial perspective on the determinants of drug abuse. That puts us now in a position to ask a key question: Can the legalization of illicit drugs be expected to have an impact upon any of the psychosocial determinants of their use and, thereby, to reduce drug abuse?

Before answering that question, it is important to mention yet another finding from the large body of psychosocial research that has accumulated. That finding is that problem behaviours come in bundles, that is, that there is co-variation among a variety of problem behaviours, including illicit drug use, problem drinking, risky driving, aggression, stealing, and the like (Jessor *et al.* 1991). Indeed, it has been demonstrated, among adults as well as adolescents, that the correlations among these various problem behaviours can be accounted for by a single underlying factor. There is warrant, then, for the notion of a problem behaviour 'syndrome' or 'lifestyle'. That finding puts us in the position to ask another key question about the legalization option: whether legalizing illicit drugs can be expected to have an impact on or reduce involvement in the other problem behaviours with which it is associated, especially in inner city populations in poverty areas.

Enlarging the perimeter around the legalization debate and introducing psychosocial theory and research have provided us with a template against which to appraise the legalization initiative, namely, the impact it is likely to have on the determinants of drug abuse. Considering that template, it is apparent that legalizing illicit drugs has no logical connection with any of the determinants established by the corpus of psychosocial studies. There is, therefore, no logical basis for expecting the implementation of a policy of legalization to result in a diminution of drug abuse. Furthermore, since the use of illicit drugs is associated with other problem behaviours, legalization could well result in amplifying involvement in those other behaviours at the same time. In view of these considerations, it seems appropriate to conclude that drug legalization has little likelihood of ameliorating committed involvement with illicit drugs.

Ameliorating poverty; the alternative to legalization

It can be argued that legalization would, nevertheless, have other salutary consequences, such as reducing drug-related crime. Any policy option, however, that fails to address directly the health- and life-compromising consequences of excessive involvement with, and commitment to, drugs is one that implicitly accepts the drug abuse *status quo*. That seems, indeed, to be the position of one proponent of legalization. Nadelmann (1989) concludes an otherwise thoughtful exposition of the likely costs and consequences of legalization with the following comment: 'Simply stated, legalizing cocaine, heroin, and other relatively dangerous drugs may well be *the only way* to reverse the destructive impact of drugs and current drug policies on the ghettos' (pp. 945–6; emphasis added).

That statement conveys an implicit acceptance of drug abuse as an inescapable component of inner city life. Such cynicism, perhaps unintended, is also unwarranted. We have tried to suggest that legalization is not 'the only way'. There is, indeed, another policy direction, one that follows logically from the findings of psychosocial research on the determinants of drug abuse, and one that is, therefore, logically compelling. That policy direction, of course, is to intervene to change the circumstances of life in the inner city, that is, to invest in the re-establishment of community institutions, to strengthen norms and the system of informal controls, to provide inner city residents with a stake in society by opening access to opportunity such as employment, to create a context in which the sense of personal efficacy is strengthened and alienation is diminished—in short, to change the psychosocial determinants of drug abuse that have been established in scientific inquiry.

To sum up, the central thesis of this chapter is that the drug policy option most likely to result in a lessening of drug abuse in the ghetto is one that addresses the psychosocial determinants of involvement in drugs. The science and policy connection is clear—reducing drug abuse depends most strongly on reducing demand for drugs, and reducing demand for drugs depends on attenuating the determinants of drug involvement. Given the association of those determinants with poverty and disadvantage and marginality in the inner city, it follows that attenuating the intensity and the concentration of poverty should be the primary objective of drug control policy.

At this point, some scientists and drug policy officials are likely to say that we have gone too far afield, that it is impractical to entertain policies that involve major social change, that the costs would be prohibitive, that our brief is properly limited to modest programmes, such as drug education in schools, or innovative treatment approaches for addicts. My reply is simply that, in making the connection between science and policy, there is an ethical responsibility to take to their conclusions the implications of the scientific knowledge that we have accumulated, wherever they lead us.

In the USA, 20 per cent of children are growing up in poverty, and the poverty rate for black children is three times that of white children. If their future is projected, using the knowledge we have accumulated about the psychosocial determinants of drug abuse, we can see that for many of them, especially those in the inner city, it is already mortgaged to later, destructive involvement with drugs. If we were able to use that same knowledge, however, to pursue the policy initiative that it logically implicates—the attenuation of poverty—the future for those children might well be far more salutary. And the legalization debate would then be seen for what it really is—a diversion that only distracts us from the urgent responsibility we have, namely, to make the real connection between science and policy.

Acknowledgement

Preparation of this paper was supported by the MacArthur Foundation Research Network on Successful Adolescent Development Among Youth in High-Risk Settings; that support is gratefully acknowledged.

References

Edwards, G. (1989). As the years go rolling by: drinking problems in the time dimension. *British Journal of Psychiatry*, **154**, 18–26.

Jessor, R., Donovan, J.E., and Costa, F. (1991). *Beyond adolescence: problem behavior and young adult development*. Cambridge University Press, New York.

Klingemann, H.K.-H. (1991). The motivation for change from problem alcohol and heroin use. *British Journal of Addiction*, **86**, 727–44.

Nadelman, E.A. (1989). Drug prohibition in the United States: costs, consequences, and alternatives. *Science*, **245**, 939–47.

Peele, S. (1987). A moral vision of addiction: How people's values determine whether they became and remain addicts. *The Journal of Drug Issues*, **17**, 187–215.

Peele, S. (1990). A values approach to addiction: drug policy that is moral rather than moralistic. *The Journal of Drug Issues*, **20**, 639–46.

Robins, L.N., Davis, D.H., and Nurco, D.N. (1974) How permanent was Vietnam drug addiction? *American Journal of Public Health*, **64**, 38–43.

Schachter, S. (1982). Recidivism and self-cure of smoking and obesity. *American Psychologist*, **37**, 436–44.

Stall, R. and Biernacki, P. (1986). Spontaneous remission from the problematic use of substances. *The International Journal of the Addictions*, **21**, 1–23.

Winick, C. (1962). Maturing out of narcotic addiction. *Bulletin on Narcotics*, **14**, 1–7.

Discussion
Research and policy connections beyond the year 2000

Chaired by Harold Kalant (Canada)

Dr Jerome Jaffe (USA): Once there is commitment by society that it wants, and has an obligation, to provide an opportunity for development and fulfilment for all its citizens, then I think one can raise certain questions. Should access to drugs be limited or not? Are legalization or decriminalization or lack of enforcement useful adjunctive policies? If we take the position that this is after all a form of income, it constitutes a kind of cynicism about the lives of people in the ghetto that is matched only by the cynicism of current American drug policy, that drug use can be stamped out by a more and more punitive kind of approach.

Is the cash-drug nexus really the economic mainstay of the ghetto? Perhaps so, but maybe only in the same sense that alcoholic beverages are the main source of calories for the alcoholic. You may not call that a balanced diet, but then you don't see the drug black market improving the housing stock of the ghetto or improving the educational circumstances. What we see are $150 sneakers, and gold chains, and Mercedes owned by people who hardly have time to drive them. The money is not going into productive investment or sustaining reasonable lifestyles. A great deal of it is probably drained away in more drugs. On the face of a balanced economic analysis there are faults in this simple characterization. There is a big cashflow going through the hands of one part of the community, but the actual wealth is running through their fingers. I doubt that there is much gain from the employment of lots of people in the drug trade.

Dr Griffith Edwards (UK): Dr Jessor said he was going to talk only about the USA, the country which he knows best. However, take the consideration beyond the ghetto or the poor of the USA and apply it to poor Africa, poor Asia, poor Latin America, and you find an applicability and a wider vision. Although we started off with some awareness of the developing world, there is a danger that this will be lost. We must consider again the seriousness and the moral commitment of that wider perspective. The inner city problem of drug use cannot be divorced from the problems of the inner city: it is cynical to suppose that by making heroin available on the corner store, you will improve the lot of the poor people who live there. If you go today to Bolivia, you will see Mercedes, you will see the money of those who are living on the fat of the cocaine trade and are living very nicely. But you will also see immense Third World poverty, with very little of the money going back into the mass of the people.

Dr Alex Wodak (Australia): My question is directed to Dr Strang. I have just heard the very good news that he has been appointed as the Chief Scientific Advisor to the erstwhile colony of Country X. They have listened to his comments about the relative importance of HIV prevention among drug users, they have recognized the truth of what he has said, and they have asked him to design a drug policy to prevent the most serious drug-related harm. Could he please reply?

Dr John Strang (UK): There may be benefit from paying more attention to this issue of price elasticity and inelasticity. In terms of one's overall strategy, it may perhaps be valuable to consider the different relationships that an individual might have with a drug. Let us stick to consideration of just one drug for the moment, then expand the consideration subsequently. If there are lessons to be learnt from alcohol and tobacco, then one would presume that by increasing the affordability of heroin, there would be an increase in consumption. That would suggest that you need to look at ways of making it less available. The problem with such a strategy is that, with those people for whom demand has already become inelastic, they will become more and more desperate about obtaining extra supplies. Perhaps you need to ensure the feasibility of a flight into therapy for those for whom the elasticity has gone. A pure control strategy would be doomed to failure because it fails to address the problems presented by those inelastic individuals. Likewise, it is a mistake to presume that all drug users need to be dealt with as if they have become inelastic. Perhaps what Country X should seek to establish, is a balance between a control policy (to reduce availability and reduce use amongst the 'elastic') and a linked care or treatment policy (to reduce the harm to self and others for those who have become 'inelastic').

Dr Eric Single (Canada): Put yourself in the place of a policy maker and think about what science has contributed to the policy debate around legalization. Mainly, it has been a wealth of technical information about adverse health affects of the various substances. To a public health specialist, the goal is to reduce the adverse consequences of substance abuse, but to a policy maker the goal is more than that. For the policy maker, it is a balance between the gains you get in reducing adverse consequences with one policy measure against the costs involved in the policy measure itself, in the attempts to reduce levels of consumption and problems associated with use. So it is always a balancing act. A number of years ago there was a literature review on the adverse health affects of cannabis and there were, about 1200 studies involved in the review—so there was a wealth of information available even then, and this was more than ten years ago. In doing a policy analysis on this issue I examined how many studies were available with regard to what is the cost of criminalizing people and I could find only two. Both involved very small samples, one was a study of cannabis offenders in Toronto, Canada, and the other was again a small sample of cannabis convicted offenders in London, UK. To my mind it was very telling, 1200 studies on the adverse health affects, two studies on the affects of criminalizing people. You cannot hold the scientists responsible, for we naturally study things in which we are trained, comfortable, familiar, and competent. But surely we need more work on the part of the funding agencies: there should be more support for the kind of work that is done by criminologist, health economists, more ethnographic kinds of methods, more work done in the ghettos themselves in the American context, to achieve a better balance. That would make the work a lot more useful to the policy makers.

The health budget of the agencies in the USA that are concerned with alcohol, drugs, and tobacco are in the orders of hundreds of millions. The Drug Institute, for example, has a budget of around 300 or 400 million. The counterpart in the Department of Justice: the National Institute of Justice has a research budget of around just 20 million. I think that ratio reflects in some ways differences and orientation in people who enforce criminal justice relative to people who are concerned with health. Those of us who are concerned with health, should not insist that we be in the position of making arbitrary judgements about criminal policy because there is no research, but we should surely be pushing that those concerned with criminal justice should invest more in, and be more informed by research.

I would like to comment on effective price. The peak of the first cocaine epidemic in the USA occurred about 1910, and it had virtually disappeared in New York according to the people who studied it in the 1930s, and it declined even more later on. I did a study recently on the price of illicit cocaine in 1907, 1908, 1909, 1910— illicit cocaine, when you could legally obtain it from a physician. There was an attempt to control cocaine: first it was legal and then it was given to the health professions to control. The involvement of the health profession had no affect at all on the illicit price, which was about that of one hour of the average industrial wage, which is almost exactly what it was in the 1980s for 100 mg. Economists estimate that the profit margins were the same in 1910, as they were in the 1980s. So, essentially, we had a market in cocaine which was equivalent in many ways to our current one. The profit margin was the same, the distribution was controlled by gangsters, children were distributing it and so on, and yet the whole thing went away. I think it's quite interesting to keep this in mind, that there is a historical progression, that things do go away. If sometimes we get too caught up with what happens within one or two years, or we put too much emphasis on the enormous margins, then it may be helpful to look at the previous epidemic and also to consider the pricing and marketing system of cocaine at that time which did not prevent its demise then, so why do we predict that it will prevent its demise now?

Dr Harold Kalant (Canada): I would like to summarize the debate so far. There is obviously agreement that calls for legalization are simplistic, and do not address properly the full cost–benefit evaluation of all the factors that go into drug use, drug abuse, and drug dependence of both licit and illicit drugs. The topic of discussion should really be not legalization versus prohibition but rather the most sane, humane, and effective set of policies to deal with drug problems. This approach should be adopted across licit and illicit drugs. The policies that relate to the use of alcohol and tobacco by the general population will necessarily have to be different from the policies that deal with the use of cocaine and other drugs by inner-city ghetto populations or by impoverished populations in countries other than the USA. One could extend the consideration beyond the USA to the populations in producer countries that to varying degrees may depend upon cocaine production for what little income they get. All of those will require different policies. If there is one single message to take away, it is not that we should be looking for the best single drug policy growing out of a cost benefit evaluation, but we should be looking for the best mix of policies, because we are dealing with different drugs and a range of problems—not one single drug problem.

Part VI A summing-up

29. Looking forward

Jerome H. Jaffe

When Sir Walter Bodmer commented that 'the future is largely unpredictable', he was referring to the process of scientific discovery. Considering the sudden and unexpected political upheavals now sweeping across Eastern Europe, it might seem foolhardy to suggest that political processes are more predictable than scientific discovery. But I believe they are, at least those processes that can be called drug and alcohol policy development. Consequently, I believe that trying to look ahead may have some value. In this chapter, I attempt to glean from the presentations and discussions that took place at this conference themes and ideas that suggest how tomorrow's world of science and policy will interact.

There were more than 60 scheduled speakers at this four-day meeting, and there were lively, insightful contributions from a very distinguished audience of scientists and policy makers. Since this chapter is intended as a response to the meeting and not as a synopsis, I make no attempt to mention the comments of each contributor, and inclusion or omission does not imply that any one contribution was more or less valuable or important than others.

Policy makers and scientists: an uneasy marriage that will endure

In opening this conference, Griffith Edwards suggested that somewhere in the darkest recesses of their hearts and minds, many policy makers believe that scientists pursue only what they are interested in, that science is too complex and overmanned, and that it is going in the wrong direction. The relevance of science to problems of alcohol, drugs, and tobacco, he concluded, still needs to be argued. Edwards' views are no doubt coloured by his own experiences with policy makers, and one of the important achievements of a meeting such as this is that, by comparing these views with those of scientists from other countries, the reader may consider the relationship between science and policy makers from a a wider perspective. For example, Thomas Babor points out that, from a world perspective, research on drugs, alcohol, and tobacco is growing exponentially; there are now 58 research centres world-wide, ranging from single laboratories with several researchers, to medium size facilities with 10–50 scientists, to major centres with more than 50 scientists. While the majority of these are in the USA, many other nations are also quite active. In addition, there are now 24 scientific journals devoted to problems in this area. Babor concludes that the present size of the infrastructure of science creates a new reality for policy makers and ensures that science will continue to play a role in the evolution of policy on drugs, alcohol, and tobacco.

Babor's description of a scientific infrastructure that is now institutionalized is not necessarily inconsistent with Edwards' view of a scientific infrastructure that needs to continually justify its right to exist. With few exceptions, publicly supported institutions and agencies have always been expected to argue for their share of public resources. And while it might seem to be wasteful of precious scientific talent to spend so much time in periodic arguments for resources, it is unlikely that an alternative system will emerge in any democratic nation in the near future.

Second only to the question, 'Will science in this area continue to exist?' is, 'What will be its relationship with the policy makers and policy-making structures?' While it is necessary for ease of discussion to subdivide these relationships into questions about how and to what degree science will be supported and encouraged in the future, and how the information generated by scientific activities will be translated into policy, such subdivisions are arbitrary. There is no way to sharply separate the way policy makers view and utilize the products of scientific activity from the way in which scientists relate to policy makers, and the way in which policy makers support and fund the scientific enterprise. Relationships will continue to be strained. Purity of motive on both sides of the divide will continue to be questioned, but not always publicly.

Among the themes that recurred most frequently at this conference was the recognition that policy makers, including those who are charged with funding science, see the world from a perspective very different from that of the scientist. Nothing discussed at this conference suggested that these differences in perspective will change in the foreseeable future. The bases for these differences include the following. Policy makers, whether within private industry, legislatures, or executive branches of government, believe it is their responsibility to weigh all views. As Laurence Lynn has put it, citizens want good public policy, but they also expect policy makers to consider not just the results, but also the costs and means used to achieve the results. Any policy that benefits one segment of the population, John Strang reminds us, is quite likely to be detrimental to another.

While experts often want privileged roles in policy formation, the policy makers must often first decide who the experts really are. The wisdom of specialists rarely goes unchallenged, even by colleagues (sometimes especially by colleagues) working in closely related areas. There was virtual unanimity among participants that, to avoid confusing policy makers, science should speak with one voice and consensus should be reached. No new ideas on how to reach such a consensus emerged. It is likely that the polyphony of today will still be heard tomorrow, especially when scientists are asked for expert opinion on how best to allocate resources across the broad range of scientific opportunities and disciplines.

Too often, policy, in the short-term, evolves on the basis of emotional appeals with little logical analysis of likely long-term effects. Such outcomes are often galling to scientists who have made careful and logical analyses of the likely results of policy options, but whose presentations did not have the emotional charge to win the day. Furthermore, scientists too often expect policy makers to be as devoid of self-interest as the scientists sometimes believe themselves to be. This is rarely the case. Policy makers have self-interest as well as public interest. Robert Kendell urges us to remember that they also may have personal experiences with problems of drug abuse and its treatment which, even if atypical, are often far more persuasive to them than the careful statistics of the experts who appear before them. And Robin Room has insightfully observed that science is not a reliable partner of policy. Scientists win admiration when they overturn a previously known 'fact'. Policy makers are more than a little disturbed when they are told that the scientific truth on which a policy had been based is no longer true. None of this is likely to change, but those who are realistic about the process are likely to be more effective in influencing it.

Another theme that presaged a continuing tense and strained relationship was the impatience of scientists with the seemingly slow process of change and with the inconsistencies which appear to characterize policies in this area. Perhaps some of the impatience stems from the way in which more than one scientist defined science: nothing but trained and organized common sense. Given such a self-perception, it is understandable that many scientists find it hard to accept the fact that in the arena of policy they are perceived, as Roger Meyer put it, as just one more interest group.

Unlike science, which can overturn long held beliefs on the basis of a few decisive experiments, social policies are often characterized by remarkable inertia. New ideas do not necessarily eclipse old ones; commonly the new are added or melded to the old. Policies will often seem inconsistent; but, it is a basic observation about policy that it is not necessarily coherent or consistent. And it would be particularly unrealistic to expect consistency across different drug categories with very different histories of social acceptance and different effects. Scientific findings about drugs or alcohol use can be used or ignored, depending on other factors that are operative.

The lag time between major scientific findings and eventual changes in social policies which reflect those findings will probably continue to shrink. While the interval will probably never be as short as the scientific community might wish, a reasonable review of history indicates that there has been substantial progress in some areas. Reginald Smart reminded us that from the time that lemon juice had been shown to prevent scurvy, it took the British

Navy more than 200 years to mandate its use. It took about 15–20 years from the time tobacco smoking was firmly linked to lung cancer (at least statistically) to mandate health warnings on cigarette packages. Recent findings about the adverse health effects of passive smoke inhalation are now being rapidly incorporated into policies that give passengers on airlines and workers in offices the right to be able to avoid passive inhalation of tobacco smoke. The history of the links between science and policy should teach us two things. Even obvious policy changes may not be made quickly and, as Dean Gerstein and others emphasized, we cannot judge the policy impact of a scientific finding without reference to a time frame. Public policy, even more than science, is a slow, cumulative process. Science, according to Edwards, may need to pull policy along, slowly.

Influencing 'policy'

To understand how science can contribute to the evolution of policy we must first understand the nature of policy itself. Policy, as it was defined by more than one speaker at this conference, is the ends and means chosen by the leadership of any collectivity. So defined, the concept of policy is broader than governmental policy. To see social policy with respect to drugs, alcohol, and tobacco, as exclusively the province of government would be to seriously misunderstand its nature. The way a society responds to the presence or use of a given drug can be shaped in the pulpits of its churches, in its classrooms, in the executive offices of its corporations, and in its popular magazines and television programmes—sometimes more effectively than in the offices of its elected officials or in the halls of its legislatures and parliaments.

To the best of my knowledge, no legislative body on either side of the Atlantic deliberated about the distribution of free cigarettes to the young men in uniform during either of the two World Wars. (The cigarettes were often generously donated by the companies that would then sell cigarettes to these same men for the next 40 years.) In the USA in the early 1960s, it was a policy of free speech, and not one favouring the use of drugs, that allowed adults in several walks of life actively to encourage young people to experiment with LSD and marijuana. It was a widely followed policy, but not an official one, for judges not to impose a prison sentence on first-time offenders solely for possession of a single marijuana cigarette (even though the police did not follow any consistent policy about arresting people for such offences).

In more and more parts of the world, non-governmental sectors of society play important roles in directly influencing drug-using behaviours, as well as influencing official or government policy. Social policy, I would argue, is best inferred from what is done, not merely what is legislated: who is hired and who is not; who is arrested and who is not. It is what is considered a legitimate reason for not showing up for work. It is who is offered medical treatment and who is not. It is who is treated courteously and who is shunned, not just by government officials such as police, but also by hospitals. It is which advertisements are accepted by which magazines and which newspapers. It is how many seats in a restaurant are set aside for those who do not smoke, or whether hospitalized patients are permitted to smoke. It is who is written about with admiration and adulation; who is considered exciting and who is not.

Many of the decisions that influence drug using behaviour are difficult to modify by government actions, but are often readily influenced by the climate of scientific ideas and beliefs. According to Herbert Kleber, the use of marijuana declined in the USA as many young people accepted scientist-generated reports on its potentially toxic effects, although there was no change in its apparent availability or price. A similar reduction in the use of cocaine occurred among middle-class users when the media gave more attention to its potentially lethal consequences, again with no substantial change in price or availability. A scientific community that looks exclusively to government as its only means to influence society and social policy is overlooking important opportunities. The focus of attention on the response to illicit drugs, such as cocaine and opioids, in many ways has distorted the perspective on the general problem of how science influences policy with respect to consumables—whether the consumables are high cholesterol cheeseburgers or low nicotine cigarettes.

I should hasten to emphasize that many scientists in the field are well aware of the diverse audiences that must be reached and influenced. For example, Robert West and Michael Russell emphasize that much could be accomplished with respect to smoking cessation if only our medical colleagues could be persuaded of the value of interventions. Kleber reminds us that science need not carry the burden of communication alone. In the USA, a private group, The Partnership for a Drug Free America, adopted a programme of massive print and electronic media campaigns to make the public aware of the toxicity of cocaine. The effort appears to have met with success, since the decline in cocaine use correlates to some degree with the intensity of media saturation.

Games and shared simplifications

Those who would influence policy need to understand the limits of policy making—the rules of the policy game—a metaphor used by both Gerstein and Lynn. It seems unlikely that either the rules or the objectives of the policy process will undergo radical change in the near future. Policy will continue to involve selective emphasis from among a range of acceptable alternatives. As Gerstein put it: 'We cannot step out of history.' (Although it does appear from the recent dissolution of the USSR that, when things get intolerable enough, the range of acceptable alternatives can expand dramatically.) Furthermore, objectives or ends cannot be reached without means, and the means used must also fall within acceptable limits. Gerstein alluded to the role in policy formation of shared simplifications. This is the idea that, in a democracy, complex or entirely novel ideas can rarely be supported; that 'There are too many people ... and too little time ... to create a shared perception of a complex structure,' (Moore and Gerstein 1981). Consequently, policy is guided by simplified groups of accepted truths, or 'governing ideas', about what causes the (drug or alcohol) problem and what needs to be done.

For the past century the three main governing ideas that have influenced policy concerning drugs, alcohol, and tobacco have been the liberal, medical, and criminal models. In my view, neither the criminal nor the medical model, the past century's dominant governing ideas, is likely to be totally abandoned in the near future. Societies will continue to believe that, to some degree, the use of illicit drugs is immoral, ruinous behaviour, and that it is the task of families, churches, and schools to teach children to behave responsibly and morally. When these institutions fail, other authorities—police, courts, prisons—must come into play. Yet these same societies will also accept the view that when some individuals use certain drugs for a while they lose flexibility about decisions for further use: they appear to have a 'disorder'. In many instances they appear to be able to overcome this disorder with help. If the history of the past century is a guide to the future, then each of these governing ideas—the criminal and the medical models—these simplified bundles of ideas about the causes and appropriate responses to problems—will continue their often uneasy co-existence.

The notion that shared simplifications generally guide policy requires an additional comment. Whether the question is about the causality of drug use, the nature of dependence, or the efficacy of treatment, the utility of the answers that science can provide to policy makers is typically limited by the sophistication of the questions that are raised. Communicating science to government and to the general public may require that we first make the concepts we use a part of the intellectual repertoire in our colleges and universities; then eventually our policy makers will understand why the road to effective policy is not paved with simple answers.

Supporting science

At this meeting there was remarkable agreement on what science in this field needs to flourish: centres of excellence where bright, talented, creative people from multiple disciplines can interact; good mentoring; adequate and stable (preferably long-term) support. In addition to such support, ideally there ought to be a shared vision, collegiality, dialogue, perhaps competition that motivates individuals to set priorities and ask questions that can be answered; and, preferably, there should be links to a University. Boris Tabakoff cautions us not to view science as homogenous—different problems require different kinds of support; and not to assume that good science means big science.

Despite the frustrations of dealing with scientists who, too often, offer only highly qualified and tentative answers to most questions dealing with alcohol, drugs, and tobacco, and despite any misgivings they may have about purity of motives, policy makers in more and more countries have been willing, over the past few decades, to help create and support conditions in which the relevant sciences can grow. There are now more research centres of excellence dedicated to problems of drugs, alcohol, and tobacco, more scientists working in these areas, more specialized journals (and more international scientific meetings) than at any time in the history of organized inquiry. The National Addiction Centre, the opening of which this conference celebrates, is one example of the willingness of society to support such centres of excellence. Babor believes that we are approaching saturation. I believe that, in some places, we may be supersaturated and we should expect some crystallization with some aggregates sinking to the bottom. But if such a falling out occurs, it ought not to obscure the more important feature of the present and likely future relationship between policy and science. In the area of drugs, alcohol, and tobacco, science is no longer an afterthought; it has been legislated into legitimacy, if not supremacy. In the USA, scientific studies have a major influence on decisions about drug regulation and control under the Controlled Substances Act. At the UN, the advice of the experts convened by the WHO plays a major role in determining which new drugs are regulated under International treaties. As Babor put it at this meeting, when the scientific infrastructure has been built to its current level, one element of policy has been fixed: science has been incorporated as a major player.

If such support is to be sustained, there must be public support, which, in turn, depends on the prestige and credibility of science. In the USA, the role of science and the work of scientists is currently under attack on several fronts. Fred Goodwin has warned us that the scientific enterprise is accused of being too costly, corrupt, cruel, and closed. From the perspective of public trust and confidence, the golden age of science may be passing, and scientists will need to find better ways to explain and justify their role. A corollary to this proposition, one emphasized by both Meyer and Goodwin, is that science needs to find better ways to reward good scientific citizens—those who take time from their careers to explain and/or defend the scientific enterprise. One way, of course, is to make public mention of those whose efforts are particularly outstanding. To be consistent with this suggestion, I need to mention Goodwin; for no one, to the best of my knowledge, has been more articulate or expended more effort in responding to the attacks by radical animal rights groups that seek to eliminate entirely the use of animals in all scientific research, but have selectively targeted the use of animals in research on drugs, alcohol, and mental health.

In defending or explaining the purpose and value of science to policy makers and the public, we may not be able to rely as much as we have in the past on a general willingness to believe in the integrity of science and scientists. There are at least two reasons for this likely erosion of trust. First, to the list of sins enumerated by Goodwin (cost, corruption, cruelty, closure),

Meyer and others have added arrogance. Those who would be future champions and spokespersons of science will need to recognize that many people see the policy positions advocated by some scientists as patently and obviously self-serving. Even the friends of science are frustrated by the seemingly insatiable need for more resources and the stereotypical response to so many policy-relevant questions: 'more research is needed'. It will require more than good citizenship to overcome such a perspective. A second and more recent threat to trust, and one which is gaining ground in the USA, is a systematic effort to root out scientific fraud and misconduct (whether it exists or not). In a process reminiscent of the Spanish Inquisition or police tactics in totalitarian states, scientists can now be subjected to interrogation about their scientific work on unspecified charges levelled by anonymous accusers who cannot be confronted, and can be interrogated by panels that can act as prosecutor, judge, and jury. Quite apart from the damage that is done to the accused scientist, the media coverage of these procedures inevitably leads to an erosion of confidence in the credibility and integrity of the scientific enterprise, and to its capacity to play an influential role in policy formation.

The stability of support that science seeks will probably not be achieved in the foreseeable future. Among the reasons are these. By its very nature, the growth of scientific knowledge is exponential—each finding raising several new questions which, if pursued, lead to still new findings. No reasonable person could expect governments around the world to allocate resources in a comparably exponential fashion. At some point, the growth of potentially fruitful and useful research opportunities will far exceed the resources needed to pursue them. Two alternative methods have evolved to cope with this inevitable situation. There can be relatively stable, long-term funding of a group of researchers of relatively fixed size, who must then prioritize the questions that seem most important. This yields a form of stability, but it largely excludes new researchers with radically new ideas from entering the field. An alternative is to have a fixed—or slowly (not exponentially) growing—pool of money for which all potential researchers must compete. Inevitably, some previously well-funded researchers will lose to others in this competitive process. This will be labelled 'instability'. Even within the first paradigm (the fixed group of researchers), as the number of questions expand, (or if the costs of research rise), priority setting is eventually required. Some researchers will receive too little to pursue what they believe are important questions. This, too, will be labelled 'instability'.

There is another variety of instability that is not inevitable, and over which policy makers and scientists can exert better control. Science now plays a role in every aspect of society. When there are pressing problems in any area it is easier for policy makers to find 'technological fixes' than to reallocate resources among competing constituencies. At times of crisis, policy makers are tempted to show they are dealing with a problem by allocating more resources to the search for a technological fix (the non-polluting automobile or energy source, the new supersmart weapons). When the focus of concern shifts to a new problem, there is a temptation again to reallocate the research resources, leaving much research unfinished. All of the onus for this second form of instability should not be placed on the heads of policy makers. Scientists have been all too willing participants, often promising quick and money saving breakthroughs if only there were adequate resources for their particular areas of interest. Policy makers under pressure from the public to 'do somethings' often provide the resources, only to turn bitter when the promised breakthroughs do not emerge. Budget reductions or freezes and the associated 'instability' ensue. The latter variety of instability, especially in its extreme form, can be devastating. While the former inevitable variety can be demoralizing, it should not obscure the more fundamental observation that the science relevant to this field has been given a solid foundation of support in many countries and is likely to be active and vital, at least for the near future.

Asking the right questions about treatment

For at least two decades policy makers have asked: 'Does treatment (or prevention) work?' Scientists have tried to answer, but the answers often have been vague and couched with so many qualifiers that they had little impact. Thomas McLellan and Kathleen Carroll told this conference about remarkable advances in methodological sophistication over the past 15 years that will allow science to give more useful answers, because we are able to reframe the questions. 'Does treatment for addiction work?' is not much better than, 'Does surgery work?' 'Does surgery work for cancer?' is only a modest advance. Today, researchers in this field, supported stably over more than a decade, have been asking: 'Does a given treatment, delivered by a specified set of procedures, and offered to particular groups of people with specified risk factors, produce changes in any of several relevant behaviours?' And we are getting answers. Moreover, we now know enough not to assume that all treatment called by the same name delivers the same services or interventions. In drawing valid inferences about which treatment 'works', we have learned to measure not just the outcome but the treatment.

More knowledge about treatment effectiveness will not necessarily make the interactions between science and policy makers less testy. Ray Hodgson suggests that many countries may be spending the most on those interventions which are the least cost-effective. Such information should confront policy makers with a need to reallocate resources among constituencies. The response will in all likelihood be far slower than could be justified by the robustness of the findings. But, as Gerstein commented, it is often more difficult to shift the means to policy objectives than to change objectives. These technological advances in the study of the efficacy of psychological treatment may even complicate the lives of other researchers and clinicians.

Researchers working on biological interventions, such as medications, not only must learn to ask equally sophisticated questions about the drugs being developed, but they also must begin to measure more carefully the quality and quantity of psychological elements of their clinical pharmacological trials, elements that until recently they had assumed could be treated as constants. Clinicians, upon learning who responds best to how much psychological intervention, must face some difficult choices in deciding how to allocate limited resources across diverse populations.

Despite this growing sophistication, there is sometimes an inverse relationship between the evidence that a particular intervention is effective and the willingness of society to accept the use of the intervention. And in connection with some approaches to treatment of addiction to illicit agents, there would appear to be, for some policy makers, no level of evidence sufficient to persuade them of the efficacy of the interventions. For example, a recent report of the Institute of Medicine (Gerstein and Harwood 1990) concluded that, of all the available interventions, methadone maintenance is the most thoroughly studied, and the evidence for its efficacy is least open to question. Yet, relative to other treatments, it is this approach that still generates scepticism and criticism from policy makers (Gordis 1991).

Some policy relevant questions for the future

The amazingly rapid growth of neuroscience makes me hesitant to predict that certain problems at the interface of science and policy are not likely soon to be solved. Despite such hesitancy, I do not believe that we can look to science to resolve the inherent conflicts between the disease and the criminal models of drug dependence. At the heart of this issue are the notions of volition, free will, and personal responsibility.

Elsewhere, Enoch Gordis has expressed the hope that neuroscience can help define some scale that would allow us to judge better when a behaviour is entirely under volitional control (Gordis 1991). I have considerable respect, if not awe, for the possibilities of positron emission tomography scanners and other *in vivo* micromeasurements of the functioning of the brain. But the finding that, on average, the brain of a person who uses a given drug differs in some way from that of a person who does not will not necessarily tell us whether a given behaviour was the result of an entirely free choice, or whether the individual should be held accountable for that behaviour before the law. The current debate about whether obvious withdrawal phenomena should be included in DSM-IV and ICD-10 as necessary criteria for the diagnosis of drug dependence (drug, alcohol, or tobacco) is driven, in part, by a longing to separate medical disorder from wilful behaviour. There has long been evidence that individuals respond differently to drugs and, more recently, evidence has accumulated that some people are genetically predisposed to develop alcoholism. I have little doubt that we shall some day find biological ways of dealing with vulnerability and tendencies toward relapse, but I do not believe that any of these will lead to more agreement on whether in any individual case we are dealing with sin or syndrome.

Conversely, it is hard to imagine how policies flowing from the criminal model will help policy makers to cope with the threat to public welfare posed by the HIV epidemic and its associated consequences. Among the most important current and future issues at the science–policy interface are related to how best to minimize the spread of HIV among drug users and from drug users to the general population; how to respond to the rapidly increasing incidence of tuberculosis among those whose immune systems are compromised by HIV infections, many of whom are drug users who are often reluctant to seek or comply with treatment; and how to protect the general public from a major reemergence of tuberculosis. Special alarms are being sounded because many of the new cases of infection are due to organisms resistant to available antibiotics. Such problems seem to cry out for new science: technological solutions rapidly achieved. It will be interesting to see who promises what to whom.

Some issues not addressed

Several issues where the science and policy related to drugs and alcohol intersect were not addressed at this conference. A few deserve brief mention because they illustrate how scientific discovery can generate a demand for new policy. The growing sophistication of our capacity to detect recent use of drugs provides one such striking example. Thirty years ago, it was difficult and expensive, if not impossible, to determine whether an individual had recently used any number of licit or illicit drugs. Consequently, in studies of treatment outcome, we were obliged to rely almost exclusively on patients' self-reports, and there was no easy way of knowing how valid such reports were. The development of quick and relatively inexpensive ways to detect drug use in body fluids not only allowed us to estimate the accuracy of self-reports under differing contingencies, but also required us to raise the standards for clinical research on drug abuse. Now, the best studies of treatment obtain biological evidence to support other data on the extent to which patients have reduced their drug, alcohol, or tobacco use. However, the analytical capacities that were developed for scientific purposes have more recently been applied in new ways that, themselves, represent new policies. For example, in the USA, drug testing prior to employment has become common; and military personnel, including officers, are tested on a random basis, and a single positive finding for an illicit drug can be grounds for discharge. These testing policies did not develop without controversy. There have been, and still are, lawsuits arguing that such procedures infringe individual privacy and liberty. There were also arguments by some scientists that the accuracy and reliability of the testing was inadequate to use for these purposes. The response of policy makers in government interested in using the technology to deter drug use, (and there is some evidence that it is an effective deterrent), was to fund further research and develop new methodologies so as to sharply reduce the likelihood of an inaccurate result. Similar policy problems are raised by the increasing ease of testing for alcohol and nicotine.

What is of interest in the context of this conference is the way in which policies about drug testing were stimulated by the evolution of scientific technology and how, once the technology was harnessed in the service of policy, further research on the technology expanded. Societies are now pondering how to respond to the availability of hair analysis that can detect drug use that occurred not within hours or days, but within weeks or months.

If we are inclined to dismiss as inconsequential this example of technology driving policy, we might consider that, in Virginia Berridge's view, it was the rise of psychiatry in the nineteenth century—a new 'technology'—that brought about a radical conceptual shift that allowed excessive drug or alcohol use to be seen sometimes as neither consumatory behaviour (the libertarian model), nor moral failure (the criminal model), but as a disorder (the medical model).

At this conference, the focus has been solidly on the areas in which scientific method can be applied to understanding the social forces that influence drug use and the efficacy of prevention and of therapeutic interventions. A curious reader might well wonder if it was by accident or by design that no voices were present to ask how best to apply scientific method to the efficacy of efforts to limit or curtail supplies of illicit drugs and deter use through criminal sanctions, and how best to incorporate the findings of such research into policy. Perhaps those policies that are based firmly on morality—people who break the law must be punished—do not require scrutiny or scientific analysis. Perhaps only those policies which derive their vitality from governing ideas (such as the medical model) that are themselves essentially a set of scientific hypotheses, need to be continually scrutinized and tested. Whatever the reason, given the resources that most societies invest in the supply control aspect of the drug problem, one might think that many policy makers would be interested in applying the methods of science to this area.

Toward globalism

International scientific conferences on drug abuse have become more frequent over the past decade. Researchers and policy makers from more than ten countries participated in this conference. There are important inferences to be drawn from this trend. First, not only are problems related to alcohol, drugs, and tobacco common to nations around the world, but policy makers and scientists are recognizing that there exists a wealth of policy relevant information available to be shared if only we invest the effort. It is in the nature of societies that we can have only one policy at a time. How can we know if some other set of policy options would bring about our objectives more effectively or at lesser cost? Without reasonable evidence we cannot make major policy shifts; but if we do not change policy, how can such evidence emerge? One way out of this dilemma is to look at the policies other nations have adopted and by considering the differences and similarities try to infer what outcomes might have emerged had they been used in our own countries. For such sharing to be useful, scientists and policy makers will have to develop common terms and reliable methods to measure both costs and outcome. Such interchanges on standardization of terms and epidemiological measurements have been taking place under the aegis of the WHO for at least two decades. Global scientific interchange can only be accelerated by the dramatic reductions in tensions that once divided East and West. Health research, said Edwards, should not be a luxury available only to developed nations. The researchers in developed nations have an ethical obligation to share information and technology with those whose resource base is smaller or non-existent. David Musto remarked that we rarely take lessons from history. Let us hope that we will be more successful in taking lessons from the experiences of other nations.

Scientists as advocates

This conference began with Griffith Edwards' proposition that the case for science still needs to be argued and ended with Richard Jessor's assertion that there is an ethical obligation to advocate for those policies we are led to by our research. Such seeming symmetry should not obscure the concerns raised during the conference about the role of the scientist as policy advocate (either for greater and more stable research funding, or for a particular set of policy options concerning drugs and alcohol.) There were no voices suggesting that scientists should limit themselves to the publication of research findings. Smart, Meyer, and others argued that science should not leave the task of policy advocacy to television, newspapers, and inside champions. Mark Taylor, Marcus Grant, and others advised that we should share our expertise, even when it is incomplete, because policy will be made with or without the input of science. Persistence is a virtue, said David Hawks: the findings of science will not necessarily be accepted the first time they are presented. Or, as Grant put it, the key players need to keep playing if they are to influence the process.

The central issues concerning advocacy at this conference were not whether scientists should speak out on matters of policy, but to what degree the mantle of science can be worn when doing so, and to what degree we should qualify our results. As Gordis has written, '. . . it is somewhat fraudulent . . . , for a scientist whose credentials bear no relationship to the area under discussion to express what amounts to the views of a public citizen while wearing the uniform of the scientist' (Gordis 1991). But Gordis also believes that policy advocacy within one's realm of scientific expertise is an appropriate and necessary part of the scientist's role. Harold Kalant, however, held out for applying an even higher ethical standard, stating that policy involves weighing values, not facts. We can often agree on facts, but when we speak on what is good policy we are by definition adding value judgements and we should recognize that we are, therefore, speaking as citizens not as scientists. George Vaillant seemed to support the role of the scientist as one who presents findings but refuses to endorse any set of policy options. The Greenwich clock, he said, earned the honour of sitting astride the zero meridian because it never told anyone which way to go, it simply offered the truth.

When Jessor argued that the focus of policy ought to be on the psychosocial determinants of drug abuse, rather than on methods directed at drug use itself, such as controlling drug supply, he added that we have an ethical obligation to advocate what we believe to be right. But, he also added an important insight into why the scientific community will continue to bring its findings forcefully to the attention of policy makers despite all of the frustrations that have been aired at this conference, and even when such findings generate antagonism between scientist and scientist and between scientist and policy maker. Jessor asserts that when scientists say they want social policy to be responsive to science, they are really saying they want their life's work to help to build a just society. There was little dissent. The building of a just society is not a new objective. The Book of Deuteronomy admonishes: 'Justice, justice shalt thou follow' (Deut. XVI:20). But the pursuit of justice is a slow and difficult process and it is not a goal sought only by those on the scientific side of the science policy divide. Policy makers believe they, too, are striving for a just society. With rare exceptions, the shaping and reshaping of policy has been and will continue to be a slow process. Sometimes we are inclined to turn away. At such times I like to remind myself of a passage excerpted from the Talmud that hung on the wall of Herbert Kleber's office at the White House Office of National Drug Control Policy:

The day is short, the work is much, the workmen are lazy . . . It is not your duty to complete the work, but neither are you free to desist from it.

References

Gerstein, D.R. and Harwood, H.J. (eds) (1990). *Treating drug problems*, Vol. 1. National Academy Press, Washington.

Gordis, E. (1991). From science to social policy: an uncertain road. *Journal of Studies on Alcohol*, 52, 101–9.

Moore, M.H. and Gerstein, D.G. (1981). *Alcohol and public policy: beyond the shadow of prohibition*. National Academy Press, Washington.

Index

AIDS

AIDS: Testing and Privacy

Martin Gunderson
David J. Mayo
Frank S. Rhame

University of Utah Press
Salt Lake City
1989

ETHICS IN A CHANGING WORLD
Margaret P. Battin and Leslie P. Francis, Editors

Library of Congress Cataloging-in-Publication Data

Gunderson, Martin, 1946–
      AIDS : testing and privacy / Martin Gunderson, David J. Mayo,
Frank S. Rhame.
            p.   cm. — (Ethics in a changing world ; v. 2)
      Bibliography: p.
      Includes index.
      ISBN 0-87480-317-9
      1. AIDS (Disease) — United States — Diagnosis — Moral and ethical
aspects.   2. Privacy, Right of — United States.   I. Mayo, David J.,
1940–   .   II. Rhame, Frank S., 1942–   .   III. Title.   IV. Series.
      [DNLM: 1. Acquired Immunodeficiency Syndrome.
2. Confidentiality.   3. Ethics, Medical.   WD 308 G975a]
RC607.A26G86   1989
174′.2 — dc19
DNLM/DLC
for Library of Congress   88-39245
                                                                    CIP

CONTENTS

v

PART TWO: SPECIFIC ISSUES

Introduction

It is now a commonplace that AIDS threatens Americans on two fronts. The disease itself threatens the health of an increasing number of Americans. The death statistics are appalling. As of January 30, 1989, over 83,000 Americans had developed AIDS. There were 20,620 new cases reported in 1987 alone. The best estimate is that 80,000 Americans will acquire AIDS in 1992.[1] There is no cure for AIDS, and virtually everyone who develops AIDS dies. The question is not whether a person with AIDS will die, but when. If left untreated, most of those who get the disease die within 24 months, although some live as long as five years.[2] The struggle to limit the number of deaths is the first front on which AIDS must be fought.

AIDS spreads panic as well as death. Persons with AIDS face a wide range of discrimination, including housing discrimination, employment discrimination, and discrimination in public accommodations.[3] When AIDS panic gets translated into political action, it poses a significant threat to civil liberties. This is the second front on which the disease must be fought. The question is how to preserve our civil liberties while the search for a means to stem the AIDS epidemic continues.

With the AIDS epidemic posing a threat on two fronts, the tests that indicate whether someone is infected with the human immunodeficiency virus (HIV), which causes AIDS, can be seen to pose problems as well as to promise help. The HIV tests have already

---

[1] The number of AIDS cases is discussed in Chapter 1 in the section entitled "Epidemiology of AIDS."

[2] Mortality statistics regarding AIDS and HIV infection are discussed in Chapter 1 in the section entitled "Health Consequences of HIV Infection."

[3] Discrimination faced by persons infected with HIV is discussed primarily in Chapter 5 in the section entitled "Testing Positive."

been of great assistance in protecting the nation's blood supply — the purpose for which they were originally developed and licensed. In addition, they allow us to gather important epidemiological data. Also, if a cure becomes available in the future, the tests will enable people who are infected but asymptomatic to verify that they are infected so that they can benefit from treatment. The tests also pose problems, however. They make possible a variety of discriminatory and repressive measures against individuals who are still healthy and productive. The tests can be used to screen people to exclude them from employment, military service, immigration, insurance, and even marriage.

Moreover, some uses of the tests pose policy questions that go well beyond AIDS and have implications for how we will handle testing for other diseases in the future. The HIV tests may in fact herald the dawning of a new age in medical testing. In the near future it will be possible to develop tests enabling us to predict with a fair degree of certainty whether a person will succumb to a variety of diseases. Insurance companies will surely be tempted to use such tests to screen applicants, just as they now screen some life insurance applicants for HIV infection. Health insurance applicants may find themselves unable to get insurance to cover the very diseases for which they will need insurance. Employers may also use such tests where legally permitted to screen potential employees, just as the military, the Peace Corps, the Job Corps, and the State Department now use the HIV tests to screen their applicants. How we deal with the HIV tests may well set a precedent for how a large number of similar tests will be handled in the future.

In the past several years, HIV testing has already presented us with an impressive tangle of ethical problems. Among the more pressing social questions are (1) whether there are any groups of people who should be required to be tested for HIV infection, (2) whether insurance companies should be permitted to do unlimited testing of prospective insurees, (3) whether persons admitted to hospitals should be tested, and (4) who should have access to the test results. On the individual level, questions include whether one ought to get tested and with whom one ought to share test results, especially if one tests positive. Is a person who tests positive, for instance, morally obligated to contact all of his or her past sexual partners?

Through this tangle of moral problems runs the thread of privacy. Many of the proposals for mandatory testing and some of the mandatory testing programs already instituted require a sacrifice of individual privacy. Legal as well as moral issues are raised regarding privacy. It is our view that privacy is a fundamentally important value and that it makes sense to speak of a right to privacy. We do not, however, believe that privacy overrides all other concerns. In dealing with the various issues surrounding HIV testing, we note the values with which privacy competes. When possible, we suggest alternatives which will preserve privacy and the competing values. When this is not possible we attempt to determine whether privacy interests are sufficiently strong to override other values. Although privacy has often figured in the public debate about HIV testing, along with cost–effectiveness, this closer look at privacy is needed, since so little attention has been given to the extent to which privacy claims are justified and deserve to be taken seriously.

Part One provides the background necessary for a discussion of ethical issues which arise concerning HIV testing. At the outset we need a basic understanding of AIDS, HIV tests, and the mechanisms by which HIV is spread. Chapter 1 provides this understanding. Chapter 2 lays out a structure for the many ethical issues concerning HIV testing. We distinguish four broad sorts of questions: (1) What groups should be tested? (2) Should the tests be mandatory or voluntary? (3) To whom should the test results be distributed? (4) What are the goals of the various testing programs?

The theme which unifies our investigation of these various issues is privacy. Chapter 3 considers the general case for privacy. We argue that privacy is a fundamental value in that it is necessary for the creation of autonomous individuals, for democracy, for a variety of individual projects, and for protection from prejudice, ignorance, and malice. We also argue that there is a right to privacy. In particular we argue that privacy covers medical information and medical testing. It is thus a fundamental value relevant to HIV testing. Chapter 4 expands on Chapter 3 in that it describes how the value we place on privacy is embodied in our legal system. We consider constitutional, statutory, and common law protections of privacy and how these might apply to HIV testing.

Part Two considers a variety of testing proposals in light of the issues dealt with in Part One. We begin by focusing on those activities which least intrude on privacy — education coupled with voluntary anonymous testing. We note that even here there may be significant sacrifices in privacy. While voluntary anonymous testing does not itself intrude on privacy, it is difficult to control the spread of information about those who test positive. Even AIDS education may infringe on privacy. The education most likely to be effective is that which deals explicitly with the activities, including sexual practices, which are most likely to spread AIDS. However, when such education is provided to a wide range of people, it intrudes on the privacy of those who would prefer not to have their sensibilities exposed to activities they find offensive. We conclude, however, that health concerns clearly override privacy concerns in the area of AIDS education. We recommend increases in spending on AIDS education and the wide availability of voluntary anonymous testing. We also note, however, that these do not constitute a panacea.

Chapter 6 deals with one of the moral problems faced by those who receive positive test results: To what extent are they morally obligated to warn their sexual partners (past and potential)? We begin with a general discussion of the duty to warn others and then apply this to the case of HIV infection. Although it seems at first glance that those who find they are HIV infected are morally obligated to warn all of their past and potential sexual partners, we argue that there are situations in which HIV-infected persons are not so obligated. We cite a number of factors on which the decision depends, including the degree of risk faced by the partner, the likelihood of harm to the person who warns, and the likelihood that the partner is aware of the risk.

We then turn to the question of whether a physician has a moral duty to warn the partners of his or her infected patients. Here the privacy of the patient must be balanced against the need to protect others. We locate the factors to be used in this balancing and argue again that while there are situations in which the physician is morally obligated to warn the partners of infected patients, there are also situations in which there is no such duty. Finally, we note the legal duties of both physicians and those who are infected.

Chapter 7 is concerned with another aspect of the doctor-patient relationship: To what extent is mandatory HIV testing justified within the health care delivery setting? We argue, in large part on grounds of privacy, that the availability of medical treatment for problems unrelated to HIV infection should not be made conditional upon the patient's taking an HIV test. Instead, we recommend that blood and body fluid precautions (e.g., wearing gloves and using safe disposal techniques for needles and other possibly contaminated objects) be taken with all patients. In those cases in which precautions could pose risks for the patient (e.g., certain surgical techniques), we recommend that the patient be given the option of either submitting to an HIV test or submitting to the precautions. We also argue that there is not sufficient evidence at the present time to require testing of health care workers. If, however, evidence comes to light which indicates that there are procedures such as surgery in which an infected physician poses a significant risk to his or her patients, then it would be morally justified to require HIV tests for those who engage in such procedures.

HIV testing has raised issues not only in the area of health care delivery, but also in the area of health care payment. Estimates of the average cost of treating a person with AIDS vary widely. One study placed the mean cost of treating an AIDS patient at more than $46,000 per year.[4] Of course, insurers are motivated to require HIV tests of prospective insurees so that premium costs will not rise dramatically because of AIDS claims. Yet those who are HIV infected, and therefore likely to get AIDS, need sufficient financial support to pay for their medical care should they get AIDS. Some states have severely limited or even forbidden the use of HIV testing as a means of determining insurability.[5]

Chapter 8 considers HIV testing by insurers and employers. We argue that the sometimes competing values of freedom of contract and adequate health care can both be preserved, along with privacy, by creating a government program to pay for AIDS care. We then turn to employment. Employers no less than insurers are motivated by economic considerations not to hire those who may be infected with HIV. We argue that states should pass laws forbidding employment discrimination on the basis of HIV infection and that employers should not be allowed to require HIV testing as a condition of employment. Chapter 8 also discusses how current laws which afford protection against employment discrimination could be applied to HIV testing.

Chapter 9 extends the discussion of employee testing to federal employment and military service. We consider mandated HIV test-

---

[4] Studies of the costs of treating AIDS patients are discussed in the introduction to Chapter 8 (see footnotes 1–4 and the accompanying text).

[5] State regulations for HIV testing are discussed in Chapter 8 (see, for instance, footnote 5 and the accompanying text).

ing of military personnel, Peace Corps and Job Corps applicants, and applicants for immigration. We also consider programs for testing federal prisoners. We argue that the testing programs instituted by the federal government are highly invasive of privacy and that many of the rationales which have been offered for the programs are inadequate. We conclude that most of the mandatory testing programs instituted by the federal government should be abandoned. We also consider mandatory premarital testing and argue against it on grounds of both cost efficiency and privacy.

Nearly all proposals for HIV testing significantly involve the issue of privacy. Of course privacy is not the only consideration. We must also consider the cost-effectiveness of various health measures, the need for epidemiological knowledge, and the need to preserve the health of individuals. But while privacy may sometimes be overridden by such competing values, it must always be taken into account.

PART ONE
The Background

1
The Medical Background

As a matter of general principle, responsible public policy on any issue must be based on reasonable belief, not fanciful opinion or hysteria. Rational policies concerning AIDS (acquired immunodeficiency syndrome) must be firmly grounded in scientific understanding and an accurate appreciation of the current limits of that understanding. One must recognize what is known, what is not known, and what is now deemed likely although not certain. Many issues require judgments even when such judgments are difficult. Some issues demand quantitative judgments. (Can a given event ever occur? Is it so rare as to be negligible? Can it occur often enough to require accommodation?) Understanding the basis of the available conclusions not only increases confidence that most are correct; it also identifies those which are most likely to require modification.

In this chapter we present an historical review and general medical information for those unfamiliar with the human immunodeficiency virus (HIV) epidemic. We also discuss (1) the virology of the HIV, (2) the health consequences and prognosis of HIV infection, (3) transmission mechanisms, and (4) various tests available for determining HIV infection. Throughout we focus on the aspects of the HIV epidemic most relevant to issues of privacy.

THE ORIGINS OF THE HUMAN IMMUNODEFICIENCY VIRUS

AIDS was recognized as a clinical entity in 1981, when diseases previously seen only among patients with immune system damage began to appear in New York, Los Angeles, and San Francisco in persons whose immune systems had no apparent reason to be weakened. Most of these diseases were not rare: Physicians had long recognized them in the immunosuppressed. But it was unusual that they should suddenly appear in persons who had no recognized basis for immune system damage and it was inexplicable that all of these persons were gay men.[1]

HIV is clearly new to the United States. Examination of large banks of stored serum specimens obtained before about 1976 practically never reveals the presence of HIV infection. Although there may have been earlier sporadic cases,[2] substantial HIV transmission did not occur in the United States before about 1976. In the United States, AIDS was recognized almost simultaneously in gay men in New York City, Los Angeles, and San Francisco and, within a few months, in IV drug abusers in New York City. However, indirect evidence suggests that substantial transmission in the United States first occurred among gay men in New York City.[3]

Although the AIDS epidemic now devastating urban central Africa was not recognized until after 1982, the available evidence suggests that HIV transmission began in rural central Africa: (1) Serum specimens obtained in Zaire near the Kenyan border in 1959 show anti-

---

[1] The early events of the HIV epidemic have been ably chronicled by Randy Shilts. See *And the Band Played On: Politics, People, and the AIDS Epidemic* (New York: St. Martin's Press, 1987).

[2] David Huminer, Joseph B. Rosenfeld, and Silvia D. Pitlik, "AIDS in the Pre-AIDS Era," *Reviews of Infectious Diseases* 9 (1987): 1104.

[3] An excess of Kaposi's sarcoma and an increase in the number of lymph node biopsies yielding nonspecific findings now known to be consistent with HIV infection were noted in New York City in 1975 and 1978, respectively, in single young men who were not IV drug users (see Robert J. Biggor, Philip C. Nasca, and William S. Barnett, "AIDS-related Kaposi's Sarcoma in New York City in 1977," *New England Journal of Medicine* 318 [1988]: 252; and Bess Miller et al., "The Syndrome of Unexplained Generalized Lymphadenopathy in Young Men in New York City: Is It Related to the Acquired Immune Deficiency Syndrome?" *Journal of the American Medical Association* 251 [1984]: 245). In addition, it may be that "gay bowel syndrome," an unfortunate term coined in New York in 1976, was partially HIV-induced diarrhea. (For a discussion of "gay bowel syndrome," see Henry L. Kazal et al., "The Gay Bowel Syndrome: Clinico-Pathologic Correlation in 260 Cases," *Annals of Clinical and Laboratory Science* 6 [1976]: 184–92.) Finally, we have evidence that HIV infection occurred in New York before it appeared on the West Coast. The AIDS development rates in cohorts of gay men established in New York City have been higher than in West Coast cohorts, perhaps because the mean durations of HIV infection at the onset of study were longer for the New York City participants.

body to the AIDS virus.[4] (2) HIV itself has been recovered from a stored serum specimen obtained in 1976 in Africa.[5] (3) Sporadic cases which appear very similar to what we now recognize as cases of AIDS occurred in Europeans who were in central Africa in the early 1960s.[6] (4) The prevalence of HIV infection exceeds 10 percent in some central African cities.

Two theories have been offered to explain the emergence of AIDS in central Africa. The first theory is that HIV circulated in remote areas of Africa at a low level for at least several centuries, and it attributes the current African problem to urbanization and an accompanying increase in sexual promiscuity. The second theory is that HIV is new to our species and first occurred within this century. There is precedent for certain human infections remaining confined to small geographic regions for prolonged periods. However, in all but one of these cases, the causative organisms do not ordinarily spread directly from person to person.[7] The absence of a precedent for a purely human pathogen remaining geographically confined makes it more likely that HIV began infecting humans relatively recently.

HIV is closely related to a retrovirus called the simian immunodeficiency virus (SIV), which has been isolated from African green monkeys and which has a similar genetic structure.[8] This degree of similarity establishes that HIV and SIV are descendants of a common ancestor but does not establish how long ago they diverged. There

---

[4] A. J. Nahmias et al., "Evidence for Human Infection with an HTLV III/LAV-like Virus in Central Africa, 1959," *Lancet*, May 31, 1986, pp. 1279–80.

[5] J. P. Getchell et al., "Human Immunodeficiency Virus Isolated from a Serum Sample Collected in 1976 in Central Africa," *Journal of Infectious Diseases* 156 (1987): 833–37.

[6] For an account of the first documented Westerner to have contracted AIDS, see Shilts, *And the Band Played On*, 3–7.

[7] They are primarily zoonoses of animals with restricted ranges (e.g., Lassa virus, Ebola virus), dependent on vectors of restricted ranges (e.g., malaria/mosquitoes), or environmental organisms dependent on specific ecological niches (e.g., Coccidioides). The exception is kuru, which remained localized because transmission required cannibalism.

[8] SIV has about 55 percent DNA base pair homology with HIV-1. See G. Franchini et al., "Sequence of Simian Immunodeficiency Virus and Its Relationship to the Human Immunodeficiency Virus," letter, *Nature* 328 (1987): 539.

is precedent for jumps between host species by viruses. But since HIV cannot infect African green monkeys, HIV has been adapted to humans for at least a moderate interval, perhaps evolving into a more virulent pathogen. Scientists are still in disagreement over the degree of difference between HIV and SIV and its significance.

Whether HIV is new to our species, an old virus which has recently mutated to a virulent form, or a virus which has only recently escaped after prolonged circulation in a remote population should not affect the issues we discuss. The AIDS epidemic in the United States today is clearly new and unprecedented.

The evidence that HIV causes AIDS is as conclusive as possible for a human pathogen which cannot be the subject of inoculation experiments:[9] (1) HIV can be recovered from virtually everyone who has AIDS. (2) A significant proportion of persons who are HIV infected develop AIDS or AIDS-related diseases; of those who are asymptomatic, many more have or develop the immunological abnormalities associated with AIDS. (3) In vivo, HIV destroys CD4 T-lymphocytes, and CD4 T-lymphocyte depletion appears to be a critical component of the immunosuppression of AIDS. (4) Animal viruses similar to HIV, such as SIV and feline leukemia virus, produce AIDS-like diseases in their respective hosts. (5) Persons without other risk activity who develop AIDS after receiving a blood donation are almost always shown upon investigation to have received blood from an HIV-infected donor.

EPIDEMIOLOGY OF AIDS

AIDS[10] is defined in detail by the Centers for Disease Control (CDC). The CDC definition has been accepted worldwide, although it can be difficult to apply in the third world, where there is often little access to complex diagnostic procedures. The definition has been amended several times. The initial definition, formulated when the etiology of AIDS was unknown, had two components: (1) the pres-

---

[9] Fulfillment of Koch's postulates requires the inoculation of animals with a pure culture of the pathogen with subsequent reproduction of the illness. Although chimpanzees and gibbons can become infected by the HIV, there is not yet a convincing demonstration that disease ensues.

[10] Acquired immunodeficiency syndrome was originally called *acquired immune deficiency syndrome*.

ence of an opportunistic condition signifying a defect in cell-mediated immunity and (2) the absence of a conventional explanation for the immune deficiency. For instance, the development of Pneumocystis carinii pneumonia in a person who had leukemia did not meet the AIDS definition; the development of Pneumocystis carinii pneumonia in a person who had no underlying leukemia or lymphoma and was not taking immunosuppressive drugs did lead to an AIDS diagnosis. The initial definition was drawn fairly narrowly because the CDC investigators wanted to study people who were certainly involved in the epidemic. It could not contain reference to HIV marker tests because they were not available. It did not even contain reference to tests of immune function because the investigators had yet to securely demonstrate that people with the syndrome were immunosuppressed.

The most recent revision of the definition was published in August 1987.[11] For the first time, the definition included reference to laboratory evidence of HIV infection, and it is also included HIV encephalopathy and HIV wasting syndrome in addition to opportunistic conditions. It makes reference to thirteen specific pathogens in the AIDS definition for adults (those over thirteen years of age) and includes additional opportunistic pathogens in the pediatric definition.

The CDC definition of AIDS has come to have significance beyond mere surveillance, which was its original purpose. Medically, if someone's condition fits the definition, that person is known to have had severe damage to the immune system and to have a prognosis that is much worse. Administratively, access is triggered to a variety of health care and social programs not available to other HIV-infected applicants. This distinction can be very frustrating: Persons with AIDS can be robust while persons with HIV-induced illness that does not precisely meet the AIDS definition can be debilitated. Under the various definitions of AIDS, 83,592 U.S. AIDS cases had been reported to the CDC as of January 30, 1989, of which 1,393 occurred in children. Of the pediatrics cases, 78 percent were attributed to maternal infection, 13 percent to blood component transfusions, and 6 percent to coagulation factor concentrate. Of the adult

---

[11] Centers for Disease Control, "Revision of the CDC Surveillance Case Definition for Acquired Immunodeficiency Syndrome," *Morbidity and Mortality Weekly Report* 36, suppl. no. 1S (1987): 3S–15S.

cases, 91 percent occurred in men. Of the adult males, 68 percent were homosexual or bisexual men who were not IV drug abusers, 9 percent were homosexual or bisexual men who were IV drug abusers, 17 percent were heterosexual IV drug abusers, 2 percent heterosexuals who had sexual contact with females at risk for HIV infection, 2 percent had blood component exposure, and 1 percent had coagulation factor concentrate exposure. Of the female adults, 52 percent were IV drug abusers, 30 percent had sexual contact with males at risk for HIV infection, and 11 percent had blood component exposure.

Regarding more recent cases, there are fewer gays and bisexuals and more IV drug abusers among the males than previously. Among the females, there are fewer with heterosexual exposure to the virus and more IV drug abusers than previously.

HIV VIROLOGY

HIV is a retrovirus. Retroviruses can be broadly separated into those which induce tumors and those which kill host cells. The second class, termed *lentiviruses*, includes the HIV. Although HIV infection can lead to tumor production, it does so as a secondary effect of the weakening of the immune system.

A cell's genes are made of DNA. Whenever cells divide, information is passed from the DNA of the parent cell to the DNA of both daughter cells. The information encoded in the DNA is used by making an RNA copy of the DNA. The RNA is then used to direct the synthesis of protein to carry out the cell's functions. Retroviruses are RNA viruses: A test tube containing HIV particles would contain RNA but not DNA. When a retrovirus enters a host cell, a viral enzyme called reverse transcriptase is inserted along with the viral RNA. This enzyme catalyzes the production of a DNA copy of the viral RNA. Reverse transcriptase takes information backwards (compared to the usual direction) from RNA to DNA—hence the term *retrovirus*. The DNA copy is inserted in the host cell's own genetic DNA; the provirus becomes part of the host cell's genes. For unknown reasons, proviral DNA may remain dormant or may activate to produce retroviral proteins, progeny HIVs, and cell destruction. Although it may someday be possible to develop therapies which keep the virus dormant, it is unlikely that a cell with incorporated HIV proviral DNA can ever be completely cured of the viral infection. It is also unlikely that the host organism could rid itself of its last HIV-infected cell. HIV infection, like a herpes infection, is probably forever.

In general, RNA viruses mutate more rapidly than DNA viruses, and retroviruses are among the most rapidly mutating RNA viruses. Mutations detected in HIV strains have been most highly concentrated in the gene that codes for production of the proteins on the surface of the virus particle. These mutations have important implications for vaccine production, because a successful vaccine may require representation of multiple strains. Strain variation may also explain the considerable difference in the rate at which HIV infection proceeds in different humans. However, it is much less likely that HIV mutations will affect transmission mechanisms. Strain variation is common among all viruses, but, within a given virus species, different strains do not differ with respect to anything as fundamental as transmission or basic pathogenic mechanisms.

Scientists have distinguished two major kinds of HIV. In the United States, AIDS is caused by what is known as *HIV-1*. In West Africa and in southern Europe, a second kind of HIV, called *HIV-2*, has been found. Although HIV-2 causes AIDS, it may be somewhat less virulent than HIV-1. In 1987, the first HIV-2 infection was detected in the United States.[12] Additional introductions will doubtlessly occur. The need to control the transmission of HIV-2 (and perhaps human retroviruses not yet discovered) may become relevant to the privacy debate. In this book, however, *HIV* refers to HIV-1.

HEALTH CONSEQUENCES OF HIV INFECTION

Within a month or two of becoming infected with HIV, many persons experience an acute mononucleosis-like illness. This may involve fever, headache, a general feeling of illness, and transient generalized lymph gland swelling. This self-limited illness can also be quite mild and may be unrecognized. Sometime during the second month after infection most HIV-infected persons begin to produce antibody to the HIV (anti-HIV antibody).[13] Thus there is regularly an interval between the onset of HIV infection (and presumably infec-

---

[12] Centers for Disease Control, "AIDS Due to HIV-2 Infection—New Jersey," *Morbidity and Mortality Weekly Report* 37 (1988): 33.

[13] Antibodies are proteins which circulate in the blood. The host makes antibodies in response to antigens, which are foreign substances.

tiousness) and the time at which the infection can be detected by the most widely used blood test, the anti-HIV serology. In some cases this interval is a year or longer.[14] The fact that people may have an HIV infection for over a year before it can be detected by our most widely used test has serious consequences for mandatory testing programs. Especially when applied to persons who are continuing to engage in HIV risk activities, the HIV antibody test may yield more false negatives than previously believed.

After HIV infection, all or almost all persons become asymptomatic chronic HIV carriers who harbor and can disseminate the virus. The ability of HIV to cause a continuously infectious carrier state in all or virtually all infected persons is quite unusual among viruses. The hepatitis B virus can accomplish this feat in about 10 percent of infected persons. There are many other viruses which can establish a chronic dormant infection, but they are only periodically infectious. For instance, after initial infection, the herpes simplex virus becomes established in a dormant state in nerve cells, coming forth periodically as cold sores or genital lesions. Affected persons are infectious while these lesions are active, but then their immune system rapidly eliminates detectable virus. Presumably, HIV is able to establish a chronic carrier state by attacking the particular part of the immune system which is involved in host defense against viral infection.

After initial HIV infection, whether or not symptomatic, a minority of HIV-infected persons progress directly to chronic symptomatic HIV infection. Most, however, become asymptomatic and many remain so for at least eight years. During this asymptomatic period, persistent generalized lymph node swelling (lymphadenopathy) may or may not be present. Lymphadenopathy is not necessarily a bad prognostic sign; it may simply reflect the host's counterattack against the virus. Those who become symptomatic typically first notice a loss of energy. Exercise tolerance decreases. Sleep requirement increases and daytime naps sometimes become necessary. The number of stools per day may increase and the stool consistency becomes less firm. The skin may become dry, flaky, and itchy. More severe

---

[14] S. Wolinsky et al., "Polymerase Chain Reaction (PCR) Detection of HIV Provirus before HIV Seroconversion." Paper presented at the 4th International Conference on AIDS, Stockholm, June 12–16, 1988.

symptoms may ensue, including fevers, night sweats, diarrhea, weight loss, and marked lassitude.

These abnormalities are often called ARC, short for *AIDS-related complex*. There is not widespread agreement on a definition of the term. Some apply it to any HIV-infected person who has illness due to HIV but who does not meet the AIDS criteria. Others use it more narrowly, applying it just to those who have had persistent generalized lymphadenopathy or have relatively severe HIV disease.

In persons whose immune systems have been sufficiently damaged, secondary or "opportunistic" conditions occur. These are termed opportunistic because they take the opportunity presented by the weakened immune system to cause illness. Opportunistic conditions do not occur or are not as severe in people with normal immune systems. These conditions include cancers and infections. The most common cancers are Kaposi's sarcoma and lymphoma. Kaposi's sarcoma occurs most often as multiple small purple-to-red nodules in the skin, mucous membranes, or internal organs. AIDS-related Kaposi's sarcoma is largely restricted to gay men. The opportunistic infections consist of a highly distinctive subset of about thirty or forty potential human pathogens.

Not all infections to which AIDS patients are predisposed are AIDS-defining infections. For instance, chicken pox is not in the AIDS definition. However, HIV-infected persons are highly predisposed to severe, even fatal, chicken pox. The reason it is not included in the AIDS definition is that chicken pox, even severe chicken pox, can occur in persons with normal immune systems. Persons with AIDS are probably at least somewhat predisposed to develop all common human infections. This may simply result from the generalized debility attendant upon AIDS. But, remarkably, this predisposition is only slight for the bulk of common human pathogens. It is generally considered advisable for HIV-infected persons to avoid exposure to the AIDS-defining opportunistic infections, tuberculosis, the varicella zoster virus (VZV, the virus which causes chicken pox and shingles), and certain other pathogens requiring intimate contact for transmission (e.g., Epstein-Barr virus, the cause of infectious mononucleosis; syphilis; CMV; and hepatitis B virus). However, persons with AIDS are not at sufficiently high risk from other pathogens to warrant efforts to avoid contagious disease beyond those appropriate for anyone else.

Consideration of the secondary infections associated with HIV infection bears on decisions about constraints on interactions between HIV-infected and uninfected persons. While casual contact with infected persons poses virtually no risk of transmitting HIV infection to uninfected persons, it might be argued that such contact should still be minimized to protect HIV-uninfected persons from secondary infections. Similarly, it might be appropriate to protect HIV- infected persons from hazardous pathogens at large in the community. As it happens, however, these considerations apply to only two of the AIDS-associated pathogens: vzv and Mycobacterium tuberculosis, the causative agent of tuberculosis.[15]

vzv causes chicken pox in persons who have never previously been infected. Thereafter, it becomes dormant in sensory nerve ganglia, subsequently coming forth in some persons one or more times as shingles. Chicken pox is highly infectious. Both vzv and Mycobacterium tuberculosis are airborne pathogens.[16] The secretions from chicken pox and shingles lesions can also cause chicken pox in persons who have never previously been infected. HIV-infected persons get particularly severe chicken pox and shingles. A common presentation of HIV disease in children is a severe case of chicken pox. Since vzv disease is readily apparent, these considerations do not provide a basis for segregating HIV-infected persons not manifesting vzv disease. However, they may provide a rationale for temporarily excluding HIV-infected persons who have never had chicken pox from places where there is a chicken pox outbreak (e.g., keep-

---

[15] Secondary pathogens do not pose a transmission hazard for several reasons. Some are acquired from the environment and cannot readily be protected against (e.g., Cryptococcus, atypical mycobacteria, Coccidioides, Histoplasma). Others are not transmitted under conditions of ordinary hygiene either because they are spread person to person only by the fecal-oral route (e.g., Cryptosporidium, Salmonella, Isospora) or because they are relatively difficult to transmit under conditions of ordinary hygiene (e.g., cytomegalovirus, herpes simplex virus). Others are readily transmissible from person to person but colonize most humans from early in life (e.g., Candida, Pneumocystis carinii). Finally, some are not spread from person to person at all (e.g., Toxoplasma).

[16] Airborne in this sense indicates the pathogen is borne long distances by the air. Transmission of pathogens by large droplets which fall to the ground in a meter or two is not considered airborne.

ing HIV-infected children out of school during a chicken pox outbreak).

Like chicken pox, tuberculosis poses a problem for HIV-infected persons. After infection due to Mycobacterium tuberculosis, most persons have a mild or inapparent, self-limited, noninfectious illness. Dormant TB foci develop. These foci may reactivate many years in the future as active tuberculosis. Active pulmonary and laryngeal TB are the infectious forms of TB. The probability of a dormant TB focus breaking down to active, infectious TB is considerably increased in persons who have HIV infection. About 2 percent of U.S. AIDS patients developed active TB. Unlike chicken pox, however, active, infectious TB can be subtle and inapparent at first.

Even though HIV-infected persons are more likely than noninfected person to have TB, there are good reasons for thinking that the threat of TB infection does not justify segregating HIV-infected persons: (1) The majority of HIV-infected persons in the United States have never been infected by tuberculosis and thus have no dormant TB foci to reactivate. (2) A totally inapparent Mycobacterium tuberculosis infection in an HIV-infected person is uncommon, and very early active TB is not very infectious. Sufficiently attentive medical care should detect the infection before more than minimal infectiousness has occurred. (3) About two-thirds of the TB arising in HIV-infected persons is extrapulmonary (which is not infectious) or disseminated (which is relatively less infectious than pulmonary disease). (4) Persons with other immunosuppressing illnesses, which are also predisposing to TB activation, are not restricted. While protecting HIV-infected persons from Mycobacterium tuberculosis infection is important, tuberculosis is a threat to HIV-uninfected persons as well. The excess threat to HIV-infected persons is only moderate, because tuberculosis, when diagnosed early, is generally one of the easiest HIV-associated opportunistic infections to treat successfully.

HIV-induced immunodeficiency has implications for immunization and international travel, and consequently on the issue of testing military and State Department personnel. Vaccines which contain only nonviable materials do not stimulate antibodies as effectively in HIV-infected persons. However, these vaccines pose no excess hazard to HIV-infected persons. In contrast, some vaccines contain live organisms which are modified, usually by successively passing them through tissue cultures or animals, to produce strains less pathogenic for humans. Live vaccines routinely in use in the United States include oral polio vaccine, measles, mumps, rubella, yellow fever, BCG (a tuberculosis vaccine), and, for military personnel, adenovirus. Vaccinia (cowpox) virus was formerly used to protect persons against smallpox. It is currently only used by U.S. and Soviet military personnel. All live virus vaccines could, in theory, produce excess illness in HIV-infected persons. However, only three have been demonstrated to cause excess disease in other immunosuppressed patients: BCG, vaccinia, and oral polio vaccine. Only the last is routinely advocated for U.S. citizens. The excess risk is not sufficiently great, however, for the U.S. Public Health Service Advisory Committee on Immunization Practices to recommend screening potential oral polio virus recipients prior to vaccination.[17]

HIV infection often results in nerve damage, both to peripheral nerves and the brain. HIV encephalopathy, with substantial deterioration of mental function, is present in a substantial fraction of AIDS patients by the time of death. Apathy and declines in cognitive function are the most prominent manifestations. Severe encephalopathy is usually restricted to the last several months of life. However, subtle declines in the ability to think can occur in persons with relatively little debility or immune system damage. The subtle declines in mental function have been invoked as a potential rationale for testing and screening HIV-infected persons to prevent them from holding certain jobs requiring the highest levels of mental capability. However, the demonstrated HIV-induced declines in mental function are small compared to the range of mental capacities among humans. More importantly, mental capability can be assessed independently of HIV infection status.

THE PROGNOSIS

Although the prognosis for HIV-infected persons is not yet fully known because of the glacial pace of HIV infection, the evidence which does exist is grim. Most studies start by assembling a group

---

[17]Centers for Disease Control, "Recommendation of the Immunization Practices Advisory Committee (ACIP): Immunization of Children Infected with Human T-Lymphotropic Virus Type III/Lymphadenopathy-associated Virus," *Morbidity and Mortality Weekly Report* 35 (1986): 595.

(cohort) of HIV-infected gay or bisexual men. The cohort is then followed for a period of time during which the development of AIDS is observed. The outcome of such studies is highly contingent on the degree of severity of the HIV-induced immune system damage at the start of the study. The degree of damage is, in turn, dependent on the duration of HIV infection prior to the study. A participant's HIV infection may have considerably antedated the creation of the cohort. Subtle effects of the way subjects are recruited may yield men who already have mild illness. Some participants may choose to enter a study because they already have early symptoms of HIV disease. Interpretation of these studies also requires cognizance of the intervals of study observation. As expected, the longer the period of observation the higher the AIDS development rate. It is not hard to see why these studies have produced a considerable range of estimates of the occurrence of AIDS. Sadly, no cohort of HIV-infected persons has stopped producing additional AIDS cases.

A study free of the usual defects is being carried out in San Francisco. A group of gay and bisexual men was recruited between 1978 and 1980 from a sexually transmitted diseases clinic (the City Clinic) for studies of hepatitis B. Serum specimens had been stored from that study. Since 1983, this group has been observed for HIV infection and AIDS. It has been possible to estimate the date of onset of HIV infection based on the stored and subsequent serum specimens. In this cohort, from the time of seroconversion (i.e., onset of HIV infection), the cumulative AIDS percentage after 1 year was 0 percent; 3 years, 5 percent; 4 years, 10 percent; 5 years, 15 percent; 6 years, 24 percent; and 7.3 years, 36 percent.[18] After 7.3 years of infection, in addition to those who had developed AIDS, 40 percent had symptoms of HIV infection. The percentage affected is disturbing enough, but the progressively steeper curve is even more ominous. Projecting these results is frightening.

A similar study of a group of hemophilia patients has produced projections not quite so disturbing. It is estimated that there are approximately 9,800 HIV-infected hemophilia patients,[19] most of

---

[18]J. W. Curran et al., "Epidemiology of HIV Infection and AIDS in the United States," *Science* 239 (1988): 610–16.

[19]Centers for Disease Control, "Human Immunodeficiency Virus Infection in the United States: A Review of Current Knowledge," *Morbidity and Mortality Weekly Report* 36, suppl. no. S6 (1987): 40.

whom became infected in 1981 or 1982.[20] Eight hundred and eighty-two had developed AIDS as of January, 1989. Thus the AIDS incidence rate was 9.0 percent at about seven years. A comparison of the hemophilia population with the San Francisco City Clinic cohort of gay and bisexual men lends support to the view that there is a cofactor, more commonly present in gay men, which aggravates the progression of HIV disease. If there is a gay-associated cofactor, it will be strongly represented in the San Francisco City Clinic cohort, probably the most sexually active large cohort of gay men studied. There is no shortage of hypothetical cofactors: repeated exposure to the HIV (more virulent strains might replace less virulent strains), increased infection due to other sexually transmitted pathogens (particularly herpes simplex virus and cytomegalovirus) that may aggravate HIV disease, inhalational nitrates, and rectal exposure to semen (animal model data suggest that injection of semen leads to certain immunological abnormalities, the clinical significance of which is not established).

Although comparisons of cohort studies as well as several in vitro virological observations support the cofactor hypothesis, in studies of HIV-infected gay men the best correlate with progression of HIV disease to AIDS is duration of HIV infection or factors which may be surrogates of duration of infection (e.g., number of sexual partners, number of sexually transmitted diseases, etc.). In short, it is not known at the present time whether there is a gay cofactor.

Even if the more optimistic prognostic projections are closer to the mark, the outcome of HIV infection is still grim. This has relevance for testing by insurance companies. Smoking, high blood pressure, and obesity are all used by insurance companies in determining availability and cost of coverage, yet these conditions carry only two- to fourfold increases in standard mortality. HIV infection probably carries a twenty-sixfold increase in mortality.[21] No single

---

[20] M. Elaine Eyster et al., "Development and Early Natural History of HTLV-III Antibodies in Persons with Hemophilia," *Journal of the American Medical Association* 253 (1985): 2220.

[21] Assuming that 20 percent of those who are HIV infected develop AIDS within five years and die within seven years, the chances of a person with HIV dying over a seven-year period is twenty-six times higher than someone in standard health. Karen Clifford and Russel Iuculano, "AIDS and Insurance: The Rationale for AIDS-related Testing," *Harvard Law Review* 100 (1987): 1814, citing an affidavit of Warren L. Kleinsasser in

test for a common condition in young, apparently healthy persons approaches having the prognostic adversity of a positive HIV test.

The prognosis after a diagnosis of AIDS, absent therapy, is also grim. When the diagnosis is based on an opportunistic condition other than Kaposi's sarcoma, less than 5 percent survive two years. Only a few survive three years and practically none survive more than four years.[22] When the diagnosis is based on Kaposi's sarcoma, survival is longer, but very few are alive after five years.

The foregoing prognoses are for untreated HIV infection. Zidovudine, marketed under the name *Retrovir* and initially called *azidothymidine* or *AZT*, has been unequivocally demonstrated to help persons who have severe ARC or are within the first four months of their first episode of Pneumocystis pneumonia.[23] It prevents most deaths in the first six months of use and increases weight and sense of well-being. Persons who have been more severely damaged by HIV often do not tolerate the drug. Whether or not it will be of benefit to persons who have milder HIV disease or are asymptomatic is the subject of intensive study. That zidovudine will be a net benefit to asymptomatic persons, most of whom have years of good health ahead of them, is far from certain.

Zidovudine is expensive, and this is relevant to policy issues. The current cost for the drug is $8,000 per year, and zidovudine is taken indefinitely — as long as the patient can tolerate it. Many patients require close medical monitoring to adjust the dose. Unfortunately, zidovudine appears to postpone illness rather than permanently prevent it. So, aside from the substantial direct cost, zidovudine will probably, over the life of a person with AIDS, increase the cost of care. If zidovudine proves advantageous to asymptomatic persons, there will be an even more profound impact on the nation's health bill.

American Council of Life Ins. v. District of Columbia, 645 F. Supp. 84 (D.D.C. 1986).

[22] Andrew R. Moss et al., "Mortality Associated with Mode of Presentation in the Acquired Immune Deficiency Syndrome," *Journal of the National Cancer Institute* 75 (1984): 1281–84.

[23] Margaret A. Fischl et al., "The Efficacy of Azidothymidine (AZT) in the Treatment of Patients with AIDS and AIDS-related Complex," *New England Journal of Medicine* 317 (1987): 185–91.

TRANSMISSION MECHANISMS

The U.S. Public Health Service has estimated that between 950,000 and 1.4 million HIV transmissions have occurred in this country.[24] Well over half of these transmissions have occurred between men during anal intercourse. In approximate descending order of frequency, other transmission mechanisms include needle sharing, vaginal intercourse, transfusion with single blood component units, transmission via coagulation factor concentrate to hemophilia patients, maternal–fetal transmissions, other sexual contact transmissions (although not yet convincingly demonstrated), and nonsexual contact transmissions.

Worldwide, vaginal intercourse has probably been the most common mechanism. HIV transmissions during anal and vaginal intercourse occur both to and from the insertive partner. The transmissions from the insertive partner are presumed by most to arise from semen and are probably facilitated by tears in rectal mucosa or ulcerative vaginal disease. Transmissions from the receptive partner to the insertive partner are presumed to occur via blood or genital secretions from the receptive partner through breaks in the insertive partner's penile skin. HIV transmission among IV drug abusers by needle sharing is particularly frequent in "shooting galleries," locations where addicts can pay to have drugs injected through needles which are used by successive clients; it is severely aggravated by "booting," the practice of drawing blood back into the syringe to wash out the last few bits of drug.

Vaginal intercourse is the main HIV transmission mechanism in Africa and has become an established mechanism of HIV transmission in the United States among Haitian immigrants and sexual partners of IV drug abusers. That vaginal deposition of semen can transmit HIV is unequivocally established from reports of artificial insemination transmissions.[25] In studies of heterosexual partners of persons who became HIV infected from a transfusion, one can establish with a high degree of confidence which partner became infected

---

[24] Centers for Disease Control, "Human Immunodeficiency Virus Infection in the United States," 40.

[25] G. J. Stewart et al., "Transmission of Human T-Cell Lymphotropic Virus Type III (HTLV-III) by Artificial Insemination by Donor," *Lancet*, September 14, 1985, pp. 581–84.

first and when the initial infection occurred. Also, unlike studies of heterosexual transmission among IV drug abusers, one can be much more confident that secondarily infected partners have a negative history regarding other HIV risk activities. It appears from these studies that female-to-male transmission is approximately half as efficient as male-to-female transmission.[26]

There are at least four possible reasons why heterosexual transmission is the predominant HIV transmission mechanism in Africa while male-to-male sexual transmission has been predominant in the United States: (1) HIV strains in Africa may be more adapted to heterosexual transmission while U.S. strains are more adapted to homosexual transmission. (2) In underdeveloped countries the prevalence of genital ulcerative disease, which permits the egress or ingress of virus, is greater. (3) Anal intercourse may be a more efficient transmission mechanism than vaginal intercourse (no direct data supporting this contention are available). (4) African heterosexuals and American gay men may have more sexual partners than American heterosexuals.[27]

Although the HIV hazard per transfused unit was never high in most parts of the United States, so many blood component units are transfused that as many as 30,000 transfusion-associated transmissions have occurred in this country.[28] HIV transmission by single blood component units has been substantially reduced since anti-HIV antibody screening of all donated blood products began in May 1985. Since HIV tests are not perfect, potential blood donors who have engaged in HIV risk activities are asked not to donate. Voluntary self-exclusion has been sufficiently effective that the hazards (including hepatitis) due to transfused blood are probably less now than before the HIV epidemic.

---

[26] Thomas A. Peterman et al., "Risk of Human Immunodeficiency Virus Transmission from Heterosexual Adults with Transfusion-associated Infections," *Journal of the American Medical Association* 259 (1988): 55–58.

[27] Daniel B. Hrdy, "Cultural Practices Contributing to the Transmission of Human Immunodeficiency Virus in Africa," *Reviews of Infectious Diseases* 9 (1987): 1112–13.

[28] Thomas A. Peterman et al., "Estimating the Risks of Transfusion-associated Acquired Immune Deficiency Syndrome and Human Immunodeficiency Virus Infection," *Transfusion* 27 (September–October 1987): 371–74.

Hemophilia patients who used coagulation factor concentrate were at extremely high risk of HIV infection because the material is made from large pools, sometimes up to 50,000 plasma units. Persons with mild hemophilia, who have been treated only with individual units of cryoprecipitate or fresh frozen plasma, are only rarely HIV infected. But, of hemophilia patients who received coagulation factor concentrate, about 70 percent with hemophilia A and 35 percent with hemophilia B are HIV infected.[29] Since mid-1985, coagulation factor concentrate has been heat-treated, probably totally eliminating HIV transmission.

Maternal-fetal transmission occurs in about 40 percent of the infants of HIV-infected mothers. Infection can occur transplacentally, as evidenced by the occurrence of a characteristic set of fetal developmental defects. Some infections doubtlessly occur from the massive exposure to maternal blood at parturition. The relative importance of these two mechanisms is unestablished. One transmission has occurred from a mother to her child after parturition.[30] The mother received a HIV-contaminated transfusion after the baby was born by cesarean section. The mother nursed the infant, and the infant was subsequently demonstrated to be HIV infected. Virus has been isolated from breast milk, and this transmission is presumed to have occurred as a result of nursing.

HIV transmission by sexual contact other than vaginal or anal intercourse has been difficult to establish. Female-to-female transmission has been demonstrated in lesbian couples whose sexual practices were sufficiently vigorous to cause vaginal bleeding.[31] Well-documented instances of HIV transmission via oral–genital sex or through kissing have not yet appeared. Such transmissions are either rare or do not occur.

Three non-sexual contact transmissions have been demonstrated outside of hospitals. In Great Britain, a transmission occurred from a dying AIDS patient to a neighbor who assisted him in his last week of life. She had extensive contact with his urine and saliva.[32] She

---

[29] Centers for Disease Control, "Human Immunodeficiency Virus Infection in the United States," 40.

[30] John B. Ziegler et al., "Postnatal Transmission of AIDS-associated Retrovirus from Mother to Infant," *Lancet*, April 20, 1985, pp. 896–97.

[31] M. Marmor et al., "Possible Female to Female Transmission of HIV Virus," letter, *Annals of Internal Medicine* 105 (1986): 969.

[32] M. Rademaker et al., "Acquired Immune Deficiency Syndrome

had a chronic hand dermatitis aggravated by washing the patient's bed linen. A transmission in the United States occurred from a baby between the ages of eighteen and twenty-four months to its mother.[33] The child had congenital short bowel syndrome, a colostomy and occasionally bloody diarrhea, and a permanent indwelling catheter. The mother had taken no particular precautions during child care but had no particular skin problem. The third occurred in Germany between siblings, both of whom were under five years old.[34] The first child was infected as a result of a transfusion. It is not known how the household transmission to the second child occurred. The last two household contact transmissions should be placed in the context of the large number of persons who have tested negative after household contact with HIV-infected persons. This number is unknown but probably exceeds ten thousand. No additional household transmissions have been reported. Non-sexual contact transmissions of virtually all pathogens occur most readily in the household. The intensity of exposure in the household is considerably higher than in the hospital. In both settings the intensity of exposure exceeds that of the workplace, school, or community.

Two transmissions have occurred to laboratory workers who were working with high concentration preparations of HIV.[35] In one the HIV strain infecting the worker was the same strain under study, ruling out unconceded HIV risk activities as the cause of the infection. A third, less well-documented laboratory transmission has been reported. In none of the cases could a specific break in technique be implicated. Clinical specimens or body secretions from HIV-infected persons probably rarely, if ever, contain virus at con-

---

without the Recognized Risk Factors," *Postgraduate Medical Journal* 63 (1987): 877–79.

[33] Centers for Disease Control, "Apparent Transmission of Human T-Lymphotropic Virus Type III/Lymphadenopathy-associated Virus from a Child to a Mother Providing Health Care," *Morbidity and Mortality Weekly Report* 35 (1986): 76–79.

[34] V. Wahn et al., "Horizontal Transmission of HIV Infection between Two Siblings," letter, *Lancet*, September 20, 1986, p. 694.

[35] Centers for Disease Control, "Occupationally Acquired Human Immunodeficiency Virus Infections in Laboratories Producing Virus Concentrates in Large Quantities," *Morbidity and Mortality Weekly Report* 37, suppl. no. S4 (1988): 19.

centrations of greater than 10^3/ml. The materials in research laboratories may exceed those concentrations by 10,000-fold.

At least seven occupational HIV transmissions to health care workers have occurred.[36] Four of them were by needle stick. It appears that needle stick exposure to a needle contaminated by HIV-containing secretions produces roughly a 1 per 200–300 chance of an HIV transmission. Three of the occupational health care worker transmissions occurred from exposure to fresh, HIV-containing blood.[37] In all three cases there was abnormal skin (severely chapped hands, severe facial acne, ear dermatitis) present in the health care worker who became infected. Even using very pessimistic assumptions, the occupational HIV transmission risk to health care workers figures to be no more than 1 per 100,000 per year for workers with the most intense exposure. This is a level of risk which is lower than many other workers face in their occupations. The vigorous effort under way in the nation's health care facilities to minimize the chance of occupational HIV transmission unfortunately has the potential to aggravate anxiety about nonsexual community contact transmission. This potential exists because of the failure to always recognize the differences between health care and community settings.

Much remains to be learned about HIV transmission. The two major gaps involve our understanding of the precise mechanism of vaginal and anal coital transmission and our understanding of the magnitude of hazard associated with other sexual interactions. But our basic understanding of HIV transmission has been unchanged for five years. That HIV transmission was very similar to hepatitis B virus transmission was predictable by the end of 1981 and established by the end of 1982. Since then, all new evidence has reinforced this view. HIV transmission is as well understood as the transmission of any pathogen.

It is critical that the public understand the implications of the ability of HIV to produce a chronic carrier state in virtually all infected

---

[36] Centers for Disease Control, "Update: Acquired Immunodeficiency Syndrome and Human Immunodeficiency Virus Infection among Health-Care Workers," *Morbidity and Mortality Weekly Report* 37 (1988): 233.

[37] Centers for Disease Control, "Update: Human Immunodeficiency Virus Infections in Health-Care Workers Exposed to Blood of Infected Patients," *Morbidity and Mortality Weekly Report* 36 (1987): 285.

persons. Because the transmission frequency per sexual contact with an HIV-infected person is probably less than 1 per 10 contacts and may be on the order of 1 per 100 contacts,[38] it might be concluded that HIV is not very efficient at transmission. However, the virus does not need to be efficient per contact, since infected persons remain infectious thereafter. Ironically, a more virulent course would not be to the advantage of the virus. Strains which rapidly kill their hosts would not have as much opportunity for subsequent transmission. Mathematical models of transmission in populations in these circumstances suggest that, when a virus is introduced into a population, only a very small, albeit increasing, fraction of the population is infectious for the first several years. As geometrical transmission proceeds, sexual contact with a randomly selected person in the population carries a higher and higher risk of infection. When a substantial fraction of the population is infected (as in the case of U.S. gay men and central African heterosexuals), even rare unprotected sexual encounters produce, over the years, an unacceptable risk of acquiring HIV infection. Persons who are having sex in these high-prevalence populations and who have reduced but not eliminated their unprotected sexual exposure still face an enormous long-term risk of becoming HIV infected.

This discussion of transmission has not taken into account the potential for variation in the degree of infectiousness of different infected persons. There is doubtless great variation in the degree of infectiousness among HIV-infected persons. Since there is no practical way to measure these differences, it is necessary to regard all HIV-infected persons as HIV infectious. Of course the degree of infectiousness must be studied indirectly. More than 90 percent of blood component transfusions from asymptomatic HIV-infected persons transmit the virus.[39] By early 1987, blood culture techniques had become sufficiently sensitive to recover viable HIV from more than 98 percent of even asymptomatic HIV-infected persons.[40] Studies of

---

[38] Norman Hearst and Stephen B. Hulley, "Preventing the Heterosexual Spread of AIDS," *Journal of the American Medical Association* 259 (1988): 2428.

[39] Herbert A. Perkins et al., "Risk of AIDS for Recipients of Blood Components from Donors Who Subsequently Develop AIDS," *Blood* 70 (1987): 1604.

[40] J. Brooks Jackson, et al., "Rapid and Sensitive Viral Culture Method

heterosexual transmission to the spouses of hemophilia patients suggest that the transmission frequency increases with the severity of HIV infection.[41]

For the reasons outlined above, there is no medically important difference between HIV *infected* and HIV *infectious*. We also reject the often used term HIV *exposed* because it is ambiguous, misleading, or both. It is ambiguous because it can refer to a person who has engaged in an HIV risk activity without reference to whether or not HIV infection occurred or it can refer to a person with anti-HIV antibody. If the term is intended to refer to persons of the latter kind, it is a euphemism which should be shunned as part of the denial process which afflicts AIDS issues. We will use the term HIV *infected*. It is an unpleasant term but unfortunately it corresponds most closely to the reality of the situation.

ASSESSING TEST ACCURACY

The accuracy of any diagnostic test involves two components. The first component is *sensitivity*, the ability of the test to correctly identify affected persons. Sensitivity is stated as the fraction of affected persons who have a positive test. The sensitivity and the false negativity rate add up to 1. A test which correctly identifies 99 out of 100 affected individuals has a sensitivity of .99 and a false negativity rate of .01. (These may also be expressed as percentages: a sensitivity of 99 percent and a false negativity rate of 1 percent.) The second component of accuracy is *specificity*, the ability of the test to correctly identify unaffected persons. Specificity is stated as the fraction of unaffected persons who have a negative test. The specificity and the false positivity rate add up to 1.

The test procedure design necessarily involves a trade-off between sensitivity and specificity. In the case of the anti-HIV enzyme immunoassay (EIA) test, currently the most commonly used test, the actual measurement is the intensity of color produced in a solution in a plastic well. The cut-off (the dividing point between a reactive

---

for Human Immunodeficiency Virus Type 1," *Journal of Clinical Microbiology*, 26 (1988): 1417.

[41]J. J. Goedert et al., "Heterosexual Transmission of Human Immunodeficiency Virus: Association with Severe Depletion of T-Helper Lymphocytes in Men with Hemophilia," AIDS *Research and Human Retroviruses* 3 (1987): 355–61.

and a nonreactive test) used in the most common test kit is twice the intensity of color produced by a panel of sera from uninfected persons. If the cutoff were raised, it would increase the specificity but decrease the sensitivity. If the cutoff were lowered, the opposite results would be produced. The use for which a test is intended influences the relative need for sensitivity and specificity. For instance, in HIV testing for purposes of protecting the blood supply, the test should have a very high sensitivity but need not have a high specificity. Insofar as blood banks want to determine which units of blood to discard because of HIV infection, they need to be sure to identify all infectious units and do not care if they discard a few uninfected units: In this situation sensitivity is everything. The problem is that blood banks also notify those whose blood is infected. Insofar as blood banks are also engaged in notifying infected people, they need to be certain that the blood really is infected: Here specificity is at least as important as sensitivity.

The sensitivity and specificity of a test are purely characteristics of the test itself. But the behavior of a test in a particular population is also a function of the prevalence of the condition being tested for in that population. To oversimplify this issue, let us consider a hypothetical HIV test with a 100 percent sensitivity and a 99.9 percent specificity. Everyone who is HIV infected will have a positive test. Of every 1000 uninfected persons, 999 will have a negative test and 1 will have a positive test. Let us now consider a population of 10,000 persons, 100 of whom are HIV infected (a prevalence of 1 percent). The 100 infected persons will have a positive test and of the 9,900 uninfected persons, 10 will have a positive test. Thus, the population will produce 110 positive tests, 100 of which are true positives and 10 of which are false positives. The so-called predictive value of a positive test would be 91 percent (100 out of 110) for this test in this population. If the same test is applied to a population of 10,000 persons, only one of whom is infected (a prevalence of .01 percent), very different results will be obtained. The single infected person will have a positive test and, again, of the approximately 10,000 uninfected persons, 10 will have a positive test. Now, of the 11 positive tests, only 1 is a true positive. The predictive value of a positive test in this population is only 9 percent (1 out of 11). To generalize, when the false positivity rate of the test is equal to the prevalence of the disease in the population to be tested, half of the positive tests are false positives.

These facts lead to two considerations which are very important for the public policy assessment of various testing proposals. First, we have the problem that even for very good tests, there is a low predictive value of a positive result in a low-prevalence population. Further, low-prevalence situations are usual when tests are used for screening generally healthy populations. Thus, screening that uses even good tests may produce results that are mostly misleading.

The second counterintuitive conclusion of this analysis is that a clinician cannot meaningfully interpret the result of a test unless he or she has, on independent grounds, made a prediction as to the probability that the patient has the condition. If the clinician judges that the condition is likely to be present, a positive test produces very helpful information. However, if the condition is very unlikely to be present the positive test is likely to be misleading.

HIV MARKER TESTS

Enzyme Immunoassay Test. The EIA test, also known as the *enzyme linked immunosorbant assay (ELISA) test*, was licensed by the FDA on March 2, 1985, and is used as an initial (screening) test for serum specimens. The test kits use a relatively pure preparation of HIV proteins. However, since the preparations are made from cell cultures, there are inevitably some contaminating antigens. The HIV antigen preparation is fixed to a solid surface (e.g., a plastic bead) that is placed in a test tube. The serum specimen to be tested is added to the test tube. Any anti-HIV antibodies in it become attached to HIV antigens fixed to the bead. The serum specimen is washed away, removing antibodies not attached to the bead. Subsequent steps produce a solution in the test tube whose color is proportionate to any remaining antibody. The appearance of color establishes that the patient specimen had an antibody to at least one of the components of the putatively pure HIV antigen preparation. Such antibodies could include an antibody to one of the non-HIV cell components or an antibody to some unrelated antigen which happened to cross-react to an HIV antigen. The EIA test is highly automated. In high-volume laboratories, the test can be performed for about three dollars, including labor and overhead but excluding specimen procurement and transport and information transfer expenses.

Western Blot Test. Western blot testing has been used since the introduction of EIA testing, although the FDA license was not extended to any Western blot tests until July 1987. The test begins with a preparation of HIV antigens similar to the EIA test, but the antigens are spread out on a special strip (a "blot") in proportion to their molecular weight. The serum specimen to be tested is applied to the strip. Again, anti-HIV antibodies become fixed to the HIV antigens which are fixed to the strip. The patient serum specimen is washed away. Developers are then placed on the strip, producing a black band wherever human antibody is adherent. Positive control strips allow one to know where on the strip the HIV proteins are located. Reactivity on a Western blot indicates the presence of an antibody to one or more proteins of precisely the molecular weights of the known HIV proteins. The more bands appearing, the more likely the tested serum is from an HIV-infected person. Antibodies to non-HIV components of the antigen preparation usually appear at the wrong spot on the blot. Cross-reacting antibody usually reacts to only one HIV antigen, thus producing only one band.

Much of the controversy about false positive Western blots has arisen from disagreement about how many bands and which bands should be present on the Western blot before it is considered positive. Over the four years that Western blot HIV testing has been done, criteria for determining when reactivity on the blot should be interpreted as a positive test result have become more stringent. The FDA-licensed Western blot, for instance, requires a moderate or strong band at the location of at least three HIV proteins. Blots which show no bands are considered negative. Blots which show some bands but do not meet the positivity criteria for the particular procedure are called indeterminate. Many previously reported false positive Western blots have shown only a single band or were not positive when repeated. These blots would not be considered positive by current criteria. Note that as criteria have become more stringent, problems associated with false positives decreased but problems associated with indeterminate results increased. An indeterminate test result can have a devastating psychological impact on the individual receiving it, causing tremendous worry and doubt.

Currently, in the United States, most HIV testing begins with an EIA test. If the EIA test is reactive, it is repeated on the same specimen either once or twice. If the repeat is reactive (or, in laboratories repeating the EIA test twice, if either of the two repeats is reactive), the specimen is considered to have a "repeatedly reactive EIA." All repeatedly reactive EIA tests should be subjected to a confirmatory test with a high specificity. Most laboratories use the Western blot, although other confirmatory tests, such as a radioimmunoprecipitation (RIP) test or an immunofluoroescence test, are sometimes adequate.

Because HIV testing was introduced to screen blood, one would expect the sensitivity of the testing procedure to be extremely high, with much less concern about the specificity. Ironically, the specificity of sequential testing (EIA followed by Western blot confirmation of EIA positive) is clearly higher than the sensitivity. Furthermore, the sensitivity in asymptomatic HIV-infected populations is not known with precision. The sensitivity of HIV testing in persons with HIV illness is less important, since such persons are less likely to be blood donors and the diagnosis of HIV infection can be made clinically. The imperfect understanding of the sensitivity in asymptomatic populations results from the difficulty in assembling a sufficiently large group of asymptomatic HIV-infected persons by some method other than the presence of anti-HIV antibody. To find a population of 1,000 HIV-infected asymptomatic persons by means of HIV cultures, for instance, would require the performance of over 10,000 cultures in an otherwise untested high-risk group. The sensitivity of the sequential test is assumed by most to be roughly 99 percent, notwithstanding the absence of direct evidence establishing it. It is apparent that at least some HIV-infected persons remain seronegative for prolonged periods.[42]

The specificity of the sequential HIV test is better determined because of the availability of large populations of tested HIV-uninfected persons. In a study of 455,000 donations from 260,000 Minnesota blood donors, 15 donors were found to be repeat EIA and Western blot positive. Fourteen of these were men, of whom 13 conceded they engaged in HIV risk activities; the female also conceded she engaged in an HIV risk activity.[43] Presuming that those who

---

[42] Wolinsky et al., "Polymerase Chain Reaction."
[43] Kristine L. Macdonald et al., "Results of a State-Wide System to

admitted HIV risks were HIV infected and that the 15th person was not, the false positivity rate would be 1 per 450,000. If the false positivity rate of HIV testing can be brought to 1 per 100,000 or lower, it would undermine arguments against screening based on concerns about the frequency of false positive results. No population in the United States has an HIV infection prevalence that low. However, a high specificity in laboratories whose quality control is extremely good cannot necessarily be extrapolated to all laboratories performing HIV serologies.

HIV Antigen Test. Recently, commercial kits have been marketed which permit the detection of free HIV antigen in the serum of infected persons. The material detected is largely or completely made up of the core protein p24, whose molecular weight is 24,000. HIV antigen appears during acute HIV infection, but, coincident with the appearance of anti-p24 antibody, it disappears in the second or third month of HIV infection. The subsequent reappearance of HIV antigen increases the probability of developing AIDS about twentyfold. The most practical way of detecting HIV infection prior to the development of HIV antibody is the HIV antigen test.

HIV Culture Test. By 1987, in selected research laboratories, HIV culture techniques had become sufficiently sensitive that more than 99 percent of all HIV-infected persons had a positive blood culture for the virus.[44] The test, however, remains quite expensive, costing $175 or more in most laboratories. In time, HIV cultures will become more widely available and may constitute the "gold standard" for establishing HIV infection. This availability will undercut arguments against widespread HIV screening based on lack of specificity and indeterminacy of results. EIA positive, Western blot negative, or indeterminate results can be sorted out by using HIV cultures.

Polymerase Chain Reaction (PCR) Test. This promising technique, also called *gene amplification*, permits the detection of specific nucleic acid (DNA or RNA) sequences. Even a single copy of an HIV sequence

---

Screen Blood Donors for Human Immunodeficiency Virus Infection: Public Health Implications," *Annals of Internal Medicine* (forthcoming, 1989).
[44] Jackson, "Viral Culture Method," 1417.

can be detected. This test may ultimately be the most sensitive of all. The best understanding of the state of HIV disease in PCR positive persons who are negative for other HIV markers is not yet known.

CONCLUSION

Several points need to be kept in mind as we turn to policy considerations concerning HIV testing. There is presently no cure for AIDS or HIV infection, and there is no vaccine. Persons who become infected with HIV are likely to develop AIDS, and, absent therapy, most persons who develop AIDS will have died within a few years. In light of this prognosis, a positive or even an indeterminate HIV test result can be psychologically devastating and, given the lack of demonstrably effective treatments, presently offers no clear health benefits to asymptomatic persons tested. The number of false positives and false negatives produced by any HIV test depends both on how the results are interpreted and on the population being tested.

While the prognosis is dim, not all of the news is black. HIV infection is not spread by casual contact. Persons who are not now HIV infected can avoid HIV infection and AIDS by not engaging in activities in which there is a risk of transmission. Those who do develop AIDS or ARC can in many cases extend their life by treatment with zidovudine, and clinical trials are presently under way to determine whether zidovudine may also benefit asymptomatic HIV-infected persons. Many other therapeutic agents are under intensive study.

In this chapter we have been concerned to present the crucial medical facts that should be taken into account when a person decides whether to seek an HIV test as well as when social policy-makers decide whether testing is to be required.

2
Four Features of Testing Proposals

INTRODUCTION

Throughout the public debate on HIV testing, attention has focused on two features of testing proposals: what group would be targeted for testing and whether testing would be voluntary or mandatory. Public opinion polls have often posed questions about testing proposals only in terms of these features. In June 1987, for instance, the *Wall Street Journal* reported that 82 percent of those questioned favored mandatory testing of all marriage license applicants, but no mention was made of what was to be done with the results of such testing.[1]

Target groups and coerciveness of testing are only two of the features of any testing policy. Two others, seldom mentioned but equally important, are the distribution and the use of test results. The evaluation of any testing policy depends on all four of these features, in part because each affects how much the policy would intrude on privacy. For instance, mandatory but anonymous premarital testing used only to enhance informed decision making by marriage license applicants is obviously less intrusive on privacy than testing whose results the state used as a basis for denying marriage licenses to infected individuals. Yet incredibly some states have considered legislative proposals which one commentator describes as "confusingly silent" about whether a positive test result would mean the license applicant would be refused.[2] Denying licenses to

---

[1]"Debate Rages over AIDS-Test Policy," *Wall Street Journal*, June 18, 1987, p. 35.

[2]Larry Gostin and Andrew Ziegler, "A Review of AIDS-related Legislative and Regulatory Policy in the United States," *Law, Medicine and Health Care* 15 (Summer 1987): 9.

infected applicants might only keep them in the "sexual market-place," where they would be apt to infect more unsuspecting part-ners than they would if locked in the monogamous bonds of holy matrimony with spouses who knew of their infection.

The distribution and the use of test results, then, are important features of any testing policy, along with the coerciveness of the policy and its target group. This chapter will be devoted to a pre-liminary discussion of each of these four variables. Our objective here is to introduce some distinctions which will be useful in the subsequent examination of particular testing policies in Part Two as well as to convey some sense of the complexity of HIV testing issues.

THE VOLUNTARINESS OF THE TESTING POLICY

Sometimes people are tested who realize what testing involves and who have made an informed decision to seek testing. Such testing is voluntary. Others are tested against their will or because they feel they have no choice, since testing is made a condition for something else they want or need, like a marriage license or admission to the armed forces. Still others — some surgery patients, for instance — are tested without their knowledge. These are all cases of involuntary testing. Since there are both degrees of coercion and degrees of ignorance, there is also a considerable range of voluntariness of test-ing. Here we will be concerned to delineate various important cat-egories of voluntariness.

Voluntary versus Mandatory Testing

There is a key distinction between voluntary and mandatory test-ing. It is one thing to offer or urge testing and quite another to require it. Mandatory testing — testing people against their will — may conflict with two different kinds of privacy. A policy requir-ing or coercing people to submit to testing against their will restricts their liberty. Thus, it intrudes on what we shall call *liberty privacy*. It is privacy in this sense of liberty or self-determination which has figured in many court decisions affirming a constitutional right to privacy.[3] Mandatory testing also typically results in others gaining

---

[3] We are taking our terminological cue here from *Griswold v. Connecticut*, 381 U.S. 479 (1965) and *Roe v. Wade*, 410 U.S. 113 (1973), in

access to personal information which the person tested might prefer to keep private. We shall say that such intrusions invade informational privacy. By *informational privacy* we mean restricted or limited access to information about a person. Both kinds of privacy figure prominently in what follows, although we shall be particularly concerned with informational privacy.

In the United States, the first wave of mandatory testing was aimed at safeguarding the nation's blood supply. The next wave of mandatory testing had as its target military personnel. Their liberty privacy is already severely attenuated so they are easy to coerce; they are also easy to identify without unwarranted intrusions into their informational privacy.[4] Although members of high-risk groups — gays, bisexuals, and needle-sharing IV drug abusers and their sexual partners — might seem to be more plausible targets of mandatory testing, mandatory testing of these groups would involve serious practical, legal, and moral problems. It would require massive intrusions into informational privacy even to identify members of these groups, and this would be in addition to the intrusions on liberty and informational privacy involved in any mandated testing. Therefore, *voluntary* testing has been urged for members of these groups.

The methods of implementing and encouraging voluntary testing are relatively straightforward. The first is to provide explicit public AIDS education (including recommending that individuals considered to be at risk seek testing). The second is to make voluntary testing and counseling widely available, preferably with absolute anonymity so people will not feel they must avoid testing in order to protect their privacy. Voluntary anonymous testing appears at first glance to pose a minimal threat to privacy of any kind. In this country it has been the standard policy recommendation made by

---

which the Supreme Court protected the right of individuals to control their reproduction. In these cases the Court was really protecting liberty, but it referred to privacy because it viewed reproduction as a "private matter" which should be free of government intrusion — hence our term *liberty privacy*. Not all of the Supreme Court's privacy decisions concern liberty privacy, however. Fourth Amendment decisions such as *Katz v. U.S.*, 389 U.S. 347 (1967) protect what we call *informational privacy*.

[4] This does not mean that there are no objectionable invasions of their informational privacy with respect to their test results, however. We return to this point in Chapter 9.

medical and public health officials and organizations, civil libertarians, and many gay rights organizations regarding high-risk group
members.[5] The only "privacy" issue seemingly involved with voluntary anonymous testing concerns the affront to "privacy" (in the
extended sense of public decency) that may occur as a result of
bringing AIDS education and recommendations for testing into the
public forum and before the public eye. We will take a closer look
at this issue in Chapter 5.

By contrast, the methods of implementing mandatory testing
are not so obvious. Minimally, mandated testing requires some
agency with mandating authority. The most obvious mandating
agency is the government, which presently mandates testing for Job
Corps and Peace Corps recruits, immigrants seeking permanent residence, some foreign service officers and federal prisoners, and all
military recruits and personnel.[6]

Even among these testing programs we see different degrees of
voluntariness, since membership in some groups is more voluntary
than membership in others. No one chooses to be a federal prisoner. By contrast, Peace Corps volunteers might be said to indirectly consent to be tested when they elect to seek participation in
the Peace Corps. Accordingly we distinguish *unconditionally mandated testing* of groups for which membership is not voluntary from
conditionally mandated testing of those who voluntarily seek membership in a group knowing that means they will be tested.

Conditionally versus Unconditionally Mandated Testing

In a March 1986 op-ed piece urging universal mandatory testing,
William. F. Buckley introduced the notion of institutional "turnstiles."[7] He pointed out that entrance into various institutions typically involves passage through a turnstile, and he suggested that if
testing were mandated as a condition of passage through enough
major turnstiles (e.g., to get into college, to get married, to get insur-

---

[5] "Debate Rages over AIDS-Test Policy."

[6] Ibid., and also "Some Federal Inmates Carrying AIDS Virus to Be
Segregated," *Star Tribune* (formerly *Minneapolis Star Tribune*), October 24,
1987, sec. A, p. 7.

[7] William F. Buckley, "Identify All the Carriers," *New York Times*,
March 18, 1986, p. A27.

ance coverage), we would all be tested sooner or later. We will adopt Buckley's terminology and speak of turnstiles at which conditionally mandated testing may take place.

Conditionally mandated testing may itself be more or less voluntary, since individuals elect passage through different turnstiles more or less freely in response to more or less urgent desires or needs. People admitted to hospitals, for instance, are by and large responding to urgent *needs*, while those who seek participation in the Peace Corps or who wish to become blood donors are typically responding to less urgent *desires*.[8] There is a range of possibilities in between (e.g., insurance or marriage license applicants). Having acknowledged this, we point out that while technically most "mandated testing" may be only conditionally mandated, nevertheless much of it is linked to such basic desires and needs that individuals are in effect coerced, since they could elect to forgo them only at considerable personal cost.

Routine Testing

Another category of voluntariness was introduced into the HIV testing debate when President Reagan called for "routine" testing, which is testing that would ordinarily be done on persons passing through certain turnstiles but that individuals could refuse without being denied passage through the turnstile. To that extent it would be "voluntary," but it would differ from most voluntary testing, since it would involve no overt volunteering. President Reagan urged

---

[8] A troublesome exception involves persons asked to make "directed" blood donations. The AIDS epidemic has led to a surge of requests for directed donations. Unfortunately, a request from a family member to make such a donation can lead to coercive pressures on an individual to donate and hence to be tested. This can lead to several serious problems. First, persons who may suspect (or even know) they are infected and who are pressured in this way find their privacy is threatened. Second, they may proceed to give blood in response to the pressure they feel, in spite of fears or knowledge they may be infected. Since most anonymous donors give blood purely out of altruism and in a way that is uncoerced and fully voluntary, the pool of anonymous donors might actually contain a lower percentage of HIV-infected people than the pool of directed donors. If this proves to be the case, persons receiving donor-directed blood may actually run a slightly higher risk of receiving infected blood that slips through screening than those receiving an anonymous donation.

routine testing of all hospital admissions and marriage license applicants.[9] Advocates argue routine testing would come to be viewed by everyone passing through the turnstile as "normal" or routine while remaining voluntary and noncoercive. We agree with critics who are suspicious of the category of routine testing. Both ignorance and coercion could compromise the voluntariness of such testing. Hospital patients are often not told explicitly about tests which are given routinely (e.g., routine blood tests), and some surgeons acknowledge they routinely test their patients for HIV without informing them. To the extent that this is so, routine HIV testing becomes a simple subversion of the requirement of informed consent.[10] Moreover, few people who are sick enough to require hospitalization, with the dependence on hospital staff which that entails, are apt to demand a full explanation of what routine tests will be done on blood which is drawn. They are even less likely to object. More typically, hospitalized patients are eager to please and to appear cooperative in order to avoid alienating any of the caregivers upon whom they are so dependent. A patient who refuses routine testing runs the risks of being perceived both as a troublesome patient and as a person with something to hide. A further penalty is that the patient will be treated as if he or she were infected. Gary Bauer, President Reagan's domestic policy advisor, even acknowledged that at least in connection with federal testing, routine was merely a euphemism for *mandatory*: "Routine testing . . . does not include the right to opt out."[11]

Some people hold that informed consent should not be required for HIV testing of hospitalized patients, but that these tests should be treated like most other blood tests and other minor procedures in

---

[9] "Reagan Urges Wide AIDS Testing but Does Not Call for Compulsion," *New York Times*, June 1, 1987, p. A1.

[10] A recent study of all HIV tests ordered within one hospital during a five-month period concluded HIV testing was routinely misused. In almost half the cases it was ordered for patients with no recognized risk factor for HIV infection. In addition, in almost half the cases there was no indication patients had either given informed consent or been counseled about HIV infection. See Keith Henry, Myra Maki, and Kent Crossley, "Analysis of the Use of HIV Antibody Testing in a Minnesota Hospital," *Journal of the American Medical Association* 259 (1987): 229–32.

[11] William Safire, "Failing the Tests," *New York Times*, June 4, 1987, p. A27.

hospitals, for which explicit informed consent has not traditionally been sought. We agree it is unrealistic to expect explicit informed consent for each and every test administered to a hospitalized patient. Because of the tremendous potential of HIV test results for altering a patient's life, however, we would argue that informed consent is morally required and should be legally required. The underlying rationale for the general requirement of informed consent is that patients have a right to refuse to undergo medical procedures which may profoundly affect their lives in ways they judge to be adverse and that this requirement is not made less stringent even if their judgment is considered foolish by others. Many medical procedures for which informed consent is traditionally required have much less impact on a patient's life than being told he or she is infected with HIV. We explore that impact in depth in Part Two.

Court-Mandated Testing

Finally, testing of particular individuals may also be court mandated. A court order might mandate testing unconditionally. A woman who has been raped, for instance, might be granted a court order requiring her assailant to submit to unconditionally mandated testing. A court might also conditionally mandate testing: An Illinois judge ruled that visitation rights a divorced gay father was seeking with respect to his child would be considered only if he submitted to HIV testing and was found to be negative.[12]

THE DISTRIBUTION OF TEST RESULTS

Test Results Which Become Public Record

For various reasons, some people have consented to revelations of their HIV status in the public media. Thus President Reagan had his negative test results announced following a routine physical a few years ago. Sometimes unauthorized disclosures in the media of a

---

[12]"Gay Father's Refusal of Test Reviewed by Fourth Judge," *AIDS Policy and Law* 1 (June 4, 1986): 3; "Court Vacates Ruling on Test for Gay Father," *AIDS Policy and Law* 1 (June 18, 1986): 2. This ruling was subsequently vacated by another judge.

person's HIV status also occur. This obviously constitutes the widest possible distribution of test results. A person's HIV status may become part of the public record in the context of legal proceedings. For example, infected persons who wish to recover damages from sex partners who infected them will need to introduce test results into the public record to establish infection. The results may then be publicized by the media. All these cases are exceptional, however.

Confidential Testing

Ordinarily, information about a person's medical status is high on the list of information we view as private, and the "right to privacy" is usually understood to encompass the right to control such information about oneself. A person's interest in privacy is even more urgent when the information is as important and potentially damaging as HIV infection. People may suffer serious harms if their HIV test results are made available to others and they lose control of that information.

The importance of privacy regarding one's medical status has long been recognized. In medical ethics, the principle of confidentiality can be traced back as far as the Hippocratic Oath. Hippocrates acknowledged that in the course of providing medical care a physician may gain access to very private information about a patient even beyond that which is strictly medical, and he stipulated that all information must be kept confidential: "Whatever, in connection with my professional practice, or not in connection with it, I see or hear, in the life of men, which ought not to be spoken abroad, I will not divulge, as reckoning that all such should be kept secret."[13]

Confidentiality has been the object of renewed interest both as the result of recent developments in medical ethics and as a by-product of various recently enacted "patients' bills of rights" and data privacy acts. The traditional argument in favor of confidentiality is that it is a precondition for optimal medical care, because without it patients would be reluctant to entrust themselves to their physicians and reveal information that would make them vulnerable. That argument assumes greater urgency than ever in connec-

---

[13]"The Oath of Hippocrates," in Robert M. Veatch, *Case Studies in Medical Ethics* (Cambridge, Mass.: Harvard University Press, 1977), 351.

tion with AIDS and other HIV-related conditions. As with any disease, headway will be difficult in the struggle against AIDS without the full trust and cooperation of those who are afflicted or are most susceptible.

Confidential testing refers broadly to testing in which the usual canons of confidentiality are observed in order to keep results confidential. We say "refers broadly" because today confidentiality is a more complicated issue than it was for Hippocrates, since the delivery of modern health care no longer involves just the patient and the physician. More typically it involves large institutions, where many people have access to an individual's "confidential" medical records. Because so much is being learned so fast about HIV, few general practitioners are apt to be as knowledgeable as specialists. Consequently a person with HIV infection is usually well advised to seek health care from a specialist, most of whom work in large medical centers. Thus the patient's "confidential" medical records will probably be routinely available to those involved in providing health care both directly (physicians, nurses, and various technicians) and indirectly (pharmacists, technicians such as lab workers, and also those involved in payment for such care). This extends beyond hospital accounting office personnel to include insurance companies. In the case of a self-insured employer, it will also include the person's employer. Moreover, in states in which HIV infection is a reportable condition, test results must also be reported to the state health department. (Presently HIV antibody positivity is a reportable condition in Alabama, Arizona, Colorado, Idaho, Minnesota, Montana, South Carolina and Wisconsin.)[14] It is acknowledged that confidentiality is important throughout this distribution of a person's test results, and assurances are given at every level that it will be preserved. Still, such a wide distribution of such "private" and potentially damaging information is unsettling. Moreover, the broader the circle of authorized distribution of an individual's confidential medical records, the greater the chance of an unauthorized breach of confidentiality. These threats to privacy posed by the routine distribution of "confidential" medical records are so great as to prompt one commentator to describe medical confidentiality as a

---

[14]Gostin and Ziegler, "AIDS-related Legislative and Regulatory Policy," 10.

"decrepit concept."[15] The confidentiality of HIV test results will be the focus of much of the discussion in Part Two.

Anonymous Testing

One strategy for trying to avoid these problems has been to provide anonymous testing—that is, testing whose results are directly known only by the individual tested. Obviously the counselor delivering test results to a tested individual at an anonymous counseling and testing site also knows the test results. However, that counselor need not know the individual's name. Thus test results are anonymous in the sense that only the individual tested knows that that individual (by name) has those test results. Even this is problematic if the counselor happens to know the individual, however. (This might often be the case in smaller communities.) Anonymous testing represents a very restrictive distribution of test results, and hence one which is minimally intrusive on informational privacy. We noted above that this makes it particularly attractive to people who are concerned about privacy but who want to know their HIV status. Because public health officials believe it is advantageous for infected people to be tested so they will know of their infection, funding has been provided for anonymous testing—and anonymous counseling—in most major cities; advocates credit these programs, along with AIDS education, with a dramatic drop in the HIV transmission rate among gays. We examine voluntary anonymous testing in depth in Chapter 5.

Notice that anonymous testing is testing in which *test results* are directly available only to the tested individual. The fact that a certain individual has been tested (either voluntarily or mandatorily) could be important information independent of his or her anonymous test results. The fact that someone sought voluntary anonymous testing usually carries with it the implication that the person considers him- or herself at some risk. (This is one reason many clients of VD clinics hope not to be recognized by acquaintances during their visits.) To our knowledge, however, there are no anonymous testing programs in which an attempt is made to document who has been tested anonymously. At anonymous testing and coun-

---

[15] Mark Siegler, "Confidentiality in Medicine—A Decrepit Concept," *New England Journal of Medicine*, 307 (1982): 1518–21.

seling sites, real names are not recorded; therefore, in theory at least, the fact that an individual has been tested remains as secret as his or her test results.

Recently, home HIV antibody test kits have become available. They are marketed as a means for making "anonymous" testing even *more* anonymous. Originally, people using these kits were instructed to have blood drawn by a physician and then to mail it to the kit marketer, with test results sent by return mail. Now kits are available which allow people to collect samples of their own blood for mailing without having to involve a physician in any way. These kits are viewed with suspicion and alarm by most advocates of voluntary anonymous testing, who have concerns about quality control and who stress the importance of counseling as an adjunct to testing.[16] They urge that counseling must be provided both before testing and as test results are given, and they believe that test results alone are much less effective in changing unsafe behavior than testing accompanied by counseling.[17] In their view, people who receive positive test results without being "prepared" for them by counseling may react badly. Several people are even reported to have committed suicide upon receiving positive test results by phone and without counseling.

Unlinked Testing

Test results can be useful for some epidemiological purposes without anyone at all knowing whose test results they are. What may be important is the number of infected individuals in a given population, or perhaps the number of infected individuals fitting various profiles which are of special epidemiological interest. The names of the infected individuals may be irrelevant. Test results which are not linked to the identity of an individual are said to be *unlinked*. In

---

[16] Such testing could cause serious harm if it omitted Western blot follow-ups on positive EIA tests.

[17] See, for instance, Alvin Novick, "Why the Burdensome Knowledge Need Not Be Imposed," *IRB: A Review of Human Subjects Research* 8 (September–October 1986): 6–7, in which Novick claims education and counseling have much more of an impact on behavior change than test results. In Chapter 5 we return to the issue of the efficacy of counseling and of testing in changing behavior.

principle, unlinked test results would also be sufficient for screening the nation's blood supply. Infected blood could simply be discarded without anyone knowing the identity of the donor. (In fact, donors of infected blood are notified of their infection as a precautionary warning.)

Strictly speaking, what distinguishes unlinked distribution of test results from other kinds of distribution is not the recipients but the nature of the information: Test results are distributed without providing the names of the tested individuals. (Indeed, test results which are reported unlinked to some persons for some purposes may also be distributed either anonymously or confidentially.)

THE USES OF TESTING

Although originally developed (and licensed) only for the screening of blood, HIV testing quickly became recognized as a tool which could serve other ends, including some which may actually be antithetical to slowing the spread of HIV. It will be useful to distinguish some of these goals and the mechanisms by which they might be achieved.

The Preventative Goal

Since HIV infection has so far proved to be irreversible, the best general strategy currently available for combating AIDS is to slow its spread. Because the goal of slowing the spread of HIV infection overall is so basic, we wish to provide a specific term for it. Henceforth when we speak of *the preventative goal* of HIV testing, we mean the goal of slowing the spread of HIV infection overall.

While there are a number of methods by which HIV testing might contribute to achieving the preventative goal, it is important to realize that some method or other is required. Mere testing by itself is not preventative. Yet, sometimes testing advocates seem to assume that any HIV testing will automatically reduce HIV transmission, even though they do not have any clear idea of the method by which this will happen and who will need to have access to test results in order for it to work. This is particularly troublesome because testing usually intrudes on privacy.

Prevention through Precautionary Warnings to Infected Individuals or to Third Parties. The most straightforward way in which HIV testing could contribute to achieving the preventative goal is by helping to engender voluntary abstention from unsafe activities. Since most HIV infection is spread through voluntary activities, infected individuals are the people in the best position to use test results to slow the spread of the disease: All they would need to do is to modify their behavior. The rationale here is that individuals who know of their infection have an added incentive to modify their high-risk behavior. This rationale will be explored in Chapter 5. We will refer to this use of testing for controlling the spread of AIDS as providing *precautionary warnings to infected individuals.*

Notice that this use of HIV testing requires only anonymous testing. Moreover, since unsafe activities are not only voluntary but also very private, it is not immediately obvious how any broader distribution of test results would serve to decrease the amount of unsafe activity by infectious individuals. At the very least, it is incumbent on advocates of nonanonymous testing for prevention to describe the methods by which third-party knowledge of someone's HIV status could serve the preventative goal of HIV testing. In Part Two we will argue that often too little attention has been given to this question, even in connection with testing programs that have already been implemented. In Chapter 9, for instance, we will argue that some federally mandated testing programs which involve significant intrusions into individual privacy cannot reasonably be held to contribute to achieving the preventative goal.

Another way in which third-party knowledge of someone's HIV status might serve the preventative goal would involve providing a *precautionary warning to third persons* who are apt to be put in contact with the infected person's blood or semen. Marriage license applicant testing, for example, might be useful for providing such warnings. (We will examine marriage applicant testing in Chapter 9.) Some people have also argued for the mandatory testing of people who will be receiving certain kinds of health care on the grounds that their caregivers need to be advised of their patients' HIV status so that they can take special precautionary measures with those who are HIV infected. Against this, others have argued that health care providers should take the same body fluid precautions with all patients and, privacy issues aside, that it would be counterproductive to inform them that certain patients are HIV infected. First, it might actually make them more nervous around patients they know are HIV positive, and hence they might be more prone to accidental exposure; second, it might create a false sense of security around other patients who may be infectious with other diseases (hepatitis B, for instance) or with undetected HIV.[18] We shall return to this debate in Chapter 7.

Prevention through Exclusionary Screening. A third method for achieving the preventative goal, as well as other goals, is exclusion. Exclusionary screening occurs when negative test results are a precondition of passage through some turnstile. Exclusionary screening of donated blood has virtually eliminated blood product transmission of HIV in the United States. Significantly, *that* goal could be achieved through testing which is not merely confidential or even anonymous, but completely unlinked.

While screening which only involves organs, semen or blood products might be unlinked, most exclusionary screening involves screening people. This occurs, for instance, when licensed prostitutes are screened for HIV infection, and other job screening has been proposed with a similar rationale. As we shall see in Chapter 9, the preventative goal has even been cited in defense of exclusionary screening for the Job Corps and the military. Any exclusionary screening of people poses severe threats to informational privacy, especially since people who have been excluded from something may find it difficult to explain to other interested parties why they have been excluded.

Other Uses of Exclusionary Screening

In addition to the preventative goal, exclusionary HIV screening can serve other goals as well. One goal might simply be to slow or prevent the spread of the virus within some screened subgroup. For example, the current U.S. immigration policy of exclusionary screening of people seeking permanent residency can hardly be construed as an attempt to promote the preventative goal — that is, to slow the *overall* spread of the virus. It is instead an attempt to prevent those people from spreading HIV in the United States rather than else-

---

[18] Dr. Molly Cook, personal communication.

where. Thus it does not protect the public health, but rather only the health of some subgroup of the public, namely, people within the United States. [19]

This distinction between exclusionary screening to serve the preventative goal and exclusionary screening to protect the health of some special group is ethically significant, because it helps us to recognize a range of cases between altruistic and ultimately moral motivations of concern for the health and welfare of "the public" at the one extreme and increasingly less altruistic and more self-interested motivations of concern for the health and welfare of just oneself and one's own group at the other. The U.S. immigration policy serves U.S. interests, but we must not pretend that this represents concern for "our fellow man" or that it is designed simply to slow the spread of the disease. More generally, when exclusionary screening is used to protect the health of some subgroup by keeping infected people out, the net effect is usually to shift the threat they pose from those within the subgroup to those outside it.

Finally, exclusionary screening may be used in ways that have nothing to do with slowing the spread of the disease, even within subgroups, but merely serve economic or other nonhealth objectives. In Chapter 9 we will argue that arguments linking exclusionary screening in the U.S. military, the Peace Corps, and the Job Corps to the preventative goal are so weak that the true goal of such testing is probably to exclude either "undesirables" or people whose medical expenses are apt to be high from federal programs.

Economic incentives of this sort cease to be covert in some contexts. In Chapter 8 we address exclusionary screening by insurance companies, which is overtly designed to protect economic interests, not health interests. In fact, the effect of such screening on health is probably negative, inasmuch as it prevents some persons from getting the insurance they must have if they are to receive first class health care. (This is not to argue that such testing is unethical, but only to acknowledge that the reasons for it conflict with health promotion.)

---

[19] Of course, such testing may slow the spread by providing a precautionary warning to the individual screened. However, the precautionary warning is not the goal of the screening, but rather a happy side benefit. If it were the goal, then screening which was not exclusionary would be sufficient.

Court-related Uses of Testing

HIV testing may be used for entirely different reasons in connection with court proceedings. We have already noted some examples of civil cases involving the use of test results. Such information might also figure in criminal proceedings. In some states it is a crime knowingly to infect another person with HIV.[20]

Epidemiological Uses of Testing

HIV testing may also be done to provide epidemiological information. The federal government announced plans in June 1987 to test 45,000 randomly selected Americans simply in order to determine the extent of the infection.[21]

However, this project will be slow to materialize — if it materializes at all. Critics within the CDC have argued that designing a meaningful study of this magnitude will take time and be expensive, and that with all the other uncertainties involving AIDS it is counterproductive to expend limited AIDS resources simply to find out how many people are infected. Thus most test results used for epidemiological purposes are unlinked results of testing done for other purposes.

The above are the important legitimate uses of testing. It is appropriate to mention, however, what we view as a misuse of testing. Since most persons who test positive are gay, and homosexuality is heavily stigmatized in our culture, it is inevitable that some testing will be driven by concerns that have less to do with health or economic goals and more to do with discrimination. We explore this issue more fully in Chapter 9 in connection with government-mandated testing programs. Such misuses of testing are by no means limited to testing mandated by the federal government, however.

----

[20]Two states, Florida and Idaho, have mandated that criminal penalization for knowingly exposing another to a sexually transmitted disease be extended to include HIV. See Gostin and Ziegler, "AIDS-related Legislative and Regulatory Policy," 12, for some of the problems associated with use of the criminal law to regulate private behavior involving consenting adults.

[21]"Government Plans Random AIDS Test for 45,000 in U.S.," *New York Times*, June 6, 1987, p. A1.

Goals or uses of testing are particularly important features of any testing policy, because they often dictate the other important features: whether testing is to be mandatory or voluntary, to whom test results are to be distributed, and what groups are to be tested.

TARGET GROUPS

Testing has been proposed for a tremendous number of different groups. Specification of its target group is the most conspicuous feature of any testing policy or proposal. As we just noted, often the specification of the target group will depend on the particular goals of a testing policy. Testing designed to prevent HIV transmission through blood products, for instance, will obviously target all donated blood (or all donors). Exclusionary screening (e.g., of insurance applicants) will require testing of those attempting passage through that particular turnstile. Sometimes testing may serve several goals simultaneously.

For these reasons, the list of target groups is probably open-ended. Here we will only list some of the more obvious target groups and categories of target groups. (These are often defined in terms of the goals of the testing.)

Universal Testing

Some people have advocated universal testing, both as a means of providing a precautionary warning to all infected individuals and for epidemiological reasons. Objections to universal testing are fairly straightforward and have been treated at length by others. Massive intrusions into both informational and liberty privacy would be required. Costs would be exorbitant—particularly if testing were accompanied by counseling, as all knowledgeable experts recommend. Moreover, individuals who had become infected too recently for detectable antibodies to have developed would receive false negative results. False negative results are problematic enough in any situation, but they would have especially severe consequences in the context of universal testing, since one of the main effects (and goals) of universal testing would be that people generally would be less concerned about "unsafe" activities unless they or their partners had tested positive. Finally, any proposal for such massive information gathering naturally invites speculation about repressive uses to which the information might be put (e.g., mass quarantines).

A Random Sample of the General Population

While universal testing would provide useful epidemiological information about how many Americans are infected, this information could be gained more easily and economically by a random sampling of the general population. Although a truly *random* sample would require invasions of liberty privacy, sampling would be useful even with unlinked test results and hence could be minimally invasive of informational privacy. However, even this more modest program has proved to be problematic.

Persons Engaging in High-Risk Activities

Testing programs calculated to provide precautionary warnings will obviously be most useful, other things being equal, when the group tested is made up of individuals at high risk. Some voluntary anonymous testing programs are geared toward high-risk individuals: those who have had unprotected anal intercourse or are sexually promiscuous, needle-sharing IV drug abusers and their sexual partners, and hemophiliacs and others who may have received tainted blood products prior to blood screening. We wish to clarify that by "high-risk group members" we do *not* mean gays, IV drug abusers, and the like, but only those people who engage in high-risk activities. A gay who never engages in unprotected anal intercourse or an IV drug abuser who always uses a clean needle is not a high-risk group member, notwithstanding the public perception to the contrary.

One question which arises in connection with such testing is how high the risk to an individual must be for testing to make sense. Early in 1987, some authorities were urging all promiscuous heterosexuals and 30 million people who had received blood transfusions between 1978 and 1982 anywhere in the United States to view themselves as "high-risk" and seek testing. One unhappy consequence was that testing and counseling centers across the country became clogged with huge numbers of persons who were at very low risk, with the result that many bona fide high-risk individuals had to wait months before they could be tested. To avoid this problem, some centers have now devised triage systems so high-risk group members can be tested more quickly.

In addition to voluntary testing of high-risk group members, testing could be mandated for members of certain easily identifiable high-risk groups, for instance, all hemophiliacs who might have received tainted blood products before 1985 or all persons arrested on gay sex, prostitution, or IV drug abuse charges. In Chapter 9 we explore the question why there has been no such proposal regarding hemophiliacs. Since most unsafe activities are private, however, it is virtually impossible for authorities to mandate testing for more than a handful of the individuals who engage in them.

Persons Entering "High-Transmission Situations"

In contrast to habitual activities that generate high-risk groups (e.g., anal sex and IV drug abuse), "high-transmission situations" involve a fairly high risk of transmission *if one person happens to be infectious*; but since most participants are not typically high-risk group members, the risk of transmission in any given case is quite low. Blood donors and persons who are thinking of entering a long-term sexual relationship (e.g., marriage) are most obviously in this category. Public support for mandatory testing of marriage license applicants is high,[22] and legislation regarding such testing had been introduced in twenty-six states as of April 1987.[23] We will discuss such testing in Chapter 9. Since roughly 40 percent of the newborns of infected women are also infected, Surgeon General Koop has also recommended voluntary testing of all women contemplating pregnancy. Some medical and dental procedures also involve a higher risk of transmission than casual contact, and proponents of testing of all hospital admissions or of all surgery patients invoke a similar rationale. Testing in health care delivery contexts will be examined in Chapter 7.

---

[22] Eighty percent of the people contacted in a February 1987 *Newsweek* poll favored testing for all people applying for marriage licenses. See "Mandatory Testing for AIDS?" *Newsweek*, February 16, 1987, p. 22.

[23] Gostin and Ziegler, "AIDS-related Legislative and Regulatory Policy," 9.

Persons Seeking Passage through Exclusionary Turnstiles

Most of the testing for the groups listed above would not be exclusionary testing. Where exclusionary testing is contemplated, the specification of the group is defined by the turnstile in question. The goal of exclusionary screening of all donated blood dictates that all donated blood will be tested, and likewise for all prostitutes seeking licenses in Nevada, aliens seeking permanent residence in the United States, and persons seeking admission to the military, the Peace Corps, the Job Corps, or certain foreign service positions. Exclusionary screening at other turnstiles (e.g., application for health or life insurance or for certain jobs or surgical procedures) would similarly define groups to be tested.

Turnstile-inspired Testing

Some testing that has been proposed seems to have as its primary rationale the mere existence of a turnstile, although there may also be some general commitment to the desirability of testing as many people as possible. When President Reagan finally spoke out on AIDS publicly on May 31, 1987, he announced mandatory testing and recommended routine testing for a number of groups, including federal prisoners, Peace Corps and Job Corps applicants, immigrants, patients being admitted to hospitals, and all marriage license applicants. A *New York Times* editorial voiced the concern, shared by many people, that in doing so President Reagan was ignoring the advice of his public health experts and was favoring testing for groups in which HIV was not particularly prevalent.[24]

Some skeptical observers suggested that President Reagan had chosen to participate in "the politics of appearance" instead of endorsing a sound public health policy: In the face of public concern that *something* be done about AIDS, President Reagan was merely going on record in favor of *something or other*, namely, lots of testing.[25] The

---

[24]"Mr. Reagan's AIDS Test," *New York Times*, June 2, 1987, p. A26.

[25]See "Reagan Urges Wide AIDS Testing," wherein the President is quoted as saying,

> AIDS is surreptitiously spreading throughout our population, and yet we have no accurate measure of its scope. It is time we knew exactly what we were facing. And that is why I support routine testing [of marriage license applicants].

most obvious common characteristic of the different groups for whom President Reagan wanted testing was simply that they all had to pass through pre-existing institutional turnstiles at which they could easily be coerced or pressured into testing. In Chapter 9 we will take a closer look at federally mandated testing.

SUMMARY

It might be well to recapitulate the four features of testing proposals we have discussed and the distinctions we have made within each.

The Voluntariness of Testing. A testing proposal could involve testing which was voluntary, conditionally or unconditionally mandated, or routine. There may also be mandatory court-ordered testing of single individuals.

The Distribution of Test Results. Test results could be distributed as matters of public record, they could be kept confidential, or they could be anonymous. In addition, for some purposes they might be unlinked with the identities of any individuals.

The Uses of Testing. HIV testing could be used in various ways to serve various goals. It may serve what we call the preventative goal: to promote the public health by slowing the spread of HIV infection. It could do so by providing precautionary warnings to either infected individuals or others who might be exposed to them in high-transmission situations. Alternatively, exclusionary screening may serve the preventative goal by simply excluding infectious individuals from situations in which they might spread the disease, either in general or within some subgroup. Exclusionary screening can also be used to exclude infectious persons from groups for other reasons (e.g., to shift the threat of infection from those within the group to those outside of it) or for economic or other nonhealth reasons. Test results also might be used in legal proceedings and for epidemiological research. Finally, testing can be misused for social or political purposes as a way of exposing gay persons or IV drug abusers.

For a skeptical analysis of Reagan's stance on testing, see William Safire, "Failing the Tests," and Nan Hunter, "Reagan's 'Weak, Coercive' AIDS Plan," *New York Times*, June 12, 1987, p. A31.

Target Groups. Testing has been proposed for the entire population, or for some random sample thereof, for epidemiological purposes. Some test policies or proposals are targeted at groups defined by high-risk activities or at persons entering high-transmission situations. Exclusionary turnstile screening would, of course, be targeted at all those seeking passage through a given turnstile. Finally, some groups may be targeted for testing primarily because they seek passage through turnstiles at which testing can easily be mandated or urged.

The cases we have described within each of the four categories may overlap, and they are not always exhaustive. Our primary aim here has been to illustrate the hidden complexities of any HIV testing policy and in the process to lay the groundwork for subsequent examination of particular testing proposals in Part Two. There we will explore thoroughly the ethics of certain prominent and representative testing proposals, with special attention given to privacy considerations. Although we obviously cannot examine all possible testing policies, we hope in the present chapter to have provided some general concepts and distinctions which readers may find useful in conducting their own assessments of particular proposals or policies, including ones we do not explore.

Because privacy is one of the main values threatened by virtually any HIV testing, we will take an in-depth look at privacy considerations before turning to particular testing policies and proposals. In Chapter 3 we will examine philosophical arguments for the claim that privacy is a fundamental value for everyone in a society which prizes freedom and individualism, not just for those with something shameful or immoral to hide. In Chapter 4 we will look at how privacy is embodied in our legal system and more specifically at how constitutional, tort, and statutory law bears on the issue of HIV testing.

3
Why Privacy Is Important

INTRODUCTION

Privacy plays a prominent role in debates over HIV testing because many think privacy and public health claims compete. Since no one denies the importance of public health, disagreement about the legitimacy of privacy claims often seems to be at the heart of HIV testing disputes. Those who argue against mandatory testing, for instance, frequently invoke a "fundamental right to privacy" in a pious tone which almost suggests the right is beyond questioning — as if it were fundamental in the sense of being axiomatic and trumping all other concerns.

This is usually rejected by their critics, who may even feel that privacy has only one use — to hide behind — and hence that it is of value only to people with something shameful, immoral, or illegal to conceal. It certainly is undeniable that privacy is tremendously useful to wrongdoers. One commentator has noted that most of the wrongdoing in the world — burglary, infidelity, spying, even war — would be difficult or impossible without privacy, and that bringing wrongdoers to justice would be greatly facilitated if they had less privacy.[1]

In this chapter we examine the philosophical credentials of privacy claims generally and of medical privacy claims in particular. Our examination proceeds in three stages. We begin by considering three clusters of arguments for privacy as a fundamental value in a free society. We then address briefly the case for privacy rights. In

---

[1] Ferdinand Schoeman, "Privacy: Philosophical Dimensions of the Literature," in *Philosophical Dimensions of Privacy*, ed. Ferdinand Schoeman (Cambridge: Cambridge University Press, 1984), 1.

the final section we discuss the scope of the right to informational privacy.

THE FUNDAMENTAL VALUE OF PRIVACY

Philosophers have given a variety of reasons for supposing that privacy is a fundamental human value and of crucial importance in an open society. In this section we review those reasons and discuss their implications for the issues surrounding HIV testing.

Privacy Is Necessary for the Creation of Autonomous Individuals and a Genuine Democracy

First of all, privacy is necessary for the pursuit of two interrelated ideals to which our culture is committed.[2] The first ideal is that of the autonomous individual. To say that an individual is autonomous is to say that he or she lives according to principles which he or she embraces on the basis of critical reflection and which therefore speak to him or her from within rather than being imposed from without by social pressure to conform.[3] An autonomous person exercises liberty in that his or her projects and life plan are freely chosen: The individual is the author of his or her life story as well as its main character. None of us, of course, is totally immune from social pressure to conform, and hence none of us is fully autonomous. Nevertheless, the idea of a fully autonomous individual may still function for us as an ideal to which we may aspire. The second ideal is that of democracy—a form of government which is at the service of its citizens, who are understood to have created it and who control it, instead of the reverse. These two ideals are interrelated. Autonomous individuals flourish best in a democracy. That, for instance, is the foundation of the claim that the government is supposed to secure for each of us the rights to "life, liberty and the pursuit of happiness." But a genuine democracy in turn is only possible to the extent that its citizens are free and autonomous—both capable of reflecting crit-

---

[2] This argument is made most forcefully by Ruth Gavison in her essay "Information Control: Availability and Exclusion," in *Public and Private in Social Life*, ed. Stanley Benn and Gerald Gaus (London: St. Martin's Press, 1983), 121–28.

[3] Gavison, "Information Control," 123.

ically on their beliefs and free to act on (and vote) their true convictions. These ideals, which are at the heart of our political heritage, combine to form the ideal of the "open society."

These ideals may emerge more clearly if we consider the contrast with a closed society. In an open society, individualism and diversity are encouraged and flourish. A crucial distinction exists between the public sphere and the private sphere, between public issues (with which governmental "public policies" are obviously concerned) and the private lives of citizens. (This is not to claim the boundary between them is always clear and distinct. We will return to this point in what follows.) Moreover, in an open society the government itself is maximally "open," that is, governmental activities are conducted with as little secrecy as possible, while citizens, as we shall argue, are by and large entitled to a presumption of both informational and liberty privacy in their personal lives.

In a closed society, on the other hand, the distinction between the public and the private is less obvious, and to the extent that it exists, the priorities of an open society regarding them may be turned upside down. Governmental activities are more apt to be conducted privately or in secret, while less privacy is accorded citizens, with a corresponding attenuation of their freedom. Thus, one of the first things that happens in fictional totalitarian antiutopias, e.g., those depicted in *Brave New World* or *1984*, is that people are deprived of their privacy.[4]

There are several specific ways in which privacy is necessary for the pursuit of the goals of fully autonomous agents in a genuine democracy, given that we are less than perfect beings. First of all, as we noted, most of us fall short of the ideal of perfect autonomy in that we look to others for affirmation of our principles and choices and we fear disapproval, criticism, and condemnation by others. In fact, we are often so sensitive to others' perceptions of ourselves

---

[4] A dramatic example of this contrast is reproductive matters in Plato's *Republic* and in the United States today. In *Griswold v. Connecticut*, 381 U.S. 479 (1965) and subsequent decisions, the U.S. Supreme Court has ruled that reproductive matters are "private" matters and that the state has no business either prohibiting or even inquiring into the use of birth control by an individual. In Plato's *Republic*, on the other hand, pairing and reproductive decisions were manipulated in secret by the state, which tricked its citizens into thinking they were being permitted to mate with particular partners as the result of a random lottery.

that we may experience ourselves or our activities radically differently if we believe that we are being observed.[5] We tend to lose our spontaneity. (Think of how strongly we would react to finding a Peeping Tom at our window. If a woman discovered that a telescope in a high rise a few blocks away was trained on her window, she would hardly shrug and go about her business.) Acts of intimacy (nonsexual as well as sexual) would be especially difficult — perhaps even impossible — if we knew we were being observed.[6] One reason for this is that when we are observed, we may imagine our observers to be judging us and may even find we are judging ourselves by what we imagine their standards to be. This will be particularly likely when a person is tentative and hence lacks self-confidence about what he or she is doing, as in the trial and error stages of learning.[7]

Several writers have suggested we are so subject to such pressures that we would lose all our individuality if we had no privacy in which to develop and maintain it. Ruth Gavison claims, for instance, that if we could keep nothing private, not even our thoughts, "we would try to erase from our minds everything we would not be willing to publish, and we would not try to do anything that would make us likely to be feared, ridiculed, or harmed. There is a terrible flatness in the person who could succeed in these attempts."[8]

Edward Bloustein concurs, stating that an individual deprived of privacy "merges with the mass. His opinions, being public, tend never to be different; his aspirations, being known, tend always to be conventionally accepted ones; his feelings, being openly exhibited, tend to lose their quality of unique personal warmth and to

---

[5] For a discussion of how our perception of ourselves changes, see, for instance, Stanley Benn, "Privacy, Freedom, and Respect for Persons," in *Philosophical Dimensions of Privacy*, 227–28.

[6] Although he overstates his case, Charles Fried has explored the connection between privacy and intimacy. See his "Privacy," *Yale Law Journal* 77 (1968): 475–93, reprinted in *Philosophical Dimensions of Privacy*, 203–22.

[7] Ruth Gavison makes this point nicely in "Privacy and the Limits of Law," in *Philosophical Dimensions of Privacy*, 364.

[8] Gavison, "Privacy and the Limits of Law," 361.

become the feelings of every man. Such a being, although sentient, is fungible; he is not an individual."[9]

Clearly such pressure would make the development of autonomous individuals nearly impossible, because at the heart of autonomy are the capacities for independent thought, critical reflection, and commitment to principles based on conclusions which are truly one's own and not just accepted because of social pressure. Privacy, then, provides the "space" (the freedom from pressures caused by observation) in which autonomy can gain a foothold and flourish.

Autonomous individuals not only *believe in* the principles they embrace as their own, however; they also *act* on those principles and govern their lives by them. In short, they have control not only over their thoughts, but also over their actions and bodies. We identify our *selves* not only with our thoughts, but also with our deeds and bodies. A part of this control consists in thinking of our thoughts and bodies (metaphorically) as *our* property.[10] You are the one who gets to decide who hears your thoughts and what your body does and what happens to it—where it is, how it is clothed, the length of its hair, the medical treatment it receives, and so on. And, as with all your property, you are the one who gets to decide who has access to your thoughts and body, and to information about them. This is what it is for our thoughts and bodies to be private, morally speaking. In his study of asylums, Erving Goffman investigated how "total institutions" such as prisons, naval ships, and mental hospitals bring about a "mortification of the self." One of the primary ways in which this is effected is through the deprivation of just this kind of privacy. Goffman claimed that individuals who are deprived of privacy suffer a loss of individuality and sense of self.[11]

This is one of the obvious reasons that persons have a privacy interest in controlling what medical tests are performed on them. Medical tests are highly intrusive not only because of the intrusion into the body but also because of the knowledge that is gleaned

---

[9] Edward Bloustein, "Privacy as an Aspect of Human Dignity," in *Philosophical Dimensions of Privacy*, 188.

[10] For an elaboration of this view, see Jeffrey Reiman, "Privacy, Intimacy, and Personhood," in *Philosophical Dimensions of Privacy*, 310–13.

[11] Erving Goffman, *Asylums* (New York: Doubleday, 1961), 3–48. Goffman's work is also cited by Reiman, "Privacy, Intimacy, and Personhood," 311.

from the tests. Learning one's own HIV status can radically alter one's view of oneself and may cast one into despair and panic. Moreover, as soon as test results are known to anyone, there is the risk that they will become known by others. Because of this, it is difficult to see how we could think of our bodies as our own and of ourselves as autonomous beings if, in the absence of overwhelming need, medical tests could be performed on us without our consent.

Privacy Is Necessary for Many Projects We Value

Even if we did not need a certain amount of "insulation" from social pressures to develop and maintain ourselves as autonomous individuals, there are other reasons for us to value privacy. One is that privacy is necessary for many of the projects or activities we want to pursue. We have in mind here especially projects which are crucially affected by information or lack of information about others and which are competitive or involve information or a "strategy" which would be undercut if others knew about them. These projects occur both in our play (jokes, surprises, and games) and in our work. Some of them are at the heart of our political and economic systems.

Privacy is necessary for a variety of personal projects — recreational competition, for instance. It has also been suggested that courtship usually involves some elements of "strategy" requiring privacy. On this view, privacy concerning intentions, desires, and expectations is essential to courtship — as is privacy within the relationship even after private information has been exchanged. Moreover, privacy plays a role in defining romantic and other social relationships. We keep certain facts private from some people, but share them with others. In this way we "modulate" the degree of intimacy of a relationship by the degree of privacy we choose to maintain. In fact, one philosopher has suggested that this selective sharing of "private" information (which is withheld from most people) is one of the building blocks of intimacy.[12] Another philosopher

---

[12] Charles Fried, "Privacy," 205–6. See also James Rachels, "Why Privacy Is Important," in *Philosophical Dimensions of Privacy*. Fried goes so far as to say that love and friendship which depend on intimacy are inconceivable without privacy. While this seems to be an overstatement, privacy is certainly important for the creation of intimacy in our culture.

argues that one of the main things that differentiates a person's various social roles is the different "face" he or she shows, that is, the different "private" information he or she reveals in each relationship.[13]

This rationale for protecting privacy is especially relevant regarding information concerning a person's HIV test results. HIV-infected persons may find it increasingly difficult to maintain control over their personal relationships as more people learn of their infection. This, of course, will make it increasingly difficult to carry out a wide range of projects. Sometimes the consequences are devastating. On September 11, 1987, a newspaper reported that Dr. Robert J. Huse, a pediatrician in Mesquite, Texas, had tested positive for HIV.[14] Within three weeks Dr. Huse's practice declined to such a degree that he was forced to abandon it. Since HIV infection is not spread by casual contact, Dr. Huse did not pose a risk to his patients. Dr. Huse lost his practice because of the ignorance and prejudice of others, and this brings us to the third reason for valuing privacy.

Privacy Protects Us from the Intolerance, Prejudice,
Ignorance, and Malice of Others

At a theoretical level we are committed, both as individuals and as a nation, to tolerance of individual differences so long as they cause no harm to others. Perhaps nowhere is this reflected more clearly than in the case law surrounding the First Amendment in the areas of freedom of speech and religion. In practice, however, most of us (imperfect beings that we are) often find ourselves uncomfortable when confronted with people who live very differently from us, especially when the difference involves the choice of other principles than those we have chosen to live by. If we are "too sure" of ourselves, we may condemn a person's choice of principles as being misguided or silly. If, on the other hand, we are unsure of our own choice of principles, we may feel threatened when confronted with another's alternative choice, but the reaction may be the same: con-

---

For a criticism of Fried's view, see Reiman, "Privacy, Intimacy, and Personhood," 304–6.

[13] Rachels, "Why Privacy Is Important," 293–95.

[14] Reported by Peter Applebombe in *New York Times*, October 1, 1987, Midwest edition, p. 16.

demnation. If such intolerance is reenforced with fear and ignorance, it may even lead to malice and malevolent actions. A third
reason privacy is valuable, then, is that in practice it helps to minimize awareness of such differences and hence to minimize intolerance, prejudice, and malice.[15] Information about a person's sexual
practices, preferences, and fantasies may be the most obvious "private information" of which others might be intolerant, but it would
be a mistake to underestimate the range of information that may
fuel intolerance. Knowledge of anything from a person's religious
convictions to spending habits to leisure time activities may trigger
intolerance.

Of course, it is not mere disapproval that we have to fear from
persons caught up in the spiral of condemnation and intolerance
and fear and ignorance. Intolerance has cost people friends, jobs,
housing, and physical well-being. In addition, privacy also helps
protect us from people who are malevolent, whether because of
intolerance or other reasons. Something as simple as leaving a light
on when going out is a mechanism for concealing that one's home is
now empty and hence vulnerable to a malevolent intruder.

A related argument for privacy can also be made. Many well-
intentioned people may find certain practices personally offensive
but realize they should tolerate them given their acceptance of the
ideal of an open society; they may find them easier to tolerate when
they are done in private.[16] The relevance of this third argument to
AIDS and HIV testing is painfully obvious. Much paranoia about AIDS
is rooted in prejudicial fear of gays and fear of death, which in turn
trigger some very irrational risk assessments. Privacy can function
here as a much-needed shield against fear, ignorance, and intolerance. This is true not only of HIV testing but of medical privacy in
general. AIDS is not the only disease which triggers prejudice. It is
not an exaggeration to say that medical privacy, then, offers fundamental psychological and even physical protection.

---

[15] W. A. Parent, "Privacy, Morality, and the Law," in *Philosophy and
Public Affairs* 12 (Fall 1983): 269–88, reprinted in *Philosophy of Law*, ed. Joel
Feinberg and Hyman Gross (Belmont, Calif.: Wadsworth, 1986),
297–307. See especially p. 300.

[16] For a similar view, but spelled out in more detail, see Gavison,
"Privacy and the Limits of Law," 367–68.

THE EXISTENCE OF PRIVACY RIGHTS

Given that individuals living in an open society have a fundamental *interest* in privacy, what reasons do we have for believing in privacy *rights*, and what do such rights encompass? Without offering a complete theory of rights, we propose to explore briefly our commitment to privacy rights. First, we will adduce a number of considerations which seem explicable only on the assumption that we do have privacy rights. Then we will address the question of the scope of such rights.

The first and most obvious consideration which suggests that we have privacy rights is that we routinely talk of such rights. A right to property, for instance, seems to entail a right to privacy. Private property is not merely property to which access is restricted, but property which the owner has a right to use as he or she will and to which the owner has a *right to control access*. It is difficult to make sense of how we could even speak of private property without speaking of rights to control access. In addition to privacy rights regarding property, we also speak of having a right to keep various personal information private, as well as a right to do certain activities in private. Of course, such talk does not constitute a compelling reason for believing in privacy rights, since we sometimes talk in ways which are misleading or just wrong. Nonetheless, it would be odd indeed if all of this talk were simply misguided — and it would be misguided if there were in fact no privacy rights.

Moreover, we use other "rights" language in talking about our privacy. We say that a person can *exercise* his or her right to privacy by refusing to divulge information upon being asked to do so, or *waive* it by telling all. A right to privacy may be *forfeited* by criminal activity. We claim our privacy has been *violated* if we find someone snooping in our correspondence (but not just if they happen to come upon us in a public place when we thought we were alone). All of these ways of speaking are ways of speaking about rights. In addition, we sometimes allude to privacy rights without using the word *rights* by using *privacy* in a normative sense, as when we speak of someone's private correspondence or property. It is difficult to understand how else reference to a "private" diary could be understood. The sort of control which we exercise over who has access to us or to information about us gives rise to a second reason for supposing that we have a right to privacy. We value not just privacy but *control* over who has access to private information. Even though privacy is of tremendous importance to each of us, it is also true that too much privacy can be as undesirable as too little. People who have no friends and are ignored by others, or whose phones are out of order, or who are lost in the woods or placed in solitary confinement suffer from too much privacy. Repressive laws prohibiting certain forms of free expression also enforce more privacy than we may want. Thus, we do not merely value privacy in itself we also value control over how much access others have. Privacy is not unique in this regard; we value food, but also value control over what and when we eat; we value travel, but again want to control where we go and when.[17]

By and large we control access to private information by giving or withholding moral permission to have access, just as we recognize an obligation not to invade the privacy of others without their permission (and feel guilty if we do). But to have moral control over the obligations of others in this manner is to have a right.[18] Thus, it is wholly appropriate to speak of a right to privacy where we speak of controlling access in this matter.

The third consideration grows out of the previous one and is based on the principle of respect for persons. To respect a person as a moral agent is to behave in ways which take account of his or her fundamental interests as an autonomous agent. We have already seen that the development of autonomous individuals requires privacy. Thus, one of the ways in which we can fail to show moral respect for a person is by violating that person's privacy. Granted that we have a right to be treated with moral respect as persons, we have a right to have our privacy respected.

---

[17] It would be a mistake, however, to identify privacy with control of access to information, as some philosophers have done. This is clear from the fact that a person on a desert island has privacy but no control over it, while a person who raises his voice unnecessarily in a restaurant or has window shades yet elects to leave them up and parade in front of the windows in his pajamas has control but not privacy.

[18] Some philosophers have gone so far as to analyze rights in terms of this sort of control. While there may be rights which cannot be controlled by the right holder (e.g., the right which children have to an education), such control is typical of most of our important rights. For a control theory of rights, see H. L. A. Hart, "Are There Any Natural Rights?" in *Rights*, ed. David Lyons (Belmont, Calif.: Wadsworth, 1979): 125–48.

One of the mechanisms which we have developed to protect our privacy depends on this sort of respect. Occasionally people lock doors to rooms they are in or lock away particularly important documents, but this way of preserving privacy seems the exception rather than the rule. More often we simply rely on others' moral respect for our privacy to keep our privacy intact. We presume, usually correctly, that others will not snoop in our (open) correspondence, eavesdrop on our conversations in restaurants, or peer through our unshaded windows.

The fourth consideration is that fundamental interests often spawn rights. Thus, our fundamental interest in liberty has arguably given rise to a number of rights, such as property rights, contract rights, and the right to try to become the kind of person one wants to be. Our fundamental interest in health and well-being has given rise to claims for rights such as the right not to be killed and even a right to adequate medical care. Those who find such arguments persuasive have good reason to believe that there are various privacy rights, since we have a fundamental interest in privacy. If we deny there are privacy rights, it would be difficult to maintain that these other rights exist.

THE SCOPE OF PERSONAL PRIVACY RIGHTS

We have seen that each of us not only has a fundamental interest in controlling personal information, but also has a right to control such information.[19] Now we turn to the difficult issue of the scope of the right to privacy.

At first glance it seems clear that not all personal information about us is covered. If I tell someone the details of Jones's medical examination, Jones may well be upset and is certainly entitled to complain. If, on the other hand, I tell someone that Jones is tall, he cannot complain that I have violated his right to privacy. Nor is he apt to want to keep this information private. In fact, people often spend time and money on their appearance, on personal grooming, for instance, precisely because they believe their appearance will be

---

[19] We use the term *personal information* to refer to all information about a person and not merely to information about a person which is considered private. We use the term in this broad manner to avoid begging the question in attempting to determine what personal information is private.

noticed—and hope it will be appreciated—even by strangers. All of us value a certain amount of publicity along with a certain amount of privacy.

Is there a reasonable principle that can be used to distinguish private personal information from other personal information which is not within the scope of an individual's right to privacy? One obvious candidate is the principle that "private information" includes only that personal information whose publication would harm or disadvantage the person the information is about. This principle seems plausible, because one reason for thinking there is a right to privacy is that people would be harmed or disadvantaged without privacy. Moreover, it seems to give clear and fairly permissive guidelines for when intrusions into privacy may be justified for reasons of public health. How could anyone object to their HIV status being made known to others if no harm or disadvantage would result from it?

There are several objections to this principle. The first lies in the difficulty of objectively determining what will be harmful or disadvantageous for someone. Who is to make such a difficult and important determination? Few of us are willing to let others make these determinations for us, especially since we ourselves may be the only ones in positions to know that certain information may prove harmful. Mothers who are tempted to read their daughters' diaries can hardly anticipate the harms that may result to the daughters, precisely because they are ignorant of what damaging information the diary may contain. Similarly, given the stigma associated with HIV infection, it is difficult for anyone to know with assurance what harms may result if someone's HIV status becomes known.

Even beyond this objection, however, there seem to be counterexamples. People who read others' diaries violate privacy rights even if they discover nothing harmful while snooping and even if there is no chance that the writers will learn of their snooping. Peeping Toms similarly violate privacy rights even if they observe nothing that could be used against their victims and even if their victims never learn they have been observed. Similarly, physicians have traditionally recognized that they would violate a patient's privacy rights if the confidentiality of medical records was breached, even if no harm came to the patient as a result.

As a final objection to this principle, consider the variations which surround what is regarded as private. First, there are radical cultural differences. Western women do not regard the appearance of their faces as a private matter, but in Arab countries, where women wear chadors, it is a highly private matter.[20] Moreover, within a single culture, what is a private personal matter may vary from context to context. If one neighbor tells another about how much or how little you mow your lawn, it does not seem to be a private matter. If, however, a person introducing you on a radio talk show told the audience the same information, the announcer might be divulging a private matter. Finally, some of us are more secretive than others about all sorts of personal matters — financial and romantic matters, for example.

It might be thought that such problems can be avoided by specifying the scope of privacy in terms of what a reasonable person would find harmful or offensive. As we will see in Chapter 4, this is the way in which several privacy torts have been specified. While this principle may suffice for instructing a jury, however, it leaves much to be desired as a philosophical principle. An initial problem, of course, is that it is not always clear what the reasonable person would find offensive or harmful. More serious, however, is that the principle begs the question. On the suggested principle we are to determine the scope of privacy on the basis of what a reasonable person would find harmful or offensive. This assumes that we can determine whether a person is reasonable independently of what he or she finds harmful, but this cannot be done. Whether a person is reasonable depends in part on what that person finds harmful.

In light of these difficulties, we propose that the scope of the right to informational privacy includes all personal information — that is, all of the information about that person. We hasten to qualify this in three ways, however. The first qualification is that, as Judith Jarvis Thomson notes, we do not have a right that entails personal information about ourselves not be known by others.[21] Rather, we have a right that entails the information not be obtained

---

[20] This example is given by Judith Jarvis Thomson in "The Right to Privacy," in *Rights, Restitution, and Risk: Essays in Moral Theory* (Cambridge, Mass.: Harvard University Press, 1986), 125.

[21] Ibid., 128.

in certain ways or used in certain ways.[22] In particular, we violate a person's informational right to privacy by thwarting that person's reasonable attempts to keep the information private. (An analysis of exactly what activities constitute a violation of the right to privacy is beyond the scope of this chapter.)

The second qualification is that there are many situations in which virtually no one stands on the right because it would be too inconvenient, too costly, or provide no benefits. Qualified in this manner, the view defended here enables us to distinguish three categories which need to be distinguished: (1) areas which are clearly regarded as private, (2) areas which almost no one bothers to keep private, and (3) areas which quite a few people choose to keep private and quite a few do not. The first category consists of information which people generally regard as private. When we speak of private information in general, we mean the sort of information which most persons generally want to keep private most of the time. A person's medical or financial records or the specifics of his or her sex life typically fall into this category. The second category consists of information which people typically do not attempt to keep private. Information about occupation, height, eye color, or the make of the car one drives typically are rarely private for any of us, since keeping these private ordinarily would be too costly and provide no benefits. Nevertheless, if for some reason a person takes steps to keep his or her eye color private, he or she would have a right to do so. Moreover, we would violate his or her right to privacy by thwarting those steps in order to learn the person's eye color. Third, there is information about which people routinely differ. People may or may not want to keep their political affiliation, sexual orientation, or charitable contributions private. Again, on our view, people have a right to keep such information private if they choose to do so.

Accommodation of such personal idiosyncrasies is at the heart of the liberal tradition and implicit in the distinction between the "public sphere" within which we are subject to governmental regulation and the "private sphere" within which we each have the liberty to act (and keep things private) as we will. Just as there is a moral presumption of liberty within the sphere of personal activ-

---

[22] Ibid., 128–30.

ity, so there is, we suggest, a moral presumption of a right to privacy. This right to privacy is the right to *control* information about ourselves—to keep it secret *if* we wish to do so. Decisions about how to control personal information will depend on many things, including where or to whom the information might be revealed. Often we will confide information to close friends that we would like to keep from others. This is only one of many possibilities, however. We may hope to keep information from friends which is a matter of public record (e.g., age or a criminal record) and we may hope the press refrains from revealing some of what we do in our personal lives but which we nevertheless do "in public."

The third qualification is that this right to privacy is only a prima facie right, in that it can be overridden by stronger countervailing moral considerations. If someone needs to know information about you in order to prevent disastrous harm to others, for instance, your right to privacy regarding that information may be overridden.[23] The force of speaking of a right to privacy is not to say it is absolute, but only to say there is a strong moral presumption in favor of privacy. The strength of that presumption is perhaps illuminated by seeing how seriously it has been taken by the law. As we shall see, fundamental interests generate rights which get taken seriously enough to require heightened judicial scrutiny. We turn now to a consideration of the legal protection of privacy.

---

[23] A full treatment of such issues as what constitutes a harm and what principles distinguish the public and private spheres is beyond the scope of this chapter. The inquisitive reader is referred to Joel Feinberg's trilogy, *Harm to Others*, *Offense to Others*, and *Harm to Self* (Oxford: Oxford University Press, 1984, 1985, and 1986) and to *Public and Private in Social Life*.

4
Relevant Aspects of Privacy Law

INTRODUCTION

The extent to which we value privacy is reflected in our legal system. In constitutional law, for instance, the Fourth Amendment's protection against unreasonable searches and seizures has been held by the Supreme Court to protect individual privacy against certain kinds of governmental intrusion.[1] The Supreme Court has also found constitutional support for several fundamental privacy rights in the areas of marriage[2] and procreation.[3] The privacy of data in the hands of the federal government is protected by the Privacy Act of 1974.[4] Even the Freedom of Information Act, which was written to give people access to data held by the federal government, has important exceptions to protect privacy.[5] State law also offers substantial protection of privacy. Several states have passed data privacy acts analogous to the federal privacy act.[6] In addition, various torts based on privacy have developed. These include torts based on intrusion into

---

[1] *Katz v. U.S.*, 389 U.S. 347, 350–52 (1967). *Katz* held that what a person said in a public telephone booth was protected by the Fourth Amendment because of the expectation of privacy. *Katz* does not, however, create a general right of privacy in the sense of a general right to be left alone.

[2] *Loving v. Virginia*, 388 U.S. 1, 12 (1967).

[3] *Griswold v. Connecticut* 381 U.S. 479 (1965); *Roe v. Wade,* 410 U.S. 113 (1973).

[4] 5 U.S.C. §552(a).

[5] 5 U.S.C. §552.

[6] See, for instance, New York's Personal Privacy Protection Law, New York Public Officials Code, §91 et seq.

solitude, publication of private data, appropriation of name or likeness for commercial purposes, and publications which place a person in a false light. All in all, the legal edifice of privacy law amounts
to a massive and intricate structure.

This chapter constitutes a general introduction to privacy law
as it applies to mandatory HIV testing. Specific legal issues regarding HIV testing will be dealt with in more detail as they arise in Part
Two. However, giving just a general account of the application of
privacy law to HIV testing is no easy task, since privacy law did not
develop for the most part to deal with epidemics, and so many questions remain unanswered. The great triumphs of privacy law were
preceded by advances in public health (e.g., sewer systems, vaccines, penicillin, and other antibiotics) that significantly reduced the
threat of epidemics. Diseases (e.g., venereal disease) that continued
to spread could at least be cured. Yet, however difficult it is to apply
privacy law to HIV testing, it is worth the attempt.

First, there are theoretical insights to be gained. Privacy law, as
we shall see, reflects our moral views and applies them to concrete
problems. Also, application of privacy law often depends on our
moral views. Thus, a study of privacy law yields moral insights
into privacy, and a study of moral issues concerning privacy facilitates legal analysis. In this way the relationship between privacy
law and the morality of privacy is synergistic rather than parasitic.
An understanding of both is enhanced by the study of either. There
are practical consequences as well. The Constitution, with its incrus-
tation of court opinions, sets limits on the types of statutes and regulations which can be passed. In this way, the Constitution limits
public policy planning in dealing with HIV infection. Also, statutes
already in place set limits on the policies which individuals and private corporations can adopt.

We will consider various legal protections of privacy which may
be relevant to HIV testing. The protections fall into three main groups:
(1) constitutional protections, (2) protections of privacy based on
federal and state statutes and local ordinances, and (3) privacy protections within tort law. We turn first to constitutional protections
of privacy.

At the outset it needs to be noted that constitutional protections
are limited. Insofar as the Constitution provides for a right of privacy, it protects individuals only from federal and state actions which

interfere with the protected privacy.[7] Generally speaking, constitutional rights protect citizens only from state actions, not from transgressions by private citizens or by private corporations; this is true of privacy as well.[8] Several amendments have been used by the courts to fashion a right of privacy. Privacy has been grounded by various Supreme Court justices in the First Amendment, the Fourth Amendment, the Ninth Amendment, and the Due Process Clauses of the Fifth and Fourteenth Amendments. The most important of these are the Fourth Amendment and the Due Process Clauses of the Fifth and Fourteenth Amendments.

THE FOURTH AMENDMENT AND MANDATORY TESTING

Nowhere does the Constitution explicitly mention privacy. As close as the Constitution comes to an explicit statement of protection of privacy is the Fourth Amendment, which protects persons against unreasonable searches and seizures.[9] The Fourth Amendment states, "The right of the people to be secure in their persons, houses, papers, and effects, against unreasonable searches and seizures, shall not be violated, and no Warrants shall issue, but upon probable cause, supported by Oath or affirmation, and particularly describing the place to be searched, and the persons or things to be seized." Until the passage of the Fourteenth Amendment after the Civil War, the Fourth Amendment limited the actions of the federal government, but it

---

[7] As we shall see, there are in fact a number of different discrete privacy rights protected by the Constitution under current Supreme Court interpretation.

[8] *State action* is a technical legal term. It applies to all laws and regulations passed by the federal government as well as the states. State action also includes ordinances and regulations passed by subunits of states, such as cities, towns, state hospitals, prisons, public schools, and state universities. Finally, state action includes the actions of individual state and federal officials acting or purporting to act in their official capacity.

[9] Surprisingly little has been written about whether HIV testing raises Fourth Amendment issues. Several writers mention the issue but do not explore it. Patricia Wagner, for instance, notes that HIV testing within prisons may violate the Fourth Amendment rights of prisoners. See "AIDS and the Criminal Justice System," in *AIDS and the Law*, ed. William H. L. Dornette (New York: John Wiley & Sons, 1987), 187–88.

did not apply to actions by state governments. The Fourth Amendment has now been interpreted to apply to the states, however, as one of the fundamental rights protected by the Due Process Clause of the Fourteenth Amendment.[10]

The first question which must be asked is whether HIV testing mandated by the government constitutes a search or seizure under the Fourth Amendment. The language of the Fourth Amendment itself seems to indicate that it does. The amendment provides that "people are to be secure in their persons . . . against unreasonable searches and seizures." Blood tests used to determine otherwise hidden facts about a person could plausibly be construed as a seizure of blood and a search of the person.

Of course, constitutional interpretation requires that we look not merely at the language of the Constitution but also at court cases which have previously interpreted the Constitution. In a Warren Court case, *Schmerber v. California*, the Supreme Court held, in part, that taking blood samples for purposes of determining alcohol content is a search under the Fourth Amendment.[11] Although *Schmerber* was a criminal case involving the gathering of evidence, it is arguable that the same principle applies in the case of taking blood for the purpose of determining whether a person has HIV antibodies. This analogy is strengthened by Supreme Court holdings to the effect that the Fourth Amendment protects the privacy of individuals from unreasonable searches and seizures even when they are not the subject of criminal investigation.[12]

Apart from specific holdings, it can be argued that mandatory HIV testing constitutes a search under the Fourth Amendment on the basis of principles developed by the Supreme Court to determine what constitutes a search. The main principle used to determine whether an action constitutes a search under the Fourth Amendment is whether the individual had a reasonable expectation of privacy concerning that which was inspected.[13] Certainly there is a

---

[10] *Wolf v. Colorado*, 238 U.S. 25, 27–28 (1949).

[11] *Schmerber v. California*, 384 U.S. 757, 767 (1966). See also *McDonell v. Hunter*, 612 F.Supp. 1122, 1127 (D.C. Iowa 1985) and *U.S. v. Granger*, 596 F.Supp. 665, 667 (D.C. Wis. 1984).

[12] *Michigan v. Tyler*, 436 U.S. 499, 504–5 (1978); *Camara v. Municipal Court*, 387 U.S. 523, 530–31 (1967); *McDonell*, 612 F.Supp. at 1127.

[13] *Katz*, 389 U.S. at 351–53.

tremendous expectation of privacy concerning those features of one's blood which would indicate the presence of a potentially life threatening condition. As scientific research shows an increasingly strong correlation between HIV seropositivity and later progression to full-blown AIDS, the expectation of privacy regarding whether one is HIV infected becomes increasingly great. Surely the expectation of privacy is sufficiently great that mandatory HIV tests are searches under the Fourth Amendment.

Once it is determined that an activity constitutes a search under the Fourth Amendment, it must then be determined whether the search is reasonable. The Fourth Amendment does not forbid all searches; it forbids all unreasonable searches.[14] It is not clear how this standard is to be applied to mandatory HIV testing, however. The problem is that case law concerning the Fourth Amendment did not evolve to take account of infectious diseases. The majority of Fourth Amendment cases concern searches and seizures in connection with criminal investigations, although a minority of cases concern administrative searches in connection with various health and safety regulations.

The Supreme Court has expressed a strong preference that searches be conducted pursuant to a warrant.[15] Warrants are to be issued by a neutral and detached judge or magistrate upon a showing of probable cause.[16] In the case of noncriminal administrative searches such as those carried out by health and fire inspectors, the warrant requirements are fairly relaxed. In *Camara v. Municipal Court*, for instance, the Supreme Court held that the probable cause necessary to obtain a warrant to search a particular dwelling exists if "reasonable legislative or administrative standards for conducting an area inspection are satisfied with respect to" the dwelling.[17] Specific knowledge about conditions within the dwelling is not required.

Such relaxed standards for the granting of search warrants would probably not apply in the case of HIV testing, however. In *Camara* the court reasoned that relaxed standards were appropriate in part because the health inspections in question had a long history of

---

[14] *Terry v. Ohio*, 392 U.S. 1, 9 (1968).
[15] *U.S. v. Ventresca*, 380 U.S. 102, 105–6 (1965).
[16] *Coolidge v. New Hampshire*, 403 U.S. 443 (1971).
[17] *Camara*, 387 U.S. at 538.

judicial and public acceptance and were not personal in nature.[18] This would not be true in the case of mandatory testing, which is, of course, highly personal.

Whatever the appropriate standard for granting a warrant, it seems clear that search warrants or court orders would be required in the case of mandatory HIV tests whenever possible. There are cases in which it would be practicable to seek a warrant for conducting a mandatory HIV test. Such a circumstance could arise, for instance, in those cases in which a rapist claimed that he had AIDS. It could also arise in certain needle stick cases. (Although these are cases in which it would make sense to seek a warrant or court order, whether a warrant should be granted would, of course, depend on the facts of the individual case.) Such warrants would not be practicable, however, where mandatory HIV tests are used as mass screening devices. Such searches would have to be accomplished without a warrant.

The general principle is that warrantless searches are per se unreasonable unless they fall within one of the narrowly defined exceptions.[19] Because of the previous development of Fourth Amendment law, all of the exceptions have arisen within the context of criminal law and administrative searches. The exceptions include searches incident to arrest,[20] searches of motor vehicles under exigent circumstances,[21] inventory searches of automobiles impounded by the police,[22] pat-down searches of persons stopped by police where the police officer observes conduct which reasonably leads to the conclusion that the person stopped is armed,[23] and administrative searches of heavily regulated businesses.[24]

Although there are no clear-cut exceptions dealing with testing for medical purposes, the most closely analogous exception is the warrantless administrative search. In *Shoemaker v. Handel* a federal appeals court held that random, warrantless urine tests of jockeys

---

[18] *Camara,* 387 U.S. at 537.

[19] *Mincey v. Arizona,* 437 U.S. 385, 390 (1978); *Tyler,* 436 U.S. at 505; *Coolidge,* 403 U.S. at 454–55.

[20] *Chimel v. California,* 395 U.S. 752 (1969).

[21] *Chambers v. Maroney,* 399 U.S. 42 (1970); *Carroll v. U.S.,* 267 U.S. 132 (1925).

[22] *South Dakota v. Opperman,* 428 U.S. 364 (1976).

[23] *Terry,* 392 U.S. at 30–31.

[24] *U.S. v. Biswell,* 406 U.S. 311 (1972).

to determine whether they had been taking drugs did not violate their Fourth Amendment rights.[25] The court noted that there were two requirements for justifying warrantless administrative searches. "First, there must be a strong state interest in conducting an unannounced search. . . . Second, the pervasive regulation of the industry must have reduced the justifiable privacy expectation of the subject of the search."[26] The court then noted that horse racing was a heavily regulated industry and that the state had a strong interest in conducting unannounced searches.

Such a standard might be used to justify some mandatory HIV testing. The state might, for instance, have a strong interest in testing prostitutes, and in those places where prostitution is legal, it is a heavily regulated business with little expectation of privacy as far as health testing is concerned. The cases of marriage license applicants and people admitted to a hospital are questionable, however. People admitted to a hospital, for instance, have a high degree of expectation of control over what medical procedures will be performed on them. Tort law has developed so that medical procedures which are administered without the consent of the person tested may constitute battery. Nonetheless, doctor-patient relationships are heavily regulated, and patients routinely sign consent forms which give consent to whatever tests the medical staff deem necessary. Similarly, while marriage license applicants generally have high expectations of privacy concerning their relationship, many states have required routine tests for venereal diseases. It is simply not clear how the courts would treat laws requiring HIV testing in such cases. The Illinois statute requiring the HIV testing of marriage license applicants, for instance, has not been tested in the courts.

Given the limits of the current exceptions to the general rule that searches are not to be conducted without a warrant, it might be thought that a new exception should be recognized in the case of mandatory HIV testing. None of the reasons for setting up the various exceptions exist in the case of HIV testing, however. Unlike blood tests for alcohol and automobile searches, there are no exigent circumstances. People who are HIV seropositive stay HIV seropositive. Unlike the exception for heavily regulated businesses,

---

[25] *Shoemaker v. Handel,* 795 F.2d 1136, 1142 (3rd Cir. 1986).
[26] *Shoemaker,* 795 F.2d at 1142, citing *Donovan v. Dewey,* 452 U.S. 594, 600 (1981).

there is typically no clearly reduced expectation of privacy. Unlike searches incident to arrest, there is typically no danger to officials or others who deal with an individual infected with HIV.

In summary, mandatory HIV testing by the government constitutes a search under the Fourth Amendment. When possible, a warrant must be obtained. In a few cases in which a warrant cannot be obtained, a warrantless search may possibly be justified under the administrative search exception which concerns heavily regulated businesses. Current principles adopted by the Supreme Court, however, do not justify carving out a new exception for health testing in general or for HIV testing in particular.

THE DUE PROCESS CLAUSE OF THE FOURTEENTH AMENDMENT AND MANDATORY TESTING

The Due Process Clause of the Fourteenth Amendment provides that no state shall "deprive any person of life, liberty, or property, without due process of law."[27] A great many laws, perhaps most, limit liberty or deprive people of property without providing for any sort of judicial process or hearing. Such laws may be held unconstitutional under the Due Process Clause unless they meet the appropriate standard of justification. Thus, any restriction of liberty by the state requires justification. What standard must be met by the state to justify the restriction depends on the type of restriction.

Some liberties such as voting, the right to travel, and certain forms of privacy have been declared by the Supreme Court to be *fundamental liberties* or *fundamental rights*. When a law which restricts fundamental rights or liberties is challenged under the Due Process Clause, the courts subject the law to *strict scrutiny*. In order to pass constitutional muster, a law subjected to strict scrutiny must be shown to be *necessary for a compelling state interest*.[28] In addition, the

---

[27] Although the Due Process Clause of the Fourteenth Amendment is directed to the states, there is also a Due Process Clause in the Fifth Amendment which applies to the federal government. Most of what we say about the Due Process Clause of the Fourteenth Amendment also applies to the Due Process Clause of the Fifth Amendment.

[28] In the case of the Equal Protection Clause of the Fourteenth Amendment, which provides that no state shall deprive any citizen of the equal protection of the laws, strict scrutiny is applied in the case of laws which discriminate on the basis of suspect classifications such as race, national origin, and alienage.

law must be drawn with precision so as to be the least restrictive alternative. Strict scrutiny is the most difficult standard for a law to meet, and most laws subjected to strict scrutiny in the context of court challenges are declared to be unconstitutional.

Although a few forms of mandatory HIV testing would be justified on this standard, many would not. Consider, for instance, mandatory tests to determine the HIV status of people planning to donate sperm or organs. Certainly there is a compelling state interest in having donated sperm and organs free of the AIDS virus. Also, at the present time some form of HIV testing is necessary to accomplish this goal. If stringent safeguards of confidentiality are used, the tests may also be the least restrictive means available. Such tests contrast sharply with mandatory tests for people admitted to hospitals and for Job Corps applicants. While the United States has a compelling state interest in limiting the spread of AIDS, it is by no means clear that mandatory tests in such cases as these are necessary. In fact, we argue in Chapter 9 that they are not necessary. It follows that if strict scrutiny is applied, mandatory testing of people admitted to hospitals and of Job Corps applicants is unconstitutional.

Strict scrutiny contrasts with *minimal scrutiny*. Laws subject to minimal scrutiny need only be *rationally related to a valid state interest*. If the legislative history does not indicate a rationale for a statute which has been challenged, the court will conjure up such a reason whenever possible. The relevant reasons need not be the reasons for which the law was actually passed. In fact, they need not be convincing or even good reasons. Only if there is virtually no conceivable rationale for the law will the court find that the law is not reasonably related to a state goal. While applying the minimal scrutiny test, the court does not sit as a super legislature to second guess legislative bodies. The federal government has a valid state interest in legislation passed so long as the legislation is within the scope of the powers explicitly conferred by the United States Constitution.[29] In the case of states, there is a valid state interest in the use of

---

[29] Such powers include the powers given to Congress under Article I, Section 8. Specific examples are the powers to regulate commerce, to coin money, and to declare war. It must be remembered, however, that even legislation passed within the scope of such powers may be unconstitutional because it is contrary to one of the amendments.

state power to promote the welfare of its residents (including their morals, safety, and health).[30] Thus, for purposes of the Due Process Clause, laws which do not encroach on fundamental rights are subject to minimal scrutiny, and laws subjected to minimal scrutiny are usually upheld.[31]

A number of laws providing for mandatory HIV testing which would not be upheld on strict scrutiny would probably pass the test of minimal scrutiny. Insofar as the rationale for mandatory antibody testing would be to limit the spread of HIV infection and therefore the spread of AIDS, there would certainly be a valid state interest. More problematic would be the issue of whether the mandatory testing is reasonably related to the spread of HIV infection. While it is obvious that some forms of HIV testing would be constitutional under minimal scrutiny, there may be some forms of mandatory testing so wholly unjustified that they arguably would not be constitutional even under minimal scrutiny (because they would not be rationally related to preventing the spread of HIV infection). In Chapter 9 we argue that a number of the federal programs mandating HIV testing are in fact wholly without justification. It is at least arguable that such programs are unconstitutional, but it is not clear what the Supreme Court would eventually hold. It makes a difference, then, whether laws and regulations requiring HIV testing are subject to strict scrutiny or to minimal scrutiny. For purposes of the Due Process Clause, this question turns on whether any particular HIV testing policy violates a fundamental right protected by the Consti-

---

[30] Such power, called state police power, is explicitly granted to the states by the Tenth Amendment to the United States Constitution which states that

the powers not delegated to the United States [the federal government] by the Constitution, nor prohibited by it to the States, are reserved to the States respectively, or to the people.

[31] For certain Equal Protection Clause cases, an intermediate form of scrutiny has also been developed to deal with laws which discriminate on the basis of certain other classifications, such as gender. The test for intermediate scrutiny is that the law at issue must be significantly related to an important state interest. See, for instance, *Craig v. Boren*, 429 U.S. 190, 197 (1976). Under the Equal Protection Clause, laws which do not discriminate on the basis of suspect classifications or on the basis of specific classifications set aside by the court for intermediate scrutiny are subjected to the rational basis test.

tution. But how do we know whether a particular law or regulation mandating testing violates a fundamental right?

In the case of mandatory testing policies, the obvious key to the issue of fundamental rights is privacy. One of the first Supreme Court cases articulating a right to liberty privacy is *Griswold v. Connecticut*, in which the court declared as unconstitutional a Connecticut law making the sale of birth control devices and prescriptions illegal.[32] Different justices offered different justifications for the constitutional right to privacy. Justice Douglas, who wrote the opinion, found the right to privacy presupposed by various amendments, including the First, Third, Fourth, and Fifth. In a concurring opinion, Justice Goldberg, joined by Justices Warren and Brennan, used the Ninth Amendment to argue that privacy was one of the fundamental rights protected by the Fourteenth Amendment Due Process Clause. The Ninth Amendment states that "the enumeration in the Constitution, of certain rights, shall not be construed to deny or disparage others retained by the people." Thus, according to Goldberg, the Ninth Amendment enables us to locate rights protected by the Due Process Clause which are not explicitly stated in the Constitution. Justices Harlan and White, in separate concurrences, also argued that privacy was a fundamental right protected by the Fourteenth Amendment Due Process Clause.

It is not perfectly clear from *Griswold* alone just how broad a privacy right had been carved out. Given the expansive language of Justice Douglas, for instance, it is arguable that the privacy right protected by *Griswold* is a general right to be left alone by the state, or at least broad enough to cover sexual and reproductive matters generally. Arguable or not, this viewpoint has not prevailed. In a recent Supreme Court case, *Bowers v. Hardwick*, the Supreme Court declared that acts of sodomy by homosexuals do not fall within the area of privacy protected by the Constitution.[33] What is more interesting from the point of view of our investigation is that the Court in *Bowers* limited previous cases concerned with privacy to rather narrow areas of privacy. Thus, *Griswold* was declared to apply to privacy in the matter of conception. Other areas of privacy concern child rearing and education, family relationships, and marriage. The

---

[32] *Griswold*, 381 U.S. at 485.

[33] *Bowers v. Hardwick,* 478 U.S. 186, *reh. den.* 478 U.S. 1039 (1986).

court found no general right to be let alone.[34] Nor has the Supreme Court carved out an area of privacy that specifically concerns mandatory medical tests to determine one's state of health.

Even though the Supreme Court has not previously held that there is an area of privacy which protects individuals from intrusive medical tests, it is arguable that there is in fact such a fundamental right covered by the Due Process Clause. In determining whether a putative right is in fact a fundamental right covered by the Due Process Clause, the Supreme Court has applied either or both of two tests. According to the first test, fundamental rights are those that are "implicit in the concept of ordered liberty," such that "neither liberty nor justice would exist if [the fundamental rights] were sacrificed."[35] According to the second test, fundamental rights are those that are "deeply rooted in this Nation's history and tradition."[36] It is unfortunate that there are two such different tests, since they may produce different results. The first test is essentially a philosophical test and concerns what *ought* to happen. The second test is essentially an historical test and concerns what *has* happened. The historical test is likely to yield more conservative results than the philosophical test, because it is tied to what has already happened. It is, of course, one of the tragedies of the human condition that the insights of moral philosophy are not always actualized in history.

Both tests sound sufficiently grand to do the job, but in fact it is not clear how either should be applied to the task at hand. Consider first the historical test. On the one hand, allowing people control over what medical tests are conducted on them certainly is deeply rooted in our nation's history and tradition. This is reflected in the tort of battery. On the other hand, throughout the twentieth century various states have required tests for venereal disease as a pre-

---

[34] *Bowers*, 106 S.Ct. at 2843. For cases dealing with privacy in the area of child rearing and education, see *Pierce v. Society of Sisters*, 268 U.S. 510 (1925) and *Meyer v. Nebraska*, 262 U.S. 390 (1923); for a privacy case concerning family relationships, see *Prince v. Massachusetts*, 321 U.S. 158 (1944); for cases dealing with privacy concerning marriage, see *Zablocki v. Redhail*, 434 U.S. 374 (1978) and *Loving v. Virginia*, 388 U.S. 479 (1965).

[35] *Bowers*, 106 S.Ct. at 2844, quoting *Palko v. Connecticut*, 302 U.S. 319 (1937).

[36] *Bowers*, 106 S.Ct. at 2844, quoting *Moore v. East Cleveland*, 431 U.S. 494 (1977).

requisite to the granting of a marriage license. In addition, physicals have long been routinely required for a variety of occupations and for insurance purposes.

How to apply the second test is not perfectly clear either. What is needed is a philosophical analysis to determine which of our rights are most fundamental. We argued in Chapter 3 that control over what medical tests one is subjected to is an integral part of control over one's body, and that this is a fundamental value which gives rise to a right. It is at least arguable on this basis that the sort of privacy at stake in the issue of mandatory HIV testing is the sort of fundamental right which passes the Supreme Court test. However, given recent Supreme Court holdings (e.g., *Bowers*), it is far from clear whether the current Supreme Court would accept such an argument.

STATUTORY PROTECTIONS

For those seeking concrete legal answers to questions concerning HIV testing and privacy, constitutional law is not completely satisfying. As often as not, we are faced with various sorts of vague balancing tests in which the individual's interest in privacy is balanced against the public's need to know. It is often unclear how any given court will weigh the items balanced. Statutory law is enticing in this regard, because of the promise of specificity. A satisfying statute will begin with definitions of various terms, state general principles, and give detailed exceptions to the principles (sometimes even including exceptions to the exceptions).

So far there are no federal privacy statutes dealing specifically with the release of AIDS information or HIV testing. There are, however, relevant statutes which can be applied. The Privacy Act of 1974 covers the release of data held by federal agencies.[37] The term *agency* as used in the Privacy Act is a technical term which includes executive departments, government corporations, government-controlled corporations, military departments, and independent regulatory agencies.[38] The Privacy Act provides that, with eleven exceptions, no agency shall release any information about an individual

---

[37] 5 U.S.C. §552a.
[38] For a complete definition of *agency* for purposes of 5 U.S.C. §552a, see 5 U.S.C. §552(e).

which contains the means for identifying that individual without the individual's prior written consent.[39] The exceptions include such things as release of information to employees of the agency which maintains the record, release of information to another agency of the United States for a civil or criminal law enforcement activity, and release of information pursuant to a valid court order.

There are two exceptions which are of interest to those concerned with the privacy of medical data relating to AIDS. The fifth exception provides for the release of information to those who produce written assurance that the information will be used for statistical research so long as the information released does not identify specific individuals.[40] In the case of AIDS-related data, this means test results could be released to epidemiologists as long as they were unlinked. The Privacy Act should not, then, significantly interfere with the research of epidemiologists.

The most interesting exception, however, is the second exception, for that exception leads to a quagmire. The second exception provides for release of information as required by 5 U.S.C. Section 552 (the Freedom of Information Act). This may initially strike one concerned with privacy as alarming, since the Freedom of Information Act is designed to give the public broad access to government information. Indeed, the Freedom of Information Act has proven to be a boon for journalists, historians, political scientists and other fact hounds.

There is no need for undue concern, however, because the Freedom of Information Act itself has nine exceptions. The one which interests us is the sixth exception, which provides that the Freedom of Information Act does not apply to "personnel and medical files and similar files the disclosure of which would constitute a clearly unwarranted invasion of personal privacy."[41] The problem we now encounter is determining what counts as a clearly unwarranted invasion of personal privacy. As might be expected, there has been litigation on the issue. The courts have generally agreed that whether information is exempted by Section 552(b)(6) is to be determined by a balancing test in which the need to know is balanced against the interest in privacy. More specifically, four factors are to be weighed:

---

[39] 5 U.S.C. §552a(b).
[40] 5 U.S.C. §552(a)(5).
[41] 5 U.S.C. §552(b)(6).

(1) the plaintiff's interest in disclosure of the information sought, (2) the public interest in disclosure, (3) the degree of the invasion of personal privacy, and (4) whether there are alternative means of getting the information.[42]

For those who turn to statutes to find clarity and precision, this is not a satisfactory state of affairs. In spite of all of the detailed statutory language specifying what information can or cannot be given out, it ultimately comes down once again to a balancing test, and so it remains unclear how a court will decide. The statutory promise of specificity has not been fulfilled in the case of the Privacy Act of 1974 in spite of all the statutory clauses and exceptions. We will argue in Part Two, however, that while it may not be clear how the courts *will* decide such issues, it is clear how they *ought* to decide them in cases of medical information concerning AIDS, ARC, and HIV seropositivity. In such cases the individual's privacy interest in preserving anonymity typically outweighs the interest of the public and the interest of the person seeking the information.

In short, while there are no federal statutes which directly protect the privacy of HIV seropositives and persons with AIDS or ARC, the Privacy Act, coupled with the Freedom of Information Act, offers some protection in the case of AIDS-related information already in the hands of the federal government. These acts can be interpreted as protecting privacy in the sense of limiting the spread of private information. The federal statutory law does not, however, clearly protect the privacy of those who suffer from AIDS or who are HIV infected.

State law is more protective, at least in some states. Several states have adopted laws dealing directly with privacy issues related to HIV testing.[43] As of this writing (August 1988), the most detailed and comprehensive law is California's. California law protects the privacy of the individual inasmuch as it gives the individual significant control over whether he or she is tested (liberty privacy) and also control over resulting information once the test is taken (informational privacy). To protect liberty privacy, California law requires that, with few exceptions, persons shall not be tested for HIV antibodies

---

[42] *Minnis v. U.S. Department of Agriculture*, 737 F2d 784 (9th Cir. 1984); *Church of Scientology v. U.S. Dept. of Army*, 611 F2d 738 (9th Cir. 1979).

[43] See, for instance, California Health and Safety Code, §199.20 et seq.; 35 District of Columbia Code, § 221 et seq.; and Wisconsin Statutes, §§20.435, 103.15, 146.023 et seq., and 631.90.

without their written consent.[44] By themselves, such consent provisions protect against unconditional mandatory testing but not against conditional mandatory testing, that is, testing in which benefits such as insurance may be withheld unless one consents to an HIV test.

California law does, however, provide protection from conditional mandatory testing on the part of insurers and employers. It provides that the results of HIV tests may not be used "in any instance for the determination of insurability or suitability for employment."[45] This law undercuts the motivation of insurers and employers for requiring HIV tests, since the results cannot be used to determine insurability or employability. It does not, however, forbid all mandatory testing. The law does not prevent employers, for instance, from requiring such tests for reasons other than determining suitability for employment. This would be conditional mandatory testing, because of the consent requirement.

Once a person is tested, California law protects the confidentiality of the test results. It provides civil penalties, criminal penalties, and civil damages for the willful or negligent disclosure of HIV test results in a manner which identifies the person tested, unless the disclosure is provided for by one of the statutory exceptions.[46] Some of the exceptions seem unproblematic. For instance, the person tested may provide written authorization for the release of the test results.[47] Other exceptions are more problematic. Hospitals, for instance, are required to report to the Health Department and County Health Officer the identity of people who are confirmed "AIDS carriers."[48] Such names are placed on a donor deferral register so that further blood donations will not be accepted.[49] No record is kept which indicates why people are placed on the list, however. Thus, persons who are seropositive cannot be distinguished from others on the list, such as those who have had hepatitis B.[50]

Some exceptions are very problematic. Although California law generally provides that no person shall be compelled in any civil,

---

[44] California Health and Safety Code, §199.22.
[45] California Health and Safety Code, §199.21(f).
[46] California Health and Safety Code, §199.21.
[47] California Health and Safety Code, §§199.21(a) and 199.21(g).
[48] California Health and Safety Code, §§199.21(a) and 199.21(g).
[49] California Health and Safety Code, §1603.1(f).
[50] California Health and Safety Code, §1603.1(f).

criminal, or administrative proceedings to identify individuals who have been tested, the court may order the release of confidential research records concerning individuals who test seropositive if the court finds that (1) there is reasonable likelihood that the information sought will be evidence of substantial value in connection with criminal charges or investigation, (2) the information cannot be obtained in any other way, and (3) there is a showing of good cause for the release of such records.[51] Whether good cause exists is to be determined by balancing "the public interest and need for disclosure against the injury to the research subject and the harm to the research being undertaken."[52] Again, as with constitutional law and the federal Freedom of Information Act, we encounter a balancing test whose outcome will depend largely on the moral views of the court doing the balancing. While the privacy protections offered by the California Health and Safety Code are not airtight, they are far more extensive and far clearer than the federal privacy act.

Unlike California, most states do not have laws that deal explicitly with privacy concerning HIV testing. Such states may, however, have more general privacy acts which can be applied to antibody testing. One of the more comprehensive of such laws is New York's Personal Privacy Protection Act.[53] This act has a general provision governing the release of information which in many respects is parallel to provisions of the federal privacy act. There is a general rule that no agency may disclose any record or personal information unless one of a long list of exceptions is met.[54] Unlike the federal privacy act, however, New York's privacy act provides that medical records shall not be disclosed by agencies unless required by law.[55] This would protect the results of AIDS tests in the hands of government agencies. The Personal Privacy Protection Act speaks only to informational privacy, however, it does not speak to liberty privacy (control over whether or not one is tested). Nor does the act speak to the issue of testing information in private hands.

---

[51] California Health and Safety Code, §§199.20, 199.35(a), and 199.35(b).
[52] California Health and Safety Code, §199.35(a).
[53] New York Public Officers Law, §§91–99.
[54] New York Public Officers Law, §96(1).
[55] New York Public Officers Law, Section 96(2)(b).

CASE LAW

Where protection of privacy from nonstate interventions cannot be found in statutes, it can often be found in case law. William Prosser has distinguished four privacy torts based on the case law in various states: appropriation of name or likeness for commercial purposes, intrusion into solitude or seclusion, public disclosure of private facts, and placement of an individual in a false light.[56] Of the four torts, two are of interest to us. The first is intrusion into solitude or seclusion. In order to establish that this tort has been committed, the plaintiff must show that the defendant intentionally intruded into a private area, that the plaintiff was entitled to privacy, and that the intrusion would be objectionable to a reasonable person. It is arguable that running unauthorized tests, such as the HIV test, on blood legitimately taken for other purposes is an intrusion. It would, of course, also be highly offensive to a reasonable person, since it would provide knowledge of the most vital details of one's present health and in some cases allow inferences about one's intimate behavior.

Public disclosure of private facts is also a relevant tort. To establish this tort, the plaintiff must show that there was a public disclose of private facts and that such a disclosure would be objectionable to a reasonable person of ordinary sensibilities.[57] The information published must be private and not part of a public record and must not be information which the plaintiff has consented to have published.[58] As Keeton and Prosser note, the cases are split on whether the disclosure must be published to a sizable number of people.[59] In those jurisdictions in which disclosure must be published to a size-

---

[56] W. Page Keeton et al., *Keeton and Prosser on Torts* (St. Paul: West Publishing Company, 1984), sec. 117. See also *Restatement of the Law 2d Torts* (St. Paul: American Law Institute, 1977), Secs. 652A–652I. Torts are injuries not resulting from breaches of contract for which damages may be recovered in civil suits. Although privacy torts have developed primarily within the context of the common law, a few states have given statutory protection to one or more of the areas of privacy. Wisconsin, for instance, protects privacy in the sense of intrusion, appropriation, and publication. See Wisconsin Statutes, §859.50(2). New York also protects privacy in the sense of appropriation of name or likeness for commercial purposes. See New York Civil Rights Code, §50.

[57] See Keeton, *Torts*, 856–57. See also *Restatement*, sec. 652D.

[58] *Cox Broadcasting Corp. v. Cohn*, 420 U.S. 469, 494–95 (1975).

[59] Keeton, *Torts*, 856.

able number of people, the usefulness of this tort is severely limited for HIV seropositives and those who have AIDS or ARC. A person who is HIV seropositive or who has AIDS or ARC is most likely to be harmed by information given to a single person, such as an employer or landlord, or to a small group of persons. This could be enough to trigger severe discrimination. Yet, the publication may not be wide enough to meet the publication requirement of the tort. In those jurisdictions which do not require such extensive publication, however, the tort offers significant protection.

Again we see the way in which legal questions regarding privacy turn on moral issues. Whether a given invasion is an invasion of a private area turns on whether the individual has a legitimate expectation of privacy. The notion of legitimate expectation here is primarily moral rather than legal. Also, whether a given invasion of privacy would be objectionable to a reasonable person turns, of course, on one's notion of what is reasonable, and this turns on one's moral views.

CONCLUSION

It should be clear from even our brief consideration of various aspects of privacy law that the extent to which we as a society value privacy is amply reflected in our legal system. Privacy law ranges from sweeping constitutional principles to rather specific statutory provisions and case law. It should also be clear that in many areas privacy law cannot be applied to HIV testing without a consideration of moral issues. The application of privacy law frequently depends, for instance, on balancing the public interest in security against individual privacy rights. While this dependency on moral considerations is expected in constitutional law, it can also be seen in the application of some of the most important statutes which protect privacy. Although privacy law in its diverse manifestations does not give us concrete answers to all of our questions regarding HIV testing, it does give us answers to some questions. Furthermore, it can be used to focus the policy debate. In the following chapters we turn to a more detailed consideration of that debate and to various legal threats to privacy arising from the AIDS epidemic.

PART TWO

Specific Issues

5
AIDS Education and Voluntary Anonymous Testing

Since nearly all HIV transmission involves voluntary activities, it would be virtually eliminated if either all those who are already infected or all those who are uninfected would abstain from high-risk activities. Since these activities are characteristically private, however, it would be virtually impossible to coerce all members of either group into abstention. While coercive measures to prevent high-risk activities may be appropriate in isolated cases, such measures stand little chance of having a major impact on high-risk activity. The sexual and needle-sharing activities of one million people would be impossible to regulate.

In this chapter we explore two noncoercive AIDS prevention measures: AIDS education, and voluntary anonymous testing and counseling. We argue briefly that explicit AIDS education should be pursued with vigor, even if some find it offensive and an invasion of their privacy. We then argue that while voluntary anonymous testing will offer a significant benefit for some individuals and should therefore be available, it should not be expected to have a major impact on the rate of HIV transmission.

AIDS EDUCATION

Public health experts and organizations, among them Surgeon General Koop, the Centers for Disease Control, the National Academy of Sciences, the American College of Physicians, and the Presidential Commission on the Human Immunodeficiency Virus Epidemic, overwhelmingly agree that explicit AIDS education is presently the most promising and cost-effective strategy available for slowing the spread of HIV.[1] Teaching people how to avoid contracting any infectious disease is a classic public health strategy. With AIDS it seems particularly appropriate since most transmission involves particular activities individuals can choose to avoid. From the point of view of uninfected individuals concerned to avoid contracting AIDS, the message of AIDS education is essential, and one of the few bright bits of news in the entire AIDS story: we know how people can avoid being exposed to HIV. Making information readily accessible about who *is* at risk, the activities by which HIV is transmitted, and how these activities can be made safer will both benefit those individuals eager to avoid exposure and promote the preventative public health goal. Public understanding of who *is not* at risk will have the further benefit of combatting "AIDS panic," which can occur when people are irrationally fearful of catching AIDS from casual contact with people they think may be infected. This in turn could reduce discrimination stemming from those irrational fears of contagion.[2] The presidential AIDS commission stressed the extent of discrimination that has occurred in connection with HIV infection and the harm it has done, and it reported that "one of the primary causes of discriminatory responses to an individual with HIV infection is fear, based on ignorance or misinformation about the transmission of the virus."[3]

While there is no debate over the desirability of AIDS education, there is considerable disagreement over what its form and content should be. Unfortunately people seldom abandon risky behaviors — especially risky behavior associated with basic drives — simply upon being informed they are unsafe.[4] Experts in behavior change argue

---

[1] See Jane Aiken, "Education as Prevention," in *AIDS and the Law*, ed. Harlon Dalton, Scott Burris, and the Yale AIDS Law Project (New Haven: Yale University Press, 1987), 90–105, notes 1, 2, 4, 42. Throughout this discussion of AIDS education we are heavily indebted to Aiken's analysis.

[2] See, for example, Tom Stoddard, "The AIDS Crisis: What the ACLU Must Do to Guard against Civil Liberties Abuses," *Civil Liberties* (Fall 1985): 1.

[3] *Report of the Presidential Commission on the Human Immunodeficiency Virus Epidemic* (Washington, D.C.: U.S. Government Printing Office, 1988): 120.

[4] People may be at their most irrational when performing informal risk assessments. For a discussion of the problems involved in informal risk assessments, see Doug MacLean, "Risk and Consent: Philosophical

compellingly that AIDS education will be optimally effective in modifying the behavior of gays and IV drug abusers only if it is in explicit, perhaps colloquial language; nonjudgmental; perceived as embodying or at least as reflecting peer values and not as presenting warnings or prohibitions from outsiders; and targeted so that it actually reaches those for whom it is intended. Several studies have concluded, for instance, that materials which can "eroticize" certain safe sex practices have a much greater impact than materials that seem to forbid certain acts. One study remarks that messages about how to make gay sex practices safer "would be better presented in the language of sex than in the language of AIDS."[5] Others have pointed out that gays are not going to listen closely to messages that do not frankly acknowledge the existence of gays.[6] Surgeon General Koop's general mailing, "Understanding AIDS," must be faulted in this regard.

Unfortunately explicit AIDS education information prompts two objections from people who oppose frank and explicit public discussion of unsafe sexual or IV drug practices. Although these objections are often presented together, they are really quite distinct. According to the first, public officials must not promote such discussion, since doing so would amount to a societal endorsement of the activities under discussion and might even encourage more people to try them. The underlying notion here seems to be that to acknowledge the existence of certain practices is to legitimize them. These critics instead favor making abstinence and restraint the predominant messages of AIDS education. This view has had some powerful advocates, including some within the Reagan administration, who have been very effective in preventing wide dissemination of targeted explicit AIDS education.[7]

Issues for Centralized Decisions," in *Values at Risk*, ed. Doug MacLean (Totowa, N.J.: Rowman & Allanheld, 1986).

[5] Aiken, "Education as Prevention," 93, note 33. See also Gina Kolata, "Erotic Films in AIDS Study Cut Risky Behavior," *New York Times*, November 3, 1987, Midwest edition, sec. 3, p. 3.

[6] Frank Rhame, "More on 'Safe Sex'," *New England Journal of Medicine* 318 (1988): 1760–61.

[7] A brochure put together by the National Institute on Drug Abuse and geared to convey to drug users the dangers of sharing needles was held up by the Administration, and a White House aide said the federal

One thread of the debate here involves a factual dispute about whether a greater reduction in high-risk activity can be achieved by encouraging persons to abstain from drug use and nonmonogamous sex or by explicit information about how to make unsafe forms of these activities safer. Public health and other experts on behavior change are convinced that the latter will prove more effective.

A somewhat different thread of this objection to explicit AIDS education is that materials acknowledging the occurrence of certain activities implies approval of them. This is not true generally: Public service announcements encouraging the use of seat belts acknowledge the fact that accidents and careless driving occur but do not legitimize careless driving. They merely try to minimize the risks created by it.

However, there is some truth to the charge that optimally targeted, explicit AIDS education may appear to endorse certain activities of the groups they target. The reason for this is that persons engaging in unsafe activities are more apt to listen to AIDS prevention messages from people who seem to be supportive and to respect them — even from people they can identify with — than from people who appear judgmental. Ultimately opponents of targeted, explicit AIDS education must realize they simply cannot have it both ways. They must choose between using AIDS education as a platform for optimally effective messages for slowing the spread of HIV and using it as a platform for public moralizing. It is extraordinary that, when lives are at stake, persons in positions of influence and responsibility can ignore the actual consensus among behavior change experts and pretend that it is otherwise.[8]

---

government would release such information "over our collective dead bodies." Aiken, "Education as Prevention," 97.

[8] In the context of an October 1987 Senate debate on federal funding for AIDS education, Senator Weicker said he doubted the majority of sexually active young people would embrace abstinence even if that became the main message of AIDS education. Senator Helms responded, "I do not believe that. I think more of our young people than that. [Your remarks] are attacks on the majority of our young people." *Congressional Record*, 100th Cong., 1st sess., October 14, 1987, p. S14208. Secretary of Education William Bennett, who evidently shares Helms's optimism about changing the sexual mores of America's single teenagers, has provided an alternative pamphlet for parents and educators, *AIDS and the Education of Our Children: A Guide for Parents and Teachers*, which stresses

The second objection which has been brought against targeted, explicit AIDS education is that many people are offended by explicit public mention of certain activities. We believe there is some merit to this charge. Persons who prefer to ignore the risks involved in their unsafe practices will not seek out AIDS education; they will only get the message if it confronts them, and this will inevitably involve also exposing other people to frank discussion of things they find offensive. Freshmen arriving on college campuses may be handed "safe sex" brochures warning of the dangers of esoteric sexual practices they have never heard of, and families gathered around the television may have to endure condom ads.

Critics hold that these mentions and discussions constitute intolerable intrusions into privacy,[9] especially when they occur in the public media and are thrust unexpectedly upon people who may not in any way be at risk for AIDS and who certainly do not want to be confronted with graphic descriptions of how it is spread. These critics have succeeded in discouraging television networks from carrying condom ads and in blocking federal funds for explicit AIDS education.[10]

---

abstinence and restraint and mentions condoms briefly, only to say they are an unreliable way to prevent the spread of HIV infection. In the same spirit, the Indiana State Board of Education is required by a 1987 statute (SB 72) to provide only AIDS education

> stressing the moral aspects of abstinence from sexual activity in any literature that it distributes. . . . Such literature must state that the best way to avoid AIDS is for young people to refrain from sexual activity until . . . marriage.

See Lawrence Gostin and Andrew Ziegler, "A Review of AIDS-related Legislative and Regulatory Policy in the United States," *Law, Medicine and Health Care* 15 (Summer 1987): 7. For further discussion of this issue, see David Mayo, "The AIDS Education Debate," in *Biomedical Ethics Reviews: 1988 AIDS*, ed. James Humber and Robert Almeder (Crescent City, N.J.: Humana, forthcoming).

[9] Notice that this is yet a third kind of privacy, namely, freedom from unwanted exposure to information.

[10] Federal funding is currently available only for AIDS education materials which are approved by local review panels, which certify the materials would not be found offensive by reasonable persons. These panels must be composed of a reasonable cross section of the community and must *not* include members of target groups. This requirement virtually guarantees that direct and explicit materials will not be eligible for federal funding. The inhibiting effect of this requirement has been so great that

It is undeniable that targeted, explicit AIDS education may offend some of the people it reaches. Where possible, its offensiveness should be minimized—by using gay publications or AIDS hotlines, for instance, so that only those who want very explicit information will receive it. However, these and other strategies to limit the offensiveness of AIDS education by limiting its distribution will also keep such education from reaching members of the public who are at risk but prefer to deny, ignore, or conceal that they are. Again the question ultimately must be asked whether saving lives is more important than avoiding the offense public AIDS education causes with its unwelcome intrusion into the privacy of people's living rooms—people who, we would note, have already endured ads on TV and in other media for toilet tissue, tampons, toilet bowl cleaners, deodorants, douches, hemorrhoid suppositories, and laxatives, ads presented not in order to save lives but simply to advance sales. The United Kingdom, Denmark, Norway, Italy, and Germany have all resolved this conflict by opting for aggressive campaigns that present on TV explicit educational messages about AIDS.[11] To date, the United States, which has a higher rate of AIDS infection than any other Western industrialized nation, has no such campaign. Instead, an uneasy compromise seems to have emerged, in which public service announcements and notices containing little specific information on how to avoid HIV advise those who are interested to call AIDS hotlines. (Imagine their effectiveness if antismoking campaigns or campaigns to prevent drunken driving or to promote early detection of breast cancer had been conducted in this way.)

Finally, we are concerned about an ominous implication of some criticism of explicit AIDS education targeted at gays and IV drug abusers. The implication is that there is no need to be concerned

---

only a small percentage of the funds set aside by Congress for AIDS education is ever actually spent for that purpose. (Aiken, "Education as Prevention," 98. See Aiken for further discussion of Administration foot-dragging on explicit AIDS education.) Instead, explicit and effective AIDS education has been funded largely by (and targeted at) the gay community itself. While this is credited with slowing the spread of HIV within the gay community, which mobilized to fight AIDS with AIDS education long before any serious attention was given to it by the federal government, one result is that effective AIDS education targeted at IV drug abusers and their sexual partners is woefully inadequate.

[11] Aiken, "Education as Prevention," 96, note 57.

with targeting *effective* AIDS education at gays and IV drug abusers, since they are only getting what they deserve; society has done its duty simply by reminding them (through totally inoffensive messages) that they should embrace abstinence and restraint. This implication is clearly evident in the remarks of a participant in the October 14, 1987, Senate debate on Senator Helms's amendment to limit federal funding for explicit AIDS education: "I guess you can say as long as this disease is confined among homosexuals, no real danger. It is bad, but they should realize this. . . . But now, when we are dealing with the other side of this coin, where children can catch it, where we know that the cases can multiply, [there is a serious problem we must address]." And also, "Of course, through that heterosexual thing, that is really one of the dangers."[12] The message here is that Senator Helms is wrong to want to limit AIDS education to ineffective preaching of abstinence to gays, since there are "good people" at risk as well, people to whom society owes a message which will actually have some impact on their behavior and do some good. The ominous implication is that ineffective messages are good enough for gays.

VOLUNTARY ANONYMOUS TESTING

Shortly after testing of the nation's blood supply began in May 1985, alternate testing and counseling sites were established throughout the country, usually at venereal disease clinics, to discourage high-risk group members from giving blood as a way of ascertaining their HIV status. Controversy over both the personal and the public health benefits of voluntary anonymous testing has continued ever since. In some communities both public health officials and spokespersons for the gay community have urged testing, while elsewhere they have not. England, for instance, has been considerably more aggressive than the United States in AIDS education, but voluntary anonymous testing is not encouraged or even available. By contrast, in the United States such testing was available at 847 sites by the end of 1985.[13] Advocates credit San Francisco's testing and coun-

---

[12] *Congressional Record*, 100th Cong., 1st sess., October 14, 1987, pp. S14210, S14205.

[13] Gostin and Ziegler, "AIDS-related Legislative and Regulative Policy," 8. Gostin and Ziegler also report that anonymous testing is specifically forbidden in Oregon.

seling program, along with an aggressive AIDS education program, with dramatically reducing the spread of HIV in that city.

Advocates of voluntary anonymous testing have argued that if large numbers of infected persons can be apprised of their HIV status through voluntary anonymous testing and counseling, a start can be made in containing the spread of AIDS. Preliminary evidence from two studies does suggest that some persons reduce their participation in unprotected insertive anal intercourse upon learning they are infected, although the reduction seems to be modest and only slightly greater than among those who participate in HIV testing studies but elect not to learn their test results.[14] Advocates also argue that such testing would not invade privacy in any way, so long as results remain truly anonymous. A final public health benefit of such testing is that it can yield important data in the form of unlinked test results about the prevalence of HIV infection.

Opponents of such testing have argued that only modest behavior changes inspired by knowledge of test results have been documented. They have also pointed out that until effective therapies have been established for asymptomatic HIV infection, there are no tangible medical benefits but very substantial privacy risks for persons who are found to be infectious.

In what follows we will explore the value of voluntary anonymous testing both for tested individuals and as a public health measure. These two issues are related, since ultimately the public health benefits cannot obtain unless large numbers of infected individuals perceive testing as beneficial to them and hence elect to be tested. Thus before we can assess the potential of voluntary anonymous testing programs for significantly slowing the spread of HIV infection, we must consider the balance of anticipated benefits and costs for individuals considering anonymous testing.

As we will see, the benefits and costs to a tested individual will depend very much on whether testing reveals the individual to be

---

[14]Robin Fox et al., "Effect of HIV Antibody Disclosure on Subsequent Sexual Activity in Homosexual Men," *AIDS* 1 (December 1988): 241–46; Jane McCusker et al., "Effects of HIV Antibody Test Knowledge on Subsequent Sexual Behaviors in a Cohort of Homosexually Active Men," *American Journal of Public Health* 78 (1988): 462–67. For an overview of research on high-risk behavior change in response to AIDS education and knowledge of HIV status, see also Carol Tauer, "AIDS: Towards an Ethical Public Policy," in *Biomedical Ethics Reviews*.

uninfected or infected. We will argue that in general, just as being uninfected is desirable and being infected is undesirable, getting anonymous negative test results is usually a benefit and getting anonymous positive results is usually a cost, at least until effective therapies are available for asymptomatic HIV carriers. Because different costs and benefits attach to different test results, and because only individuals uncertain of but concerned about their HIV status would seek testing, a decision about whether to seek testing will ordinarily involve a kind of gamble for the individual. The first variable in this gamble is the individual's perceived chances of testing one way rather than the other, and the second is the perceived balance of costs and benefits of each possible outcome. In order to understand more fully these costs and benefits, we will examine in some detail the different benefits and costs of anonymous testing associated with the different outcomes, starting with those of negative test results. We can then assess the attractiveness of voluntary anonymous testing for persons considering such testing and hence the extent of the impact which voluntary anonymous testing programs are likely to have on the spread of HIV infection. We should clarify that here we are only addressing voluntary anonymous HIV testing of individuals who are asymptomatic. Obviously testing is advisable for persons who are manifesting symptoms which could be HIV related, for such would facilitate accurate diagnoses and appropriate treatments of secondary infections which might develop.

Testing Negative

Benefits for Negatives. The most obvious benefit of testing negative is relief from fear and peace of mind. The prospect of this payoff is undoubtedly the single factor which has motivated most people who have in fact sought such testing.

A second benefit for someone for whom safe sex guidelines have been burdensome and who is in or seeking a monogamous relationship is that these guidelines may now be ignored if the partner is also known to be uninfected.[15] The promise of this benefit has also

---

[15] People in this situation should bear in mind, however, that there may be as much as a year between infection and the time at which the

inspired the use of conditionally mandated testing as a screening device for membership in "safe sex clubs"; if all members are (allegedly) certifiably "clean," then any member supposedly can have unrestricted sex with any other member without concern for HIV infection.

Common sense would suggest that persons receiving negative test results get a third benefit in the form of additional motivation for modifying unsafe activities and hence remaining uninfected. Surprisingly, two studies found that while gay men receiving negative test results who had engaged in unprotected receptive anal intercourse did reduce the amount of this unsafe activity, the reduction was no greater than for those who elected not to be given their test results. In one of the studies, those receiving negative test results actually reduced the amount of very unsafe behavior *less* than those who elected not to be given their test results.[16] This suggests that while beneficial behavior change results from either the counseling or the soul-searching that comes with deciding to be tested, negative results per se do not typically provide additional motivation to avoid unsafe behaviors.

Costs for Negatives. Costs for those who test negative are very low but not absolutely zero. Some of the stigma associated with being infected with HIV carries over to being suspected of being infected, and, as we noted in Chapter 2, anonymity of test results does not entail privacy with respect to the fact that one has sought testing. Anyone who seeks even anonymous HIV testing risks exposure as a person who thinks he or she is at high risk for HIV infection. This risk of exposure may be modest, but it is not negligible. (Hospital workers who have suffered needle sticks typically react by immediately telling co-workers who are close at hand, but then they reportedly have regrets about doing so, since they subsequently find some of these co-workers are uneasy around them.) Although the potential for being stigmatized as a result of seeking testing has decreased as more people at low risk have done so, anyone who attends a VD clinic for anonymous HIV testing still

infection can be detected by antibody tests currently in use. See Chapter 1 for further discussion of this point.

[16] Fox et al., "Effect of HIV Antibody Disclosure"; McCusker et al., "Effects of HIV Antibody Test Knowledge."

runs some risk of having this fact discovered, and some people will not accept even this minimal risk. Some avoid it by seeking such testing from private physicians,[17] but in doing so they forgo the benefits of anonymous testing, since both the fact of testing and their test results presumably appear in their medical records, and this usually leads to a wider dissemination of the information. Awareness of these risks may prompt some concerned high-risk individuals to forgo testing, although some physicians who are sensitive to these concerns have gone out of their way to minimize these risks. We will return to these issues shortly.

The weighing of all these costs and benefits for people contemplating voluntary anonymous testing will, of course, vary with individual and circumstance. People who find it difficult to live with uncertainty will be more inclined to seek reassurance from testing than those who are comfortable with uncertainty or capable of extensive denial. Moreover, individuals who do not have monogamous relationships with partners who are negative will not reap the benefit of being able to ignore safe sex guidelines if they test negative. While the third alleged benefit — the additional incentive to avoid unsafe activities — looms large in the public debate, the evidence to date suggests that knowledge of one's freedom from infection from HIV provides little motivation to avoid unsafe activities beyond that derived from AIDS education and counseling.

In spite of these variables, by and large most individuals who test negative benefit overall from testing. Generally, testing will be attractive to thoughtful individuals who expect to test negative but want to eliminate any trace of gnawing uncertainty. Individuals who are reasonably sure they are negative and have this confirmed when they elect to be tested have in effect gambled and won (they've at least gained peace of mind). This presumably explains the flood of persons seeking testing early in 1987, when the press showered attention on the possibilities of heterosexual infection and of infection through transfusion (which became a cause for worry for the thirty million Americans who had such transfusions before screening of the blood supply began in May 1985).

---

[17]Tauer cites a study showing that fully 75 percent of those seeking voluntary testing in Minnesota opted to forgo the advantages of anonymous testing and sought testing instead from their private physicians or other health care providers. See Tauer, "AIDS."

While voluntary anonymous testing may be very attractive to concerned individuals who realize they are probably negative, the testing of uninfected individuals does nothing toward the preventative goal of alerting those who are *infected* of the threat they pose to their partners if they engage in unsafe activities. Let us turn, then, to the question of how the costs and benefits of testing positive will appear to individuals contemplating testing who have more reason to believe they are infected.

Testing Positive

Benefits for Positives. In the case of most sexually transmitted diseases, those who test positive receive a quick and effective cure for a potentially life-threatening condition. This is obviously the primary benefit that testing for sexually transmitted diseases offers these people. Until therapies for HIV infection which have been proven effective are routinely available, HIV testing offers no comparable benefit. The payoffs of testing for those who are positive are much more modest, but still not zero. There are four obvious possible benefits: (1) Positive test results may provide them with additional motivation to modify unsafe activities, this time to avoid infecting others. (2) They may be able to plan better for the future. (3) If the hopes for early therapies for controlling HIV infection are realized, they will be in a better position to seek such treatments. (4) They may be in a position to help future victims of HIV infection through participation in experimental treatment protocols now under way. Let us consider each of these four benefits.

Any minimally decent person wants to avoid putting innocent persons at unnecessary risk of serious harm. This concern will extend not only to sex partners within committed loving relationships, but to short-term sexual and drug contacts as well. Although being infected with HIV is certainly a liability, knowledge of infection can be a benefit to infected persons in that it may provide both the information and the incentive needed to protect partners from infection. Happily, the preliminary evidence suggests that knowledge of test results has its greatest impact on the sexual activity of infected persons who engage in the sexual activity most apt to infect others, insertive anal intercourse. Unfortunately, studies again suggest that even here the behavior change above and beyond that experienced by persons who undergo counseling and testing but do not elect to receive test results seems to be modest.[18]

Even though these studies suggest that knowledge of one's test results per se does not have a dramatic impact on unsafe behavior, they also suggest that involvement with voluntary HIV testing does have a considerable impact. This may be due to the one–on–one counseling which accompanies testing. Alternatively, we suggest the availability of anonymous testing may itself confront people with a decision about whether or not to opt for it and in that way may help break through denial and prompt the kind of soul-searching conducive to behavior change. One physician described the case of a patient who wanted to "play it safe" but was anxious because he did not always manage to do so; he was actually per-suaded to seek testing by the argument that either test result would strengthen his resolve to respect safe sex guidelines.[19]

As for the second benefit, all of us must develop our life plans against a background of uncertainty; in general, the more uncer-tainty we can dispel, the more reasonably we can plan. Persons infected with HIV are no exception; those who learn they are infected might benefit by looking after their health with plenty of rest and good nutrition, by not committing limited time and energy to projects they will be unable to complete, and by anticipating finan-cial and other special needs they will have when they become ill. So long as any private health or life insurance is available without HIV testing, persons who learn anonymously that they are infected face an opportunity (and an ethical dilemma) in connection with seek-ing insurance coverage. In Chapter 8 we will look at these and other insurance issues.

HIV infection may never be reversible. One of the most promis-ing avenues of treatment may involve keeping the virus from repli-cating and hence keeping HIV infection under control. Although presently there are no proven therapies for asymptomatic HIV infec-tion, a number of therapies are on the horizon, and by the time this appears in print, some of them may be established. During 1987, AIDS Treatment Evaluation Units began clinical trials involving

---

[18] Fox et al., "Effect of HIV Antibody Disclosure"; McCusker et al., "Effects of HIV Antibody Test Knowledge."

[19] Dr. Molly Cook, personal communication.

zidovudine treatment of asymptomatic HIV infection. As soon as any therapeutic benefits of zidovudine or other treatments for asymptomatic persons infected with HIV are established, the prospect of such treatment will provide the best reason to be tested for people who think they may be infected with HIV.

As for the final benefit, at this time asymptomatic infected volunteers are needed to participate in treatment protocols. People who learn they may have a terminal condition often find their priorities shift dramatically, and may find they can get great satisfaction from participating in projects which previously would have struck them as hollow or silly. Many of the persons who are now probably terminally ill might find meaning in their circumstances if they felt they were somehow able to make a significant contribution to research which will ultimately benefit future HIV patients. The opportunity to participate in these protocols could well prove a significant benefit to persons once they learned they were infected.

Costs for positives. Unfortunately the costs of learning one has tested positive for HIV infection are considerable and often not appreciated by proponents of large-scale HIV testing. A positive test result is much more than just a useful piece of information which facilitates more intelligent and responsible decision making. Even though we generally make better decisions when we have more relevant information, that does not mean we will always *benefit* from important information about ourselves and our future. Most of us would probably be happy to forgo advance knowledge of the exact time or circumstances of our deaths, even if such knowledge were available and would undeniably facilitate better planning on many of our most important personal projects. This is because there can also be serious costs associated with having certain kinds of knowledge.

The major costs associated with learning one is infected with HIV involve, first, the direct psychological impact and, second, various problems associated with privacy regarding the information about one's infection. Such information could be very damaging in the wrong hands, yet individuals may have very good practical or moral reasons for informing others. We will consider each of these two costs in turn.

Someone who understands the full implications of receiving a positive test result is confronted first and foremost with his or her own mortality — with the very strong possibility that death will come soon, preceded by a series of painful losses, often including cherished relationships, economic well-being, job and home, and mental capacity, and of course physical well-being. Uncertainty surrounding all of this can aggravate its painfulness. Severe stress, anxiety, and depression are not uncommon reactions, particularly for a person in the physical and creative prime of life. Ironically, the best medical advice for such people presently seems to be to take good care of themselves, get plenty of rest, and maintain a positive attitude — while waiting and watching for early symptoms to develop. (It is ironic that one of the mechanisms by which psychological stress leads to physical illness is by weakening the immune system.)

Beyond the direct psychological reaction to the news of positive test results, an individual also faces various privacy issues in connection with sharing this information with others. The highly charged nature of the information and its potential for harming an individual's interests make privacy a major issue for most people in this situation. At the same time, most people will have strong motives for wanting to share it with others, as well as obligations to do so.

First, people receiving bad news about their health typically turn to family or friends for support. There are many risks associated with such informal sharing of news of HIV infection, however. Many persons tell family members with the expectation they will respond with support; instead they turn out to be in the grip of a panic about AIDS and respond with fear and even hostility. Some of them have even felt it was their duty to warn others of the danger their infected relative posed! Moreover, the revelation that one is infected will usually have to be accompanied by an explanation of how one became infected, and this can obviously involve additional problems. Thus a gay man, for instance, may be reluctant to turn to family members if he has not already discussed the issue of his sexual orientation with them. He may, of course, decide to "come out" in order to discuss his medical status, but unfortunately that process usually has a positive result only if he can project satisfaction with his own sexual identity as he does so. "Coming out" to one's family is apt to have a negative result if the gay man conveys the impression he is miserable because he is gay. HIV infection, of course, makes it very difficult to achieve or maintain a positive self-image. IV drug abusers face analogous problems.

More generally, an infected individual who turns to others often cannot be sure how the news will be received and has no guarantee that the confidantes will not reveal his or her condition to others. In short, the danger of gossip is very real. The fact that someone is infected and speculation about the cause of infection will be of some interest to mutual acquaintances, and a confidante may easily succumb to the temptation to pass information along. The rumor mill may whir well out of control at this point, since people often feel less obligation to respect confidences if the person who has confided in them has already violated the integrity of the original confidence in doing so. At the point one's HIV status and accompanying speculation achieves the status of gossip, it has the potential for dramatically changing one's social standing among family and friends and eventually among casual acquaintances. Many people have become social "lepers" in this way, even within their own families. The cases involving children — Ryan White in Kokomo, Indiana, or the Ray children in Arcadia, Florida, whose classmates' parents were completely in the grip of a panic about AIDS — may be the most notorious, but they are by no means unique. And as with these children and their families, there may be more tangible costs for anyone whose infection becomes generally known, such as the loss of a job, exclusion from school, destruction of property, and even threats to physical well-being.

These risks will vary considerably, depending, for instance, on one's geographical location and social milieu. Persons living in San Francisco risk less in being open about their HIV infection than persons in communities in which there is less understanding of AIDS and more panic about AIDS and homophobia.[20] Nevertheless, even in major metropolitan centers with large gay communities, HIV dis-

---

[20] An *Oprah Winfrey Show* broadcast during the week of November 16–20, 1987, featured an AIDS victim who said he was "hounded out of Williamson, West Virginia, after going for a swim in . . . the town pool." On the show he was confronted by the angry town mayor, also a guest on the show, who had closed the pool because of the "one chance in a million" there might have been a transmission. The mayor expressed outrage that the person with AIDS expected compassion from the very townspeople he was putting at risk. The indignant audience indicated their sympathies were entirely with the mayor. See also "School Officials Sued in AIDS-related Case," *Star Tribune* (formerly *Minneapolis Star Tribune*), November 17, 1987, sec. A, p. 13.

crimination is very much an issue. The presidential AIDS commission reported that "at virtually every Commission hearing, witnesses have attested to discrimination's occurrence and its serious repercussions for . . . the individual who experiences it" and that reports of such discrimination show a sharp increase.[21] "For example, HIV-related cases handled by the New York City Commission on Human Rights have risen from three in 1983, to more than 300 in 1986, to almost 600 in 1987." As a result, "individuals infected with the HIV face two fights: the fight against the virus and the fight against discrimination."[22] And again, "aside from the illness itself, it is discrimination that is most feared by the HIV infected."[23]

Beyond these costs of informal dissemination of health status information, infected individuals stand to suffer additional costs if and when this information is disseminated through more official channels, usually beginning with their medical records. Individuals who receive positive test results anonymously are counseled to see their private physicians for further information and for monitoring of their health status. As soon as they do this, their test results are no longer anonymous but become part of official records and hence subject to whatever "confidential" distribution such records routinely receive. As we saw in Chapter 2, that distribution may be considerable. Even the patient who sees a physician in a small, private office will have his or her HIV status entered into medical records at that point. In addition, the patient will either have to pay for the visit out of pocket, or authorize release of these records to a third party payer. Some states have no statutes which prohibit the third party payer from providing others—the person's employer, for instance—with information about the person's health status. Moreover, if the person works for a company which is self-insured, there may not be adequate safeguards to prevent medical information about the person from being made available to his or her supervisors within the corporation. As we shall see in Chapter 8, self-insurers present a special problem, since state insurance regulations typically do not apply to them.

---

[21] *Report of the Presidential Commission on the Human Immunodeficiency Virus Epidemic*, 119.
[22] Ibid., 120.
[23] Ibid., 126.

From a strictly medical point of view, an infected person would probably do well to seek out a specialist in HIV infection. Most specialists work in the larger medical centers. Thus, if the person does go to a specialist, even more people will have access to his or her records. The primary purpose of such records is to provide physicians and other health care providers with ready access to a patient's medical history and conditions. Even in an ordinary hospital, as many as seventy-five persons routinely have access to a patient's chart, that is, his or her complete records.[24] In most major medical centers, anyone wearing a white coat who approaches a nurses' station and reaches for a patient's chart authoritatively will probably not be challenged. Moreover, parts of that record are computerized. It would be very difficult logistically to restrict access to the computerized records of any given patient so that only those who had a legitimate need for information about that patient could obtain it, and few major medical centers have attempted to do so. At best, different individuals are given access to only some "screens" or special subcategories of information on patients, e.g., those dealing directly with medical conditions, the pharmacy, the x-ray department, the clinic most recently visited, the billing department, etc. Anyone with access to certain screens of any patient's computerized records usually has access to the corresponding screens for all patients. The fact that a patient has seen an HIV specialist will be reflected in many of these screens, and his or her HIV status could be inferred from any of them. Those with access to some of these screens include not only the health care professionals directly and indirectly involved in delivering health care, whose primary responsibility (and *sense* of responsibility) will be to the welfare of the patient, but also those who are involved in securing or providing third party payment and whose relations with the patient are more distant than those of the patient's caregivers, perhaps even adversarial. In some medical centers, literally thousands of people have access to computerized records from which a patient's HIV infection could be inferred. Moreover, the records are often accessible to authorized personnel by phone from outside the hospital.

Thus the "anonymous" test results of an infected individual who decides to see an HIV specialist in a large medical center quickly find

---

[24] Mark Siegler, "Confidentiality in Medicine — A Decrepit Concept," *New England Journal of Medicine* 307 (1982): 1519.

their way into "confidential" records—usually the computerized records—of the physician, the medical center, the insurance company, and the employer (if the employer is self-insured) and even into the computer of the Medical Information Bureau maintained by the American Council on Life Insurance for the purposes of sharing medical information about policy holders and applicants. In states in which HIV infection is a reportable condition (as it is presently in Alabama, Arizona, Colorado, Idaho, Minnesota, Montana, South Carolina, and Wisconsin), physicians and health labs must report the names of infected patients to the state health departments.[25] Moreover, a further threat to privacy exists in that an individual's medical records might be successfully subpoenaed from many of these sources. It is easy to see why people anxious to keep their HIV infection private feel concern about so wide an authorized distribution of supposedly private information.

Because distribution of information about HIV infection can be so damaging, special efforts have been made by various parties to enhance confidentiality. Some persons seeking medical care have done so using false names, although this will not be possible if they are seeking care from doctors who know them or if they expect third party payment. Some physicians, usually those in larger metropolitan areas, who see many patients about HIV-related conditions and who are thus more sensitive to the importance of confidentiality and privacy of HIV-related information, may actively encourage or conspire with patients to help keep such information out of their official records. Some physicians have referred patients coming to them for HIV testing to anonymous test sites. Some occasionally keep parallel "informal" records in addition to their official records or attach false names to blood samples sent for testing to labs required to report positive test results. While these practices suggest these physicians feel the urgency of protecting the privacy of their patients' HIV-related information, they are not without their own costs, since they frustrate the very legitimate medical ends served by complete and accurate records.

Confidentiality of HIV-related records has also been the focus of legislative concern. Many states traditionally provide very strong protection for information they acquire when sexually transmitted

---

[25] Gostin and Ziegler, "AIDS-related Legislative and Regulatory Policy," 10.

diseases are reported to them, but unfortunately HIV infection is not classified as a sexually transmitted disease in most of these states.[26] Several states have passed legislation specifically protecting the confidentiality of HIV test results in the belief that the public health is best served by doing so.[27] Several others, in an attempt to address dilemmas involving confidentiality and the duty to warn, have passed statutes requiring notification under certain conditions.[28] To enhance the confidentiality of health records provided to third party payers, the National Association of Insurance Commissioners has adopted the Insurance Information and Privacy Protection Model Act. To date this act has also been adopted by eleven states.[29] Even Vice President Bush spoke of the importance of confidentiality when he addressed the Third International Conference on AIDS in Washington, D.C., in June 1987.[30]

The presidential AIDS commission also made extensive recommendations in connection with the confidentiality of HIV records, urging legislation at both the state and federal level to protect such records from indiscriminate distribution to parties with no real need to know, and it also urged public health organizations, health care institutions, insurance companies, and even the military to pay closer attention to the importance of the confidentiality of medical records.[31]

---

[26] Just about the time Alabama's reporting law went into effect, the Associated Press reported that police in Montgomery, Alabama, were maintaining a list of AIDS victims; the mayor defended this as necessary so that police and firefighters will know when they are in contact with HIV. The report did not explain how they got the list, nor was it clear whether it was a list of HIV-infected people or a list of persons with AIDS. See "Secret List of AIDS Victims Criticized," *Star Tribune*, (formerly *Minneapolis Star Tribune*), September 25, 1987, sec. A, p. 19.

[27] These include California, Florida, Hawaii, Kentucky, Maine, Massachusetts, and Wisconsin. See Gostin and Ziegler, "A Review of AIDS-related Legislative and Regulatory Policy," 13.

[28] Ibid.

[29] Russell P. Iuculano, "Life Insurance," in *AIDS and the Law*, ed. William H. L. Dornette (New York: John Wiley & Sons, 1987), 211.

[30] "Bush Tells Big AIDS Meeting That Testing Is Necessary," *New York Times*, June 2, 1987, C2.

[31] *Report of the Presidential Commission on the Human Immunodeficiency Virus Epidemic*, 127–28.

In spite of these efforts, most persons who receive positive test results anonymously will find it extraordinarily difficult to prevent them from receiving wide authorized confidential distribution. The circle of confidentiality, which originally included only the patient and physician, has undergone radical extension as the physician has come to be replaced by a "health care team" and as third party payers have become routine. Thus, for the vast majority of persons who receive positive "anonymous" test results and who follow counseling recommendations to consult a physician for follow-up, anonymous testing is truly a short-lived will-o'-the-wisp. Few patients are able to see physicians under assumed names and pay for such follow-up visits out of pocket.

In addition to problems of confidentiality relating to the *authorized* confidential distribution of test results from medical records to hospitals, insurance companies, employers, and state health officials, there is also the risk of *unauthorized* distribution as a result of breaches of confidentiality—a risk which grows as the number of people included in the circle of authorized distribution grows. Often persons with legitimate access to someone's records may be relatives, friends, or acquaintances or know people who are. As we noted earlier, in smaller communities, those working in the anonymous testing and counseling centers will often be acquainted with those being tested. Moreover, the famous also get sick, and information about them may strike some as "fair game."[32] Sometimes even health care workers themselves fail to take seriously the confidentiality of their patients' medical status or discount the possibility that they will be overheard by people who know the patients whose conditions they discuss wherever they can, including in elevators, cafeterias, or other public areas of medical centers. This tendency may be aggravated by the fact that people often do not choose to keep private medical information which they are entitled to keep private. A

---

[32] An interesting instance of "leaked" computerized health care records was the subject of "Faint Light, Dark Print," an ambivalent article by Jack Anderson associate Dale Van Atta which appeared in *Harpers Magazine*, November 1986, pp. 54–57. The article is half expose, half critique of the secrecy surrounding the AIDS death of a prominent Washington, D.C., figure, and it consists of a copy of part of the patient's computerized medical record, with annotations of remarks that imply—but never actually state—the patient had AIDS.

person entering a hospital for routine surgery is usually more inclined to hope for visitors during convalescence than to stand on his or her right to privacy. If physicians are sometimes lax about their patients' privacy concerns, how much less likely is it that confidentiality will be taken seriously by hospital recordkeepers, who never have contact with patients, whose training may not emphasize the importance of confidentiality, and whose daily routine of sitting at a computer terminal in the billing department might occasionally be made more personal as a familiar name flickers across the terminal screen? The President's Commission on AIDS also recognized this problem and urged, among other things, that health care education programs should emphasize the special sensitivity of HIV-related information.[33]

So far we have been considering costs an infected individual may incur in confiding in others with whom he or she will tend to share test results for reasons of self-interest. We have argued the reasons are nearly always sufficient to prompt infected individuals to divulge their HIV status to both acquaintances and medical personnel. This means that for those who test positive, the results of anonymous testing are soon no more private than the results of confidential testing; hence for them the advantages of anonymous testing over confidential testing are largely illusory. Moreover, we believe that these privacy considerations, combined with the direct psychological costs to individuals that result from learning they are infected, are sufficient to make voluntary anonymous testing unattractive to many of those who believe they may well be infected.

In Chapter 6 we will consider additional reasons that those who test positive may have for divulging their HIV status to others, in particular, moral considerations involving the duty to warn. To anticipate briefly, all of us have a general prima facie duty to warn others when we know of risks they may be exposed to unknowingly. Knowledge that one is infected provides a stronger reason than mere suspicion to warn others whom one may have exposed or whom one may expose in the future. While some persons who suspect they may be positive will see the need to warn partners as a reason

---

[33] *Report of the Presidential Commission on the Human Immunodeficiency Virus Epidemic*, 128.

for testing, we believe many will view the prospect of incurring such a painful obligation as an additional cost of testing positive and hence as an additional reason not to seek such testing.

CONCLUSION

We believe voluntary anonymous testing should be available to those who wish to know their HIV status. It can provide peace of mind to those who are uninfected and enable people to plan their futures more confidently — or more carefully — and make more intelligent choices about needle sharing, sex, marriage, and parenting. People should be able to obtain such information with as little intrusion into their privacy as possible. Moreover, studies suggest that testing and counseling do have a significant impact on unsafe behavior, even if actually learning one's HIV status, positive *or* negative, has only a modest additional impact. At the very least, the availability of voluntary anonymous testing prompts some individuals who engage in high-risk activities to confront the possibility of being infected, which in turn may break through denial and contribute to behavior change.

In light of the costs and benefits of anonymous testing for persons who perceive themselves to be at high risk of HIV infection, however, we believe that voluntary anonymous testing will be attractive to a significant percentage of people who suspect they are infected only when effective therapies become available for asymptomatic persons infected with HIV. Until then, many will feel they have little to gain and much to lose by having their fears confirmed. For this reason, we are fairly skeptical of the efficacy of voluntary anonymous testing as a preventative public health measure. Unfortunately our analysis suggests it will be most attractive to those who are at very low risk and hence reasonably certain they are uninfected, but who are also very uncomfortable with uncertainty and want to dispel lingering doubts. For individuals who realize they may well be infected, on the other hand, there are formidable risks involved in testing and confirming their fears that they are infected. The presidential AIDS commission put this point even more forcefully: "As long as discrimination occurs, and no strong national policy with rapid and effective remedies against discrimination is established, individuals who are infected with the HIV will be reluctant to come forward for testing, counseling, and care."[34]

Unlike other creatures, we are above all reasoning beings capable of planning, and our states of knowledge contribute crucially to our well-being, both directly (in terms of our immediate psychological states) and indirectly (by defining our choices and ultimately our projects). Some thoughtful persons who believe they may well be infected will prefer the certainty, either because they are tormented by uncertainty or so they can plan their limited futures more realistically. We believe, however, that most will not seek testing, because they will feel that confirmation of their fears of HIV infection would result in more costs than benefits. If this is so, voluntary anonymous testing will not have a major preventative impact.

---

[34] Ibid., 119.

6
Warning Patients, Warning Partners

INTRODUCTION

We saw in Chapter 5 that the person who tests positive for HIV faces serious social risks as well as medical problems. The social risks increase dramatically as more people learn that he or she is infected. The risks include loss of job, loss of housing, and, perhaps worst of all, alienation from former friends and from family. It is not an exaggeration to say that a person who is HIV infected may risk social death long before he or she faces physical death. HIV-infected persons have powerful prudential reasons for not wanting knowledge of their health status to fall into the wrong hands. Yet, they also have prudential reasons for telling family, friends, and health care professionals. Moreover, they may have moral and legal reasons for warning others whom they have less reason to trust. In this chapter we explore reasons for warning others.

We begin with a general discussion of reasons for warning people who face risks. We argue, for instance, that the risk that harm will occur and the fact that the person who warns has knowledge which the person warned does not have constitute reasons for warning. We also argue that the strength of these reasons depends on the severity of the harm risked, the probability of its occurring, and the degree of certainty of the warner compared with the uncertainty of the person warned. On the other hand, we argue that some factors constitute reasons for not warning. The fact that the warner may thereby expose him or herself to risk, for instance, constitutes a reason for not warning. This reason for not warning will be strengthened if the warning is unlikely to be heeded. Finally, we argue that the relationship between warner and the person warned, as well as the relationship between the warner and the person who threatens harm, may also provide reasons for warning or not warning.

In light of these general considerations, we then discuss whether HIV-infected persons ought to warn their sexual partners. We consider both past partners and partners with whom HIV-infected persons are about to have sexual relations.[1] In particular, we argue that there are morally compelling reasons for warning some sexual partners, but not others. We then explore the legal duty to warn partners that one is HIV infected, and we note that failure to warn potential sexual partners who are at risk of being infected may expose one to liability for negligence, battery, and misrepresentation.

Next we turn to the dilemma faced by the physician who believes that an HIV-infected patient will not warn sexual partners. We argue that the physician must weigh the same factors as the infected individual, but that these must be balanced against his or her reasons for preserving the confidentiality of the patient. We also note that a physician who fails to warn persons who may be infected by his or her patient may risk legal liability. In addition, physicians may be legally required to report cases of AIDS or even HIV infection to state officials.

Finally, we explore the constitutionality of reporting laws and contact-tracing laws that provide for contacting past partners of those who have AIDS or who test positive for HIV. We argue that while reporting laws are probably constitutional, contact-tracing laws are probably unconstitutional.

GENERAL MORAL REASONS TO WARN

As a general rule we have a moral reason to warn those we know are in danger. Warnings of danger serve as a means of preventing harm. Since as a general rule we have a moral reason to prevent harm, we also have a moral reason to warn. Warnings of danger also serve to alert those warned of dangers of which they might not

---

[1] Although we focus our attention on sexual partners, the factors we consider could also be applied to other situations in which warnings might be thought appropriate; for example, in the case of an HIV-infected patient considering whether to warn a dentist or surgeon prior to an invasive procedure or an HIV-infected drug abuser considering whether to warn those who have shared needles with him or her.

be aware. Those warned are then in a position to act with more complete knowledge of the consequences of their actions. In this way warnings serve to enhance the individual autonomy of those warned. Insofar as enhancing the autonomy of those warned provides a moral reason for acting, warning others of danger also provides a moral reason for acting.

The general rule that we have a moral reason for warning others applies on an individual level. It is a rare person who would not warn a child about to dash in front of a car and a still rarer person who would think it morally permissible not to warn the child. The rule also applies on a societal level. As a society we believe, for instance, that people ought to be warned of public health hazards such as water pollution and smoking. Certainly the rule applies in the case of AIDS. Much of AIDS education can be viewed as a public warning about high-risk activities and the danger of HIV infection. The disputes concerning AIDS education are disputes over what people should be told to do in order to avoid infection. There is no dispute over whether people should be warned.

While it is generally true that we ought to warn those in peril, this is not always true. There are exceptions to this general rule, and reasons for warning may be overridden. Consider some exceptions. We should not warn wrongdoers about those who threaten to foil their plans. For example, we should not warn a thief that he or she is about to be captured by the police. It is not that our duty to warn the thief is overridden; rather, we have no duty whatever to warn a thief of the threat of apprehension. Additionally, there are cases in which we should not warn people who will be harmed in a competitive situation into which they have voluntarily entered. Poker players are under no obligation to warn each other of their good hands; and, as mere bystanders to the game, we not only have no duty to warn, but are expected not to warn. Similarly, as mere bystanders, we may have no duty whatever to warn a businessman that his competition is about to make a takeover bid for his corporation. There are also situations in which our reasons for warning another of impending danger are overridden by more weighty reasons. A priest's reasons for warning a woman that her husband is intending to be unfaithful, for example, is overridden by the priest's duty to preserve the confidentiality of the husband's confession.

The outright exceptions in cases of wrongdoing and competition typically do not apply in cases where people are at risk of being infected with HIV. Such people are typically innocent victims, even if the infection is transmitted as a result of voluntary actions. It may be, however, that the reasons for warning those at risk of being infected with HIV are overridden by more stringent reasons. In order to determine whether this is so, we need to consider both the reasons which incline one to think that one ought to warn another and the reasons which might count as stronger countervailing reasons. In short, we need to consider factors which strengthen reasons for and against warning others of danger.

Successful warnings alert people to dangers of which they are not aware or not taking into account. This assumes both that there is a danger and that the warner is more aware of the danger than the person warned. Because people can be more or less aware of a risk, the strength of this reason for warning depends, in part, on the extent to which the warner is certain and on the extent to which the person warned lacks certainty. There is also no duty to warn unless there is a risk of harm. Without the risk of harm, there is nothing about which to warn the person. Other things equal, the greater the risk of harm, the stronger the reason to warn. In determining the degree of risk, we need to take into account both the probability the harm will occur and its severity.

Also, one has no duty to warn if one knows the person being warned is fully aware of the harm risked or at least is consciously taking the risk into account. If one encounters a rock climber who is checking and rechecking climbing equipment before attempting a difficult climb, it is just silly to warn the climber of the danger of falling. It would not, however, be silly to warn the climber that an unexpected storm had just been forecast. As noted above, we may be more or less aware of a risk. Thus, the person who merely has a hunch that there might be a storm has less of a reason to warn the climber than the person who hears the entire weather forecast and knows with certainty that a storm has been forecast.

The strength of the duty to warn also varies with the extent to which the person warned is able to act on the warning and avert risk. As we have noted, one justification for warning others is the prevention of harm. If a person, upon being warned, could not act to avoid the harm risked, then the warning could not prevent the harm. On the other hand, if the person warned could act to prevent the harm, then the warning may help to prevent the harm.

Another justification for warning is that it enables people to act freely by giving them information about risks which they might not otherwise have. If the person warned is not in a position to act on the warning, then the warning does not serve to enhance the autonomy of the person warned. Consequently, there is little reason based on autonomy for warning in such a case. In short, whether one bases the justification for warning on the prevention of harm or the enhancement of individual autonomy, there is little point in warning a person if harm cannot be avoided or even mitigated. If a man is hopelessly trapped in a cave, warning him that the cave will soon be flooded will only make him more nervous.

In some cases warning another poses a risk to the warner. The law-abiding citizen who warns a shop owner that the person who made such an attractive offer is a really a Mafia agent runs a risk of danger because of that warning. Such risks to the person in a position to issue a warning constitute a legitimate reason for not warning and weaken the overall justification for warning. While we generally expect people to warn others, we do not expect them to be heroes.

The relationship between the warner and the person warned also makes a difference. Those who are in some way responsible for potential harm to another have a stronger reason to warn than do mere bystanders who know that harm is being risked.[2] For example, it seems obvious that an HIV-infected man, for example, who infects another without warning does something which is worse than the mere bystander who fails to warn.

There are several likely explanations of this. One such explanation is in terms of rights. In at least some cases, the person who causes the harm thereby violates the rights of the person harmed. The mere bystander who does not warn of potential harm may fail

---

[2] One can be responsible for harm either because one is likely to cause harm oneself (e.g., one is subject to bouts of madness or is using a very dangerous machine) or because one is in charge of a person or animal that is likely to cause harm (e.g., one is the guardian of a madman, owns a vicious pet, or supervises a man who uses a dangerous machine). In addition, one can be responsible for harm either because one is likely to cause the harm oneself or because it is one's duty to prevent harm. In any of these cases, one ought to warn those who might be harmed.

to do something which he or she should do, but he or she does not thereby violate the rights of the person harmed. When a person about to cause harm to another warns that person, the warner may avoid violating that person's rights in one of two ways, depending on the reaction of the person imperiled. On the one hand, the person at risk may be able to take steps to avoid the harm altogether. For instance, if an HIV-infected person warns a potential sexual partner, the potential partner may refuse to engage in risky sexual activities. On the other hand, the potential partner may decide that it is worth the risk to engage in some unsafe sexual activities. In that case, the person who causes harm does not violate the rights of the partner. This constitutes an additional reason for the person about to cause harm to warn the person about to be harmed.

Even if there is no question of a violation of rights, an explanation might be offered using the principle that it is worse to cause harm to people than to fail to prevent harm.[3] The bystander who sees that someone is likely to harm another person and who does not warn the imperiled person merely fails to prevent harm. The person who is likely to cause harm actually does the harm if he or she fails to warn the person in peril. In the event that harm occurs, the bystander is guilty only of the lesser offense of failing to prevent harm.

Other relationships also provide an additional reason to warn those in danger. Some such relationships are based on agreements. The lawyer who agrees to represent a person in negotiations concerning a lease, for instance, has a duty to warn the client of any legal problems which can arise from the proposed lease. When an attorney agrees to represent a client concerning a certain matter, it is understood that within the area of representation the attorney will warn the client of dangerous courses of action which the client might be inclined to take. Such warnings are a large part of what the lawyer is paid for. Similarly a doctor who takes on a patient has

---

[3] The moral distinction between doing and allowing to happen is philosophically controversial. See, for instance, Raziel Abelson, "To Do or Let Happen," *American Philosophical Quarterly* 19 (1982): 219–28; Bruce Russell, "On the Relative Strictness of Negative and Positive Duties," *American Philosophical Quarterly* 14 (1977): 87–97; James Rachels, "Active and Passive Euthanasia," *New England Journal of Medicine* 292 (1975): 78–80.

a duty to warn the patient of health problems which the patient faces. Such duties are based on explicit or implicit agreements. When such agreements give rise to a duty to warn, we may also claim that the person at risk has a right to be warned in virtue of the agreement or understanding. Thus, the relationship may actually alter the moral situation to the extent that failure to warn involves not only a wrongful action, but also a violation of a right.

Professional relationships are also built on reliance. Typically a person who hires a lawyer relies on the lawyer to warn of legal problems, and the lawyer knows that the client is relying on him or her. Such reliance can also arise independently of any agreement. If a Boy Scout stops to help a blind man across the street, the Scout knows that the blind man will rely on him even if the Scout does not explicitly guarantee his safety. If the Scout leaves him alone in the middle of the street or gives him bad advice about the traffic, the Scout will have been at least partially responsible for any resulting mishap. Note, however, that this only occurs when the Scout has reason to believe that another is relying on him. If someone relies on a Boy Scout without his knowledge, the reliance does not give rise to an additional duty or additional reasons to warn the person of danger or to keep the person out of danger. If the Scout learns that a person is relying on him to warn of dangers concerning some matter, it does not follow that he or she has a duty to warn that person of dangers within the scope of his reliance. He may instead warn the person not to rely on him. Still, if he knows that someone is relying on him, then he has a moral reason for either warning the person not to rely on him or for warning the person of dangers within the area in which the person relies on him. It is this sort of reliance and trust which gives those who are lovers such a strong moral reason to warn their partners of dangers. Failure to warn one's lover that one has AIDS may be a serious breach of trust.

While a relationship of trust or reliance may give the person who is relied on a stronger reason to warn those who rely on him or her, such a relationship sometimes also provides a reason for not warning others. A lawyer should not warn a tenant that his or her client, the landlord, is planning to raise the rent. The lawyer is an agent of his or her client and has a special duty in virtue of that relationship not to warn others of the client's activities. Similarly, as previously noted, the relationship of trust between the priest and someone who confesses to him provides a compelling reason for not warning those who may be harmed by that person. As we shall see, the physician of an HIV-infected patient has reason not to warn others of the patient's infection if it will be detrimental to the patient. To at least some extent, the physician is an agent of the patient, and the patient trusts and relies on the physician. We will consider the question of when, if ever, such reasons are overridden by counter-vailing reasons.[4]

FIRST PERSON WARNINGS

Consider now a man who learns that he has tested positive for HIV. On top of all of the physical and practical worries faced by such a man, there are moral worries. Should the man warn his past sexual partners? As noted in Chapter 5, if he warns his past partners himself, he faces potentially heavy costs. Those he notifies may be angry and may attach little value to respecting his confidentiality. If so, he may face a major loss of privacy and the whole range of recrimina-tions and discriminations which such a loss can entail. These can include housing and employment discrimination. Just when money is most needed, the man, if he tells others that he is infected, may lose his job. In short, by warning past partners, he may sacrifice some privacy and risk further severe losses of privacy if those whom he tells do not keep his confidence, as often happens. Although such factors do not always override the reasons for warning past part-ners, they do indicate that the reasons for warning them must be balanced against certain contrary reasons.

In addition, there may be several considerations that may weaken the man's reasons for warning others. First, he must calculate the amount of risk under which he has placed his past partners. If he frequently had unsafe sexual relations with a particular partner, the risk to that partner may be great. If he had infrequent sexual rela-

---

[4]The examples given in this section assume that the warning is given so that the person warned may protect him- or herself from risk. Of course, warnings may also be issued to prevent someone from harming another person. Thus, a passenger may shout at the driver to watch the road. As far as the various factors which we discuss are concerned, however, it makes no difference whether the warning is issued to prevent harm to the person warned or to prevent the person warned from harming another. Yet it might be noted that doctors certainly have a strong reason to warn their HIV-infected patients of the danger of infecting others.

tions or wore a condom and engaged in oral rather than anal or vaginal sex, the risk may be small.[5] Even if there is a fairly high risk that he has infected past partners, however, the reason for warning is weakened by the fact there is little that the partners can do now about the health threat. There is no cure for AIDS and no way to get rid of HIV infection.

Such considerations do not, however, wholly destroy the reasons for warning. There are things that past partners can do if, after being warned, they get tested and find out that they are infected. They can attempt to join experimental programs in which they receive treatments, such as zidovudine, that promise to prolong the lives of infected persons. They can also engage in financial planning for the eventuality of AIDS and prepare themselves psychologically. Moreover, they can in turn protect future sexual partners. Still, from the point of view of the persons warned, the benefits of being warned are insignificant when compared with the benefits of being warned about other sexually transmitted diseases, where actual cures are possible.

The crucial factor in deciding whether to warn may be the knowledge differential between the warner and the person warned. In the case of gay men, for instance, there is already widespread knowledge of the risks of various sexual activities. Past gay partners may already be aware of the risk under which they have placed themselves. In San Francisco's gay community, for instance, as many as 75 percent may be HIV infected. Warning past partners may expose someone to potential discrimination while providing them with little additional knowledge. As we have seen, risking discrimination constitutes a reason for thinking that it is permissible not to warn a past partner.

---

[5] There is no solid evidence that HIV is transmitted by oral-genital contact. For instance, in a study of 2,507 gay and bisexual men over a six-month period, Dr. Lawrence A. Kinsley was unable to detect any risk associated with oral sex. While 95 men seroconverted (became HIV infected), no one seroconverted who engaged in receptive oral intercourse while refraining from anal intercourse. Kinsley warns, however, that while there is no proof that HIV is transmitted through oral-genital contact, the sample considered is too small to infer that oral-genital contact is safe. See Lawrence A. Kinsley et al., "Risk Factors for Seroconversion to Human Immunodeficiency Virus among Male Homosexuals," *Lancet*, February 14, 1987, pp. 345–48.

The situation is radically different for married bisexuals. The wife or former wife of such a bisexual may have no idea that she has been exposed to the risk of HIV infection. Similarly, gay men in monogamous relationships may not suspect that their partners are infected, especially if they have been tested previously. Being told that they have been exposed to HIV infection may provide such people with important new knowledge—knowledge which may prompt them to seek testing, to refrain from unsafe conduct, and, if they test positive, to seek experimental treatments such as zidovudine. Women who find that they are HIV infected may also want to refrain from bearing children.

The relationship between spouses or long-term lovers is also a special relationship, for both partners typically agree to be sexually faithful and come to rely on each other for at least a high degree of sexual faithfulness. As we have seen, such relationships of reliance and trust provide reasons for supposing that an infected person ought to warn past partners with whom he or she has been in such relationships.

Monogamous relationships are also special from the point of view of warning others so that they will not harm third parties. When a person's monogamous relationship dissolves, there may be no reason for that person to suspect that infection has occurred. He or she will then be in a position to spread the infection to other persons unknowingly. Again there is good reason to suppose that one ought to warn past partners with whom one has been in a largely monogamous relationship. This contrasts with the case of past partners with whom one has had casual, high-risk sexual relations. Informing such past partners may not provide any news that is likely to change behavior.

In short, while those who are infected often have moral reasons for warning past partners, they do not always have compelling reasons. When one has practiced unsafe sex with past partners who themselves are promiscuous, warning them may provide little information they don't already have.

The case seems clearer concerning potential partners, as opposed to past partners. There certainly are good reasons for warning a person before exposing the person to the risk of infection. The warning may prevent serious harm. A person warned that a sexual partner is HIV infected can effectively avoid being infected. If the person decides to enter into some sort of sexual relation even after being warned, the risk of infection can be minimized or even eliminated completely.

Apart from preventing harm, warning one's potential partner enables the partner to make a more informed choice. Even in communities in which 75 percent of the people are infected, knowing that there is a 100 percent chance that one's partner is infected can be sobering. Also, it is not clear what counts as safe sex. While some practices (e.g., mutual masturbation) are quite safe, there is some doubt concerning the safety of other practices (e.g., sexual intercourse using a condom). What someone considers to be safe sex may depend on that person's estimate of the likelihood that his or her partner is infected. Finally, a potential sexual partner may be looking for a more permanent relationship and would want to know whether *his or her* potential partners were infected.

While it would appear that persons who know that they are infected always ought to warn future partners, we wish to argue that this may not always be true. There are certainly heavy costs to warning all of one's potential partners, and these should not be overlooked. Infected persons who warn all of their potential partners not only run all the risks of discrimination which those who warn past partners run, they also risk being unable to have any sexual relations, regardless of how safe the sex is.

In light of such risks, it may be morally permissible for persons who practice safe sex not to warn their partners. Suppose, for instance, that a man who knows that he is HIV positive meets another man in a San Francisco gay bar and they decide to engage in safe sex. The partner of the infected man knows that if he picks up men in gay bars, he will periodically pick up someone who is infected. He also knows that if he engages in safe sex, the chances of being infected are very slim. In short, he assumes the risk in order to lead a lifestyle which, for him, is worth the risk. The infected man can assume that his partner has already decided to risk having safe sex periodically with infected persons.

The question is whether the reasons for supposing HIV-infected persons ought to warn their partners are strong enough to override the reasons for not telling which are generated by the risks faced by infected persons. As in the case of warning partners generally, this depends, in part, on who the future partners are. If one is in a long-term, stable relationship or is contemplating such a relationship, the reasons for warning may indeed outweigh the risks, since, as we have seen, such relationships may involve a high degree of trust and vulnerability. On the other hand, when potential partners are already likely to know the risks they face and to have accepted those risks and when the activities engaged in are very safe, the reasons for warning are probably overridden by the dangers of warning.

In short, in those cases in which one has a strong reason for warning a potential partner about one's infection before engaging in unsafe sex, one has a weaker reason for warning before engaging in safe sex. This weaker reason is often overridden by the risks faced by the infected person. In general, the strength of the moral reasons for warning one's partner is proportional to the degree to which the partner can be trusted to keep the information confidential.

Suppose now that a man who might have been exposed to HIV infection decides to enter into a sexual relation in which he would clearly be obligated to warn his partner if he knew he was infected. Is such a person morally required to find out whether he is in fact infected? The duty to warn is incurred only when there is a differential in knowledge. If both people are equally aware or equally ignorant of the risk, the duty to warn simply does not arise. Suppose that Jones has not been tested for HIV infection but engages in high-risk sexual activity with a partner who has no reason to suspect that Jones has previously engaged in high-risk sexual activity. Jones is then confronted with a choice. He must either tell his partner of his high-risk status or get tested to find out whether he is positive. If he chooses the latter and is positive, he must then inform his partner of this. He has no obligation to find out whether he is infected, however, as long as his partner is as knowledgeable as he is about the risk.

THIRD PERSON WARNINGS

So far we have been dealing with reasons for the infected person to warn others of his or her own infection. Others who know of someone's infection may also have reasons to warn those who may become infected. As with first person warnings, the value of privacy is clearly pitted against the value of preventing danger by warning. The dilemma is perhaps most pressing in the case of the physician who learns that an HIV-infected patient has a sexual partner who is unaware of the infection.[6] If the patient refuses to tell the partner of the infection, what should the physician do? Certainly the physician has a reason to respect the confidentiality of medical information about patients. But the physician also has a reason for warning the partner of the risk. It thus becomes a question of which reason has more weight.

Several reasons have been given for thinking that overall the physician ought to preserve the confidentiality of the information. Sheldon Landesman claims that there are two reasons why doctors should not be legally required to warn those at risk. First, it may discourage voluntary testing.[7] This consideration may be especially troubling for physicians who treat a great many AIDS patients. Landesman claims that doctors with an "AIDS practice" should not warn the partners of HIV-infected patients because it would make it more likely that people with AIDS or who are HIV positive would not seek medical attention.[8] This, of course, is an empirical question, and it is difficult to know to what extent the practice of informing sexual partners at risk would really discourage people from seeking medical attention. There are several reasons, however, to think that the discouragement may not be as great as Landesman fears. Spouses and other sexual partners would be warned only if the physician was convinced that the infected person would not tell the sexual partner but would continue to have unsafe sex with him or her. Thus, not all of the physician's AIDS patients would have need to fear a breach of confidence. The only people discouraged would be those willing to tell the physician both that they had sexual partners who were ignorant of their infection and that they would refuse either to have safe sex in the future or to tell their partners of the risk they faced. Moreover, any person concerned enough about this problem would be more apt to deceive a physician about the partner's ignorance of the infection than to forgo medical care altogether.

---

[6] Although we will deal primarily with the duty of the physician, we believe that health care workers employed by the physician or acting as agents of the physician have the same duty as the physician to preserve confidentiality. However, they might not have the same duty to warn third parties, because they are not in charge of the overall treatment of patients to the same extent as physicians.

[7] Sheldon H. Landesman, "AIDS and a Duty to Protect," *Hastings Center Report* (February 1987): 23.

[8] Ibid.

The second reason mentioned by Landesman is that such a legal requirement would be difficult to implement fairly.[9] This is because it is unclear which sexual partners should be informed. However, this is not as unclear as Landesman seems to think. As we shall see, there are a number of factors which the physician can use to make a reasonable determination concerning whether a particular sexual partner should be warned (assuming the physician is aware of them). These factors include such things as whether the patient will engage in unsafe sexual practices, whether the patient will warn the partner, whether the partner is already likely to be aware of the risk, and whether the partner is probably already infected.

There are other reasons for thinking that the physician ought not to warn the partner. Perhaps the strongest reason for preserving confidentiality even in such situations is that spreading confidential information would be a violation of the patient's privacy. It is also a violation of the relationship of trust which the doctor and patient have established. This relationship is one of the most important social supports of the practice of medicine. It is trust which enables the patient to tell the physician those private things which are necessary for a proper diagnosis, and it is trust which gives the patient the confidence to take prescribed treatments even when they are unpleasant.

The fact that the patient and the partner are in a sexual relationship also makes a difference. Since they are in an intimate relationship, the physician must intrude on the privacy of the relationship in order to warn the partner. The physician runs the risk of meddling with a delicate and private relationship about which he or she may know little. It may be, for instance, that the patient will have to be careful in telling the partner in order to keep the relationship going. A heavy-handed call from the physician could needlessly destroy a relationship which the patient needs.

These reasons for preserving confidentiality conflict with reasons for warning the partner. The most obvious reason for warning the partner is that the physician may thus save the life of a person in peril, assuming that the partner has not already been infected. In the case of heterosexual relationships, it could also prevent the conception of a baby that might be born infected with HIV. If the phy-

---

[9] Ibid.

sician knows that his or her intervention may well save a life, there is a strong case to intervene, for saving a life generally overrides keeping a confidence. The case for intervention is weakened somewhat, however, by the fact that the physician must weigh the certainty that the patient's privacy will be violated against the mere likelihood that the partner will become infected. While this weakens the case, it does not destroy it. Surely preventing a substantial risk to life is far more weighty than the certainty of a violation of privacy.

In short, there are cases in which the physician ought to warn a partner who may be adversely affected, but such cases are much more rare than might be supposed at first glance. Since knowledge that there are sexual partners who might be at risk from the patient's activity puts the physician in an uncomfortable moral position, it might be tempting to avoid the moral problem by avoiding the knowledge which triggers it. This can be done in several ways. The physician can warn the patient that he or she regards it as morally obligatory to warn sexual partners whom the patient refuses to warn. This would allow the patient the opportunity to refuse to answer questions concerning partners whom the patient does not want the physician to contact. If the patient answers the questions, there is clearly a waiver of the right to privacy, since the patient knows the consequences of answering. The physician might also refrain from asking questions about sexual partners who might be at risk. While there is reason for thinking that the physician ought to warn the patient's sexual partners, it is by no means clear that the physician ought to attempt to find out whether there are sexual partners who are at risk. A physician's patients may be harming others in all sorts of ways. Surely the physician has no duty to ferret out all of this harm. Only if knowledge of the harm to others arises quite naturally in the course of treatment does the physician have good reason for inquiring further.

Obviously, the physician could also attempt to protect other persons at risk by explaining to the patient that the patient's sexual partners are at risk and should be warned, leaving it up to the patient to act on the physician's advice. This strategy has the additional advantage of enhancing the relationship of trust between the physician and the patient. The physician trusts the patient to act morally, while expecting the patient to trust him or her to respect confidentiality. Such a course of action seems especially justifiable in states in which there are mandatory reporting laws and contact tracing, since the physician can then rely on the state to warn partners. (Later we shall see that this actually constitutes one reason, though a minor one, for reporting laws and contact tracing.) In states without such laws this course of action seems justifiable only if the physician has reason to trust the patient.

Before deciding whether to warn the sexual partners of a patient, the physician must go through a complex balancing act, taking into account the various factors mentioned above. Because of the complexities of individual cases, it is difficult to specify general rules to cover all of the cases. It seems plausible in light of the above discussion, however, that at least the following conditions must be met before the physician is morally obliged to warn a sexual partner of an HIV-infected patient. The doctor must know with a high degree of certainty that (1) the infected patient will have unsafe sexual relations with a partner, (2) the patient will not warn the partner, (3) the potential partner is unaware of the risk which he or she faces, and (4) warning the partner will not so destroy the trust of other patients that more harm than good will result.

So far we have been concerned with the moral duty of a physician. Third persons other than health care workers may be in much the same position as physicians. However, two factors usually involved in the patient–physician relationship are often not relevant in the case of other third persons. The first is that physicians have a moral reason for preserving confidentiality. The physician learns about the infection of a patient because the patient allowed the physician to run tests with the expectation that, except for reports required by law, the results would be kept confidential. The physician learns about the patient's partners because the patient confides in the physician. While such confidential information may be given to nonphysicians, others may learn the relevant facts without being in a confidential relationship with the infected person.

The second factor is that physicians have a counseling role and their advice can be expected to carry weight with their patients. While other third parties may also have influence, it is standard that patients respect their physicians' advice (which is not to say that such respect is universal).

Other than these two, the factors are much the same in both cases. The medical expertise of the physician does not by itself create a special duty to warn others. While other third parties are not likely to know as much about the infection suffered by the person infected with HIV, they may know as much about the person's life and much more about the person's relationship with the partner. Nothing that has been said above would indicate that third parties who are not health care workers always have less of a reason to warn partners than physicians. In fact, they may have a stronger reason, because there are not the countervailing reasons based on trust and confidentiality which typically attend the patient–physician relationship.

THE LEGAL DUTY TO WARN

So far we have been exploring the complex moral issues concerning the duty to warn. The issues are morally complex and not easily resolved, at least in part because there are often conflicting values. Compared to the moral issues, the legal issues are relatively straightforward. Overall, the case law indicates that one who knowingly exposes another to a venereal disease through sexual contact without warning that person is open to a variety of tort suits, including negligence, battery, and misrepresentation.[10] Plaintiffs have recovered sizable damage awards from those who have infected them with venereal diseases, including herpes.

A person who negligently exposes another to an infectious disease is civilly liable for negligence.[11] The person is negligent if he

---

[10] *Kathleen K. v. Robert B.*, 150 Cal. App. 3d 992, 198 Cal. Rptr. 273 (1984). Although the facts of *Kathleen K.* concerned herpes, the court made it clear that its holding would apply to HIV infection as well (*Kathleen K.* at 276, note 3). For other cases upholding causes of action for transmission of venereal disease, see *De Vall v. Strunk*, 96 S.W. 2d 245, 246 (1936); *Crowell v. Crowell*, 180 N.C. 516, 105 S.E. 206, 208 (1920); *State v. Lankford*, 29 Del. 594, 102 A. 63, 64 (1917). For an excellent article on theories of liability in tort law and defenses, see Paula Murray and Robert Prentice, "Liability for Transmission of Herpes: Using Traditional Tort Principles to Encourage Honesty in Sexual Relationships," *Journal of Contemporary Law* 11 (1984–1985): 67–103.

[11] See, for instance, *Duke v. Housen*, 589 P.2d 334, 340 (1979), reh. den. 590 P.2d 1340 (1979); *Earle v. Kuklo*, 26 N.J. Super. 471, 98 A.2d 107, 109 (1953); *Kliegel v. Aitken*, 94 Wis. 432, 69 N.W. 67, 68 (1896).

or she failed to exercise the standard of care which a reasonable person would exercise. In the case of HIV infection, having unsafe sex with an unknowing partner would certainly be negligent. It is not always clear, however, what counts as negligence. For instance, suppose an infected person uses a condom and still infects the partner. It is not clear whether that would count as negligence, for it is not perfectly clear whether a reasonable person would regard the use of a condom as an appropriate level of care.

There are defenses against the charge of negligence. The relevant one from our point of view is assumption of risk. If the infected person warns the partner about the infection and the partner agrees to have sexual relations anyway, then the partner has assumed the risk of infection and the infected person is not liable for negligence.

An infected person who has sexual relations without warning the partner may also be liable for battery. Battery is offensive touching which is not consented to. It can be argued that the partner did not consent to have sexual relations with a person who is HIV infected. A recent California case, *Kathleen K. v. Robert B.*, held in part that failure to warn one's partner that one has a venereal disease, including AIDS and herpes, vitiates consent.[12] Although a person will be assumed to have consented to an act even if the consent was based on mistaken beliefs, a person does not consent to an act where the mistake concerns those aspects of the act which make it offensive and is the result of misrepresentation by the defendant. The misrepresentation can consist of untrue statements on which the plaintiff relies or it can consist of remaining silent when the plaintiff knows that the defendant is relying on a mistake.[13]

In general, third persons who merely know of risks but do not themselves expose others to harm have no legal duty to imperiled persons. Thus, a neighbor who learns that an HIV-infected husband has not told his wife of the infection has no legal duty to warn the wife. There are exceptions to this general rule, however. One such exception is the physician who has a patient with a contagious or infectious disease. Physicians have a legal duty to exercise reasonable care to protect others from infections transmitted by their patients, and this duty includes a duty to warn those who may become infected when it is necessary to do so to prevent harm. The

---

[12] *Kathleen K.*, 198 Cal. Rptr. at 277.
[13] See, for instance, *Crowell, supra* note 9.

physician-patient relationship, which tended to reduce the moral justification for warning others, increases the legal justification.

Doctors and other health workers may also have a duty under tort law to warn the sexual partners of those who test seropositive. A number of cases from a variety of jurisdictions have held that doctors have a duty to warn family members who may be in danger from a patient's contagious disease.[14] Although most previous cases have dealt with contagious disease which can be spread without voluntary conduct, courts have begun to hold medical professionals liable for the voluntary acts of their clients in cases other than those involving contagious disease. The most famous case in this respect is *Tarasoff v. Regents of the University of California*, in which a man killed a woman, Ms. Tarasoff, two months after confiding to his psychotherapists that he intended to kill her. No one warned Ms. Tarasoff that she was in danger. The court held that "a doctor or a psychotherapist treating a mentally ill patient, just as a doctor treating physical illness, bears a duty to use reasonable care to give threatened persons such warnings as are essential to avert foreseeable danger arising from his patient's condition or treatment."[15] Thus, in jurisdictions following *Tarasoff*, doctors and other health care providers have a duty to use reasonable care to protect others who may be threatened by their patients, including warning the sexual partners of patients who test HIV seropositive when it is necessary to do so in order to prevent foreseeable transmission of HIV. Failure to do so may make the doctor or health care provider liable for negligence.

Not just every health worker has such a duty to warn, however. In order for there to be a duty to warn, there must be a special relationship between the person with the duty and either the potential victim or the person likely to do the harm. While the notion of such a special relationship has not been given precise definition by the courts, it is clear that such a relationship exists between doctors and their patients. Such a relationship probably also exists between

---

[14] *Wojcik v. Aluminum Co. of America*, 18 Misc.2d 740, 183 N.Y.S.2d 351, 357–59 (1959); *Jones v. Stanko*, 118 Ohio St. 147, 160 N.E. 456, 458 (1928); *Davis v. Rodman*, 147 Ark. 385, 227 S.W. 612, 614 (1921); *Skillings v. Allen*, 143 Minn. 323, 173 N.W. 663, 664 (1919).

[15] *Tarasoff v. Regents of the University of California*, 118 Cal. Rptr. 129, 529 P.2d 553, 559 (1974).

patients and any health care workers, such as nurse practitioners, who have roles similar to those of physicians.

Threats to privacy arising from the duty to warn will be increasingly significant in the future as those who are diagnosed as HIV seropositive are increasingly motivated to sue. The tendency to sue is being fuelled by several factors. First, many scientists now believe that virtually everyone who is infected will eventually develop AIDS or ARC and die as a result. This is significant because people infected with HIV, unlike many people with AIDS, have time to bring suit on their own behalf. Such people are likely to live beyond the two or so years it takes to get a case to court. Second, insurance companies more and more, are refusing to insure people who are HIV infected and demanding that prospective insurees be tested. This means that an infected person may be facing uninsured expenses as high as $150,000 in caring for his or her illness. People facing such expenses are highly motivated to find sources for the needed funds. Third, as the threat of AIDS induces people to be less promiscuous, people who do become HIV infected will have a better chance of determining the source of the virus. Fourth, case law has been developing since the advent of herpes that makes such suits possible under a variety of tort theories.

The possibility of such suits and the increasing motivation for bringing them threatens privacy in several ways. Doctors who foresee the possibility of such suits will attempt to warn the sexual partners of their patients who are diagnosed with HIV infection. Also, those who bring suits will attempt to subpoena various test and other medical records in order to establish the causal claims necessary for their suits.

REPORTING LAWS AND CONTACT TRACING

Most states require the reporting of confirmed cases of AIDS and several states require the reporting of HIV infection. Many states also have contact tracing or partner notification programs. In some programs, such as those in Connecticut, Delaware, Maine, and Michigan, persons who are HIV infected are encouraged to notify their own partners, and state assistance is provided if requested. However, in some states, such as Colorado, Idaho, and North Carolina, named partners are contacted by state officials if the HIV-infected person does not agree to notify them.[16] All states with such programs protect the confidentiality of the infected person. The Centers for Disease Control (CDC) recommends that

> persons who are HIV-antibody positive should be instructed in how to notify their partners and to refer them for counseling and testing. If they are unwilling to notify their partners or if it cannot be assured that their partners will seek counseling, physicians or health department personnel should use confidential procedures to assure that the partners are notified.[17]

On the surface, reporting laws and contact tracing have a number of benefits. In theory, reporting laws enable state epidemiologists to compile comprehensive lists of people with AIDS or HIV infection. This data can be used in a variety of studies that yield important knowledge. Reporting laws also facilitate contact tracing. We have already touched briefly on one of the benefits of contact tracing. Physicians who must warn partners of their HIV-infected patients are faced with the difficult choice of either violating the patient's trust or allowing an innocent person to be placed in avoidable peril. Reporting laws and contact tracing can be helpful in alleviating the problem. If the doctor tells the patient about these laws at the outset, he or she can make clear the terms of the doctor-patient relationship — that there is an exception to the duty of the physician to keep medical information about patients confidential. This means that the doctor is not violating the trust of the patient when he or she reports the patient's name to the state, since there was no expectation that such information would be kept confidential in the first place. In order for this benefit to occur, however, doctors must inform their patients of the relevant laws at the outset. Contact tracing can also mean that the doctor does not have to question the patient about his or her sexual partners. This is left to the state. When the state official arrives to ask questions about sexual partners, the infected

---

[16] See David Goodman, "Questions Raised about Contact Tracing for AIDS," *American Medical News*, March 18, 1988, p. 2.

[17] "Partner Notification for Preventing Human Immunodeficiency Virus (HIV) Infection — Colorado, Idaho, South Carolina, Virginia," *Morbidity and Mortality Weekly Report* 37 (1988): 393, citing Centers for Disease Control Public Health Service guidelines for counseling and antibody testing to prevent HIV infection and AIDS, *Morbidity and Mortality Weekly Report* 36 (1987): 509–15.

person is certainly on notice about what will be done with the information. Thus, unlike the case of physicians who warn, the potential for deception and manipulation does not exist.

There are also benefits for those people who test positive and feel that they are morally obliged to warn past partners but who also fear a loss of confidentiality. If the contacts are made by state officials who preserve confidentiality, then those who are warned may be unaware which of their partners was infected. Of course, such contact tracing by the state will actually preserve confidentiality only in those cases in which past partners have themselves had several partners. The faithful and unsuspecting wife of an HIV-infected bisexual will be able to infer without difficulty who exposed her to the virus. Nonetheless, there is a benefit. It should be noted that this benefit can be secured with a program of voluntary contact tracing in which an infected person is allowed to decide whether to use the services of the state.

Some people who learn that they have been exposed to HIV infection may want to get tested so that they can make plans for the future with full knowledge of their state of health. Such plans may include financial planning and, if possible, making use of experimental treatments which promise a lengthened life, if not a cure. As Chapter 5 makes clear, however, for other people, this rather small benefit will not be worth the risk. Unlike other venereal diseases, there is no prospect of a cure for HIV infection that would motivate one to learn of the disease. Also, the person who learns that he or she is positive faces all of the costs noted in Chapter 5.

Contact tracing may also help to slow the spread of the disease by motivating people to change their behavior. As noted in Chapter 5, if people who are warned get tested and find that they are negative, they may be motivated to refrain from risky behavior in the future. Nothing makes one watchful while crossing streets like nearly being struck by an automobile. If, on the other hand, they find that they are positive, they may well be motivated not to engage in unsafe activities in order to protect others. In order to be effective in this regard, contact tracing must be combined with a serious counseling program. This benefit is not as strong as might at first appear, however. Unlike other venereal diseases, AIDS does not usually manifest symptoms shortly after the time of infection. It may be a number of years before a person who has become HIV infected develops symptoms of AIDS. This means that it is more difficult to stamp out infection or even dramatically reduce the incidence of the infection with contact tracing than in the case of other venereal diseases. This is because many people may be infected by a sexually active person in the long period before the appearance of symptoms. Also, the lack of a cure means that those who are found to be positive may still infect others. The spread must be stopped with behavior change rather than with a "magic bullet."

From what has been said so far, it may appear puzzling that not every state has adopted both reporting laws for HIV infection and a rigorous program of contact tracing. There are, however, burdens imposed by reporting laws and contact tracing as well as benefits. Reporting laws and some contact tracing programs pose a threat to privacy in that they amass information in government hands and thus enable other uses of the information. These dangers will be aggravated if hysteria over AIDS increases to the point where the state itself may use the information for discriminatory purposes. Also, the information might be subpoenaed for use in criminal and civil suits. Once subpoenaed, there is danger that the information will become public by being made part of a public trial. The judge granting the subpoena may, however, issue orders designed to protect confidentiality. Apart from such legal threats to the confidentiality of the information, there is also the possibility of accidental or illicit release.

Thus the most obvious problem with contact tracing is that it is a tremendous incursion into privacy. As we have noted in Chapter 3, sexual matters are among the things which we regard as most private. For contact tracing to be successful, the infected person must tell the identity of his or her sexual partners to a total stranger. When contact tracing is combined with psychological counseling, it may become even more invasive. One is not only suddenly thrust into a situation in which one is expected to identify sexual partners, but one must also deal with a counselor skilled at worming his or her way into the personality. While some counselors may be sensitive to the fears and needs of people who have recently learned that they are HIV infected, others may not. Names gleaned by the contact tracers are part of state files that those named have no control over. It is not unreasonable for someone to fear being put on a state list of people who have a disease which has triggered tremendous discrimination. Such fear may motivate HIV-infected persons to lie to contact tracers or withhold information in order to protect past partners about whom they are concerned.

Even if the state preserves confidentiality, a person may still have reason to believe that past sexual partners will be able to determine that he or she is infected. This occurs when the person can be relatively certain that these sexual partners have themselves had only one or two sexual partners. People enmeshed in the net of contact tracing are then placed in a situation in which their disease may be publicly exposed even when the state sedulously maintains confidentiality.

These burdens are alleviated, at least to some extent, in contact-tracing programs in which state officials provide counseling and contact partners only upon the request of the HIV-infected person. Such programs minimize the intrusion into privacy while obtaining at least some of the benefits of the more active programs of contact tracing.

THE CONSTITUTIONALITY OF REPORTING LAWS AND CONTACT TRACING

The Supreme Court has not dealt with the constitutionality of laws requiring the reporting of AIDS or HIV infection. Nor has it dealt with contact tracing. The Supreme Court has, however, dealt with several medical reporting laws. In *Whalen v. Roe*, the Supreme Court held that a New York statute which required physicians to report to the state the names and addresses of all persons receiving prescriptions for various drugs was not a violation of privacy or liberty guaranteed by the Fourteenth Amendment.[18] Justice Stevens, writing for the majority, noted that legislation having some effect on liberty or privacy was not to be found unconstitutional merely because the court found it unnecessary.[19] In upholding the particular legislation in question, Justice Stevens found that the legislation was a reasonable exercise of police powers.[20] In short, Justice Stevens applied the rational basis test, according to which laws are to be upheld if they are reasonably related to a legitimate state interest.

---

[18] *Whalen v. Roe*, 429 U.S. 589, 603 (1977).
[19] Ibid., 596–97.
[20] Ibid., 598.

This suggests that the rational basis test will be applied to minor restrictions of liberty or even privacy. The Court also pointed out that there was little chance of public disclosure of the information collected.[21] Yet, the Court also said that it was not deciding the question presented by unwarranted disclosure of accumulated data. Finally, the Court pointed out that "disclosures of private medical information to doctors, to hospital personnel, to insurance companies, and to public health agencies are often an essential part of modern medical practice."[22] The Court gave as a specific example the statutory reporting requirements concerning venereal disease.

Reporting requirements have also been upheld in abortion cases provided that they were reasonably directed to the preservation of health and respected the patient's confidentiality. In particular, the reports should not include personal information about the patient or information about the basis for the medical judgment, and they should be used solely for statistical purposes and be kept confidential except with respect to public health officers.[23]

Given Justice Stevens's use of the rational basis test, it is probable that state laws requiring the reporting of AIDS and even HIV infection will be upheld as long as confidentiality is preserved. While reporting laws may not be necessary for stemming the spread of AIDS, we have seen that such laws are reasonably related to slowing the spread of AIDS.[24]

It does not follow from anything that has been said above, however, that contact tracing is constitutional. In fact, it is arguable that programs of contact tracing in which partners are contacted with-

---

[21] Ibid., 601–2.

[22] Ibid., 602.

[23] *Thornburgh v. American College of Obstetricians and Gynecologists*, 476 U.S., 747 (1986); *Planned Parenthood of Central Mo. v. Danforth*, 428 U.S. 52, 80 (1976).

[24] For an argument that reporting laws which require identification of people who test positive are unconstitutional in spite of *Whalen*, see Donna Costa, "Reportability of Exposure to the AIDS Virus: An Equal Protection Analysis," *Cardozo Law Review* 7 (Summer 1986):1125–26. On the other hand, several writers have thought that reporting laws would be found constitutional under the *Whalen* standard. See, for instance, Lawrence Gostin, William Curran, and Mary Clark, "The Case against Compulsory Casefinding—Testing, Screening and Reporting," *American Journal of Law and Medicine* 12 (1987): 52.

out the consent of the infected person who provides the names are not constitutional. First, the intrusion into privacy is much greater than in the case of reporting laws. It is arguable that the intrusion is sufficiently significant that strict scrutiny or at least an intermediate test should be applied rather than the rational basis test. While contact tracing may, as we have seen, be reasonably related to slowing the spread of AIDS and HIV infection, it is not necessary for slowing the spread of AIDS. Even in the case of the rational basis test, it could be argued that active programs of contact tracing do not adequately preserve confidentiality.[25] As we have seen, it is reasonable to suppose that there will be numerous cases in which a partner who is contacted will be able to infer which one of his or her partners or former partners is HIV infected.

CONCLUSION

The duty to warn constitutes a significant threat to the privacy of those who are infected with HIV. There may be a legal duty to warn partners, but some of those warned will inevitably not keep the information confidential. Should one infect a partner who then brings suit, one's HIV status will become part of the public record. An HIV-infected person's own physician may be legally obliged to report the patient's infection to state officials and even to warn sexual partners. Even when there is no legal duty to warn others, an infected person may have a moral duty to inform sexual partners. However, these partners may fail to keep the confidence. All of this constitutes a major threat to the privacy of a person who desperately needs to keep it intact.

---

[25] For a similar argument regarding mandatory reporting laws which require that the identity of the AIDS carrier be reported, see "The Constitutional Rights of AIDS Carriers," *Harvard Law Review* 29 (1986): 1288.

7
Testing and Health Care Delivery

INTRODUCTION

In an address in which he criticized doctors who refuse to treat AIDS patients, Surgeon General C. Everett Koop stated, "In some ways the purely scientific issues pale in comparison to the highly sensitive issues of law, ethics, economics and social cohesion that are beginning to surface."[1] Dr. Koop is right. The moral problems which AIDS poses for the delivery of health care are daunting. There has been heated discussion, for instance, concerning what steps should be taken to protect health care workers from HIV-infected patients and to protect patients from HIV-infected health care workers.

In this chapter we argue for several controversial theses. We argue (1) that competent patients should never be tested for HIV seropositivity without their consent, (2) that medical treatment for problems unrelated to HIV infection or AIDS should not be made conditional upon taking an HIV test, and (3) that health care workers such as surgeons should be tested for HIV positivity if it can be shown that they perform procedures in which there is a significant risk that they could, if infected, transmit the infection to patients. We note, however, that there is not sufficient evidence of risk to require testing of health care workers at the present time.

Although we are concerned with health care delivery in general, we will concentrate mainly on the hospital setting. It is in the hospital that the issues and competing values come most sharply into focus.

---

[1] C. Everett Koop, Address to the Presidential Commission on the Human Immunodeficiency Virus Epidemic, as reported by Philip Boffey in the *New York Times*, September 10, 1987, A1.

THE HOSPITAL SETTING

Hospitals differ from other institutions for which mandatory HIV testing has been proposed. First, unlike institutions such as the armed forces and the Job Corps, procedures are routinely performed in hospitals during which it is possible to spread the AIDS virus. Such procedures include surgery, emergency procedures involving massive bleeding, intubation of patients, hemodialysis, and some dental work. Even so routine a procedure as giving an injection could be a means of transmitting the virus when an accidential needle stick occurs with a needle which has just been used on an HIV-infected person. Even a brief list of the procedures which could possibly spread the AIDS virus makes it appear that hospitals are fraught with danger. In fact, the probability of the virus being transmitted in a hospital setting is extremely low. Although millions of surgeries have been performed since the AIDS virus was detected in 1981, there is no known case of a surgeon being infected by a patient or of a patient being infected by a surgeon. Indeed, only a handful of health care workers have been identified who can be presumed to have been infected through job-related mishaps such as needle stick injuries or exposure of mucous membranes to infected body fluids.[2]

It is helpful to compare HIV with hepatitis B, since they are spread in similar ways. The risk of hepatitis B transmission in the health care setting far exceeds the risk of HIV transmission.[3] If a health care worker gives an injection to a person infected with hepatitis B and then accidentally sticks him- or herself, the probability of the health care worker acquiring hepatitis B is between 6 and 30 percent. The probability of HIV transmission resulting from a needle

---

[2] As of July 10, 1987, the CDC national surveillance system had located 1,875 health care workers with AIDS. Yet, as of August 21, 1987, the CDC had identified fewer than 20 HIV-infected health care workers whose exposure to HIV could not be accounted for by risk factors other than health care work. See "Centers for Disease Control Recommendations for Prevention of HIV Transmission in Health-Care Settings," *Morbidity and Mortality Weekly Report* 36 (August 21, 1987): 4S-5S. It should, of course, be noted that there may be other infected individuals not identified by the CDC.

[3] "Centers for Disease Control Recommendations for Preventing Transmission of Infection with Human T-Lymphotropic Virus Type III/Lymphadenopathy-associated Virus in the Workplace," *Morbidity and Mortality Weekly Report* 34 (1985): 681-86, 691-95.

stick with a contaminated needle is less than 1 percent.[4] It is interesting to note that in spite of the higher probability of transmission, the CDC has never recommended screening all patients or health care workers for hepatitis B infection. In short, the overall picture gives no cause for alarm. Nonetheless, the possibility of transmitting infection, however slight, warrants prudence.

Some of the risks faced in hospitals also occur in small clinics and in the offices of private practitioners. A nurse giving an injection in a small clinic can accidentally stick him- or herself as easily as a nurse in a large metropolitan hospital. However, some risks, such as those involved in surgery, are associated primarily with hospitals.

A second way in which hospitals differ from certain other institutions is that in hospitals there is a reduced expectation of privacy. Hospitals share this feature with prisons and the military service. Patients who enter a teaching hospital know that they may not only be physically examined by their own doctors, but also be asked to consent to examination by strangers or in the presence of strangers, such as nurses or interns not directly involved in the treatment. Patients also know that a battery of tests are likely to be performed and records kept indicating a variety of personal facts about their state of health. The loss of privacy experienced by patients in hospitals is far greater than the loss of privacy experienced by patients in small clinics or within the offices of their own doctors. Even in these settings, however, patients must sacrifice privacy in order to be treated effectively.

Closely associated with the diminished expectation of privacy is the diminished control over their lives which patients experience. This is the third way in which hospitals differ from certain other institutions. Again there is an analogy between hospitals on the one hand and prisons and the military on the other hand. Patients admitted to a hospital enter a tightly controlled, hierarchical environment dominated by people with expertise in fields about which most patients know little. It is impossible for patients to deal with such professionals on equal terms during the process of determining the course of treatment. The doctor shares with the patient knowledge he or she thinks is relevant and directs the patient's attention to

---

[4] Ibid.

issues which the doctor has decided merit the patient's concern. The difficulties faced by the patient are exacerbated by the hospital setting, where doctors and nurses wear uniforms, where doctors are called "doctor" while patients are called by their first names, and where patients are often placed on a schedule determined by the convenience of others. These are problems faced by patients who are calm and in control of their faculties. Patients brought into an emergency room may be overwhelmed by pain and fear. They may be unconscious, or barely conscious, or incoherent. Such patients have little autonomy.

Patients often have more autonomy in dealing with small clinics or private doctors. The bureaucracy is not as large and impersonal, the setting is less forbidding, and the patient may have a well-established relationship with those treating him or her. Even in such benign settings, however, the patient is still dealing with professionals on uneven terms.

Finally, hospitals differ from some other institutions for which testing has been proposed in that the health care workers who staff hospitals are committed to a deeply held ethic of care. In this way hospitals differ dramatically from prisons and the military. There are, however, a number of competing values faced by health care professionals, and it is worthwhile considering these briefly.

HEALTH CARE VALUES

The debate over HIV testing in the health care setting takes place against a background of various health care values. While there is no need to explore all of these values or to provide a philosophical defense for them, it will be helpful to call attention to several of them which are generally accepted.[5]

In light of recent reports about physicians who have refused to treat HIV-infected people, perhaps the most relevant value is the value of providing treatment to those who are ill or injured. No one would deny that one of the primary values served by the medical profession is the provision of medical treatment to those who require it. The controversy arises not over the value of providing medical

---

[5] For the sake of simplicity we will concentrate on physicians, but much of what we say applies to other health care professionals such as nurses and therapists.

treatment but over whether there is also a duty to provide it. While few would deny that physicians, taken as a group, ought to provide medical treatment to those who require it, there is significant controversy over whether individual physicians have a duty to provide treatment. It is certainly false that individual physicians have a duty to treat everyone requesting treatment. They do not, for instance, have a duty to treat people outside their areas of competence. Nor do they have a duty to treat more patients than they can comfortably handle, assuming those turned away can get help elsewhere. Physicians also do not have a duty to treat those requesting treatments which they reasonably believe to be ill-advised.

Notwithstanding all of these limitations, many would agree that physicians have at least a prima facie duty to treat those within their areas of competence who require treatment and who cannot readily get the treatment elsewhere, especially in the case of emergencies.[6] Although the issue of when individual physicians have a duty to treat those who are ill or injured is beyond our scope, we note that those who fail to treat patients in need of medical treatment when other physicians are not available sacrifice one of the foremost values of the medical profession.[7]

We also place a high degree of value on preserving patient autonomy. The extent to which we value autonomy and its relationship to privacy was discussed in Chapter 3. Although there is significant controversy over whether individual physicians have a duty to treat

---

[6] See, for instance, the International Code of Medical Ethics adopted by the Third General Assembly of the World Medical Association, London, England, 1949, which provides that

> a doctor must give emergency care as a humanitarian duty unless he is assured that others are willing and able to give such care.

Reprinted in Robert M. Veatch, *Case Studies in Medical Ethics* (Cambridge, Mass.: Harvard University Press, 1977), 355–56. Section 7 of the American Hospital Association's Patient's Bill of Rights states that

> the patient has the right to expect that within its capacity a hospital must make reasonable response to the request of a patient for services. The hospital must provide evaluation, service and/or referral as indicated by the urgency of the case.

Reprinted in Veatch, *Medical Ethics*, 352–54.

[7] For a discussion of the duty to treat patients with HIV infection, see Abigail Zuger and Steven H. Miles, "Physicians, AIDS, and Occupational Risk," *Journal of the American Medical Association* 258 (1987): 1924–28.

patients, most would agree that physicians have a duty to respect the autonomy of their patients.[8] That is, the patient's desires and choices need to be taken into account in determining the appropriate course of treatment. The disagreement arises over just what this principle entails. How much information do patients need to be given before their consent to a particular treatment should be considered informed? How do we determine when a patient is competent to consent to a procedure? However these questions are resolved, it is at least clear that the patient's desires are to be given substantial weight in decisions about how the patient is to be treated. This principle of respect has the corollary that patients ought to be informed of the significant facts concerning their condition and of the significant risks involved in various alternative treatments.[9]

Another corollary of this principle is that there is a duty to preserve patient confidentiality. Medical professionals generally recognize this duty and attempt to keep the conversations and records of their patients confidential.[10] As we have seen, this is especially important for patients who are HIV seropositive. Unfortunately, as we have also seen, the duty to preserve confidentiality is sometimes overridden by compelling moral reasons based on the need to warn others of danger posed by a patient.

Apart from moral duties to patients and to the public generally, health care workers who employ others have duties to their employees. Like other employers, health care employers have a duty to

---

[8] This duty is given voice in the American Hospital Association's Patient's Bill of Rights. Sections 3, 4, and 5 provide that the patient shall receive the information necessary for informed consent, shall have the right to refuse treatment and shall have his or her privacy respected. Reprinted in Veatch, *Medical Ethics*, 353.

[9] See, for instance, Sections 2 and 3 of the American Hospital Association's Patient's Bill of Rights, reprinted in Veatch, *Medical Ethics*, 352.

[10] See Sections 5 and 6 of the American Hospital Association's Patient's Bill of Rights and Section 9 of the American Medical Association's Principles of Medical Ethics, reprinted in Veatch, *Medical Ethics*, 352–54. Section 9 of the Principles of Medical Ethics states the following:

A physician may not reveal the confidences entrusted to him in the course of medical attendance, or the deficiencies he may observe in the character of patients, unless he is required to do so by law or unless it becomes necessary in order to protect the welfare of the individual or of the community.

provide their employees with as safe a workplace as possible and to warn employees of risks which cannot be eliminated. Such moral considerations are given legal force through the Occupational Safety and Health Act (OSHA).[11] OSHA regulations require employers not only to provide a safe workplace and to warn employees of unavoidable risks, but also to protect employees who refuse to do certain jobs because they reasonably and in good faith believe that the jobs pose a danger of death or serious injury.

TESTING PATIENTS

Some have argued that hospitals should test patients for HIV infection to gain epidemiological knowledge and to allow precautions to be taken with those who test positive. Depending on the procedure, such precautions might include wearing gloves, masks, goggles or impervious gowns, using staples instead of sutures, and using electrocautery devices in surgery instead of scalpels.[12] Such proposals may take one of three general forms. First, it might be proposed that all patients admitted to a hospital be tested. Second, it might be proposed that patients from high-risk groups be tested. Third, it might be proposed that patients about to undergo procedures where there is the possibility of transmitting HIV infection be tested. As we shall see, problems arise for some of these proposals but not others. (There are also some problems that arise for all of the proposals.)

Several reasons are given for testing patients. First, it is argued that by testing patients hospitals will be able to gain valuable knowledge about the spread of AIDS. Hospitals are one of the turnstiles at which it is convenient to test large numbers of people. As we have noted above, hospitals and health care workers serve the important social function of contributing to knowledge concerning public health. This gives at least some support to this reason for testing. Yet the reason is much weaker than might at first appear. The vast majority of people admitted to hospitals are elderly and not HIV infected. Mass testing of such people results in little benefit consid-

---

[11] See 29 U.S.C., §254 of the Occupational Safety and Health Act.

[12] For lists of precautions to be taken in various health care settings, see "Centers for Disease Control Recommendations for Prevention of HIV Transmission in Health-Care Settings."

ering the expense. Attempting to test people admitted from high-risk groups would have a higher yield of seropositives. However, it is not clear how hospitals could accurately determine who is in a high-risk group.

The second reason which is given for testing is that it is important to determine who is HIV infected in order to protect hospital health care workers. Health care workers can take precautions to protect themselves from HIV-infected patients that they would not take with patients generally. We have seen that employers have a duty to provide a safe working environment, and it has been argued that HIV testing would be the best way to provide such an environment.

This reason, too, is weaker than it might at first appear. Very few health care workers have been infected with HIV through job-related transmissions. As of August 1987, fewer than twenty health care workers had become infected with HIV in cases in which no other risk factors were present.[13] Moreover, there have been no documented cases of surgeons being infected by transmission of the virus during surgery. The risk of HIV infection can hardly be said to have turned the hospital into a dangerous place.

Also, the reason does not support testing all hospital patients or even all patients from high-risk groups. At best, it supports testing patients who are about to undergo procedures in which there is some risk of transmission. However, there are two problems even with this variation. First, there is a problem with false negatives. People who are infected with HIV may take as long as a year to develop antibodies at levels which can be detected by antibody tests such as ELISA and the Western blot test. Testing does not, then, provide fail-safe protection. Second, precautions can be taken without testing. If precautions pose no risk to the patient, they can be taken for all patients (universal precautions). The CDC, for instance, recommends that blood and body fluid precautions be taken for all patients, since "medical history and examination cannot reliably identify all patients infected with HIV or other blood-borne pathogens."[14] If, however, the precautions do pose some risk to the patient (e.g., by slowing down a surgical procedure or making the sur-

---

[13] See note 2.

[14] "Centers for Disease Control Recommendations for Prevention of HIV Transmission in Health-Care Settings," 5S.

geons less efficient), then the precautions can be taken only for those who decline to take the test or who test positive. The patient can be given the choice whether to take the test or take the risk of a procedure performed with precautions. We will return to this proposal later where we argue that it provides an acceptable alternative to mandatory testing of patients.

A third reason for testing persons admitted to a hospital is that those who test positive can be counseled to change their behavior so as not to infect others. This is not a negligible benefit. Surely some people would be detected who are HIV infected and unaware of their infection, and surely some of these could be persuaded to change their behavior.

Nonetheless, the vast majority of those tested would have very little chance of being infected. Concentrating on the testing of high-risk groups admitted to the hospital would be more efficient. But again, it is not clear how it could be determined whether a patient admitted to a hospital was a member of a high-risk group without a massive violation of privacy. As for reaching HIV positives who are unaware of their status, it would simply be more efficient to attempt to educate and counsel gays and IV drug abusers.

These rather weak reasons for requiring patients to be tested must be weighed against very powerful reasons for not requiring testing. To begin with, many patients have good reason to resist being tested for HIV. The most obvious reason is that hospital confidentiality cannot in fact be guaranteed. We have noted in Chapters 2 and 5 how easy it is for unauthorized persons to gain access to a patient's physical records. It is difficult for hospitals to create the security necessary to guarantee privacy, because treatment of patients is more efficient when those who need access to records and facts about patients can get the records easily and quickly. When large numbers of health care workers and even hospital staff not directly involved in treatment can gain access to a patient's records, there is of course a chance that information will leak outside the bounds of the hospital.

Apart from the unauthorized release of confidential information, those who test positive for HIV also need to fear releases of information which they may later be forced to authorize. If a patient is planning to buy insurance, he or she might not want to be tested until the insurance is purchased. If a patient already has insurance, the test results may be released when the bill for tests and various treatments is sent to the insurance company. Also, patients who later become involved in lawsuits in which their health is an issue may be required by the court to release medical records.

Patients may also reasonably resist being tested upon entrance to a hospital because they are not psychologically ready to be tested at that time. We have already noted that news of a positive HIV test can create a tremendous psychological and moral crisis. It is important that those who are tested be adequately counseled and be ready for the test.

The strength of the reasons against mandatory tests can also be clearly seen by considering the choices faced by a hospital which requires testing. Suppose that a patient is told that he or she must be tested for HIV infection and is asked to sign a consent form for the test. If the patient refuses to "consent" to the test, then the hospital is faced with a serious problem. There are three possibilities: (1) Hospital staff can simply force the patient to take the test unwillingly. (2) Hospital staff could threaten to refuse to provide treatment unless the patient consents. (3) The hospital could run the test on the patient without the patient's knowledge.

The first alternative is obviously unacceptable. Forcing a patient to undergo a test unwillingly is a form of battery and would expose the hospital to legal liability. Moreover, as we have seen, testing should be done in a supportive environment in which counseling has a chance to be effective. Testing which results from threats or outright coercion destroys the relationship of trust between the doctor and patient which is crucial to effective health care.

While the second alternative is less drastic than simply forcing the patient to take the test, it too has serious problems. First, testing should be done with adequate counseling and in an atmosphere of trust. Patients who are required to take an HIV test in order to get treatment at all are responding to threats, and this will detract from the effectiveness of counseling. In addition, when a patient is injured or requires treatment, it is not clear that consent to an HIV test is genuine consent. Severely ill patients who must consent to HIV testing in order to get treatment are being subjected to a form of coercion. The second alternative also puts the hospital in the position of having to deny treatment in the event that the patient refuses to consent or withdraws the consent originally given. This is justified only if the test is required as part of the treatment or to protect others. But whatever precautions would be taken if the person tested positive can be taken if the person refuses to be tested. In this case, however, the patient should be informed of the precautions that will be taken if any of the precautions create a risk for the patient.

It might be thought that a hospital could avoid any serious problems by adopting the third option and simply testing the patient without the patient's knowledge.[15] Yet, like the first option, this too would expose the hospital to legal liability. Moreover, if the test is positive, then the hospital has a legal duty to warn the patient. It also has, as we have seen, a duty to ensure that others whom it knows will be placed at risk by the patient are warned. Finally, when the doctor tells the patient that he or she has been surreptitiously tested for HIV and has tested positive, the relationship of trust which is necessary for effective counseling and the exploration of possible treatments has been severely damaged.

We have supposed up to this point that the patient refuses to give his or her consent to mandatory testing. Even if the patient signs a consent form for the HIV test, however, it is not clear that the consent is genuine. For example, if a patient is told that the doctor will refuse to perform needed surgery unless the patient "consents" to participate in a research experiment conducted by the doctor, then the consent is not genuine but coerced. We are inclined to say that the consent to participate in the experiment was not genuine in part because the experiment was not reasonably related to the success of the surgery. If, however, that which is consented to is reasonably related to the procedure, then the consent is genuine. For instance, if a patient about to undergo needed surgery is told that the surgery will not be performed unless the patient consents to a blood transfusion because it is necessary for the success of the surgery, the patient cannot claim that he or she was coerced into consenting to the transfusion. The question concerning HIV testing now becomes whether the HIV test is reasonably related to the patient's treatment.

There are cases in which conditionally mandated HIV testing is perfectly reasonable. In some cases there is reason to believe that the patient is HIV infected and that an HIV test is needed for diagnosis so that appropriate forms of treatment can be undertaken. No

---

[15] This actually happens. See Keith Henry, Myra Maki, and Kent Crossley, "Analysis of the Use of HIV Antibody Testing in a Minnesota Hospital," *Journal of the American Medical Association* 259 (1987): 229–32.

one would claim that a physician who requires an HIV test before prescribing zidovudine is unreasonable or that the consent to the test is not genuine.

Unfortunately, this is not what those who propose conditionally mandatory testing have in mind. If all persons admitted to a hospital are required to be tested, much of the testing will obviously be unrelated to any treatment which the patient is receiving. This will even be true if tests are required of all persons in high-risk groups. In addition, if all hospitals require tests, then there may be no option of receiving treatment elsewhere. Under such circumstances, the consent given will not be genuine.

Whether it is ethical to test patients about to undergo procedures where there is a possibility of transmitting infection is less clear. Since there is a possibility of transmitting the infection, there is at least some reason to require tests so that precautions can be taken or the treatment denied. At first glance it may appear that the hospital is in a dilemma. It must either refuse to treat patients needing help or force them to take a test without fully voluntary consent.

The way out of the dilemma is to go between the horns. Hospitals can come close to balancing the various values involved by requiring their workers to take the same precautions with all patients that they would take with those who are HIV seropositive, unless the precaution would pose a risk to the patient. As we have noted, this is the recommendation of the CDC. In those cases in which precautions would be taken for a patient who is HIV infected but not for other patients because the precautions pose a slight risk to the patient, the physician should point out to the patient what precautions are taken when the HIV status of the patient undergoing the procedure is not known. The physician should point out both the risks to the patient of the precaution and the risks which may result from breaches of confidentiality regarding a positive HIV test. The patient can then decide whether to consent to an HIV test and take the chance that there will be a positive result and a breach in confidentiality or instead to withhold consent and accept the slightly increased risk brought about by the precautions taken by the surgeons.

The adoption of such a policy has several advantages. First, it does not require medical professionals to withhold treatment or to threaten to withhold treatment. Second, for adult patients it also provides that the patient's consent will be secured before being subjected to HIV testing or to any risks resulting from precautions which may have to be taken. In the case of children, consent will have to be given by their parents or guardians. While there are problems concerning consent given by parents because of potential conflicts of interest between parent and child, parental consent for HIV testing is no more problematic than parental consent for other medical procedures. It is certainly preferable to universal HIV testing or universal precautions. Third, the policy also does not require invasions of privacy or discrimination against gays or other high-risk groups. Finally, the policy offers protection to health care workers.

TESTING HEALTH CARE WORKERS

The vast majority of health care workers do not engage in procedures in which there is the possibility of infecting a patient. There are some procedures, however, in which it may be possible for infected health care workers to infect patients. Some argue that surgeons who cut themselves during surgery, for instance, may infect the patient as well as be infected by the patient. If this is true, there is reason to test health care workers who perform invasive procedures in which the patient could become infected just as there is reason to test the patient. (For the moment we shall assume that there is a significant risk of transmitting HIV infection from health care workers to patients in order to consider some of the ethical implications of this assumption.)

Assuming that there is a significant risk of transmitting infection, the reasons against mandatory testing of health care workers involved in invasive procedures are not as compelling as the reasons against testing patients. If a patient tests positive, health care workers, as we have seen, are still obliged to provide treatment. As we have also seen, this obligation significantly undercuts the rationale for the mandatory testing of patients. On the other hand, patients who do not want to accept the risks imposed by an infected doctor are under no obligation to allow themselves to be treated by the doctor. Thus there is a crucial asymmetry between doctors and patients.

On the assumption that HIV-infected physicians who perform certain procedures pose a significant risk of infection to their patients, the physicians ought either to refrain from performing the procedures or to inform their patients of the risk which they face. Failing to inform a patient of a material risk posed by the procedure would invalidate the patient's consent to the procedure. In effect, the physician would be committing battery against the patient. Physicians who expose their patients to a significant risk of infection may also be liable for negligence should a patient become infected.

The costs of informing patients that a physician is HIV infected should not be underestimated. Unlike physicians, patients do not typically take themselves to be under a duty to preserve the confidentiality of information about their physicians. As word spreads that a hospital or clinic employs an infected physician, there is genuine danger that fear will cause people not to use the hospital or clinic. Patients might also refuse to be treated by the infected physician, even in cases in which there is no risk of transmission. We already saw in Chapter 3 how Dr. Huse lost his pediatrics practice in less than three weeks after a local newspaper published that he was HIV infected. Certainly, in the vast majority of cases, patients would ask for a new doctor if a risky procedure was required, and a large number of infected doctors would simply be unable to perform certain procedures.

The risks to a hospital or clinic of informing patients about to undergo certain procedures that there is a possibility of being infected with HIV because the physician is infected are so great that virtually all hospitals and clinics would simply refuse to allow the physician to perform the procedure. This is unfortunate, for there are cases in which it would be rational for a patient to accept the risk and even some in which a patient would do well to accept the risk. In some cases, an infected doctor may be so skilled in certain techniques that a patient would be willing to accept the slight risk of being infected. In other cases, a patient who had a well-established relationship with a doctor might be willing to accept the risk.

It does not follow from anything said above that hospitals or other health care facilities should require that all of their health care employees be tested for HIV infection. It does, however, follow that health care facilities should require that health care workers be tested for HIV infection before engaging in procedures in which it can be established that there is a significant risk of transmitting HIV infection to a patient.

This, of course, poses a problem for those health care workers who must be tested. Health care workers have a great deal to fear from being tested by the facility in which they are employed or given privileges. Confidentiality may not be secure, and those in the facility may restrict the health care worker more than is necessary to prevent the spread of infection. Individual health care workers who wish to engage in procedures for which they must be tested can avoid some of the dangers by consenting to anonymous testing elsewhere. In the event of a positive test result, the health care worker could refrain from doing any of the procedures for which the facility requires HIV testing. Of course, this in itself might involve great hardship for the health care worker.

An important caveat must be noted at this point. The foregoing discussion assumed that there are procedures such as surgery which pose a genuine risk of transmitting infection from an infected physician to a patient. Since physicians do cut themselves during surgery at times, this assumption seems plausible. However, since there have been no reported cases of physicians infecting patients with HIV virus in spite of the millions of surgical operations which have been performed since the discovery of AIDS, it may turn out that there is little risk after all. In the balance are the careers and reputations of excellent physicians and surgeons. Therefore, a policy of mandatory testing for medical personnel should not be adopted until there is good evidence that there is, in fact, a risk of transmitting infection to the patient. At the present time, that risk has not been established.

TESTING AS A DIAGNOSTIC TOOL

We have already touched briefly on the issue of requiring HIV tests as a diagnostic device in dealing with suspected cases of HIV infection. If a patient seeks a treatment which is specifically related to HIV infection, the doctor may require that a proper diagnosis be established using an HIV test before embarking on a treatment program. Some drugs, such as zidovudine, that are given to AIDS patients and in some cases to persons who are HIV infected may have serious side effects. The use of such drugs is warranted only when the physician is certain of the diagnosis. In this respect, AIDS is no different from many other diseases.

The second diagnostic use of the test involves pregnant women who might be HIV infected. A recent study in New York City found that in one inner-city hospital 2 percent of the women giving birth were infected with HIV.[16] An HIV-infected woman has roughly a 50 percent chance of transmitting the infection to the fetus. Even if the child is not born with HIV infection, the infection can be transmitted from the mother to the child through breast milk.[17] There is nothing that an HIV-infected pregnant woman can do to lessen the chance that her HIV infection will be transmitted to her fetus. She must choose between having an abortion and risking that her child will be born HIV infected. Once the child is born, however, the HIV-infected mother can prevent transmitting HIV to her child by refraining from nursing.

In light of such evidence, it might be asked whether pregnant women should be required to take an HIV test. There are several reasons for not mandating tests for pregnant women, even when they are members of groups in which there have been a large number of HIV-infected women. To begin with, a pregnant HIV-infected woman needs a great deal of sensitive counseling. She will, of course, need counseling to enable her to come to grips with her own disease and the possibility of contracting AIDS in the near future. In addition, she will need counseling to help her decide what to do concerning her pregnancy. She needs to be counseled about whether to have an abortion and about the risks of future pregnancies. She also needs to be counseled about the care of her new baby, especially the risks of nursing. If this counseling is to be successful, it needs to be done in a context in which a high degree of trust has been established between the woman and the professionals with whom she deals. Establishing this trust is often especially difficult for inner-city minority women, who may be alienated from, or even view themselves as victimized by, the professionals whose help they now need. In order to establish the trust necessary for adequate counseling, the medical tests to which the woman is subjected, including any HIV test, must be done with the consent of the woman. For

---

[16] Sheldon Landesman et al., "Serosurvey of Human Immunodeficiency Virus Infection in Parturients," *Journal of the American Medical Association* 258 (1987): 2701–3. This study was conducted on 602 women who gave birth in an inner-city municipal hospital in New York City. Twelve women were found to be HIV infected.

[17] John B. Ziegler et al., "Postnatal Transmissions of AIDS-associated Retrovirus from Mother to Infant," *Lancet*, April 20, 1985, pp. 896–97.

pregnant women who irrationally refuse to take an HIV test, the appropriate response is counseling, not coercion, which is likely to make further counseling difficult or even impossible.

Quite apart from considerations of trust and counseling, there is no morally acceptable way in which mandated testing of pregnant women could be enforced effectively. It would be unconscionable to deny care to pregnant women who refuse to consent to an HIV test. The threat of criminal sanctions might make inner-city minority women who are already mistrustful of the medical establishment still more distrustful. Forcing women to take the test or testing them surreptitiously would give rise to all of the problems which have already been noted. Such considerations constitute powerful reasons for not mandating HIV testing of pregnant women.

We recommend making HIV testing available to all pregnant women, along with appropriate counseling. In areas in which there are a large number of women who are HIV infected, pregnant women and those contemplating pregnancy should be encouraged to get tested so that they can make fully informed, relevant decisions regarding the fetus. While strong encouragement is surely justified in such cases, fully voluntary consent and counseling should be prerequisites for all HIV testing of pregnant women.[18]

CONCLUSION

There is virtually never a compelling reason for testing a patient or potential patient for HIV seropositivity without his or her consent. There is, however, a good reason for requiring tests of health care workers if they are involved in procedures for which it can be shown that there is a danger of transmitting the HIV infection from health care workers to patients. At the present time, however, this cannot in fact be shown. Until evidence establishes that there is a risk, health facilities should adopt a policy of testing medical personnel only at their request. In the meantime, universal blood and body fluid precautions should provide sufficient protection for both patients and health care workers.

---

[18] For a similar recommendation, see Landesman et al., "Serosurvey of Human Immunodeficiency Virus Infection," 2703.

8
Testing Mandated by Insurers and Employers

INTRODUCTION

AIDS is costly as well as deadly. Estimates of the cost of treating an individual with AIDS vary widely. One study places the mean cost of treating a person with AIDS in Massachusetts in 1986 at $46,505 per year.[1] Another study estimated the costs of hospital care alone run as high as $147,000.[2] Interestingly, a survey of 372 insurance corporations indicated that in 1986 the average health insurance claim paid for people with AIDS was $36,159 and that the average life insurance claim was $33,471.[3] The cost of treatment with zidovudine is between $8,000 and $10,000 per patient per year.[4] Apart from the cost of medical treatment, there are indirect costs (e.g., loss of earnings and the cost of needed support services other than medical treatment) as well as the costs of research and education. One estimate figured the total direct and indirect costs of AIDS in 1986 to

---

[1] George Seage III et al., "Medical Care Costs of AIDS in Massachusetts," *Journal of the American Medical Association* 256 (1987): 3108.

[2] Ann M. Hardy et al., "The Economic Impact of the First 10,000 Cases of Acquired Immunodeficiency Syndrome in the United States," *Journal of the American Medical Association* 255 (1986): 210.

[3] Benjamin Schatz, "The AIDS Insurance Crisis: Underwriting or Overreaching?" *Harvard Law Review* 100 (1987): 1795, citing an unpublished survey of member companies conducted by the American Council of Life Insurance and the Health Insurance Association of America, on file at the Harvard Law School Library, August 19, 1986, pp. 3–4.

[4] Robert Buchanan, "State Medicaid Coverage of AZT and AIDS-related Policies," *American Journal of Public Health* 78 (1988): 432.

have been nearly 8.7 billion dollars, and costs of over 66 billion dollars were projected for 1991.[5]

This has dramatic implications for the insurance industry. Few individuals with AIDS are wealthy enough to pay for their own treatment. As a result, people who believe that they are at risk for AIDS may attempt to offset the direct health care costs of the disease through private health insurance. In addition, individuals may attempt to offset indirect costs associated with loss of future income through life and disability insurance. The cost of AIDS also has dramatic implications for employers. Employers who provide group insurance to their employees may find their insurance rates increasing rapidly if they have employees with AIDS. In addition, employers of persons with AIDS are faced with all of the costs associated with employees who become ill and eventually die. Such costs include lost work time due to illness and the costs of retraining new employees as employees with AIDS eventually become unable to work.

Both insurers and employers have good reason to try to protect themselves by finding out who is at risk of contracting AIDS. Methods for protection include attempting to determine who is in a high-risk group (e.g., who is gay), attempting to determine who engages in high-risk behavior, and attempting to determine who is HIV infected by checking medical records or by requiring HIV testing. The fact that insurers and employers are gravely tempted to protect themselves from the costs of AIDS is not lost on the various state legislatures and insurance commissioners, and several states have enacted legislation or regulations forbidding insurance companies and employers from using HIV antibody tests for the purpose of determining insurability or employability.[6]

---

[5] Anne Scitovsky and Dorothy Rice, *The Internist: Health Policy in Practice* 28 (April 1987): 10. The projected costs for 1991 include $8.5 billion in personal medical costs, $2.3 billion in nonpersonal costs such as blood screening and research, $3.3 billion in indirect costs such as the value of lost productivity, and $52.3 billion in indirect mortality costs such as the loss of future earnings by those who die prematurely.

[6] States which have such laws or regulations include Arizona, California, Delaware, District of Columbia, Massachusetts, Michigan, New Jersey, and New York. See Ruth Faden and Nancy Kass, "Health Insurance and AIDS: The Status of State Regulatory Activity," *American*

In this chapter we are primarily concerned with whether insurers and employers ought to be forbidden from requiring HIV testing as a precondition of insurance or employment. In asking this question, we will be primarily concerned with privacy issues. Concerning insurers, we argue (1) that insurers do not violate individual privacy rights by requiring HIV testing or inquiring into high-risk behavior, (2) that such tests and inquiries do intrude into privacy even if they do not constitute a violation of the right to privacy, (3) that the costs of the treatment of AIDS should be borne by the state. Concerning employers, we argue that employers should not be allowed to require HIV tests as a condition of employment because of both privacy and public policy considerations. We consider the issue of insurance first and then turn to the issue of employment.

BACKGROUND VALUES

Our insurance system has evolved to meet several important and sometimes competing values. The first is the value which we place on providing health care. As a society, we are committed to providing necessary health care to citizens who are unable to finance their own health care. Conservatives as well as liberals agree on this commitment, though they differ over what care is necessary and over who can afford to finance their own health care. Few conservatives argue that we should allow those who are desperately sick and unable to afford health care to die without treatment. Those who do argue for such positions are rarely elected to public office. The debate between liberals and conservatives over just what health care is necessary is puzzling, and it is not clear what principles should be adopted. The debate need not detain us, however, for clearly some treatment for AIDS is necessary, at least to minimize the suffering of the patient. This is because persons with AIDS are desperately ill and often unable to afford treatment. Even according to the most conservative criteria, people with AIDS who cannot afford medical care must be provided with treatment. Treating the opportunistic infections in terms of which AIDS is defined prolongs life and alleviates misery despite the ultimate deadliness of the disease. Thus the treatment of AIDS has as much claim to being necessary as does

Journal of Public Health 78 (1988): 438. This study updates a survey of state regulations conducted by the National Gay Rights Advocates.

the treatment of fatal cancers. Also, the cost of treating AIDS is so high that few individuals can afford it without some form of health insurance.

In the case of insurance, there is another general value which needs to be taken into account. This second value is sometimes called *contractual freedom* or *freedom of contract*.[7] As a society we believe that, other things being equal, people ought to be allowed to enter freely into agreements with others. We believe that this freedom is enhanced when all of the contracting parties know the relevant facts concerning the agreement. We also believe that this freedom is enhanced when both parties are in a roughly equal bargaining position. Such values are reflected in the law of contracts. Courts may modify or even refuse to enforce contracts which are so one sided as to be unconscionable.[8] In addition, courts will typically allow minors and mental incompetents to void contracts into which they have imprudently entered. There are also cases in which courts will modify or refuse to enforce a contract because one or both of the parties were mistaken as to the relevant terms of the contract. Thus, if one party relies on fraud or misrepresentation of the other party to enter into a contract, courts will not enforce the contract against the victim of the fraud.

In the specific case of health insurance, these values are sometimes in tension. The insurance company that knows all of the relevant facts about a person's health may refuse to enter into an insurance contract with that person, leaving him or her without financial access to adequate health care. It is arguable that states which forbid insurers to require HIV tests are restricting freedom of contract in order to enhance health care. It is also arguable that states which allow insurers to require HIV tests are in effect placing a higher priority on freedom of contract than on provision of health care. While these values may conflict, such conflict is not necessary, and it is

---

[7] For an article which places significant emphasis on the contractual freedom of insurance companies, see Joyce Nixson Hoffman and Elizabeth Zieser Kincaid, "AIDS: The Challenge to Life and Health Insurers' Freedom of Contract," *Drake Law Review* 35 (1986–1987): 709–71.

[8] Today courts modifying or refusing to enforce an unconscionable contract rely on Section 2–302(1) of the *Uniform Commercial Code*, which has been adopted by various states. Historically courts relied on common law doctrine regarding unconscionability.

reasonable to hope for resolutions which enable us to achieve both values.

ECONOMIC INCENTIVES

Before getting down to specific moral arguments concerning whether insurers should be forbidden to consider HIV seropositivity and high-risk behavior in underwriting insurance, it needs to be noted that there are significant economic pressures on insurance companies to determine who is at risk for AIDS. First, there are economic pressures to treat people with roughly equal risks in a roughly equal manner for purpose of insurance underwriting.[9] Indeed, this is the single most fundamental principle of underwriting.[10] This principle is given legal instantiation in the National Association of Insurance Commissioners Model of Unfair Trade Practices Act, some version of which has been adopted by every state.[11] If an insurance company requires healthy persons to subsidize those who are less healthy, then, in a free market system, the healthy will either band together to insure themselves or choose insurance companies which base premiums on risk.[12] Thus, in a free market system, insurance companies are forced to treat people at roughly equal risk equally. Of course, such pressure can be avoided by state legislation that forbids any insurance company from denying insurance to specific groups.[13] For example, a state law forbidding all insurers from using

---

[9] Underwriting is the process by which degree of risk is assessed for the purpose of determining insurability and setting premiums.

[10] See, for instance, Karen Clifford and Russel Iuculano, "AIDS and Insurance: The Rationale for AIDS-related Testing," *Harvard Law Review* 100 (1987): 1807–12; Phillip Stano and Russel Iuculano, "AIDS Related Testing of Insurance Applicants: Fear vs. Fairness," *Journal of Insurance Regulation* 5 (1987): 319–20.

[11] National Association of Insurance Commissioners, "An Act Relating to Unfair Methods of Competition and Unfair and Deceptive Acts and Practices in the Business of Insurance," in *Proceedings of the National Association of Insurance Commissioners* (Kansas City, Mo.: NAIC, 1972), 493–511, cited in Stano and Iuculano, "AIDS Related Testing," 320.

[12] This argument was given, for instance, by Michael J. Cowell, Vice President and Actuary of State Mutual Life Assurance Company of America in his testimony before the Massachusetts Insurance Commissioner on August 5, 1987.

[13] This argument is also made by Mark Scherzer. See Mark Scherzer,

AIDS or HIV seropositivity as a factor in underwriting will prevent competitive advantage from being gained by companies who do not insure those who are infected with HIV. Whether such legislation is justified will be explored shortly. For now, it is enough to note that without such legislation, insurance companies have an economic incentive to try to determine who is at risk for AIDS and to base underwriting decisions on the test results.

A second economic consideration arises from the fact that people who are HIV infected can in most states find out that they are positive at anonymous test sites. Such people, of course, have good reason to purchase large quantities of life and health insurance. Purchasing insurance when one knows that a claim will likely be made while keeping this from the insurance company is called *antiselection* or *adverse selection*. Antiselection has already occurred among persons with AIDS and HIV. According to a 1985 survey conducted by the American Council on Life Insurance and the Health Insurance Association of America, 44 percent of the total amount paid on AIDS life insurance claims are for claims made within two years of the issuance of the life insurance policy.[14] By contrast, only 7.6 percent of the total amount paid on non-AIDS claims are for claims made within two years of the issuance of a policy.[15] Even though persons with AIDS die at a much younger age than the general population, it is doubtful that this can account for such large discrepancies in the number of people dying within two years of purchasing life insurance. In addition, one insurance company reported that for 1984 its life insurance claims for deaths from AIDS were five times higher than its claims generally.[16] Insurance companies faced with the pros-

---

"Insurance," in *AIDS and the Law*, ed. Harlon Dalton, Scott Burris, and the Yale AIDS Law Project (New Haven: Yale University Press, 1987): 194.

[14]Stano and Iuculano, "AIDS Related Testing," 330–31, citing an unpublished survey of member companies by the American Council of Life Insurance and the Health Insurance Association of America, August 19, 1986. See also Clifford and Iuculano, "AIDS and Insurance," 1817.

[15]Stano and Iuculano, "AIDS Related Testing," 331. Stano and Iuculano note, however, that on individual life insurance policies, as opposed to group policies, issued to people under fifty years of age, of the total amount of claims paid on the non-AIDS claims, 25.2 percent of the total claim amount occurred within the two years after the issuance of the policy.

[16]Mark Scherzer, "Insurance," 191, citing a report by the General Reassurance Company.

pect of antiselection have a strong economic incentive to require HIV tests for prospective insurees.

The third economic factor which motivates insurance companies to determine a prospective insuree's risk for AIDS is the simple fear that insurance companies will be overwhelmed with AIDS-related claims. In his report "AIDS and Life Insurance," Michael Cowell projects that the total amount for AIDS-related life insurance claims could reach $2 billion annually, or about 15 percent of individual life insurance claims for all U.S. companies by the mid-1990s.[17] Cowell also notes, however, that without effective screening for HIV, the level of projected AIDS claims by the middle to late 1990s could be double the level at which some insurance companies would face financial difficulties.[18]

Positive tests results will be used by life insurance companies to screen out those who are HIV infected rather than to increase insurance rates to cover the risk. While estimates of the number of HIV-infected persons who eventually get AIDS vary, the best evidence indicates that during the next five years approximately 20–30 percent of those who learn that they are HIV infected will develop AIDS.[19] If present trends continue, approximately 75 percent will progress to AIDS within fifteen years.[20] Assuming that only 20 percent of those who are HIV infected develop AIDS within five years and die within seven years, the chances of a person HIV infected dying over a seven-year period is twenty-six times higher than for someone in standard health.[21] By contrast, people who smoke are two times more likely to die than those in standard health; people with diabetes, four times; and people who have had heart attacks, five times.[22] Most life insurance companies will not insure people

---

[17] Michael J. Cowell, "AIDS and Life Insurance," Report to the Society of Actuaries Task Force on AIDS, August 1987, p. 23.

[18] Ibid., 24.

[19] Clifford and Iuculano, "AIDS and Insurance," 1813.

[20] Cowell, "AIDS and Life Insurance," 12.

[21] Clifford and Iuculano, "AIDS and Insurance," 1814, citing an affidavit of Warren L. Kleinsasser in *American Council of Life Ins. v. District of Columbia*, 645 F. Supp. 84 (D.D.C. 1986).

[22] Taken from Michael J. Cowell's testimony before the Massachusetts Insurance Commissioner on August 5, 1987. See Cowell, "AIDS and Life Insurance"; Stano and Iuculano, "AIDS Related Testing," 326.

whose mortality rate is more than five times the standard mortality rate. This is because the cost of the premiums would be so high that only those who know that they are about to die would be willing to buy the insurance. Clearly this is also true of persons with AIDS where the mortality rate is even higher than five times standard mortality.[23]

The situation is somewhat different with health insurance. Insurance companies usually do not test the health of prospective insurees applying for group health insurance, and group insurance accounts for 90 percent of all health insurance policies. Thus, at the present time, health insurers are not heavily involved in HIV testing. In the case of individual health insurance policies, companies do not always deny insurance to those who have various health problems. They sometimes charge higher rates for those who engage in risky behavior such as smoking. They also exclude various pre-existing health problems from coverage for a certain period of time. With HIV-infected persons, however, it is so likely that some of the many health problems will occur that health insurance underwriters simply refuse insurance altogether.

This does not necessarily mean that those who test positive go without health insurance. Roughly a dozen states have assigned risk pools into which those who are uninsurable are placed by a state agency.[24] People in assigned risk pools are then assigned to various insurance companies and given insurance at a much increased premium. In states where there are no assigned risk pools, those who are denied health insurance because they are HIV infected are faced with the prospect of having to exhaust their resources before becoming eligible for Medicaid. Since Medicaid is managed and regulated by the states, the level of income below which one becomes eligible for Medicaid and the exact benefits vary from state to state. Medicaid has played a major role in financing AIDS treatment. Although nationally Medicaid provides health financing for only 9 percent of the population, it currently provides financing for 23 percent of the AIDS cases.[25] It is also estimated that approximately 40 percent of

[23] Cowell, "AIDS and Life Insurance," 19.

[24] Clifford and Iuculano, "AIDS and Insurance," 1822. The states include Connecticut, Florida, Illinois, Indiana, Iowa, Minnesota, Montana, Nebraska, North Dakota, Tennessee, and Wisconsin.

[25] Buchanan, "State Medicaid Coverage of AZT," 432, citing the

AIDS patients will eventually exhaust their resources and become dependent on Medicaid.[26] Because of the means test for Medicaid, persons with AIDS must be driven into poverty before becoming eligible for health care financing through Medicaid.

OPTIONS AND PRACTICAL PROBLEMS

We have seen that insurance companies have a strong economic reason to find out which of their prospective insurees are at risk for AIDS. There are several ways in which insurers could attempt to gain this knowledge. Insurers could attempt to find out who is in a high-risk group. Such groups notably include gay men and IV drug abusers. (Insurers can afford to be less concerned about IV drug abusers, as they are not significant consumers of insurance.) Using high-risk group status as a criterion of insurability is both overinclusive and underinclusive. It is overinclusive because not all people who identify themselves as gay, for example, engage in high-risk behavior. Those who didn't would be denied life insurance under this criterion, even though they were not at a higher risk for contracting AIDS than heterosexuals. The criterion is underinclusive because there are self-identified heterosexuals who do engage in high-risk behavior. These people would be granted insurance under the criterion even though they are at risk for HIV infection.

Not only are overly inclusive criteria inefficient from an economic standpoint, they give rise to the moral charge of unfair discrimination. In the case of criteria based on sexual preference, such criteria are especially odious, since they tend to contribute to the oppression of an already oppressed group. We will examine questions of fairness shortly.

In addition, there are practical problems, because prospective gay insurees could simply lie about their sexual orientation; insurance companies do not have the resources to do thorough investi-

---

testimony of William L. Roper before the Senate Subcommittee on Social Security and Family Policy, September 10, 1987.

[26] Buchanan, "State Medicaid Coverage of AZT," 432, citing "Methodology of the Health Care Financing Administration Medicaid AIDS Estimates," prepared by the U.S. Department of Health and Human Services, Health Care Financing Administration, Office of the Actuary, June 22, 1987, p. 4.

gations of all insurance applications. If insurance companies attempt to use, for example, occupation, address, sex, and marital status to determine who is gay, the test becomes even more overinclusive. Many people who work in occupations or who live in neighborhoods with a high percentage of gays never engage in sexual practices likely to transmit HIV. In light of such problems, the National Association of Insurance Commissioners adopted a policy recommendation that sexual preference and the various indices of sexual preference should not be used for purposes of underwriting insurance.[27] The NAIC policy recommendation has been adopted by the American Council of Life Insurance. Unfortunately, not all insurance companies follow the NAIC recommendations. A recent survey conducted by the Office of Technology Assessment found that of the seventy-three commercial insurers responding to their survey, thirteen companies use sexual orientation in underwriting individual health insurance and five consider it important or very important.[28]

Insurers might attempt to base underwriting decisions on whether or not a prospective insuree engages in high-risk behavior. This criterion is not overinclusive. By definition, high-risk behavior is behavior in which there is a high risk of becoming HIV infected and eventually contracting AIDS. The criterion is, however, somewhat underinclusive. There are people who become HIV infected without engaging in high-risk behavior. Examples include the rare instances when hospital workers have become infected by handling contaminated blood or through needle stick injuries and the less rare instances when people have become infected through blood transfusions. Such examples are now sufficiently rare so as not to pose a major practical problem.

There are, however, more serious practical problems. First, it is not always clear just when a person is engaging in high-risk behav-

---

[27] Benjamin Schatz, "AIDS Insurance Crisis," 1789, citing the National Association of Insurance Commissioners Advisory Committee on AIDS, "Medical/Lifestyle Questions on Applications and Underwriting Guidelines Affecting AIDS and ARC," December 11, 1986, Section I(B).

[28] Jill Eden, "AIDS and Health Insurance: An OTA Survey," U.S. Congress, Office of Technology Assessment, February 1988, pp. 1–2. Four of the sixteen responding health maintenance organizations which issued individual policies considered sexual orientation a "key to insurability"; however, none of the Blue Shield or Blue Cross plans surveyed used sexual orientation as a basis for underwriting.

ior. For example, a person can engage in unprotected sexual intercourse in the context of what he or she incorrectly believes is a monogamous relationship. Second, prospective insurees might lie about their sexual activities, and it is extremely difficult and costly to attempt to find out what sexual practices a prospective insuree engages in. Insurers can attempt to determine who engages in high-risk behavior by checking medical records to see whether there is a history of venereal disease, but this is not a good indication of whether the person engages in high-risk behavior at the present time.

Insurers might also use HIV testing as a way of determining risk. Of the seventy-three commercial insurers responding to the recent Office of Technology Assessment survey, thirty-one companies routinely test at least some individual health insurance applicants, but only seven test all individual applicants.[29] HIV testing is not overinclusive. As we have seen, the tests, when done in combination, are extremely accurate, and those who are HIV infected are at high risk for getting AIDS. It should be noted that the cost of HIV testing means that it will not be economically worthwhile to test people applying for low levels of insurance. In any case, the practical problems associated with HIV testing are not so great as to rule out use of the tests at the outset. We turn now from practical problems to a consideration of moral problems.

SPECIFIC MORAL PROBLEMS

Insurers present three arguments based on fairness for requiring HIV testing and for inquiring about high-risk behavior. The arguments differ depending on which groups are being compared. The first argument is that since people can determine for themselves whether or not they are infected with HIV, it is unfair not to allow insurers also to make this determination before insuring a person for risks including those associated with HIV seropositivity.[30] We have already seen that there is evidence of antiselection and that

---

[29] Ibid., 3. Only one of the fifteen responding Blue Shield or Blue Cross plans routinely tests some of its individual applicants and only two of the fifty responding health maintenance organizations do.

[30] Mark Scherzer also notes this argument. See Scherzer, "Insurance," 193.

those who find that they are HIV infected have good reason to load up on insurance. This provides at least a reason for allowing insurers to require HIV testing before granting insurance. There are other reasons as well.

We have noted that it is a fundamental principle of insurance that equal risks should be treated in the same fashion for purposes of insurance underwriting. We have also seen that in a free underwriting market there is an economic reason for using this principle. Moral reasons might be offered as well. It has been argued, for instance, that it is unfair for low-risk insurees to pay higher rates to subsidize high-risk insurees.[31] The alleged unfairness here is that people who are relevantly different are being treated in the same fashion. Those who use this argument may find such inequitable treatment especially galling when it is a person's voluntary behavior which leads to the higher risk. It might be replied, however, that it is not unfair to any significant degree, because insurees voluntarily sign insurance policies knowing full well what the costs are. If I know that in a game of blackjack the odds are in favor of the house but I choose to play anyway, I can hardly complain that the game is unfair when I lose.

There is another argument based on fairness. If smokers, diabetics, and others with great health risks are forced to pay higher premiums, it might be claimed that it is unfair to them not to take HIV positivity into account, for HIV positives are also at high risk.[32] Here the alleged unfairness results from treating classes which are not relevantly different in radically different ways. Of course, a major disanalogy between HIV-infected persons and people who pay higher rates because of health risks is that HIV seropositivity, if taken into account, would result not merely in higher rates or, in the case of health insurance, exclusion of a pre-existing condition, but in denial of any insurance whatever. The argument is thus better stated in terms of the unfairness of treating people denied insurance coverage because of, for example, a previous severe heart attack differently from people infected with HIV.

---

[31] Clifford and Iuculano, "AIDS and Insurance," 1817. See also Hoffman and Kincaid, "AIDS," 765.

[32] Michael Cowell, for instance, gave this argument in his testimony before the Massachusetts Commissioner of Insurance, August 5, 1987. See also Cowell, "AIDS and Life Insurance."

Assuming that there are no relevant differences between people with health risks resulting from their HIV status and people who are denied insurance coverage for other health-related reasons, it could plausibly be claimed that an insurer who did not also exclude HIV-infected persons from health coverage is acting unfairly. Of course, there is little danger that the insurance companies will act unfairly in this manner if left to their own devices. Insurers would gladly exclude HIV-infected persons, as well as others at extreme risk, from various forms of insurance coverage. The real question is whether those states which forbid screening for HIV infection are acting unfairly in protecting some people at extreme health risk, but not others.

Whether the difference in protection accorded persons with HIV and others who have serious health risks is in fact unfair depends on whether there are morally relevant differences between the two groups. Consider, first, questions concerning high-risk behavior. There is a significant disanalogy between dangerous sexual practices and other forms of high-risk behavior. I would feel perfectly free to ask the man sitting next to me on the city bus whether he engaged in rock climbing but not whether he engaged in anal intercourse. What accounts for the difference, of course, is that, at least in our culture, asking whether he climbs mountains, sky dives, or the like does not require an answer involving a great sacrifice of privacy. In fact, such activities are usually carried out in public. We do, however, seek an answer which would involve considerable sacrifice of privacy when we ask about someone's sexual behavior.

The disanalogy is not so great when insurance companies require HIV tests or check medical records for the results of any HIV testing. It could be argued that just as insurance companies have a right to know whether a prospective insuree suffers from cancer or heart disease, insurance companies also have a right to know whether a prospective insuree suffers from AIDS or is HIV infected. That someone has cancer or heart disease is nearly as much a private matter as whether someone has AIDS or is infected with HIV. The difference seems to be more one of degree than of kind. The degree of difference can be significant, however, if the information becomes general knowledge. People who are HIV infected have been evicted from their homes and fired from their jobs. In one case, townspeople destroyed the home of three boys who were HIV infected. Cancer and heart patients, whatever their problems, do not face such serious discrimination.

In short, there are significant privacy claims which can be offered against the fairness claims made by insurance companies and in favor of state laws prohibiting insurers from HIV testing or making under-writing decisions based on HIV status. There are, however, several reasons for thinking that such privacy considerations are not, in fact, overriding.

To begin with, even though there may be a sacrifice of privacy, there is no violation of the right to privacy, since in answering ques-tions concerning high-risk activity or in consenting to HIV testing, a person waives the right to privacy. This, of course, assumes that the consent is genuine and not in some sense coerced. It might be claimed that the consent is in fact not voluntary, at least in the case of health insurance, because insurance is a necessity given the high cost of medical treatment. People have no choice but to purchase insurance and therefore no choice but to do what is necessary to purchase it. A similar, though less forceful, argument could be given concerning life insurance. It could be argued that it is necessary to provide for dependents in the case of death and that, for most people, life insurance is the only way in which this can be done. This argu-ment is less forceful, because there are more ways to provide for dependents than through insurance. Also, AIDS is most prevalent among gays, who are less likely than heterosexuals to have such typical dependents as children and spouses, though certainly some gays have married and have children.

There are several problems with the above argument. First, it is by no means clear that health and life insurance are in fact necessi-ties. In those states that have assigned risk pools for health insur-ance, people who otherwise would have been denied health insur-ance are provided with health insurance at an increased rate. Even in those states without assigned risk pools, Medicaid and Aid to Families with Dependent Children ensure that at least the minimal health and sustenance requirements will be met. The benefits are provided by welfare programs administered by the states, though, as we noted, eligibility is restricted to those whose assets and income fall below a certain level (which varies among the states). As a result, those who would rely on these benefits must first exhaust their resources. Nonetheless, the existence of such programs means that private health insurance is being used not so much to provide needed health financing as to ensure a certain level of income. This in turn means that it is difficult to argue that health insurance, much less life insurance, is required for meeting genuine necessities.

Second, even if health insurance were necessary for adequate health care, it would not follow that someone's consent to insurance company requirements is not voluntary. People who are in the position of being the sole suppliers of something which someone needs do not necessarily coerce that person by demanding that conditions be met before receipt is made. Suppose, for example, that a starving person walks out of the wilderness into a restaurant and orders a meal. The fact that the starving man must pay a reasonable price for the meal does not mean that he did not pay voluntarily. If, however, the restaurant owner demanded that the starving man have sex with her before she would feed him, then there would be coercion. The difference is that in one case the price is reasonable and in the other it is not. In the case of insurance, the question turns on whether requiring an HIV test or asking whether the person engages in high-risk behavior is reasonable in light of the insurance sought. There are three considerations which suggest that it is in fact reasonable. First, the insurance companies are setting requirements concerning the very conditions for which insurance is being sought. Second, there is a high likelihood of antiselection if insurance companies do not screen. Third, there is a safety net for those denied insurance, even if it is not what it should be.

What follows from the above is that insurance companies do not violate the right to privacy by requiring HIV testing and inquiring about high-risk behavior before granting insurance. This is because the right to privacy is voluntarily waived by those seeking insurance. Even if the right to privacy is waived, however, it is nonetheless true that insurance must be purchased at a sacrifice of privacy. The fact that this privacy is voluntarily sacrificed does not mean that it is not a genuine cost. It is not pleasant revealing one's sexual activities to an insurance agent. Nor is it pleasant to reveal one's HIV status to others, even if they are medical professionals. Given that the loss of privacy is a genuine cost, it is an important question how the interests of insurance companies should be balanced against such a loss, even if the right to privacy is not violated.

ALTERNATIVES

There are alternatives to the present system which require little sacrifice of privacy while preserving the background values of freedom of contract and public health. Perhaps the most extreme alternative is to institute a national health insurance program. Such a program would provide for most of our health needs yet would not require extensive medical and health checks of those wanting to obtain insurance. It could be coupled with various private insurance plans for those who sought benefits or medical programs not available within the national health insurance plan. It would also have the advantage of spreading the risks over an extremely wide pool — far wider than any pool available to private insurance companies. Tests developed in the next few decades to predict diseases other than AIDS thus would not cause a health care crisis, at least as far as finances are concerned. The feasibility of national health insurance has been extensively debated over the past several decades, and we need not concern ourselves with a full discussion of the benefits and costs of various national health insurance plans. National health insurance is not at the present time a political possibility. We wish merely to note that one benefit of such a plan would be that it could be structured to better preserve privacy than existing arrangements.

A more realistic alternative is to bring AIDS treatment under the Medicare program in the way in which end-stage renal disease was brought under Medicare so that people could obtain dialysis. Health insurance companies could then be forbidden from requiring HIV testing and allowed to exclude coverage of AIDS. Such a policy would have the advantage of (1) requiring few changes in the present health insurance industry, (2) protecting private insurers from potentially disastrous financial losses, and (3) preserving individual privacy. While the costs of such a program would be significant, some costs cannot be wholly avoided so long as we have a moral commitment to treatment. As we have seen, it is already projected that the government will pay for 40 percent of the treatment of AIDS through Medicaid. In addition, such a program would have the further advantage of spreading costs of the other 60 percent over a much wider population.[33]

---

[33] It is not clear just how much more such a program would cost than the amount society now pays for the treatment of AIDS. A full economic analysis would have to consider such questions as whether a government program of the sort advocated here would make it likely that doctors would prescribe treatments which they would not prescribe if a patient or a private insurer bore the cost. A consideration of such economic issues is, of course, beyond the scope of this book.

Such government programs hold out the promise of providing for health care while at the same time preserving privacy. If such programs are not adopted, at least the loss of privacy suffered by persons with HIV infection can be kept to a minimum. Laws explicitly forbidding insurance companies and medical professionals from divulging HIV test results or the HIV status of applicants and patients could be passed. Laws preserving the confidentiality of information in the hands of insurance companies and medical professionals could be extensions of the data privacy acts which protect medical information in the hands of government agencies. Laws could also be passed explicitly providing for civil suits based on a violation of privacy in cases in which others release confidential information regarding a person's HIV status. Such laws would help to preserve confidentiality without preventing insurance companies from HIV screening. A good start along these lines is the National Association of Insurance Commissioner's Insurance Information and Privacy Protection Model Act, already adopted by eleven states. The act protects medical information in the hands of insurance corporations and also provides for civil remedies in the event of disclosure.[34]

It should be noted, however, that laws of this sort need to cover both employers who are self-insurers and private insurance corporations. At the present time, 42 percent of those who receive health insurance through their employers are covered by employers who self-insure rather than rely on plans offered by insurance corporations.[35] This is significant, since self-insurers are not regulated by state insurance commissioners.[36] As a result, state insurance regulations fail to protect a large number of insurees.

Laws permitting civil suits for violation of privacy would codify and strengthen already existing tort law on privacy. We have already noted in Chapter 4 that a person can bring suit for violations of privacy due to the publication of private facts. Although consent to publication is a defense, people who consent to HIV test-

---

[34] NAIC Insurance Information and Privacy Protection Model Act, Proceedings of the National Association of Insurance Commissioners (Kansas City, Mo.: NAIC, 1981): 267–313, cited in Stano and Iuculano, "AIDS Related Testing," 334.

[35] Faden and Kass, "Health Insurance and AIDS," 437.

[36] The significance of this is also emphasized by Faden and Kass, "Health Insurance and AIDS," 437–38.

ing and reveal high-risk behavior to medical professionals and to insurers do not consent to the general publication of this information. Such tort law could be strengthened by statutory law requiring written consent for any sharing of information regarding a persons's HIV status.

On the whole, then, there are far less costly means of balancing the various values at stake than forbidding insurers from requiring HIV testing as a condition of insurance. For this reason, we oppose laws which forbid insurers from mandating HIV tests.

EMPLOYMENT

Like insurers, employers have a number of reasons for screening people who are infected with HIV or at risk for AIDS. Some of these reasons concern insurance. Employers themselves may provide insurance to their employees, in which case the economic benefit of keeping out those at risk for AIDS is obvious. If, on the other hand, the employer relies on group insurance, the insurance rates may rise to unacceptable levels if there are too many claims against the insurance company.[37]

Employers who hire persons infected with HIV or people at high risk for contracting AIDS face costs associated with an ill employee. These include the costs associated with lost work time due to illness and eventually the cost of training a new employee. Sadly, in some cases it also includes the cost of prejudicial reaction by other employees or by customers. Perhaps the most obvious example is a restaurant which would lose customers if it became generally known that one of its employees was infected with HIV. In very few cases, however, will HIV infection itself be relevant to job performance. The most notable exception to this are certain medical occupations, which were dealt with in Chapter 7.

With the possible exception of employers who are self-insurers, it is arguable that it is unreasonable for employers to demand that a person take an HIV test or answer questions about his or her sexual history before being accepted for employment. In fact, HIV seropositivity and sexual behavior are seldom relevant for employment.

---

[37]Eighty percent of private insurance is currently handled through group policies and most of these are through employer policies. See Faden and Kass, "Health Insurance and AIDS," 437.

The fairness considerations which form a significant part of the justification for insurance screening those at risk for AIDS do not apply to employment. There is no analogy to antiselection. Potential employees are contracting with employers concerning matters to which their sexual behavior and HIV status is by and large irrelevant. In addition, other employees are not being asked to subsidize the employee infected with HIV. If an employer screens out health risks generally, it may be unfair not to screen out those at risk of AIDS as well, but it is by no means clear that employers are justified in screening out health risks in the first place.

Regarding employers who are self-insurers, it might be claimed that the insurance aspect justifies screening for those at risk for AIDS. The obvious solution is to keep the insurance and employment aspects separate. Thus, applicants could be hired without regard to whether they are at risk for AIDS, but they could be screened before being offered insurance. An equally obvious problem is that when those in the firm responsible for the insurance learn that a new employee is HIV positive or engages in high-risk behavior, they are likely to inform others in the firm. There are two ways in which this could be prevented through legislation. First, legislation could require that screening by self-insurers be done by people outside the firm who inform the firm whether the person should be granted insurance but do not give the reason. Second, legislation could forbid employers from firing those infected with HIV.

In short, there do not seem to be compelling arguments to support the view that employers are justified in using HIV tests as a means of screening potential employees. There are, however, two general arguments which can be given to support the view that employers are not justified in HIV screening. The first is an economic argument. If employers generally were to screen applicants for HIV infection, it would put otherwise able people on welfare, thereby increasing an already serious state problem. It would also make it impossible for people at risk to arrange their finances to be able to withstand the financial burden of eventual treatment for AIDS. This would mean even greater state expenses incurred for the treatment of AIDS.

The second argument is based on considerations of fairness. As a society we have committed ourselves to protecting the handicapped from employment discrimination. At the federal level this protection is embodied in the federal Rehabilitation Act of 1973. As far as reasons for protecting the handicapped are concerned, there is no significant difference between handicapped persons and those who have HIV infection. Thus, it would be unfair not to accord those who are HIV infected the same protections afforded others who have medical problems which do not significantly affect their job performance.

There is a strong analogy between HIV infection and more traditional handicaps as far as employment discrimination is concerned. Just as many people with handicaps can perform their jobs competently, so too can many people with HIV infection. Just as handicapped persons pose no threat to their co-workers because of their handicaps, those who are infected with HIV pose no threat to their co-workers because of their infection (we saw in Chapter 1 that HIV is transmitted only through intimate sexual contact or the exchange of body fluids in other ways). Just as handicapped persons typically need employment in order to achieve a high level of personal autonomy, HIV-infected persons typically need employment to achieve autonomy. Finally, both HIV-infected persons and handicapped persons are likely to be subjected to irrational discrimination unless they are given legal protection.

On the basis of the analogy between HIV infection and traditional handicaps, it can be argued that those who are HIV infected ought to be given protection under the legislation which protects handicapped persons. We begin by asking whether current legal analysis allows us to apply federal protections to those who are HIV infected. The Rehabilitation Act of 1973 promises protection, especially in light of recent case law. If this act, which prohibits discrimination against the handicapped by certain employers, can be interpreted to cover persons with HIV infection, it will protect privacy in two ways. It will help prevent outright discrimination against those with HIV infection, since such discrimination would be illegal. It will also protect privacy by undercutting the temptation of certain employers and administrators to test those they supervise for the HIV antibodies. Employers who cannot discriminate against those with AIDS, ARC, or HIV infection will have less motive to test for the HIV antibodies. However, if AIDS and ARC are covered but not HIV infection, then employers will be motivated to require tests, since they can then get rid of employees who are HIV infected before they develop AIDS or ARC and receive the protection of the rehabilitation act.

The rehabilitation act provides that no person who is handicapped and otherwise qualified shall "be subjected to discrimination under any program or activity receiving Federal financial assistance or under any program or activity conducted by any Executive agency or by the United States Postal Service."[38] The crucial question concerns who is a handicapped individual for purposes of the act. Section 794, formerly Section 504, of the act defines a handicapped person as "any person who (i) has a physical or mental impairment which substantially limits one or more of such person's major life activities, (ii) has a record of such an impairment, or (iii) is regarded as having such an impairment."[39]

A plaintiff bringing suit under the rehabilitation act must show four things.[40] First, the plaintiff must show that the person who discriminated against the plaintiff was covered by the rehabilitation act. Not all private employers are covered, but only those who receive federal funds. Employment by executive agencies such as the State Department are covered. Thus, the rehabilitation act is relevant to the HIV screening of State Department employees and their families.

Second, the plaintiff must show that he or she is handicapped. Section 794, quoted above, makes it clear that it is sufficient to show that the plaintiff has a physical or mental impairment which substantially limits at least one major life activity. For our purposes it is relevant to note that impairments include physiological disorders of the reproductive, genitourinary, hemic, and lymphatic systems.[41] Major life activities include "functions such as caring for one's self, performing manual tasks, walking, seeing, hearing, speaking, breathing, learning, and working."[42] A plaintiff can also be

---

[38] 29 U.S.C. §794. Many writers still refer to this section as §504, which was its designation in Statutes at Large under 87 Stat. 394.

[39] 29 U.S.C. §706(8)(B).

[40] *Doe v. New York University*, 666 F.2d 761 (2nd Cir. 1981).

[41] 45 C.F.R. §84.3(j)(2)(i). The definition of *impairment* is embodied in regulations passed by the Department of Health and Human Services pursuant to the Rehabilitation Act of 1973. Each executive agency is empowered by the rehabilitation act to pass regulations for implementing the act. Although strictly speaking §84.3j(2)(i) applies only to the Department of Health and Human Services, courts would use it for guidance in interpreting the rehabilitation act in suits involving other employers.

[42] 45 C.F.R. §84.3(j)(2)(ii).

shown to be handicapped if he or she has a record of such an impairment even when the plaintiff has been misclassified as having an impairment.[43] A plaintiff can also be shown to be handicapped if it can be shown that the plaintiff is treated by an employer as having an impairment which substantially limits major life activities even when the plaintiff has no such impairment.[44] Finally, a plaintiff can be shown to be handicapped if it can be shown that the plaintiff has an impairment and that impairment substantially limits life functions because of the attitudes of others even when the impairment would not otherwise substantially limit life functions.[45]

Third, the plaintiff must show that he or she was discriminated against solely because of the handicap. Fourth, the plaintiff must show that he or she is otherwise qualified for the job or program. This means that the plaintiff can perform the job with reasonable accommodation by the employer.[46]

Until recently it was not clear how the rehabilitation act applied to persons with contagious or communicable diseases. In *School Board of Nassau County v. Arline*, however, the Supreme Court held that "a person suffering from the contagious disease of tuberculosis can be a handicapped person within the meaning of the Section 504 of the Rehabilitation Act of 1973."[47]

---

[43] 45 C.F.R. §84.3(j)(2)(iii).

[44] 45 C.F.R. §84.3(j)(2)(iv).

[45] Ibid.

[46] 45 C.F.R. §84.3(k)(1).

[47] *School Board of Nassau County v. Arline*, 480 U.S. 273 (1987). A number of recent articles have dealt with the relevance of *Arline* to discrimination against persons with AIDS. Virtually all of the law review writers have argued that AIDS victims are handicapped for purposes of the rehabilitation act. For an excellent overview, see R. P. Wasson, Jr., "AIDS Discrimination under Federal, State and Local Law after Arline," *Florida State University Law Review* 32 (September 1986): 221–78.

Some commentators argue, however, that HIV infection is not in itself a handicap. See, for instance, Mary Landolt, "Are AIDS Victims Handicapped?" *Saint Louis University Law Journal* 31 (1987): 740–41; J. D. Powell, J. H. White, and R. K. Robinson, "Contagious Disease in the Workplace: The School Board of Nassau County v. Arline," *Labor Law Journal* 38 (1987): 707.

Others argue that HIV infection is in itself a handicap. See, for instance, J. H. Carey and M. M. Arthur, "The Developing Law on AIDS in the

Certainly many persons suffering from AIDS or ARC meet the definition of a handicapped person. All persons with AIDS and ARC have disorders of the hemic and lymphatic systems which count as impairments for purposes of the rehabilitation act. In addition, many persons with AIDS have one or more of the debilitating diseases (e.g., pneumocystis pneumonia) that substantially limit major life functions (e.g., the ability to breathe). People with ARC have one of several severe physical symptoms, such as serious weight loss (wasting) and prolonged fever, that also affect major life activities, such as the ability to work. Even when persons with AIDS or ARC are not substantially limited by their disease, they are often regarded as being substantially limited by their employers or are treated by others in such a way that they are substantially limited in major life activities. In spite of these limitations, persons with AIDS and ARC are often qualified for employment with reasonable accommodations by their employers.

The case of asymptomatic persons who have HIV infection is less clear. In an important footnote, the Court in *Arline* specifically noted that it did not reach the question "whether a carrier of a contagious disease such as AIDS could be considered to have a physical impairment, or whether such a person could be considered, solely on the basis of contagiousness, a handicapped person as defined by the Act."[48]

The reasoning of the Court in *Arline* supports the view that many asymptomatic persons with HIV infection, as well as many persons with AIDS or ARC, are handicapped under the act. The act defines as handicapped not only those persons who actually have a physical or mental impairment which limits major life activities, but also those who are regarded as having such an impairment. The Court stated in *Arline* that in defining "handicapped person" in this

---

Workplace," *Maryland Law Review* 46 (Winter 1987): 293–94; Michael E. Hilton, "Civil Rights — Rehabilitation Act of 1973 — Individual Affected with Contagious Disease Held 'Handicapped' and Entitled to Protection of Section 504," *St. Mary's Law Journal* 19 (1987): 231–36; Terry L. Pabst, "Protection of AIDS Victims from Employment Discrimination," *University of Illinois Law Review* 1987 (1987): 369.

[48] *School Board of Nassau County v. Arline* at 1128, note 7. It should be noted that, strictly speaking, AIDS is not contagious. It is not spread by casual contact. It is, rather, a communicable disease spread by transfer of some body fluids (e.g., blood and semen).

manner, Congress "acknowledged that society's accumulated myths and fears about disability and disease are as handicapping as are the physical limitations that flow from actual impairment."[49] The Court also noted that misapprehension about contagion is especially productive of fear.[50] Certainly the fear of AIDS and HIV seropositivity has reached near hysteria in some quarters. Political leaders and major columnists have proposed everything from quarantine of persons with AIDS to tattooing those who are HIV infected. Many who are HIV infected have suffered serious employment, education, and housing discrimination. The effects of this fear and discrimination are certainly as handicapping as actual physical limitations. Given the Court's rationale in *Arline*, asymptomatic persons infected with HIV infection may qualify as handicapped individuals for purposes of the rehabilitation act. All in all, after *Arline* the Court would have to be wholly irrational not to count AIDS or ARC as a handicap but merely unreasonable not to count HIV seropositivity as a handicap.

There are also state statutes modeled on the federal rehabilitation act which protect handicapped persons against employment discrimination.[51] State statutes have the advantage that the protection they offer is not restricted to employers who receive federal funds. *Arline* does not, however, apply to state statutes, and it is not clear whether state courts will regard a contagious disease as a handicap for purposes of their antidiscrimination statutes.

In light of the fact that the Rehabilitation Act of 1973 does not unequivocally apply to those who are HIV infected, we believe that new federal legislation is warranted which clearly prohibits employment discrimination against HIV-infected persons. At the federal level it would be most easy simply to amend the Rehabilitation Act of 1973 to include HIV infection. It is important that state legislation also be passed, however. The federal rehabilitation act applies only to employers who receive federal funds. State laws can expand such protection to cover a far wider range of employers.

CONCLUSION

There are a number of reasons for allowing insurance companies to require HIV testing as a condition of insurability, and these reasons

---

[49] *School Board of Nassau County v. Arline* at 1129.
[50] *School Board of Nassau County v. Arline* at 1129.
[51] See, for instance, Minnesota Statutes, Chapter 363.

are not overridden by privacy concerns. The various values at stake can best be balanced by federal legislation modifying Medicare to provide for AIDS treatment in the manner in which it now provides for dialysis. While employers also have self-interested reasons for requiring HIV testing as a condition of employment, these reasons do not override the privacy and public policy considerations which militate against such screening.

9
State-mandated Testing

In the preceding chapters we have seen that the most effective means presently available for combatting AIDS is to slow the rate of HIV transmission. Because nearly all HIV transmission involves voluntary activities, mandatory testing and proscriptions on these activities for those found to be infected might at first glance seem straightforward. As we have seen, however, this is not the case. This is partly because HIV infection is so widespread and partly because of privacy considerations. We have argued that privacy is a fundamental value in a liberal democracy. The activities by which HIV is spread are characteristically private and defy effective large-scale governmental regulation. More specifically, we have argued that the indiscriminate use of HIV testing to identify infected persons constitutes a severe infringement of the right to privacy and can result in very real harms, especially given the stigmas associated with some HIV-related activities and the level of fear and panic AIDS has generated.

Nevertheless, there is widespread popular support in this country for aggressive mandatory testing. A June 1987 Gallup poll found that 52 percent of those polled favored testing everyone, 90 percent favored testing immigrants, 88 percent favored testing federal prisoners, 83 percent favored testing military personnel, and 80 percent favored testing all marriage license applicants.[1] We believe this reflects a failure on the part of the general public to think carefully about how exactly mass testing would enhance prevention and what

---

[1] "Widespread Tests for AIDS Virus Favored by Most, Gallup Reports," *New York Times*, July 13, 1987.

the implications of testing would be for privacy. Again, public health officials have consistently favored AIDS education as the best strategy for prevention and opposed most mandatory testing.

To all of this, the federal government has responded by mandating massive testing for a wide range of individuals over whom it has jurisdiction. President Reagan recommended massive testing for other groups as well. In this chapter we will first explore the most prominent of the large-scale mandatory testing programs, including programs targeted at the nation's blood supply and at immigrants, federal prisoners, and those seeking admission to Veterans Administration hospitals, the military, the Peace Corps, the Job Corps, and certain foreign service programs. We will then explore the proposal that testing should be mandated for all marriage license applicants.

Before we consider particular programs, it will be useful to reiterate briefly the two primary criticisms which have been brought against many of them: (1) that they are not cost-effective in slowing the spread of AIDS and (2) that they intrude into the privacy of those tested, who are sometimes harmed as a result.

Regarding the lack of cost-effectiveness, critics argue that, given limited financial resources for the pursuit of some goal, it is irrational (other things being equal) to spend some of those resources in one way when another would be more cost-effective. We share this view. Resources for preventing the spread of HIV are limited, and unless there are good reasons for doing otherwise, the rational place to spend them is where the marginal cost per prevented transmission is lowest. Figures on this are hard to develop, but the advocates of AIDS education claim that dollars spent on AIDS education will almost certainly provide a greater return in terms of transmissions prevented than dollars spent on almost any of the mandatory testing programs we will be considering in this chapter. If this is so, any justification of such programs would have to be grounded in considerations other than prevention.

The second general objection to most mandatory testing programs is that they intrude into the privacy of the individuals who are tested. We have already seen that people whose HIV infection becomes known to others may suffer serious harm, including social ostracism, loss of jobs and housing, and even physical violence. The dangers are real enough, even when the infected person has initial control over the distribution of test results obtained through an anonymous testing program. They are obviously exacerbated when the person lacks even this minimal control — when test results first appear on some list or are entered into a data bank (usually computerized) even before they are given to the person tested.

Given these costs, it is certainly incumbent on advocates of any mandatory testing program to indicate precisely what ends the program is to serve, how it is to serve them, and who will have to be provided with test results to achieve them. If, for instance, the goal of a mandatory testing program was simply to provide a precautionary warning to infected individuals, no more than anonymous mandatory testing would be necessary. Interestingly, no mandatory testing program has ever been instituted (nor, to our knowledge, seriously proposed) which would involve only anonymous distribution of positive test results. Broader distributions of positive test results have been part and parcel of all mandatory testing programs instituted or proposed to date. Mandatory testing by definition intrudes on liberty privacy and nearly always threatens informational privacy as well. One can only ask on a policy-by-policy basis what goals are served by such testing and whether the policy offers benefits sufficient to outweigh the intrusions into liberty and informational privacy.

The screening of the nation's blood supply began immediately after the test for that purpose was licensed in May 1985.[2] Federally mandated testing began shortly thereafter, when the Department of Defense decided to test all military personnel, reservists, and potential recruits.[3] On May 31, 1987, President Reagan announced that he was ordering or recommending mandatory testing for a wide range of individuals over whom the federal government had jurisdiction, including federal prisoners and immigrants, and that he had asked for a review of mandatory testing for all V.A. hospital patients. He also recommended "routine" testing for other groups. We will begin our examination of these testing programs with relatively brief discussions of the testing of donated blood and the mandatory

---

[2] Such testing is not presently mandated by the federal government, but it is the universal practice of blood collection agencies and is required for certification by the American Association of Blood Banks.

[3] Rhonda Rivera, "The Military," in *AIDS and the Law*, ed. Harlon Dalton, Scott Burris, and the Yale AIDS Law Project (New Haven: Yale University Press, 1987), 221–34.

testing of immigrants and illegal aliens seeking permanent residency and of persons admitted to V.A. hospitals. We will then consider federally mandated testing programs affecting federal employees and persons in federal employment programs, i.e., military, Peace Corps, Job Corps, and foreign service personnel. We will then examine testing programs for federal prisoners.

THE NATION'S BLOOD SUPPLY

The one massive testing program which has been subject to virtually no criticism is the screening of the nation's blood supply. Concern about blood product–related transmission of HIV has been so great that it initially inspired the development of the HIV antibody tests. Doubtless one reason for this is that receiving a blood product is not voluntary in the way that sex and IV drug abuse are. Even for people who have no sympathy for those who become infected with HIV through voluntary behaviors, the situation is quite different with those who became infected through blood products, and victims of blood product infection strike some as paradigmatically vulnerable and innocent. Moreover, people who know they are not at risk for infection through high-risk behaviors may still fear the possibility of infection from blood products. Finally, HIV is transmitted more efficiently through blood products than through any other means. Blood products were responsible for considerable HIV infection before blood screening began in 1985.[4] In particular, factor VIII coagulation concentrate is estimated to have infected as many as 85 percent of the hemophilia A patients who use it. This is because it is made from pools containing plasma from as many as 50,000 donors and because those who need it typically receive material from multiple lots.

Eisenstaedt and Getzen did a careful cost-benefit analysis of the screening of blood donors in 1986. According to their analysis, approximately 10 million donors were screened in 1986, at a total

---

[4]The Public Health Service estimates that as of 1987 there were 11,000 Americans still living who had been infected by blood products before testing began. See T. A. Peterman et al., "Estimating the Risks of Transfusion-associated Acquired Immune Deficiency Syndrome and Human Immunodeficiency Virus Infection," *Transfusion* 27 (1987): 371–74.

cost of approximately $36 million. As a result of the screening, 292 cases of transfusion-related HIV infection were prevented. This works out to a cost of approximately $124,000 per prevented transmission.[5]

One remarkable feature of these statistics is the low rate of HIV infection among blood donors. This indicates that voluntary self-screening by blood donors is working. Another remarkable feature is the high cost per prevented transmission. Eisenstaedt and Getzen, taking account of both costs of therapy and loss of earnings for HIV-infected persons, argue that each expenditure of $124,000 for a prevented transmission yields a savings of $149,000. Hence, such testing has a benefit to cost ratio 1.2:1, which entails that it is cost-effective. These economic considerations, according to them, prove that money spent on screening is money well spent.

We wish to dispute this claim. It is not enough to know that the money is being spent in a way that is cost-effective. What must be argued is that it is being spent in a way that is *optimally* cost-effective — that is, more cost-effective than alternative strategies for preventing the transmission of HIV. Without having hard figures to back up their claim, advocates of explicit AIDS education, with whom we concur, submit that $133,000 worth of explicit AIDS education ads and brochures geared to gays, teens, and needle-sharing IV drug abusers would certainly lead to enough behavior change to prevent many more than just one transmission.[6]

Even if it is true that universal testing of donated blood in low-prevalence areas is less cost-effective as a means of preventing HIV

---

[5] Richard Eisenstaedt and Thomas Getzen, "Screening Blood Donors for Human Immunodeficiency Virus Antibody: Cost-Benefit Analysis," *American Journal of Public Health* 78 (1988): 450–54. These figures are remarkably close to those for Minnesota, for instance, where testing of the first 455,725 units of donated blood identified only 15 infected units, at a cost of approximately $2,000,000; the cost per prevented transmission was roughly $133,000. See Kris MacDonald et al., "Survey of a Statewide Program to Identify Blood Donors Infected with HIV: Minnesota, USA" (Paper delivered at the Third International AIDS Conference, Washington, D.C., June 3, 1987).

[6] The Education Program of the Minnesota AIDS Project, for instance, reached 417,468 individuals through lectures, brochures, and hot-line calls during 1987, at a cost of $348,662, or $.83 per contact. (This information was obtained by personal communication with Pat Humbert.)

transmission than AIDS education or other prevention measures, we believe, with Eisenstaedt and Getzen, that it is justified, albeit by other considerations, the most prominent of which is the comfort and reassurance it provides to people who receive blood products. (Eisenstaedt and Getzen point out that many individuals would be willing to pay for these added protections and psychological benefits.[7] If this is true, such benefits could also be construed as economic benefits of testing.) Still other considerations, to which we will return in connection with discussion of testing proposals involving marriage license applicants, involve privacy.

IMMIGRANTS SEEKING PERMANENT RESIDENCY

The U.S. Immigration and Naturalization Service has traditionally screened immigrants seeking permanent residency and ultimately citizenship in the United States and excluded those who had dangerous diseases. AIDS was put on the list of such diseases in June 1987, and two months later it was replaced by HIV infection. Since December 1, 1987, the United States has also tested applicants to the amnesty program for illegal aliens in order to exclude those with HIV infection.[8]

Whether or not this is defensible depends largely on more general ethical issues involving U.S. immigration policy, and specifically on how the interests of persons seeking permanent residency should be balanced against the interests of those who already have it. This question is obviously well beyond our present scope. We wish only to point out that while the exclusionary screening of applicants on the basis of HIV may be defensible, the defense cannot consist of an appeal to the preventative goal. The policy is not designed to slow the spread of HIV infection by itself, but only to ensure that some of the spread and some of the HIV-related deaths that might otherwise have taken place in this country will instead take place elsewhere. This exclusionary testing program does serve this nation's self-interest, yet presumably does so at the expense of other nations. Moreover, to the extent that persons infected with HIV would be

---

[7]Eisenstaedt and Getzen, "Screening Blood Donors," 453.

[8]James L. Buck, Regional Commissioner, Northern Region, U.S. Immigration and Naturalization Service, personal communication, November 16, 1987. For the Federal Regulations, see 42 C.F.R. §34.2(b).

more apt to receive good counseling and AIDS education here than in the countries of their origin, there is reason to believe that the exclusionary testing policy may ultimately result in *more* HIV transmissions overall than would occur if HIV-infected aliens were allowed permanent residency in this country.

VETERANS ADMINISTRATION HOSPITAL ADMISSIONS

The Veterans Administration operates 172 hospitals, which treat 3.5 million patients a year. Shortly after May 31, 1987, when President Reagan called for a review of mandatory testing of all persons admitted to V.A. hospitals, he received a memorandum from Dr. John A. Gronvall, chief medical officer of the V.A., stating that he and other V.A. administrators favored voluntary testing for those patients who felt they were at high risk. However, they opposed mandatory or even routine testing of all patients, both because, at an estimated cost of $60 million a year, it would lack cost-effectiveness or even be counterproductive, and because they felt such testing would pose unacceptable threats to the right of privacy of V.A. patients. They wondered by what authority they could test patients without their consent, and they noted that problems of confidentiality would arise concerning information that was so sensitive that patients' interests could be severely compromised. They even noted that some veterans who needed health care might choose to forgo care rather than be subjected to such threats to their privacy. In short, Dr. Gronvall, speaking for V.A. administrators, presented the two classic criticisms of mandatory testing in opposing such testing for all V.A. patients.[9]

We have already addressed the general issues involved in testing all persons admitted to hospitals. We feel that Dr. Gronvall's response is significant for two reasons. First, it includes unequivocal statements of both of the standard criticisms of all federally mandated testing programs. Second, it represents the considered assessment by knowledgeable medical personnel—personnel possessing both superior understanding of the medical facts and firsthand experience of the importance of patient trust in the caregiver-patient relationship and hence of confidentiality and respect for patient pri-

---

[9] "Mandatory Test for AIDS Virus Opposed by Doctors at the V.A.," *New York Times*, June 24, 1987, A1.

vacy — of the only federal testing proposal involving a setting which is essentially dedicated to health care delivery and the welfare of patients.

FEDERAL EMPLOYMENT AND EMPLOYMENT PROGRAMS
TESTING AND SCREENING: THE MILITARY, THE PEACE
CORPS, THE JOB CORPS, AND THE STATE DEPARTMENT

Most of the nonvoluntary testing done in this country has been mandated by the federal government for people it employs. Most of this has involved exclusionary screening; individuals who are found to be infected are excluded from the federal program at issue. The Peace Corps screens out all infected invitees and volunteers, and the State Department screens out infected applicants from employment and retests current employees about to undergo a change of tour of duty, restricting those who are infected from overseas assignments except to certain designated posts where "adequate medical care is available." This latter restriction applies to their family members as well.[10] Even infected applicants to the Job Corps, a federally funded domestic job training program which usually involves live-in housing, are screened out unless they are seeking entrance to one of the few non–live-in training programs. Prevention of transmission of HIV is cited as one goal of each of these screening programs, although other goals are also sometimes given.

The most extensive mandatory testing and screening program in this country, apart from that for donated blood, is the program of the U.S. military. Within a year of the development of the HIV antibody test, the Department of Defense decided to extend its mandatory testing policy to include over 3 million persons, including 300,000 yearly recruits, 2.1 million personnel on active duty, and 1.1 million military reservists.[11] During the first year of testing, 976 recruits were excluded from the armed forces on the basis of positive HIV tests. Personnel on active duty are to be tested every two years. As of this writing, those who test positive are not automatically discharged, although they may be assigned to different duties

---

[10] This policy was passed pursuant to federal regulation. See 22 C.F.R. 11.1(e) (1)–(5).

[11] Rivera, "Military," 226. We are heavily indebted to Rivera throughout this section.

or may even be discharged if it emerges that they became infected through gay activities.[12]

The costs of this policy in terms of privacy are obviously considerable. Recruits who are rejected when testing reveals they are infected have their lives disrupted and suffer all of the costs we mentioned earlier. In addition, they may feel forced to reveal their HIV infection to family and acquaintances in order to explain their rejection. Although theoretically the medical records of personnel on active duty are confidential, privacy is just one of the rights which are severely attenuated within the armed forces.[13] While there may be good reasons for this arising from the nature of the military, it means that the risks that individuals must bear in connection with private information about themselves are correspondingly greater. Consequently, careful thought should be given to what information needs to be generated in the first place. Unfortunately, the infected status of HIV carriers within the military is not always a well-kept secret, and dissemination of this information within the military can have very painful consequences and may eventually lead to dishonorable discharge. These costs, of course, are above and beyond the general trauma experienced by anyone who learns of HIV infection. Sometimes personnel who test positive are sent for two weeks of clinical evaluation. At the very least, this requires the individual to provide some explanation to associates within and without the military. Moreover, U.S. Navy policy requires that commanders of individuals who test positive receive a letter indicating as much and instructing them to

> ensure the member is aware that he is being retained on active duty despite statistics which indicate that 90% of all individuals having the HIV antibody are homosexual or drug abusers. He is not being labeled as such unless his actions reflect otherwise. If his actions reflect such behavior, he will be subject to disciplinary action and/or administrative separation.[14]

There are a number of cases on record of military personnel who came down with AIDS and were subsequently discharged as a result

---

[12] Ibid., 222–23.

[13] Ibid.

[14] COMNAVMILPERSCOM LETTER, from: Commander, Naval Military Personnel Command, 1300 Ser. N453/, at (2)(d), quoted in Rivera, "Military," 231, and cited in her footnote 107.

of betrayal by their military doctors. Their doctors had elicited information about risk factors from them after giving assurances of confidentiality; then they reported these patients to their commanders for admitting to gay activity prior to enlistment.[15]

What rationales have been given for these federal testing and screening policies instituted by our government? Although the cases differ slightly from program to program, there are more similarities than differences, so it will be useful to proceed by rationale rather than by program.

One rationale that has been offered for exclusionary screening of military draftees and Peace Corps invitees is that those who are accepted are given vaccines which could be dangerous for persons suffering immunosuppression. Although prior to HIV testing there was one celebrated case of an HIV-infected recruit who did have a severe reaction to a vaccine,[16] this rationale is weak, as we noted in Chapter 1. First, not all infected individuals are immunosuppressed. Second, only two live vaccines, live polio vaccine and smallpox vaccine, are believed to present a threat to those who are. Smallpox has been effectively eradicated: Presently it can be found only in freezers in government laboratories in Moscow and at the Centers for Disease Control in Atlanta. The only possible threat of exposure to smallpox would be in the event of germ warfare involving smallpox agents. This, however, is very unlikely. Even assuming serious involvement by the superpowers in biological warfare, smallpox is hardly a reasonable candidate for use in such warfare. It is inefficient, and a vaccine could be administered quickly which would block its effectiveness in the event it was used. For these reasons, and because both nations, along with forty-eight others, signed the Biological Weapons Convention of 1972, which requires renouncing such weapons and destroying existing stocks, some observers have argued that both superpowers should destroy their samples of the virus and stop vaccinating their troops. Nevertheless, both superpowers continue to vaccinate all their troops against smallpox. The

---

[15] Rivera, "Military," 224–26. See also *Doe v. Lehman*, U.S.D.C., M.D. Fla, No. 86-971-Civ-J-16, March 15, 1988, in which a recruiter for the Naval Reserve challenged his dismissal from the Naval Reserve on the basis of a positive HIV test.

[16] Rivera, "Military," 228.

Department of Defense spends $1.5 million a year on smallpox vaccine.[17]

Finally, recruits are given a live adenovirus vaccine. Again, not all HIV-infected persons are suffering immunosuppression. Moreover, it is not obvious that the additional risk of live vaccines for infected persons is not outweighed by the additional benefit they may promise. Originally, the Public Health Service's Immunization Practices Advisory Committee recommended that attenuated live vaccines not be given to immunosuppressed persons, even though there had been no case reports of excess illness associated with any live virus vaccines except smallpox and oral (live) polio vaccines. Recently, however, it reversed part of that recommendation and now urges vaccinating asymptomatic HIV-infected children with live measles, mumps, and rubella vaccines.[18]

Another rationale offered for exclusionary testing of military draftees is that it prevents the spread of HIV through direct blood transfusions. While the Department of Defense insists such transfusions occur routinely on board Navy ships and were common during the Vietnam War and the Granada and Beirut episodes, others insist they must be extraordinarily rare, partly because they are objectionable for other medical reasons and partly because they are needed less as a result of the development of artificial blood expanders. In any case, if preventing the very remote possibility of HIV infection by direct transfusion is a high priority of the Department of Defense, one must ask why an equally high priority was not assigned to preventing the possibility of hepatitis B infection through direct blood transfusions; exclusionary screening was never undertaken for that condition, even though a test became available in 1972. Although hepatitis B does not carry the high mortality rate associated with AIDS, it is much more infectious, was more widespread until recently, and, prior to 1987, caused more deaths in this country than AIDS.

---

[17] Linnea Capps, Sten Vermund, and Christine Johnsen, "Smallpox and Biological Warfare: The Case for Abandoning Vaccination of Military Personnel," *American Journal of Public Health* 76 (1976): 1229–31.

[18] "Recommendations of the Immunization Practices Advisory Committee (ACIP), Immunization of Children Infected with Human Immunodeficiency Virus—Supplementary ACIP Statement," *Morbidity and Mortality Weekly Report* 37, (1988): 181–83.

A third rationale, offered on behalf of military draftees and personnel on active duty, Peace Corps volunteers, and State Department foreign service personnel, is that persons suffering immunosuppression must not be exposed to threatening diseases which may be common elsewhere in the world. This argument too is of questionable merit. Again, most infected persons do not have clinically significant immunosuppression. More importantly, one of the great enigmas of HIV infection is that infected people usually retain their immunity to most diseases. They become especially susceptible to only thirty or forty opportunistic infections. Some of these involve pathogens which colonize most of us as children, so that subsequent exposure is inconsequential. Others are environmental, so that we are all exposed on a daily basis. Infection with nearly all of the others is preventable by ordinary hygiene. The only important exception, a disease less common in the United States than elsewhere in the world, is tuberculosis. However, as we noted in Chapter 1, even tuberculosis is relatively rare. It is also one of the more treatable of the opportunistic infections associated with AIDS.

These first three arguments involve the issue of protecting of various federal personnel. Only one of them involves the issue of slowing the spread of HIV infection. Each argument is weak in that it rests on an extraordinarily remote possibility of medical harm. We feel it is significant that in August 1985 the Armed Forces Epidemiological Board (AFEB) was asked by the Department of Defense to make a recommendation about whether to institute mandatory testing of recruits and military personnel. Ultimately AFEB's recommendation was against universal testing because of its lack of cost-effectiveness. Instead they urged more limited testing and AIDS education to reduce irrational fears within the military. Presumably they felt the universal testing proposals they had been asked to evaluate had been inspired by such fears. Unfortunately, the Department of Defense reached a decision to institute testing three weeks before they received the AFEB recommendations they had requested.[19]

The final argument given for exclusionary screening in the military, the Peace Corps, the Job Corps, and the State Department has nothing to do with slowing the spread of HIV. It is, quite simply, that HIV infection is a pre-existing condition which may ultimately

---

[19] Rivera, "Military," 227–28.

lead to problems that would prevent those infected from performing their jobs, or finishing their commitments, and that would involve
major costs the federal program in question wishes to avoid. However, given the unusually long incubation period for AIDS, this argument begins to make these testing programs sound like job discrimination pure and simple.

We argued in the previous chapter for legislation prohibiting
such discrimination for both economic reasons and reasons of justice. There is a sad irony that the same federal government which
claims to protect the handicapped from job discrimination should
itself practice job discrimination against persons infected with HIV.

The military, of course, has long maintained that there are, and
must be, no active gays within its ranks, and it has always been
quicker to protect our rights and liberties than to instantiate
them.[20] Moreover, the courts have traditionally shown great defer-
ence towards the military in this and other matters. Our dismay at
the discriminatory policies of the Peace Corps and the Job Corps is
accompanied by genuine puzzlement that these federal programs,
which are dedicated to the ideals of self-actualization and independence, are as quick to exclude persons infected with HIV as the military.

Of all these federal programs, employment by the State Department is most commonly the result of a career choice. Here, then,
one might have the highest hopes that the antidiscrimination protections guaranteed to the handicapped by the federal government
would come into play for individuals handicapped by HIV infection.
Unfortunately these expectations have been disappointed. Shortly

---

[20] Ibid., 222. Rivera notes that the military's opposition to gays in its
ranks dates back to 1943; she quotes a 1981 regulation in this connection
(DOD 1332.14), which states that the presence of gay

> members adversely affects the ability of the Military Services to maintain
> discipline, good order, and morale; to foster mutual trust and confidence
> among service members; to ensure the integrity of the system of rank and
> command; to facilitate assignment and worldwide deployment of service
> members who frequently must live and work under close conditions affording
> minimal privacy; to recruit and retain members of the Military Services; to
> maintain the public acceptability of military service; and to prevent breaches
> of security.

It is ironic that the antipathy to gays expressed by this regulation creates
the very problems it lists.

after the State Department began its exclusionary screening in January 1987, the American Federation of Government Employees, which represents State Department Employees, brought suit in Federal District Court seeking a preliminary injunction banning State Department testing. The suit was based on the Fourth Amendment and the Rehabilitation Act of 1973.[21] The preliminary injunction was denied on the grounds that the State Department policy was reasonable, since HIV-infected persons are more susceptible to diseases which are more prevalent in some foreign countries and because there is generally a higher medical risk in some foreign countries.[22] The court also stated that there was no violation of the rehabilitation act, because employees with HIV infection were not otherwise qualified for foreign service duty.[23] We believe this opinion is incorrect and that the policy is a violation of the rehabilitation act as interpreted by *Arline*. An HIV-infected person who is asymptomatic and who is not suffering immunosuppression is as qualified for foreign service work as for any other work. The only way in which HIV infection is relevant for foreign service work is as an indicator that at some future time the HIV-infected individual may become ill, be unable to perform adequately or complete the tour of duty, and incur medical expenses which the federal government would have to pay. We believe all the arguments concerning job discrimination against HIV-infected individuals which were discussed in Chapter 8 apply to the State Department policies on HIV screening, including the argument that such discrimination is a violation of both the spirit and the letter of the federal rehabilitation act on any reasonable interpretation of the act and of the medical facts.

PRISONS

There are over 500,000 persons in state and federal prisons in this country. Another 8 million are jailed annually.[24] Between January 1981 and October 1987 there were a total of 1964 AIDS cases in vari-

---

[21] *Local 1812, American Federation of Government Employees v. U.S. Department of State*, 662 F. Supp. 50, 53 (D.D.C. 1987).

[22] Ibid., 52–53.

[23] Ibid., 54.

[24] Urvashi Vaid, "Prisons," in *AIDS and the Law*, 236–37.

ous prisons and jails,[25] the majority of them IV drug abusers in prisons in New York, New Jersey, and Florida. Undoubtedly many times that number are infected. Several states test all prisoners,[26] and a few segregate those who are positive.[27]

Contrary both to a vote of the National Association of State Corrections Administrators in 1986 against mandatory testing of all inmates and to a recommendation that the Public Health Service had made to the White House just weeks before, President Reagan, on May 31, 1987, announced a program to test all federal prisoners for HIV infection. It soon became clear that the decision to test had been made before any clear rationale had been arrived at for such testing and even before it had been determined what would be done with test results. For example, after a White House spokesman announced that "our desire is to separate any federal prisoner who tests positive,"[28] a Justice Department spokesman indicated it had not been decided whether all prisoners would be tested, much less segregated.[29] In the weeks that followed, such a variety of arguments were offered that suspicions that they were only afterthoughts were aroused. In the words of one commentator, "Only the politics of appearance can explain this selection of the politically voiceless and the legally vulnerable."[30]

During the first three months of universal testing, 16,372 prisoners were tested; only 3 percent were found to be positive. In October 1987, the Bureau of Prisons announced it was scrapping the universal testing program and was substituting a more restricted program that involved testing only certain groups: (1) inmates who ask to be tested; (2) inmates with clinical indications of HIV infection; (3) 5 percent of incoming inmates, randomly selected; (4) inmates

---

[25] "10,000 New Inmates to Be Tested to Gauge Spread of AIDS Virus," *New York Times*, May 28, 1988, A8.

[26] Vaid reports that Nevada, Colorado, and South Dakota either do or are about to test all state prisoners. See Vaid, "Prisons," 239.

[27] Vaid, "Prisons," 235, 237. Throughout this section we are heavily indebted to Vaid's account of AIDS and prisons.

[28] "Problems Seen in Reagan Testing Plan," *New York Times*, June 3, 1987, B8.

[29] The American Medical Association came out in favor of such testing on the assumption that infected prisoners would be segregated. See *American Medical News*, July 3–10, 1987, p. 43.

[30] Hunter, "Reagan's 'Weak, Coercive' AIDS Plan," A31.

involved in community activities; (5) inmates within sixty days of release; and (6) promiscuous or "predatory" inmates (i.e., rapists).[31]

There are several reasons why AIDS transmission may be a special problem in prisons. First, in some areas prison populations include a disproportionately high percentage of HIV-infected persons, since many persons are imprisoned for high-risk (drug-related) activities. Second, if an infected person is a prisoner, others may be at an increased risk of exposure. Prisoner-to-prisoner transmission may occur through sex (including rape), the sharing of needles for IV drugs and tattooing (which is a common prison ritual),[32] and possibly even through bloody violence. Prison guards have expressed concern that prisoner-to-guard transmission may occur through urine, feces, or blood tossed at guards by hostile or sociopathic prisoners; through wounds from sharp, HIV-contaminated objects which prisoners leave hidden in creases in mattresses and blankets and which may cause cuts during room searches, and even through injuries guards sustain while breaking up bloody fights between inmates. Although some authorities discount the risk of prisoner-to-guard transmission, unfortunately very little is known about how great the risk really is, or about how much HIV transmission actually occurs in prisons generally.[33] Third, effective AIDS education and counseling in a prison setting will be especially difficult, since prisoners are skeptical about any warnings from "authorities." Fourth, prison officials are reluctant to provide condoms or clean needles to prisoners, since, as we noted earlier, some people believe that is tantamount to endorsing proscribed activities.

Widespread mandatory testing would have a legitimate role in ameliorating the threat of transmission within prisons only if it could contribute to minimizing these risks and could do so without imposing costs that outweigh the benefits of such testing. Not only is it uncertain how much HIV transmission occurs within prisons, it is not obvious how universal testing would significantly reduce the threat of transmission in any of the contexts enumerated above.

---

[31]"Some Federal Inmates Carrying AIDS Virus to Be Segregated," *Star Tribune* (formerly *Minneapolis Star Tribune*), October 24, 1987, sec. A, p. 7.

[32]Vaid, "Prisons," 239.

[33]Ibid., 238. The lack of information itself provides a reason for repeated testing of some prisoners, but it does not require that all prisoners be tested.

Anonymous testing is unlikely to have much impact. The effectiveness of precautionary warnings to infected prisoners would depend on the prisoners' good sense *and* goodwill, and both may be in short supply in prisons, particularly among malevolent, psychopathic, violent, or predatory prisoners. Precautionary warnings to uninfected inmates might have some impact on potential iv drug abusers, but since many prisoners who are receptive in anal intercourse are coerced in some degree or another into that role,[34] they are unlikely to have the power to benefit from a precautionary warning by insisting on safer sex practices. Precautionary warnings to guards would of course require that test results be distributed to the guards. Even if confidentiality could be maintained, such use of the test results would provide no precautionary warning, and hence little protection, to other prisoners. Moreover, in practice it would be virtually impossible to maintain confidentiality: Standards of confidentiality are notoriously low in prisons, and it would be impossible for guards to take special precautions in handling infected prisoners without that fact being obvious to other prisoners. Any prisoner whose infected status became known to other prisoners would face a very serious risk of violence from other prisoners. That risk might even be greater than the risk he would pose to others if his infected status was never detected.

At the same time that confidentiality of prison medical records may be a will-o'-the-wisp, one of the rationales for the fundamental value of privacy is especially strong with respect to the prison setting: Without privacy regarding their hiv status, prisoners may suffer both significant physical harm and unjust disadvantages as a result of the ignorance and malice of fellow prisoners, prison guards, and even administrators. While we would stop short of arguing against all hiv testing of prisoners, we urge great caution and would favor testing only when the strictest precautions have been taken against the harms we have been discussing and when some clear benefit can reasonably be expected.

Although the rights of prisoners are attenuated, they are not eliminated. This is true of both moral and legal rights. It is clear that prisoners do not sacrifice the moral right to be treated humanely or the moral right to be protected from random violence.

---

[34] Vaid, "Prisons," 238.

These important moral rights are reflected at several points in our legal system.[35] The most important constitutional protection for prisoners is the Eighth Amendment, which protects against cruel and unusual punishment.[36] The Cruel and Unusual Punishments Clause not only reflects our moral concerns, but has been interpreted so that it incorporates current moral views. The Supreme Court has held that penalties which transgress today's "broad and idealistic concepts of dignity, civilized standards, humanity, and decency are prohibited."[37] The basic principle is that the "conditions of confinement must not involve the wanton and unnecessary infliction of pain."[38] Specifically, "deliberate indifference to serious medical needs of prisoners constitutes the 'unnecessary and wanton infliction of pain' proscribed by the Eighth Amendment."[39] In addition, the Eighth Amendment provides protection against violent attacks by other inmates.[40] Unfortunately, these constitutional embodiments of our basic moral commitment to treat other human beings decently are seriously attenuated by the requirement that inmates who bring suits against prison officials for failure to provide Eighth Amendment protections must prove not merely that the officials were negligent or failed to exercise due care, but that they acted with "obduracy and wantonness."[41]

Other potentially relevant constitutional protections are the Due Process Clause and the Equal Protection Clause of the Fourteenth Amendment. The Due Process Clause protects prisoners against deliberate or reckless deprivations of life or property without due

---

[35] For an overview of constitutional issues affecting prisoners, see Laura J. Moriarity, "AIDS in Correctional Institutions: The Legal Aspects," *Criminal Law Bulletin* (1987): 533–49.

[36] Specifically, the Eighth Amendment states that "excessive bail shall not be required, nor excessive fines imposed, nor cruel and unusual punishments inflicted."

[37] *Estelle v. Gamble*, 429 U.S. 97, 102, reh. den. 439 U.S. 1122, quoting *Jackson v. Bishop*, 404 F.ed 571, 579 (8th Cir. 1968).

[38] *Rhodes v. Chapman*, 452 U.S. 346, 347 (1981).

[39] *Estelle v. Gamble*, 429 U.S. 97, 104 (1976).

[40] *Benny v. Pipes*, 799 F.2d 489, 495 (9th Cir. 1986); *Johnston v. Lucas*, 786 F.2d 1254, 1259 (5th Cir. 1986); *Watts v. Laurent*, 774 F.2d 168, 172 (7th Cir. 1985); *Martin v. White* 742 F.2d 469, 474 (8th Cir. 1984).

[41] *Davidson v. Cannon* 474 U.S. 344 (1986); *Daniels v. Williams*, 474 U.S. 327 (1986); *Whitney v. Albers*, 475 U.S. 312 (1986).

process.[42] The Due Process Clause also protects inmates against restrictions of liberty that are not within the sentence imposed on them.[43] The Equal Protection Clause protects prisoners and groups of prisoners from being arbitrarily singled out for disadvantageous treatment.

We believe that segregating HIV-infected prisoners from the general prison population is suspect practically, morally, *and*, because the Constitution is responsive to moral considerations here, also constitutionally. It is suspect practically because even segregated prisoners need to be guarded; therefore, it is not clear that segregation would reduce the risk of prisoner-to-guard transmissions. It is suspect morally for several reasons. HIV infection carries with it a stigma and it can mark a person — especially a prisoner — for discriminatory and sometimes violent treatment if it becomes known to others. Segregating prisoners who test positive will typically serve to put other prisoners on notice that these prisoners are infected. Apart from the stigma, however, there are several other reasons why segregating infected prisoners is morally objectionable. First, it is expensive, and in a world of very scarce prison resources, this means either that other programs will suffer or, more likely, that prisoners who are segregated will be made to endure substandard conditions. Moreover, in prisons having only a few infected prisoners, segregation would amount in practice to isolation. It is reported that HIV-infected inmates have been isolated for long periods in small medical observation cells "under twenty-three or twenty-four hour-a-day lock down conditions and denied access to law libraries, outdoor exercise, and educational, vocational and work-release programs."[44] In addition, infected prisoners who are segregated or isolated are often supervised by guards whose fear of contracting AIDS puts the prisoners at a further disadvantage. The most dramatic deprivations, however, involve parole opportunities. Isolated prisoners may be denied opportunities to participate in special programs which qualify participants for early parole.[45] Former Attorney General Meese even suggested that one "benefit" of widespread

---

[42] *Parratt v. Taylor*, 451 U.S. 527 (1981); *Hudson v. Palmer*, 468 U.S. 517 (1984).

[43] *Hewitt v. Helms*, 459 U.S. 460, 468 (1983).

[44] Vaid, "Prisons," 241.

[45] Ibid.

prisoner testing might be that positive test results could be used as a basis for denying parole to prisoners who were otherwise eligible.[46] Morally speaking, any benefits of such segregation appear to be outweighed by the burdens placed on those segregated. For a variety of reasons, HIV-infected prisoners who have been segregated have simply not been treated fairly and humanely.

Such segregation is also suspect constitutionally because it would presumably be indefinite or permanent. The Supreme Court held in *Sutto v. Finney* that if conditions of segregation differed materially from the general conditions, the length of segregation would be a factor in determining whether the conditions constituted cruel and unusual punishment.[47] Thus it is arguable that segregation of HIV-infected inmates is cruel and unusual punishment because the conditions of segregation are severe and the segregation will last the entire length of their incarceration.

It could also be argued that the sort of segregation described above is arbitrary treatment in violation of the Equal Protection Clause of the Fourteenth Amendment. Laws or state actions which disadvantage some persons but not others raise equal protection issues. Even though AIDS and HIV infection do not constitute suspect classifications triggering strict scrutiny, actions and laws which disadvantage people on the basis of either are still subject to minimal scrutiny, which requires that they must be rationally related to a valid state interest.[48] While slowing the spread of HIV infection is undeniably a valid state interest, it could be argued in light of current medical evidence that treating prisoners with AIDS or HIV infection in this manner is not rationally related to it.

Unfortunately, the few court cases which have dealt specifically with the segregation of prisoners with AIDS have produced holdings unfavorable to prisoners with AIDS and HIV infection. In *Codero v. Coughlin*, for instance, a federal court held that it is not a violation of the Equal Protection Clause to segregate prisoners with AIDS, because there is a rational basis for the segregation.[49] Interestingly,

---

[46]"Many Questions Cloud Start of AIDS Testing," *New York Times*, June 10, 1987, A29.

[47]*Hutto v. Finney*, at 687–88.

[48]See Chapter 4 for a discussion of the different levels of scrutiny to which government action may be subject.

[49]*Cordero v. Coughlin*, 607 F. Supp. 9, 10 (S.D.N.Y. 1984).

the primary rational basis offered by the court was not that the inmates with AIDS might infect other inmates, but that the fear of AIDS among the general prison population might lead to disturbances.[50] *Codero* also held that segregation of prisoners with AIDS was not cruel and unusual punishment, because they were not deprived of necessities.[51]

It is also doubtful that, in the present climate, a case could succeed on due process grounds. In *Hewitt v. Helms*, the Supreme Court held that it was not a violation of the Due Process Clause to transfer an inmate to the "less amenable and more restrictive quarters" of administrative segregation for nonpunitive reasons, because it was within the terms of confinement ordinarily contemplated for a prison sentence.[52] It might be argued that persons who are segregated because of HIV infection will be segregated for the duration of their incarceration and that, because such long-term segregation is not within the terms of confinement ordinarily contemplated for a prison sentence, *Hewitt* should not be controlling. Unfortunately, the strong language of *Hewitt* suggests that presently this argument would have little chance of success.

In general, the emerging precedent would seem to suggest that segregation of inmates who are HIV infected or who have AIDS will probably be upheld by the courts even if the conditions for those segregated are inferior to the conditions for the general prison population. It should be clear that we deplore this trend on both moral and constitutional grounds. Prisoners who also suffer HIV infection are doubly stigmatized; unfortunately they are thus doubly subject to being treated as less-than-fully human.

In light of the problems with widespread mandatory testing in prisons, we believe that even the more restricted federal testing program substituted in October 1987 is objectionable. Instead, we would urge the adoption of the following policies for slowing the spread of HIV infection within prisons. First, in spite of prisoners' skepticism about "advice" from prison authorities, prisons should adopt thorough and explicit educational programs, which include instruction on cleaning needles. The evidence is overwhelming that explicit and nonjudgmental AIDS education is presently our most effective

---

[50] Ibid., 10.
[51] Ibid., 11.
[52] *Hewitt v. Helms* at 468.

weapon against the spread of HIV. Second, condoms and clean needles should be made available to prisoners. Condoms are already made available in Vermont state prisons.[53] Neither explicit AIDS education nor the distribution of condoms need carry messages of endorsement or approval of proscribed activities; they simply acknowledge the fact that unsafe activities are occurring and attempt to make them safer. Disapproval — even legal proscription — is perfectly compatible with both. Any lingering doubts on this point might be resolved by packaging such condoms and needles in wrappers bearing not only warnings about risks of HIV infection, but also the statutes or regulations which proscribe the relevant high-risk activities. Third, HIV testing should be done only when requested by the prisoner or when medically appropriate as a diagnostic tool (i.e., when an inmate has symptoms indicating possible HIV infection.) Fourth, all such testing should be combined with counseling, as it often is elsewhere. Finally, all prisoners likely to assault other prisoners should be placed in administrative segregation without regard to whether they are infected with HIV.

The difference between this final recommendation and the current testing policy for promiscuous or predatory prisoners is instructive. The Justice Department has indicated that federal prisoners who are found to be promiscuous or predatory (i.e., rapists and other sexually aggressive prisoners) will be tested; those found to be infected will be isolated. We commend this policy at least for acknowledging that some prisoners face the risk of sexual assault. The threat of prison rape is even more troubling now, when it may carry with it the additional threat of HIV infection, and it would be to the credit of any program if it could eliminate this additional threat.

But if prison officials are really able to identify predatory prisoners, as the policy presupposes, should only *infected* rapists be isolated? While rape by an infected rapist is obviously worse than rape by an uninfected rapist, prisoners are surely entitled — morally and constitutionally — to protection from sexual assault by anyone.

Making the isolation of all rapists a higher priority than it has been up until now is a better way of preventing HIV infection via rape than the existing policy. It would not only avoid all of the problems associated with testing, but would also provide prisoners

---

[53] "White House Decides against Condoms for Federal Inmates," *Minneapolis Star-Tribune*, June 29, 1987, sec. D, p. 20.

with more protection from violence, protection to which they are entitled by any civilized standard. This all seems so obvious that it raises the question of why the Bureau of Prisons has *not* opted for this strategy. We suspect the reason is that prison resources are so scarce that it is impossible to maintain many prisoners in minimally acceptable conditions of segregation or isolation. If this is correct, it reenforces our case against the segregation of all prisoners infected with HIV.[54]

PREMARITAL TESTING

On the face of it, the debate over mandatory premarital testing mirrors the debate over general mandatory testing. On the one hand, support is widespread, with 80 percent of the public in favor. President Reagan also spoke out in favor of routine premarital testing in his talk on May 31, 1987. Such testing has received considerable attention from state legislatures: Gostin and Ziegler report that as of April 1987, thirty states had considered sixty-two bills dealing with premarital screening, some of which were not even explicit about the consequences of a positive test result.[55] Yet only Illinois and Louisiana had adopted mandatory premarital screening as of January 1988. Indeed, within months of the passage of its law, Illinois even considered repeal in light of the high cost to marriage license applicants and the resulting drop in marriage license applications in Illinois as couples went to neighboring states to be married.[56]

As with most proposals for massive mandatory testing, there is a sharp contrast between the favorable attitude of the general pub-

[54] Lawrence Gostin, William Curran, and Mary Clark, "The Case against Compulsory Casefinding in Controlling AIDS—Testing, Screening and Reporting," *American Journal of Law and Medicine* 12 (1987): 43. Gostin, Curran, and Clark also argue that prison officials should direct their attention to the behavior that spreads HIV infection and segregate HIV-infected inmates.

[55] Larry Gostin and Andrew Ziegler, "A Review of AIDS-related Legislative and Regulatory Policy in the United States," *Law, Medicine and Health Care* 15 (Summer 1987): 9.

[56] Within four months of the passage of the Illinois law requiring HIV testing of marriage license applicants, a number of bills to repeal the law were introduced into the Illinois House of Representatives. See *AIDS Update* 2 (May 1988): 3.

lic and negative attitude of public health experts. Again, most public health officials, including Surgeon General Koop and the American Medical Association, have all gone on record against such testing on the grounds that it is not cost-effective.

A recent study has documented the claim that national mandatory premarital testing would not be a cost-effective way to slow HIV transmission.[57] Cleary and his associates painstakingly took into account careful estimates of a large number of relevant variables (the number of marriages per year in the United States, the probable infection rates of the men and women involved, the sensitivity and specificity of various tests, the costs of testing and counseling, the percentage of infected couples who had not had sex prior to marriage, the percentage of those couples whose members both tested positive, etc.). Their figures led them to the following estimates: Of the 3,800,000 persons marrying each year, only 1348 will be infected. Testing and counseling all of them would cost $100,000,000 and would identify only "1,200 infected persons who had not already transmitted the virus to their partner . . . each year."[58] This means a cost of approximately $83,000 per prevented transmission. In addition, another 100 infected persons would be assured they were not infected and as many as 350 persons would be told incorrectly that they were infected. They concluded such testing was not cost-effective and ought not to be implemented: "The more resources that we devote to such marginally effective ventures, the fewer resources we will have to develop truly effective public health programs. A comprehensive public health education program, in which premarital counseling and voluntary testing is one component, has the greatest potential for reducing the spread of infection."[59] This study is the most elaborate and careful attempt to date to assess the cost-effectiveness of mandatory premarital testing.

We agree with the stand of Cleary and his associates and of other public health experts against mandatory testing but question their claim that considerations of cost-effectiveness alone warrant

---

[57] Paul Cleary et al., "Compulsory Premarital Screening for the Human Immunodeficiency Virus: Technical and Public Health Considerations," *Journal of the American Medical Association* 258 (1987): 1757–62.

[58] Ibid., 1760.

[59] Ibid., 1761.

its rejection. We do so because we are struck by analogies between screening marriage applicants and screening blood donors — the one massive testing program which has received virtually no criticism from either cost-conscious public health officials or civil rights groups concerned about privacy. Gays and IV drug abusers are under-represented among blood donors and marriage applicants. They have been urged not to donate, and low percentages of contaminated blood suggest these urgings have been heard. (Again, in Minnesota only 1 unit per 30,000 has been found to be infected, at an estimated cost of $133,000 per identified infected unit.) Moreover, while the surest route of HIV transmission is through blood products, repeated exposure to an infected partner as a result of frequent sexual inter-course, such as would normally occur between newlyweds, also puts an uninfected partner (and any child by an infected partner) at very high risk. Thus, while mandatory premarital testing would be a very expensive undertaking and would identify only a very small percentage of HIV-infected persons, the same can be said of the widely acclaimed blood-testing program. We conclude that if cost-effectiveness considerations were to be determinative in both cases, as the remarks of public health officials have consistently suggested they should, both programs should either be implemented or rejected. The fact that public health officials do not take this view suggests to us that there must be other factors at work in their thinking which distinguish the two cases but which do not surface in the public debate. We wish to argue here that those factors involve privacy.[60]

Intuitively, and quite properly in our view, we all tend to view governmental intrusions into marriage with great suspicion. Marriage is, above all, an intensely personal relationship whose delicate fabric partners create and work through for themselves on the basis of mutual concern, respect, and trust. It is a relationship into which people enter freely, as self-determining agents. Many people do as much to shape the course of their lives by their decisions to marry (and related decisions to parent) as they do by any decisions they

---

[60] See also Gostin, Curran, and Clark, "The Case Against Compulsory Casefinding," 35, where they note that "more important than the economic cost of implementing a system of pre-marital screening is the personal cost to individual privacy."

will ever make. For many people, marriage and family life are at the core of "personal" or "private" life. It has even been suggested that marriage provides a private sanctuary into which one may retreat from the pressures of social life.[61]

In light of these assumptions, government intrusions into "family matters" quite properly should be resisted. Indeed, one of the first cases in which the Supreme Court spoke of a right to privacy involved just such an intrusion into a married couple's birth control practices. In *Griswold v. Connecticut,* Justice Douglas wrote, "We deal with a right of privacy older than the Bill of Rights—older than our political parties, older than our school system. Marriage is a coming together for better or for worse, hopefully enduring, and intimate to a degree being sacred."[62]

All of this is in stark contrast to the relation which obtains between blood donors and recipients. Persons receiving blood products hardly do so as a result of free and unfettered decisions. Rather, they need them desperately—usually to stay alive. Their relationship to their caregivers is one of dependency, and if they become infected through contaminated blood products, they strike us as totally innocent and hapless victims. At the same time, the organizations that provide health care are radically less personal than is a marriage. They are, in effect, offering products and services. Their relationships with both blood donors and recipients are business-like, not personal. Marriage partners, on the other hand, do not offer a product or service, and those who infect their spouses are viewed quite differently than blood donors who infect blood recipients.

It should be noted that the kind of privacy at issue here is not just informational privacy: The argument is not simply that married people are entitled to *secrets* within their relationship and that some particular harm would come to persons planning marriage should it become known they were infected with HIV. We strongly believe that in the area of matrimony people's liberty privacy should

---

[61] For a dissenting discussion of this view, see John McMurtry, "Monogamy: A Critique," in *Philosophy and Sex,* ed. Robert Baker and Frederick Elliston (Buffalo, N.Y.: Prometheus Books, 1984), 107–18.

[62] *Griswold,* 381 U.S. at 479, 486.

also be respected; barring very strong reasons to the contrary, they should be free of paternalistic state intervention.

This is not to say that there could never be such reasons. Does the possibility of HIV infection of one of the partners constitute a sufficiently strong reason? Undoubtedly some small percentage of marriage partners present a detectable threat, in virtue of their HIV infection, to the lives and welfare of people they are about to marry. Moreover, there is another consideration which weighs in favor of mandatory premarital testing. The very fact that marriage is supposed to be founded on trust may discourage some persons from asking (or requiring) a fiancé to submit to testing. A woman who suspects her fiancé *may* have had previous drug or sexual experiences which put him at risk, for instance, may also feel she is in no position to insist that he (or they) submit to HIV testing. To do so would imply distrust. To the extent that this is so, mandatory premarital testing would not amount to *paternalistic* state intervention to protect individuals from themselves, but would empower persons planning marriage to protect themselves by making more informed decisions. Short of refusing to marry someone, a person might otherwise have no means of getting the requisite information for making an informed choice.

How are all these considerations to be weighed against each other? There will never be a mechanical formula for determining how that is to be done. (Aristotle warns us against asking for more precision than the subject allows.) Obviously, however, as the rate of HIV infection increases in a certain geographical area, so does the case for mandatory premarital testing. Already, for instance, premarital testing in high-risk areas (e.g., New York City) would obviously be many times more cost-effective than the figures Cleary and his associates arrive at for national mandatory testing. As cost-effectiveness increases and the case for mandatory premarital testing becomes stronger, however, it should be borne in mind that a person anticipating marriage will probably still face a much greater (and detectable) threat to his or her welfare in virtue of the fiancé's medical problems and tendency toward alcoholism, violence, depression, and just plain irresponsibility than in virtue of possible HIV infection. Nevertheless, governmental intrusions designed to "protect" spouses by testing for the presence of any of these dangers would strike us as coarse, inappropriate, and quite antithetical

to the spirit of mutual concern and trust on which marriage is supposed to be predicated. One commentator has even noted that testing of marriage license applicants for syphilis — a requirement many
states have abolished — might be found unconstitutional given today's
heightened respect for privacy.[63]

---

[63] However, abolishment has usually occurred because of lack of
cost-effectiveness. See Cleary et al., "Compulsory Premarital Screening,"
1761.

10
Privacy and Perceptions of AIDS

Throughout our analysis we have claimed that considerations of privacy should be given more weight in debates about HIV testing than many people have acknowledged. We also argued, in Chapter 3, that one indication of the value of privacy is the great importance we attach to it in other contexts and as a precondition of other goods, such as autonomy and tolerance. At this point it might well be asked, If the importance of privacy is really generally recognized, why have so many people failed to give it due consideration in their thinking about HIV testing?

We wish at this point to offer some speculations about why this is so. Very briefly, we want to suggest that the right to privacy of HIV-infected persons is often not given proper moral consideration because most HIV infections are acquired by stigmatized activities — IV drug abuse and gay sex. To develop this thesis, we must look closely at the notions of stigma and of the limits of the moral community.

One issue which any moral theory must address is how membership in the moral community is determined: Which creatures are to be thought of as having interests or rights entitled to moral consideration and protection?[1] Some theories hold moral consideration is due all creatures capable of consciousness (e.g., utilitarianism and recent animal rights theories). More typically, moral consideration is held to be due just to creatures who are themselves capable of moral agency. In any case, most moral theories agree that moral respect is due others who are *like us* in the relevant ways. Whether stated in the language of compassion and empathy for fellow persons, as in the golden rule, or in the more austere Kantian language

---

[1] Thus, for example, the abortion debate could be construed as a debate over whether fetuses are to be included in the moral community.

of autonomy and capacity for reasoned self-determination, all theories consider our recognition of and identification with beings like
ourselves to be the foundation for determining who is within the
moral community.

Stigmatization, on the other hand, is the process of viewing
persons with certain characteristics as essentially alien or *different
from* us. A stigmatized person is the "other," unlike us, the "normal"
ones. When people bear stigmas perceived as unrelated to free choice
(e.g., physical handicaps or disfigurement), others may experience
only psychological discomfort or revulsion. When a stigma occurs
as a result of seemingly voluntary behaviors, however, the stigmatized person is often perceived as being outside the moral community — as a creature whose rights and interests warrant no consideration in moral deliberations.

Which characteristics are stigmatizing will depend among other
things on what is perceived as threatening or harmful. In a repressive, closed society an individual may be stigmatized for mere non-
conformity, that is, just for engendering diversity where uniformity for its own sake is expected and demanded. A pluralistic, open
society such as ours, on the other hand, sees diversity not as a threat
but as a desideratum, a corollary of personal freedom. However,
given the natural tendency to be less comfortable around things
that are alien to us and our way of life, we, as members of an open,
pluralistic society, must live with a tension. On the one hand, we
must identify with others and see them as fundamentally *like ourselves* if we are to be bound together with them into a society or
moral community. At the same time, if our society is to be an open
one, in which freedom and individuality can flourish, we must tolerate important differences. It was argued earlier that protections of
privacy based on morality, law, and even etiquette help to deal with
this tension. Privacy helps resolve it by enabling each of us to have
space in which to develop and exercise our individuality free from
the scrutiny and judgment of others and, conversely, to avoid having to confront features of others that could make it difficult to
identify with them as we must if we are to constitute a moral community. Of course, there is a difference between individuality which
should be tolerated and antisocial behavior which should not. But
moral disapproval differs from the kind of extreme stigmatization
we are discussing here, which puts others beyond the bounds of the

moral community. Moral condemnation can only be leveled against individuals who are still granted the status of moral beings.

IV drug abuse and gay sexuality are stigmatized activities. Perhaps nowhere are deviations from "normalcy" viewed as more threatening than in the area of human sexuality. The advent of AIDS has only intensified the stigmatization of gays. One obvious manifestation of this was the reluctance of the government and the news media (both of which are responsive to public perceptions) to "take AIDS seriously" as long as it was seen as only a disease of stigmatized minorities. This lack of concern continued even after AIDS had claimed many more lives than other "epidemics" such as legionnaire's disease and toxic shock syndrome, each of which received much more attention.[2] We saw in Chapter 5 that even after the government and the media recognized the seriousness of AIDS, they both continued to resist public discussion essential to effective, explicit AIDS education. Another manifestation of this stigmatization is the extent to which the rights of gays and IV drug abusers, including the right to privacy, have been discounted by many people in the debate about AIDS and HIV testing.

If we are right, then two puzzling phenomena immediately become explicable. The first phenomenon is the absence of any public clamor for mandatory testing of the group with highest risk of all those for which testing might be mandated: hemophilia patients at high risk for HIV infection. The second phenomenon is the surprising consistency with which the lines have been drawn on so many HIV testing proposal debates: Much of the general public and most conservatives, that is, those whose main agenda is political, on one side and those whose main agenda is medical on the other. We will consider each of these phenomena briefly.

Imagine for a moment a federally mandated HIV testing program targeted at all hemophilia patients who had been given factor VIII coagulation concentrate prior to April 1985. There are approximately 15,000-18,000 Americans with coagulation disorders,[3] 9,800

---

[2] See Shilts, *And the Band Played On*; 109–10.

[3] For a discussion of the epidemiology of AIDS among hemophiliacs, see Jeanette K. Stehr-Green et al., "Hemophilia-associated AIDS in the United States, 1981 to September 1987," *American Journal of Public Health* 78 (1988): 439–442.

of whom are believed to be infected with HIV.[4] This group is at higher risk for HIV infection than the target group of any mandatory testing proposal that has ever been taken seriously. From a practical point of view, a testing program for hemophilia patients would be relatively cheap and easy to implement: Legislation making hemophilia a reportable condition would oblige doctors to report all the hemophilia patients in their care to the state. Alternatively, they could be traced through prescription records, which would note who had been given factor VIII coagulation concentrate medications. Because of the high percentage of those infected, the cost per identified infected person would be literally hundreds of times less than in mandatory premarital testing programs. Moreover, in most cases it would be a simple matter to identify and warn uninfected individuals (e.g., spouses) who had a very high risk of infection from hemophiliacs who tested positive.

For these reasons, most health care professionals working with hemophiliacs agree they should be urged in the strongest possible terms to undergo *voluntary* testing. What we find instructive, however, is that so very little has been heard about hemophiliacs as a target group in the public and political debate about *mandatory* testing. This is so even though, given the preventative goal, hemophiliacs are probably a more logical target group than any of those which are under public discussion. We suggest the reason for this is that a program of mandatory testing of the nation's hemophiliacs would so obviously intrude on the rights of people who do not bear the stigma of AIDS-related behaviors.

Unlike gays and IV drug abusers, hemophiliacs are not stigmatized; they are perceived by everyone as normal, decent citizens, at risk through no fault of their own. Those hemophiliacs who are infected are viewed as *innocent* victims. The double misfortune of their hemophilia and their infection would only be compounded by the intrusion of testing mandated by the state (and to what end, exactly?). Ironically, people who view all adult singles with suspicion may view married hemophiliacs as worthier of having their rights respected than single ones, in spite of the fact that they probably pose greater threats to their regular sex partners — and certainly to children they may conceive. Nevertheless, these threats are not

---

[4] See the discussion of hemophilia in Chapter 1.

viewed as strong enough to override hemophiliacs' right to privacy. The public perception in this case seems to be that the government has no business "rounding up" respectable citizens and intruding into their privacy by testing them, especially since any benefit from such testing could only be mandated by even grosser intrusions into the private (sexual) activities of those found to be infected.

By contrast, nearly all persons found to be infected by other mandatory testing programs which have widespread public support are neither normal, decent folk nor innocent victims in the eyes of many people. Rather, they are almost all people who have chosen to engage in stigmatized activities, and hence they are morally disenfranchised and considered to be beyond the pale. As such, their privacy and other moral claims deserve no moral consideration, especially if they conflict with what are perceived as legitimate interests of members in good standing. At worst, they may even be viewed as perverts who have gotten what they deserve and who should receive no sympathy. On this view, most massive testing programs are seen as desirable because the only privacy they threaten is the privacy of those who are really not entitled to it in the first place — the others, passing among us undetected as if they were "normal." One commentator has even gone so far as to argue that the real motive for requiring premarital HIV testing is not to slow the spread of AIDS, but to purge marriage, the very embodiment of heterosexual orthodoxy, of pollution by gays.[5]

The second phenomenon our hypothesis explains is the remarkable consistency with which those whose careers and fundamental goals are in medicine and public health have opposed the massive mandatory testing programs for which there is so much popular enthusiasm. Perhaps more than anywhere else, medicine and public health are areas in which confidentiality and respect for privacy are recognized as absolute preconditions of trust and hence of the professional enterprise. Public health officials are especially aware that progress has been made in the treatment of other sexually transmitted diseases and, more recently, in the research and treatment of

---

[5] Richard Mohr, "Policy, Ritual and Purity: Mandatory AIDS Testing" (Paper delivered to the Chicago Area AIDS Task Force, July 14, 1987). Whatever else may be said for that view, it is certainly true that many unhappy gay men have sought to escape the stigma of homosexuality by marrying and having families.

AIDS only because a bond of trust has been forged between themselves and those at risk. Without that trust, there will be no cooperation; without cooperation, medical and public health enterprises become impossible. In the words of the Presidential Commission on AIDS,

> HIV-related discrimination is impairing this nation's ability to limit the spread of the epidemic. Crucial to this effort are epidemiological studies to track the epidemic as well as the education, testing, and counseling of those who have been exposed to the virus. However, public health officials will not be able to gain the confidence and cooperation of infected individuals or those at high risk for infection if such individuals fear [discrimination].[6]

The re-emergence of syphilis during the 1960s teaches us that not even an HIV vaccine or a sure cure would end the AIDS epidemic unless there was sufficient understanding and trust on the part of those at risk that they would be willing to come forward and seek help from the medical and public health professions. As Allan Brandt put it, "even 'magic bullets' need to be effectively delivered."[7]

Targeted, explicit AIDS education and voluntary HIV testing and counseling are not only the most promising avenues presently available for slowing the spread of HIV infection, they are also symbolic embodiments of trust. Privacy is not a supreme value, and we have argued that at some point it is rational to subordinate it to other values. What is irrational, immoral, and imprudent is to discount privacy claims altogether because they are usually made by or on behalf of stigmatized individuals who are at high risk for HIV infection. These are precisely the people whose privacy claims may be the most legitimate.

---

[6] *Report of the Presidential Commission on Human Immunodeficiency Virus Epidemic* (Washington D.C.: U. S. Government Printing Office, 1988), p. 119.

[7] Allan Brandt, "AIDS in Historical Perspective: Four Lessons from the History of Sexually Transmitted Diseases," *American Journal of Public Health* 78 (1988): 371. See also Allan Brandt, *No Magic Bullet: A Social History of Venereal Disease in the United States since 1880* (New York: Oxford University Press, 1987) and Alfred Yankauer, "AIDS and Public Health," *American Journal of Public Health* 78 (1988): 364–66, for further development of the theme that cooperation is essential for the success of any treatments for sexually transmitted diseases and that moralizing about the sexual activity is often an obstruction to success.

Selected Bibliography

Aiken, Jane. "AIDS — Pushing the Limits of Scientific and Legal Thought." *Jurimetrics Journal* 27 (Fall 1986): 1–7.

———. "Education as Prevention." In *AIDS and the Law: A Guide for the Public*, edited by Harlon Dalton, Scott Burris, and the Yale AIDS Law Project. New Haven: Yale University Press, 1987.

Banks, T. L., and R. R. McFadden. "Rush to Judgment: HIV Test Reliability and Screening." *Tulsa Law Journal* 23 (1988):1–35.

Bayer, Ronald. *Private Acts, Social Consequences: AIDS and the Politics of Public Health.* New York: The Free Press, 1989.

Benn, Stanley. "Privacy, Freedom, and Respect for Persons." In *Philosophical Dimensions of Privacy*, edited by Ferdinand Schoeman. Cambridge: Cambridge University Press, 1984.

Benn, Stanley, and Gerald Gaus. *Public and Private in Social Life.* London: St. Martin's Press, 1983.

Bloustein, Edward. "Privacy as an Aspect of Human Dignity." In *Philosophical Dimensions of Privacy*, edited by Ferdinand Schoeman. Cambridge: Cambridge University Press, 1984.

Brandt, Allan. "AIDS in Historical Perspective: Four Lessons from the History of Sexually Transmitted Diseases." *American Journal of Public Health* 78 (1988): 367–71.

———. *No Magic Bullet: A Social History of Venereal Disease in the United States since 1880.* New York: Oxford University Press, 1987.

Buchanan, Robert. "State Medicaid Coverage of AZT and AIDS-related Policies." *American Journal of Public Health* 78 (1988): 432–36.

Burns, Robert. "AIDS: A Legal Epidemic?" *Akron Law Review* 17 (1984): 717–37.

Carey, John Howard, and Megan M. Arthur. "The Developing Law on AIDS in the Workplace." *Maryland Law Review* 46 (Winter 1987): 284–319.

"Centers for Disease Control Recommendations for Prevention of HIV Transmission in Health Care Settings." *Morbidity and Mortality Weekly Report* 36, suppl. no. 2S (1987): 3S–18S.

"Centers for Disease Control Recommendations for Preventing Transmission of Infection with Human T-Lymphotropic Virus Type III/Lymphadenopathy-associated Virus in the Workplace." *Morbidity and Mortality Weekly Report* 34 (1985): 681–95.

Cleary, Paul, Michael J. Barry, Kenneth H. Mayer, Allan M. Brandt, Larry Gostin, and Harvey B. Fineberg. "Compulsory Premarital Screening for the Human Immunodeficiency Virus: Technical and Public Health Considerations." *Journal of the American Medical Association* 258 (1987): 1757–62.

225

Clifford, Karen A., and Russel P. Iuculano. "AIDS and Insurance: The Rationale for AIDS-related Testing." *Harvard Law Review* 100 (1987): 1806–25.

Closen, Michael, Susan Marie Connor, Howard L. Kaufman, and Mark E. Wojcik. "AIDS: Testing Democracy; Irrational Responses to the Public Health Crisis and the Need for Privacy in Serologic Testing." *John Marshall Law Review* 19 (1986): 835–928.

"The Constitutional Rights of AIDS Carriers." *Harvard Law Review* 29 (1986): 1274–92.

Costa, Donna. "Reportability of Exposure to the AIDS Virus: An Equal Protection Analysis." *Cardozo Law Review* 7 (1986): 1103–39.

Cowell, Michael J. "AIDS and Life Insurance." Society of Actuaries, Worcester, Mass., August 1987.

Dalton, Harlon L., Scott Burris, and the Yale AIDS Law Project, eds. *AIDS and the Law: A Guide for the Public.* New Haven: Yale University Press, 1987.

Damme, Catherine J. "Controlling Genetic Disease Through Law." *University of California Davis Law Review* 15 (1982): 801–37.

Dornette, William H. L., ed. *AIDS and the Law.* New York: John Wiley & Sons, 1987.

Eden, Jill. "AIDS and Health Insurance: An OTA Survey." Report prepared for the U.S. Congress, Office of Technology Assessment. 100th Cong., 2d sess., 1988.

Eisenstaedt, Richard, and Thomas Getzen. "Screening Blood Donors for Human Immunodeficiency Virus Antibody: Cost-Benefit Analysis." *American Journal of Public Health* 78 (1988): 450–54.

Faden, Ruth, and Nancy Kass. "Health Insurance and AIDS: The Status of State Regulatory Activity." *American Journal of Public Health* 78 (1988): 437–38.

Fontana, V. R. "The Ramifications of the AIDS Crisis for Local Governments." *Tort and Insurance Law Journal* 23 (Fall 1987): 195–214.

Fried, Charles. "Privacy." *Yale Law Journal* 77 (1968): 475–93.

Gavison, Ruth. "Information Control: Availability and Exclusion." In *Public and Private in Social Life,* edited by Stanley Benn and Gerald Gaus. London: St. Martin's Press, 1983.

———. "Privacy and the Limits of Law." In *Philosophical Dimensions of Privacy,* edited by Ferdinand Schoeman. Cambridge: Cambridge University Press, 1984.

Gillett, Grant. "AIDS and Confidentiality." *Journal of Applied Philosophy* 4 (1987): 15–20.

Goodman, David. "Questions Raised about Contact Tracing for AIDS." *American Medical News,* March 18, 1988; p. 1.

Gostin, Lawrence O., William J. Curran, and Mary E. Clark. "The Case against Compulsory Casefind in Controlling AIDS—Testing, Screening and Reporting." *American Journal of Law and Medicine* 12 (Spring 1987): 7–53.

Gostin, Lawrence O., and Andrew Ziegler. "A Review of AIDS-related Legislative and Regulatory Policy in the United States." *Law, Medicine and Health Care* 15 (Summer 1987): 5–16.

Gray, Alexander G. "The Parameters of Mandatory Public Health Measures and the AIDS Epidemic." *Suffolk University Law Review* 20 (Fall 1986): 505–22.

Gray, Joni, and Gary Melton. "The Law and Ethics of Psychosocial Research on AIDS." *Nebraska Law Review* 64 (1985): 637–88.

Hammond, J. D., and A. F. Shapiro. "AIDS and the Limits of Insurability." *The Millbank Quarterly* 64 (1986): 143–67.

Hardy, Ann M., Kathryn Rauch, Dean Echenberg, W. Meade Morgan, and James W. Curran. "The Economic Impact of the First 10,000 Cases of Acquired

Immunodeficiency Syndrome in the United States." *Journal of the American Medical Association* 255 (1986): 209–11.

Henry, Keith, Myra Maki, and Kent Crossley. "Analysis of the Use of HIV Antibody Testing in a Minnesota Hospital." *Journal of the American Medical Association* 259 (1987): 229–32.

Hermann, Donald H. J. "AIDS: Malpractice and Transmission Liability." *University of Colorado Law Review* 58 (Winter 1986–1987): 63–107.

Hermann, Donald H. J., and Robert D. Gorman. "Hospital Liability and AIDS Treatment: The Need for a National Standard of Care." *University of California Davis Law Review* 20 (1987): 441–79.

Hilton, Michael E. "Civil Rights — Rehabilitation Act of 1973 — Individual Affected with Contagious Disease Held 'Handicapped' and Entitled to Protection of Section 504." *St. Mary's Law Journal* 19 (1987): 231–36.

Hoffman, Joyce Nixson, and Elizabeth Zieser Kincaid. "AIDS: The Challenge to Life and Health Insurers' Freedom of Contract." *Duke Law Review* 35 (1986-1987): 709–71.

Iglehart, John. "Financing the Struggle against AIDS." *New England Journal of Medicine* 317 (July 16, 1987): 180–84.

Landesman, Sheldon H. "AIDS and a Duty to Protect." *Hastings Center Report* 17 (February 1987): 22–23.

Landolt, Mary. "Are AIDS Victims Handicapped?" *St. Louis University Law Journal* 31 (1987): 729–47.

"Law, Social Policy, and Contagious Disease: A Symposium on Acquired Immune Deficiency (AIDS)." *Hofstra Law Review* 14 (Fall 1985): 1–209.

Leader, Janet H. "Running from Fear Itself: Analyzing Employment Discrimination against Persons with AIDS and Other Communicable Diseases under Section 504 of the Rehabilitation Act of 1973." *Willamette Law Review* 23 (Fall 1987): 857–936.

Leonard, Arthur. "Employment Discrimination against Persons with AIDS." *University of Dayton Law Review* 10 (1985): 681–703.

Loscalzo, Theresa E. "AIDS in the Workplace: How Should Corporate America Cope?" *Delaware Journal of Corporate Law* 12 (1987): 527–61.

McCusker, Jane, et al. "Effects of HIV Antibody Test Knowledge on Subsequent Sexual Behaviors in a Cohort of Homosexually Active Men." *American Journal of Public Health* 78 (1988): 462–67.

Marco, Carey H. "AIDS 1986: A Medical-Legal Explosion," *Medical Trial Technique Quarterly* 33 (1987): 360–75.

Mayo, David, "The AIDS Education Debate." In *Biomedical Ethics Reviews: 1988 AIDS*, edited by James Humber and Robert Almeder. Crescent City, N.J.: HUMANA, FORTHCOMING.

Mercola, Joseph. "AIDS Update." *Medical Trial Technique Quarterly* 34 (1987): 45–58.

Merritt, Deborah Jones. "Communicable Disease and Constitutional Law: Controlling AIDS." *New York University Law Review* 61 (1986): 739–99.

Mohr, Richard D. "AIDS, Gays and State Coercion." *Bioethics* 1 (January 1987): 35–50.

———. "Mr. Justice Douglas at Sodom: Gays and Privacy." *Columbia Human Rights Law Review* 18 (Fall-Winter 1986-1987): 43–110.

———. "Policy, Ritual, Purity: Gays and Mandatory AIDS Testing." *Law, Medicine and Health Care* 15 (Winter 1988): 178–85.

Moriarity, Laura J. "AIDS in Correctional Institutions: The Legal Aspects." *Criminal Law Bulletin* 23 (1987): 533–549.

Murray, Paula C., and Robert A. Prentice. "Liability for Transmission of Herpes: Using Traditional Tort Principles to Encourage Honesty in Sexual Relationships." *Journal of Contemporary Law* 11 (1984–1985): 67–103.

Myers, D. W., and P. S. Myers. "Arguments Involving AIDS Testing in the Workplace." *Labor Law Journal* 38 (1987): 582–90.

Nanula, Peter J. "Protecting Confidentiality in the Effort to Control AIDS." *Harvard Journal on Legislation* 24 (Winter 1987): 317–46.

National Academy of Sciences Institute of Medicine. *Confronting AIDS: Update 1988.* Washington D.C.: National Academy Press, 1988.

Orland, Leonard, and Sue L. Wise. "The AIDS Epidemic: A Constitutional Conundrum." *Hofstra Law Review* 14 (Fall 1985): 137–62.

Osterholm, Michael T., and Kristine L. MacDonald. "Facing the Complex Issues of Pediatric AIDS: A Public Health Perspective." *Journal of the American Medical Association* 258 (1987): 2736–37.

Pabst, Terry L. "Protection of AIDS Victims from Employment Discrimination under the Rehabilitation Act." *University of Illinois Law Review* 1987 (1987): 355–78.

Parent, W. A. "Privacy, Morality, and the Law." *Philosophy and Public Affairs* 12 (Fall 1983): 269–88.

"Partner Notification for Preventing Human Immunodeficiency Virus (HIV) Infection — Colorado, Idaho, South Carolina, Virginia." *Morbidity and Mortality Weekly Report* 37 (1988): 393–401.

Pascal, Richard J. "Statutory Restrictions of Life Insurance Underwriting of AIDS Risk: With Special Emphasis on Restrictions in the District of Columbia." *Defense Counsel Journal* 54 (July 1987): 319–29.

Peter, Arnold P., and Heribento Sanchez. "The Therapist's Duty to Disclose Communicable Diseases." *Western States University Law Review* 14 (1987): 465–78.

Peterman, T. A., et al. "Estimating the Risks of Transfusion-associated Acquired Immune Deficiency Syndrome and Human Immunodeficiency Virus Infection." *Transfusion* 27 (1987): 371–74.

Powell, J. D., J. H. White, and R. K. Robinson. "Contagious Disease in the Workplace: The School Board of Nassau County v. Arline." *Labor Law Journal* 38 (1987): 702–7.

Rachels, James. "Why Privacy Is Important." In *Philosophical Dimensions of Privacy*, edited by Ferdinand Schoeman. Cambridge: Cambridge University Press, 1984.

"Recommendations of the Immunization Practices Advisory Committee (ACIP), Immunization of Children Infected with Human Immunodeficiency Virus — Supplementary ACIP Statement." *Morbidity and Mortality Weekly Report* 37 (1988): 181–83.

Reiman, Jeffrey. "Privacy, Intimacy, and Personhood." In *Philosophical Dimensions of Privacy*, edited by Ferdinand Schoeman. Cambridge: Cambridge University Press, 1984.

Report of the Presidential Commission on the Human Immunodeficiency Virus Epidemic. Washington, D.C.: U. S. Government Printing Office, 1988.

Ritter D. B., and R. Turner. "AIDS: Employer Concerns and Options." *Labor Law Journal* 38 (February 1987): 67–83.

Rivera, Rhonda. "The Military." In *AIDS and the Law: A Guide for the Public*, edited by Harlon Dalton, Scott Burris, and the Yale AIDS Law Project. New Haven: Yale University Press, 1987.

Rosencranz, Holly A., and Warren G. Lavey. "Treating Patients with Communicable Diseases: Limiting Liability for Physicians and Safeguarding the Public Health." *St. Louis University Law Journal* 32 (Fall 1987): 75–101.

Rothstein, Mark A. "Medical Screening of Workers: Genetics, AIDS, and Beyond." *The Labor Lawyer* 2 (1986): 675–82.

Schatz, Benjamin. "The AIDS Insurance Crises: Underwriting or Overreaching?" *Harvard Law Review* 100 (1987): 1782–1805.

Scherzer, Mark. "Insurance." In *AIDS and the Law: A Guide for the Public*, edited by Harlon Dalton, Scott Burris, and the Yale AIDS Law Project. New Haven: Yale University Press, 1987.

Schoeman, Ferdinand. "Privacy: Philosophical Dimensions of the Literature." In *Philosophical Dimensions of Privacy*, edited by Ferdinand Schoeman. Cambridge: Cambridge University Press, 1984.

———, ed. *Philosophical Dimensions of Privacy*. Cambridge: Cambridge University Press, 1984.

Seage, George, III, Stewart Landers, Anita Barry, Jerome Groopman, George A. Lamb and Arnold M. Epstein. "Medical Care Costs of AIDS in Massachusetts." *Journal of the American Medical Association* 256 (1986): 3107–9.

Shilts, Randy. *And the Band Played On: Politics, People, and the AIDS Epidemic*. New York: St. Martin's Press, 1987.

Siegler, Mark. "Confidentiality in Medicine—A Decrepit Concept." *New England Journal of Medicine* 307 (1982): 1518–21.

Stano, Phillip E., and Russel P. Iuculano. "AIDS-related Testing of Insurance Applicants: Fear vs. Fairness." *Journal of Insurance Regulation* 5 (1987): 314–39.

Stehr-Green, Jeanette K., Robert C. Holman, Janine M. Jason, and Bruce L. Evatt. "Hemophilia-associated AIDS in the United States, 1981 to September 1987." *American Journal of Public Health* 78 (1988): 439–42.

Stein, R. E. "Strategies for Dealing with AIDS Disputes in the Workplace." *The Arbitration Journal* 42 (September 1987): 21–29.

Tauer, Carol. "AIDS: Towards an Ethical Public Policy," in *Biomedical Ethics Reviews: 1988 AIDS*, edited by James Humber and Robert Almeder. Crescent City, N.J.: Humana, forthcoming.

Thomson, Judith Jarvis. "The Right to Privacy." In *Rights, Restitution and Risk: Essays in Moral Theory*. Cambridge, Massachusetts: Harvard University Press, 1986.

Tyburski, E. "AIDS and the Workplace: An Annotated Bibliography, 1984–1986." *Legal Reference Services Quarterly* 7 (Spring 1987): 15–33.

Vaid, Urvashi. "Prisons." In *AIDS and the Law: A Guide for the Public*, edited by Harlon Dalton, Scott Burris, and the Yale AIDS Law Project. New Haven: Yale University Press, 1987.

VanDeVeer, Donald, and Christine Pierce, ed. *AIDS: Ethics and Social Policy*. Belmont, Calif.: Wadsworth, 1987.

Wagner, Patricia. "AIDS and the Criminal Justice System." In *AIDS and the Law*, edited by William Dornette. New York: John Wiley & Sons, 1987.

Wasson, R. P., Jr. "AIDS Discrimination under Federal, State and Local Law after Arline." *Florida State University Law Review* 15 (Summer 1987): 221–78.

Wilson, Carole W. "From AIDS to Z: A Primer for Legal Issues concerning AIDS, Drugs, and Alcohol in the Workplace." *The Labor Lawyer* 2 (1986): 631–74.

Yankauer, Alfred. "AIDS and Public Health." *American Journal of Public Health* 78 (1988): 364–66.

Zuger, Abigail, and Steven H. Miles. "Physicians, AIDS, and Occupational Risk." *Journal of the American Medical Association* 258 (1987): 1924–28.

Index

8680